HUMAN SEXUAL AGGRESSION: CURRENT PERSPECTIVES

ANNALS OF THE NEW YORK ACADEMY OF SCIENCES
Volume 528

HUMAN SEXUAL AGGRESSION: CURRENT PERSPECTIVES

Edited by Robert A. Prentky and Vernon L. Quinsey

The New York Academy of Sciences
New York, New York
1988

Library of Congress Cataloging-in-Publication Data

Human sexual aggression.

(Annals of the New York Academy of Sciences, ISSN 0077-8923; v. 528)
Papers presented at a conference held by the New York Academy of Sciences in New York, N.Y., on Jan. 7-9, 1987.
Bibliography: p.
Includes indexes.
1. Rape—United States—Congresses. 2. Child molesting—United States—Congresses. 3. Sadism—United States—Congresses. 4. Sex offenders—Rehabilitation—United States—Congresses. 5. Rape victims—United States—Congresses. 6. Sexually abused children—United States—Congresses. I. Prentky, R. A. II. Quinsey, Vernon L. III. New York Academy of Sciences. IV. Series.
Q11.N5 vol. 528 500 s 88-17912
[HV6561] [364.3′6]
ISBN 0-89766-451-5
ISBN 0-89766-452-3 (pbk.)

PCP
Printed in the United States of America
ISBN 0-89766-451-5 (cloth)
ISBN 0-89766-452-3 (paper)
ISSN 0077-8923

ANNALS OF THE NEW YORK ACADEMY OF SCIENCES

Volume 528
August 12, 1988

HUMAN SEXUAL AGGRESSION: CURRENT PERSPECTIVES[a]

Editors and Conference Organizers
ROBERT A. PRENTKY AND VERNON L. QUINSEY

CONTENTS

[a] The papers in this volume were presented at a conference entitled Human Sexual Aggression: Current Perspectives, which was held by the New York Academy of Sciences in New York, New York on January 7-9, 1987.

Part III. Biological Issues

Part IV. Treatment and Prevention

Part V. Victim Issues

Part VI. Social Policy

Financial assistance was received from:

- THE HARRY FRANK GUGGENHEIM FOUNDATION

Preface

ROBERT A. PRENTKY

Research Department
Massachusetts Treatment Center
Bridgewater, Massachusetts 02324

VERNON L. QUINSEY

Research Department
Mental Health Centre
Penetanguishene, Ontario L0K 1P0, Canada

Over the past several decades the enormous cost of sexual aggression, both to victims and to society at large, has become increasingly apparent. The long-term psychological impact of sexual assault on adult and child victims has been documented many times. The costs incurred by society include a network of medical and psychological services provided to aid victim recovery, the investigation, trial, and incarceration of offenders—often in segregated units or special facilities—and the invisible blanket of fear that forces potential victims to schedule normal daily activities around issues of safety. Simple questions for parents, such as choosing day care or babysitters, or permitting unsupervised outside play; and equally common questions for adult women, such as when to leave work in the evening, what mode of transportation to use, where to park the car, where it is safe to walk or jog, and whether to use their first name on the mail box or in the phone book, become major concerns. Society's recognition of this danger is reflected in the special legislation many states have passed to deal specifically with such offenders, as well as in a number of recent commissions and conferences (e.g., the Attorney General's Commission on Pornography, Washington, D.C., June 1985; the Surgeon General's Workshop on Violence and Public Health, Leesburg, Virginia, October 1985; and the New York Academy of Sciences Conference in January 1987). Indeed, the ambiguity and controversy surrounding the appropriate societal and legal response to sexual offenses is evidenced by the number of special statutes that were rescinded during the sixties and seventies.

The evidence that has provoked such concern is, however, only the tip of the iceberg. In 1977 the Battelle Law and Justice Study Center suggested that less than 3% of rape *reports* are disposed as rape convictions. If victimization estimates are reliable, the number of actual rapes is about four times the number reported. Thus, of the estimated 250,000 incidents per year, only about 7,500 eventuate in a rape conviction. And whatever the "real" victimization rates are for adult women (incidence estimates vary considerably), the prevalence of child molestation may be twenty times greater. Incidents of child sexual abuse range from 500,000 to 5,000,000 cases per year. At this point, a crude estimate of prevalence suggests that about one-third of all adults were sexually exploited by an adult male during their childhood or adolescence.

The lack of sound empirical data addressing the problem of sexual aggression is certainly noteworthy, though perhaps not surprising. The relative absence of empirical research in this area may be attributable to historical scientific timidity about most aspects of sexual behavior. In 1922 Dr. Robert L. Dickinson wrote in the *Journal of the American Medical Association,* "In view of the pervicacious gonadal urge in human beings, it is not a little curious that science develops its sole timidity about the pivotal point of the physiology of sex. . . ." Indeed, the first studies explored the sociological/psychological aspects of sexuality. It was not until 1948 that the entomologist Alfred C. Kinsey and his colleagues first published *Sexual Behavior in the Human Male.* The Kinsey reports, based upon extensive interviews and the files of Dr. Dickinson, probably remain the largest collection of data on sexual experience in the world.

Physiological studies of human sexual behavior lagged behind even these preliminary excursions. The laboratory research of William Masters and Virginia Johnson, appearing only twenty short years ago, described for the first time the fundamental sexual physiology of females and males. Thus, while humans have been reproducing for thousands of years, only in the last twenty years or so have we had other than sparse and anecdotal information about reproductive physiology.

And if the domain of sexual physiology, as a medically "pure" topic of inquiry, has, until recently, been "off limits" for investigators, the area of sexual aggression has been even more neglected, discredited as a subject of respectable science, or reserved for social and political sparring. Despite the seriousness of the problem, the amount of empirical research directed at the etiology, pathogenesis, and prognosis of rape and child molestation has been minimal. When deciding what treatments are most appropriate for a given offender and when making crucial management and dispositional decisions, clinicians have had to rely predominantly on their experience. Such experience has limitations and lacks the validation that empirical research can provide. Although many writers have stressed the insufficiencies of our knowledge about sexual aggression, until recently there has been very little empirical research.

The past decade, however, has witnessed major scholarly contributions to this field. It was the intention of the Academy conference to marshal "state of the art" research on sexual aggression, focusing on (1) assessing and reviewing treatment and dispositional options for different types of sex offenders, with the ultimate goal of improving management decisions and increasing predictive accuracy of social adaptation, dangerousness, and recidivism; (2) assessing the recent evaluative research on the assessment and treatment of victims of sexual abuse; (3) developing critical need statements for future research; and (4) providing a forum for the exchange of ideas and information among disparate, often isolated, members of the research community (e.g., victim researchers, biologically oriented investigators, sociologists, anthropologists, and variously trained mental health investigators). The overriding mission of this conference was to give research on human sexual aggression a priority that is commensurate with the magnitude of the problem and the depth of public concern. The reader of this volume will note that scientific progress is currently being made on a wide spectrum of issues relating to sexual aggression. Many of the findings reported here have relevance not only to ongoing research but also, importantly, to the development of social policy.

On behalf of the community of scholars striving to advance our understanding of sexual aggression, we would like to extend our gratitude to the many members of the Academy through whose vision and support the conference became a reality. It is our hope that this proceedings will mark the beginning of a continuing collective effort to tackle the problem of sexual aggression. The Massachusetts Treatment Center and the Commonwealth of Massachusetts deserve a note of thanks for the ongoing support and encouragement provided to the first editor. We would like to thank the Harry Frank Guggenheim Foundation for assisting with conference expenses. The National Institute of Justice and the National Institute of Mental Health deserve special acknowledgment for underwriting much of the excellent research reported in this volume.

Introductory Comments

VERNON L. QUINSEY

Mental Health Centre
Penetanguishene, Ontario L0K 1P0, Canada

The papers reported in Part I address issues in the general area of experimental psychopathology. Past attempts to examine the motivation and etiology of sexually aggressive behavior have been from essentially three perspectives: (A) psychodynamic, (B) psychodiagnostic (e.g., Diagnostic and Statistical Manual of Mental Disorders I, II, III), and (C) psychometric (particularly projectives and self-report inventories). The psychodiagnostic studies have revealed that sex offenders are, by and large, not psychotic and quite characterologically heterogeneous. The psychometric studies have been somewhat more fruitful. Despite numerous methodological shortcomings, they provide tentative support for speculations that various distinct personality styles distinguish certain groups of sex offenders. Overall, however, very few inroads have been made in understanding the familial and developmental origins of sexually aggressive behavior and in identifying more precise and reliable methods for discriminating among sex offenders.

During the past decade there have been several new contributions to this area of inquiry. The first two papers in Part I (Knight; Prentky, Knight, and Rosenberg) describe efforts to develop taxonomic systems for the classification of child molesters and rapists, respectively. This research is important for a number of reasons. First, in a methodological context, heterogeneity of offender characteristics within offense-based categories can obscure important differences between sex offenders and nonoffenders. A reliable and valid typology of sex offenders would allow differences between different subtypes of sex offenders and nonoffender subjects to be studied. Second, a good typology may have fundamental treatment implications (i.e., some forms of treatment may be appropriate for only certain types of offenders). Third, the variables upon which the typology is based are appropriate candidates for etiological theories pertaining to the various subtypes. Etiological theories can ultimately lead to strategies of prevention.

The second set of papers in Part I address phallometry, with the first paper (Earls) providing an overview of the measurement of sexual preferences using phallometric techniques. The second paper (Quinsey) describes a new method designed to obtain more accurate phallometric data through the minimization of faking (i.e., a method of obtaining a valid measurement of a subject's sexual preferences under conditions where the subject attempts to conceal his real sexual interests). Phallometry is an increasingly used method of precisely identifying the deviant and nondeviant cues that elicit sexual arousal in individual sexual offenders. In addition to its use in selecting specific areas of deviant sexual arousal to be targeted in treatment interventions, it has led to theories of sexual deviance that employ sexual preferences as a central explanatory construct.

Phallometry dovetails with taxonomic research in a mutual and converging effort to reduce heterogeneity by creating theoretically meaningful, homogeneous subgroups. While the approaches are quite dissimilar, both areas of research share a common goal of identifying nuances of the core pathology, enhancing treatment efficacy, and improving outcome prediction.

A Taxonomic Analysis of Child Molesters[a]

RAYMOND A. KNIGHT[b]

Department of Psychology
Brandeis University
Waltham, Massachusetts 02254
and
Massachusetts Treatment Center
Bridgewater, Massachusetts 02324

The prominent role that taxonomic considerations play in the theorizing about child molesters[1,2,3] has been supported both by clinical observations of the heterogeneity of these offenders and by empirical data corroborating the diversity of men who abuse children.[4] Despite such support and despite the recognition that an erroneous conceptualization of child molesters as homogeneous could mask differences that might be critical for treatment and management,[5] no adequately operationalized, reliable, empirically validated child molester typology has been developed.

Our research program at the Massachusetts Treatment Center has been addressing this important taxonomic question. In this paper I will present a brief overview of our efforts over the last decade to generate a reliable and valid typology for child molesters. I will be focusing on the process we employed to generate our typology, because it clarifies the relation of our final typology to previous typologies and demonstrates the validity of the system. Those interested in the specific criteria for the system can find them in other sources.[6] FIGURE 1 depicts a flow diagram of the research program we developed to tackle this taxonomic problem. I will first give a brief overview of the program and then describe in more detail some of the critical aspects of our typology-generation process.

We employed both rational/clinical and empirical/clustering strategies simultaneously, hoping that the two approaches would dovetail and ultimately converge on valid taxonomic models. In typology generation, the deductive/rational and inductive/empirical strategies differ most in their points of departure. Their goal is the same, and ultimately their methods should coalesce. The rational approach begins by generating or choosing a taxonomic structure, operationalizing that structure, and putting it at severe risk for disconfirmation. The empirical approach focuses on data acquisition. Because the very determination of what data to gather requires some theoretical notions about what variables are important, some initial theory is also necessary in this approach. The difference is that the initial theory can be substantially less structured than the theories employed in the rational approach. Here one chooses dimensions hypothesized to be critical by clinicians and researchers or shown to have some

[a]This work was supported by grants from the National Institute of Mental Health (MH 32309) and the National Institute of Justice (82-IJ-CX-0058).

[b]Address for correspondence: Raymond Knight, Research Department, Massachusetts Treatment Center, Box 554, Bridgewater, MA 02324.

discriminating power in the empirical literature, and hopes that analysis of the critical variables with methods that are reasonable and consistent will make the organizing structures we are seeking become obvious.

As can be seen in FIGURE 1, the implementation of both strategies followed parallel stages. After target types had been chosen for the rational strategy and meaningful dimensions had been selected for the empirical strategy, the process of reliably operationalizing these types and dimensions ensued. When we had a reliable rational system, we assigned cases to the types and tested the validity of the typological scheme. After we had abstracted the most relevant dimensions, we used them to generate types with cluster analysis. The validity of these cluster analytic types was also investigated.

With luck the validity analyses for each strategy will yield data that are also helpful in restructuring the results of the other strategy. Corroboration and disconfirmation of specific rational types can suggest neglected, important dimensions that should be considered in the empirical domain. Cluster solutions can in turn suggest new types. The integration of the results from these two strategies leads inevitably to a cycling back to Stage III. In our program we encountered such cross-fertilization of strategies while we were still developing our rational scheme. When we were attempting to establish the reliability of our rational types, our cluster analyses suggested changes that permitted a more reliable operationalization of our rational scheme. I will describe this particular cross-fertilization after I summarize the work that preceded it.

STAGE I

The first stage of implementing both approaches involved the assessment of the current status of theory and research in the area and the specification of the domains that were the focus of our analyses. For the purpose of this exposition I simply want to illustrate the process that we followed in choosing our initial types, in abstracting important dimensions from these types, and in examining the empirical literature to determine dimensions for our empirical analyses.

FIGURE 2 illustrates our comparative analysis of the available schemes. Because there were virtually no studies of the extant schemes, we had to depend solely on the clinical descriptive literature. Note that the typological system that we chose as our initial point of departure, the model developed by Cohen, Seghorn, and their colleagues,[7] posited four types that have counterparts in many other systems. Indeed, these are the types most consistently described in the literature, and therefore appear to be the types most salient to clinicians. They include the Fixated type, the Regressed type, the Exploitative type, and the Aggressive or Sadistic type. The details of this comparative analysis and the descriptions of the types we chose have been presented elsewhere.[4] It should be noted that in Fitch's scheme,[8] which proposed types similar to the ones described by Cohen *et al.*,[7] the corresponding types were crossed with categories based on the sex of the victim(s) (homosexual, heterosexual, and bisexual). Some data suggest that this categorization has some prognostic utility.[8–11] However, because this victim-gender trichotomy would have greatly increased the number of subgroups assessed, we decided to keep this categorization separate and to relate it later, in Stage IV, to the Cohen *et al.* system.

FIGURE 3 illustrates how we extracted dimensions from these typologies for our cluster analyses. Because the typologies described in the literature have focused on identifying particular prototypic groups, these dimensions had to be abstracted from the descriptions of their types. The major discriminators included:

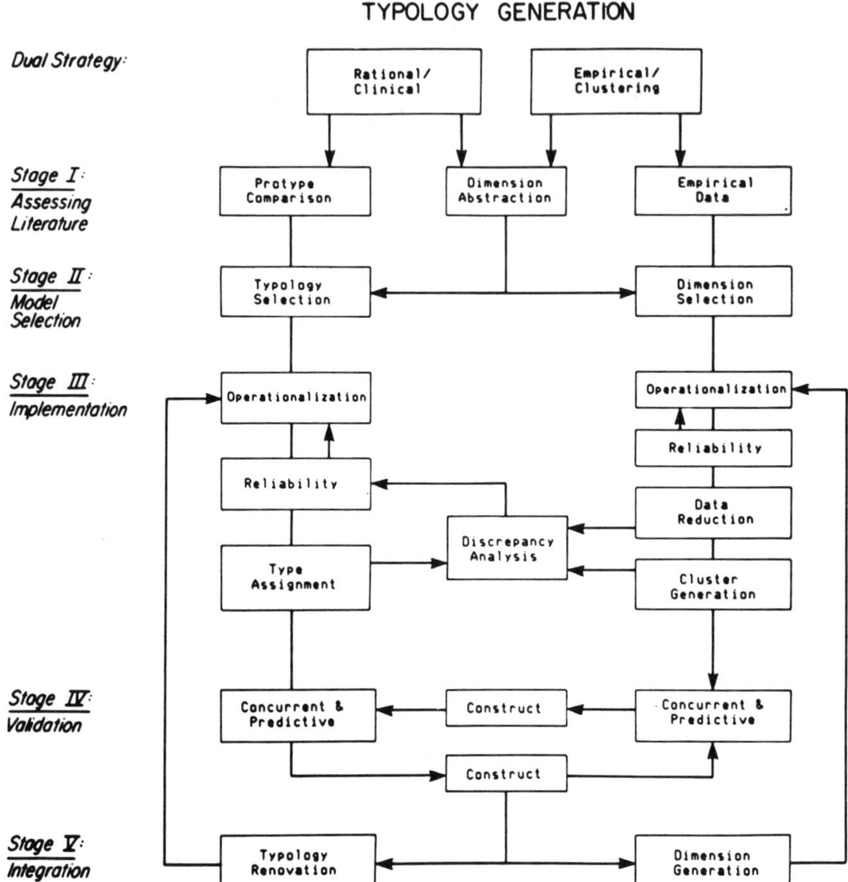

FIGURE 1. A flow diagram of the taxonomy research program at the Massachusetts Treatment Center.

Fitch (1962)	Kopp (1962)	Gebhard et al. (1965)	McCaghy (1967)	Swanson (1971)	Groth (1978)	Cohen et al. (1979)
Immature	Type I (Timid, passive, immature)	Sociosexually Underdeveloped	High Interaction Molester	Classic Pedophiliac	Sex-Pressure Offender	Fixated-Passive Offender
		Pedophile				
Frustrated	Type II (Self-righteous, self-important, man of the world)	Situational		Situational Violator	Regressed	Regressed
			Asocial Molester		SADISTIC: No — Sex-Force Exploitative Offender	Exploitative
Sociopathic		Amoral Delinquent		Inadequate Sociopathic Violator		
			Spontaneous Aggressive Molester		SADISTIC: Yes — Sex-Force Sadistic Offender	Aggressive Pedophile
Pathological		Mentally Defective		Brain damaged		
		Senile Deteriorate	Senile Molester			
		Psychotic	Incestuous Molester			
Miscellaneous		Drunken	Career Molester			

FIGURE 2. A comparative analysis of various child molester classification schemes.

1. the identification of various factors aimed at selecting offenders whose sexual offending is secondary to other problems (e.g., psychosis, alcoholism, brain damage, or mental retardation),
2. the achieved level of social relationships,
3. general lifestyle impulsivity, and
4. the amount of aggression or sadism in the crime.

TABLE 1 summarizes our survey of the discriminatory power of a number of variables with respect to five areas of research on sexual offenders. The details of this survey have been presented elsewhere.[4] In establishing our database, which was generated from a careful coding of the detailed clinical and criminal files at the Massachusetts Treatment Center for sexual offenders at Bridgewater, Massachusetts, we made certain that we created scales for as many of the variables found to have discriminatory power as our sources permitted. It is noteworthy that our review indicated that the empirical literature supported the discriminating power of the major differentiating characteristics proposed in the rational typologies. For example, the degree of violence was found to be an important discriminator in four research areas. Consequently, both the clinical and empirical literature converged on the dimensions that were the focus of our cluster analytic studies.

	Typology Dimensions				
	Primary Diagnostic Consideration				Secondary Diagnostic Consideration
	Achieved Level of Relations				
	High Fixation	Low Fixation (regressed)			
		Antisocial Lifestyle			
		Absent	Present		
Swanson (1971)	Classic Pedophile	Situational Offender	Inadequate (Sociopathic) Offender		Brain-Damaged
			Sadistic		
			No	Yes	
Groth (1978)	Sex-Pressure Offender	Regressed	Sex-Force: Exploitative	Sex-Force: Sadistic	
Cohen et al. (1979)	Fixated-Passive Offender	Regressed	Exploitative	Aggressive	

FIGURE 3. An example of how major discriminating dimensions were abstracted from a comparison of child-molester typologies.

TABLE 1. Ratings of the Empirical Support within Five Research Domains for Potential Typological Discriminators

	Sociological	Legal	Psychiatric	Psychometric	Physiological/ Behavioral
Cultural influences	***				
Offense variables					
Degree of planning	**	**		*	
Time	**				
Location	**	**			
Number of offenders	**	**			
Degree of violence	**	***		**	***
Sexual acts in offense	**	***		**	
Coincidence with nonsexual offense	**				
Alcohol in offense	**	**			
Victim characteristics					
Age	**	***		***	***
Sex	**	***			***
Relation to offender	**	***		**	
Offender characteristics					
Age	**	***		**	
Nonsexual criminal history	**	***		***	
Sexual criminal history		**		**	**
Occupational status/stability	**	**		**	
Education	*	*		**	
Social skills/adjustment		***		***	***
Assertion skills		**			*
Social anxiety		**			
Empathy					*
Heterosexual adaptation	**	***		**	
Alcohol use/abuse		***	***	***	
Intelligence	*	*	***	*	
Sexual arousal/motivation				*	***
Level of psychopathology		*	***	***	
Antisocial personality		*	***	*	
Personality styles			***	***	
Hostility/aggressiveness		*		*	
Activity level				*	
Compensatory motivation				*	

NOTE: The number of asterisks indicates the relative amount of evidence for the discriminatory power of each variable in the specific area of research rated.

STAGE II

The clinical and empirical literatures we surveyed converged on a typological scheme to serve as a point of departure for our rational strategy and numerous dimensions for our cluster analyses.

STAGE III

We began the third stage, implementation, by attempting to operationalize both the rational typology we had chosen and our preliminary dimensions, and by testing the reliability of each on a sample of committed sexual offenders. These child molesters were all repetitive and/or violent offenders who had been declared "sexually dangerous." A detailed description of our sample has been provided elsewhere.[12]

Rational Typology

To help us establish criteria for our preliminary rational typology, we compared two different approaches to classifying a sample of child molesters. First, we created summative scales that listed the major characteristics hypothesized as essential for each type. Two trained assistants rated each of 15 offenders on these scales. Second, three clinicians who were familiar with the typology assigned these same 15 offenders to each type, using detailed abstracts from the offenders' clinical files. Each clinician classified ten offenders, so that all offenders were typed by two clinicians.

FIGURE 4 depicts the four types of the original system and the major reliability problems that we encountered in this pilot study. These included:

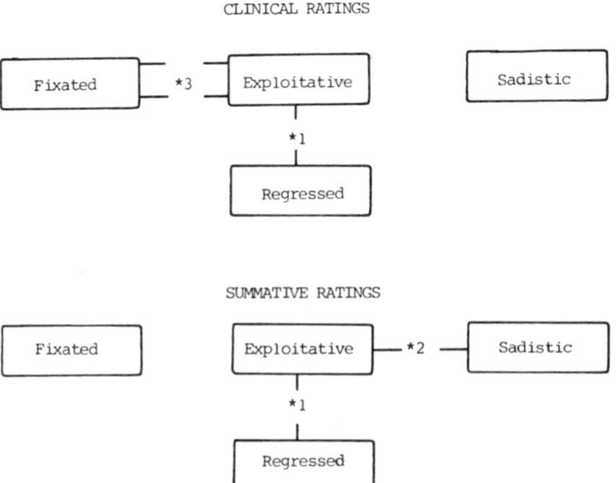

FIGURE 4. The three major reliability problems encountered in the preliminary study of the four types in the original Cohen *et al.* typology.

TABLE 2. Criteria Hypothetically Differentiating the Fixated Child Molester from the Exploitative Child Molester

Discriminator Domain	Offender Type	
	Fixed	Exploitative
1. Relationship	Relationship oriented—offender knows child	Narcissistically oriented—offender does not know child
2. Sexual aim	Passive—pregenital	Active—orgasm, genital
3. Style of approach	Planned, seductive	Impulsive, deceptive
4. Personality	Passive-dependent, avoidant	Passive-aggressive, antisocial, borderline
5. Work history	Stable, low aspirations	Unstable
6. Offense history	Absence of nonsexual crimes	Presence of nonsexual crimes
7. Internalization	Good parent	Bad parent

1. Regressed/Exploitative problem (cf. problem #1 in both sets of ratings). We tried to correct this problem by specifying the criteria for achieved level of social competence and focusing on this aspect of the Fixated-Regressed distinction in making our judgments.
2. The Exploitative/Sadistic distinction seemed to be a problem only for the summative scale raters (#2). We attempted to correct this by making more explicit the apparently successful criteria of the clinicians.
3. The Fixated/Exploitative problem (#3) created major difficulties. From an intensive study of the discrepancy cases and the rating criteria, I argued that a new type had to be established to occupy the hypothetical space between these two.

TABLE 2 presents the criteria hypothetically differentiating the Fixated and Exploitative types. I made the following suggestions about reorganizing these criteria:

1. We do not have the data to assess #7 (in TABLE 2), so drop it.
2. Delete #4, #5, and #6 as typological discriminators. They were theoretically less important discriminators. Thus, we could determine their relation to the types empirically.
3. That left three discriminators. I hypothesized that the relationship with the child and the style of approach should be highly correlated, because it is difficult to seduce someone with whom you have no relationship at all. These two could, therefore, be reduced to a single variable—aim-inhibited relationships with children, that is, having relationships with children in nonsexual contexts. We would then have the two variables depicted in FIGURE 5.

If we dichotomize these two remaining discriminators and cross them, we generate the four types shown in FIGURE 5. In our pilot study we had not come upon one of these types, an exclusively pregenital offender with an absence of aim-inhibited relations, and we could find no instances of this type in our sample. Thus, this structuring of discriminators yielded a three-type solution that could serve as a working model for isolating the middle offender type between Fixated and Exploitative. This new

		Offense Sexual Activities: Pregenital	Offense Sexual Activities: Genital
Aim-Inhibited Relations	Present	True "Fixated" "Interpersonal"	"Narcissistic"
	Absent	?	Exploitative

FIGURE 5. The generation of four types from the dichotomization and crossing of offense sexual activities and aim-inhibited relations with children.

type was labeled Narcissistic. FIGURE 6 depicts a new structure for a child molester typology that I proposed as a scheme for incorporating this new type. Its initial decision separated out the small number of regressed individuals in our sample on the basis of higher social competence. All remaining offenders would be considered "fixated" in the narrower sense that they both had lower social competence and a

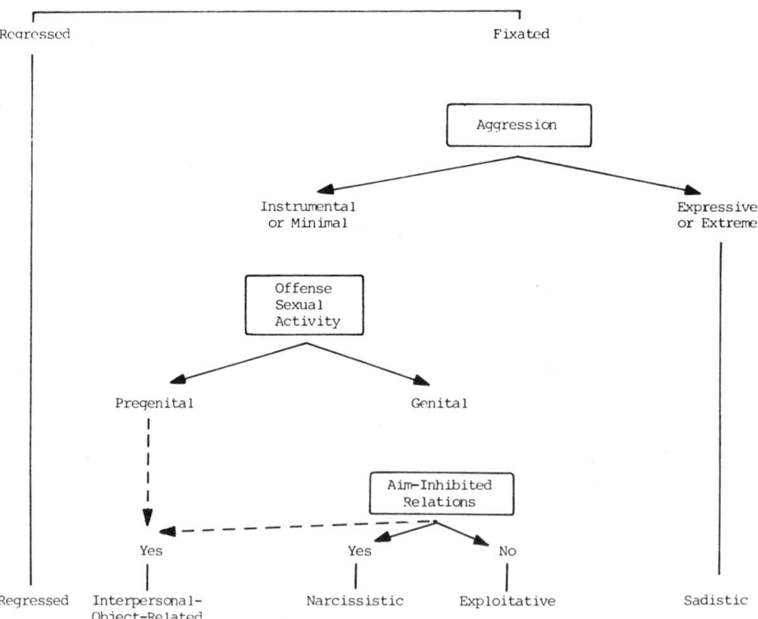

FIGURE 6. An alternative typology proposed to incorporate the results of our preliminary discrepancy analysis of the original Cohen *et al.* scheme.

chronic focus on children as sexual objects. These fixated offenders would be further differentiated by a judgment of low versus high aggression. Within the low aggression offender group the nature of offense-related sexual activity and the presence or absence of aim-inhibited relationships would define the types listed on the bottom of the figure.

The other members of my team accepted neither my new type nor my new structure. Because there were not sufficient data available at that time to convince them of the viability of such a radical departure from the original system, we arrived at the compromise shown in FIGURE 7. This compromise typology essentially kept the Fixated (Instrumental, Object-Related in FIGURE 7), Exploitative, and Sadistic types intact, and crossed each with a Regressed/Fixated discrimination, thereby allowing us to test empirically the relation of social competence to the other characteristics. As can be seen in FIGURE 7, we agreed to use aggression (instrumental versus expressive) as a primary discriminator.

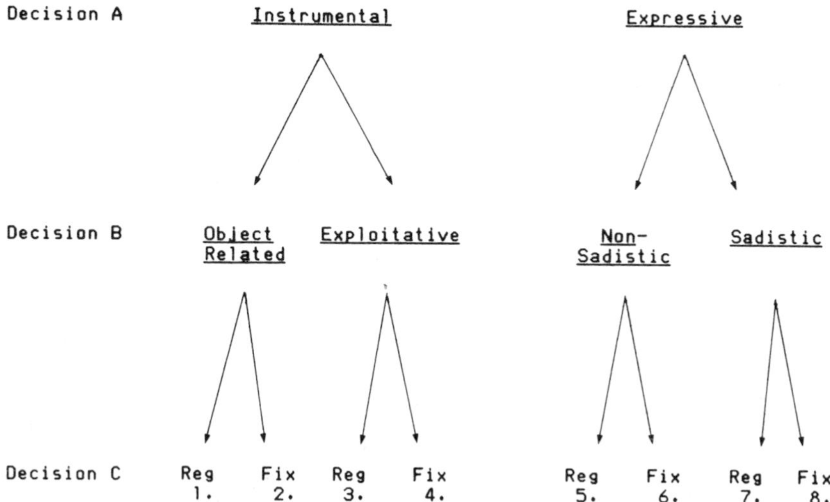

FIGURE 7. The compromise, first revision of the Cohen *et al.* scheme.

In deference to my desire to investigate my newly hypothesized type, my colleagues agreed to limit the type originally called Fixated, but now referred to as Object-Related, to only offenders who had aim-inhibited relationships with children. Thus, my hypothesis about the Narcissistic type could be tested, because we were also encoding in another part of the project all the sexual acts in the crime. This enabled the subdivision of the Object-Related group by the nature of these sexual acts.

It is also obvious from this figure that we dropped the summative scale technique for determining type assignment, and settled on a hierarchical decision tree. A number of results of this pilot study suggested that a tree scheme mirrored the sequential and conditional nature of the clinicians' method of case assignment better than the summative approach.

Unfortunately, this compromise system failed to attain adequate reliability. After subtyping a large number of child molesters, we discovered that we still had problems in the same three areas:

1. The old Object-Related/Exploitative problem still existed.
2. The Regressed and Fixated offenders were still not being adequately differentiated by social competence.
3. The Sadistic offenders were still not being differentiated from the instrumental, Exploitative offenders.

The low level of reliability meant that the revised typology could not serve adequately as a point of departure. Because we were about to undertake a generalization study at another site, it had to be revamped quickly. The difference between this second revision and our first attempt was that we now had a substantial amount of data in the computer to help us solve the discrepancy problems. Therefore, when arguments arose, we were usually able to resolve them empirically. Also, a set of cluster analyses gave some initial boundaries to our investigation. I will first describe our cluster analyses and then our discrepancy analyses.

Cluster Analysis

While we were operationalizing our typology, we were engaged in a similar process of operationalizing dimensions for cluster analyses. Cluster analysis is a generic term for a group of statistical techniques that share the common characteristic of separating a group of individuals into subgroups on the basis of a set of variable scores. The intent is to separate the individuals into subgroups whose members are both similar to each other and different from members of other subgroups.

Since I have already summarized how we selected the input variables for our cluster analysis, I will move directly to the data reduction phase. Because of space limitations, I will only highlight the critical aspects of our cluster analyses. A complete description of this phase of our program can be found in Rosenberg and Knight.[13] After an arduous weeding out process in which we attempted to assemble the most relevant set of variables that we could assess reliably, we arrived at the variables listed on the left side of TABLE 3. For cluster analysis these variables had to be reduced to a smaller number of theoretically meaningful, homogeneous scales. This was accomplished through a principal components analysis with rotation to Varimax criteria. This analysis yielded the four factors shown in TABLE 3—Substance Use, Unsocialized Behavior, Life Management, and Offense Impulsivity. We created summative scales for these four factors, and for the cluster analyses added to these, Sexual Aggression, a theoretically important measure. This variable, which differentiates levels of sexual aggression, including that manifested in nonoffense sexual behavior, remained unique through a series of principal component analyses and was retained as a separate scale because of the considerable discriminatory power it had shown in the empirical literature.

We cluster analyzed the resident population at Massachusetts Treatment Center, both rapists and child molesters, on these five scales using Ward's method. A 12-cluster solution was chosen for interpretation. Three of these clusters were important for the revision of the rational child molester typology—two clusters that included predominantly child molesters and a high aggression type whose profile closely resembled that of the consensus Sadistic molester.

FIGURE 8 presents the profile of the first of these clusters, called the Fixated child molester type. As the profile indicates, the molesters in this cluster were non-substance abusing, marginally competent offenders, who were not typically antisocial, and whose offenses were neither impulsive nor aggressive. This cluster was composed almost exclusively of child molesters, most of whom were judged Object-Related on the revised typology presented in FIGURE 7. The rest were judged Exploitative, suggesting that there were still some difficulties in the Object-Related/Exploitative distinction in the first revised typology. On personality dimensions these offenders were rated as more detached, passive, and dependent than other offender groups.

The second cluster of interest is shown in FIGURE 9. This cluster was called the Low Competence Antisocial type and was comprised mostly of Exploitative types with one Object-Related type. This group was moderately antisocial, with low scores

TABLE 3. Principal Components Analysis of the Variables Selected for Cluster Analysis: Varimax Rotated Component Pattern

	Components			
Items	Substance Use	Unsocial Behavior	Life Management	Impulsivity in Offenses
Alcohol use	*.94*[a]	.12	−.08	.14
Recent alcohol use	*.94*	.12	−.10	.10
Substance use in offenses	*.82*	.10	−.15	.01
Alcohol/acting out linked	*.92*	.06	.06	.19
Frequency of drinking	*.90*	.21	.08	.08
Problems—grammar school	.00	*.85*	−.08	.01
Problems—middle school	.04	*.85*	−.09	−.01
Family instability	.13	*.55*	−.06	.20
Childhood maladjustment	−.02	*.65*	−.26	.02
Unsocialized aggression	.21	*.70*	.03	.05
Impulsivity/recklessness	.25	*.61*	−.02	.03
Achieved skill level	−.05	−.34	*.64*	−.22
Consistency of skill level	−.04	−.22	*.63*	−.18
Independence	.01	−.05	*.81*	−.08
Pair bonding—achieved	−.03	.04	*.89*	.20
Pair bonding—at offense	−.09	.00	*.85*	.22
Modal offense impulsivity	.15	.13	−.05	*.89*
Highest offense impulsivity	.07	.14	−.05	*.80*
Lowest offense impulsivity	.16	−.07	.10	*.84*

[a] Loadings > .60 are italicized.

on substance use, social competence and life management, offense impulsivity, and sexual aggression. This cluster is noteworthy because the somewhat planned nature of their offenses, coupled with their low sexual aggression, suggested that it might be the Narcissistic group that I had suggested bridged the gap between the Fixated and Exploitative types in the original typology. This cluster was differentiated from the Fixated child molester cluster by the greater activity of its personality style and its greater ambivalence rather than dependence in interpersonal relationships.

The last cluster, depicted in FIGURE 10, was distinguished by its high sexual aggression. Because it comprised predominantly Sadistic child molesters and Displaced Anger rapists, and had a low life management score, we called it the Low-Competence

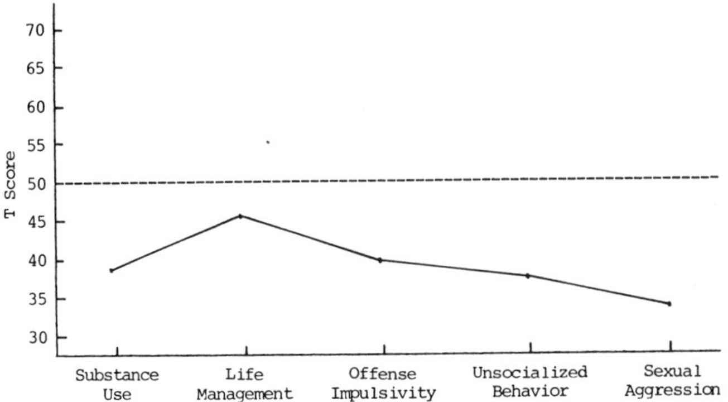

FIGURE 8. The mean profile of the Fixated Child Molester cluster on the five cluster-analysis input scales.

Aggressive type. It is important for the revision of the typology because of its similarity to the profile of the consensus Sadistic child molesters.

These clusters gave some initial boundaries for our attempts to revise our hierarchical child molester typology. These analyses suggested that:

1. The Object-Related type seemed well established. Whatever changes we made, this type had to remain intact.
2. The Exploitative type was a hodgepodge that needed major revision.
3. There was some preliminary evidence for the proposed Narcissistic type.
4. Some Sadistic offenders seemed to have similar profiles, but as a group they were not adequately differentiated.

We began our assessment of the reliability problems of our typology by doing discrepancy analyses of the major areas of unreliability. For each of the three problem

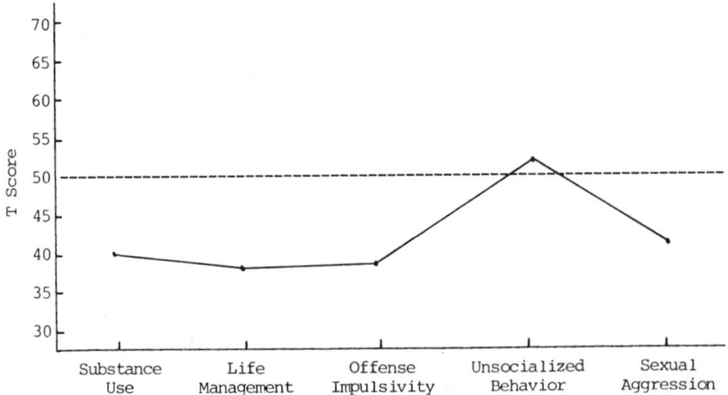

FIGURE 9. The mean profile of the Low Competence Antisocial Child Molester cluster on the five cluster-analysis input scales.

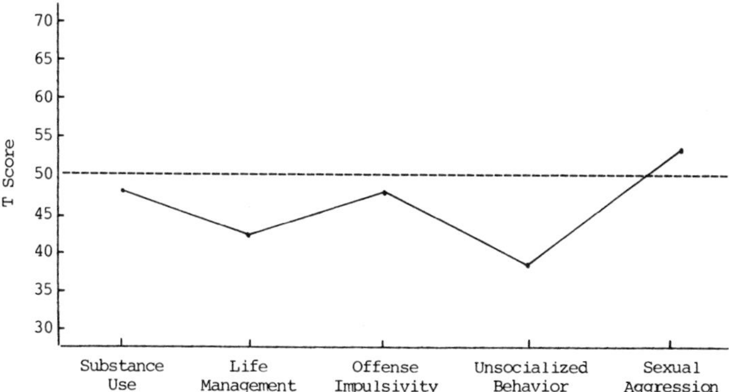

FIGURE 10. The mean profile of the Low Competence Aggressive Child Molester cluster on the five cluster-analysis input scales.

areas we generated mean profiles for the agreed cases and the discrepancy cases on the scales we had used for the cluster analysis. Then, we compared the agreed cases in the unreliable types to the cases that fell between the types. This helped us to identify the case assignment problems and directed us toward possible solutions.

Because of space limitations, I cannot describe in detail how our discrepancy analyses helped resolve each of the three major reliability problems. Instead, I will focus on the first problem, the Object-Related versus Exploitative differentiation, and simply summarize the other two solutions. FIGURE 11 depicts the first stage of our discrepancy analysis. What is striking about these data is the similarity between two of these profiles and the profiles of two of the clusters that emerged from our cluster analysis. FIGURE 12 presents the mean profiles of the consensus Object-Related type and the Fixated child molester cluster. The similarity between the two is undeniable. Almost as similar are the profiles of the Object-Related/Exploitative discrepancy cases and the Low-Competence Antisocial cluster shown in FIGURE 13. These typological

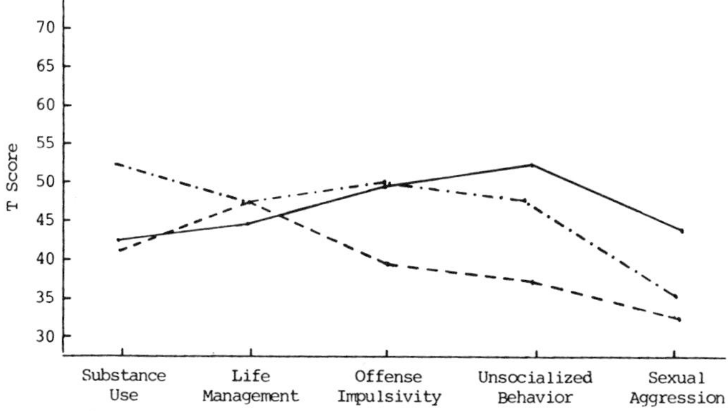

FIGURE 11. Fixated offenders: Object-Related vs. Exploitative. The mean profiles on the five cluster-analysis input scales of the Revision I Object-Related (— — —) and Exploitative (— • —) types and the cases in which there was a discrepancy in assignment between these two types (——).

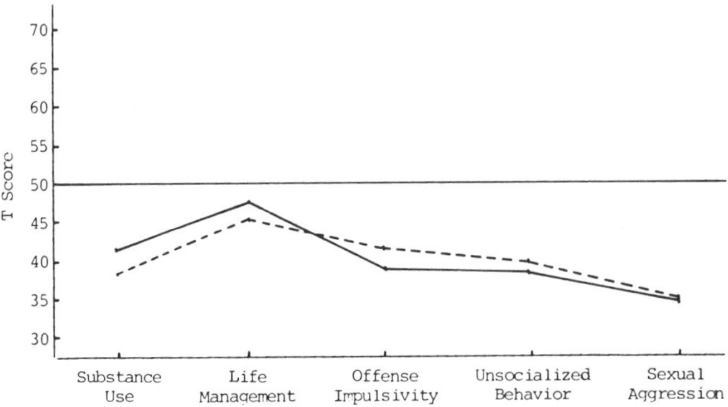

FIGURE 12. Interpersonal type. A comparison of the mean profiles of the consensus Object-Related type (*solid line*) and the Fixated Child Molester cluster (*broken line*).

similarities across two different methods support the viability of these two types and suggest that the Narcissistic type that I had proposed earlier needed to be considered seriously as a real type that occupied the theoretical space between the Object-Related and Exploitative types.

Subsequent detailed analyses of the discrepant cases suggested a clearer picture of the Narcissistic offenders. These were offenders who, like the Object-Related offender (whom we now refer to as the Interpersonal type), seek more extensive contact with children. For the Narcissistic offender, however, the motivation for contact is almost exclusively sexual; that is, they do not seek a personal relationship with the child. It turns out that the nature of the relationship of the offender with the victim is highly correlated with the nature of the sexual acts in the offense. The less close the relationship, the greater the genital activity. The Narcissistic molesters seek the company of children only to increase their opportunities for sexual contact. They also molest children whom they do not know well; this explains their slightly higher offense impulsivity. They did not fit into either the original typology or the first revision, because they appear to have substantial aim-inhibited contact with children (in other words, contact outside of the offense); but they also molest children whom they do not know, and their sexual acts are not limited to fondling and caressing, but include genital penetration. Thus, their offenses are clearly more exploitative. By providing a category for this type of offender, the new system solved this reliability problem.

The other two major reliability problems were solved in a similar fashion. Our discrepancy analyses of the Regressed-Fixated decision clearly revealed that fixation, or the focus on children as primary sexual objects, and the achieved level of social competence of the offender had to be assessed separately. These results corresponded closely with the problems we experienced in our attempts to apply the Regressed-Fixated distinction. We encountered offenders with long-standing fixations on children, who entered pathetic marriages or got married in attempts either to compensate for their fixations or to gain access to their wives' children. We also found offenders who not only showed poor social competence, but also presented little evidence of any fixation on children. Thus, both the empirical data and the reported difficulties in reaching consensus on this judgment indicated that these two components had to be rated separately. Making these separate judgments and clarifying the criteria for each decision addressed this problem.

The last problem, which involved the differentiation between the Exploitative and Sadistic types, was also clarified both by our profile analysis of the discrepant cases and by the reported problems in consensus. The analyses revealed that symbolic or "muted" sadism could occur in the absence of physical damage, and high physical damage could occur for nonsadistic reasons (for example, because of anger or clumsiness). We addressed this rating problem by making the assessment of the physical injury done to the child and the amount of sexual sadism present separate dimensions, and by specifying more concretely the criteria for sadism.

These changes required a major reorganization of the child molester typology. FIGURE 14 illustrates how these changes were integrated into a single system. Note that the fixation and social competence ratings are now done separately as Axis I. On Axis II the first discrimination to be made is the amount of contact with children. Here we do not attempt to judge whether the nature of that contact is aim-inhibited. For those judged high in contact we attempt to discriminate the meaning of that contact. For those judged low in contact we first discriminate the amount of physical damage done to the victim and then the meaning of that aggression.

This system has increased the reliability of type assignment to acceptable levels. Reliabilities of the previous system ranged from .40 to .50. Interrater reliabilities of two samples assigned to the revised typology were substantially higher. For the current residents of Massachusetts Treatment Center ($n = 66$) the reliability of Axis I was .75 and that of Axis II was .79. For the discharged sample ($n = 111$) the reliability of Axis I was .70 and that of Axis II was .74.

STAGE IV

Recent data indicate that the system has reasonably good validity. A path analytic study of the validity of the major discriminators in the typology[14] indicates that the three major changes we made in the typology yield types with distinguishable developmental histories and differences in adult adaptation. For instance, on Axis I whereas high fixation was predicted by less school-related acting out, more academic and

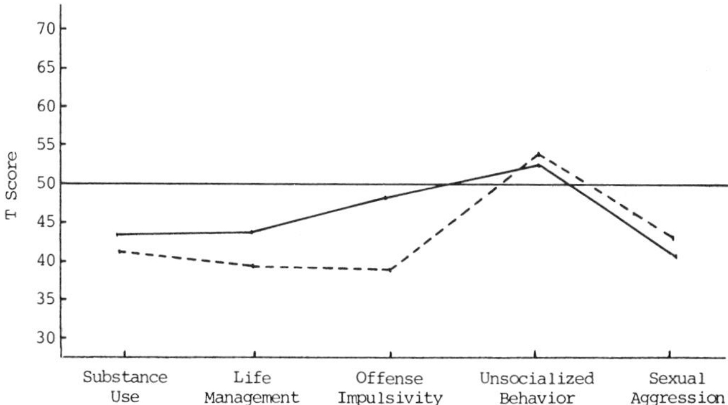

FIGURE 13. Narcissistic type. A comparison of the mean profiles of the Object-Related/Exploitative discrepancy cases (*solid line*) and the Low-Competence Antisocial cluster (*broken line*).

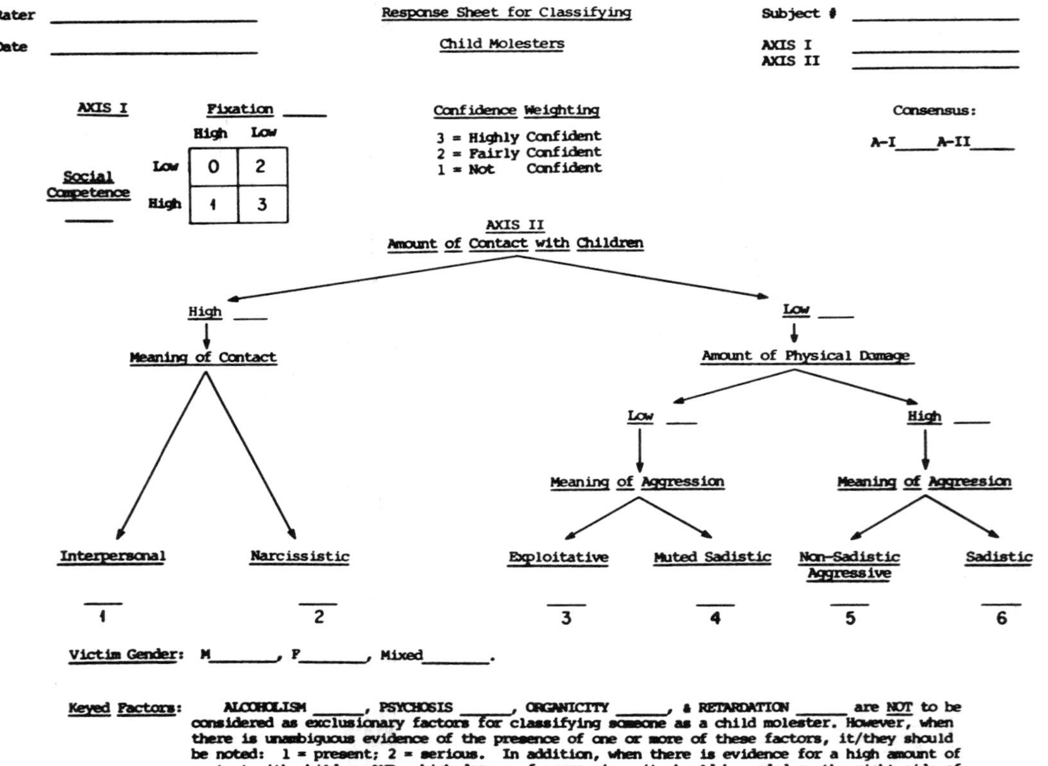

FIGURE 14. A flow diagram of the decision structure for Axis I and Axis II of Revision II of the Massachusetts Treatment Center Child Molester Typology.

interpersonal problems, and greater emotional and behavioral instability in childhood and adolescence, and by less alcohol abuse in adulthood, lower social competence was predicted only by less school-related acting out in childhood and adolescence and by lower interpersonal competence in adulthood. Thus, the two dimensions we created were correlated with different aspects of adaptation. Likewise, the amount of injury in the offense was predicted by higher emotional and behavioral instability in childhood and adolescence and by the amount of alcohol abuse in adulthood, but sadism was predicted by greater school-related acting out and lower interpersonal competence in adulthood. Finally, the Narcissistic type looked more like the Interpersonal type than like the Exploitative type in developmental history and adult adaptation. The major differences between the Narcissistic and the Interpersonal types appear to be in interpersonal style, frequency of sexual offenses, and sexual deviance in their families. If the Narcissistic type had not been introduced, not only would reliability have been adversely affected, but the substantial differences in developmental course and adult adaptation that were evident between the Interpersonal and Exploitative types would have been masked.

STAGE V—CONCLUSIONS

Tracing the generation of our rationally guided, empirically driven typology illustrates the importance of the interplay of the rational and empirical approaches in developing reliable and valid typologies. In this instance they have coalesced to produce a reasonably reliable typology that appears to have some evidence of postdictive (etiological) and concurrent validity. Moreover, we currently have the data on line to test its predictive validity. It is critical to point out that the interplay of these strategies has produced a typology that represents a radical departure from the theoretical system that served as our point of departure. The original Cohen *et al.* typology was created within a psychoanalytic framework and focused on intrapsychic dynamics. Our revision clearly emphasizes interpersonal dynamics and has moved away from many of the original psychoanalytical constructs.

Our revised typology is important because it provides an implementable and disconfirmable model from which we can move to enhance our knowledge of child molesting. The data presented here illustrate the importance of creating such disconfirmable typological models. Without the generation and testing of imprecise and even ultimately incorrect first guesses about typological structure, we would miss many of the interactions among dimensions that have been revealed in our studies. We must, however, also remain constantly cognizant of the transience of our models. The validity testing of Stage IV inevitably leads to the integration of Stage V, which in turn begins once again the cycle of revision, refinement, and retesting.

Finally, it is important to emphasize the need to develop multiple typologies and to pit them against each other. The rational typology on which I have focused represents only one possibility. It is unlikely that any one typology is going to be adequate for all purposes—etiology, treatment, prognosis—and only a multitude of perspectives is going to help explain the extremely complex problem of child molesting.

ACKNOWLEDGMENTS

Leonard Bard, Richard Boucher, Daniel Carter, David Cerce, Murray Cohen, Ralph Garofalo, Alison Martino, Denise Marvinney, Robert Prentky, Beth Schneider, Theoharis Seghorn, Harry Strauss, and Ruth Rosenberg collaborated with me in this research.

REFERENCES

1. CONTE, J. R. 1985. Clinical dimensions of adult sexual abuse of children. Behav. Sci. Law **3:** 341-354.
2. LANYON, R. I. 1986. Theory and treatment in child molestation. J. Consult. Clin. Psychol. **54:** 176-182.
3. QUINSEY, V. L. 1986. Men who have sex with children. *In* Law and Mental Health: International Perspectives, Vol. 2. D. Weisstub, Ed. Pergamon Press. New York, NY.
4. KNIGHT, R. A., R. ROSENBERG & B. SCHNEIDER. 1985. Classification of sexual offenders: Perspectives, methods and validation. *In* Rape and Sexual Assault: A Research Handbook. A. Burgess Ed., Garland Publishing. New York, NY.
5. EARLS, C. M. & V. L. QUINSEY. 1985. What is to be done? Future research on the assessment and behavioral treatment of sex offenders. Behav. Sci. Law **3:** 377-390.
6. KNIGHT, R. A., D. L. CARTER & R. A. PRENTKY. 1988. A system for the classification of child molesters: Development and application. Submitted for publication.
7. COHEN, M. L., R. J. BOUCHER, T. K. SEGHORN & J. MEHEGAN. 1979. The sexual offender against children. Presented at a Meeting of the Association for Professional Treatment of Offenders, Boston, Massachusetts.
8. FITCH, J. H. 1962. Men convicted of sexual offenses against children: A descriptive follow-up study. Br. J. Criminol. **3**(1): 18-37.
9. FRISBIE, L. V. & E. H. DONDIS. 1965. Recidivism among Treated Sex Offenders. Research Monograph Number 5. California Department of Mental Hygiene. Sacramento, CA.
10. FRISBIE, L. V. 1969. Another Look at Sex Offenders in California. Research Monograph Number 12. California Department of Mental Hygiene. Sacramento, CA.
11. QUINSEY, V. L. 1977. The assessment and treatment of child molesters: A review. Can. Psychol. Rev. **18**(3): 204-220.
12. BARD, L. A., D. L. CARTER, D. D. CERCE, R. A. KNIGHT, R. ROSENBERG & B. SCHNEIDER. 1986. A descriptive study of rapists and child molesters: Developmental, clinical and criminal characteristics. Behav. Sci. Law **5:** 203-220.
13. ROSENBERG, R. & R. A. KNIGHT. 1988. Determining male sexual offender subtypes using cluster analysis. Submitted for publication.
14. PRENTKY, R. A., R. A. KNIGHT, R. ROSENBERG & A. LEE. 1988. A path analytic approach to the validation of a taxonomic system for classifying child molesters. Submitted for publication.

Validation Analyses On a Taxonomic System for Rapists: Disconfirmation and Reconceptualization[a]

ROBERT A. PRENTKY, RAYMOND A. KNIGHT, AND RUTH ROSENBERG

Research Department
Massachusetts Treatment Center
Bridgewater, Massachusetts 02324
and
Department of Psychology
Brandeis University
Waltham, Massachusetts 02154

A principal objective of programmatic research at the Massachusetts Treatment Center over the past ten years has been to organize a large database on sexually aggressive offenders into homogeneous and reliable scales and dimensions for the purpose of generating and validating clinically and heuristically useful classification systems for rapists.

The original version of the Treatment Center classification system[1] focused on the relative contribution and interaction of sexual and aggressive motivations in men who sexually assault adult women. Cohen, Seghorn, and their colleagues argued that although all rape includes both motivational components, for some rapists the aim is primarily aggressive—to humiliate, defile, or injure—whereas for others the aim is primarily sexual, with a relative absence of violence and brutality. The dichotomization and crossing of these two motivational components yielded four types. These four types are presented in relation to other classification systems in TABLE 1.

In the Compensatory type, the aim is hypothesized to be primarily sexual, with minimal aggression facilitating the gratification of the sexual fantasy. In the Displaced-Aggression type, the aim appears to be primarily aggression, with sexual behavior being used to degrade, defile, and physically harm the victim. In the Sex-Aggression Defusion type, sexual and aggressive feelings are synergistically intertwined, and there is a sadistic quality to the assault. Finally, in the Impulse type, the assault is predatory and neither sexual nor aggressive motives appear to be important.

Subsequent studies using this system suggested that simply looking at the two primary motives (sex and aggression) failed to capture the heterogeneity of the offenders observed at the Treatment Center. The need to examine multimotivational

[a]This work was supported by the National Institute of Justice (82-IJ-CX-0058), the National Institute of Mental Health (MH32309), and the Commonwealth of Massachusetts.

TABLE 1. Rapist Classification Schemes

Guttmacher & Weihofen (1952)	Kopp (1962)	Gebhard *et al.* (1965)	Groth *et al.* (1977)	Cohen *et al.* (1971); Seghorn & Cohen (1980)
True Sex Offenders	Type I Compliant		Power-Reassurance	Sexual Aim/ Compensatory
		Double Standard	Power-Assertive	
Aggressive Offender	Type II Aggressive Psychopaths	Amoral Delinquents		Impulsive
		Explosive	Anger-Retaliation	Aggressive Aim/ Displaced anger
Sadistic Rapists		Assaultive-Sadistic	Anger-Excitation	Sex-Aggression Defusion/Sadistic

themes and how they are lived out in the offenses was discussed by Seghorn and Cohen,[2] but no concrete resolution to this problem was proposed.

Partial resolution came from a pilot study that examined the reliability of the original four-type system. The analyses of interrater agreement on subtype assignment yielded unsatisfactory results and led to fundamental changes both in the content of the classificatory system and in the assignment process. The majority of disagreements in this study were confined to cases that fell between the Compensatory and Impulse types. Detailed examination of the discrepant cases suggested that a mixed or borderline group might constitute a distinct, cohesive type. The attempts to specify the variables that distinguished this hybrid type from the related types in the original scheme led to a focus on the scheme's underlying constructs. A three-step decision tree structure evolved in part from the efforts to reduce within-group heterogeneity and increase interrater agreement through successive applications of finer distinctions (FIG. 1).

The resulting model yielded eight subtypes. It required an initial decision about the meaning of aggression in the offense, followed by a decision about the meaning of sexuality in the offense, and finally a decision about the relative amount and quality of impulse control in the life history of the offender.[3,4] Inclusion of the third-level decision on lifestyle impulsivity allowed us to specify a type whose offenses were compensatory but who was impulsive in nonoffense contexts (the type observed in the pilot study), and also generated types not previously considered but logically possible—such as offenders who manifest displaced aggression in their offenses but show higher levels of general impulsivity than previously hypothesized for this type.

Since the adoption of this revised system, more than 200 offenders have been classified, and a series of validity studies have been carried out. The present report will attempt to synthesize the results of all these studies. We will crystallize these results into suggestions for important changes in the conceptualization and refinement of the Treatment Center taxonomy.

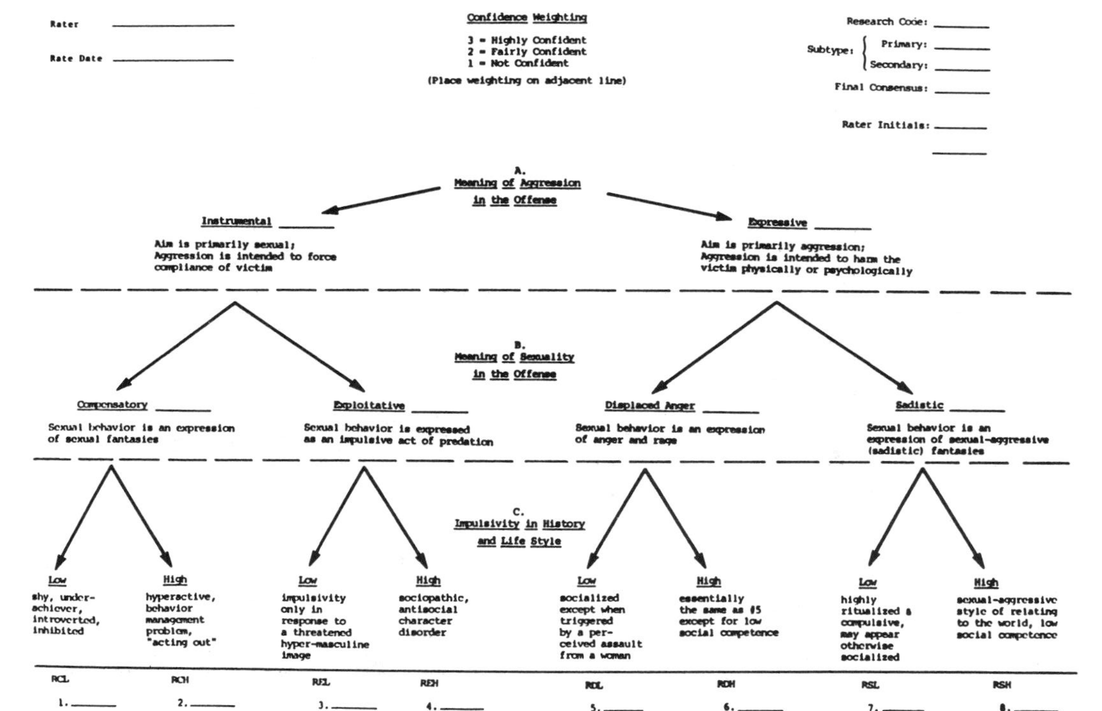

FIGURE 1. Decision tree for subtyping rapists. From Prentky *et al.*[4] Reprinted by permission from *The Bulletin of the American Academy of Psychiatry and the Law.*

METHOD

Subjects

The subjects examined in the studies described in this report comprise two subsamples selected from the population of sex offenders committed to the Treatment Center. Subsample #1 (Resident Patients) consists of 107 convicted male rapists who were committed to the Treatment Center as "sexually dangerous" and were institutionalized there at the time of the studies. Subsample #2 (Released Patients) consists of 94 convicted male rapists who were also committed to the Treatment Center as "sexually dangerous" but have been released from the Center after varying lengths of treatment. Demographic characteristics of both subsamples are provided in TABLE 2. The remarkable similarity between the resident and discharged offenders on these demographic variables permitted the collapsing of the two subsamples to yield a larger group ($n = 201$) for purposes of analysis. Detailed descriptions of the demographic characteristics of the resident population at the Treatment Center may be found elsewhere.[5]

Procedure

File Coding

The primary data source for each subject was his clinical file, which included all information gathered during his evaluation and commitment periods at the Treatment Center. Postcommitment information routinely available included such Treatment Center records as treatment summaries, behavioral observation reports, work reports, summaries of program participation, and results of any diagnostic assessments. Information collected during the subject's observation period included—in addition to reports of diagnostic assessments and clinical interviews conducted as part of the evaluation itself—data from multiple sources external to the Treatment Center, such as past institutionalization records, school and employment reports, police reports, court testimony, parole summaries, probation records, and social service notes. These reports not only originated from different agencies, but also were written at different points in the subject's life to describe events as they were occurring at the time. In many cases, social service and school reports were available that predated the subject's first arrest or legal involvement. Access to these original reports helped to counteract the retrospective biases inherent in file research based largely on summary reports of a subject's life written after events of particular importance have already taken place (in the case of these studies, after the onset of criminal activity).

Reliability

To maximize the accuracy of the coded information, two trained research assistants, blind to hypothesized relationships among the variables under study, rated each file and then met to resolve all discrepancies through a consensus procedure. Since the consensus codings served as the basis for all analyses, the reliability estimates reported in each study are the Spearman-Brown transformations of the Pearson correlations of the preconsensus ratings.[6] The reliability estimates for the validating variables in each study may be found elsewhere.[5,7–10]

TABLE 2. Demographic Characteristics of the Sample

	Combined (n = 201)	Resident Patients (n = 107)	Released Patients (n = 94)
Race			
White	84.6%	81.3%	88.3%
Nonwhite	15.4%	18.7%	11.7%
IQ			
$\overline{X}$	101.14	100.76	101.51
SD	13.81	12.30	15.23
Range	61-138	61-128	69-138
Education (grade)			
$\overline{X}$	9.15	9.40	8.90
SD	1.99	1.90	2.10
Range	3-16	6-16	3-13
Achieved skill level (0 = unskilled)			
$\overline{X}$	1.35	1.40	1.29
SD	1.27	1.28	1.27
Range	0-5	0-5	0-4
Juvenile penal record	41.9%	47.6%	35.5%
Number of juvenile penal offenses			
$\overline{X}$	2.32	2.28	2.36
SD	1.96	1.88	2.10
Range	1-12	1-12	1-12
Adult penal record	93%	94.4%	91.3%
Number of adult penal offenses			
$\overline{X}$	2.31	2.16	2.49
SD	1.82	1.57	2.07
Range	1-14	1-10	1-14
Adult penal time (years)			
$\overline{X}$	3.33	3.30	3.36
SD	3.81	3.28	4.38
Range	0-27	0-15	0.1-27
Marriage (never)	53.5%	57.0%	49.5%

Classification Procedure and Reliability. The lengthy clinical files of each subject were condensed into research files, which included diagnostic and evaluative information, school and employment reports, police reports and court testimony, parole summaries, probation records, social service notes, past institutionalization records, and complete Treatment Center records on familial and developmental history. The research files were read and subtyped independently by two senior clinicians who were familiar with the subject population. When there was disagreement in primary subtype, the raters met to resolve discrepancies and reach consensus. In the event that discrepancies could not be resolved, a third clinician made an independent rating. If this third judgment failed to promote a consensus of agreement, the case was omitted. Consensus was obtained in 95% of the cases.[b]

Reliability estimates, based upon the Spearman-Brown transformations of the Pearson correlations of the preconsensus ratings,[6] are: Decision A = .73; Decision B = .69; Decision C = .71. The details of the development, application, and reliability of this classification system may be found elsewhere.[3,4]

Data Analysis

Data analytic strategies have either employed parametric and nonparametric statistics for univariate contrasts,[7–9] or multivariate statistics using path and survival models or cluster analysis.[10–13] To conserve space the details of the analyses for each study have been omitted and may be found in the individual reports. Brief descriptions of each study discussed have been incorporated into the RESULTS section.

RESULTS AND DISCUSSION

The first decision in the classification system ("A" in FIG. 1) was intended to capture the quality and degree of aggression in the offense. It was a decision that, at the time it was established, made clinical and rational sense. One-third of all of the interrater disagreements, however, were due to difficulties in assessing the qualities of expressive aggression.[4] It was clear from this initial interrater discrepancy analysis that manifest behavior is not always sufficient for making a reliable instrumental/expressive differentiation. It was often necessary to make a clinical inference regarding the internal motivational state of the offender—a highly speculative task, given the nature of most archival data sources. A subsequent validation study employing stepwise logistic regression analysis[10] found that alcohol abuse in adulthood was the *only* component that significantly discriminated between expressive and instrumental aggression. In this case alcohol abuse increased the probability of an expressive aggressive outcome ($\gamma = .37$, SE $= .16$, $p < .05$). In another study, the Mantel-Haenszel (M-H) chi-square (-2 log (likelihood ratio)) was used to examine the failure distributions for a discharged sample of rapists.[12] Six separate survival analyses were performed, using release to the street as the start date and subsequent charge of a specific category of crimes as the failure date. In no analysis was there a significant difference between instrumental and expressive offenders with respect to reoffense

[b] The total resident sample (including child molesters) of 184 was reduced by nine cases (5%) where consensus could not be reached. The total discharge sample (including child molesters) of 270 was reduced by 30 cases (11%) where consensus could not be reached. The remaining discharge sample of 111 rapists was reduced by 17 double commitments. These were 17 cases who were discharged, reoffended, and were recommitted at the time of analysis. These cases were included as part of the current (resident) sample rather than the discharge sample.

rates. Thus, although the initial distinction between aggression that is instrumental in forcing the compliance of the victim and aggression that is intended to brutalize, humiliate, and injure the victim made intuitive sense, it was difficult to render judgments reliably, contributing to a major source of error at the next level of decision making.

The second decision ("B" in FIG. 1) was intended to capture the meaning of sexuality in the offense. If the person was rated as instrumental in Decision "A," the B-level decision distinguished between Compensatory and Exploitative. In the *Compensatory* case, sexual behavior is hypothesized to be an expression of sexual fantasies, with the offenses representing a "compensatory" defense against low self-esteem and pervasive feelings of inadequacy. In the *Exploitative* case, sexual behavior is hypothesized to be an impulsive, predatory act. The rape is conceptualized as an impulsive act determined more by contextual and immediate antecedent factors than by fantasy. if the person was rated as expressive in Decision "A," than the B-level decision distinguished between Displaced Anger and Sadistic. In the *Displaced Anger* case, sexual behavior appears to be used in the service of physically harming, degrading, and humiliating the victim, with the victim purportedly representing, in a displaced fashion, the hated individual (hypothetically, the mother; however, the assault may reflect a cumulative series of experienced or imagined insults from many women). In the *Sadistic* case, sexual behavior is hypothesized to be an expression of sexual-aggressive (sadistic) fantasies. Clinical descriptions of the Sadistic offender suggest a synergistic relationship between sexual and aggressive drives, so that increases in sexual arousal elicit increases in aggressive feelings and, similarly increases in aggressive feelings heighten sexual arousal. These four types are discussed in detail elsewhere.[4]

The first major validity study focused on this B-level decision by examining group differences on variables rationally grouped into five areas, covering the family, the developmental period, educational and occupational variables, the adulthood period, and eight paraphilia variables (TABLE 3).[9] Group differences were tested using the chi-square or analysis of variance along with range comparisons (Newman-Keuls). There were important areas of disconfirmation for the Compensatory rapists. Contrary to hypothesis, this group had the highest level of heterosexual adaptation, the highest employment skill level, the most benign developmental histories, and, overall, significantly better social adaptation. It is noteworthy, however, that a small group of these offenders turned out to be *low* in social and interpersonal competence, as predicted by the model, and that the Compensatory rapists, as a group, engaged in more paraphilias than any of the other types.

There was additional evidence that the Compensatory type may be confounding two different offender types. In a series of cluster analyses, Rosenberg and Knight[13] also found a smaller group that coincided with the prototypic description of the Compensatory type as low in social and interpersonal competence. A larger Compensatory group was characterized by high social competence. Because the second type was far more frequent, the Compensatory offenders at the Treatment Center were, contrary to hypothesis, found to be the most socially competent rapist types in our validity analyses. The logistic regression study[10] did provide some support for the discriminability of the Compensatory and Exploitative types. The presence of antisocial acting out during adolescence ($\gamma = 1.26$, SE $= .34$, $p < .001$) and adulthood ($\gamma = 1.42$, SE $= .46$, $p < .005$) increased the probability of being an Exploitative rapist when compared to Compensatory rapists. In general, however, the most serious reliability problems in the classification system continued to be the discrimination between Compensatory and Exploitative offenders.[4] Thus, the introduction of the distinction between impulsivity in the offense and lifestyle impulsivity, which had been aimed at making the discrimination between these two types more reliable,[3,8] did not solve the problem it was intended to address.

TABLE 3. Developmental, Competence, and Behavior Management Variables[a]

	Type				
	Compensatory	Exploitative	Displaced Anger	Sadistic	
	% Present				Chi-Square
Parental marriage *not* intact[b]	40.0	68.8	80.0	60.0	22.16 ($p < .01$)
Subject adopted[b]	2.5	0.	20.0	0.	13.28 ($p < .01$)
Subject foster child[b]	10.0	31.3	52.6	13.3	14.46 ($p < .01$)
Subject physically abused[b]	37.9	73.9	56.3	63.6	7.09
Subject neglected[b]	19.0	56.3	58.3	57.1	7.79 ($p < .05$)
	Mean/SD				F Value
Family stability[c]	1.48/ .95	2.24/ .73	2.21/ .76	2.13/ .88	6.34 ($p < .005$)
Last grade level	10.25/2.1	8.58/1.26	9.50/1.93	8.60/1.35	6.41 ($p < .001$)
Highest achieved skill level[d]	2.00/ .94	0.94/ .95	1.11/ .90	1.23/1.30	4.98 ($p < .005$)
Problems in grammar school[e]	0.83/ .92	1.62/1.01	1.25/1.23	1.69/1.18	3.86 ($p < .01$)
Problems in junior high school[e]	1.42/1.08	2.20/ .85	1.25/1.21	2.07/1.07	5.03 ($p < .005$)
General aggression[f]	2.06/1.13	3.05/ .94	2.66/1.56	3.33/1.37	5.95 ($p < .001$)
Sexual aggression[f]	1.91/ .69	2.23/ .51	3.27/ .59	3.30/ .70	31.77 ($p < .001$)

[a] $n = 107$.
[b] Dichotomous.
[c] 0 = secure and stable; 3 = severely chaotic.
[d] 0 = unskilled; 6 = high-level professional.
[e] 0 = no problems; 3 = severe problems.
[f] 0 = no evidence of aggression; 6 = extreme aggression (sexual aggression: 0-4).

As a group, the Exploitative rapists had the highest percentage of childhood physical abuse (74%), nonintact parental marriage (69%), youth service board contact (66%), juvenile penal history (65%), and the lowest achieved skill level (note TABLE 3).[9] Furthermore, this group of rapists demonstrated almost as much general aggression as the Sadistic rapists, and more than the Compensatory and Displaced Anger rapists. Overall, the Exploitative group failed to cohere in a hypothetically predicted fashion. Offenders so assigned splintered into multiple clusters in a cluster analysis on the entire sample,[13] and serious reliability problems plagued the classification process.[4] A separate cluster analysis on just the Exploitative offenders identified three interpretable subgroups. FIGURE 2 illustrates clearly that the major differences among these three clusters were in the areas of social competence and offense impulsivity. One of the most salient findings was that, as noted, the Exploitative offenders evidenced far more aggression than had been predicted. In a study that examined the relation between victim response and aggression by the offender, it was found that more Exploitative

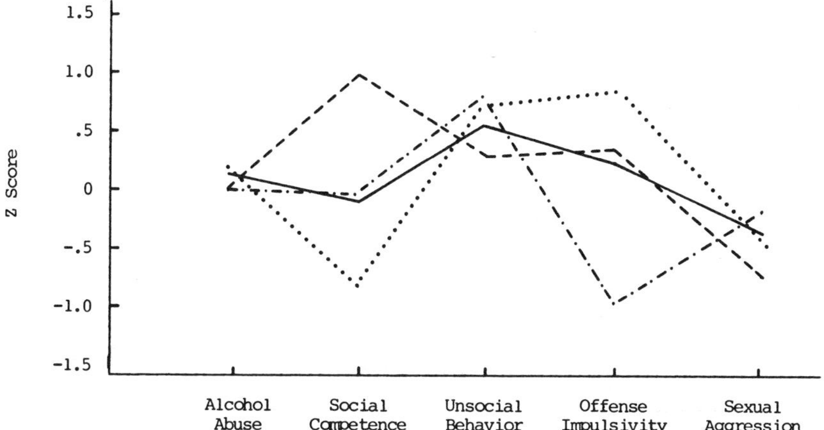

FIGURE 2. Cluster analysis on exploitative rapists. Three-group solution, Ward method. n = 47. *Solid line* = sample mean; *dotted line* = Cluster 1; *broken/dotted line* = Cluster 2A; *broken line* = Cluster 2B.

rapists committed brutal physical aggression against noncombative victims than did any of the other groups.[7] It was also found that more Exploitative rapists committed nonbrutal physical aggression *after* the sexual act than did any other group. It is noteworthy, and confirmatory of the contextual nature of exploitative offenses, that more victims were using alcohol at the time of the offense (37%) than were victims of any of the other three rapist types.[7] Presumably, this finding supports the hypothesis that exploitative offenses more often begin in social settings (e.g., parties, bars/pubs, etc.). There is also some evidence that the involvement of alcohol in the actual commission of the offenses of Exploitative rapists had a significant impact on the acts in the offenses. The correlation between alcohol use and the amount of instrumental aggression used *before* the rape was .52 for the Exploitatives, compared to .28 for the Compensatory, −.05 for the Displaced Anger, and .18 for the Sadistic offenders. In a series of interrater discrepancy analyses, time spent with biological father emerged as an unexpected correlate of this type (i.e., one that was not predicted a priori).

Exploitative rapists spent the *least* amount of time with their biological fathers ($\overline{X}$ = 7.2 years), compared with Compensatory ($\overline{X}$ = 14 years), Displaced Anger ($\overline{X}$ = 10.6 years) and Sadistic ($\overline{X}$ = 9 years) offenders. Interestingly, the Exploitative offenders spent *more* time with their biological mothers than did any of the other rapist types, though the mean group differences were unremarkable (range: 12.7-14.1 years).

The Displaced Anger offenders were originally hypothesized to be low in lifestyle impulsivity. The initial pilot study undertaken to operationalize assignment criteria indicated, however, that there were Displaced Anger rapists with highly impulsive lifestyles. When the revised system was applied to a much larger sample, it was discovered that in fact the highly impulsive Displaced Anger offender was far more frequent in our sample than was the low impulsive counterpart. Interrater discrepancy analyses based on this larger sample confirmed within-group differences in impulsivity. It may be noted in these discrepancy analyses (FIGS. 3 and 4) that Type 6 Displaced Anger rapists were much higher than Type 5 Displaced Anger rapists on both childhood and adult antisocial behavior, as well as Hare ratings of psychopathy.[15] The Type 6s were higher in lifestyle impulsivity than the Type 5s, which was reflected in a much higher incidence of school-related behavior problems.

Another area of disconfirmation within the Displaced Anger group was in the domain of social competence. The combined Displaced Anger groups in the resident sample (i.e., Types 5 and 6) were *low* in social competence,[9] thus failing to confirm

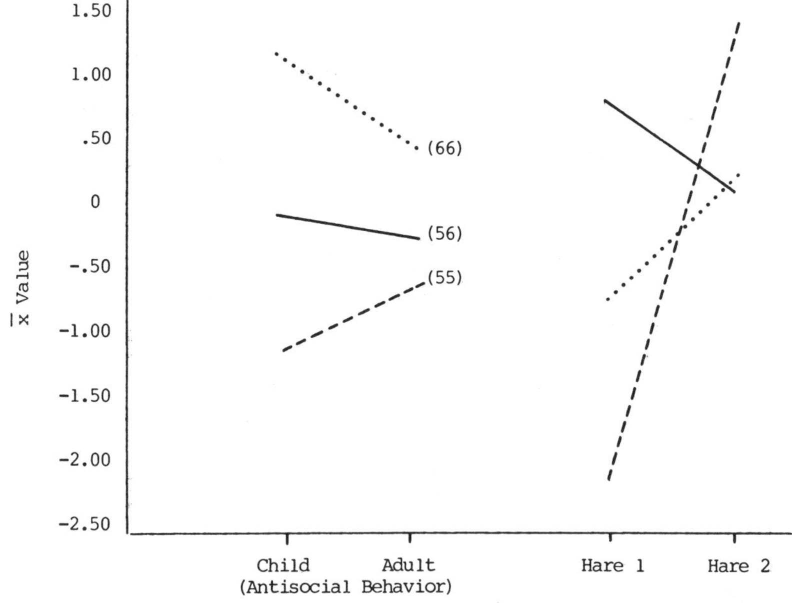

FIGURE 3. Discrepancy analysis of displaced-anger types: antisocial behavior. For this figure and FIGURES 6 and 8, Hare Factor 1: callous, lack of remorse, low frustration tolerance, and lack of long-term goals; Hare Factor 2: glib, grandiose, narcissistic personality. For this figure and FIGURE 4, identical numbers in parentheses indicate preconsensus agreement on that type; different numbers in parentheses indicate preconsensus disagreement on that type (e.g., "56" refers to instances in which one coder rated the case "5" and the other coder rated the case "6").

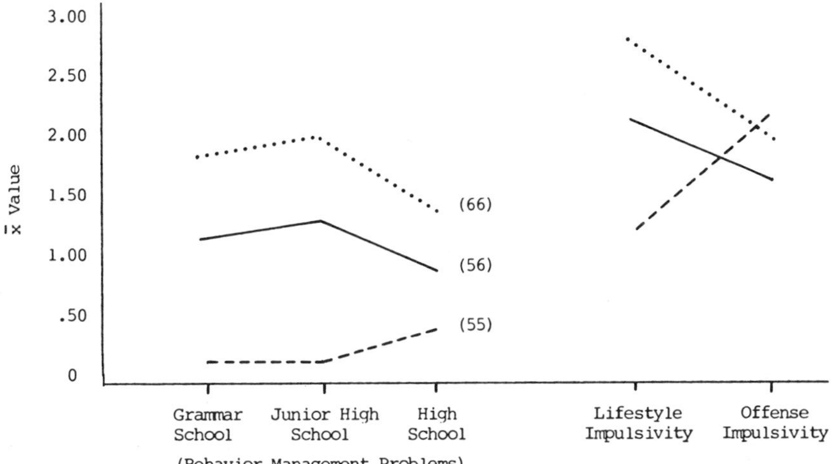

FIGURE 4. Discrepancy analysis of displaced-anger types: impulsivity. For numbers in parentheses, see caption to FIGURE 3.

the prototypic description of this type. The cluster analyses revealed that the Displaced Anger group split into two clusters.[13] One cluster was similar to the clinical description of the Displaced Anger group in that the crimes were committed impulsively, without planning, and a significant amount of physical injury was inflicted. Offenders in this group did not, however, show either the low lifestyle impulsivity or the high social competence anticipated by the model.[1,4] The second cluster captured the low incidence of antisocial behavior hypothesized to be characteristic of the Displaced Anger type, but contrary to hypothesis, the group was also characterized by low social competence and more offense-related planning than had been predicted.

The generally low level of social competence found among the Displaced Anger rapists is consistent with the finding that these offenders experienced the most chaotic, unstable childhoods. For example, 80% of them came from broken homes, 20% were adopted, and 53% were foster children.[9] Overall, the data from the validity analyses suggest that there may be two Displaced Anger types, characterized by different aspects of the one hypothesized type. One group is characterized by a much higher incidence of childhood antisocial behavior and behavior management problems throughout the childhood and adolescent years; a higher incidence of childhood learning disabilities, psychiatric disturbance, high lifestyle impulsivity, and criminal impulsivity; a high degree of independence in interpersonal relationships; and a high amount of physical injury to the victims. With the exception of low social competence, which was moderate in the first group and very low in the second, the second group is a mirror image, evidencing more offense planning, a low incidence of antisocial behavior, and a high degree of dependence in interpersonal relationships.

Despite clinical, behavioral, and offense-related profiles that suggest clear hypothetical differences between Displaced Anger and Sadistic offenders, our validity analyses failed to recover many of these presumptive differences. The path analytic study revealed only that Sadistic rapists have a higher probability of impulsive antisocial acting out in adulthood than Displaced Anger rapists have ($\gamma = 1.28$, SE $= .42$, $p < .005$).[10] The recidivism study indicated that Sadists reoffended sooner than did Displaced Anger rapists (M-H $\chi^2 = 3.83$, $p < .05$), as well as all nonsadistic rapists

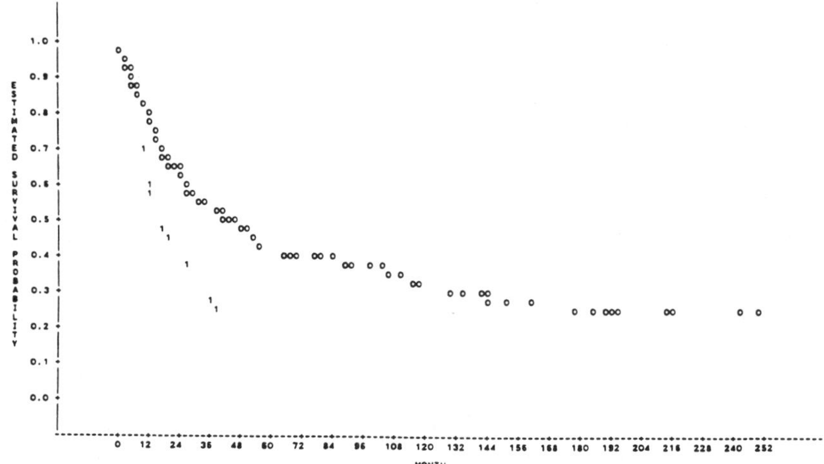

FIGURE 5. Survival functions for all traffic and criminal charges: sadistic versus nonsadistic types. 0 = nonsadistic (Types 1-6); 1 = sadistic (Types 7, 8).

combined (M-H $\chi^2 = 3.69$, $p < .05$) (FIG. 5).[12] The discrepancy analyses (FIGS. 6 and 7), based on a larger sample, clearly indicated that Displaced Anger offenders engaged in more antisocial behavior in childhood and adolescence than the Sadistic offenders. There were no differences between the groups in lifestyle impulsivity. The Sadists were much higher on Hare psychopathy ratings,[15] which reflect greater adult behavior management problems. When the Sadistic and Exploitative offenders were compared in the discrepancy analyses (FIGS. 8 and 9), it became evident that the

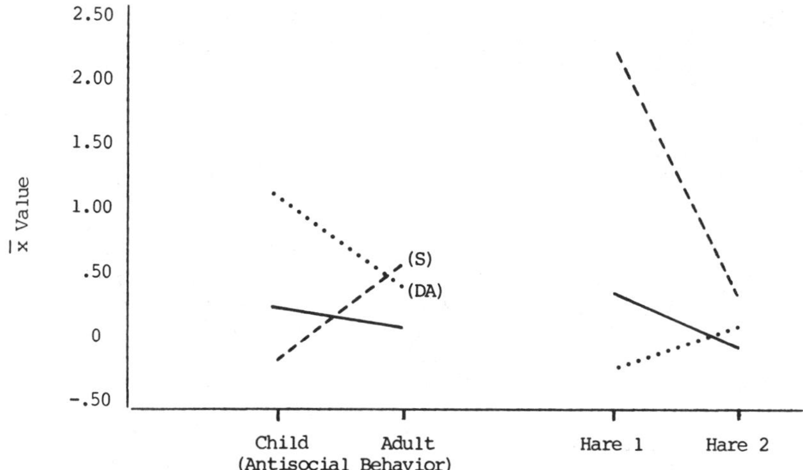

FIGURE 6. Discrepancy analysis of sadistic versus displaced-anger types: antisocial behavior. *Broken line* (S) = sadistic; *dotted line* (DA) = displaced anger; *solid line* = discrepancies. For Hare Factors, see caption to FIGURE 3.

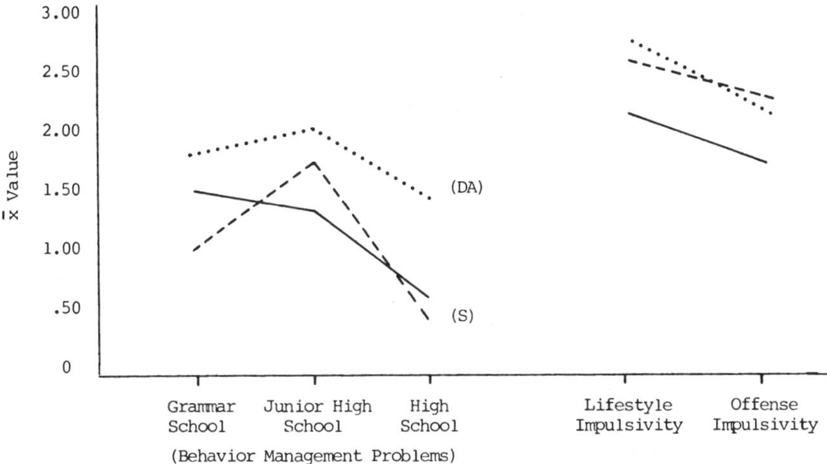

FIGURE 7. Discrepancy analysis of sadistic versus displaced-anger types: impulsivity. *Broken line* (S) = sadistic; *dotted line* (DA) = displaced anger; *solid line* = discrepancies.

Exploitatives engaged in more antisocial behavior during childhood and adolescence than the Sadists. By adulthood, there were no differences between the two groups. The Exploitatives were higher in lifestyle impulsivity, though lower in Hare ratings of psychopathy, than the Sadists. These analyses suggest that specifying the developmental stage at which impulsivity becomes manifest may assist in differentiating certain offender types.

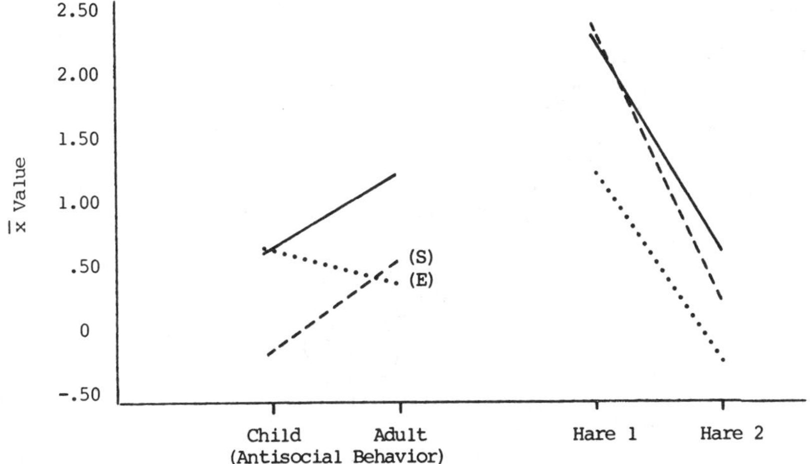

FIGURE 8. Discrepancy analysis of sadistic versus exploitative types: antisocial behavior. *Broken line* (S) = sadistic; *dotted line* (E) = exploitative; *solid line* = discrepancies. For Hare Factors, see caption to FIGURE 3.

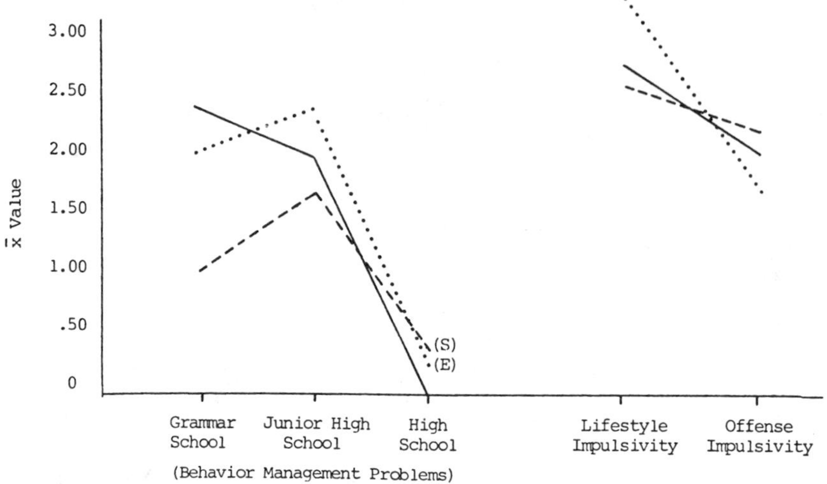

FIGURE 9. Discrepancy analysis of sadistic versus exploitative types: impulsivity. *Broken line* (S) = sadistic; *dotted line* (E) = exploitative; *solid line* = discrepancies.

The major characteristics that seem to define most uniquely the Sadistic group involved sexual deviation and abuse. The Sadists were twice as likely to come from a family in which there was sexual deviation (46%, compared with 19% for the Displaced Anger group), and, as adults, engaged in paraphilias (e.g., voyeurism, fetishism, promiscuity, and exhibitionism).[9] The Sadists were more likely to have been sexually assaulted at some time in their lives than any of the other offender types. They also attained the lowest level of heterosexual pair bonding ($\bar{X}$ = 1.9, compared to 3.1, 3.5, and 4.2 for the other groups) and the highest level of homosexual pair bonding ($\bar{X}$ = 3.3, compared to 1.2, 1.5 and 1.8 for the other groups).[9] In addition, the Sadists had the highest percentage of victims who were close friends or family (19%, compared to 2.5%, 3.2% and 8% for the other groups).[7] Despite some interesting and unexpected differences between the Displaced Anger and Sadistic groups, serious reliability problems and the failure of the validity studies to distinguish consistently between expressively aggressive rapists suggest the need to reconceptualize this subdivision of offenders.

The addition of a lifestyle impulsivity dimension to the classification model is predicated upon the observed need to address major sources of interrater disagreement, particularly involving Compensatory and Exploitative types, in the original system. This dimension did not emerge as an effective group delimiter, because approximately three-quarters of all offenders classified were rated as high in impulsivity.[4] There were, nevertheless, some informative results from the validity studies. The study that examined three measures of impulsive behavior found that judgments of higher impulsivity were associated with a wide variety of noncriminal antisocial behavior, particularly during adolescence, and a number of criminal offense variables (TABLE 4).[8] These findings were especially noteworthy because the lifestyle impulsivity decision concentrates on preadolescent problems in mastery of life's tasks. Early aberrations in adaptation and maturation antecede a pattern of antisocial acting out in adolescence and adulthood. Importantly, this pattern includes an increased frequency of adult rapes. Thus, although some of the offenses may appear more compulsive than impulsive due to the frequency of sexual assault, the early developmental styles of the offenders clearly reflect a more impulsive than inhibited adaptation. This conclusion is supported not only by the aforementioned study[8] but also by a subsequent logistic regression study,[10] in which three separate analyses yielded longitudinal paths emerging from antisocial acting out in childhood and leading directly to a taxonomic outcome of high impulsivity (FIG. 10). In addition, when examining the proportional hazards for high versus low impulse offenders,[12] it was noted in three separate analyses that the rapists with a highly impulsive lifestyle reoffended earlier (FIG. 11). Such findings are not intuitively obvious, because the measure of impulsivity being examined is assessed from data in the early developmental years and is not intended to capture offense-related impulsivity. Indeed, Prentky and Knight[8] found that planning in the sexual offense was unrelated to lifestyle impulsivity. Sexual offense planning was highest in rapists whose motivation was relatively more sexual (i.e., the Compensatory type). The unplanned, spontaneous rape was more common in the Displaced Anger type, whose motivation was more aggressive and angry. Prentky and Knight[8] found that the Sadistic offender evidenced a moderate level of planning, as would be anticipated when sexual fantasies are an important component of the offenses. Subsequent discrepancy analyses suggested, however, that the Sadists were fairly impulsive. It was also reported in Prentky and Knight,[8] and confirmed in later analyses on a larger sample, that the Exploitative offender evidenced little planning in his offenses.

Importantly, our original hypothesis about the equivocality of the construct of impulsivity was generated from discrepancy analyses of the taxonomy. This hypothesis has been supported in a number of studies, underscoring the typological implications of specifying more univocal components of the impulsivity construct. The results of the various studies reviewed clearly indicate the need to tighten our definition of lifestyle impulsivity. Adopting a more precise definition may, alone, resolve interrater assignment problems between Types 1 and 2 and between Types 2 and 4. The discrepancy analyses further suggest that examining the time period at which impulsivity becomes blatantly manifest may help to resolve interrater assignment problems between Types 4 and 8 and between Types 6 and 8.

TABLE 4. Lifestyle Impulsivity and Antisocial Behavior[a]

	Impulsivity		
	Low	High	Chi-Square
Youth service board contact	10	90	7.43 ($p < .01$)
Running away	8	92	9.86 ($p < .005$)
Juvenile assaults on peers	13	87	10.90 ($p < .001$)
Juvenile assaults on teachers	7	93	7.66 ($p < .01$)
Juvenile instigating fights	11	89	11.18 ($p < .001$)
Adult assaults on peers	12	88	5.81 ($p < .05$)
Adult instigating fights	13	87	12.25 ($p < .001$)
	Mean		Value[b]
General aggression	1.86	2.90	3.60 ($p < .001$)
Adult nonsexual victimless offenses	2.23	4.34	3.69 ($p < .001$)
Adult nonsexual victim involved	0.71	1.95	2.91 ($p < .01$)
Adult serious sexual offenses	2.28	3.11	2.08 ($p < .05$)

[a] $n = 107$.

[b] Two-tail probability based on separate variance estimate.

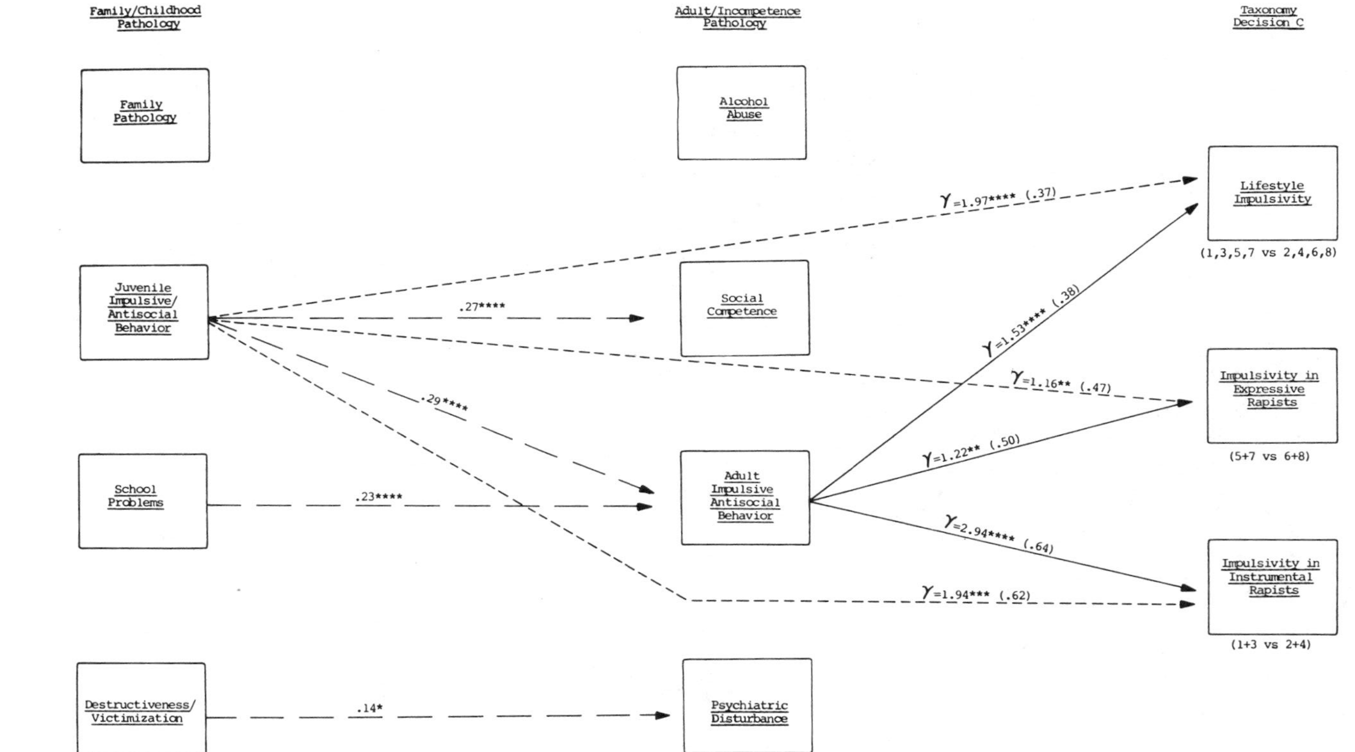

FIGURE 10. Probabilistic outcomes for lifestyle impulsivity using stepwise logistic regression analysis. $*p < .05$; $**p < .01$; $***p < .0005$; $****p < .001$. All betas derived from stepwise regression analyses. Logistic regression (γ): $\log \frac{P}{1-P} = \gamma_0 + \gamma_1 x_1 + \gamma_2 x_2$.

CONCLUSIONS

The data from these studies indicate that even though we did not always find support for the speculations about the various proposed types, and indeed sometimes uncovered surprising disconfirmations, the types we have analyzed appear to capture some important taxonomic invariance. It appears that the major distinctions in this taxonomy (instrumental versus expressive aggression, sexual versus aggressive or opportunistic motivation, and lifestyle impulsivity) have some discriminatory power. These constructs require definitional fine tuning, and impulsivity needs to be subdivided according to the developmental stages in which acting out first becomes manifest. It was also evident from these studies that the structuring of these discriminators is not optimal. One such structural modification would remove the third-level decision of lifestyle impulsivity and place it on a separate, independent axis. Finally, social competence emerged as a major, unspecified discriminator whose role must be clearly defined if the reliability and validity of the system is to be improved.

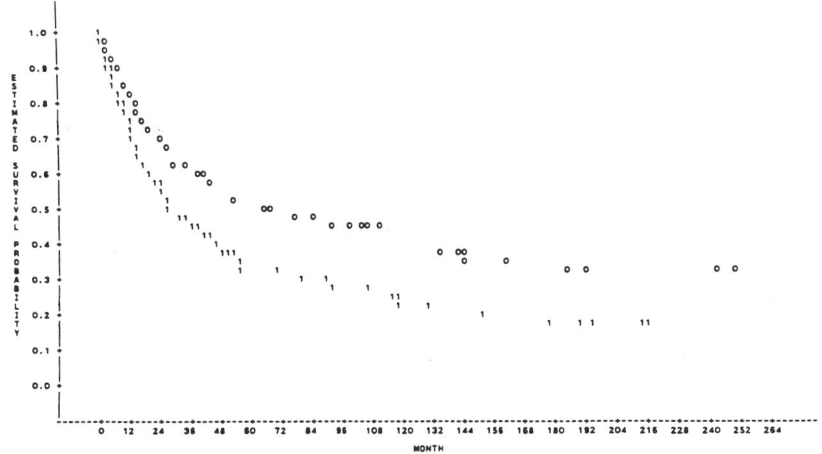

FIGURE 11. Survival functions for all traffic and criminal charges: low versus high lifestyle impulsivity. 0 = low impulsive (Types 1, 3, 5, 7); 1 = high impulsive (Types 2, 4, 6, 8).

At present, it is possible to provide no more than tentative conclusions as to how the foregoing findings will translate into a revised system. At this point we anticipate making the following changes:

1. Create a separate axis with which to examine lifestyle impulsivity (note FIGS. 12 and 13).
2. Precisely define lifestyle impulsivity as it is manifest at two points in the life cycle (childhood and adulthood).
3. Incorporate social competence as an additional discriminator on that same axis.
4. Create a separate independent axis that will focus on the sexual offenses.
5. Replace Instrumental/Expressive Aggression with Degree of Physical Injury sustained by the victim as the preemptory decision on that axis.

Lifestyle Impulsivity: Childhood	Adulthood	Social Competence: Moderate	Social Competence: Low
Y	Y	Empirically-determined Exploitative Type ("4") & Compensatory Type ("2")	Low Competence Antisocial Cluster
N	Y	Clinically-described Exploitative Type ("3")	
N	N	Empirically-determined Compensatory Type & High Competence Non-aggressive Cluster	Clinically-described Compensatory Type ("1")

FIGURE 12. Axis I hypothetically applied to instrumental (less violent) rapists. "Clinically-described" refers to types discussed in the literature. "Empirically-determined" refers to results from our own studies.

6. Provide categories for Displaced Anger and Sadistic rapists who cause a low Degree of Physical Injury (through muted, symbolic acts).
7. Provide a category for an offender who causes a high Degree of Physical Injury but evidences none of the characteristic Displaced or Sadistic motives.

These changes have been incorporated into a hypothetical revised model depicted in FIGURES 12, 13 and 14. FIGURES 12 and 13 illustrate the application of a hypothetical

Lifestyle Impulsivity: Childhood	Adulthood	Social Competence: Moderate	Social Competence: Low
Y	Y	Empirically-determined Impulsive Aggressive Cluster & Impulsive Displaced Anger Type ("6")	?
N	Y	?	Empirically-determined Predatory Antisocial Aggressive Cluster & Sadistic Type ("8")
N	N	Empirically-determined Displaced Anger Type ("5")	Empirically-determined Low Competence Aggressive Cluster

FIGURE 13. Axis I hypothetically applied to expressive (more violent) rapists. "Empirically-determined" refers to results from our own studies.

Axis I to offender types identified in our analyses. This model is not presently operational and is subject to further modification and fine tuning.

The anticipated revised system, while differing radically from the original structure, retains many of the important clinical themes that characterized the original taxonomy. It should be apparent that this system, like any viable taxonomy, provides an a priori structure serving a time-limited purpose, awaiting further modification. As such, this report represents a critical step in the evolutionary and disconfirmatory process of taxonomy development.

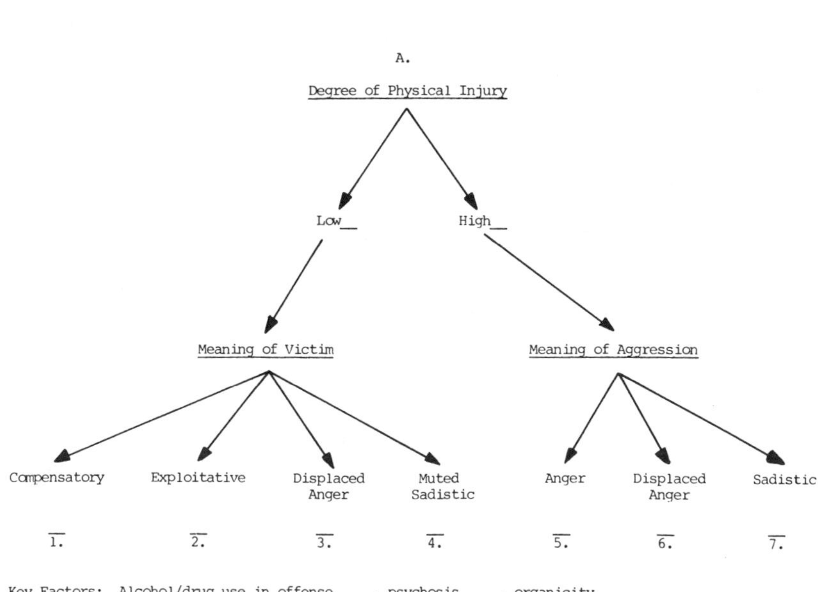

FIGURE 14. Hypothetical Axis II for revised rapist taxonomy.

REFERENCES

1. COHEN, M. L., T. SEGHORN & W. CALMAS. 1969. Sociometric study of sex offenders. J. of Abnor. Psychol. **74:** 249-255.
2. SEGHORN, T. & M. COHEN. 1980. The psychology of the rape assailant. *In* Modern Legal Medicine, Psychiatry, and Forensic Science. W. Cerran, A. L. McGarry & C. Petty, Eds. F. A. Davis. Philadelphia, PA.
3. KNIGHT, R., R. ROSENBERG & B. SCHNEIDER. 1985. Classification of sexual offenders: Perspectives, methods and validation. *In* Rape and Sexual Assault: A Research Handbook. A. Burgess, Ed. Garland Publishing. New York, NY.

4. Prentky, R. A., M. L. Cohen & T. K. Seghorn. 1985. Development of a rational taxonomy for the classification of sexual offenders: Rapists. Bull. Am. Acad. Psychiatry Law. **13:** 39-70.
5. Bard, L. A., D. L. Carter, D. D. Cerce, R. A. Knight, R. Rosenberg & B. Schneider. 1987. A descriptive study of rapists and child molesters: Developmental, clinical and criminal characteristics. Behav. Sci. Law. **5**(2): 203-220.
6. Roff, J. D. 1981. Reminder: Reliability of global judgments. Percept. Mot. Skills **52:** 315-318.
7. Prentky, R. A., A. W. Burgess & D. L. Carter. 1986. Victim responses by rapist type: An empirical and clinical analysis. J. Interpersonal Violence **1**(1): 73-98.
8. Prentky, R. A. & R. A. Knight. 1986. Impulsivity in the lifestyle and criminal behavior of sexual offenders. Criminal Justice Behav. **13:** 141-164.
9. Knight, R. A. & R. A. Prentky. 1987. Motivational components in a taxonomy for rapists: A validational analysis. Criminal Justice Behav. **14**(4): 403-426.
10. Rosenberg, R., R. A. Knight, R. A. Prentky & A. Lee. 1986. Validating the components of a taxonomic system for rapists: A path analytic approach. Bull. Am. Acad. Psychiatry Law. In press.
11. Knight, R. A., R.A. Prentky, B. Schneider & R. Rosenberg. 1983. Linear causal modeling of adaptation and criminal history in sexual offenses. *In* Prospective studies of Crime and Delinquency. K. Van Dusen & S. Mednick, Eds. Kluwer-Nijhoff Publishing. Boston, MA.
12. Prentky, R. A., R. A. Knight & A. Lee. 1987. Failure rate and Bayesian analyses of types of rapists. Manuscript in preparation.
13. Rosenberg, R. & R. A. Knight. 1986. Determining male sexual offender subtypes using cluster analysis. Submitted for publication.
14. Knight, R. A., R. Fleming, A. Ames & H. Straus. Antisocial Personality Disorder and Hare assessments of psychopathy among sexual offenders. Manuscript in preparation.

Aberrant Sexual Arousal in Sexual Offenders

CHRISTOPHER M. EARLS [a]

Department of Psychology
Université de Montréal
and
L'Institut Philippe Pinel
Montréal, Québec, Canada

The technology for the direct measurement of continuous changes in human male sexual arousal was first developed by Kurt Freund.[1] His initial work consisted of the presentation of photographic slides depicting nude adults of both sexes while measuring changes in penile volume. Soon after, this procedure was extended to include stimuli in which both sex and age were systematically varied. The results of these experiments have consistently shown that it is possible not only to differentiate among men having homo- versus heterosexual preferences but also to identify inappropriate sexual age preferences among child molesters.[2,3] These findings have since been replicated in other laboratories using penile circumferential measurements.[4,5]

However, one of the drawbacks to the methodology, as originally conceived by Freund, is that the static nature of photographic slides can prove limiting if we wish to present stimuli in which the interaction of one or more persons is involved. A case in point is the physiological evaluation of arousal to sexually aggressive cues.

Abel, Blanchard, Barlow, and Guild[6] solved this problem by developing a series of audiotaped descriptions of sexual interactions between an adult male and an adult female in which the level of aggression was varied over three levels: mutually consenting sex, rape, and nonsexual aggression. Using these audiotapes, Abel demonstrated that rapists and nonrapists could be differentiated on the basis of their sexual arousal to stimuli describing the rape of an adult woman.

At around this same time, investigators from a variety of fields began to reconsider previous conceptions of child molesters as relatively harmless individuals.[4] Evidence from a number of demographic studies,[7,8] clinical studies,[9] and historical accounts[10] suggest that, for some men, sexual interest in children can be aggressive and violent.

The purpose of the present paper is to present an overview of the work concerning deviant sexual arousal to sexually aggressive and nonsexually aggressive cues in rapists and child molesters. In addition, recent recommendations regarding the interlaboratory standardization of procedures and stimulus material are considered. It is argued that such recommendations reflect a misunderstanding of the state of the art of research in this area and should, at present, be discouraged. Finally, suggestions are made concerning future areas of inquiry.

[a] Address for correspondence: C. M. Earls, Departement de psychologie, Université de Montréal, Case Postale 6128, Succursale "A", Montréal, Québec, Canada, H3C 3J7.

SEXUAL AGGRESSORS AGAINST WOMEN

At present, there are a number of studies concerning sexual arousal in rapists.[6,11–16] The basic strategy in these experiments is to sample from two or more distinct groups: the experimental group consists generally of incarcerated rapists; the control group(s) usually consist of university students, inmates in the same institution convicted of nonsexual crimes, community volunteers (equated with the rapist sample in age and socioeconomic status), or finally, various combinations of these three comparison groups. All subjects are presented with sexually explicit stimuli, in the form of videotapes, audiotapes, or a combination of both. During these presentations, changes in penile tumescence are measured using appropriate instrumentation.[17,18] While the number and exact content of these stimuli varies over experiments, there are two themes that are consistently present and of direct experimental interest: a scene describing a mutually consenting interaction between an adult male and an adult female; and, a scene describing the rape of an adult female. The data are then analyzed in a variety of fashions but invariably include a statistical analysis between groups as well as an individual analysis in terms of a "rape index."

The results in terms of group differences usually indicate no significant differences between groups in response levels to mutually consenting episodes. However, groups are distinguished in terms of responses to rape episodes, that is, "normals" respond significantly less to descriptions of rape while rapists respond to rape episodes at the same levels as they do to mutually consenting scenes. Most authors are careful to point out that it is *not* that rapists are more aroused to rape than to mutually consenting scenes, but that they fail to differentiate physiologically between the two. Recently, however, there has been one experiment[15] in which rapists were, in fact, significantly more aroused by descriptions of rape than of mutually consenting sex. Several explanations of the differences in penile response between rapists and nonrapists have been offered,[11,19,20] but none as yet have been adequately tested experimentally.

The rape index is a measure first introduced by Abel and his associates[6] and is arrived at by dividing the average response to rape stimuli by the average response to mutually consenting stimuli. The chief advantage of the rape index is that it eliminates differences between subjects in terms of absolute levels of response. Indices theoretically can range between 0 and 100 (when using percentage of full erection) but are generally situated between .10 and 5.0 in practice. While there appears to be a strong relationship between the rape index and previous rape history,[21] the cutoff index for discriminating rapists from nonrapists varies considerably between experiments. In almost all of the work done to date, the most accurate cutoff ranges between .70 and 1.0 (note that a cutoff of 1.0 reflects the within-group finding of no significant differences between consenting sex and rape in rapists).

We have recently completed an experiment[12] in which the stimuli used by Abel and his collaborators were translated into French. These stimuli were then presented to 20 men: 10 incarcerated for rape or indecent assault and 10 nonincarcerated men equated with the experimental group in age and socioeconomic status. Our results indicated no significant differences in response between groups to mutually consenting sexual episodes; as in previous experiments, the rapists and nonrapists were distinguished with respect to their responses to rape descriptions (nonsexual offenders responded significantly less to descriptions of rape, while the rapists responded equally to both stimulus categories). In addition, using a cutoff for the rape index of 1.0, we were able to identify correctly all of the rapists and 8 of the 10 nonrapists.

It would appear, then, that despite variability between laboratories, experimenters, stimulus material (while stimulus content is comparable, few of the experiments reported here have used the same stimuli), and language, the results are reasonably homogeneous. Nevertheless, there have been two published reports of failure to identify rapists using erectile measures. In one study,[22] rapists were found to respond significantly less to rape episodes than to scenes of mutually consenting sex. Unfortunately, these data are difficult to interpret, since a control group of nonsexual offenders was not included. While it may be possible to argue that a control group was not required because the results failed to show the characteristic pattern of response in rapists (i. e., statistical equivalence between mutually consenting and rape stimulus episodes), it remains difficult to predict how nonsexual offenders would have responded in the same experimental setting.

The second experiment[23] reporting an inability to identify rapists did include a control group of nonsexual offenders. However, this experiment differs in one other important aspect from all other experiments cited above in that stimuli were presented in the form of videotape recordings. Videotapes tend to generate higher levels of arousal than either audiotapes or photographic slides.[24] In addition, it has previously been shown that when depictions of rape and mutually consenting sex are presented on videotape, the discrimination that "normals" generally make between these two stimulus categories is disrupted.[21] These results suggest that if we wish to increase the accuracy of discrimination between rapists and nonrapists, we should rely more heavily on data obtained using audiotaped stimuli.

Before turning to the research on child molesters, there is one additional aspect of interest concerning deviant sexual arousal among rapists. As we have already seen, there is a correspondence between measures of sexual arousal and past behavior (i. e., differences between rapists and nonrapists). However, given the aggressive nature of rape, we might also expect there to be some relation between response and a more specific aspect of past behavior, namely, levels of aggression used during the rape. In order to examine this hypothesis, estimates of physical force used during the rape have been compared to either the rape index or an aggression index (mean responses to nonsexual violence divided by mean responses to mutually consenting sex). Abel and his associates[21] reported a positive relationship between the rape index and the likelihood of victim injury as well as number of victims. However, the authors did not describe the manner in which they estimated victim injury. Using a more objective scale and independent raters, Quinsey and Chaplin[25] found significant differences between rapists and nonrapists with respect to aggression indices. These results suggest a relationship between responses to nonsexual violence and victim injury. However, as the authors point out, "the relationship is not large and . . . it does not appear to be linear" (p. 378). In a subsequent study,[15] these same investigators found a significant correlation ($r = .42$) between the aggression index and a dichotomized victim injury score (death or hospitalization versus lesser injury); no significant correlations were found between the aggression index and number of victims, number of arrests for sexual crimes, or victim injury for the most serious offence.

Although the correlation reported above between the aggression index and victim injury is small, it is nevertheless encouraging: as Quinsey and Chaplin[25] note, victims can sustain injury for reasons other than the sexual intentions of the offender—for instance, fortuitous injury or unwillingness to leave a witness.

CHILD MOLESTERS

As mentioned earlier, observations from a number of sources have recently led researchers to question the previously held view that men with sexual interest in children were physically nonabusive. In an effort to explore this observation experimentally, Abel, Becker, Murphy, and Flanagan[26] applied the same strategy used with rapists and developed a series of six audiotaped stimuli describing interactions between an adult male and a female child in which the level of force required to obtain victim compliance was systematically varied. Using penile tumescence as the dependent variable, these investigators identified (among a group of heterogeneous sexual offenders) a percentage of child molesters who were more sexually excited by descriptions of sexual violence than of "mutually consenting" sex with a child. While no between-group statistical analyses were provided, indices of aggression were calculated (penile responses to descriptions of aggressive sexual interactions with children divided by responses to descriptions of nonaggressive sex) that appeared to be related to sexual offense history.

In a subsequent experiment Avery-Clark and Laws[27] also developed a series of five audiotape stimuli describing various nonviolent and violent interactions between an adult male and a child. Two sets of audiotapes were constructed: one for homosexual child molesters and a second for heterosexual child molesters. Stimuli were presented to two groups of sexual offenders previously classified on the basis of offense history as being either "more dangerous" or "less dangerous." In this experiment the focus of the data analysis was a presentation of aggression indices. The data show that child molesters classified as more dangerous responded at significantly higher levels to the aggressive cues than did the child molesters classified as less dangerous.

In a recent and well-controlled study, Marshall and his associates[4] included a control group of non-child molesters and compared their penile responses to those of a group of heterosexual child molesters and a group of incest offenders. Although heterosexual child molesters evidenced less arousal to descriptions of nonsexual violence than to episodes describing sexual interactions with children, they responded at higher levels over all stimulus categories than did the non-sexual offender group (there were no significant differences between the non-child molesters and the incest offenders). Also reported was a significant correlation ($r = .40$) between degree of force used by these men in previous sexual encounters with children and the ratio of responses to forced sex to "consenting" sex with children (pedophile aggression index). However, there was an indeterminate proportion of the variance in this correlation that was shared by other variables, most notably the number of previous victims for each offender. As with the studies concerning nonsexual aggression in rapists, such correlations must, for the moment, be viewed with some caution. This may be particularly true for child molesters (who tend to have more victims than rapists),[28] simply because as the number of victims increases, so does the probability of fortuitous victim injury.

In summary, the experimental data to date indicate that we are able to identify both rapists and child molesters on the basis of their erectile responses to descriptions of sexual violence. It may be also possible to identify individuals having sadistic sexual interests; however, further research using larger sample sizes and more precise victim injury scores is necessary before this issue can be directly addressed. In addition, it would be worthwhile to attempt to control for the variance attributable to the number of previous victims and to distinguish between fortuitous and intentional injury.

CLINICAL, PRACTICAL, AND EXPERIMENTAL ISSUES

To this point, the existing research regarding human aggressive sexual behavior has been discussed from an experimental perspective. However, given the current pressing need to design effective assessment and treatment programs, it is only natural that penile measurement has found its way into immediate clinical application. For example, although it is far from evident that erections due to nonsexual violence predict future behavior, most clinicians would find it difficult to ignore such information when deciding upon possible intervention strategies. This may be for the best, since as has been previously noted,[25] "The worst outcome in the event of an error would be that [an individual] receives a short term treatment that he does not need" (p. 380).

Because of the need objectively to identify and target relevant behaviors in treatment, there appears to be an increasing number of individuals and institutions conducting routine assessments of sexual arousal in sexual offenders. The necessary equipment is reasonably inexpensive; erotic stimuli are not difficult to obtain, and the recording procedures are relatively straightforward. It is perhaps the growing popularity of these assessment procedures that has led to recent recommendations that a certain degree of standardization of procedures and assessment stimuli be established and adopted.[29,30] Such recommendations are at best premature and at worst misinformed; standardization should not be confused with a careful description of the methodology used and the operational definition of dependent, independent, and extraneous variables.

As I have already discussed, there are quite a number of experiments concerning deviant sexual arousal in rapists and child molesters. Considerable work has also been done concerning identification of sex and age preferences using erectile measures.[10] What is surprising when one considers these results is the remarkable homogeneity among experiments. In Campbell and Stanley's[31] terms, there appears to be a reasonable degree of internal validity and a high degree of external validity in experiments concerning deviant sexual arousal. Equivalent results in the face of interlaboratory differences should be viewed as positive and encouraging and not as a source of variance to be controlled. Of course, some form of standardization is necessary to facilitate communication between clinicians and researchers; however, at present we should be wary of discouraging research concerning new stimuli and procedures. Standardized stimuli and procedures will also be of considerable value when one presents data in court; but it would be unwise, for the moment, to oversell the utility of erectile measurements in assessment and treatment. There are still a great many unanswered questions to explore empirically before we begin to think of standardizing our stimuli and collecting normative data. For example, we are as yet uncertain regarding the effect of many parametric variables in the assessment setting.[32] We do not know if the sex of the experimenter can have an influence on the results. It is unclear that circumferential measurements, as currently used, are the most sensitive means of measuring male sexual arousal.[18] The physiological mechanisms of penile tumescence are not completely understood.[33] There is conflicting evidence concerning the ideal stimulus duration.[15,27] The effect on subsequent responses of exposing subjects to "warm-up" stimuli needs to be addressed.[34] Work is required concerning the predictive validity of erectile measurements both in assessment and treatment.[10] Although recently there have been some promising results with respect to the voluntary control of erection,[35] considerably more work is required. The list could go on.

If we wish to introduce some form of standardization, we might consider standardizing the statistical analyses used and the manner in which results are presented. For example, as discussed earlier, most experiments concerning the differentiation of known groups, such as rapists and child molesters, include analyses in the form of various indices reflecting individual relative responses to sexually violent, nonsexually violent, and sexually nonviolent stimuli. This practice has allowed at least some degree of comparison between laboratories.

We could also consider the manner in which we transform raw data. In an effort to permit comparisons in terms of responding both between and within subjects, most investigators using circumferential measurements typically transform the data to percentage of full erection or Z scores. We have recently completed an experiment[36] in which various methods of data scoring were statistically compared with respect to the proportion of variance accounted for by each data method. A total of 19 males were presented with photographic slides from 5 stimulus categories: neutral, female adult, female adolescent, male adult, and male adolescent. The data were then analyzed in terms of raw scores, percentage of full erection, and Z scores. The results indicated a clear superiority for the Z-score transformations with respect to the proportion of variance captured by each data set. We suggest that, because Z scores eliminate between-subject variability and highlight differences in response among stimuli, they are the most appropriate method of data analysis for the types of research questions currently being posed (i.e., our ability to differentiate between known groups of sexual offenders). An added benefit of using Z scores is that calculating them does not require that subjects attain full erection during assessment (a requirement necessary for the transformation to percentage of full erection).

All of this is not necessarily to argue in favor of the immediate and unilateral adoption of Z-score data analyses; but instead to recommend that the establishment of procedural, analytic, and stimulus-material standardization be based on empirical research. The direct measurement of sexual arousal is, at present, the best technology available for the identification of sexual preferences among sexual offenders. However, there are many aspects of this technology that are not clearly understood. In order to maintain the validity of these assessment procedures, it will be necessary that future research proceed carefully and methodically.

SUMMARY

The present article has reviewed the experimental work concerning deviant sexual arousal to sexually aggressive and nonsexually aggressive cues in rapists and child molesters. To date, the results of this work are encouraging and indicate that we are able to identify these two offender groups on the basis of their erectile responses to sexual violence despite variability due to laboratories, stimulus material, and language. In addition, recent suggestions regarding the standardization of procedures and stimulus material have been considered. It has been argued that while standardization has a number of advantages, we must be careful not to discourage the development of new procedures nor to oversell current assessment procedures. Finally, some directions for future research have been outlined and suggestions based on empirical findings made for ways in which we might begin standardization.

ACKNOWLEDGMENTS

I wish to thank V. L. Quinsey and Louis-Georges Castonguay for their comments on an earlier version of this manuscript.

REFERENCES

1. FREUND, F., F. SEDLACEK & K. KNOB. 1965. A simple transducer for mechanical plethysmography of the male genital. J. Exp. Anal. Behav. **8:** 169-170.
2. FREUND, K. 1967a. Diagnosing homo or heterosexuality and erotic age-preference by means of a psychophysiological test. Behav. Res. Ther. **5:** 209-228.
3. FREUND, K. 1967b. Erotic preference in pedophilia. Behav. Res. Ther. **5:** 339-348.
4. MARSHALL, W. L., H. E. BARBAREE & D. CHRISTOPHE. 1986. Sexual offenders against female children: Sexual preferences for age of victims and type of behavior. Can. J. Behav. Sci. **18:** 424-439.
5. QUINSEY, V. L., C. M. STEINMAN, S. G. BERGERSEN & T. F. HOLMES. 1975. Penile circumference, skin conductance, and ranking responses of child molesters and "normals" to sexual and nonsexual visual stimuli. Behav. Ther. **6:** 213-219.
6. ABEL, G. G., D. H. BARLOW, E. B. BLANCHARD & D. GUILD. 1977. The components of rapists' sexual arousal. Arch. Gen. Psychiatry **34:** 895-903.
7. DE FRANCIS, V. 1969. Protecting the child victim of sex crimes committed by adults. American Humane Association, Children's Division. Denver, CO.
8. EARLS, C. M., L. BOUCHARD & J. LABERGE. 1984. Etude descriptive des délinquants sexuels incarcérés dans des pénitenciers québécoise. Cahier de Recherche No. 7. Institut Philippe Pinel. Montreal, Canada.
9. MARSHALL, W. L. & M. M. CHRISTIE. 1981. Pedophilia and aggression. Crim. Justice Behav. **8:** 145-158.
10. QUINSEY, V. L. 1986. Men who have sex with children. *In* Law and Mental Health: International Perspectives, Vol. 2. D. N. Weisstub, Ed.: 140-172. Pergamon Press. New York, NY.
11. BARBAREE, H. E., W. L. MARSHALL & R. D. LANTHIER. 1979. Deviant sexual arousal in rapists. Behav. Res. Ther. **17:** 215-222.
12. EARLS, C. M. & J. PROULX. 1986. The differentiation of francophone rapists and nonrapists using penile circumference measures. Crim. Justice Behav. **13:** 419-429.
13. HINTON, J. W., T. M. O'NEILL & S. WEBSTER. 1980. Psychophysiological assessment of sex offenders in a security hospital. Arch. Sex. Behav. **9:** 205-216.
14. QUINSEY, V. L. & T. C. CHAPLIN. 1984. Stimulus control of rapists' and non-sex offenders' sexual arousal. Behav. Assess. **6:** 169-176.
15. QUINSEY, V. L., T. C. CHAPLIN & D. UPFOLD. 1984. Sexual arousal to nonsexual violence and sadomasochistic themes among rapists and non-sex-offenders. J. Consult. Clin. Psychol. **52:** 651-657.
16. QUINSEY, V. L., T. C. CHAPLIN & G. VARNEY. 1981. A comparison of rapists and non-sex-offenders' sexual preferences for mutually consenting sex, rape, and physical abuse of women. Behav. Assess. **3:** 127-135.
17. ROSEN, R. C. & F. J. KEEFE. 1978. The measurement of human penile tumescence. Psychophysiology **15:** 366-376.
18. EARLS, C. M. & W. L. MARSHALL. 1983. The current state of technology in the laboratory assessment of sexual arousal patterns. *In* The Sexual Aggressor: Current Perspectives on Treatment. J. G. Greer & J. R. Stuart, Eds.: 336-362. Van Nostrand Reinhold. New York, NY.
19. MARSHALL, W. L. & H. E. BARBAREE. 1984. A behavioral view of rape. Int. J. Law Psychiatry. **7:** 51-77.
20. WYDRA, A., W. L. MARSHALL, C. M. EARLS & H. E. BARBAREE. 1983. Identification of cues and control of sexual arousal by rapists. Behav. Res. Ther. **21:** 469-476.
21. ABEL, G. G., E. B. BLANCHARD, J. V. BECKER & A. DJENDEREDJIAN. 1978. Differentiating sexual aggressives with penile measures. Crim. Justice Behav. **5:** 315-332.
22. BAXTER, D. J., W. L. MARSHALL, H. E. BARBAREE, P. R. DAVIDSON & P. B. MALCOLM. 1984. Differentiating sex offenders by criminal history, psychometric measures, and sexual response. Crim. Justice Behav. **11:** 477-501.
23. MURPHY, W. D., J. KRISAK, S. STALGAITIS & K. ANDERSON. 1984. The use of penile tumescence measures with incarcerated rapists: Further validity issues. Arch. Sex. Behav. **13:** 545-554.

24. ABEL, G. G., D. H. BARLOW, E. P. BLANCHARD & M. MAVISSAKALIAN. 1975. Measurement of sexual arousal in male homosexuals: Effects of instruction & stimulus modality. Arch. Sex. Behav. **4:** 623-629.
25. QUINSEY, V. L. & T. C. CHAPLIN. 1982. Penile responses to non sexual violence among rapists. Crim. Justice Behav. **9:** 372-381.
26. ABEL, G. G., J. V. BECKER, W. D. MURPHY & B. FLANAGAN. 1981. Identifying dangerous child molesters. *In* Violent Behavior: Social Learning Approaches to Prediction, Management, and Treatment. R. B. Stuart, Ed.: 116-137. Brunner/Mazel. New York, NY.
27. AVERY-CLARK, C. A. & D. R. LAWS. 1984. Differential erection response patterns of sexual child abusers to stimuli describing activities with children. Behav. Ther. **15:** 71-83.
28. ABEL, G. G., J. V. BECKER, J. CUNNINGHAM-RATHNER, J. L. ROULEAU, M. KAPLEN & J. REICH. 1984. The Treatment of Child Molesters. Department of Psychiatry, Emory University School of Medicine. Atlanta, GA.
29. FARRALL, W. 1986. A proposal for guidelines for phallometric and plethysmographic assessment. Presented at the Florida Mental Health Institute Conference on the Assessment and Treatment of Sex Offenders, Tampa, Florida, February 1986.
30. FARRALL, W. & R. D. CARD. 1987. Advancements in physiological evaluation of assessment and treatment of the sexual offender. Ann. N.Y. Acad. Sci. This volume.
31. CAMPBELL, D. T. & J. C. STANLEY. 1963. Experimental and Quasi-experimental Designs for Research. Rand McNally. Chicago, IL.
32. EARLS, C. M. & V. L. QUINSEY. 1985. What is to be done? Future research on the assessment and behavioral treatment of sex offenders. Behav. Sci. Law **3:** 377-390.
33. NEWMAN, H. F. & J. D. NORTHUP. 1981. Mechanisms of human penile erection: An overview. Urology **17:** 399-408.
34. MARSHALL, W. L. 1986. Personal communication.
35. QUINSEY, V. L. & T. C. CHAPLIN. 1987. Preventing faking in phallometric assessments of sexual preference. Ann. N.Y. Acad. Sci. This volume.
36. EARLS, C. M., V. L. QUINSEY & L. G. CASTONGUAY. 1987. A comparison of three methods of scoring penile circumference changes. Arch. Sexual Behav. **6:** 493-500.

Preventing Faking in Phallometric Assessments of Sexual Preference

VERNON L. QUINSEY [a] AND TERRY C. CHAPLIN

Mental Health Centre
Penetanguishene, Ontario, L0K 1P0, Canada

The measurement of penile responses to various sexually relevant stimuli has become a widely accepted method of determining the direction of male sexual interest.[1] It has been employed in many studies to determine preferred partner gender, preferred partner age, and degree of interest in coercive or sadistic sexual activities. Despite this wide and growing acceptance, however, it has been known for many years that some men can fake phallometric assessments of sexual preference; that is, to indicate that they prefer certain sorts of sexual partners or activities when their sexual histories provide strong evidence that they do not. Concern about the issue of sexual response faking has spawned a variety of strategies to minimize its effects or to eliminate it.

There have been a large number of studies that indicate that at least some (but certainly not all) men can both inhibit and enhance their penile responses to various stimuli in accord with instruction under various conditions.[2–13] Although some of these studies have attempted to prevent penile response faking through the use of brief stimuli, trying various modalities of stimulus presentation, or the use of "priming" techniques (in which a stimulus that is preferred or said to be preferred by the subject is presented immediately before the stimulus of interest), none have been completely successful in eliminating instructional control or in preventing faking by motivated subjects.

The present study is a continuation of a line of research on the faking problem that was begun very early. Laws and Rubin[14] reasoned that, if penile tumescence changes are partly "voluntary," subjects should be able to modify their responses in accord with instructions. Normal subjects were shown several ten-minute erotic films and were required to press a button when a light appeared at irregular intervals at the top or bottom of the viewing screen in order to ensure attention to the screen. Subjects were able to inhibit their responses to the films, and this inhibition was not due to fatigue or boredom with the film; they reported engaging in competitive cognitive tasks, such as mental arithmetic, to accomplish this inhibition. Subjects were less successful in developing and maintaining an erection when instructed to do so in the absence of any erotic stimulus.

Henson and Rubin[15] observed that there was no guarantee in the above study that subjects actually attended to the relevant aspects of the stimulus; indeed, subjects reported using distracting cognitive tasks in order to prevent an erection. To circumvent this problem, Henson and Rubin required subjects to describe the activity on the film as the film was played. As in the first study, a ten-minute film was shown repeatedly.

[a] Address for correspondence: Dr. V.L. Quinsey, Research Department, Mental Health Centre, Penetanguishene, Ontario, L0K 1P0, Canada.

The conditions were: normal instructions (with the light vigilance task), inhibit instructions (with light), inhibit and describe instructions (without light), normal and describe instructions (without light), and normal instructions (with light). Briefly, the subjects could inhibit their erectile responses whenever asked. Neither the subjects nor the experimenters could explain how this inhibition was accomplished when the subjects were required to describe the story. In addition, observers could not differentiate between audiotapes of the subjects' descriptions generated in the inhibit and the noninhibit instructional conditions.

The investigators hypothesized that the "verbal description might have functioned as a competing behavior that resulted in reduction of penile erection." This hypothesis received some support in that the description task resulted in diminished erections even without inhibit instructions. Subsequently, it has been found that the amount of erection elicited by an erotic audiotape declines with the difficulty of a competing cognitive task. [16]

The above two studies indicate that the penile response is voluntary in the sense that it can be brought under instructional (or self-instructional) control. However, the reflexive link between erotic stimuli—if attended to—and penile tumescence has never been questioned. Subjects who intentionally influence their penile responses apparently do so by not attending to or not processing the erotic material that is presented to them, focusing their attention elsewhere. In order to prevent such intentional influence, therefore, it is necessary to ensure that the subject processes only the relevant information that is presented. It is clearly insufficient to ensure that the subject looks in the direction of a visual stimulus or attends to possibly irrelevant aspects of an auditory or visual stimulus and not to its sexual meaning. Unfortunately, it is not clear, even in the Henson and Rubin study,[15] that subjects attended only to the sexual aspects of the stimulus; we know only that the subjects instructed to inhibit described the general activity shown on the film and that this description was not differentiable from that given by subjects who were not instructed to inhibit.

The approach taken in the present experiment was to examine instructional control in the context of a semantic task (c.f. References 17-19) of pressing a button during an auditory stimulus presentation whenever sexual material was described and a second button whenever violence was described (both buttons were to be pressed when violent sexual behavior was described). This kind of task ensures that, in order to be accurate, subjects must attend to the critical dimensions of the stimulus as they must process the very stimulus dimensions to which sexual arousal is to be measured. In addition, it was expected that the task would not be distracting since it involved focusing on the relevant stimulus dimensions and indicating this focus with a very simple motor response.

METHOD

Subjects

Fifteen male subjects were recruited from the local community through newspaper advertisements. They were paid a minimum of ten dollars per session for four sessions. None of these subjects had been tested in our laboratory before, and none admitted to previous convictions or sexual offences. One maximum security psychiatric institution patient with a history of economic offences was also recruited. The subjects' average age was 24.88 years (SD = 5.69). Four of the subjects were fully employed, 4 were employed part-time, and 8 were unemployed. They had completed an average of 12.13 (SD = 2.75) years of education.

Apparatus

The Sexual Behavior Laboratory was located at the end of a maximum-security psychiatric ward. Within the laboratory, subjects were seated in a reclining chair located in a sound-attenuated and electrically shielded room equipped with a one-way mirror and intercom. Penile responses were measured using a mercury-in-rubber strain gauge that the subject fitted on the shaft of his penis. The closed-loop gauge was periodically calibrated, and the relationship between circumference and deflection was found to be linear within the working limits of the gauge. The leads from the gauge were connected to a Parks Electronics Model 270 Plethysmograph. Penile responses were recorded at two levels of amplification on a Beckman R511A Dynograph; as well, penile responses were monitored on a digital voltmeter. Auditory stimuli were presented by a programmable tape recorder through a speaker in the subject's chamber. All programming and recording equipment (except the plethysmograph) was located outside the subject's chamber.

When the subject was seated and the gauge was in place, a plywood sheet was placed over the arms of the reclining chair so that the subject could neither see nor manipulate his penis. One button was located at the right side and another at the left side of the board.

Stimuli

The stimuli employed by Quinsey, Chaplin, and Varney[20] were used in the present study because we have had the most experience using this assessment tape with rapists, and the stimuli discriminate non-sex offenders from rapists quite well.

There were 18 stimuli in this set, each narrated by a male in the first person, present tense, and describing some interaction with an adult female. The stimuli averaged 100 sec in duration and were presented in a fixed random order, with the restriction that no more than two stimuli from the same category could be immediately adjacent. There were 4 categories of story: 3 neutral stimuli (involving a nonsexual interaction between a male and female), 5 consenting sex stimuli (explicit descriptions of sexual activity), 5 rape stories (involving brutal, forced sex with physical violence), and 5 nonsexual violence stories describing extremely violent mugging scenes. These stories are described in more detail by Quinsey, Chaplin, and Varney.[20]

Procedure

Each subject participated in four sessions held on separate days. In each session the stimuli were the same. The first 8 subjects received the following sequence of sessions: normal, fake, fake with buttons, and normal. The second 8 received a different sequence: normal, normal with buttons, fake, and fake with buttons. The sessions differed in one or both of two ways. First, they could differ as to whether normal or fake sets were given. To induce the normal set, a subject was instructed to relax, listen to the stimuli, and pretend that he was the person "saying it." These are the standard and vague instructions used in our laboratory (e.g., References 20 and 21).

To induce the fake set, subjects were instructed to appear as if they were sexually interested in rape and in nonsexual violence but not consenting sexual activity. Based upon the faking literature and our previous research, subjects were given some advice about how this faking might best be accomplished, although they were free to invent their own techniques if they wished. Thus, subjects were advised that they could think about something else when the stimulus was presented (sexually exciting or not, depending on whether they were trying to indicate arousal or not) or to concentrate only on sexually interesting or uninteresting aspects of the stimulus story.

Subjects were instructed before each session in which they were asked to fake preferences that they would be paid double for that session if they were successful.

The second way in which the sessions could differ was in whether the semantic tracking task was used. In the tracking task the subject was instructed to depress the right button (marked "S") whenever sexual activity was occurring in the story and the left button (marked "V") whenever violence was being described. Thus, neither, one, or both buttons could be pressed at a given time.

Only subjects who showed normal preferences (specifically, lower responses to the neutral category than to any of the sexual story categories and a rape index[20] of less than .85) and who produced a reasonable magnitude of response to the consenting sexual category in the first session were included in the study. Six other subjects did not meet these criteria.

Treatment of the Data

Penile data were analyzed in the form of raw scores (mm circumference change from story onset to the largest reading in the period from 2 sec after story onset to 30 sec after the story finished) and Z scores. The Z scores were calculated for each subject and for each session separately, based on the 18 responses for that session. As the results were essentially the same for both types of scores, only the Z scores are reported on in the principal analyses. The raw data did, however, indicate that there was no great decrease in overall responsiveness with repeated assessments or with the semantic tracking task. Among the first 8 subjects' raw scores there was no significant difference between the first and last session ($F(1,7) = 4.40$, $p < .10$) and no difference between sessions 1 and 2 for the second group of subjects ($F(1,7) = 2.25$, $p > .10$). Finally, for the entire group of subjects there were no differences among sessions in the raw scores when the normal instructions, fake, and fake with buttons conditions were compared ($F(2,30) = 1.46$, $p > .10$).

Prior to the principal analyses of variance, the two normal sessions for the first 8 subjects and the normal and normal-with-buttons sessions for the second 8 subjects were compared. The variables in these analyses were session and stimulus category; no simple effect of session was possible because of the Z-score transformation. Among the data from the first 8 subjects there was a large stimulus category effect ($F(3,21) = 193.24$, $p < .001$) and no significant interaction. The analysis comparing the normal instructions with and without the tracking task (for the second group of subjects) yielded a large stimulus category effect (F (3,21) = 115.07, $p < .001$) and no session by stimulus category interaction. As these analyses indicated no differences between the sessions with normal instructions, these sessions were averaged for each subject. A repeated-measures analysis of variance was then computed for all 16 subjects using the variables session type (normal, fake, and fake with buttons) and stimulus category (neutral, consenting sex, rape, and nonsexual violence).

Four Wilcoxon Signed Ranks tests were computed for each subject separately. These tests employed Z scores and compared: (a) the first normal session with the last normal session for the first group of subjects and the first normal session with the second normal-with-buttons session for the second group; (b) the first normal session with the fake session; (c) the first normal session with the fake-with-buttons session; and (d) the fake session with the fake-with-buttons session. In these analyses the neutral stimuli were discarded, and the sign of change for the rape and nonsexual violence categories were reversed so that a faking change, if present, was in the same direction for all of the categories. A one-tailed test of significance at the .025 level was employed, because our laboratory uses this criterion for deciding whether a patient has successfully modified his phallometric responses during treatment.

The accuracy of subject tracking was evaluated by comparing it to the performance of 4 external male raters who completed the tracking task without undergoing penile plethysmography. Raters were carefully instructed and were allowed to listen to the tape as often as required. A template was constructed by marking "sex" or "violence" as occurring in the tapes whenever at least 2 raters indicated it was present. In order to calculate kappa coefficients, each second of each stimulus (excluding neutrals) was included as an observation for a given session. Violence was not scored for the consenting sex scenarios.

RESULTS

The principal results are shown in FIGURE 1. As can be seen in the figure, the two groups exhibited normal preferences during all nonfake sessions, were able to successfully fake preference for rape, and could increase their responses to nonsexual violence when there was no semantic task. The semantic task prevented faking. These effects are shown more clearly in the combined data of FIGURE 2.

The analyses of variance confirmed these visual impressions. There were significant effects for stimulus category (F (3,45) = 59.93, $p < .001$) and stimulus category by session (F (6.90) = 67.14, $p < .001$). Planned contrasts showed that subjects responded differently in the fake session than in the normal session for the consenting-sex (F (1,90) = 224.10, $p < .001$), rape (F (1,90) = 51.78, $p < .001$), and nonsexual-violence categories (F (1,90) = 61.74, $p < .001$). The fake session also produced responses different from those of the fake-with-button session for consenting sex (F (1,90) = 143.82, $p < .001$), rape (F (1,90) = 49.42, $p < .001$), and nonsexual violence (F (1,90) = 24.63, $p < .001$). The normal and fake-with-buttons sessions were not significantly different for the rape category (F < 1) but showed significant, although relatively small effects for the consenting sex (F (1,90) = 8.87, $p < .005$) and nonsexual violence categories (F (1,90) = 8.38, $p < .01$).

Of course, the data of individual subjects are of greater concern in actual clinical work. Wilcoxon Signed Ranks tests on individual subjects provide detailed support for the inferences drawn from the analyses of variance. There were no significant

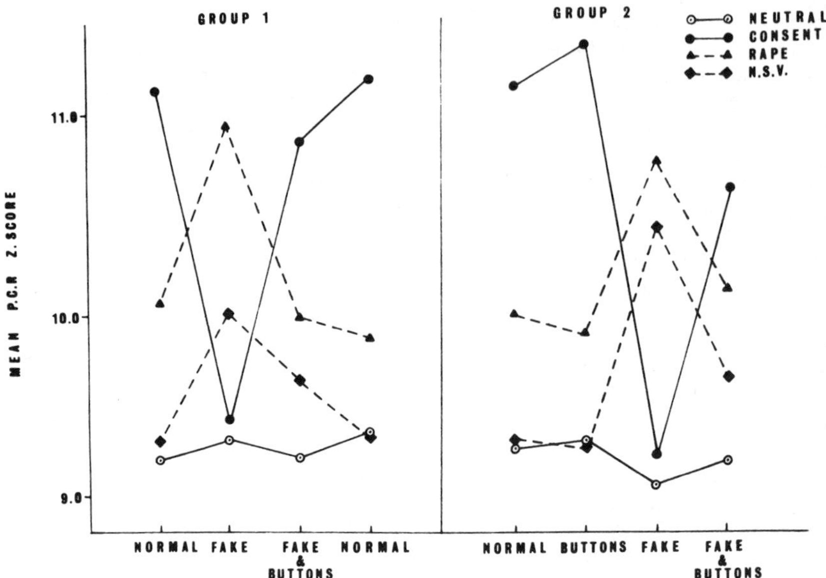

FIGURE 1. Mean penile circumference Z scores as a function of stimulus category and session for each group.

differences among the sessions with normal instructions for any of the subjects. Although 15 of the 16 subjects significantly altered their responses in the fake condition (p's $< .05$), only 2 subjects in the second group succeeded in the fake-with-button session. The fake-with-buttons condition was significantly different from the fake session for 14 of the subjects. In summary, 12 of the 16 subjects were perfect: they each exhibited significant differences neither between the 2 normal instruction sessions nor between the normal and fake-with-buttons conditions, but did show significant differences between the normal and fake conditions and between the fake and fake-with-buttons conditions.

The subjects who could, or could almost, fake with the semantic task are of particular interest. Two subjects in the first group successfully earned their extra ten dollars in the fake-with-buttons condition (all subjects earned this money in the fake condition without the semantic task). For Subject 7 the shift was marginally significant with a Wilcoxon Signed Ranks test ($t = 26$, $n = 15$, $p < .05$, 1-tailed, as it was for Subject 8 ($t = 30$, $n = 15$, $p = .05$, 1-tailed). However, Subjects 12 and 15 in the second sequence significantly and clearly altered their responses during the fake-with-buttons session ($t = 3$, $n = 15$, $p < .001$ and $t = 12$, $n = 15$, $p < .005$, respectively, both 1-sided).

Subjects were asked to describe their strategies at the end of each faking session. During the faking sessions without the tracking task, all subjects reported using the suggested strategy of substituting their own fantasies for the auditory material; none of the subjects reported any difficulty in discriminating among the stimulus categories. All subjects reported that it was very difficult to fantasize about something else when required to press the buttons in order to track the stimulus content. The reports of the subjects who succeeded or nearly succeeded in faking during the fake-with-buttons session are illuminating. Subject 7 stated that he found a small nail on the board that the buttons were on and jammed his finger into to it in order to "turn himself off" when the consenting sex stories were presented and that he concentrated on the sexual aspects of the rape stories in order to generate sexual arousal. Subject 8 commented that, although it was more difficult to fake when required to track the stimulus content, he was able to perform the task because he was trained as a pilot and was used to doing two things at once. Subject 12 memorized the stories (note that for the second group of subjects, the fake-with-buttons session was last), so that he knew when to press the buttons without having to attend very closely. Subject 15 also used a similar strategy, reporting that, since he knew "what was coming," he could block out the story. Based on the differential effectiveness of these 4 subjects, memorization of the stimulus material appears to be the best strategy; none of the other subjects reported using memorization to try to counteract the tracking task.

The analysis of the agreement data for the tracking task is hindered by missing data caused by the intermittent failure of the polygraph pen used to monitor the violence theme. Nevertheless, these preliminary data indicate that subjects showed modest but better agreement with the rater template in tracking the sex than in tracking the violence theme. There was no diminution of accuracy in the fake as opposed to the nonfake condition. The average kappas were as follows: Group 2, session 2 (nonfake instructions), K (sex) = .56, range .46 - .63, n = 8, and K (violence) = .37, range .34 - 43, n = 3; Group 1, session 3 (fake instructions), K (sex) = .49, range .27 - .63, n = 7, and K (violence) = .29, range .18 - .39, n = 5; Group 2, session 4 (fake instructions), K (sex) = .55, range .33 - .67, n = 8, and K (violence) = .33, range .16 - .47, n = 3. Of the two subjects who could successfully fake, Subject 12 showed as good agreement on both sex and violence in the fake as in the nonfake condition; Subject 15, however, showed a marked decrease in agreement for the sex theme under the fake condition (.63 to .33); no data were available for this subject on the violence theme because of pen failure.

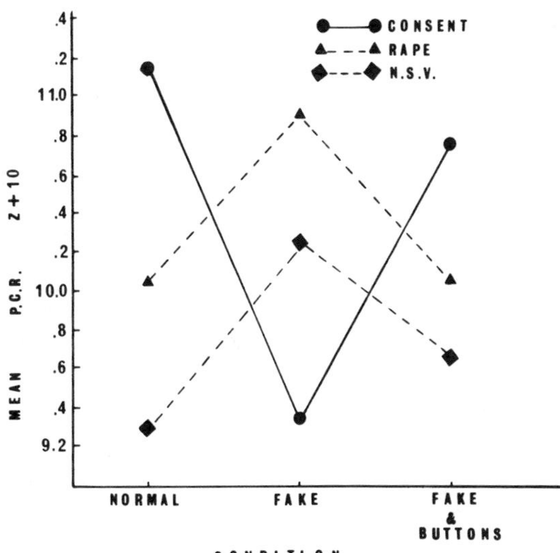

FIGURE 2. Mean penile circumference Z scores as a function of stimulus category and condition for both groups combined.

DISCUSSION

One of the most striking results of this study is how well subjects could fake an ordinary sexual preference assessment when given the expectation that they could do so and some advice about strategy. In our earlier faking research[8,9] we gave our normal subjects no advice or expectations, and a substantial proportion of them did not fake successfully. The present results do not, of course, necessarily mean that paraphiliacs can produce a particular sexual preference profile at will, but they do indicate that subject naiveté might be related to more accurate results. Accuracy in this context is usually assessed by agreement with the subjects's sexual history. Clearly, however, paraphiliacs cannot always control their penile responses in phallometric assessment. As part of treatment efforts in our laboratory, even though rapists and child molesters are instructed to control their penile responses to visual stimuli and are given biofeedback in order to help them, few patients are successful with biofeedback alone.[22] In addition, it is very common for pedophiles to deny any sexual interest in children but to exhibit plainly such a preference in phallometeric testing (e.g., see Reference 23). Nevertheless, even though there is some reason to believe that paraphiliacs might have more difficulty than normals in faking their preferences, at least in the case of pedophiles tested with visual stimuli, the exquisite instructional control exhibited by these normal subjects raises grave questions about the accuracy of phallometric assessments of individuals who are highly motivated to fake and are housed in institutions where knowledge of faking strategies is widespread. Some patients from our institution have in fact been advised by other patients to adopt the strategies we coached our subjects to adopt in the present study. It is for this reason that most of our phallometric research is based on subjects new to the institution.

The semantic tracking task appears to be a promising method for minimizing the effects of faking in phallometric assessments of sexual preference that employ audiotaped stimuli. Presumably, it was more effective than the ongoing description of the stimuli employed by Henson and Rubin[15] because the button pressing task is less effortful and focuses the subject's attention on the critical elements of the stimulus. While this approach requires extensive further testing and validation on paraphiliacs, the possible development of a method to prevent faking raises a number of ethical and theoretical questions.

One of the ethical questions has to do with the danger that sexual behavior laboratories will become more policelike in their functioning. While most person who perform phallometric assessments prefer to use them for research and treatment, there is pressure from others who, understandably, want assistance in making dispositional decisions relating to community security. The potential development of a fakeproof sexual preference assessment would undoubtedly increase this pressure.

To turn to theoretical issues, while nobody believes that penile tumescence *is* male sexual arousal or that relative penile responsiveness to sexual cues constitutes sexual preference, the discriminative power and face validity of phallometric technology make it easy to forget these distinctions, particularly inasmuch as paraphiliacs' reports of their sexual preferences are much more likely to be at variance with their actual histories of sexual behavior than are the results of phallometric assessments. The distinction between the phallometric measure of sexual preference and the psychological construct of sexual preference itself is of paramount importance in interpreting changes in sexual preference, reflected by penile measurements, that are occasioned by behavioral treatments. The question of whether these treatment-induced changes are due to faking can profitably be considered in this context. Of course, in order to conclude that treatment-produced changes are due to faking, one would have to demonstrate that the client consciously set out to deceive the therapist. I rather doubt that this is invariably the case, although it certainly occurs. Nevertheless, the stimulus control acquired during behavioral treatment and that exerted by subjects in faking studies may well be very similar. According to this view, clients who improve as a result of a behavioral intervention should not demonstrate this improvement in phallometric assessments that employ a semantic tracking task.

Whether the acquisition of appropriate stimulus control via behavioral intervention is worthwhile, however, cannot be determined by finding out whether it is similar to faking but can be evaluated only through lengthy treatment outcome studies. It could well be that the only difference between faking and treatment lies in whether the client attributes the change to his ability to deceive or his ability to learn. Viewing the acquisition of stimulus control in treatment as similar to that involved in instructional control, however, has a number of merits. First, it means that we view stimulus control as something that the client actively performs. Second, it simplifies the issue of change, because change must be interpreted strictly behaviorally (i.e., its quality is not dependent on how it is produced). And, third, it emphasizes the artificiality of the treatment situation and focuses the therapist on issues of generalization—particularly, teaching the client to exert the control of the inappropriate sexual arousal that he has demonstrated in the laboratory in real-life situations. It could even be that new cognitive-behavioral interventions could be discovered through the investigation of instructional control paradigms.

SUMMARY

This study evaluated a method of preventing sexual preference faking in phallometric assessments employing audiotaped stimuli. The stimuli were stories describing neutral heterosocial interactions, consenting heterosexual activity, rape, and nonsexual violence. Sixteen normal heterosexual males were each tested with ordinary instructions, with fake instructions (i.e., to appear sexually interested in rape and nonsexual violence but not in consenting sex), and with fake instructions while performing a secondary semantic tracking task. The tracking task was to press one button whenever sexual activity was being described and another button whenever violence occurred. This simple task was designed to focus subjects' attention on only the critical elements of the stories. Group data indicated that subjects could fake inappropriate preferences when instructed to do so without the semantic tracking task but could not when the task was required. The implications of these findings for ethical practice and for the theoretical interpretation of phallometric assessment data were discussed.

ACKNOWLEDGMENTS

We wish to thank C. Earls, G. Harris, and M. Rice for their comments on an earlier version of this manuscript.

REFERENCES

1. FREUND, K 1981. Assessment of pedophilia. *In* Adult Sexual Interest in Children. M. Cook & K. Howells, Eds.: 139-179. Academic Press. Toronto.
2. ABEL, G. G., D. H. BARLOW, E. B. BLANCHARD & M. MAVISSAKALIAN. 1975. Measurement of sexual arousal in male homosexuals: the effects of instructions and stimulus modality. Arch. Sexual Behav. **4:** 623-629.
3. ABEL, G. G., BLANCHARD, E. B. & D. H. BARLOW. 1981. Measurement of sexual arousal in several paraphilias: The effects of stimulus modality, instructional set and stimulus content on the objective. Behav. Res. Ther. **19:** 25-33.
4. ALFORD, G. S., D. WEDDING & S. JONES. 1983. Faking "turn-ons" and "turn-offs": the effects of competitory covert imagery on penile tumescence responses to diverse extrinsic sexual stimulus materials. Behav. Modification **7:** 112-125.
5. FREUND, K., S. CHAN & R. COULTHARD. 1979. Phallometric diagnosis with "nonadmitters". Behav. Res. Ther. **17:** 451-457.
6. LAWS, D. R & M. L. HOLMEN. 1978. Sexual response faking by pedophiles. Criminal Justice Behav. **5:** 343-356.
7. MALCOLM, P. B., P. R. DAVIDSON & W. L. MARSHALL. 1985. Control of penile tumescence: the effects of arousal level and stimulus content. Behav. Res. Ther. **23:** 272-280.
8. QUINSEY, V. L. & S. G., BERGERSEN. 1976. Instructional control of penile circumference in assessments of sexual preference. Behav. Ther. **7:** 489-493.
9. QUINSEY, V. L. & W. F. CARRIGAN. 1978. Penile responses to visual stimuli: Instructional control with and without auditory sexual fantasy correlates. Criminal Justice Behav. **5:** 333-341.
10. ROSEN, R. C. 1973. Suppression of penile tumescence by instrumental conditioning. Psychosom. Med. **35:** 509-513
11. ROSEN, R. C., D. SHAPIRO & G. E. SCHWARTZ. 1975. Voluntary control of penile tumescence. Psychosom. Med. **37:** 479-483.
12. RUBIN, H. B. & D. E. HENSON. 1975. Voluntary enhancement of penile erection. Bull. Psychon. Soc. **6:** 158-160.
13. WYDRA, A., W. L. MARSHALL, C. M. EARLS & H. E. BARBAREE. 1983. Identification of cues and control of sexual arousal by rapists. Behav. Res. Ther. **21:** 469-476.
14. LAWS, D. R. & H. B. RUBIN. 1969. Instructional control of an autonomic sexual response, J. Appl. Behav. Anal. **2:** 93-99.
15. HENSON, D. E. & H. B. RUBIN. 1971. Voluntary control of eroticism. J. Appl. Behav. Anal. **4:** 37-44.
16. GEER, J. H. & R. FUHR. 1976. Cognitive factors in sexual arousal: the role of distraction. J. Consult. Clin. Psychol. **44:** 238-243.
17. HYDE, T. S. & J. J. JENKINS. 1973. Recall for words as a function of semantic, graphic, and syntactic orienting tasks. J. of Verbal Learn. Verbal Behav. **12:** 471-480.
18. MATHEWS, R. C. 1977. Semantic judgments as encoding operations: The effects of attention to particular semantic categories on the usefulness of interitem relations in recall. J. of Experimental Psychology: Hum. Learn. Mem. **3:** 160-173.
19. TULVING, E. 1972. Episodic and semantic memory. *In* Organization of Memory. E. Tulving & W. Donaldson, Ed.: 381-403. Academic Press. New York, NY.
20. QUINSEY, V. L., T. C. CHAPLIN & G. W. VARNEY. 1981. A comparison of rapists' and non-sex offenders' sexual preferences for mutually consenting sex, rape, and physical abuse of women. Behav. Assessment **3:** 127-135.
21. QUINSEY, V. L., T. C. CHAPLIN & D. UPFOLD. 1984. Sexual arousal to nonsexual violence and sadomasochistic themes among rapists and non-sex-offenders. J. Consult. Clin. Psychol. **4:** 651-657.
22. QUINSEY, V. L., T. C. CHAPLIN & W. F. CARRIGAN. 1980. Biofeedback and signaled punishment in the modification of inappropriate sexual age preferences. Behav. Ther. **11:** 567-576.
23. QUINSEY, V. L., C. M. STEINMAN, S. G. BERGERSEN & T. F. HOLMES. 1975. Penile circumference, skin conductance, and ranking responses of child molesters and "normals" to sexual and nonsexual visual stimuli. Behav. Ther. **6:** 213-219.

Clinical Reflections on Sexual Aggression

EUGENE REVITCH [a]

Robert Wood Johnson Medical School
Piscataway, New Jersey 08854

LOUIS B. SCHLESINGER

University of Medicine and Dentistry of New Jersey
Newark, New Jersey 07103

Most sexual offenses are nonviolent and noncoital. Out of the first 1,206 cases examined at the New Jersey State Diagnostic Center, only 110 used force,[1] and only 4.5% of the sample were rapists. Groth and Birnbaum[2] and Groth and Hobson[3] conceptualized rape as a sexual expression of aggression rather than the aggressive expression of sexuality. They divided rape into three categories, based on the underlying emotions fueling the act: (1) anger rape, (2) power rape, and (3) sadistic rape. These concepts may apply to all types of sexual violence. Groth and Burgess[4] found a prevalence of erectile and ejaculatory dysfunctions in the rapist, and such dysfunctions were found to be more frequent in the rapist than in the general population. In our experience, rapists admit to an absence of sexual excitement or sexual satisfaction during the act of rape. Seventy-five percent of Groth and Burgess's[4] victims sustained genital and bodily injury. All of this supports the role of aggression rather than sexual satisfaction in sexual violence.

Sexually motivated burglaries[5,6] may end with attacks on, or even murder of, female occupants. Banay[7] mentioned burglars who achieve orgasm as they enter the premises in breaking through the window or door. A 12-year-old boy with a history of break-ins revealed under the influence of sodium amobarbital (amytal) that he hoped to see a "naked lady" in the house. His burglaries continued into young adulthood. Some burglars defecate and urinate on the premises or vandalize the house. Voyeuristic impulses are common and are expressed directly through peeping through the windows, or indirectly through exploring the premises and contents of the drawers with a strong feeling of curiosity. A notorious case is that of William Heirens,[8] who

[Editors' Note: The contributions of Dr. Revitch to the clinical literature on sexual aggression are well known. His writings, along with those of his colleague Dr. Schlesinger, have provided fertile ground for the development of theory and the generation of hypotheses. Accordingly, we have asked Drs. Revitch and Schlesinger to provide some brief comments on issues of concern to them. In particular, we asked them to highlight areas of importance that have been neglected in the research literature.—R. A. P. and V. L. Q.]

[a] Address for correspondence: Eugene Revitch, M.D., 40 Stephenville Parkway, Edison, New Jersey 08820.

had a history of breaking into homes since the age of nine. At the age of 17, he killed two women on separate occasions, and his rampage ended with abducting a 6-year-old girl from her home, killing her, and dismembering the body. A 37-year-old man broke into several homes, where he attacked and raped, or attempted to rape, several elderly women just one month after his release from prison, where he had served a long sentence for burglaries. A 42-year-old man who spent half his life in various prisons because of repeated burglaries stated in a light hypnotic trance that on one occasion, for no apparent reason, he followed a woman on the street and hit her on the head with a stick. This man revealed a strong hatred for cats, which he tortured and threw into flames while experiencing a feeling of triumph and euphoria. He compared cats with women in their looks and action. The cat is a female symbol, and we found extreme abuse of cats in many violent sex offenders.

Not all sexual assaults openly display a sexual component. The sexual aspect of the assault is covert in many cases, and the offense is usually perceived as a crime for monetary gain. Some cases of purse snatching as well as burglary belong to this category. Valuables are misappropriated in order to justify and provide a logical reason for the offense. The sexual underpinnings of the cases described above are obvious. In the following case, the sexual dynamics are much more covert: A 30-year-old male with a history of purse snatching since childhood was referred to us for therapy by a private psychiatric hospital. He was married, had a well-paying job, and was the proud father of a baby son. He was doing well for the three years in psychotherapy, but then, on one occasion, he admitted that he had to force himself to leave a department store where he noticed a woman's purse on the counter. A month or so later he attacked three woman while on the way home from his job. He threw them violently to the ground and forcibly took their purses. This took place just after he received an unfriendly letter from his mother. Confused relationships with mother are commonly seen in the violent male sex offender, particularly in sex murderers. Mothers are seen as either rejecting or overprotective and seductive. The cases of adult burglars mentioned above reportedly had rejecting and hostile mothers. In fact, the 42-year-old man started killing cats after severing all ties with his mother.

The consensus is that the prognosis of violence, in general, is tenuous and unreliable. Stone[9] considered most cases of violence as being situational and therefore not easily predictable. The psychiatric diagnosis per se rarely explains the offense, and a "good" psychiatric diagnosis does not mean a good prognosis in terms of reoffense. For this reason, we[10,11] elaborated a system of classification of antisocial activities based on a motivational spectrum of stimuli ranging from purely exogenous to purely endogenous forces leading to the commission of the offense. The spectrum is divided into: (1) environmental-sociogenic, (2) situational, (3) impulsive, (4) catathymic, and (5) compulsive. Sexual violence may occur in all the categories. Rapes by soldiers during war, for example, are due generally to environmental stimuli more than to psychopathology. Of interest to us are catathymic and compulsive cases of sexual aggression.

The concept of catathymic crisis was introduced into the psychiatric aspects of criminology by Wertham.[12] He defined catathymic crisis as "the transformation of the stream of thought as the result of certain complexes of ideas that are charged with a strong affect, usually a wish, a fear or an ambivalent striving" (p. 975). Catathymic crisis occurs within a relationship to another person, usually a boyfriend or girlfriend, although there are other combinations that are of less interest to our present concern with sexual violence. The relationship itself disrupts the psychic homeostatis of the future offender through stimulating underlying homosexual and/or incestuous reminiscences or fantasies. A state of depression often develops—with confused feelings about the relationship and suicidal ideas (later mixed with fantasies of killing the future victim)—which finally results in homicide and the relief of the accumulated tension. In compulsive homicides, situational influences are less prominent. Eventually, in serial killings committed under the pressure of the compulsion, a victim is sought out, and the situational component plays almost no role. These are the most dangerous offenders; and offenses of a similar nature may be repeated after years of imprisonment. A man who murdered and mutilated the body of a 15-year-old girl attacked another woman while on parole, following the commutation of his sentence after 15 years on death row. In another of our cases, a 40-year-old man stalked and killed two young women, mutilated the body of one, and performed necrophilia with the other. He had previously served many years in prison for two other murders of women.

In this paper we attempted to review briefly some of the variety of sexual aggression that we have experienced clinically. This experience suggests that distinctions among sexual offenders that are based only on manifest behavior may well be misleading. As Groth[2] has indicated, and we agree, rape is a sexual expression of underlying aggression, rather than an aggressive expression of sexuality. Other types of offenses that on the surface do not appear sexually motivated, such as certain cases of break-in, purse snatching, or apparently nonsexual, physical attacks on women, such as choking, hitting with a stick, or knifing, may also have serious sexual underpinnings. The covert sexual aspect of these crimes is usually unrecognized, and the offenders are treated as nonsexual offenders; while aggressive sexual fantasies and other important historical information, such as mistreating animals (particularly cats) remain unexplored. It is critical in creating classifications of sexual offenders that these underlying motivations be explored and taken into account.

REFERENCES

1. BRANCALE, R., D. MCNEIL & A. VUOCOLO. 1965. A profile of the New Jersey sex offender: a statistical study of 1206 male sex offenders. Welfare Rep. **16:** 3-9.
2. GROTH, A. N. & H. J. BIRNBAUM. 1979. Men Who Rape: The Psychology of the Offender. Pergamon Press. New York, NY.
3. GROTH, A. N. & W. F. HOBSON. 1983. The dynamics of sexual assault. *In* Sexual Dynamics of Anti-Social Behavior. L. B. Schlesinger & E. Revitch, Eds.: 159-172. Charles C. Thomas Publisher. Springfield, IL.
4. GROTH, A. N. & A. W. BURGESS. 1977. Sexual dysfunction during rape. N. Engl. J. Med. **27:** 764-766.
5. REVITCH, E. 1978. Sexually motivated burglaries. Bull. Am. Acad. Psychol. Law **6:** 277-283.
6. REVITCH, E. 1983. Burglaries with sexual dynamics. *In* Sexual Dynamics of Anti-Social Behavior. L. B. Schlesinger & E. Revitch, Eds.: 173-191. Charles C. Thomas Publisher. Springfield, IL.
7. BANAY, R. S. 1969. Unconscious motivation in crime. Med. Aspects Hum. Sexuality **3:** 91-102.
8. FREEMAN, L. 1956. Catch me before I kill more. Pocket Books. New York, NY.
9. STONE, A. A. 1985. The legal standards of dangerousness for injury and practice. *In* Dangerousness. E. D. Webster, M. H. Ben Aron & S. J. Hicks, Eds. Cambridge University Press. Cambridge University Press. Cambridge, MA.
10. REVITCH, E. 1977. Classification of offenders for prognostic and dispositional evaluation. Bull. Am. Acad. Psychol. Law **5:** 45-50.
11. REVITCH, E. & L. B. SCHLESINGER. 1981. Psychopathology of homicide. Charles C. Thomas Publisher. Springfield, IL.
12. WERTHAM, F. 1937. The catathymic crisis: a clinical entity. Arch. Neurol. Psychiatry **37:** 974-977.

Social and Cross-Cultural Issues: Introduction

MARGARET T. GORDON

*Center for Urban Affairs
and Policy Research
Northwestern University
Evanston, Illinois 60201*

The papers in Part II shift the focus to social and cross-cultural issues in human sexual aggression. While the preceding papers emphasized individual beliefs, attitudes and behaviors, (usually of perpetrators of violence), in this part the focus is on sexual aggression and violence in the context of widespread cultural norms. The studies reported this afternoon offer support for:

- a theory arguing that sexual aggression and violence in the United States are related to a widespread acceptance of legitimate (and even criminal) violence in dealing with a range of problems
- a theory positing connections among sexual aggression, domestic/family violence, street violence, capital punishment, and war
- a policy approach to interventions with offenders that takes into consideration that sexual aggression may be "normal" (rather than "abnormal") behavior because it may be a rational, learned response to cultural norms.

Two papers in Part II report on studies of sexual violence on college campuses in the United States (Sandy and Koss). One takes an epidemiological approach to child molestation and suggests that it may be related to some social and cultural norms of childrearing methods in the United States (Finkelhor). Another focuses on the effects of sexual child abuse on the subsequent sexual functioning of adolescents, and the differences between Afro-American and white women (Wyatt). Another paper looks at the increased variance explained in sexual aggression when both cultural and individual measures are included in analyses of the causes of sexual aggression (Malamuth). A final study uses a "spillover theory" to explain patterns of relationships between acceptance of "legitimate violence" and incidence of rape in the 50 states (Baron). Thus, all the papers illustrate the role of current, accepted social norms and practices in human sexual aggression in the United States.

Although none of the data in the studies reported this afternoon are cross-cultural, they beg us to ask whether the findings would hold if the studies were conducted in other countries with different cultural norms, especially with respect to violence. That is, is there greater incidence of sexual violence of the types examined here in the United States than elsewhere? And, if so, to what extent are our problems of sexual violence the result of the way our country has chosen to organize (socially, economically, and politically); and, conversely, to what extent are they universal problems?

If we believe the United States has special problems of culturally supported sexual violence, further policy questions must be raised about the effectiveness of current prevention and treatment strategies. Policy issues are confronted more specifically later in the volume.

An Epidemiologic Approach to the Study of Child Molestation[a]

DAVID FINKELHOR

Family Research Laboratory
University of New Hampshire
Durham, New Hampshire 03824

I. A. LEWIS

Los Angeles Times Poll
Los Angeles, California 90012

In the last decade, research on sexual assault has increasingly shifted from an orientation that was clinical and criminologic toward one that was epidemiologic. In concrete terms, studies from prisons, police blotters, and hospital emergency rooms have been replaced by surveys. The clinical and criminologic studies have provided and continue to provide rich findings for the field. But there is increasing recognition that samples from prisons, police, and hospitals do not represent the whole picture. Concern has grown about the large quantity of rape, child sexual abuse, and sexual harassment that goes unreported and undetected.

The shift to epidemiologic methods has been matched by a shift to more social psychological concepts. Talk of sociopaths, the criminal personality, pedophilia, sadism, and masochism has given way to talk about rape myths, peer pressure, media exposure, attitudes, and beliefs. The new sense of the scope of the problem has been reflected in a new level of analysis.

As much as the field has changed, however, it has not changed uniformly. The epidemiologic shift has been more advanced in the study of victims than of offenders. For example, there has been a large increase in the number of new victims surveys,[1–4] while efforts to study undetected offenders or rape-prone individuals are still fairly new. And within offender research, the shift has been much less developed in the area of child sexual abuse than in the area of rape. A number of techniques have been developed and refined for gaining self-reports from undetected rapists and many analyses treat rape as a behavior of "ordinary" men;[5–8] but almost no such devices and analyses have been developed for child sexual abusers.

In this paper, we will begin to delineate more of the elements of an epidemiologic and social psychological approach to the problem of child molesting. We will try to show that it may be indeed feasible to look at child molesting in this way. In the first section of paper, we will present a study that illustrates how feasible it may be to

[a]This work was supported by Grants 90CA1155/01 and 90CA1215/01 from the National Center on Child Abuse and Neglect.

gather data on undetected molesters using an epidemiologic approach. In the second part of the paper, we will discuss some possible social-psychological concepts that could be applied to child molestation, focusing particularly on its relationship to normal male socialization.

A NATIONAL SURVEY OF CHILD SEXUAL ABUSERS

The idea that there are a significant number of undetected child molesters in the population at large could be inferred from the data on the prevalence of victimization. Numerous retrospective surveys of the general population suggest that a quarter to a third of all females and a tenth or more of all males were molested during childhood.[9] In the one national survey to date,[10] 22% of all respondents (27% of females and 16% of males) reported such victimization. If the average molester victimizes only 1-4 children, as suggested by a recent study,[11] then a sizeable percentage of the population could conceivably have committed molestations. Although the exact numbers cannot be ascertained, the large number of victims does tend to imply a large number of abusers.

Another indication that significant numbers of the general population may have had sexual contact with children comes from efforts by Freund and colleagues[12] and Malamuth[13] to detect signs of an interest in child molesting among "normal" men. Freund,[14] using slides of naked children, recorded sexual arousal using the plethysmograph in many men with no admitted history of and no expressed preference for sexual contact with children. In his studies, Malamuth has asked ordinary subjects (mostly psychology students), "If you could be assured of not being caught or punished, how likely would you be to engage in pedophilia, that is, sexual activity with a child." Fifteen percent of male subjects indicated at least some likelihood to engage in such behavior. However, it is impossible to extrapolate from such arousal or expressed interest to actual behavior.

This study reports on an attempt to identify child molesters in the general population using self reports with the Randomized Response Technique (RRT).[15,16] Presumably one of the key barriers to gaining self-reports from child molesters is fear of detection and embarrassment. The Randomized Response Technique has been developed to deal with this problem by creating additional anonymity for the respondent beyond that which is usually afforded in a survey situation.

In the most general form of the technique, respondents are presented with two simultaneous questions, a sensitive one and an innocuous one. Some randomizing device (a coin toss or spinner) is used by the respondent to decide which question to answer, without the interviewer knowing which it is. The key to the technique is for the researcher to know the prevalence in the population being studied of the responses to the innocuous question, either from another survey or from archival sources. (Thus the innocuous question could be one like, "Do you own a General Motors car?" or "Is your birthday in June, July, or August?") Since the researcher knows the prevalence of responses to the innocuous question and the overall likelihood the respondent is responding to it (50% in the case of the coin toss), it is possible to calculate the prevalence of responses to the sensitive question.

The RRT is still a highly experimental technique. Questions have been raised about whether respondents understand the instructions, whether it assuages suspicions, or whether its complexity may, in fact, increase them. Although in a half dozen comparison studies RRT obtained generally higher estimates of sensitive behavior than other methods (direct questioning or anonymous questionnaires), in the four true validational studies cited in a recent review,[15] only two found unambiguously superior results for RRT. However, there are a variety of random response techniques, and their effectiveness may differ intrinsically and may also differ according to the population surveyed and question being asked. The utility of the technique is still being explored.

The present study used a variation of the RRT developed by Folsom *et al.*[17] The sample was randomly divided in half. Sample 1 was presented with these two simultaneous questions:

1. Have you ever sexually abused a child at any time in your life, or not?
2. Do you rent the place where you live, or not?

Sample 2 was presented with a different pair:

1. Have you ever sexually abused a child at any time in your life, or not?; and
2. Are you a member of a labor union or a teacher's organization, or not?

In order to know the distribution of the innocuous question in the population, Sample 1 was asked directly the question about union membership at another point in the interview, and Sample 2 was asked directly the question about renting.

These questions were inserted into a survey conducted by the Los Angeles Times Poll in August 1985. The study consisted of half-hour telephone interviews with a probability sample of 2627 Americans 18 years of age or older. The subject of the survey was child sexual abuse—people's attitudes toward the problem, their experiences with the problem, and their recommendations about what should be done. The questionnaire included questions about whether the respondents had been sexually victimized in childhood themselves. The randomly dialed respondents were not identifiable to the researchers by either name or address. The refusal rate for the survey was 24%.

Findings

The findings and estimates derived from this question are shown in TABLE 1. Using the randomized response question from the first sample and the direct question from the second, we can estimate (with a formula provided in Tracy and Fox)[15] the responses of men in the first sample who were answering the question about sexual abuse by itself. Finally, it is possible to calculate a standard error for this estimate, and from that a 95% confidence interval for the estimate.

The findings should be interpreted as follows. Of the men responding to the question "Have you ever sexually abused a child . . .?" an estimated 17% in Sample 1 and 4% in Sample 2 said yes. The true figure for all men in the United States should fall, in 95 out of 100 cases, between 13% and 21% according to Sample 1 and between 1% and 7% according to Sample 2. Based on 1985 population estimates, this could be between 10.9 and 17.6 million men for Sample 1 and between 840,000 and 5.9 million men for Sample 2.

These are large estimates of undetected child molesters. Unfortunately, we have no independent source of information, as there is in some other RRT studies, against which to check the estimates. However, there are some internal comparisons that can be made within the study to make some assessment of whether the RRT worked here in arriving at an estimate of the number of molesters.

A first source of internal validation is the comparison between the two samples. Although the estimates from Samples 1 and 2 are both large, the difference between them (quite large and statistically significant) is a puzzle. In theory, the samples should have produced identical estimates. Both were independent random samples from the same population. The RRT technique, if it works properly, should produce the same estimate when any innocuous question is paired with the sexual abuse question, as long as the frequency distribution of the innocuous question is known. This difference should not, in theory, have occurred.

A possible explanation of the difference is as follows. The whole point of the RRT is to give the respondent confidence that the interviewer cannot identify him clearly

TABLE 1. Randomized Response Technique (RRT) Estimate of Self-Disclosed Sexual Abuse By Males

	Sample 1 (n = 647)	Sample 2 (n = 588)
RRT question	Abuser + rent	Abuser + union member
% yes	22	12
% no	73	84
% refused	5	4
Direct question	Union member	Renter
% yes	20	27
% no	79	72
% refused	1	1
Estimated sexual abusers		
% yes	17	4
% no	74	89
% refused	9	7
95% confidence interval		
% yes	13–21	1–7

as a possible child molester. However, if the respondent fears for some reason that a yes answer will make him conspicuous, he many answer no to whichever question he is supposed to answer. There are a number of reasons to believe that the simultaneous questions in Sample 2 (pairing the sensitive question with labor union question) was more threatening than in Sample 1 (pairing with the rent question).

1. Because of certain other questions in the survey, respondents probably felt that their membership or nonmembership in a labor union was more transparent than whether they were a renter. The study asked at an earlier point for information on their job in some detail. Remembering this earlier question, respondents may well have feared that the interviewer or researcher had a way (perhaps a devious way) of knowing or guessing whether they really belonged to a union. The noes to the RRT question in Sample 2 were especially substantial among

blue collar workers, a group that may have particularly suspected that their membership or nonmembership was a matter of record.

2. Belonging to a labor union is, and also is likely to be perceived as, a lower-frequency attribute than renting. Sixteen percent of the men in the survey were union members, while 27% were renters. But more importantly, union membership is probably perceived, especially among some social groups, as a very-low-frequency attribute. Most adults have had the experience of being a renter at some time in their lives. Most have *not* had the experience of belonging to a union. Thus to say yes to either question in the abuse/labor pairing probably felt more conspicuous and likely to create suspicion because both attributes were perceived to be of such low frequency.
3. Finally, it seems likely that membership in a labor union is in itself, for some people, a more stigmatizing attribute than being a renter. The combination of two stigmatizing questions in Sample 2 (union membership and child abusing) may have particularly increased the threat of the question and thus inflated the number of noes.

These reasons might be an argument for considering the Sample 1 estimate more accurate than Sample 2.

Another way of trying to validate internally the RRT findings is to look at their relationship to other variables in the survey. From other literature and from clinical studies certain observations have been made about detected child molesters that could lead to hypotheses about how child molesters in general might tend to respond to other items in the questionnaire. We selected a broad range of items—any item that might have a plausible connection to molesting. These items fall into a number of categories.

1. Family background characteristics. There are some clinical suggestions of family disturbance in the backgrounds of child molesters.[18] Thus we looked at variables related to not having a close relationship with one's mother, being raised in a single-parent family, reporting an unhappy family climate, inadequate sex education, or very strict parental authority.
2. Prior victimization. Among the most widely replicated of findings is that child molesters report unusually large amounts of sexual victimization in their own backgrounds.[18]
3. Social isolation. As there is substantial research suggesting that child molesters feel awkward relating to peers,[18] we looked at whether or not the respondent reported having few friends in childhood.
4. Current marital status. Research suggests that child molesters have difficulties in adult heterosexual relationships, either experiencing conflict or finding them altogether aversive.[18] We looked at a questionnaire item inquiring about the respondents' level of current satisfaction with his sexual relationships in addition to his current marital status.
5. Sympathy for abusers. Presumably a molester would hold more positive, sympathetic attitudes toward the situation of other abusers. Thus we included items that (a) asked if in court trials concerning abuse the respondent was more concerned about protecting the child from psychological harm or protecting the legal rights of defendants; (b) measured the severity of punishment the respondent would mete out to abusers; and (c) asked if they were in favor of fingerprint checks for those who work with children.
6. Rationalizations for abuse. Molesters are reported frequently to disclaim responsibility for abuse,[19] or to not see their activity as antisocial or harmful.[20]

Thus we examined items that asked (a) whether the respondent saw children as in part to blame for abuse that occurred; (b) whether the respondent thought sex between an adult and a child prostitute or a consenting 14-year-old constituted abuse; and (d) whether abused children suffer much immediate or long-term harm.

7. Miscellaneous. We also included: (a) an item asking whether the respondent suspected that other people he knew among his relatives, friends, and neighbors had ever sexually abused a child, assuming that a person who abuses will be more likely to know other abusers or at least to suspect that others share his proclivities; and (b) an item that asked whether the talk about sexual abuse nowadays had made him change the way he treated children in some way, assuming that a molester might be more worried than other people about hiding his proclivities in the current climate of interest in sexual abuse.

TABLE 2 summarizes the relationship between the RRT items and these other questions in the survey. Both bivariate and multivariate analyses are possible with the RRT technique.[15] In evaluating the bivariate relationships shown here, estimates of the percentage of molesters were calculated for each subcategory of the independent variable, using the same formula as in the sample as a whole. These subcategory estimates were then compared to one another using a formula from Fox and Tracy.[15]

Of the forty-six possible relationships that were expected between the two samples, only one was confirmed. There was a higher estimate of the number of molesters in Sample 2 among those who themselves had been victims of sexual abuse. Three of the significant relationships were in the opposite direction to what was expected. Higher numbers of molesters were estimated among those in Sample 1 reporting happy family life in childhood, among those who believed that it is abuse even when a 14-year-old consents to sex with an adult and among those who see sex abuse as having many permanent effects.

The absence of these expected relationships does undermine confidence that the RRT questions were truly estimating the number of individuals who had committed acts of child molestation. However, two caveats must be kept in mind. First, the power of tests of association using the RRT question is very low because of the measurement error that is a consequence of the randomized structure of the procedure. Thus it is very difficult to find relationships without a much larger sample. Second, it is quite within the realm of possibility that undetected child molesters are quite different from, and do not have the characteristics and attitudes that might be expected from studies based on, identified molesters.

Discussion

Is the RRT the key to an epidemiological approach to child molesting? The findings of this experiment have to be considered mixed. The RRT did produce estimates for the proportion of the adult male population that had sexually abused a child according to self reports. These estimates, although high, are not beyond the realm of possibility, given the rates of self-reported victimization.

They are consistent, for example, with estimates one might make by comparing the number of victims with estimates of the number of victims per perpetrator. Here is an example of such a calculation. Abel and Becker, reviewing data on 652 sex offenders (both self-reported and referred through criminal justice) found that for all but male-object extrafamily abusers, the median number of victims per perpetrator was 1.3.[11] For male-object pedophiles it was 4.4. They did find a number of extremely-high-volume perpetrators, but such individuals are undoubtedly very overrepresented in samples of people seeking treatment or referred from the criminal justice system. If approximately 22% of all children are victimized (the figure on prevalence obtained by the survey reported here), men commit 90% of the abuse, on average each molester is responsible for 2 victimizations, and the population of potential victims at any given

TABLE 2. Background Factors and Characteristics Expected to Characterize Child Molesters

	Sample	
	1	2
Raised in single parent family	-	-
Unhappy family life as child	x	-
Not close to mother as child	-	-
Strict parental authority	-	-
Inadequate sex education	x	-
Victim of sexual abuse	-	y
Fewer friends as child	-	-
Not married	-	-
Unsatisfied with current sex relationships	-	-
Opposes finger-print checks for child care workers	-	-
Favors rights of defendants in sex abuse cases	-	-
Favors lenient punishment for abusers	-	-
Victims are responsible for abuse	-	-
Consenting sex between 14 year old and adult is not abuse	x	-
Sex with 14-year-old prostitute is not abuse	-	-
Indecent suggestion to child is not abuse	-	-
Taking naked photos of child is not abuse	-	-
Exposing to child is not abuse	-	-
Sex abuse does not usually involve force	-	-
Sex abuse does not cause much harm	-	-
Sex abuse does not have many permanent effects	x	-
Suspects that friends or relatives have abused children	-	-
Current talk about sexual abuse has changed way they treat children	-	-

NOTE: y = expected relationship, x = opposite relationship, - = no relationship.

time (children under 16) is one-fourth the population of potential perpetrators (persons 12 and older), then very approximately 5% of the male population should have committed a molestation. If rates of victimization are higher and the ratio of victims per perpetrator is lower, then this figure could easily be doubled. This suggests that the mean of the two estimates in the current survey, 10%, is on the high side but within the realm of plausibility.

However, various internal criteria do cast some doubt on the validity of the estimates obtained in this survey. First, the two samples produced divergent estimates, when they should have been the same. Second, the group of identified child molesters manifested very few of the characteristics or attitudes that might have been predicted from prior knowledge about molesters.

These considerations lead us to have some misgivings that the percentage for sexual abusers obtained in this survey is an unbiased one. However, we are still optimistic about the potential utility of the RRT. The current study was an exploratory attempt at obtaining self-reports of abusers from a survey. More such experiments need to be done using other forms of the RRT with a variety of modifications.

1. The RRT question about sexual abuse needs to be paired with innocuous questions that are less potentially threatening. A common techniques is to ask if the respondent's birthday falls in June, July, or August.
2. The technique should be tried in conjunction with a face-to-face interview method. In a face-to-face interview, the interviewer's presence insures that the respondent actually flips the coin or performs some other randomizing procedure.
3. When RRT is tried in conjunction with telephone interviewing, precautions should be taken to try to increase compliance with the randomization procedure. A suggestion from Fox[21] is to ask respondents over the telephone to write down answers to both questions, and then to flip the coin. Since they have both answers before them, lazy respondents would be less tempted simply to listen, remember, and answer the question of his/her choice.
4. Some attempts need to be made to validate an RRT-type question about child molesting using external criteria. The question can be pretested using prison inmates.
5. Other internal checks on validity need to be built into these efforts. Respondents need to be asked at the end of the survey whether they complied with and answered honestly all questions.
6. Efforts must be made to improve upon the wording of a question asking for a self-report of child molesting behavior. It is often observed among child molesters that they tend to deny that their behavior is abuse. They may have rationalized their behavior as normal affection, harmless play, or sex education, or as a situation in which they were themselves victimized by a child. A question that simply asks about sexual contact with a child or that has a clear preamble defining what behaviors are of interest to the researcher might overcome some of these definitional problems.

TOWARD A SOCIAL PSYCHOLOGY OF CHILD MOLESTING

The RRT may not yet be perfected as a method for obtaining prevalence estimates about the number of child sexual abusers, but it strongly suggests, as does the other research cited earlier, that such behavior is of epidemiological proportions. Such proportions are an argument in favor of a move to social-psychological rather than simply psychopathological concepts in efforts to understand the sources of the behavior. When a behavior is thought to be uncommon, then idiosyncratic elements in an individual's experience and psychology are adequate explanations. When a behavior is found to be widespread, social institutions, large group processes, and common socialization patterns are more likely to be important factors. The social-psychological concepts being used to analyze sexual assault appear to grow out of these kinds of assumptions:

1. Social groups, including the family and peer groups, and social institutions, such as the media, are influential in fostering sexual assault.
2. The behavior of sexual assault, although discouraged by some social sources, receives endorsement and support from others; and this support is an important factor in explaining individual behavior.
3. The main vehicle through which social groups and institutions foster and endorse sexual assault and discourage alternative behaviors is the transmission of attitudes and beliefs.

Social psychological concepts growing out of these assumptions have been fairly well articulated in the area of rape. For example, a great deal of success has been achieved in identifying sets of beliefs and attitudes that characterize rapists and a rape-prone men. These include myths about rape and its effect on victims,[22] attitudes of hostility toward women,[23] and attitudes that endorse the use of interpersonal violence in general.[23] Excellent work has been done on some of the social groups and institutions that appear to support rape—for example, studies suggesting that peer endorsement[5,6] and possibly media exposure[24] promote assault. How much of this work can be transferred to the analysis of child sexual abuse?

Unfortunately, some of the social-psychological concepts that have been developed for analysis of rape do not seem entirely transferable. Take, for example, hostility toward women. Hostility toward women may be a factor in some child sexual abuse, but it does not seem to be the central factor. Slightly modified to "hostility toward children," it still does not seem to fit. It appears, from the clinical literature, that some child sexual abusers feel some genuine affection for their victims, and most are probably calloused rather than hostile.[25] For some of the same reasons, acceptance of interpersonal violence also does not seem to be transferable to child sexual abuse. Most child sexual abuse does not involve violent attacks on children, but rather the use of authority or misrepresentations to manipulate children into sexual contact.[26]

However, two other social psychological concepts from the rape literature—peer groups and media—are perhaps more useful. Child sexual abusers will possibly report more peer support for child molestation than will non-child molesters. However, the overall role of this factor seems different in sexual abuse. The picture painted in some of the research on rape is that of an influential peer subculture, where gender-adversarial attitudes are rife and members are encouraged to have sexual relations with women by any means.[6] The situation is not parallel for child sexual abuse. There are rings of pedophiles who support one another's predations,[27] and there may be some adolescents who as a group exploit younger children. But for most child molesters, even adolescent offenders—the majority of whom are described as isolates[28]—the socialization into such behavior seems to occur alone, not among peers.

The situation is similar for the role of child pornography. Exposure to child pornography is certainly associated with some sexual abuse. In fact, the production and viewing of child pornography is the key component for some molesters.[27] But pornographic depictions of children are not as widely available as depictions of rape and violence against women.[29] Exposure to such images is not part of normal socialization. More probably child pornography is consumed by those with an already-established sexual interest in children. Its importance in fostering child sexual abuse is not known.

The concept from the social-psychological approach to rape that has the most clearcut relevance to child sexual abuse is the idea of rape myths. Child sexual abusers as a group would seem likely to endorse such child sexual abuse myths as: affectionate sexual contact with an adult can be a healthy form of sex education for a child; children often use their sex appeal to get things they want to from adults; or the taboos on sex between adults and children are part of obsolete puritanical sexual beliefs.

However, the search for social-psychological concepts to apply to child molestation has to go deeper than this. The simple transfer of ideas from research on rape is not enough. One cue can be taken from the analysis of rape. In trying to understand rape, researchers looked for characteristics of the male socialization experience. Rape was analyzed as male behavior that had roots in the social construction of masculinity. Child sexual abuse is also a predominantly male behavior, and can also be plausibly analyzed as having roots in the social construction of masculinity. What follows is speculation about three aspects of masculine socialization that might be associated with child sexual abuse and might form the basis of concepts aimed at analyzing the contribution of that socialization to the likelihood of such abuse.

The Oversexualization of Needs

One characteristic of male sexuality that has been noted by many observers is the importance that men place on having many sexual opportunities.[30,31] Sex seems more important for men than for women. Sex assumes such importance not simply because sex becomes equated with masculinity and status in peer groups and in the popular culture. Sex takes on this importance because it is one of the few acceptable vehicles through which most men can meet certain fundamental emotional needs.

Developmental psychologists have noted, for example, that young girls are touched and held more than young boys.[32] Physical contact is withdrawn from boys at an earlier age. Along with this goes a variety of attitudes that discourage physical affection and emotional dependency among boys. Boys are not supposed to need comforting. Boys are not supposed to be dependent and clingy. Thus boys are thwarted in the pursuit of needs that are normal in young children.

Later, when young boys become adolescents and then young men, they are offered the opportunity to meet these needs, but now through sex. In sexual interactions a man can be touched, a man can be nurtured, a man can be clingy, a man can be close. These needs are acceptable in a sexual context. To fulfill them in this way does not diminish his manliness. The result is that when all kinds of natural human emotional needs arise, men are more likely to try to fulfill them in a sexual context. Thus men give great importance to creating sexual contexts, because it is only there that many of these emotional needs can be met.

There are some dysfunctional aspects to this training. One is that many men find it difficult to disentangle sex from other distinct emotional needs. This creates problems in a range of situations. For example, when an adolescent and his best friend go hiking together and are enjoying themselves, the feelings of closeness that arise may prompt panic and withdrawal because the situation feels sexual. The inability to differentiate creates conflicts between men and women, too, when men equate closeness in relationships to having sexual intimacy.

This difficulty plays an important part in child sexual abuse, as well. Children often spontaneously seek physical closeness with adults. They evoke tender feelings of nurturance. They remind men of unfulfilled needs for closeness. All of this creates problems. Closeness for men has strong sexual connotations, as do nurturance and dependency. When these feelings arise in relationships with children, they often bring along with them sexual associations. Men deal with such associations in different ways. Some recognize their inappropriateness, are frightened by them, and choose to distance themselves from children. We see this pattern particularly in fathers who retreat from closeness with their daughters as they approach puberty. Some men recognize the inappropriateness of these sexual associations and are able to find ways around them so as to have nonsexual closeness with children. Others, however, succumb to them. When closeness with children brings up sexual fantasies, these men look for ways to rationalize and develop these fantasies and make them real. This seems especially likely, we hypothesize, among men who are deprived of other sources of physical closeness and nurturance. Thus, we would argue, sexual abuse often grows out of normal emotional needs evoked by children that become oversexualized through the process of masculine socialization.

Obviously, not all men are socialized alike. The oversexualization of emotional needs is more prominent in some men than in others. Such oversexualization, we would argue, should be an important predictor of a proclivity to abuse children sexually. Among the ideas involved in such oversexualization might be: (1) all touching has sexual connotations; (2) it is not manly to be vulnerable, except in sexual situations; (3) sex is the most important thing to make me feel good; (4) being close to children prompts sexual fantasies. The relationship between sexual abuse and these elements of masculine socialization needs to be explored.

Sexualization of Subordination

A second theme in masculine socialization that appears to be related to child sexual abuse is what might be called the sexualization of subordination. That is, many of the attributes that are given high sexual value by males in our culture are attributes of inferiority or subordination. Clearly, smallness, youthfulness, and vulnerability are generally valued over largeness, maturity, and powerfulness. There are also themes of various importance in various subcultures that give sexual qualities to inexperience, dependency, acquiescence, and helplessness. These themes are common in male-oriented pornographic literature, in current modes of fashion, and in social statistics (e.g., male preference for pairing with women who are younger, smaller, and of lower social status). All these attributes are variations on a theme: there is a hierarchical dimension to sexual attractiveness.

The sources of this dimension are debatable. Some components may have evolutionary roots; men's choice of youthful partners may be adaptive, although the key should be health, not inferiority. In a social system traditionally organized around gender inequality, attributes that challenge the hierarchical relationship should be less attractive. From a psychoanalytic perspective, it is argued that due to the nature of the mother-infant son bond, men choose sexual objects that are minimally threatening, minimally like the powerful mother. All these factors, and others, may play a role. The sexualization of subordination is important for child sexual abuse because children are the ultimate subordinates. Virtually every attribute that acquires sexual valence according to this principle applies even more strongly to children. Children are small, young, vulnerable, inexperienced, dependent, acquiescent. It is not surprising that socialization into a value system that sexualizes subordination will end up sexualizing children.

Children are not the only victims here. The problems created by the sexualization of subordination extend to other hierarchical relationships. We see men as physicians inappropriately sexualizing relationships with patients, therapists with their clients, and employers with their employees. It is important to note that the vulnerability to abuse in these hierarchical relationships is not simply that superiors have the power to coerce and manipulate subordinates into sexual compliance. For some men, the characteristics of subordination—dependency and vulnerability, for example, are sexually arousing.

We think this can be an important social-psychological concept in understanding child sexual abuse. We hypothesize that the men who have a greater tendency to find subordinate statuses sexually arousing will be those most likely to abuse children sexually. Here again there are probably some individual components to this construct. We suggest that elements of this construct might be: (1) youthfulness as sexually attractive; (2) smallness as sexually attractive; (3) helplessness/vulnerability as sexually attractive; (4) maturity as sexually unattractive; (5) largeness as sexually unattractive; (6) powerfulness as sexually unattractive.

Empathy-with-Children Deficiency

A third element of male socialization that is a good candidate as a social-psychological concept to be studied in connection with sexual abuse concerns the attitudes and beliefs men acquire about children. We would argue that a number of factors in male socialization can block the development of empathy toward children. In the absence of empathy, sexual exploitation of children is possible and more likely.

Men face a number of barriers to empathy with children. One lies in the nature of their anticipatory socialization for adulthood. Boys are not encouraged to consider parenting and caretaking as two of their most important roles, so they develop little interest in learning about children, their needs, and how to care for them. Since interest in children is seen as quintessentially a female characteristic, it acquires a strongly negative connotation for many boys. Even when men become parents, the division of labor in many families is such as to discourage men from learning about child care. They are encouraged to be breadwinners and disciplinarians, two functions that do not require—in fact may be better performed without—empathy.

Another important barrier to empathy with children may be men's alienation from their own childlike vulnerabilities. Among the requirements that masculinity imposes early on boys is renunciation of openly felt dependency, fear, and hurt. The emphasis on acquiring power, status, and competence pushes boys to adopt adult coping styles prematurely. They come to assign negative value to the characteristics of children—their neediness and immaturity. This also may make it difficult to empathize later with the vulnerability of children.

Inability to empathize seems to be a component in the sexual abuse of children. Research by Parker and Parker[33] on incestuous fathers has shown that they were more likely than a comparison group of nonincestuous fathers to be relatively uninvolved in the early care of their children. Some of the statements and rationalizations commonly used by offenders betray this lack as empathy as well. "She wasn't hurt," "I didn't rape her," "It was just play," and similar statements all reflect an inability to observe or consider that the children were or might be frightened, upset, or otherwise traumatized by the sexual contact. An adult's ability clearly to imagine and empathize with the kind of hurt, upset, or confusion that a child could experience would likely deter the impulse to sexual exploitation. Moreover, for a moderately empathic person, the actual discomfort displayed by a child should interfere with the enjoyment of sexual activities.

Obviously, empathy with children is part of a more generalized capacity for empathy. The lack of this generalized capacity plays a role in all forms of sexual coercion. But the issue of empathy with children is worthy of consideration as a separate entity, because otherwise-empathic men sometimes sexually exploit children.

We hypothesize that a deficiency of empathy for children would characterize many, if not most, child molesters. This concept might be thought of as having a number of components: (1) absence of protective feelings toward children; (2) denial that children occupy a special status and qualify for special treatment; (3) disdain for childlike emotional characteristics—neediness, spontaneity, ignorance; (4) lack of interest in children; (5) feeling of inadequacy in a caretaking role.

CONCLUSION

This paper has attempted to illustrate how the study of child molestation can move away from an analysis that is primarily clinical and criminologic toward one that is more epidemiologic. A first task is to develop research methods that are better able to identify and describe the aspect of child molestation that is not identified by law enforcement or child welfare—what might be called "normal child molesting." A second task is to develop new concepts for understanding the sources of such behavior—concepts that derive from social psychology rather than clinical psychopathology. These concepts would benefit well from theorizing about masculinity and male socialization, given the strong gender bias for child molestation. The development of these new methods and new concepts is an exciting challenge for future social scientists—one that offers the possibility of new advances in efforts to reduce the toll of this disturbing social problem.

ACKNOWLEDGMENT

The authors would like to thank Donna Wilson for help in preparation of the manuscript.

REFERENCES

1. Badgley, R., H. Allard, N. McCormick, P. Proudfoot, D. Fortin, D. Oglivie, Q. Rae-Grant, P. Gelinas, L. Pepin & S. Sutherland. 1984. Sexual Offenses against Children, Vol. 1. Canadian Government Publishing Centre. Ottawa.

2. KILPATRICK, D. G. 1984. Assessing victims of rape: Methodological issues (final report). National Institute of Mental Health, Department of Health and Human Services. Rockville, MD.
3. KOSS, M. P. & C. J. OROS. 1982. Sexual experiences survey: A research instrument investigating sexual aggression and victimization. J. Consult. Clin. Psychol. **50:** 455-457.
4. RUSSELL, D. E. H. 1986. The Secret Trauma: Incest in the Lives of Girls and Women. Basic Books. New York, NY.
5. AGETON, S. S. 1983. Sexual Assault among Adolescents. Lexington Books. Lexington, MA.
6. KANIN, E. J. 1985. Date rapists: Differential sexual socialization and relative deprivation. Arch. Sexual Behav. **14(3):** 219-231.
7. KOSS, M. P. & K. E. LEONARD. 1984. Sexually aggressive men: Empirical findings and theoretical implications. *In* Pornography and Sexual Aggression. N. Malamuth & E. Donnerstein, Eds.: 213-232. Academic Press. New York, NY.
8. MALAMUTH, N. M. 1981. Rape proclivity among males. J. Soc. Issues **37:** 138-157.
9. PETERS, S. D., G. E. WYATT & D. FINKELHOR. 1986. Prevalence. *In* A Sourcebook on Child Sexual Abuse. D. Finkelhor, Ed.: 15-59. Sage Publications. Beverly Hills, CA.
10. TIMNICK, L. 1985. 22% in survey were child abuse victims. Los Angeles Times, August 25, p.1.
11. ABEL, G. & J. BECKER. 1985. Eighteen years and 652 sex offenders later: research conclusions. Presented at the Society for Sex Therapy and Research, Minneapolis, Minnesota, June 28-30, 1985.
12. FREUND, K., C. MCKNIGHT, R. LANGEVIN & S. CIBIRI. 1972. The female child as a surrogate object. Arch. Sexual Behav. **2:** 119-133.
13. MALAMUTH, N. M. 1987. Personal communication.
14. FREUND, K. 1981. The assessment of pedophilia. *In* Adult Sexual Interest in Children. M. Cook & K. Howells, Eds.: 139-179. Academic Press. London.
15. FOX, J. A. & P. E. TRACY. 1986. Randomized Response: A Method for Sensitive Surveys. Sage Publications. Beverly Hills, CA.
16. WARNER, S. L. 1965. Randomized response: A survey technique for eliminating evasive answer bias. J. Am. Stat. Assoc. **60:** 63-69.
17. FOLSOM, R. E., B. G. GREENBERG, D. G. HORVITZ & J. R. ABERNATHY. 1973. The two alternative questions randomized response model for human surveys. J. Am. Stat. Assoc. **68:** 525-530.
18. ARAJI, S. & D. FINKELHOR. 1986. Abusers: A review of the research. *In* Sourcebook on Child Sexual Abuse. D. Finkelhor, Ed. Sage Publications. Beverly Hills, CA.
19. MCCAGHY, C. H. 1986. Drinking and deviance disavowal: The case of child molesters. Soc. Prob. **16:** 43-49.
20. GROTH, N. 1982. The incest offender. *In* Handbook of Clinical Intervention in Child Sexual Abuse. S. Sgroi, Ed. Lexington Books. Lexington, MA.
21. FOX, J. 1987. Personal communication.
22. BURT, M. R. 1980. Cultural myths and supports for rape. J. Pers. Soc. Psychol. **38:** 217-230.
23. MALAMUTH, N. M. 1983. Factors associated with rape as predictors of laboratory aggression against women. J. Pers. Soc. Psychol. **45(2):** 432-442.
24. MALAMUTH, N. M. & J. V. P. CHECK. 1981. The effects of mass media exposure on acceptance of violence against women: A field experiment. J. Res. Pers. **15:** 436-446.
25. HOWELLS, K. 1979. Some meanings of children for pedophiles. *In* Love and Attraction. M. Cook & F. Wilson, Eds. Pergamon Press. London.
26. BURGESS, A. & L. HOLMSTROM. 1978. Accessory to sex: Pressure, sex, and secrecy. *In* Sexual Assault of Children and Adolescents. A. Burgess, A. Groth, L. Holmstrom & S. Sgroi, Eds. Lexington Books. Lexington, MA.
27. BURGESS, A. 1984. Child Pornography and Sex Rings. Lexington Books. Lexington, MA.
28. FEHRENBACK, P., W. SMITH, C. MONASTERSKY & R. DEISHER. 1986. Adolescent sexual offenders: Offender and offense characteristics. Am. J. Orthopsychiatry **56(2):** 225-233.
29. DIETZ, P. E. & B. EVANS. 1982. Pornographic imagery and prevalence of paraphilia. Am. J. Psychiatry **139:** 1493-1495.
30. GROSS, A. E. 1978. The male role and heterosexual behavior. J. Soc. Issues **34:** 87-107.

31. PERSON, E. S. 1980. Sexuality as the mainstay of identity. Signs **5:** 605-630.
32. BLACKMAN, N. 1980. Pleasure and touching: Their significance in the development of the preschool child—an exploratory study. *In* Childhood and Sexuality: Proceedings of the International Symposium. J. M. Samson, Ed. Editions Vivantes. Montreal.
33. PARKER, H. & S. PARKER. 1986. Father-daughter sexual abuse: An emerging perspective. Am. J. Orthopsychiatry **56(4):** 531-549.

Legitimate Violence, Violent Attitudes, and Rape: A Test of the Cultural Spillover Theory[a]

LARRY BARON[b]

Department of Sociology
Yale University
New Haven, Connecticut 06520

MURRAY A. STRAUS

Family Research Laboratory
University of New Hampshire
Durham, New Hampshire 03824

DAVID JAFFEE

Department of Sociology
State University of New York, New Paltz
New Paltz, New York 12561

This article examines the relationship between cultural support for violence and the incidence of rape in the 50 American states and the District of Columbia. Legitimate violence was measured with a Legitimate Violence Index that combines 12 indicators of noncriminal violence and a Violence Approval Index that combines 14 indicators of the social approval of violence. A theoretical model hypothesizing the relationship of these two measures of legitimate violence and seven control variables to rape was developed and tested using path analysis. The results show that legitimate violence is directly related to the rape rate. The degree of social disorganization, urbanization, and economic inequality, and the percent of single males are also directly related to rape. The population's youthfulness and percent of blacks affect rape indirectly through their association with legitimate violence. These findings are interpreted as providing support for structural explanations of the origins of cultural support for violence and for a *cultural spillover* theory of rape.

[a]This work was supported by the Graduate School of the University of New Hampshire and the National Institute of Mental Health (Grant T32MH15161 and Yale Training Grant T32MH15123).

[b]Present address: Center for the Study of Women, 236A Kinsey Hall, University of California, Los Angeles, Los Angeles, California 90024.

INTRODUCTION

Rape is such a heinous crime that it is difficult for most people to accept the idea that there may be covert or implicit cultural norms that encourage some men to rape. The existence of such norms was brought to public attention by members of the feminist movement[1-3] and later substantiated by research on rape myths, such as the belief that women expect or enjoy being forced to have sex.[4-7]

In addition to beliefs and values that directly refer to rape, there may be other aspects of the culture that indirectly serve to increase the probability of rape. The presence of norms that legitimate nonsexual violence could be implicated in rape. This might occur if a positive evaluation of physical force in one aspect of life were to be extrapolated by part of the population to relationships between the sexes. To the extent that such extrapolations occur, violence for nonsexual and socially legitimate purposes will be associated with phenomena such as rape.

While cultural theories of criminal violence, such as the subculture of violence theory[8] or the southern culture of violence theory,[9-11] have attained a moderate degree of influence in the social sciences, these explanations have been the subject of considerable controversy and have not been adequately tested.[12,13] A major obstacle in testing such theories is the lack of an independent measure of the purported "culture" that supports crimes of violence. In order to avoid the circular reasoning of inferring cultural support for violence from high rates of violent crime, it is necessary to use a measure of cultural approval of violence that is conceptually and empirically distinct from the measure of criminal violence. As a step in that direction, this paper describes the development of two measures of cultural support for violence. These measures will be used to test the theory that within the United States the large differences between states in the incidence of rape are partly the result of state-to-state differences in cultural support for nonsexual and legitimate violence.[c]

THE CULTURAL SPILLOVER THEORY OF CRIMINAL VIOLENCE

We refer to the theory tested in this paper as cultural spillover theory. The distinctive feature of cultural spillover theory is the idea that cultural support for rape may not be limited to beliefs and attitudes that directly condone rape and other criminal violence. There could be cultural elements that indirectly legitimate sexual violence. The central proposition of this theory is that the more a society tends to endorse the use of physical force to attain socially approved ends—such as order in the schools, crime control, and military dominance—the greater the likelihood that this legitimation of force will be generalized to other spheres of life, such as the family and relations between the sexes, where force is less approved socially.

[c] Despite the importance of the concept of culture to sociological analysis there is little agreement about what it is and how it should be defined.[14] The aspect of culture that is relevant to this paper is the constellation of norms, values, and beliefs shared by the members of society. This is not to say that all members of society have the same degree of commitment to particular norms and values. There are person-to-person variations as well as group differences. This paper examines differences between states in one aspect of violent cultural norms and their relationship with rates of rape.

Although this may seem tenuous, there are a number of empirical studies that can be interpreted as supporting cultural spillover theory. Lambert, Triandis, and Wolf's study of nonliterate societies showed that societies that have a religious system in which deities are punitive tend to rely on physical punishment in child rearing.[15] Studies of modern nations show that the implicit cultural support for killing inherent in war tends to be reflected in a higher murder rate,[16] a higher rate of child abuse,[17] and more violence in fiction.[18]

Sanday's cross-cultural study of 156 tribal societies[19] can also be interpreted as showing spillover effects. She found strong support for an association between the level of nonsexual violence in the society (e.g., whether warfare is frequent or endemic) and rape. Sanday concluded that "where interpersonal violence is a way of life, violence frequently achieves sexual expression" (p. 18). This suggests that rape is partly a spillover from cultural norms that permit and condone violent behavior in other areas of life.

Another illustration of cultural spillover theory comes from LeVine's analysis of rape among the Gusii of southwestern Kenya.[20] According to LeVine the marital sexual script, which encourages men to force sex on their wives, is carried over into premarital relationships, resulting in a comparatively high rape rate. LeVine concludes that: "Rape committed by Gusii men can be seen as an extension of this legitimate pattern to illegitimate contexts under the pressure of sexual frustration" (p. 221).

Amir's study of rape also suggests a spillover effect.[21] Amir found a positive correlation between arrests for rape and arrests for other crimes of violence and interprets this as showing the existence of subcultural norms approving of rape:

> Because the highest rates of the offenses studied occurred among relatively homogenous groups, it is, therefore, assumed that these groups situated in a subculture, hold a particular set of conduct norms which emphasize and condone aggressive behavior, and have also the least "resistance potential" toward aggressive sexual behavior. Thus, under special circumstances, violence, including sexual violence toward women, is more likely to occur (pp. 319-320).

It should be noted that since Amir does not provide evidence of beliefs and values that specifically approve or promote rape, his findings can just as appropriately be interpreted as supporting cultural spillover theory. In actuality, Amir's subcultural explanation of rape is not supported by the data. This is because he did not directly investigate the extent to which violent offenders accept norms that advocate and legitimate violence. Instead, he *infers* the existence of such norms from their violent behavior. This is an example of the circular reasoning that has given the subculture of violence thesis its notoriety.

The controversy over the subculture of violence theory and other cultural theories of violence[d] cannot be resolved without data that directly reflects shared beliefs, values, and norms—that is, data on the relevant aspects of culture itself. Moreover, such

[d] We define violence as an act carried out with the intent of causing physical pain or injury to another person. There are many different dimensions which must be taken into account in research on violence. For example, the pain or injury of an attack can vary from little or none to death. Another critically important aspect is whether the acts are normatively legitimate as in the case of the physical punishment of a child and execution of a murderer, or illegitimate as in the case of rape or homicide. As explained elsewhere,[22] these critically important aspects of violence are deliberately omitted from the definition so that they can be treated as variables. This paper treats *legitimate violence* as a variable and investigates its relationship to rates of rape.

research needs to include controls for variables that might confound the relationship between violent cultural elements and rape. The balance of this paper reports the results of a study that was designed with these criteria in mind.

DATA AND METHODS

Unit of Analysis

The 50 American states and the District of Columbia are the units of analysis for the study. The main reason for choosing states as the units of analysis is that most of the data for the variables of central theoretical interest are available only for states. Another reason for focusing the study on states is that there are large differences between the states in the incidence of violent crime, including rape (see TABLE 1), and also substantial variation among the states on a number of variables of theoretical interest relating to crime. The large differences between states in respect to these variables permits empirical tests of the cultural spillover theory. These differences also hold out the possibility that an understanding of why rape occurs so much more often in states like Alaska and Nevada than in such states as North Dakota and South Dakota might suggest ways of reducing the national average rape rate.[e]

[e]There are also a number of reasons for skepticism about macro-sociological research using states as the units of analysis; these reasons cannot be discussed here due to space limitations. One concern is the ecological fallacy. We do not think this applies because our objective is to test a theory of the macrostructural aspects of society, and this can be done only by using societal units such as nations, states, cities, Standard Metropolitan Statistical Areas, (SMSAs), and counties. A second concern is that state-level data reflects aggregation bias. This is an important concern that we share. Consequently, readers need to keep in mind that the estimates to be reported are based on the assumption that aggregation to the state level does not lead to substantial bias in parameter estimates.

Assumptions of this type need to be tested, and we are engaged in a variety of studies with that objective. For example, we have done an analysis of the extent to which rural and urban parts of the states share common sociocultural characteristics. This was done by disaggregating to the metropolitan and nonmetropolitan level all the state-level variables in the 1983 *County and City Data Book,*[23] which resulted in two statistics for each variable: one for the population residing in the SMSAs of each state and the other for the non-SMSA population of each state. Correlations between these two measures were then computed. All were found to be statistically significant, and 41% were .80 or higher. These correlations can be interpreted as evidence supporting the view that despite differences in the absolute values of these variables, the metropolitan and nonmetropolitan areas within each state are influenced by being part of the same state, at least to the extent that they share the same rank, relative to other states, in respect to a number of key sociocultural characteristics.

Variables

The UCR Rape Rate

The dependent variable is the incidence rate per 100,000 population of rapes known to the police, as reported in the annual FBI Uniform Crime Reports (UCR). A number of criticisms have been made of the UCR data. Many of these criticisms, such as failure to include all police departments and failure to update the population denominators used to compute the rates, are no longer valid. Perhaps the most serious criticism of the UCR is that only a fraction of all rapes are reported to the police, resulting in an underestimation of the incidence rate. Despite this problem, methodological studies comparing the UCR data with data collected through victim surveys have shown similar regional variations and comparable rural/urban distributions.[24] These findings led Hindelang[24] to conclude "that the UCR data provide robust estimates of the relative incidence of index offenses known" (p. 14). Hindelang's findings and conclusion are particularly relevant to the present analysis because our central concern is the relative ranking of the states in respect to rape. Specifically, our objective is to investigate whether certain theoretically selected variables are associated with state-to-state differences in the incidence of rape, not to ascertain the absolute number of rapes committed.[f] (See Reference 27 for a comprehensive analysis of the validity of UCR data.)

[f]Readers should keep in mind that this study is predicated on the assumption that the large differences between states in the incidence of rapes reported to the police reflect, for the most part, differences in the true incidence of rape, not just differences in the willingness of women to report rape. However, there are grounds for believing that differences exist between states in the willingness of victims to report rape. For example, rape victims everywhere are reluctant to report because they might be stigmatized. Yet it is possible that victims are less likely to report a rape in stable rural areas such as North Dakota than in a state like California, for example, where there is greater anonymity and a more liberal and tolerant sexual climate.

Since the rate of reported rape might reflect differences in reporting, rather than differences in the incidence of rape, it is necessary to have empirical evidence on this issue. Consequently, we conducted a series of analyses, each of which approaches the issue from a different perspective. In a previous paper we reported three such analyses.[25] The first entailed a correlation between UCR data on rapes reported to the police and National Crime Survey interview data. A correlation of .49 was found for the 10 largest states (the only ones for which state data has been released). Given the fact that these sources of data are known to have different errors, this correlation suggests that reported rapes correspond to the presumably more complete data derived from interviews with a representative sample of the population.

The second analysis in the Baron and Straus paper utilized five indicators of the willingness of women to report rape to the police: rape crisis services per 100,000 females, membership in the National Organization For Women (NOW) per 100,000 females, number of NOW chapters per 100,000 females, the circulation rate per 100,000 females of *Ms* magazine, and the number of battered women's shelters per 100,000 females. The rationale for these measures is given in Baron and Straus. Assuming that each of these variables does partly reflect willingness to report rape, the results suggest that reporting effects play a minimal role in accounting for state-to-state differences in the UCR rape rate. Three of the five correlations were not significant. As for the two variables that were significantly correlated with the UCR rape rate (rape crisis service availability and NOW membership), when these were introduced into the regression equation, the results did not suggest any modification of the model being tested (i.e., the correlates

Cultural Support for Violence

The theoretical model, which is described in a later section, includes eight variables, each of which is hypothesized to be associated with state-to-state variation in the incidence of rape. Two of these variables, the Legitimate Violence Index and the Violence Approval Index, are intended to measure cultural support for legitimate violence. The analysis will be replicated for the two measures. Since these are newly developed measures and are crucial for testing the cultural spillover theory, they will be described in separate sections.

Other Independent Variables

The other seven independent variables have been shown in previous research to be significant in explaining the incidence of rape. Since the theoretical focus of this paper is the cultural spillover theory, these seven variables are conceptualized as control variables, even though they are also important in their own right. While our central focus is the relationship between the cultural legitimation of violence and the incidence of rape, it is also necessary to control for competing explanations by testing for spuriousness. The theoretical and empirical literature on rape was reviewed to determine which variables to include as controls.

Studies show that the incidence of rape is higher in urban than in rural areas of the United States.[28,29] Therefore, states that are more urbanized than others might be expected to have a higher rape rate. The degree of urbanization was operationalized as the percent of the population residing in SMSAs. Research also shows that a disproportionate number of both victims and offenders are likely to be relatively young,

---

of rape found in the original model did not hinge on differences in reporting behavior as indexed by these two variables).

The third analysis investigated the possibility that state-to-state differences in the rape rate reflects, at least in part, the assiduousness of reporting effort by police departments. However, using the percent of the population covered by the UCR as a measure of police reporting effort, none of the four correlations between the state as a whole, metropolitan areas, other cities, rural areas and the UCR rape rate were significant.

Finally, Jaffee and Straus present another analysis focused on estimating the degree to which the UCR rape rate reflects reporting differences rather than differences in the actual incidence of rape.[26] This analysis correlated a measure of nontraditional sex-role attitudes and a measure of sexual permissiveness with the UCR rape rate. The authors reasoned that high scores on these two measures would indicate a *sexual climate* in which all aspects of sex, including sexual violence, can be more openly discussed, increasing the willingness of women to report rape to the police. However, when the analysis presented in Baron and Straus[25] was replicated with the two sexual climate variables in the equation, the model again remained essentially unchanged.

The aforementioned methodological tests do not rule out the possibility that the findings reported in this paper might be the result of confounding with differences in the tendency to report rape. However, our attempts to demonstrate such confounding have not been successful despite our approaching the issue from several perspectives and with a variety of measures. Thus, while reporting effects probably exist, they do not seem to be large enough to confound importantly the results of the causal model tested in this paper.

black, and economically deprived.[21,28-32] The measures used to represent these variables are the percent of the population aged 18-24, the percent of the population black, and the Gini Index of income inequality.[g]

As might be expected from the large proportion of young men involved in rape, a high percentage of them are single.[21,33] Some researchers suggest that the lifestyle of many single men includes a number of activities such as dating and going to bars that may be "conducive to rape." [31,34,35] As a result, we included a variable measuring the percent of single males. Other investigators have speculated that rape may be a

TABLE 1. Ranking of the States on the Legitimate Violence Index

Rank	State	Index Score	Rank	State	Index Score
1	Wyoming	98	27	Washington	45
2	Montana	87	28	Hawaii	45
3	Mississippi	85	29	Tennessee	44
4	Utah	83	30	Nebraska	42
5	Idaho	83	31	Ohio	41
6	Georgia	78	32	Iowa	41
7	Nevada	77	33	West Virginia	38
8	Arkansas	60	34	Kentucky	36
9	Vermont	71	35	Pennsylvania	35
10	Louisiana	66	36	Maine	34
11	Alaska	64	37	Illinois	34
12	Florida	63	38	California	33
13	Oklahoma	62	39	Minnesota	32
14	Alabama	62	40	Indiana	31
15	Texas	61	41	New Hampshire	30
16	Arizona	60	42	Missouri	30
17	South Carolina	60	43	Michigan	29
18	South Dakota	59	44	Connecticut	29
19	North Dakota	57	45	Wisconsin	27
20	Oregon	56	46	New York	27
21	New Mexico	54	47	Maryland	26
22	Colorado	54	48	New Jersey	22
23	Delaware	54	49	Massachusetts	19
24	Kansas	52	50	Rhode Island	18
25	North Carolina	47	51	D.C.	MISSING
26	Virginia	47			

NOTE: The index score is the percent of the maximum possible score.

function of the sexual composition of the population.[1,33,36-38] Thus, an unequal distribution of the sexes, skewed in the direction of considerably more men than women, might result in some men forcing sex upon women. This was measured as the ratio of males to females aged 15-24. Finally, studies have shown a relationship between marital dissolution and rape.[39,40] Consequently, we included the percent of divorced

[g] The Gini Index was computed using 1979 census data on family income. Scores on the Gini Index can range from 0 to 100, with higher scores indicating a greater degree of income inequality. Conceptually, the Gini Index is used as an indicator of relative deprivation.

males as one of our measures. A complete list of the variables and their sources can be found in APPENDIX I.

THE LEGITIMATE VIOLENCE INDEX

Conceptual Basis of the Index

The indicators included in the Legitimate Violence Index (LVX) (completely described in Reference 41) were selected on the assumption that if there are group differences in values concerning violence, this should be observable in many different activities, including education, recreation, and law enforcement. Consequently, we searched for indicators that might reflect an underlying belief in the efficacy and desirability of physical force. However, to avoid the circularity involved in inferring cultural support for violence from high rates of violent crime, such indicators must be restricted to violent activities that are noncriminal and socially approved. The LVX was constructed to measure this aspect of cultural support for violence.

It should be noted that the indicators comprising the LVX are aggregate behaviors (such as membership in the armed services or subscription to violent magazines) or cultural products (such as legislation authorizing corporal punishment in the schools) rather than verbal expressions of beliefs, attitudes, and values. This corresponds roughly to Durkheim's "collective representations" [42,43] and is consistent with much anthropological research (such as that by Geertz,[44] especially chapters 1 and 15) as well as with the ethnomethodological studies done by Garfinkel.[45] The choice of behavioral and cultural product indicators was based partly on the lack of comparative opinion survey data for states, but also on the limitations of such data. Specifically, there are cultural contradictions in the evaluation of violence that make it extraordinarily difficult for people to verbalize their true beliefs and attitudes.[46,47] Therefore, public opinion survey data, even if it were available for states, might not accurately reflect the extent to which there are proviolence elements in American culture.

Before describing the measure itself, four conceptual points need to be clarified. First, the measure is called the Legitimate Violence Index rather than the Subculture of Violence Index, because it is intended to refer to only one aspect of cultural support for violence—legitimate violence. Second, the term "subculture" was avoided because we do not think that what the Index measures is restricted to limited groups in American society. This does not discount the possibility that cultural support for violence may be relatively more characteristic of some groups and geographic areas than of others. What it does suggest is that norms legitimating violence are widely diffused; therefore, the measure should be one that is widely applicable. Third, the use of "legitimate" in the name of this index does not indicate our evaluation of these activities as desirable or morally acceptable. Finally, it was not our intention to use indicators of approval or tolerance of rape itself, and none of the indicators in the index have any manifest relation to rape. Rather, the theory we are testing asserts that there is a carry-over, or diffusion, from legitimate violence to criminal violence. Hence the hypothesis that there is a higher incidence of rape in sectors of society characterized by a high level of legitimate violence.

The Indicators

The indicators included in the Legitimate Violence Index are summarized below. The rank order of the states on the 12 indicators of legitimate violence and their source documents are presented in APPENDIX II. They fall into three broad categories.

Mass Media

The mass media indicators serve two purposes. The first was to use a group of indicators that measures the extent to which a population is interested enough in violence to choose television programs and magazines with a high violence content. Two such indicators were used: the readership rate per 100,000 population of violent magazines, and the Neilson ratings for the six most violent network television programs. Use of these indicators assumes that the larger the readership or audience for media violence, the greater the interest in and fascination with violent behavior. The second purpose was to use a group of indicators that measures the military and veteran population in a particular geographic area.

Governmental Use of Violence

The second group of indicators is based on the idea that socially shared beliefs about the utility of violence can be expressed in laws and government actions that seek to attain socially desirable ends through the use of physical force. The indicators in this category include state legislation permitting corporal punishment in the schools, race-specific measures of prisoners sentenced to death per 100,000 population, and executions per 100 homicide arrests for the years 1940-1959 and 1960-1978.

Participation in Legal or Socially Approved Violent Activities

The third group of indicators is the rate of participation in violent but legal or socially approved activities. The indicators in this group are hunting licenses per 100,000 population, the state of origin of college football players, National Guard enrollment per 100,000 population, National Guard expenditures per capita, and lynchings per million population during the period 1882-1927.

Indexing Method and Reliability of the LVX

The LVX was computed by Z scoring each of the indicators, summing the 12 Z scored indicators, and dividing by 12. The resulting variable is easily mistaken for a

Z score because it also has a mean of zero. However, the standard deviation is less than one and the index scores, such as +1.2 or −.89, do not indicate the number of standard deviation units above or below the mean. To achieve that, the index must be standardized. A number of standardizations are possible, such as percentiles, Z scores, and T scores. We decided to use a modification of the Z score, called the "ZP" score.[h,48]

The SPSS reliability program was used to analyze the internal consistency reliability of the LVX. The reliability program computes the sum of the items as the index score and reports a variety of statistics on the resulting composite index. One of the most important of these summary statistics is the alpha coefficient of reliability. The LVX has an alpha coefficient of .71. The ranking of each state on the LVX is presented in TABLE 1. The regional and divisional breakdown of the states is displayed in FIGURE 1.

THE VIOLENCE APPROVAL INDEX

Since the Legitimate Violence Index is a new and unvalidated measure, a test of the cultural spillover theory using the LVX might result in no support for the theory, either because the theory is incorrect, or because the measure is not valid. Consequently, it is desirable to test the theory with an alternative measure. We therefore developed a second indicator of cultural support for violence—the Violence Approval Index (VAX).

The VAX differs fundamentally from the Legitimate Violence Index (LVX) because it is based on directly expressed attitudes regarding the circumstances under which it is appropriate to use physical force. More specifically, the VAX is based on the percentage of persons in each state who endorsed the use of violence under each circumstance. This measure has the disadvantage, as noted above, of being dependent on self-report data. Nonetheless, it has the advantage of being a direct measure of shared beliefs and therefore of the norms and values of society.[14,49] Finding parallel results using a measure based on attitudinal data will enhance confidence in the validity of the cultural spillover theory and also in the validity of both the Legitimate Violence Index and the Violence Approval Index. Thus, we expect to find a significant relationship between the VAX and the LVX, although not a perfect correlation. Moreover, since the attitudes expressed in the VAX are directly related to the social approval of violence, the VAX is expected to be related to rape in the same way, and for the same reasons, as the LVX.

[h] ZP scores accomplish two things. First, as with Z scores, the transformation creates a variable in which the units have a known meaning (i.e., deviation from the mean). Second, ZP scoring includes an additional transformation designed to avoid negative numbers. These transform the Z score into a score with a mean of 50 and a range of 0-100. Zero is assigned to cases that are 2.5 or more standard deviations below the mean, and 100 is the ZP score for cases which are 2.5 or more standard deviations above the mean.

The interpretation of ZP scores can focus on either the fact that each change of one ZP-score point is a change of one percent of the 0-100 score range, or focus on the fact that each change of 20 ZP score points is a change of one standard deviation. Thus, statistically trained readers can interpret ZP scores in terms of standard deviation units and other readers can interpret ZP scores as showing the percentage of the maximum score.

```
              30        40        50        60        70        80
REGION    :....:....:....:....:....:....:....:....:....:....:....:
          :
West      :XXXXXXXXXXXXXXXXXXXXXXXXXXXXXXXXXXXXXXXX
          :
          :
South     :XXXXXXXXXXXXXXXXXXXXXXXXXXXXXXX
          :
          :                                    F = 10.07, p < .001
North     :XXXXXXXXXXXXXXX
Central   :
          :
North     :XXXXXXX
East      :
          :....:....:....:....:....:....:....:....:....:....:....:
              30        40        50        60        70        80
```

```
              30        40        50        60        70        80
DIVISION  .....:....:....:....:....:....:....:....:....:....:....:
          :
Mountain  :XXXXXXXXXXXXXXXXXXXXXXXXXXXXXXXXXXXXXXXXXXXXXXXXX
          :
          :
West S.   :XXXXXXXXXXXXXXXXXXXXXXXXXXXXXXXXXXXXXXXXX
Central   :
          :
East S.   :XXXXXXXXXXXXXXXXXXXXXXXXXXXXXXXX
Central   :
          :
South     :XXXXXXXXXXXXXXXXXXXXXXXXXXXX
Atlantic  :
          :
Pacific   :XXXXXXXXXXXXXXXXXXXXXXXX
          :
          :                                     F = 6.39, p < .001
W. North  :XXXXXXXXXXXXXXXXXXXX
Central   :
          :
New       :XXXXXXXX
England   :
          :
E. North  :XXXXXXX
Central   :
          :
Middle    :XXX
Atlantic  :
          :....:....:....:....:....:....:....:....:....:....:....:
              30        40        50        60        70        80
```

FIGURE 1. Mean score of Legitimate Violence Index by region and division.

It should be emphasized that even though the VAX was constructed by aggregating individual attitudes, it is a measure of the extent to which the population of each state *shares* these views and is therefore intended as a measure of social norms and values that characterize the culture of each state. It cannot be used to make inferences about the relationship between an individual's attitudes and his propensity to commit rape. Rather, we are interested in establishing whether cultural support for nonsexual and socially approved forms of violence contributes to a social climate that increases the risk of rape.

Construction of the Violence Approval Index

The Violence Approval Index is based on 14 questions from the General Social Survey (GSS) that deal with attitudes toward the use of violence and force that were reported in surveys from 1972 to 1984.[50] For each of the individual items included in the index we computed the percentage of respondents in each state who responded to questions indicating approval of the use of violence. The 14 questions can be grouped into three categories:

Policy Opinion. The three items in this group are the percentage of respondents in each state who support greater military spending, support the death penalty, and oppose gun permits. For example, 74% of the respondents opposed gun permits.

Approve of Punching Adult Male Stranger. The six items in this group are based on the percentage of respondents who approve of punching an adult male stranger under a variety of different circumstances. For instance, 10% of the respondents would approve of punching a man who was drunk and bumped into someone on the street.

Approve of Police Striking an Adult Male Citizen. The remaining five questions ask respondents whether they would approve of a policeman striking an adult male citizen under a number of different conditions. Twenty-three percent of the respondents, for example, approved if a man said vulgar and obscene things to a policeman.

The VAX score for each state was obtained by summing the 14 percentages and dividing by 14. This yields the mean percentage of approval. We interpret this score as an indicator of the extent of social approval for violence. The alpha reliability coefficient for the Violence Approval Index is .68.

It is reasonable to expect that if the VAX is a valid measure it will be related to the Legitimate Violence Index. In fact, this is what was found. The zero-order correlation between the LVX and the VAX is .40. This correlation can be taken as evidence of the validity of both measures of cultural support for violence.

Although the VAX provides a needed additional method of testing the cultural spillover theory, it has certain disadvantages, and we therefore regard it as a supplemental test. First, the sample design for the General Social Survey is intended to provide a nationally or regionally representative sample, rather than a representative sample for each state. Second, even though we used the cumulative file of approximately 15,000 cases, the number of respondents per state is low for the smaller states. Third, the sample for the General Social Survey includes 40 states and the District of Columbia rather than all 50 states. For these reasons, despite the excellence of the General Social

Survey at the individual level, findings based on state-aggregated GSS data must be regarded as highly tentative.

RAPE IN AMERICAN STATES AND REGIONS

The first question that needs to be answered about the incidence of rape is whether the differences between states are large enough to warrant subsequent analysis. As TABLE 2 clearly shows, there is substantial variation between the states. In 1980, the

TABLE 2. Ranking of the States on Rapes Known to the Police per 100,000 Population, 1980

Rank	State	Rape Rate	Rank	State	Rape Rate
1	D.C.	75.6	27	Vermont	29.1
2	Nevada	67.2	28	Wyoming	28.6
3	Alaska	62.5	29	Utah	27.7
4	California	58.2	30	Virginia	27.4
5	Florida	56.9	31	Massachusetts	27.3
6	Washington	52.7	32	Illinois	26.9
7	Colorado	52.5	33	Arkansas	26.7
8	Texas	47.3	34	Mississippi	24.6
9	Michigan	46.6	35	Delaware	24.2
10	Arizona	45.2	36	Nebraska	23.2
11	Louisiana	44.5	37	Minnesota	23.2
12	Georgia	44.3	38	Pennsylvania	23.0
13	New Mexico	43.3	39	North Carolina	22.7
14	Oregon	41.5	40	Idaho	22.4
15	Maryland	40.1	41	Connecticut	21.6
16	South Carolina	37.5	42	Montana	21.0
17	Tennessee	37.4	43	Kentucky	19.2
18	Oklahoma	36.3	44	New Hampshire	17.3
19	Hawaii	34.7	45	Rhode Island	17.1
20	Ohio	34.3	46	West Virginia	15.8
21	Indiana	33.1	47	Wisconsin	14.9
22	Missouri	32.6	48	Iowa	14.3
23	Kansas	31.5	49	Maine	12.9
24	New York	30.9	50	South Dakota	12.5
25	New Jersey	30.7	51	North Dakota	9.5
26	Alabama	30.0			

District of Columbia led the rest of the country with a rape rate of 75.6 per 100,000 population. The rate for the District of Columbia is approximately eight times greater than that for North Dakota (9.5 per 100,000 population), which has the lowest rape rate. This means that women in the District of Columbia are approximately eight times more likely to be sexually assaulted than are the women in North Dakota. An examination of the upper level of the distribution suggests that the high-rape states are concentrated in the West. In fact, six of the top ten states are situated in the

West. Conversely, the states with the lowest rape rates represent a mixture of North Central and North Eastern states.

In order to determine more accurately the extent of such regional differences, we categorized the states into the four census regions and the nine census divisions and computed an analysis of variance (ANOVA). FIGURE 2 shows that there are large and statistically significant differences between the regions. As might be expected from the state rankings, the Western region has the highest average rape rate (42.9 per 100,000 population), followed by the South (35.9 per 100,000 population), the North Central (25.2 per 100,000 population), and the North East (23.3 per 100,000 population). According to these calculations, women living in the West are approximately twice as likely to be sexually assaulted as are women living in the North East.

The large differences among states and regions in the incidence of rape require explanation. One possibility is that the high rates of rape reflect a cultural context that tolerates and condones a wide range of violent activities. The analyses that follow are designed to examine this hypothesis.

TESTS OF THE THEORETICAL MODEL

The Theoretical Model

FIGURE 3 presents the hypothesized relationships of the model to be tested. In the proposed model, the variables representing various aspects of the social organization of society are on the far left, the measure of cultural support for violence (LVX) is in the center, and the rape rate is on the far right. Moving from left to right, all of the variables that precede a given variable are presumed to be antecedent. The seven control variables are exogenous, which means that their antecedents are not examined in the present study. Two endogenous variables are postulated: they are the LVX and the rape rate. Endogenous variables are the outcome variables, although in many instances they can become predictors of other endogenous variables. This is the case for the LVX, which is both endogenous to the set of control variables and a predictor of rape. The arrows indicate the hypothesized direction of causation from one variable to another. It should also be noted that the model is fully recursive. That is to say, all of the arrows point in one direction with no reciprocal relationships or feedback loops.

Violation of Assumptions

We began the analysis by inspecting the data for departures from linearity, and checking for outliers and multicollinearity. Linearity was examined by plotting the decile version of each independent variable against the rape rate and the LVX. The test of linearity provided by the SCSS breakdown procedure indicated that none of the bivariate plots of the rape rate significantly deviated from linearity. This was not the case for the LVX, however. The joint distribution of percent black and the LVX was U-shaped, suggesting that a polynomial model might provide a more adequate

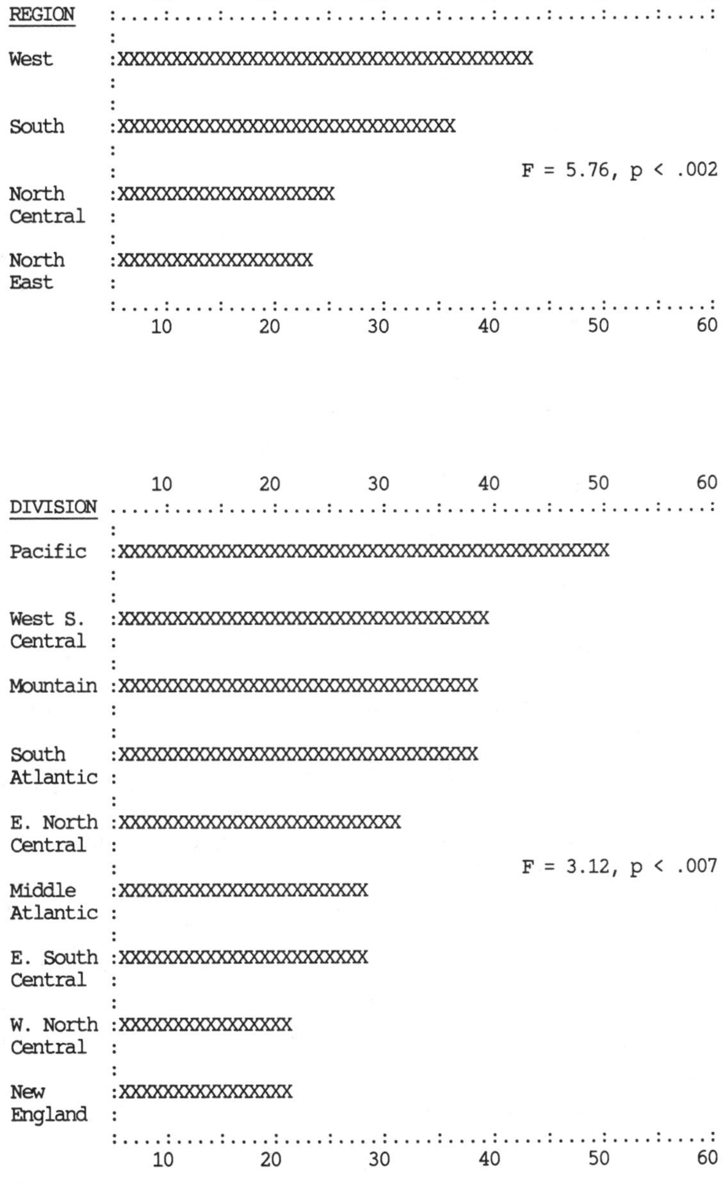

FIGURE 2. Rapes known to the police per 100,000 population by region and division, 1980.

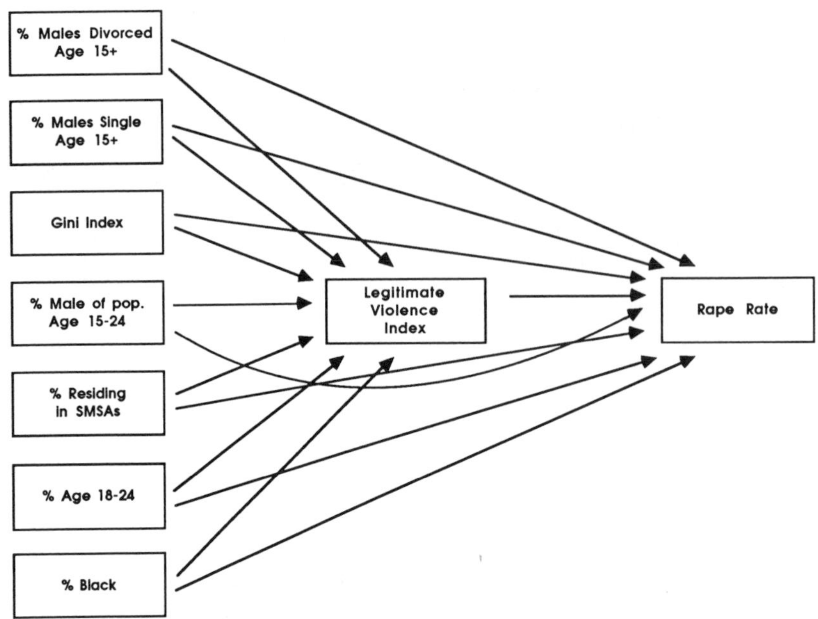

FIGURE 3. Theoretical model of variables antecedent to rape.

description of the data. Further analysis showed that the quadratic of percent black provided the best fit. However, a comparison of two separate regressions of the LVX on percent black and the other control variables, one using the linear equation and the other using the quadratic equation, yielded similar results. As a result, the linear equation was retained and employed in the following analysis.

Outliers were checked by examining frequency distributions, residual scatterplots, and Cook's D statistic, but no extreme scores were located. Zero-order correlations of the control variables and the LVX were examined for any excessively high coefficients that might indicate a problem with multicollinearity. A substantial correlation ($r = .93$) was observed between percent of the population below poverty level incomes and the Gini Index of income inequality. A correlation of such magnitude suggests that these variables are likely to be measuring the same underlying construct. Since the inclusion of both variables would inflate the standard error and produce unstable regression coefficients, it was decided to exclude percent below the poverty level from the analysis.

Test of the Model Using the Legitimate Violence Index

The approach employed in this study is path analysis.[51-53] The regressions were performed using the SCSS regression procedure with backward elimination. We chose the backward solution because our objective was to isolate the best prediction equation and estimate the partial regression coefficients based on a model that includes the significant variables only. The regression results were inspected for linkages that could be excluded from the theoretical model.[53] Direct paths that were not statistically significant at the .05 level were deleted, and the regressions were recalculated with the nonsignificant paths omitted.

Associations between the exogenous variables may be found in TABLE 3. FIGURE 4 displays the path coefficients of the trimmed model, and TABLE 4 presents the unstandardized regression coefficients and standard errors.

The central question guiding this research is whether legitimate violence is related to the incidence of rape. As FIGURE 4 clearly shows, the Legitimate Violence Index has a direct effect on the rape rate. This means that as the magnitude of support for legitimate violence increases, the rape rate increases. In other words, the social approval of nonsexual and noncriminal violence has a significant relationship to rape, independent of those effects contributed by the control variables. This finding provides support for the cultural spillover theory.

The path coefficients, presented in FIGURE 4, measure the relative contribution of individual predictor variables after the effects of the other predictor variables in the equation have been partialed out. It can be seen that the percent of divorced males and the degree of urbanization figure more prominently than the social approval of violence in the incidence of rape. However, legitimate violence is more influential in the prediction of rape than either the percent of single males or the degree of economic inequality. The coefficient of multiple determination indicates that a linear combination of the variables directly associated with rape accounts for 81% of the state-to-state variation in the UCR rape rate (adjusted $R^2 = .81$).

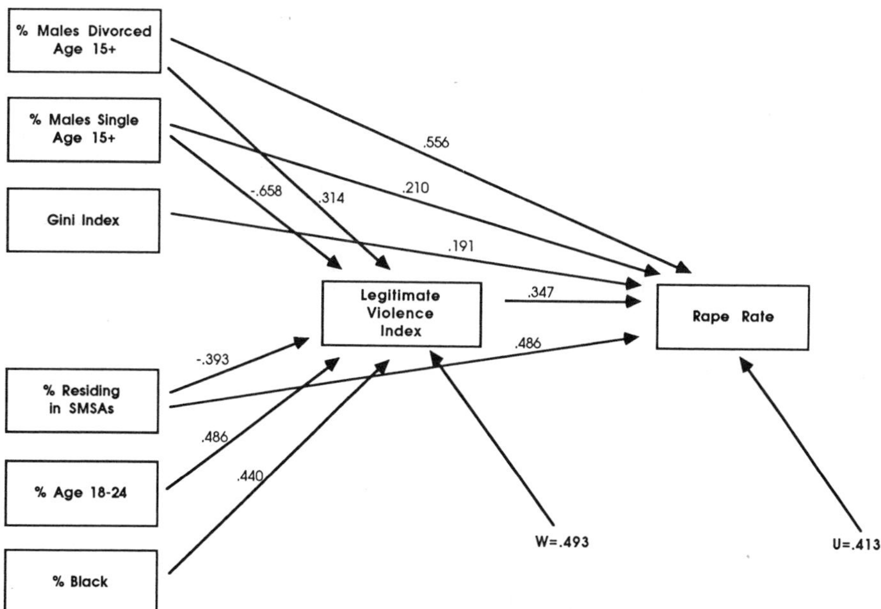

FIGURE 4. Trimmed model of variables antecedent to rape. Correlations among the exogenous variables are reported in TABLE 3.

TABLE 3. Basic Correlation Matrix

Variable	1	2	3	4	5	6	7	8	9
1. Rape rate	1.00								
2. Legitimate Violence Index	.20	1.00							
3. % residing in SMSAs	.49[a]	−.53[a]	1.00						
4. Gini Index	.27[b]	.29[b]	−.05	1.00					
5. % black	.40[c]	.11	.29[b]	.71[a]	1.00				
6. % age 18-24	.20	.29[b]	−.09	.06	.14	1.00			
7. % male of population age 15-24	.07	.23	−.22	−.20	−.37[c]	.33[c]	1.00		
8. % males single age 15+	.30[b]	−.42[c]	.44[a]	.15	.45[a]	.46[a]	−.14	1.00	
9. % males divorced age 15+	.73[a]	.27	.19	−.05	.01	.03	.22	−.01	1.00
Mean	32.95	50.04	62.13	35.00	10.34	13.49	50.38	29.65	5.43
Standard Deviation	14.90	19.96	23.25	2.00	12.52	.78	1.19	3.58	1.37

NOTE: Since pairwise deletion was used, all correlations with the Legitimate Violence Index exclude D.C., but all others include it.
[a] $p < .001$.
[b] $p < .05$.
[c] $p < .01$.

TABLE 4. Regression Analysis Using the Legitimate Violence Index ($n = 51$)[a]

Independent Variables	Legitimate Violence Index				Rape			
	Regression Coefficient	Standard Error	Beta	$p<$	Regression Coefficient	Standard Error	Beta	$p<$
% black	.702	.133	.440	.001				
% age 18-24	12.392	2.301	.486	.001				
% residing in SMSAs	−.337	.078	−.393	.001	.311	.054	.486	.001
% males single age 15+	−3.676	.595	−.658	.001	.879	.311	.210	.007
% males divorced age 15+	4.568	1.116	.314	.001	6.032	.786	.556	.001
Gini Index					1.430	.520	.191	.009
Legitimate Violence Index					.259	.069	.347	.001

[a] Final estimates after elimination of the nonsignificant variables from the model.

In addition to the direct effects, FIGURE 4 shows that several variables influence the rape rate indirectly through the cultural approval of violence. Contrary to what would be expected from previous research,[21,31,54] the youthfulness of the population and the proportion of blacks do not effect rape directly; rather, their effects are mediated by an environment favoring violence. Thus, a disproportionate number of oppressed minorities and young people are instrumental in shaping the violent cultural norms that precipitate rape.

In light of the direct effect of legitimate violence on rape, it is interesting to point out that the zero-order correlation of the LVX and rape is low and not statistically significant (see TABLE 3). Analysis of the first-order partial correlations (not reported here) showed that the variables acting to obscure the relationship between the LVX and the rape rate were the percent of single males and the percent of the population living in SMSAs. The magnitude of the relationship between the LVX and the rape rate increased once the moderate inverse effects of these two variables were held constant.

One finding, worthy of special mention, is that the percent of divorced males proved to be the best parameter estimate of rape. This result is consistent with the research done by Blau and Blau[39] on the 125 largest SMSAs. In their study, the Blaus used the percent divorced and separated as an indicator of social disorganization and found it to be a better predictor of rape than economic inequality, racial inequality, percent black, and population size. To the extent that marital dissolution involves the severing of an important social tie, it is highly plausible that a heavy concentration of divorced men produces a social context of disorder and confusion. This finding suggests that social disorganization increases the probability of rape. The percent of divorced males also affects the rape rate indirectly through its association with a cultural milieu supporting violence.

Replication Using the Violence Approval Index

To provide an additional test of the theoretical approach linking the social approval of violence to the incidence of rape, we replicated the analysis with an alternative indicator of violence approval, described earlier—the Violence Approval Index. If parallel results are found using this measure, which is based on attitudinal data aggregated by state, greater confidence can be placed in the validity of the Legitimate Violence Index, as well as of the general theoretical model.

The results of the regression analysis are presented in TABLE 5. There are some differences in the exogenous variables that predict the Violence Approval Index as compared to those which predict the Legitimate Violence Index.[i] The most critical issue, however, is the effect of the exogenous variables and the Violence Approval Index on the incidence of reported rape. On this question, the results using the VAX are remarkably similar to the original model. Like the Legitimate Violence Index, the

[i] The differences could be due to differences in the two measures of cultural support for violence, or to the fact that the replication uses a sample size of 41 instead of 51. To check on this we replicated the analysis of the Legitimate Violence Index shown in TABLE 4 using the same sample of 40 states and the District of Columbia as was used for analysis of the Violence Approval Index. The results showed that although the regression coefficients are slightly different, there are no differences in the independent variables that are significantly related to rape.

TABLE 5. Regression Analysis Using the Violence Approval Index ($n = 41$)[a]

Independent Variables	Violence Approval Index				Rape			
	Regression Coefficient	Standard Error	Beta	$p<$	Regression Coefficient	Standard Error	Beta	$p<$
% age 18–24	2.148	.634	.450	.002				
% males of population, age 18–24	1.287	.609	.270	.042				
% males single age 15+	−.692	.195	−.670	.001				
% residing in SMSAs	.043	.023	.250	.079	.322	.056	.540	.001
Gini Index	−.570	.200	−.310	.009	2.570	.580	.400	.001
% males divorced age 15+					5.903	1.047	.520	.001
Violence Approval Index					.822	.344	.230	.022

[a] Final estimates after elimination of the nonsignificant variables from the model.

VAX has a significant relationship to the rate of reported rape. In addition, with the exception of the percent of single males, the same exogenous variables (i.e., the Gini Index of economic inequality, the percent of divorced males, and the percent of the population residing in SMSAs) remain significant predictors of state-to-state differences in the incidence of rape.

SUMMARY AND CONCLUSIONS

Depending on the year, there are seven to ten times more rapes per 100,000 population in the top ranking states than in states at the low end of the distribution. This research investigated factors that might help explain these large differences between states in the incidence of rape, with particular emphasis on what we call the cultural spillover theory. This theory holds that the legitimate use of violence to achieve socially acceptable or desirable goals tends to be diffused to other social contexts and is therefore associated with an increased rate of rape.

Measures of Cultural Support for Violence

A serious limitation of previous research on cultural and subcultural theories of criminal violence has been the absence of a conceptually and empirically distinct measure of cultural support for violence. A methodological contribution of this investigation is the introduction of two indexes intended to measure state-to-state differences in legitimate violence. The first of these, the Legitimate Violence Index was created by combining 12 indicators of aggregate behavior (such as enrollment per 100,000 population in the National Guard) and cultural products (such as legislation authorizing corporal punishment in the schools). The second index, the Violence Approval Index, was computed by combining responses to 14 questions on situations in which the respondents approve of using violence. The two indexes, although based on very different types of data, have a correlation of .40, which provides evidence of the concurrent validity of both indexes. The LVX and the VAX made it possible to perform a direct test of the extent to which rape is a reflection of cultural support for violence.

Tests of Cultural Spillover Theory

A structural model of the cultural spillover theory was tested using the Legitimate Violence Index and replicated using the Violence Approval Index. Both tests showed that cultural support for violence has a direct and non-spurious association with the incidence of rape. Since the LVX and VAX measure socially legitimate and nonsexual aspects of violence, rather than beliefs about rape, the findings provide support for the cultural spillover explanation of sexual violence. This suggests that legitimate violence tends to be diffused to relations between the sexes, resulting in an increased probability of women being raped.

The Structural Basis of Cultural Support for Violence

This study also provides information on the social conditions that might account for the wide variation between states in cultural support for violence. Wolfgang and Ferracuti[8] suggested that norms endorsing violence tend to be generated in social settings characterized by poverty, youthfulness, and disadvantaged minorities. The path analysis provides some support for this conjecture.[j] States that are high in respect to legitimate violence tend to have a larger representation of men in the violence-prone ages of 18 to 24 and a higher proportion of black residents. However, the analysis shows that much more is involved, since it was also found that legitimate violence is more prevalent in rural states and in states that have a disproportionate number of divorced and nonsingle men.

Of the eight independent variables, the percent of males divorced emerged as the most powerful predictor of rape. Since marital dissolution represents a significant disruption in an individual's life, it could be argued that a heavy concentration of divorced men contributes to a social context that is conducive to rape. This interpretation is consistent with Blau and Blau's[39] social-disorganization explanation of rape. A related explanation assumes that divorced men tend to harbor feelings of anger, contempt, and hostility toward their estranged spouses. These feelings may become generalized to other women as well and create a climate of antagonism between the sexes. Whatever the underlying processes, it is clear that a large proportion of divorced men increases the risk of rape.

Theoretical and Practical Implications of the Model

The finding that legitimate violence is associated with rape has both theoretical and practical significance. However, as in the case of all cross-sectional research, the evidence must be treated as being consistent with the theory, rather than proving it. Nevertheless, the findings carry us a step beyond prior research on the cultural antecedents of criminal violence, because no previous study employed a measure of socially approved violence that was empirically independent of the criminal violence that it sought to explain. Therefore, the model we tested not only suggests a cultural spillover effect, but may also be regarded as providing the strongest support to date for cultural theories of violent crime. At the same time, the results also suggest that the distinction between cultural and structural theories may present a false dichotomy. Specifically, the path model provides evidence that is consistent with cultural and structural explanations of the etiology of rape (e.g., social disorganization and economic inequality) and therefore implies that rape is an expression of both influences.

[j] Our discussion is limited to the Legitimate Violence Index because, for the reasons given earlier, we have more confidence in this measure than in the Violence Approval Index.

There are also important practical implications of this research. The findings suggest that if rape is to be reduced, attention must be paid to the abundance of socially approved violence, not just to criminal violence, and to the structural conditions that underlie a reliance on violence for socially approved ends. This will be a formidable task, considering that economic and racial inequality, corporal punishment of children, violent sports, mass-media violence, capital punishment, and other forms of legitimate violence are woven into the fabric of American culture.

ACKNOWLEDGMENTS

It is a pleasure to acknowledge the important contributions of the members of the Family Violence Research Program seminar and of Colin Loftin, Steven Messner, Albert J. Reiss, Sally Ward, and Kirk R. Williams, for insightful and critical comments, not all of which could be included in this paper.

REFERENCES

1. BROWNMILLER, S. 1975. Against Our Will: Men, Women, and Rape. Simon and Schuster. New York, NY.
2. GREER, G. 1973. Seduction is a four-letter word. Playboy **20** (January): 80-82, 164, 17B, 224-228.
3. GRIFFIN, S. 1971. Rape: The all-American crime. Ramparts (September): 26-35.
4. BURT, M. R. 1980. Cultural myths and supports for rape. J. Pers. Soc. Psychol. **38:** 217-230.
5. CHECK, J. & N. MALAMUTH. 1983. Sex role stereotyping and reactions to depictions of stranger versus acquaintance rape. J. Pers. Soc. Psychol. **45:** 344-356.
6. FIELD, H. S. 1978. Attitudes toward rape: A comparative analysis of police, rapists, crisis counselors, and citizens. J. Pers. Soc. Psychol. **36:** 156-179.
7. SCULLY, D. & J. MAROLLA. 1985. "Riding the bull at Gilley's": convicted rapists describe the rewards of rape. Soc. Probl. **32:** 251-263.
8. WOLFGANG, M. E. & F. FERRACUTI. 1967. The Subculture of Violence: Towards an Integrated Theory of Criminology. Tavistock. London.
9. GASTIL, R. D. 1971. Homicide and a regional culture of violence. Am. Sociol. Rev. **36:** 412-427.
10. HACKNEY, S. 1969. Southern violence. Am. Hist. Rev. **74:** 906-925.
11. MESSNER, S. F. 1983. Regional and racial effects on the urban homicide rate: The subculture of violence revisited. Am. J. Sociol. **88:** 997-1007.
12. LOFTIN, C. & R. H. HILL. 1974. Regional subculture and homicide: An examination of the Gastil-Hackney Thesis. Am. Sociol. Rev. **39:** 714-724.
13. NETTLER, G. 1984. Explaining Crime. 3d edit. McGraw-Hill. New York, NY.
14. WALLACE, W. L. 1983. Principles of Scientific Sociology. Aldine. New York, NY.
15. LAMBERT, W. W., L. M. TRIANDIS & M. WOLF. 1959. Some correlates of beliefs in the malevolence and benevolence of supernatural beings: A cross-societal study. J. Abnorm. Soc. Psychol. **58:** 162-169.
16. ARCHER, D. & R. GARTNER. 1984. Violence and Crime in Cross-National Perspective. Yale University Press. New Haven, CT.
17. SHWED, J. A. & M. A. STRAUS. 1979. The Military Environment and Child Abuse. Mimeographed manuscript.
18. HUGGINS, M. B. & M. A. STRAUS. 1980. Violence and the social structure as reflected in children's books from 1850 to 1970. *In* The Social Causes of Husband-Wife Violence.

M. A. Straus & G. T. Hotaling, Eds.: 51-67. University of Minnesota Press. Minneapolis, MN.

19. SANDAY, P. R. 1981. The socio-cultural context of rape: A cross-cultural study. J. Soc. Issues **37:** 5-27.
20. LEVINE, R. A. 1977. Gusii sex offenses: A study in social control. *In* Forcible Rape: The Crime, the Victim, and the Offender. D. Chappell, R. Geis & G. Geis, Eds.: 189-226. Columbia University Press. New York, NY.
21. AMIR, M. 1971. Patterns in Forcible Rape. University of Chicago Press. Chicago, IL.
22. GELLES, R. J. & M. A. STRAUS. 1979. Determinants of violence in the family: Toward a theoretical integration. *In* Contemporary Theories about the Family. W. R. Burr, R. Hill, F. I. Nye & I. L. Reiss, Eds.: 549-581. Free Press. New York, NY.
23. STRAUS, M. A. 1985. The validity of U.S. states as units for sociological research. Presented at the Meeting of the American Sociological Association, San Antonio, Texas, August 28, 1985.
24. HINDELANG, M. J. 1974. The Uniform Crime Reports revisited. J. of Crim. Justice **2:** 1-17.
25. BARON, L. & M. A. STRAUS. 1984. Sexual Stratification, Pornography, and Rape in the United States. *In* Pornography and Sexual Aggression. N. M. Malamuth & E. Donnerstein, Eds.: 185-209. San Francisco, CA.
26. JAFFEE, D. & A. STRAUS. 1985. Sex-roles, sexual liberation, and reported rape. Presented at the Annual Meeting of the Society for the Study of Social Problems, Washington, DC, August, 1985.
27. GOVE, W., M. HUGHES & M. GEERKEN. 1985. Are Uniform Crime Reports a valid indicator of the index crimes? An affirmative answer with minor qualifications. Criminology **23:** 451-501.
28. BROWN, E. J., T. J. FLANAGAN & M. MCLEOD EDS. 1984. Sourcebook of Criminal Justice Statistics—1981. U. S. Department of Justice, Bureau of Justice Statistics. Washington, DC.
29. HINDELANG, M. J. & B. L. DAVIS. 1977. Forcible rape in the United States: A statistical profile. *In* Forcible Rape: The Crime, Victim, and the Offender. D. Chappell, R. Geis & G. Geis, Eds.: 87-114. Columbia University Press. New York, NY.
30. KATZ, SEDELLE & M. A. MAZUR. 1979. Understanding the Rape Victim. John Wiley and Sons. New York, NY.
31. RABKIN, J. G. 1979. The epidemiology of forcible rape. Am. J. Orthopsychiatry **49:** 634-647.
32. SCHWENDINGER, J. R. & H. SCHWENDINGER. 1983. Rape and Inequality. Sage. Beverly Hills, CA.
33. SVALASTOGA, K. 1962. Rape and social structure. Pacific Sociol. Rev. **5:** 48-53.
34. GOODCHILDS, J. D. & G. L. ZELLMAN. 1984. Sexual signaling and sexual aggression in adolescent relationships. *In* Pornography and Sexual Aggression. N. Malamuth & E. Donnerstein, Eds.: 233-243. Academic Press. San Francisco, CA.
35. MACNAMARA, D. E. J. & E. SAGARIN. 1977. Sex, Crime, and the Law. Free Press. New York, NY.
36. HARRIES, K. D. 1974. The Geography of Crime and Justice. New York: McGraw-Hill. New York, NY.
37. SHORTER, E. 1978. On writing the history of rape. Signs **3:** 471-482.
38. VON HENTIG, H. 1957. The Criminal and His Victim. Yale University Press. New Haven, CT.
39. BLAU, J. R. & P. M. BLAU. 1982. The cost of inequality: Metropolitan structure and violent crime. Am. Sociol. Rev. **47:** 114-128.
40. SMITH, M. D. & N. BENNETT. 1985. Poverty, inequality, and theories of forcible rape. Crime and Delinquency **31:** 295-305.
41. STRAUS, M. A. The Index of Legitimate Violence. Unpublished manuscript.
42. DURKHEIM, E. 1901. The Rules of Sociological Method. Translated, 1938. Free Press. Glencoe, IL.
43. LUKES, S. 1972. Emile Durkheim: His Life and Work. New York: Harper and Row. New York, NY.
44. GEERTZ, C. 1973. The Interpretation of Cultures. Basic Books. New York, NY.

45. GARFINKEL, H. 1964. Studies of the Routine Grounds of Everyday Activities. Soc. Probl. **11:** 225-250.
46. DIBBLE, U. & M. A. STRAUS. 1980. Some social structure determinants of inconsistency between attitudes and behavior: The case of family violence. J. Marriage Fam. **42:** 71-80.
47. GREENBLAT, C. S. 1983. A hit is a hit is a hit. . . or is it? Approval and tolerance of the use of physical force by spouses. *In* The Dark Side of Families. edited by D. Finkelhor, R. J. Gelles, G. T. Hotaling & M. A. Straus, Eds.: 235-260. Sage. Beverly Hills, CA.
48. STRAUS, M. A. 1981. The 'ZP' Scale: A percentaged Z score. Unpublished manuscript.
49. WILLIAMS, R. M. JR. 1970. American Society: A Sociological Interpretation. Knopf. New York, NY.
50. DAVIS, J. A. & T. W. SMITH. 1985. General Social Surveys, 1972-1984 Cumulative Codebook. National Opinion Research Center. Chicago, IL.
51. ASHER, H. B. 1983. Causal Modeling. 2d ed. Sage University Paper Series on Quantitative Applications in the Social Sciences, Series 07-003. Sage. Beverly Hills, CA.
52. DUNCAN, O. D. 1975. Introduction to Structural Equation Models. Academic Press. New York, NY.
53. HEISE, D. R. 1969. Problems in path analysis and causal inference. *In* Sociological Methodology 1969. E. F. Borgatta & G. W. Bohrnstedt, Eds. Jossey-Bass. San Francisco, CA.
54. HINDELANG, M. J. 1978. Race and involvement in common law personal crimes. Sociol. Rev. **43:** 93-109.
55. SHRYOCK, H. S. & J. S. SIEGEL. 1980. The Methods and Materials of Demography. U. S. Government Printing Office. Washington, DC.

APPENDIX I

References to Data Sources

The identification codes for variables listed under the "Variable Name" column are those used in the State and Regional Indicators Archive (SRIA). The SRIA variable names are used so that persons interested in this data can obtain SRIA holdings. All SRIA data is available for public use. An article describing the SRIA,[23] and information on codebooks, subject index, and other materials may be obtained by writing to the Program Assistant, State and Regional Indicators Archive, University of New Hampshire, Durham, New Hampshire, 03824.

The letters following the number part of some variable names indicate that the original variable has been transformed in one of the following ways:

r The source document variable was transformed to a rate.
z ZP scored version of a variable.[g]

Variable Name	Variable Label and Source Document
xcv12zp	Legitimate Violence Index 1882-1980 See APPENDIX II for the variables and sources used to construct the index.
blk80	Percent Black of the Population 1980 Bureau of the Census. 1982. State and Metropolitan Area Data Book. Washington, D.C.: U.S. Government Printing Office.

Variable Name	Variable Label and Source Document
c78s	Percent Male of the Population Age 15-24 1980 Bureau of the Census. 1982. State and Metropolitan Area Data book. Washington, D.C.: U.S. Government Printing Office.
ckf29	Rapes Known to the Police Per 100,000 Population 1980 Bureau of Justice Statistics. 1981. Sourcebook of Criminal Justice Statistics—1980. Washington, D.C.: U.S. Government Printing Office.
cp62r	Percent Male of the Population Single Age 15+ 1979
cp66r	Percent Male of the Population Divorced Age 15+ 1979 Bureau of the Census. 1982. State and Metropolitan Area Data Book. Washington, D.C.: U.S. Government Printing Office.
gini79fx	Gini Index of Income Inequality 1979 Bureau of the Census. 1979. Provisional Estimates of Social Economic, and Housing Characteristics of States and Selected Standard Metropolitan Areas (Publication No. PHC80-S1-1). Washington, D.C.: U.S. Government Printing Office. The index was computed using family income data. The calculations were done following the procedures given in Shryock and Siegel.[55]
met80	Percent of the Population Residing in SMSAs 1980 Bureau of the Census. 1982. State and Metropolitan Area Data Book. Washington, D.C.: U.S. Government Printing Office.
yng80	Percent of the Population Age 18-24 1980 Bureau of the Census. 1982. State and Metropolitan Area Data Book. Washington, D.C.: U.S. Government Printing Office.
xgs2a	Violence Approval Index 1972-1984 Davis, James A., and Tom W. Smith. 1985. General Social Surveys, 1972-1984: Cumulative Codebook. Chicago, IL: National Opinion Research Center. The statements used to construct the Violence Approval Index are listed below.

Variable Name	GSS Question	Response	Label
GS14T1	68I	1	Spending too little on military
GS18T1	79	1	In favor of death penalty for murder
GS19T2	80	2	Oppose requiring gun permits
GS69T1	185	1	OK for a man to punch an adult male
GS70T1	185RA	1	OK for a man to hit a protestor with opposing views
GS71T1	185RB	1	OK for a man to hit a drunk who bumped into him and wife
GS72T1	185RC	1	OK for a man to hit someone who hits your child
GS73T1	185RD	1	OK for a man to hit a male if male beat a woman
GS74T1	185RE	1	OK for a man to hit a male if he is breaking in
GS80T1	186R	1	OK for police to strike an adult male
GS81T1	186RA	1	OK for police to hit male saying obscene things to police
GS82T1	186RB	1	OK for police to hit murder suspect
GS83T1	186RC	1	OK for police to hit male attempting escape
GS84T1	186RD	1	OK for police to hit male attacking police with fists

APPENDIX II

Indicators Included in the Legitimate Violence Index

	Violent Television Viewing Index		Violent Magazine Circulation Index		NATIONAL GUARD Enrollment		NATIONAL GUARD Expenditures	
Rank	State	cv16a	State	xvmc	State	v474r	State	v475r
1	South Carolina	2269	Alaska	5.29	Vermont	7.35	Alaska	47.38
2	Louisiana	2235	Wyoming	2.33	Alaska	6.81	D.C.	32.76
3	Georgia	2085	Nevada	1.56	Wyoming	5.90	Hawaii	31.57
4	North Carolina	2063	Hawaii	1.05	Alabama	5.87	Wyoming	30.51
5	Montana	2008	Kansas	0.74	South Dakota	5.83	Idaho	28.28
6	Tennessee	1990	Idaho	0.72	Delaware	5.67	Vermont	28.15
7	West Virginia	1898	Arizona	0.69	Hawaii	5.64	Delaware	28.01
8	Alabama	1860	Colorado	0.67	Mississippi	5.52	South Dakota	26.68
9	Mississippi	1859	Montana	0.52	Arkansas	5.22	Montana	25.23
10	Kentucky	1858	Washington	0.34	North Dakota	4.98	Mississippi	23.92
11	Wyoming	1798	Oregon	0.33	D.C.	4.70	North Dakota	22.55
12	Idaho	1797	Texas	0.27	Utah	4.64	Nevada	22.46
13	Arkansas	1733	D.C.	0.26	Idaho	4.45	Alabama	17.90
14	Maryland	1712	North Dakota	0.25	Rhode Island	3.99	Rhode Island	17.80
15	Illinois	1708	New Mexico	0.24	Montana	3.85	Maine	17.76
16	Ohio	1699	California	0.17	South Carolina	3.83	Utah	16.86
17	Texas	1670	South Dakota	0.06	Maine	3.74	Arkansas	16.12
18	Oklahoma	1663	New Hampshire	0.04	Oklahoma	3.65	New Mexico	16.01
19	South Dakota	1656	Virginia	0.03	New Mexico	3.42	Kansas	15.02
20	Wisconsin	1645	Delaware	-0.07	New Hampshire	3.41	New Hampshire	14.96
21	Indiana	1639	Vermont	-0.14	Tennessee	3.25	Arizona	13.96
22	Virginia	1634	Maine	-0.18	Oregon	3.22	Oklahoma	13.27
23	New Mexico	1628	Georgia	-0.22	Nevada	3.11	Oregon	13.18
24	Missouri	1609	Louisiana	-0.24	Kansas	3.30	Iowa	12.47
25	Kansas	1602	Nebraska	-0.32	Nebraska	2.96	Nebraska	12.43
26	Utah	1592	Michigan	-0.34	Iowa	2.89	Tennessee	12.03
27	Delaware	1583	Iowa	-0.42	Minnesota	2.72	West Virginia	11.86
28	North Dakota	1557	Maryland	-0.43	Indiana	2.58	South Carolina	11.66
29	Florida	1541	Utah	-0.43	West Virginia	2.58	Minnesota	11.05
30	Colorado	1539	Illinois	-0.46	Louisiana	2.47	Colorado	10.53
31	Michigan	1538	Ohio	-0.47	Georgia	2.45	Georgia	10.08
32	Iowa	1536	Indiana	-0.47	Missouri	2.30	Missouri	9.77
33	Minnesota	1523	Florida	-0.48	Arizona	2.29	Washington	9.66
34	Maine	1495	North Carolina	-0.50	North Carolina	2.29	Massachusetts	9.21
35	Vermont	1465	Kentucky	-0.50	Wisconsin	2.26	Indiana	8.47
36	D.C.	1403	Wisconsin	-0.51	Connecticut	2.21	Louisiana	8.20
37	Pennsylvania	1399	Arkansas	-0.54	Massachusetts	2.17	Connecticut	8.15
38	New York	1395	West Virginia	-0.55	New Jersey	2.09	Wisconsin	7.81
39	Nebraska	1353	Pennsylvania	-0.55	Washington	1.99	New Jersey	7.63
40	Oregon	1333	South Carolina	-0.55	Kentucky	1.87	Michigan	7.46
41	Connecticut	1328	Missouri	-0.58	Maryland	1.81	Maryland	6.66
42	Washington	1313	Connecticut	-0.60	Ohio	1.72	Kentucky	6.62
43	Nevada	1250	Alabama	-0.69	Pennsylvania	1.62	Ohio	6.59
44	California	1183	Tennessee	-0.70	Colorado	1.59	North Carolina	6.42
45	Massachusetts	1163	Minnesota	-0.70	Virginia	1.57	Texas	6.08
46	Hawaii	1155	New York	-0.73	Texas	1.51	Virginia	6.04
47	Arizona	1099	Massachusetts	-0.83	New York	1.32	Pennsylvania	5.90
48	Rhode Island	1086	Mississippi	-0.83	Michigan	1.26	California	5.04
49	Alaska	Missing	New Jersey	-0.91	Florida	1.19	New York	4.69
50	New Hampshire	Missing	Rhode Island	-1.06	California	1.09	Florida	3.84
51	New Jersey	Missing	Okalahoma	Missing	Illinois	0.97	Illinois	3.82

	Football Player Production		Hunting Licenses Sold Per 100,000 Pop.		Corporal Punishment Permission Index		Lynchings Per Million Population	
Rank	State	cv53	State	cv49er	State	xvcp1	State	v1829r
1	Texas	2.01	Wyoming	324.6	New Mexico	9	Florida	520.83
2	Louisiana	1.90	Montana	232.8	North Carolina	8	Wyoming	445.65
3	Mississippi	1.77	Idaho	230.5	Nevada	8	Montana	366.26
4	Montana	1.68	Vermont	209.6	Vermont	7	Mississippi	361.70
5	Idaho	1.68	Utah	188.6	Colorado	7	Louisiana	295.95
6	Ohio	1.48	South Dakota	182.3	North Dakota	7	Arizona	252.03
7	North Dakota	1.38	Maine	180.6	Delaware	6	Georgia	247.74
8	Georgia	1.29	Alaska	163.6	Texas	6	Arkansas	238.75
9	Florida	1.25	Wisconsin	148.6	Oregon	6	New Mexico	194.87
10	South Carolina	1.19	Oregon	147.4	New York	6	Alabama	194.64
11	Viriginia	1.16	Arkansas	141.2	Florida	6	Oklahoma	178.48
12	Oregon	1.12	West Virginia	141.0	Illinois	6	Texas	175.14
13	Pennsylvania	1.12	North Dakota	138.0	Virginia	6	Nevada	139.53
14	Oklahoma	1.10	Minnesota	120.3	Minnesota	5	Tennessee	132.67
15	Hawaii	1.08	Tennessee	108.7	Ohio	5	Idaho	130.43
16	Alaska	1.08	Mississippi	104.2	Washington	5	South Carolina	129.85
17	California	1.05	Pennsylvania	102.3	Georgia	5	Colorado	126.16
18	South Dakota	1.04	Michigan	101.7	Michigan	5	Kentucky	108.52
19	Massachusetts	1.03	Nebraska	98.2	Arkansas	5	South Dakota	59.85
20	Utah	1.00	Oklahoma	98.2	Oklahoma	4	Virginia	58.79
21	Illinois	0.99	New Mexico	97.3	Montana	4	West Viginia	56.31
22	Washington	0.98	Missouri	93.6	California	4	Nebraska	54.36
23	Kansas	0.98	Louisiana	89.4	Louisiana	4	Washington	54.05
24	Arizona	0.97	Iowa	89.2	Pennsylvania	4	North Carolina	52.80
25	Tennessee	0.97	Kansas	88.9	South Dakota	4	Oregon	48.31
26	Kentucky	0.96	Colorado	87.3	South Carolina	3	Missouri	37.66
27	Arkansas	0.91	Washington	86.4	Hawaii	3	Kansas	37.39
28	New Jersey	0.89	Kentucky	82.0	Arizona	2	North Dakota	34.48
29	Indiana	0.88	Virginia	80.7	Nebraska	2	California	33.65
30	Iowa	0.81	New Hampshire	80.5	Connecticut	2	Utah	28.88
31	New Hampshire	0.80	Arizona	71.1	Alabama	2	Maryland	22.73
32	Alabama	0.79	Alabama	70.6	Utah	1	Indiana	20.67
33	Nebraska	0.77	Georgia	68.2	Kentucky	1	Iowa	8.06
34	D.C.	0.74	Texas	64.6	Wyoming	1	Illinois	6.64
35	North Carolina	0.74	South Carolina	64.3	New Hampshire	1	Ohio	6.25
36	Colorado	0.74	Indiana	62.5	Indiana	1	Delaware	5.41
37	Connecticut	0.74	Nevada	61.2	Kansas	1	Minnesota	5.14
38	Wyoming	0.73	North Carolina	58.6	Iowa	1	Michigan	3.30
39	West Virginia	0.72	Ohio	44.9	Missouri	1	Wisconsin	2.90
40	Michigan	0.70	Delaware	41.3	Mississippi	1	Maine	1.44
41	Minnesota	0.70	New York	40.9	Tennessee	1	Pennsylvania	1.27
42	Vermont	0.63	Maryland	36.0	Idaho	1	Connecticut	1.10
43	Maryland	0.59	Illinois	30.3	West Virginia	1	New Jersey	0.53
44	Missouri	0.57	Connecticut	26.6	Wisconsin	1	New York	0.41
45	Rhode Island	0.55	Florida	25.8	Alaska	1	Vermont	0.00
46	New Mexico	0.53	New Jersey	23.6	Rhode Island	1	Rhode Island	0.00
47	Wisconsin	0.52	California	22.7	Maine	0	New Hampshire	0.00
48	Delaware	0.51	Massachusetts	19.7	Massachusetts	0	Massachusetts	0.00
49	Nevada	0.50	Rhode Island	13.4	New Jersey	0	Alaska	0.00
50	Maine	0.47	Hawaii	11.5	Maryland	0	Hawaii	0.00
51	New York	0.38	D.C.	Missing	D.C.	Missing	D.C.	Missing

	PRISONERS UNDER SENTENCE OF DEATH				EXECUTIONS PER 100 HOMICIDE ARRESTS			
	Per 100,000 White Pop.		Per 100,000 Black Pop.		1940-1959		1960-1978	
Rank	State	z266r2	State	z267r2	State	cv59	State	cv60
1	Georgia	21.14	Idaho	100.00	Nevada	100.00	Utah	5.45
2	Florida	15.54	Utah	100.00	Vermont	76.36	Kansas	5.29
3	Alabama	15.48	Arizona	75.00	Utah	69.79	Arkansas	5.25
4	Mississippi	14.29	Montana	56.00	Georgia	42.84	Wyoming	4.96
5	Nebraska	7.14	Wyoming	56.00	Connecticut	42.70	Iowa	4.11
6	Delaware	6.25	Nevada	37.50	New York	39.07	Mississippi	4.04
7	Illinois	6.03	Oklahoma	33.87	South Carolina	37.16	Colorado	3.92
8	Arkansas	5.81	Nebraska	31.58	Arkansas	36.68	Nevada	3.70
9	Oklahoma	5.30	Oregon	25.00	Oregon	35.12	Oklahoma	3.42
10	Utah	5.00	Florida	19.35	North Carolina	34.70	Arizona	2.77
11	Louisiana	4.43	Washington	16.67	Arizona	33.47	South Carolina	2.48
12	Texas	4.00	Georgia	11.44	Maryland	32.83	Texas	2.39
13	Indiana	3.42	Delaware	10.53	California	32.73	Georgia	2.31
14	Montana	3.33	Texas	7.77	Mississippi	32.25	California	1.76
15	Virginia	3.28	Arkansas	6.32	Florida	31.13	Virginia	1.63
16	Arizona	2.92	Mississippi	4.90	Washington	31.03	Florida	1.60
17	South Carolina	2.65	Alabama	4.11	Colorado	30.65	Washington	1.46
18	North Carolina	2.01	Tennessee	3.74	Louisinana	30.30	Connecticut	1.23
19	Tennessee	1.66	Kentucky	3.57	New Jersey	25.70	Alabama	1.15
20	Missouri	1.36	South Carolina	3.38	D.C.	25.39	Ohio	1.14
21	Pennsylvania	1.21	California	1.98	Ohio	25.23	New Mexico	1.11
22	California	0.36	Louisiana	1.74	Pennsylvania	23.81	Missouri	1.08
23	South Dakota	0.00	Virginia	1.57	Iowa	23.04	Oregon	1.03
24	Kentucky	0.00	North Carolina	1.45	Delaware	21.79	New Jersey	0.88
25	Washington	0.00	Indiana	1.32	Texas	20.96	New York	0.74
26	West Virginia	0.00	Illinois	1.08	Virginia	20.22	Pennsylvania	0.55
27	Kansas	0.00	Missouri	0.72	Idaho	19.53	Indiana	0.38
28	North Dakota	0.00	Pennsylvania	0.59	Kentucky	18.69	Kentucky	0.37
29	Colorado	0.00	Maryland	0.43	Kansas	18.01	Maryland	0.30
30	Idaho	0.00	West Virginia	0.00	Alaska	17.45	Tennessee	0.27
31	Maryland	0.00	Colorado	0.00	Wyoming	17.08	Louisiana	0.25
32	Nevada	0.00	North Dakota	0.00	West Virginia	16.97	Illinois	0.22
33	Iowa	0.00	Kansas	0.00	Oklahoma	16.58	North Carolina	0.19
34	New Mexico	0.00	New Mexico	0.00	Massachusetts	15.86	Idaho	0.00
35	Wyoming	0.00	South Dakota	0.00	Nebraska	15.32	Nebraska	0.00
36	Ohio	0.00	Ohio	0.00	Tennessee	13.48	Massachusetts	0.00
37	Minnesota	0.00	Minnesota	0.00	New Mexico	12.70	West Virginia	0.00
38	Michigan	0.00	Michigan	0.00	South Dakota	10.23	South Dakota	0.00
39	Wisconsin	0.00	Wisconsin	0.00	Missouri	9.37	D.C.	0.00
40	Maine	0.00	Maine	0.00	Indiana	6.78	Delaware	0.00
41	Oregon	0.00	Iowa	0.00	Illinois	6.68	Vermont	0.00
42	Connecticut	0.00	Connecticut	0.00	Montana	4.82	Montana	0.00
43	New Jersey	0.00	New Jersey	0.00	North Dakota	0.00	North Dakota	0.00
44	New York	0.00	New York	0.00	Wisconsin	0.00	Wisconsin	0.00
45	Vermont	0.00	Vermont	0.00	Michigan	0.00	Michigan	0.00
46	Rhode Island	0.00	Rhode Island	0.00	Rhode Island	0.00	Rhode Island	0.00
47	New Hampshire	0.00	New Hampshire	0.00	New Hampshire	0.00	New Hampshire	0.00
48	Massachusetts	0.00	Massachusetts	0.00	Maine	0.00	Maine	0.00
49	Alaska	0.00	Alaska	0.00	Alaska	0.00	Alaska	0.00
50	Hawaii	0.00	Hawaii	0.00	Hawaii	0.00	Hawaii	0.00
51	D.C.	Missing	D.C.	Missing	Minnesota	0.00	Minnesota	0.00

References to Variables Used to Construct the Legitimate Violence Index

Variable Name	Variable Label and Source Document
cv16	Violent TV Viewing Index 1980 A.C. Nielson Company. 1980. "Network Programs by Designated Market Area, Average Week Audience Estimates," October 30–November 26. The audience estimates are for the six most violent programs in the Fall of 1980.
xvmc	Violent Magazine Circulation Index 1979 The items in this index are the 1979 circulation rates for the following magazines: *Easy Riders, Guns and Ammo, Heavy Metal,* and *Shooting Times;* and *Army, Airforce,* and *Navy Times* (combined circulation). The circulation rates come from the Audit Bureau of Circulation. These five magazines were selected from a larger group of magazines on the basis of a principal components analysis. The magazines included in the principal components analysis were chosen either because they indicate the relative population of military personnel and veterans (*Army, Airforce,* and *Navy Times*) or because they have a high violence content. The magazines selected all had high loading coefficients on the first factor. This subset of magazines was factor analyzed a second time, and the factor score option in the SCSS program was used to compute a factor score index for each state. The factor score option multiplies the Z-scored version of each variable by its factor score coefficient, sums the products, and transforms the sum to a Z score.
v474r	National Guard Enrollment Per 100,000 Population 1976
v475r	National Guard Expenditures Per Capita 1976 Bureau of the Census. 1977. Statistical Abstract of the United States. Washington, D.C.: U.S. Government Printing Office.
c53	State of Origin of College Football Players 1972 Rooney, John F. 1975. "Sports From a Geographical Perspective." Pp. 51–115 in Sport and Social Order: Contributions to the Sociology of Sport, edited by Donald W. Ball and John W. Loy. Reading: Mass. This measure is based on the state of origin of NCAA football players.
cv49er	Hunting Licences Sold Per 100,000 Population 1980 Federal Aid to Fish and Wildlife Restoration. 1980. U.S. Fish and Wildlife Service. Washington, D.C. U.S. Department of the Interior.
xvcp1	Corporal Punishment Permission Index 1979 Friedman, Robert H., and Irwin A. Hyman. 1979. "Corporal Punishment in the Schools: A Descriptive Survey of State Regulations." Chapter 9 in Corporal Punishment in American Education: Readings in History, Practice, and Alternatives, edited by Irwin A. Hyman and James H. Wise. Philadelphia, PA: Temple University Press. The Corporal Punishment Permission Index is based on the number of circumstances, specified by state law, under which school officials have the right to hit a child.
v1829r	Persons Lynched Per Million Population 1882–1927 White, Walter. 1929. Rope and Faggot. New York: A. A. Knopf.
z266r2	Whites Sentenced to Death Per 100,000 White Homicide Arrests 1980

Variable Name	Variable Label and Source Document
z267r2	Blacks Sentenced to Death Per 100,000 Black Homicide Arrests 1980 Bureau of Justice Statistics. 1981. Sourcebook of Criminal Justice Statistics—1980. Washington, D.C.: U.S. Government Printing Office.
cv59	Ratio of Execution Rate to Homicide Rate 1940–59 Grove, Robert D., and Alice M. Hetzel. 1968. Vital Statistics Rates in the United States, 1940–1960. Washington, D.C.: U.S. Government Printing Office.
cv60	Ratio of Execution Rate to Homicide Rate 1960–78 Bureau of the Census. 1960–1978. Statistical Abstract of the United States. Washington, D.C.: U.S. Government Printing Office.

The Relationship between Child Sexual Abuse and Adolescent Sexual Functioning in Afro-American and White American Women[a]

GAIL ELIZABETH WYATT [b]

Department of Psychiatry and Biobehavioral Sciences
University of California at Los Angeles
Los Angeles, California 90024

The adjustment of child sexual abuse victims later in life has been found to be affected in a variety of ways. Clinical studies with adults who were victimized as children have identified poor sexual functioning as one of the most pervasive effects of sexual abuse. The most common problems that have been associated with child victimization are promiscuity, dissatisfaction, and sexual dysfunction.[1–12] Indeed, as a result of sexual abuse, women may experience impaired sexual functioning,[13–17] which can, in turn, contribute to relationship problems, avoidance of men, and negative attitudes about them.[18] Several recent empirical studies have compared the sexual functioning of abused and nonabused women and found that abused women begin intercourse at earlier ages, have higher numbers of partners, and engage in a wider variety of sexual behaviors.[4,19–21]

Researchers have also identified sexual problems in recent victims of child sexual abuse.[22–24] Friedrich[25] has reported increased preoccupation with sexual thoughts, fantasies, and behaviors in male and female children.

While the above-noted studies have identified a variety of sexual problems, there is little indication as to whether altered sexual patterns in childhood persist into adolescence and adulthood. While there is a consensus that adolescence is the period in which the onset of sexual activity occurs,[26,27] factors affecting adolescent sexual behaviors have just begun to be identified in the last 10 to 15 years. Research has indicated that adolescent decision making about sexual activity often includes inadequate knowledge of what sex will be like[28] and a poor understanding of the consequences of being sexually active (e.g., unplanned pregnancies).[29] However, not enough is known about a full range of social, environmental, and sexual experiences affecting sexual activity that often begins at such a crucial developmental period. Some adolescents' initiation into sexual activity may not be of their own volition, but a result

[a]This research was funded by The Center for Prevention and Control of Rape, NIMH (MH33603) and through a Research Scientist Career Development Award (MH00269).

[b]Address for correspondence: Dr. Gail Elizabeth Wyatt, Neuropsychiatric Institute, 760 Westwood Plaza, Los Angeles, California 90024.

of sexual abuse. Furthermore, aspects of their sexual activity patterns may be influenced by sexually abusive experiences.

Finkelhor and Browne[30] have recently proposed a conceptual model with four traumagenic dynamics that can account for some of the lasting effects of child sexual abuse. One of those dynamics is traumatic sexualization, which includes: (1) an increased preoccupation with and knowledge of sex and sexual behaviors; (2) an altered understanding of the role that sex plays in relationships; and (3) an increase in sexual activities. Although this dynamic has been noted in recent victims of sexual abuse,[25] the ages of children included in recent studies[25,31] frequently do not extend into adolescence, the age at which the onset of sexual activity most likely occurs. Research that incorporates abusive as well as voluntary sexual experiences before age 18 is needed to better understand the relationship of child sexual abuse to later sexual functioning.

Although previous research has been helpful in identifying the nature of sexual problems that can occur in child abuse victims, most of this research includes clinical samples, which often have a variety of other psychological problems in addition to their sexual abuse histories. This is particularly true for ethnic groups included in clinical samples. By virtue of their utilization of public health care facilities, these ethnic group samples tend to be poor, undereducated, and at risk for other individual and family problems.[28] Consequently, the examination of a variety of factors affecting child abuse victims has been limited by the samples and the methodologies in previous studies.

Identifying the relationship between child sexual abuse and the onset and pattern of sexual activity in a community sample, which includes Afro-American women, would also accomplish other purposes. First, the findings would confirm that the effects of child sexual abuse are pervasive in a nonclinical sample and add to the growing empirical documentation that traumatic sexualization does occur. Second, although no significant differences between ethnic groups have been found in the prevalence of child sexual abuse before age 18 for Afro-American and white American women,[32] differences in the proportion of Afro-American women becoming sexually active in early adolescence has been noted.[28,29,33] In light of these ethnic differences, it is important to determine if child sexual abuse has similar or different influences upon the adolescent sexual behaviors of these two ethnic groups.

This study will examine the relationship between child sexual abuse and adolescent sexual functioning in a community sample of women,[c] almost half of whom reported at least one incident of child sexual abuse before age 18.[32] One of the advantages of utilizing retrospective data from women about their voluntary and abusive sexual experiences in childhood and adolescence is that a comprehensive, longitudinal sexual history, with the full range of adolescent sexual experiences, can be examined. Thus, any possible linkages between abuse and voluntary sexual experiences can be established and tested on adolescent subjects in future research.

[c] Afro-American women were of African descent, whose parentage also included a variety of other ethnic and racial groups found in America. White women were of Caucasian descent, whose parentage included women of Jewish heritage, as well. Women in both ethnic groups spent at least 6 of the first 12 years of their childhood in the United States.

METHOD

In order to obtain a sample of Afro-American and white American women with comparable demographics on age (18 to 36 years), education, marital status, and the presence of children, a multistage stratified probability sample of 248 women was recruited by random in digit dialing in Los Angeles County. (For more discussion of the sampling procedure, see Reference 32.) They were interviewed face to face for three to eight hours at the location of their choice by trained female interviewers who matched their ethnicity. Subjects were reimbursed twenty dollars for their time, and a baby-sitting and transportation allowance was offered to those who required those services. Information about women's voluntary and abusive sexual experiences from childhood to the present was obtained through a structured interview, The Wyatt Sex History Questionnaire (WSHQ). Details about the interval validity and reliability of the WSHQ and the techniques utilized to facilitate the recall of retrospective information are available elsewhere.[32]

Definition of Child Sexual Abuse

Child sexual abuse required contact of a sexual nature before age 18, with both familial and nonfamilial perpetrators. Incidents were considered abusive depending upon the perpetrator's age and the victim's willingness to participate. Experiences with victims 12 or younger were included if the perpetrator was older, even if she willingly participated, because children do not understand to what they are consenting and are not free to refuse an adult.[37] The experiences of adolescent victims (13 to 17 years) were considered if the perpetrator was older and if the experiences were unwanted. If the perpetrator was an adolescent-age peer, the experience had to be unwanted.

Among the sample of 126 Afro-American and 122 white women, only three women were virgins at the time of the interview. Although 20 women's first coitus was as a result of child sexual abuse, only women's age of voluntary coitus was used. (For further discussion of how voluntary and abusive first intercourse were separated, see References 28 and 33.)

Organization of Data

Because of the range of sexual behaviors included in abuse incidents, a further distinction was made: (1) noncontact abuse incidents included verbal propositions, exposure, and masturbation; and (2) contact abuse incidents involved fondling and vaginal and oral intercourse. Data from women who were sexually abused before age 18 were separated into the above-mentioned categories. Those women who reported only abuse that did not involve body contact prior to age 18 were included in the noncontact abuse group. Those who experienced some form of abuse that involved body contact prior to age 18 were included in the contact abuse group, along with women who experienced both contact and noncontact abuse.

RESULTS

The mean ages of first coitus for Afro-American and white American women was 16.7 and 17.2 years, respectively—a six-month, but nonsignificant difference between ethnic groups. The average age of first coitus for the overall group was 16.9 years.

A series of analyses of variance (ANOVA) were conducted to examine several aspects of women's abuse experiences and their adolescent sexual activity. First, a two-way ANOVA was conducted, with contact and noncontact abuse and ethnicity as the independent variables and age of first voluntary coitus as the dependent variable. The overall analysis was highly significant [$F(5,231 = 4.07, p < .002]$, due to the main effect of abuse [$F(2,231 = 7.63, p < .001]$, but not to ethnicity or the interaction. (See FIG. 1.)

Comparisons of least squares means, collapsing over ethnicity, revealed that women who had experienced contact abuse had a lower mean age of first intercourse than the nonabused women ($p = .003$, adjusting for multiple post-hoc comparisons, using the Bonferroni's inequality[38]). Overall, women in the contact abuse group had intercourse 15.4 months earlier on the average, than women in the nonabused group. However, women who had experienced noncontact abuse were not significantly different from either the contact-abuse or the nonabused groups.

Although the main effect of ethnicity was not significant, it is interesting to note the pattern of ethnic differences and similarities within abuse groups. Within both the contact-abuse group and the noncontact-abuse groups, the mean age of first intercourse is nearly identical for the two ethnic groups.

Examining differences within each ethnic group, the relationship between abuse and onset of intercourse appears to be stronger for white than for black women. While the contact-abused black women did begin intercourse earlier (16.3 years) than the noncontact abused (16.9 years) or the nonabused women (17 years), the differences between groups were not statistically significant. Among white women, those who experienced contact abuse began intercourse significantly earlier (16.5 years) than those with no abuse (18.3 years, $p = .0006$, adjusting for multiple post-hoc comparisons). The difference between the noncontact-abuse and nonabused groups did not attain statistical significance when adjustments were made for multiple comparisons.

Second, the temporal relationship between abuse and first intercourse was examined, and the number of abuse incidents occurring prior to or after the age of first coitus were identified for each woman. When the abuse occurred in the same year as the age of first intercourse ($n = 6$), abuse incidents were assumed to have occurred after first coitus.

TABLE 1 illustrates that the majority of women experienced their first abuse incident prior to intercourse. Using a more restrictive criterion, the proportion of cases in which at least half of the abuse incidents preceded intercourse remains very high. Furthermore, in roughly two-thirds of the cases, *all* of the sexual abuse incidents reported by a woman preceded her first voluntary experience with intercourse. Although these findings do not demonstrate a causal link between sexual abuse and early onset of intercourse, the fact that the large majority of abuse incidents reported occurred before a woman engaged in intercourse suggests that sexual abuse may be a contributing factor to early coitus.

Third, an analysis was conducted to determine whether women abused early in childhood would begin sexual activity at earlier ages than women who were abused later in adolescence.

The age at which sexual abuse first occurred was separated into two categories—11 or younger and 12 or older. This age break corresponded to the point at which children typically move from the stage of concrete operations to the stage of formal operations.[34] Thus, children who first experienced abuse at a later age might be better able to

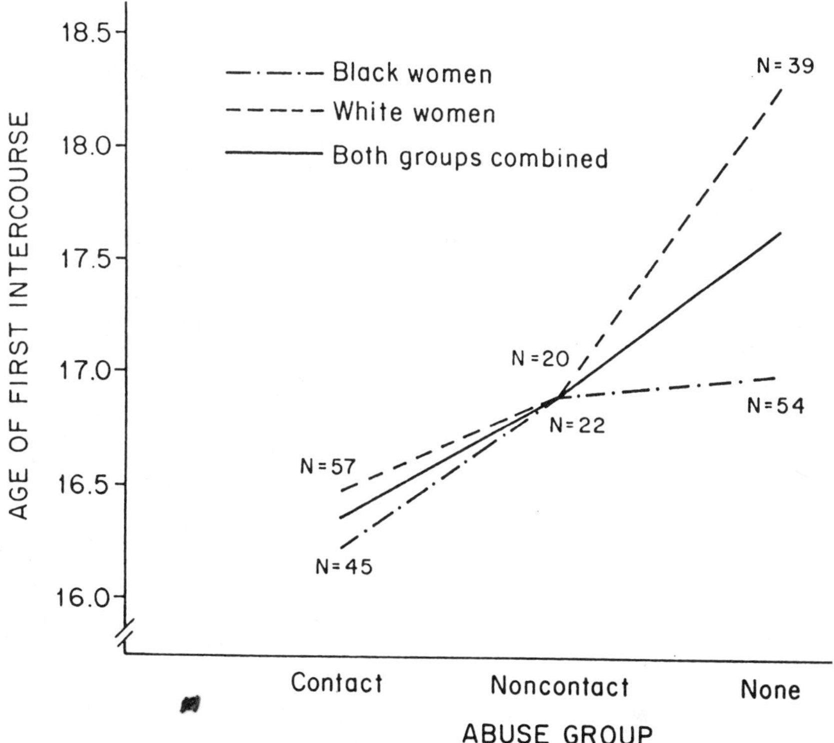

FIGURE 1. Sexual abuse and onset of intercourse.

understand and cope with the experience than younger children, who, because of their ages, might not have the cognitive processes to incorporate the experience. However, no effect of age of first abuse on onset of intercourse was found, and the means failed to reveal any trends regarding differences between the age groups.

Thus, it appears that while the occurrence of sexual abuse before age 18 is associated with earlier onset of intercourse, the age at which the abuse first takes place does not appear to be related to the age at which voluntary intercourse begins. Sexual abuse probably does have different effects on children depending on their age, but these effects appear to be manifested in areas other than the age of onset of sexual activity.

TABLE 1. The Temporal Relationship between Sexual Abuse and First Voluntary Intercourse

	First Abuse Occurred before First Intercourse	Half of Abuse Occurred before First Intercourse	All Abuse Occurred before First Intercourse
Contact abuse			
Black (n = 45)	43 (95.6%)	43 (95.6%)	31 (68.9%)
White (n = 58)	53 (91.4%)	49 (84.5%)	37 (63.8%)
Noncontact abuse			
Black (n = 22)	20 (90.9%)	20 (90.9%)	19 (86.4%)
White (n = 20)	17 (85.0%)	17 (85.0%)	13 (65.0%)

The severity of child sexual abuse was rated by interviewers on a scale of 1 to 10, incorporating aspects of the experience, the type of abuse perpetrated, the age of the victim, the relationship of the victim to the perpetrator, and the victim's reaction to the abuse. Values for the overall severity of abuse were derived mathematically from ratings made by the interviewers at the conclusion of each interview. Interrater reliability was established on a weekly basis among the interviewers, and the average coefficient correlation between raters on the severity of child sexual abuse was .90. This assessment of the severity of sexual abuse differs from other studies examining the seriousness of abuse.[35–37] In these studies, seriousness tended to be based upon the type of sexual behavior that occurred rather than an incorporation of the circumstances of the abuse experience and the victim's reaction.

At the completion of data collection, incidents were divided into least, moderate, and most severe incidents. When severity of abuse and ethnicity were examined as independent variables and age of voluntary first coitus as the dependent variable, the relationship was highly significant [$F(7,228 = 4.01, p < .001$], due to the main effect of abuse [$F(3,228 = 6.00, p < .001$]. The mean age of first coitus for Afro-American and white women with the most severe types of abuse was 15 years and 16 years, respectively, as compared to their nonabused peers (17 and 18 years, respectively). When adjusted for multiple comparisons, these differences were significant at the .05 level for Afro-American women and at the .01 level for white women.

Child Sexual Abuse and Other Adolescent Sexual Behaviors

In addition to the onset of intercourse, other aspects of adolescent sexual behavior and sexual abuse were examined.

In order to examine adolescent sexual behavior, six behaviors—ages of necking, petting including breasts and genitals, petting including breasts only, first voluntary coitus, the length of sexual relationships during adolescence, and the numbers of partners—were entered into a factor analysis that performed a principal component solution and varimax rotation.[39] Number of partners was translated into a rate, in order to account for differences between the age of subjects (18 to 36 years) and the length of time they were sexually active.

Two factors were established to assess various aspects of the subjects' sexuality in adolescence. The first factor, sexual behavior related to first intercourse, consisted of the age of necking (.80), breast (.90) and genital petting (.93), and intercourse (.88). The second factor, adolescent sexual behavior, consisted of the length of sexual relationships (.86) and the number of sexual partners (.45). These factors accounted for 75% of the common variance.

A series of ANOVAs were conducted with abuse and ethnicity as independent variables and the two adolescent factors as dependent variables. The overall relationship was marginally significant [$F(5,231) = 2.16$, $p = .05$], due to the main effect of abuse and Factor 1 (necking, petting, and first coitus) [$F(2,231) = 3.99$, $p < .02$], but not to ethnicity or the interaction. Women who experienced contact sexual abuse had significantly lower factor scores on ages of necking, petting, and first coitus, indicating that their ages of necking and petting were younger than women who experienced noncontact abuse or no abuse. (See TABLE 2)

Furthermore, the relationship between abuse and Factor 2 (short term relationships and numbers of sexual partners) was highly significant [$F(5,231) = 3.15$, $p < .01$], due to the main effect of abuse [$F(2,231) = 4.43$, $p < .02$], and to ethnicity [$F(1,231) = 5.54$, $p < .02$]. Women with contact abuse experiences had lower factor scores, indicating that they had more sexual partners and briefer relationships with their partners, than women with no child sexual abuse histories ($p < .05$, see TABLE 2).

Additionally, white women had more sexual partners and briefer relationships than their black peers. However, the interaction between abuse and ethnicity was not significant.

When severity of sexual abuse was examined with other adolescent sexual behaviors, a relationship similar to child sexual abuse was found. While the overall relationship was marginal [$F(7,229) = 1.76$, $p = .09$], the main effect of severity of abuse and Factor 1 was significant [$F(3,229) = 2.89$, $p < .04$]. Women whose child sexual abuse was rated most severe had significantly earlier ages of necking, petting, and coitus than women with least severe, moderately severe, or no abuse ($p < .05$, see TABLE 3) No ethnic or interaction effects were noted. Furthermore, the relationship between severity of abuse, ethnicity, and Factor 2 was highly significant [$F(7,229) = 3.12$, $p < .01$], due to severity of abuse [$F(3,229) = 5.73$, $p < .001$]. Women with the most severe incidents had more sexual partners and shorter-termed relationships than women with least severe, moderately severe, or no abuse experiences. ($p < .02$). The main effects of ethnicity and Factor 2 and the interaction were not significant at the desired confidence level. (See TABLE 3).

TABLE 2. The Means of Child Sexual Abuse and Adolescent Sexual Behaviors

	Factor 1		Factor 2	
Type of Abuse	Afro-American ($n = 121$)	White ($n = 116$)	Afro-American ($n = 121$)	White ($n = 116$)
Contact	−.234	−.172[a]	−.032	.392[a]
Noncontact	.102	−.019	−.228	.185
No Abuse	.059	.392[a]	.259	−.144[a]

[a] Significant at .01 when adjusted for multiple comparisons.

CONCLUSIONS

This study examined relationships between several aspects of women's child sexual abuse experiences and their voluntary sexual behavior before age 18.

Significant relationships were found between women who experienced contact sexual abuse and earlier coitus, as compared to women with noncontact abuse or those with no abuse histories. Likewise, women with sexual abuse that was most severe—including experiences that were rated as highly negative by victims and that may have involved family members and long term relationships with the perpetrators, also had earlier coitus than women who reported noncontact or no abuse. However, abuse that began earlier in childhood (before age 12) did not appear to be related to early coitus. Knowledge of the age at which abuse first occurred reveals very little about a woman's voluntary sexual experience. It may be that other aspects of the abuse history, such as the severity of the experience, are more salient to its impact on sexual abuse than the age at which the abuse began.

TABLE 3. The Means of Interviewers' Ratings of the Severity of Child Sexual Abuse and Adolescent Sexual Behaviors

	Factor 1[a]		Factor 2[b]	
Type of Abuse	Afro-American (n = 121)	White (n = 116)	Afro-American (n = 121)	White (n = 116)
No abuse	.056	.392	−.241	−.144
Least severe	.039	−.042	−.279	.179
Moderately severe	−.321	−.072	.097	.183
Most severe	−.495	−.302	.289	.685

[a] Factor 1 includes ages of necking, petting including the breasts only, breast and genital petting, and first voluntary coitus.

[b] Factor 2 includes the numbers of sexual partners and numbers of sexual relationships during ages 13 to 17 years.

Significant relationships were also found between women with contact-abuse incidents and other adolescent sexual behaviors, such as earlier ages of necking and petting, more sexual partners, and shorter-termed sexual relationships. Similarly, relationships were found between the most severe child-sexual-abuse incidents and earlier onset of sexual behaviors (i.e., necking, petting, and coitus, as well as briefer relationships and more sexual partners). Both women's contact abuse and most severe experiences appeared to influence a variety of adolescent sexual behaviors.

The finding regarding ethnic differences between white and black women's numbers of sexual partners during adolescence has also been noted in other studies.[40,41] These findings suggest that there are some aspects of women's voluntary sexual experiences that may be related to their ethnicity or to values regarding how and with whom sexual behaviors should be engaged in. It is interesting to note that when variables such as age, education, and, to a large extent, income are controlled in a sample such as this, ethnic differences between ages of first coitus diminish markedly between groups, but differences in other variables, such as the numbers of sexual partners and the length of sexual relationships, do not. More research on factors influencing women's voluntary sexual patterns is needed.

These findings confirm results from nonclinical studies regarding the increase in the number and kind of sexual experiences noted in women with abuse histories.[5,19–21] There are two clinical interpretations offered. One describes sexual abuse victims learning about their own sexual arousal in such a way as to create a precocious interest in sex, early in their psychosexual development.[30] This interest in sex is expressed through the variety and frequency of sexual behaviors in which victims engage. Another, more psychodynamic interpretation is that female victims replicate sexual encounters in an effort to gain control or mastery of an experience in which they felt violated and powerless.[42] Both of these conceptual formulations are similar in that they stress that the effects of child sexual abuse can alter women's subsequent sexual patterns. The data presented here adds to the literature that confirms that relationship.[1–19,22–24]

It appears that certain types of sexual behaviors may have more influence upon voluntary sexual behaviors than others. Contact sexual abuse, including fondling, and attempted or completed oral or vaginal intercourse, appears to be more consistently related to adolescent sexual behaviors than noncontact abuse or no child abuse. Apparently, observing an individual engaging in self-stimulatory sexual behavior (as in noncontact abuse) does not influence one's own interest in sex.

Women's sexual abuse histories also appear to be related to ages of necking, petting, and first coitus in a way that their ethnicity is not. Patterns of relationships within ethnic groups were found to be quite similar in relation to child sexual abuse. However, the relationship of child sexual abuse to the age of first coitus appears to be stronger for white women, possibly because they begin coitus six months later than Afro-American women.

While these findings suggest that adolescent sexual behaviors, and particularly first coitus, may be influenced by child sexual abuse histories, some of these results do not necessarily imply a causal relationship. For some of the behaviors, such as necking and petting, it has not been ascertained that the sexual behavior followed, rather than preceded, the abuse. However, since abuse typically precedes onset of intercourse, and first intercourse must precede number of partners and length of relationships, the temporal relationship between abuse and sexual behavior is clearer for these indicators of sexual activity.

More longitudinal research with multiethnic samples controlled on critical demographic variables can confirm these relationships and further describe the extent of traumatic sexualization that occurs in child sexual abuse victims. Research that examines the sexual patterns of child abuse victims in adolescence as well as adulthood is also needed to determine the more pervasive effects upon later sexual functioning in adulthood.

Even as more research is being conducted, it is hoped that researchers and social policy makers will begin to incorporate child sexual abuse as a factor that can influence the sexual decision making of adolescents. Mental health professionals need to examine more carefully the sexual histories of young adolescents for abusive experiences that may affect their present and future sexual patterns. Because we know that abuse victims are at risk for revictimization,[37] these findings raise questions as to whether sexual patterns established in adolescence may continue or even escalate in adulthood, with continued or repeated sexual abuse. Before we view adolescents as solely willful participants in the decisions that they make about their sexuality, we need far more information about the myriad of influences upon them, including sexual victimization.

SUMMARY

This study has examined the relationship between child sexual abuse and adolescent sexual functioning in a community sample of 245 Afro-American and white American women, most of whom became sexually active during adolescence. Significant relationships between several aspects of women's child abuse experiences and their voluntary sexual behavior before age 18 revealed that women who reported contact sexual abuse (fondling, and attempted and completed oral and vaginal intercourse) had voluntary sexual intercourse 15.4 months earlier than women with noncontact (e.g., observing exhibitionists) or no abuse. Likewise, women with contact abuse engaged in necking and petting behaviors at earlier ages, and had more sexual partners during adolescence and briefer sexual relationships than women with noncontact or no abuse. Similar relationships between interviewers' ratings of the severity of child sexual abuse and women's adolescent sexual behaviors were noted.

These findings stress that child sexual abuse, rather than women's ethnicity alone, may contribute to the early onset and frequency of adolescent sexual behaviors. Conceptual formulations that address these relationships and the implications for future research and social policy have been discussed.

ACKNOWLEDGMENTS

The author wishes to thank Stefanie Peters, Ph.D., for her valuable assistance with this manuscript, The Women's Project Staff, Gwen Gordon, Donald Guthrie, Ph.D., and Ray Mickey, Ph.D., for data programming and analysis.

REFERENCES

1. BRIERE, J. 1984. The effects of childhood sexual abuse on later psychological functioning: Defining a "post-sexual abuse syndrome." Presented at the Third National Conference on Sexual Victimization of Children, Washington, D.C.
2. BROWN, M. E. 1979. Teenage prostitution. Adolescence **14:** 665-680.
3. COURTOIS, C. 1979. Characteristics of a volunteer sample of adult women who experienced incest in childhood or adolescence. Diss. Abstr. Int. **40:** 3194A-3195A.
4. DEYOUNG, M. 1982. Sexual Victimization of Children. McFarland. Jefferson, NC.
5. BENWARD, J. & J. DENSEN-GERBER. 1975. Incest as a causative factor in antisocial behavior: An exploratory study. Contemp. Drug Probl. **4:** 323-340.
6. HERMAN, J. 1981. Father-daughter Incest. Harvard University Press. Cambridge, MA.
7. JAMES, J. & J. MEYERDING. 1977. Early sexual experiences and prostitution. Am. J. Psychiatry **134:** 1381-1385.
8. JEHU, D., M. GAZAN & C. KLASSEN. 1984-1985. Common therapeutic targets among women who were sexually abused. J. Soc. Work Hum. Sexuality **4:** 46-69.
9. MEISELMAN, K. C. 1978. Incest: A Psychological Study of Causes and Effects with Treatment Recommendations. Jossey-Bass. San Francisco, CA.
10. SILBERT, M. H. & A. M. PINES. 1981. Sexual child abuse as an antecedent to prostitution. Child Abuse and Neglect **5:** 407-411.

11. Tsai, M. & N. Wagner. 1978. Therapy groups for women sexually molested as children. Arch. Sexual Behav. **7:** 417-429.
12. Westermeyer, J. 1978. Incest in psychiatric practice. A description of patients and incestuous relationships. J. Clin. Psychiatry **39:** 643-648.
13. Burgess, A. W. & L. L. Holmstrom. 1974. Rape: Victims in Crisis. Robert J. Brady Co. Bowie, MD.
14. Finch, S. M. 1967. Sexual activity of children with other children and adults (Commentaries). Clin. Pediatr. **3:** 1-2.
15. McGuire, L. & N. Wagner. 1978. Sexual dysfunctions in women who were molested as children: One response pattern and suggestions for treatment. J. Sex Marital Ther. **4:** 11-15.
16. Rosenfield, A., C. Nadelson, M. Krieger & J. Backman. 1979. Incest and sexual abuse of children. J. Am. Acad. Child Psychiatry. **16:** 327-339.
17. Steele, B. & H. Alexander. 1981. Long-term effects of sexual abuse in childhood. *In* Sexually Abused Children and Their Families. P. B. Mrazek & C. H. Kempe, Eds. Pergamon. Oxford.
18. Wyatt, G. E. & M. R. Mickey. 1987. Ameliorating effects of child sexual abuse: An exploratory study of support by parents and others. J. Interpers. Violence **2:** 403-414.
19. Fromuth, M. E. 1983. The long term psychological impact of childhood sexual abuse. Ph.D. dissertation, Auburn University, Auburn, Alabama.
20. Seidner, A. L. & K. S. Calhoun. 1984. Childhood sexual abuse: Factors related to differential adult adjustment. Presented at the Second National Conference for Family Violence Researchers, Durham, New Hampshire, August 1984.
21. Tsai, M., S. Feldman-Summers & M. Edgar. 1979. Childhood molestation: Variables related to differential impact of psychosexual functioning in adult women. J. Abnorm. Psychol. **88:** 407-417.
22. Yates, A. 1982. Children eroticized by incest. Am. J. Psychiatry **139:** 482-485.
23. Friedrich, W. N., A. J. Urquiza & R. Beilke. 1986. Behavior problems in sexually abused young children. J. Pediatr. Psychol. **11:** 47-57.
24. Gomes-Schwartz, B., J. M. Horowitz & M. Sauzier. 1985. Severity of emotional distress among sexually abused preschool, school-age, and adolescent children. Hosp. Community Psychiatry. **36:** 503-508.
25. Friedrich, W. N. 1987. Children from sexually abusive families: A behavioral comparison. J. Interpers. Violence **2:** 391-402.
26. DeLamater, J. & P. MacCorquodale. 1979. Premarital Sexuality. University of Wisconsin Press. Madison, WI.
27. Zelnik, M. & J. F. Kantner. 1980. Sexual activity, contraceptive use and pregnancy among metropolitan-area teenagers. 1971-1979. Fam. Plann. Perspect. **12:** 230-237.
28. Wyatt, G. E. 1988. Factors affecting adolescent sexuality: Have they changed in 40 years? *In* Adolescence and Puberty. J. Bancroft, Ed. Oxford University Press. New York, NY. In press.
29. Hofferth, S. 1988. Trends in adolescent sexual activity, contraceptive use and pregnancy. *In* Adolescence and Puberty. J. Bancroft, Ed. Oxford University Press. New York, NY. In press.
30. Finkelhor, D. & A. Browne. 1985. The traumatic impact of child sexual abuse: A conceptualization. Am. J. Orthopsychiatry **55:** 530-541.
31. Conte, J. 1987. The effects of sexual abuse on children: A multidimensional view. J. Interpers. Violence **2:** 380-390.
32. Wyatt, G. E. 1985. The sexual abuse of Afro-American and White women in childhood. Child Abuse and Neglect **9:** 507-519.
33. Wyatt, G. E. 1987. Factors affecting Afro-American and White-American women's first coitus. Submitted for publication.
34. Elkind, D. 1974. Children and adolescence: Interpretive essays on Jean Piaget. 2nd ed. Oxford University Press. New York, NY.
35. Bagley, C. & R. Ramsey. 1985. Disrupted childhood and vulnerability to sexual assault: Long-term sequels with implications for counseling. Presented at the Conference on Counseling the Sexual Abuse Survivor, Winnipeg, February 1985.

36. FINKELHOR, D. 1984. Child sexual abuse: New theory and research. Free Press. New York, NY.
37. RUSSELL, D. 1984. The prevalence and seriousness of incestuous abuse: Stepfathers versus biological fathers. Child Abuse and Neglect **8:** 15-22.
38. MILLER, R. G. 1984. Simultaneous Statistical Inference. 2nd ed. Springer-Verlag. New York, NY.
39. SAS, INTERNATIONAL. 1982. SAS User's Guide: Statistics. Cary, NC.
40. BELCASTRO, P. A. 1985. Sexual behavior differences between Black and White students. J. Sex Res. **21:** 56-67.
41. ELLIOTT, D. S. & B. J. MORSE. 1985. Drug use, delinquency and sexual activity. *In* Drug Abuse and Adolescent Sexual Activity, Pregnancy and Parenthood. C. Jones & E. McAnarney, Eds. NIDA Research Monograph Series. U.S. Government Printing Office. Washington, DC.
42. GREEN, A. H. 1985. Children traumatized by physical abuse. *In* Post-Traumatic Stress Disorder in Children. S. Eth & R. S. Pynoos, Eds. American Psychiatric Press. Washington, DC.

A Multidimensional Approach to Sexual Aggression: Combining Measures of Past Behavior and Present Likelihood

NEIL M. MALAMUTH[a]

Departments of Communication Studies and Psychology
University of California, Los Angeles
Los Angeles, California 90024

Researchers have recognized the inadequacy of studying the general topic of sexual aggression by relying exclusively on samples of rapists identified by the judicial system.[1,2] Not only is it well known that a small percentage of rapes are reported to the police,[3,4] but there are various sexually aggressive acts that do not necessarily meet the legal definition of rape or sexual assault. Acts reported to the police may be only the "tip of the iceberg" of sexual aggression. Researchers have therefore sought to obtain samples from the general population in addition to identified rapists.

Two types of self-report measures have been used to study heterosexual sexual aggression in general population samples. In the first, men indicated whether they had committed various forms of sexual aggression.[5–7] In the second, they reported the likelihood that they would engage in forced sex if they could be assured of not being identified or punished.[8–11] This latter measure appears to assess some aspect of the attraction or desire to commit sexual aggression (if there were no negative consequences to the aggressor). These two measures have at times been described as alternative approaches,[2] and researchers have relied on one or the other. The present article contends that rather than being differing ways of assessing the same continuum, these two approaches represent different dimensions, and that combining them results in more comprehensive information than using either one alone.

Theoretically, it may be expected that somewhat different information would be derived from the two variables of past sexual aggression and of desire to commit forced sex, as assessed by the likelihood of forcing sex measure. For the purposes of explication, consider crossing these two variables, with each having two levels, a low versus a high score, thereby yielding the following four cells: First, some men may not have engaged in any sexual aggression and may have no desire or attraction to do so. Second, some men may not have committed any sexual aggression, but may have some desire to do so if they could avoid punishment. Such desire may not have been expressed in actual behavior for various reasons. These could include fear of the consequences, the lack of opportunity to aggress, or having certain attributes or

[a]Address for correspondence: Neil M. Malamuth, Communication Studies, 334 Kinsey Hall, University of California, Los Angeles, Los Angeles, California 90024

emotions (e.g., empathy) that are incompatible with acting out aggressively. Third, some men have been sexually aggressive in the past but may now report relatively little desire for forcing sex. Some may regret their previous aggression or have changed their attitudes, emotions, or other characteristics. Others may not recognize or admit to themselves that their past behavior constitutes coercive sex or, in certain instances, rape. Fourth, some men who have been sexually aggressive still have considerable attraction and desire to engage in such behavior.

Although it is convenient for the purposes of explication to think of these two variables in the low versus high dichotomy, such a division may be too limited. Previous research has shown that more elaborate gradations are needed. For example, even though Malamuth and associates found that a two-level classification based on men's reported likelihood of raping was very useful,[8] later research showed that a three-level classification was preferable.[11] This classification was based on two questions. The first asked the likelihood that the man would force a female to do something sexual she didn't want to if "... assured that no one would know and that you could in no way be punished." The second question was similar, but the word "rape" was used instead of referring to forced sex. On the basis of these items, subjects were classified into one of three groups: (1) no likelihood of forcing or raping (LF−/LR−), (2) some likelihood of forcing but no likelihood of raping (LF−/LR+), and (3) some likelihood of both forcing and raping (LF+/LR+). Analyses of subjects' scores on measures of attitudes pertaining to aggression against women showed a linear pattern that provided support for this classification scheme: force-only subjects (i.e., LF+/LR−) were intermediate in their support of various types of violence against women, falling between those indicating no likelihood of either forcing or raping, and those indicating some likelihood of both.

Similarly, Koss and associates[6] found a four-level scheme useful for classifying the responses of college males to a questionnaire assessing different degrees of past sexual aggression: No Sexual Aggression, Sexually Coercive, Sexually Abusive, and Sexually Assaultive groups. (These categories are described in greater detail later in this article.) A discriminant analysis revealed significant differences among these groups on attitude measures assessing such areas as Adversarial Sexual Beliefs, Rape Myth Acceptance, and Relationships as Gameplaying.

In the present study, subjects are classified on both their past sexual aggression and reported likelihood of coercive sex. These two dimensions are factorially crossed, such that within each of the four levels of past sexual aggression there are three levels of likelihood of forcing sex.[b]

To examine the usefulness of this classification approach, I will present here analyses using variables available in two data bases we gathered earlier.[7,12,13] The past sexual aggression and likelihood of forcing sex dimensions are used here as the independent variables to examine their relations to variables referred to as "predictors" in earlier research.[7] Since the findings were very similar on the two data bases, they were combined in the analyses reported below. The new contribution of the present article is in revealing the theoretical and empirical utility of combining the measures of past sexual aggression and likelihood of forcing sex.

[b] Instead of using the classification schemes described here, the full range of responses on the sexual aggression and likelihood of forcing sex dimensions could have been used. That would have certain advantages,[14] such as increased statistical power. Due to the skewness of the distributions and for consistency with the existing literature, I decided to utilize the classification approach described here.

METHOD

The methods used (e.g., recruitment of subjects, instruments and procedures, etc.) have been described in detail elsewhere.[7,12] To summarize briefly here, the data for a total of 453 male subjects were analyzed from the two data bases. For all subjects, scores were available on a self-reported sexual aggression scale.[5] I used it to classify subjects according to the categories developed by Koss and associates:[6]

1. The Sexually Nonaggressive men did not admit to having engaged in any coercive, abusive, or assaultive sexual behavior toward women.
2. The Sexually Coercive men indicated that they had obtained sexual intercourse with a woman by using extreme verbal pressure (e.g., false promises, insistent arguments, or threats to end the relationship).
3. Men classified as Sexually Abusive reported either of two experiences. The first was having obtained some sexual contact (e.g., petting) by the use of threats of force or actual force. The second was having attempted to obtain sexual intercourse by the same means, but for various reasons intercourse did not occur.
4. The Sexually Assaultive men admitted coercing vaginal, oral, or anal intercourse either by the threat of harm or by actual physical force, such as twisting a woman's arm or holding her down.

Scores were also available on self-reported likelihood of sexual force (LF) and likelihood of rape (LR) if the man could be sure that others would not know and that he would not be punished. On the basis of these responses, subjects were classified into three levels of Likelihood of Forcing Sex (LFS) as described earlier in this article and elsewhere.[11]

The dependent measures were five "paper and pencil" scales that have been linked, on both theoretical and empirical grounds, to aggression against women. These included three of Burt's[15] attitude measures—the Acceptance of Interpersonal Violence (AIV) against women, the Rape Myth Acceptance (RMA), and the Adversarial Sexual Beliefs (ASB) scales. Also included were Nelson's[16] measure assessing dominance as a motive for engaging in sexual acts and Check and Malamuth's[12,13,17] Hostility Toward Women (HTW) scale.

RESULTS

Classification of Subjects

The Sexual Aggression (SA) and Likelihood of Forcing Sex (LFS) variables were not strongly correlated, $r(452) = .15$, $p < .005$. TABLE 1 presents a frequency distribution classifying the 453 subjects on the basis of the four SA and the three LFS levels. As can be seen in this table, the use of the latter variable enabled considerable differentiation within each of the sexual aggression levels. For example, of the 301 subjects not reporting any sexual aggression, 64 (or 21%) indicated that there was

TABLE 1. Frequency Distribution According to Sexual Aggression and Likelihood of Forcing Sex Dimensions

Likelihood of Forcing Sex	Sexual Aggression Category				
	Nonaggressive	Coercive	Abusive	Assaultive	Totals
LF−/LR−	196	59	15	4	274
LF+/LR−	64	28	13	3	108
LF+/LR+	41	18	8	4	71
Totals	301	105	36	11	453

NOTE: LF−/LR− = no likelihood of forcing or raping; LF+/LR− = some likelihood of forcing but no likelihood of raping; LF+/LR+ = some likelihood of both forcing and raping.

some likelihood that they would force a woman into sexual acts if they could be assured of not being punished (LF+) and another 41 (or about 14%) also reported some likelihood of raping (LR+). A similar distribution occurred within the Coercive group. As expected, within the Abusive and Assaultive groups, there appear to be somewhat higher percentages of LF+/LR− and of LF+/LR+ men than within the lower sexual aggression categories.

Overall Effects

An assessment of overall effects was obtained by a 4 (Sexual Aggression) by 3 (Likelihood of Forcing Sex) Multivariate Analysis of Variance (MANOVA) on the five dependent scales. To account for unequal sample sizes and nonorthoganality of the independent variables, an exact least-squares analysis was performed (on this and all other MANOVAs and ANOVAs in this article) by assessing each effect after first adjusting for its relationship to all other effects.[18] The results showed significant main effects for both the SA and LFS dimensions ($p < .0001$). The interaction was not significant.

Regression Analyses

To assess directly whether using both classifications increased the amount of variance accounted for on each of the five dependent measures, regression analyses are presented in TABLE 2. The SA variable was "forced" entered first, followed by entering the LFS variable. On all five variables SA entered significantly and LFS increased significantly the overall amount of accounted variance. Entering interactions after the two "main effects"[14] did not significantly add to the accounted variance on any of the dependent measures. Examination of the squared semi-partial correlations on all the dependent variables suggests that the LFS variable may have accounted for a higher percentage of unique variance than SA, although both dimensions contributed significantly (see TABLE 2). The simple correlations are also shown in this table.

Mean Scores

The importance of using both classification dimensions is further shown by examining the mean scores on the dependent variables. As presented in FIGURE 1, they are separated into the four SA levels (Nonaggressive, Coercive, Abusive, Assaultive) and, within the first three of these, also separated by the LFS classification (LF−/LR−; LF+/LR−; LF+/LR+). Due to the small number of Sexually Assaultive men, however, and since the analyses reported below did not show significant differences within this group, their mean data are not divided into the three LFS levels. On the whole, though, their pattern of means on the dependent variables was similar to that of the other groups when separated by LFS levels.

TABLE 2. Simple Correlations and Regression Analyses on Dependent Variables Using Sexual Aggression and Likelihood of Forcing Sex Dimensions (n = 453)

Independent Variable	r[a]	Multiple R	sr^2[b]
		AIV	
SA	.21[c]	.21[c]	.03[c]
LFS	.29[c]	.34[c]	.07[c]
		ASB	
SA	.13[d]	.13[d]	.01[d]
LFS	.20[c]	.22[c]	.03[c]
		HTW	
SA	.20[c]	.20[c]	.03[c]
LFS	.23[c]	.28[c]	.04[c]
		RMA	
SA	.18[d]	.12[d]	.01[e]
LFS	.28[c]	.30[c]	.07[c]
		DOM	
SA	.26[c]	.26[c]	.04[c]
LFS	.32[c]	.40[c]	.10[c]

NOTE: SA = Sexual Aggression; LFS = Likelihood of Forcing Sex; AIV = acceptance of interpersonal violence (against women) scale; RMA = rape myth acceptance scale; ASB = adversarial sexual beliefs scale; DOM = dominance motive; HTW = hostility toward women scale.

[a] Pearson product-moment correlation coefficient.

[b] Squared semipartial correlation coefficient indicating unique contribution of independent variable to dependent variable after both independent variables have been entered.

[c] $p < .0001$.

[d] $p < .05$.

[e] $p < .07$.

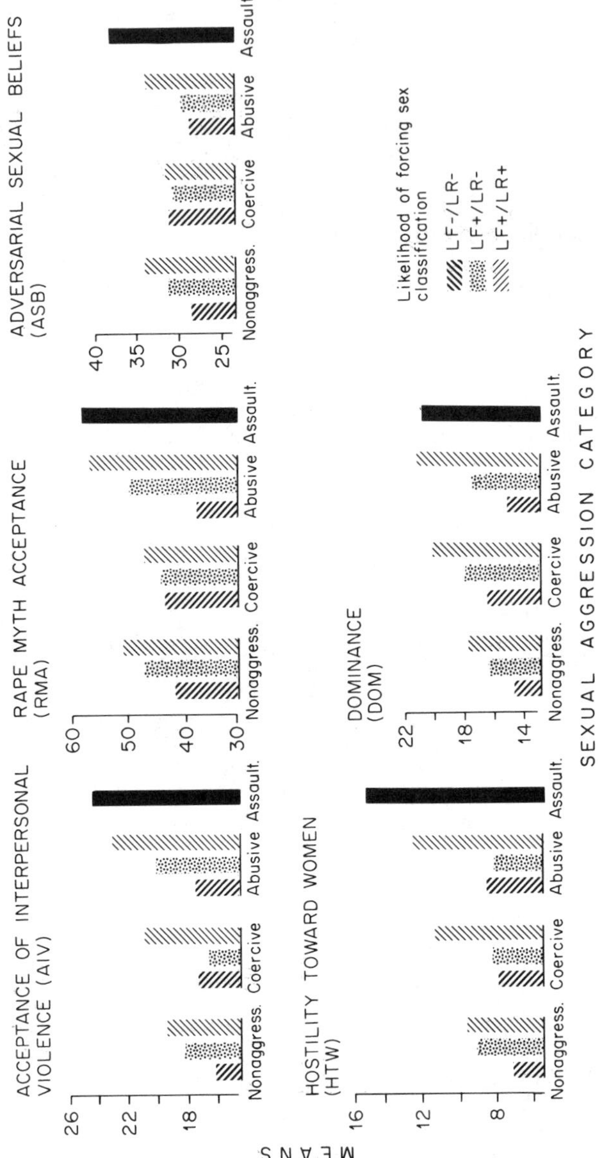

FIGURE 1. Means of dependent variables as a function of Sexual Aggression and Likelihood of Forcing Sex dimensions.

In keeping with the regression results, the means suggest that (a) higher levels of sexual aggression are associated with higher scores on the dependent measures, and that (b) within the Sexual Aggression categories, higher Likelihood of Forcing Sex levels show higher scores on the dependent variables. To assess these latter differences statistically, additional analyses within each of the SA levels are reported below.

Analyses within Sexual Aggression Categories

Using only the Sexually Nonaggressive group, a MANOVA was performed on the five dependent variables with LFS as the independent variable. This analysis yielded a highly significant effect, Wilks' Lambda = .85, $F(10, 588) = 4.91$, $p < .0001$. Univariate analyses also showed significant effects ($p < .001$) on all the dependent variables. Post-hoc comparisons among individual means using the conservative Scheffé[19] test (particularly suited for unequal n's) indicated that in all instances the LF+/LR+ group was significantly higher than the LF−/LR− group. Further, except for ASB, the LF+/LR− group was always significantly higher than the LF−/LR− group. These data show that using the LFS measure enabled very clear discrimination among sexually nonaggressive men.

Similar analyses were performed on the Sexually Coercive group. Here, as well, a significant MANOVA effect was obtained for LFS, Wilks' Lambda = .79, $F(10, 196) = 2.51$, $p < .007$. Significant univariates were found on the AIV, HTW, and Dominance variables. Scheffé follow-ups showed that the LF+/LR+ group was significantly higher than the LF−/LR− group on all of these three variables, and higher than the LF+/LR− group on the AIV measure.

Similar analyses on the Sexually Abusive group yielded a significant MANOVA for LFS, Wilks' Lambda = .50, $F(10, 58) = 2.44$, $p < .02$. Significant univariates were found on the RMA, Dominance, and HTW variables. Scheffé comparisons showed the LF+/LR+ group significantly higher than the LF−/LR− group on the RMA and Dominance variables, and higher than the LF+/LR− group on the HTW measure.

No significant effects were obtained within the Sexually Assaultive group. This may be due to the small sample ($n = 11$) and/or because once men have committed acts that would legally be defined as rape, a "ceiling effect" may occur.

Overall, these analyses show consistently that using the LFS classification yields statistically significant differences within levels of sexual aggression. This is particularly important for the lowest level of sexual aggression, in which the majority of men are classified. Previous research using a classification typology based only on the SA dimension[6] did not enable differentiation within this majority.

Sexually Experienced Only

In their analyses, Koss and associates[6] excluded subjects who had not engaged in mutually consenting intercourse. In order to perform a similar assessment here, the analyses reported above were also conducted using only those subjects who were relatively highly sexually experienced in heterosexual relations, as indicated by Bentler's[20] sexual experience scale. The results were very similar to those reported above for all subjects.

DISCUSSION

The findings show very clearly that using information derived from both the dimensions of past sexual aggression and reported likelihood of forcing sex resulted in a much more comprehensive account of men's attitudes, dominance motives, and hostility toward women than using either dimension alone. It appears, then, that focusing either only on actual aggressive behavior or only on attraction to such aggression is insufficient. Both dimensions are important, although the data suggest that the LFS dimension may generally account for more of the variance on the type of dependent variables used here. It is reasonable that with these variables (e.g., attitudes) there would be stronger links with attraction to sexual aggression rather than with actual behavior.

On the basis of the data patterns appearing in FIGURE 1, however, we might speculate that two of the measures used here, the Hostility Toward Women and the Adversarial Sexual Beliefs scales, might be most capable of differentiating between those men who actually commit the highest levels of sexual aggression (i.e., the Assaultive Group) and those who may be strongly attracted to such aggression but are not actually assaultive. Examining the items of these two scales, as well as statistical assessments of their overlap,[12] suggest that both scales tap a hostile-emotional reaction to women. Future research should systematically assess whether such a reaction may be a crucial contributor to converting a high attraction for sexual aggression into actual assault, at least in the type of subjects we have studied here.

The findings advance considerably the goal of developing multivariate models of sexual aggression. In order to develop such models within a structural equations context,[21,22] it is important to use a multivariate approach both to assess the factors leading to aggression and to measure aggression itself. While previous work documented the desirability of the former,[7] the present article demonstrates the usefulness of the latter as well. It is hoped that future research will combine both, employing a multivariate approach at both "sides of the equation." Such an approach should use both multiple indicators of the same dimensions[21] as well as multiple dimensions.

In future research, it may be useful to go beyond even the two dimensional approach described here. For example, researchers might measure (1) past sexual aggression, (2) how the person feels about his past behavior, (3) an estimate of the likelihood that he will aggress in the future,[23] and (4) his likelihood of doing so if assured of not being punished. It may be useful also to obtain more detailed information than is usually gathered about the type of sexual aggression the person is attracted to or has engaged in. This may enable better comparisons with taxonomies being developed with incarcerated sexual offenders.[24,25] Such a multidimensional approach will, it is hoped, contribute to understanding the factors leading to attraction to various forms of sexual aggression, and when such attraction is or is not expressed in actual behavior.

ACKNOWLEDGMENTS

I would like to acknowledge the collaboration of James V. P. Check in collecting some of the data and to thank Ricky Eng for his assistance in the data gathering.

REFERENCES

1. WEIS, K. & S. S. BORGES. 1983. Victimology and rape: The case of the legitimate victim. Issues Criminol. **8:** 71-115.
2. KOSS, M. P. & K. E. LEONARD. 1984. Sexually aggressive men: Empirical findings and theoretical implications. *In* Pornography and Sexual Agression. N. M. Malamuth & E. Donnerstein, Eds. Academic Press. New York, NY.
3. Law Enforcement Assistance Administration. 1975. Criminal Victimization Surveys in 13 American Cities. U. S. Government Printing Office. Washington, DC.
4. RUSSELL, D. E. H. 1984. Sexual exploitation: Rape, child sexual abuse and workplace harassment. Sage Publications, Beverly Hills, CA.
5. KOSS, M. P. & C. J. OROS. 1982. Sexual experiences survey: A research instrument investigating sexual aggression and victimization. J. Consult. Clin. Psychol. **50:** 455-457.
6. KOSS, M. P., K. E. LEONARD, D. A. BEEZLEY & C. J. OROS. 1985. Nonstranger sexual aggression: A discriminant analysis of psychological characteristics of nondetected offenders. Sex Roles **12:** 981-992.
7. MALAMUTH, N. M. 1986. Predictors of naturalistic sexual aggression. J. Pers. Soc. Psychol. **50:** 953-962.
8. MALAMUTH, N. M. 1981. Rape proclivity among males. J. Soc. Issues **37:** 138-157.
9. MALAMUTH, N. M., S. HABER & S. FESHBACH. 1980. Testing hypotheses regarding rape: Exposure to sexual violence, sex differences, and the "normality" of rapists. J. Res. Pers. **14:** 121-137.
10. MALAMUTH, N. M. & J. V. P. CHECK. 1980. Penile tumescence and perceptual responses to rape as a function of victim's perceived reactions. J. Appl. Soc. Psychol. **10:** 528-547.
11. BRIERE, J. & N. M. MALAMUTH. 1983. Self-reported likelihood of sexually aggressive behavior: Attitudinal versus sexual explanations. J. Res. Pers. **17:** 315-323.
12. CHECK, J. V. P. 1984. The Hostility Toward Women Scale. Diss. Abstr. **45 (12).**
13. CHECK, J. V. P. & N. M. MALAMUTH. 1983, June. The Hostility Toward Women Scale. Presented at the Western Meetings of the International Society for Research on Aggression, Victoria, Canada.
14. COHEN, J. & P. COHEN. 1983. Applied Multiple Regression/Correlation for the Behavioral Sciences. Erlbaum. Hillsdale, NJ.
15. BURT, M. R. 1980. Cultural myths and support for rape. J. Pers. Soc. Psychol. **38:** 217-230.
16. NELSON, D. A. 1979. A sexual functions inventory. Ph.D. dissertation, University of Florida, Gainesville, FL.
17. CHECK, J. V. P., N. M. MALAMUTH, B. ELIAS $_0$ S. BARTON. 1985. On hostile ground. Psychol. Today **19:** 56-61.
18. OVERALL, J. E., D. K. SPEIGEL & J. COHEN. 1975. Equivalence of orthogonal and nonorthogonal analysis of variance. Psychol. Bull. **82:** 182-186.
19. SCHEFFÉ, H. A. 1953. A method for judging all possible contrasts in the analysis of variance. Biometrika **40:** 87-104.
20. BENTLER, P. M. 1968. Heterosexual behavior assessment—I: Males. Behav. Res. Ther. **6:** 21-25.
21. BENTLER, P. M. & D. G. BONNETT. 1980. Significance tests and goodness of fit in the analysis of covariance structures. Psychol. Bull. **88:** 588-606.
22. KENNY, D. A. & C. M. JUDD. 1984. Estimating the nonlinear and interactive effects of latent variables. Psychol. Bull. **96:** 201-210.

23. MALAMUTH, N. M., J. V. P. CHECK & J. BRIERE. 1986. Sexual arousal in response to aggression: Ideological, aggressive and sexual correlates. J. Pers. Soc. Psychol. **50:** 330-340.
24. PRENTKY, R. A. & R. A. KNIGHT. 1986. Impulsivity in the life-style and criminal behavior of sexual offenders. Crim. Justice Behav. **13:** 141-164.
25. PRENTKY, R. A., M. L. COHEN & T. K. SEGHORN. 1985. Development of a rational taxonomy for the classification of sexual offenders: Rapists. Bull. Am. Acad. Psychiatry Law **13:** 39-70.

Predictors of Sexual Aggression among a National Sample of Male College Students

MARY P. KOSS [a] AND THOMAS E. DINERO

Department of Psychology
Kent State University
Kent, Ohio 44242

Recent studies have concluded that a history of sexual violence is highly prevalent among nonclinical, general population samples of women.[1,2,3] The notion that violence of such magnitude could be the work of a "psychopathic fringe" has been rejected, yet most studies of sexual aggression involve men who are convicted rapists incarcerated in prisons or in prison hospitals for the mentally ill.[4] Recently, attempts have been made to extend research on sexual aggression to undetected offenders.[5,6]

Research on rapists has been guided by several theoretical models that have focused on various realms of behavior (e.g., psychopathology, attitudes supportive of rape, hostility toward women, deviant arousal) and developmental stages (e.g., victimization as children, heterosexual dating skills, marital adjustment). Presently, integrative models of rape are appearing, stimulated by Finkelhor's conceptual work on child abusers.[7,8] He has proposed that five preconditions must be satisfied for the occurrence of sexual violence: assault must be emotionally congruent with the perpetrator's beliefs; sexual arousal must be possible in the presence of nonconsent and resistance; obstacles that block access to consenting partners must exist; "releasers" that allow behavior to occur that is typically inhibited must be present; and environmental settings that preclude assault, including the victim's resistance, must be overcome. Because Malamuth has provided a succinct review of sexual aggression research relevant to each of these contentions, this material will not be reiterated here.[6]

While this conceptualization of preconditions and releasers provides the broad outlines for an integrative theory of sexual violence, the interrelationships of the variables have not yet been specified, nor has a time sequence been proposed for the development of the preconditions during a subject's history. To date, empirical research has focused on current time measures of personality and attitudes. Sexually aggressive men's early backgrounds and the presence of releasers of sexual violence in their current behaviors have not been studied systematically. The present study was designed to sample a large, representative group of undetected sexually aggressive men regarding the presence of the preconditions and releasers of sexual aggression in their histories and to determine those variables that are predictive of self-reported sexual aggression. Unlike our earlier research on undetected offenders,[5] inquiry was not limited to subjects' psychological characteristics. Their early background as well as their current behavior were explored. In addition, a suggested developmental sequence was followed

[a] Present address: Department of Psychiatry, University of Arizona, Tucson, Arizona 85724.

in data analysis so that the effects of later variables could be examined after the effects of earlier variables had been controlled. The imposition of temporal ordering is necessary before a set of preconditions and releasers of sexual violence can involve into a hypothesized causal model.

METHOD

The data for the present study were collected during a nationwide survey via self-report questionnaire of a sample of 6,159 students in 32 U.S. institutions of higher education (data from the women respondents are not reported here). The methods of sample design, institutional recruitment, questionnaire construction, validity and reliability checks, and administration procedures have been described in detail elsewhere.[2,9] Thus, they are only summarized below.

Sampling Procedures

The sampling goals of the project were to represent the universe of the higher education student population in the United States in all its diversity. No sampling design could be expected to result in a purely random or representative sample, however, because the subject matter is sufficiently controversial that some schools targeted by a systematic sampling plan can be expected to refuse to participate. The U.S. Department of Education Office of Civil Rights maintains records of the enrollment characteristics from the 3,269 institutions of higher education in the United States.[10] The Office of Civil Rights provided a copy of their information for 1980 (the latest available) on data tape to the survey consultants, Clark/Jones, Incorporated of Columbus, Ohio.

On the basis of these data, the institutions in the entire nation were sorted by location in the ten Department of Education regions of the United States (i.e., Alaska, Hawaii, New England, Mideast, Great Lakes, Plains States, Southeast, Southwest, Rocky Mountain, and West). Within each region, institutions were placed into homogeneous clusters according to five criteria: location inside or outside of a standard metropolitan statistical area (SMSA) of a certain size; enrollment above or below the national mean percentage enrollment of minority students; control of the institution by private secular, private religious, or public authority; type of institution, including university, other four-year college, two-year junior college, and technical/vocational institution; and total enrollment within three levels. Every *x*th cluster was sampled according to the proportion of total enrollment accounted for by the region. Replacements were sought from among other schools in the homogeneous cluster if the original target proved uncooperative.

The amount of time required to obtain a sample of cooperating institutions was very extended; some schools required 15 months to arrive at a final decision regarding participation. During that period, 93 schools were contacted, and 32 institutional participants were obtained. Nineteen of the institutions were first choices, the remaining 13 were solicited from among 43 replacements. The actual institutional participants cannot be listed, because they were guaranteed anonymity. A random selection process based on the entire catalogue of course offerings from each institution was used to choose target classes and alternates in the case of schedule conflicts or refusals. The questionnaire was administered in classroom settings by 1 of 8 post-master's level psychologists (2 men and 6 women), who used a prepared script and were trained by the first author in standard procedures to handle potential untoward effects of participation. The questionnaire was completely anonymous and was accompanied by a cover sheet that contained all the elements of informed consent. Only 91 persons (1.5%) indicated that they did not wish to complete the survey.

Subjects

The final sample consisted of 6,159 persons, including 2,972 men students. They were characterized as follows: *M* age = 21.0; 91% single, 9% married, 1% divorced; 86% White, 6% Black, 3% Hispanic, 4% Asian, and 1% Native American; and 40% Catholic, 34% Protestant, 5% Jewish, and 22% other or none. Four variables were examined to determine the extent to which the sample was representative of the U.S. higher education enrollment: institution location, institution region, subject ethnicity, and subject family income. Region in which the institutions were located was the only variable on which significant discrepancy was observed (no statistical tests were performed because even minute differences would attain significance given the large sample sizes). The present sample underrepresented the West and overrepresented New England and the Southwest. In many respects, the regional disproportion is unimportant, since the individual participants in the sample still closely resembled the national enrollment in terms of ethnicity and family income. Nevertheless, for purposes of data analysis, the present sample was weighted using the proportions of enrollment in each of the federal regions. Whereas 12.7% of the present sample were attending institutions in New England, only 6.3% of the national enrollment is represented by that region. Thus, the responses from students in New England were weighted to be equivalent to 6.3% of the present sample. Likewise, the responses of the 20.6% of the subjects in the present sample who were attending Southwestern schools were weighted to be equivalent to 9.8% of the sample. Finally, only 6.0% of the subjects in the present sample were attending western schools, whereas 18.3% of the nationwide enrollment is in the West. Therefore, the responses from subjects in the West were weighted to be equivalent to 18.3% of the present sample.

Survey Instrument

All data were obtained via a self-report questionnaire entitled "National Survey of Inter-Gender Relationships." This title was selected to avoid the word *sex* so that participants would not prejudge the content of the survey before explanations were given. However, the inside coversheet of the questionnaire described the content explicitly. The survey consisted of 329 items divided into 7 sections and had a branching format. The factor of sexual aggression was measured by the 10 items that compose the Sexual Experiences Survey.[11,12] The following sample item is typical of the item content: "Have you engaged in sexual intercourse with a women when she didn't want to by threatening or using some degree of physical force (twisting her arm, holding her down, etc.)?" Those subjects who have not been involved in sexual aggression were instructed to skip subsequent sections relevant to those experiences. All subjects responded to items pertaining to demographic characteristics, preconditions for sexual violence (e.g., early family instability, parental strictness, family violence, delinquent involvements), and current behaviors that could serve as releasers of sexual violence (e.g., drinking habits, use of pornographic magazines, participation in sexually oriented discussions of women, sexual values, number of sexual partners, sexual satisfaction, and conflict tactics as measured by Strauss' Conflict Tactics Scale[13]). The content of items was guided by a review of relevant literature on the etiology of sexual aggression and by appropriateness for use with college students.[5,6,14] Psychological characteristics were measured through the use of standardized measures selected from previous research on sexual aggression including Check's 30-item Hostility Toward Women Scale,[15,16] the 28 items of the short-form MMPI Psychopathic Deviate Scale,[17] Burt's 36 items reflective of Rape Supportive Beliefs,[18,19] and the Extended Personal Attributes Scale.[20] MMPI Scale 4 and the Hostility Toward Women Scale each yield one score. Using the scoring directions of the original authors, four scores were obtained from Rape Supportive Beliefs (Adversarial Beliefs, Acceptance of Violence, Sexual Conservatism, and Rape Myths), three scores were derived from the Extended Personal Attributes (Positively Valued Masculinity, Negatively Valued Masculinity, and Androgyny), and three scores were derived from the Conflict Tactics Scale (Violent Aggression, Symbolic Aggression, and Reasoning).

Reliability and Validity

Many investigators have questioned the validity of self-reported sexual behavior. The accuracy and truthfulness of self-reports on the Sexual Experiences Survey have been investigated.[12] Significant correlations have been found between men's level of aggression as described by self-report and as given in the presence of an interviewer ($r = .61, p < .001$). A further validity study was conducted in conjunction with the present study. The Sexual Experiences Survey items were administered both by self-report and by one-to-one interview on the same occasion and in one setting. The interviewer was a fully trained, licensed, and experienced male Ph.D. clinical psychologist. Subjects were 15 male volunteers, identified by first name only, recruited through newspaper advertisements on the campus of a major university. Participants gave their self-reports first and then were interviewed individually. The intent was to match the participants' verbal responses with their self-reports on the Sexual Experiences Survey. The results indicated that 14 of the participants (93%) gave the same responses to the Sexual Experience Survey items by self-report and in interview.

Scoring and Data Reduction Procedures

The Factor of Sexual Aggression

The content and response frequencies for each item of the Sexual Experiences Survey are presented in TABLE 1. All items are specified to have occurred after the

TABLE 1. Frequencies of Individual Sexual Experiences since Age 14 Reported by Male Postsecondary Students

Sexual Behavior	Percent Yes (N = 2,972)	Mean Number of Incidents	SD
1. Have you engaged in sex play (fondling, kissing or petting, but not intercourse) with a woman when she didn't want to by overwhelming her with continual arguments and pressure?	19	2.9	1.5
2. Have you engaged in sex play (fondling, kissing, or petting, but not intercourse) with a woman when she didn't want to by using your position of authority (boss, teacher, camp counselor, supervisor)?	1	2.5	1.5
3. Have you engaged in sex play (fondling, kissing, or petting, but not intercourse) with a woman when she didn't want to by threatening or using some degree of physical force (twisting her arm, holding her down, etc.)?	2	2.3	1.5
4. Have you attempted sexual intercourse with a woman (got on top of her, attempted to insert penis) when she didn't want to by threatening or using some degree of force (twisting her arm, holding her down, etc.), but intercourse *did not* occur?	2	2.0	1.2
5. Have you attempted sexual intercourse with a woman (got on top of her, attempted to insert your penis) when she didn't want to by giving her alcohol or drugs, but intercourse *did not* occur?	5	2.2	1.4
6. Have you engaged in sexual intercourse with a woman when she didn't want to by overwhelming her with continual arguments and pressure?	10	2.4	1.4
7. Have you engaged in sexual intercourse with a woman when she didn't want to by using your position of authority (boss, teacher, camp counselor, supervisor)?	1	2.0	1.4
8. Have you engaged in sexual intercourse with a woman when she didn't want to by giving her alcohol or drugs?	4	2.5	1.5
9. Have you engaged in sexual intercourse with a woman when she didn't want to by threatening or using some degree of physical force (twisting her arm, holding her down, etc.)?	1	2.3	1.5
10. Have you engaged in sex acts (anal or oral intercourse or penetration by objects other than the penis) with a woman when she didn't want by threatening or using some degree of physical force (twisting her arm, holding her down, etc.)?	1	2.5	1.5

subjects' 14th birthday. "Sexual intercourse" is defined for the subjects as "penetration no matter how slight, ejaculation is not necessary." For the present study, the factor of sexual aggression was scored according to the following procedure. The groups labeled "rape" (yes responses to items 8, 9, and/or 10 and any lower-numbered items) and "attempted rape" (yes responses to items 4 and/or 5 but not to any higher-numbered items) included individuals whose behavior met legal definitions of these crimes, such as that of Ohio, which is similar to that of many states. Here, rape is defined as "... Vaginal intercourse between male and female, and anal intercourse, fellatio, and cunnilingus between persons regardless of sex. Penetration, however slight, is sufficient to complete vaginal or anal intercourse.... No person shall engage in sexual conduct with another person ... when any of the following apply: (1) the offender purposely compels the other person to submit by force or threat of force, (2) for the purpose of preventing resistance the offender substantially impairs the other person's judgment or control by administering any drug or intoxicant to the other person...."[21] A total of 4.4% of the men were classified in the rape group, and 3.3% of the men were classified in the attempted-rape group.

The group labeled "sexual coercion" (yes responses to items 6 and/or 7 but not to any higher-numbered items) included subjects who engaged in sexual intercourse subsequent to the use of menacing verbal pressure or misuse of authority. No threats of harm or direct physical force were used. The group labeled "sexual contact" (yes responses to items 1,2, and/or 3 but not to any higher-numbered items) consisted of individuals who had engaged in sexual behavior such as fondling or kissing that did not involve attempted penetration, subsequent to the use of menacing verbal pressure, misuse of authority, threats of harm, or actual physical force. Men who were labeled sexually nonaggressive responded no to all of items 1-10. The percentages of men who were classified into the sexual coercion, sexual contact, and sexually nonaggressive groups were 7.2%, 10.2%, and 74.8%, respectively.

Discriminating Variables

Inferential analyses were based on sets of variables that were constructed by a rational process informed by empirical procedures. First, the adjusted correlations of items were calculated. These values are pooled correlations that reveal the relationships of the items free of differences due to level of sexual aggression. Then, the adjusted correlation matrices were used to identify homogeneous subsets of variables that were highly intercorrelated. Items that were found to be of similar content and to be intercorrelated ($> r = .20$) were aggregated by simple summation. Values from standardized instruments were *not* summed.

The 16 variables used have been arranged into blocks according to the point in time to which they refer, and each block has been given a rationally determined name. The first block, named *early experiences,* includes the summed variables of Family Violence and Early Sexual Experiences. These variables refer to historical information about the subjects' background and early years in their parents' home, including exposure to family violence, childhood sexual experiences both forced and voluntary, and age of sexual initiation. Questions regarding childhood sexual experiences were specified to have occurred on or before the subjects' 14th birthday. The second block of variables, named *psychological characteristics,* reflects the subjects' personal characteristics at the time of the survey. These characteristics are assumed to have been influenced by the subjects' early experiences and to have developed in the years that have intervened between childhood and the present. Included in this set of variables are MMPI Scale 4, Hostility Toward Women, Adversarial Beliefs, Acceptance of Violence, Sexual Conservatism, Rape Myths, Positive Masculinity, Negative Masculinity, and Androgyny. The third block, named *current behavior,* includes the summed variables of Releasers and Adult Sexual Behavior that reflect the subjects' practices at the time of the survey. These variables are composed of items regarding the subjects' current frequencies of alcohol use, intoxication, pornographic magazine use, exposure to conversation in which women are sexually objectified, values regarding the intimacy necessary to justify sexual intercourse, and number of different sexual partners, as well as the typical amount of alcohol consumed. The three scores describing conflict tactics complete the current behavior block. The current behavior variables are assumed to be influenced by both early experiences and psychological characteristics.

RESULTS

Blockwise discriminant function analysis was performed to determine the least redundant set of variables predictive of the level of self-reported sexual aggression. The analysis allowed the role of each set of variables to be examined with the effect of earlier variables controlled and also had the advantage of following the course of subjects' histories. The analyses were accomplished by entering variables in blocks, with those blocks that operate earliest in time entering first. Specifically, in the first step the early experience variables were entered stepwise. In the second step, the early experience variables that entered the model in step one were forced in first, then the psychological characteristics were allowed to enter the model stepwise. In the third step, those early experiences and psychological characteristics that entered the model in steps one and two were forced in, then all current behavior variables were entered stepwise. The blockwise discriminant analysis was performed once using all variables, and then run a second time with only the most powerful variables included. The method of minimizing Wilks' lambda was used for inclusion of variables, the criterion of $p < .001$ was set, and the $SPSS^X$ statistical package for discriminant analysis was used. Weighting factors as described earlier were used to correct regional imbalance. Missing data were replaced if the amount missing on a variable did not exceed 20% of the total sample for single items or no more than 20% of an individual respondent's items on standard scales. Where these requirements were met, the mean for the entire sample was substituted for missing values. To aid in the interpretation of the results, the raw means and standard deviations of the 16 variables used in the analysis are found in TABLE 2.

Early Experiences Block

In step one, the early experience variables were allowed to enter stepwise. The Wilks' lambda of .94 (approximate $\chi^2 = 194.67$, df $= 8$, $p < .001$) indicated that the five groups differed significantly. The first discriminant function accounted for 94% of the discriminating power. The canonical correlation of .25 indicated a slight

TABLE 2. Raw Means and Standard Deviations on Summed Variables among Men

Discriminating Variable	Nonaggressive		Sexual Contact		Sexual Coercion		Attempted Rape		Rape	
	M	SD	*M*	SD	*M*	SD	*M*	SD	*M*	SD
I. Early Experiences										
Violence	4.73	1.80	5.33	2.19	5.08	1.85	5.72	2.67	5.76	3.00
Early sex experiences	3.59	1.54	3.86	1.56	4.36	1.70	4.72	1.93	4.80	1.82
II. Psychological Characteristics										
MMPI scale 4	7.92	3.36	9.01	4.82	8.33	3.46	9.01	3.23	9.74	3.69
Hostility toward women	7.09	4.70	8.63	5.29	8.44	5.16	9.84	5.03	9.59	4.98
Adversarial beliefs	21.97	6.29	22.92	6.06	23.33	6.57	24.33	6.46	26.36	6.22
Acceptance of violence	12.66	3.85	13.46	3.68	13.49	4.05	14.70	3.21	15.13	3.55
Sexual conservatism	25.96	6.18	25.77	5.77	24.09	6.43	26.94	5.90	26.23	5.73
Rape myths	22.49	7.14	23.90	7.59	22.30	7.22	25.12	6.57	26.93	8.11
Positive masculinity	22.95	4.35	23.23	4.14	23.94	4.12	22.64	4.27	23.35	4.18
Negative masculinity	8.23	5.14	9.97	5.27	9.13	5.44	10.59	5.85	12.48	6.13
Androgyny	15.31	3.95	14.84	4.03	15.82	4.65	14.38	3.55	15.22	3.94
III. Current Behavior										
Releasers	13.96	3.81	14.89	3.23	15.50	3.18	15.85	3.75	17.07	3.06
Adult sex behavior	18.05	4.86	19.34	3.89	20.82	2.99	20.15	4.14	22.20	3.04
Reasoning	51.70	25.85	54.37	26.48	54.06	25.14	56.401	25.85	58.39	28.58
Violent aggression	4.95	11.77	8.45	18.30	8.13	15.77	8.16	16.03	14.61	24.82
Symbolic aggression	20.97	20.13	25.52	21.27	24.88	21.57	31.12	24.92	35.20	27.11

degree of association between the five groups and the first discriminant function; approximately 6% of the variance in the function was redundant with group membership. After the first function had been derived, analysis of the residuals resulted in a second discriminant function with a Wilks' lambda of .99 (approximate $\chi^2 = 11.92$, df = 3, $p < .01$). The canonical correlation of .06 indicated that less than 1% of the variance on the function was redundant with group membership. After the first two functions had been derived, analysis of the residuals indicated no further significant functions. Early Sexual Experiences was the first variable to enter the model, and its correlation with the first discriminant function was r = .85. Family Violence was most highly correlated with the second discriminant function (r = .86). When just these two variables were used to classify the men into levels of sexual aggression, 47.21% of the cases could be grouped correctly. These data are summarized in TABLE 3.

Psychological Characteristics Block

In step two, the early experience variables were forced in as a block, then the psychological characteristics were allowed to enter stepwise. The Wilks' lambda of .88 (approximate $\chi^2 = 356.29$, df = 40, $p < .001$) indicated that the five groups differed significantly. The resulting discriminant function accounted for 82% of the discriminating power. The canonical correlation of .31 suggested a mild degree of association between the five groups and the first discriminant function; approximately 10% of the variance in the function was redundant with group membership. After the first function had been derived, analysis of the residuals resulted in a second discriminant function with a Wilks' lambda of .98 (approximate $\chi^2 = 65.53$, df = 27, $p < .001$). The canonical correlation of .12 indicated that just 2% of the variance of the second function was redundant with group membership. After the first two functions had been derived, analysis of the residuals indicated no further significant functions. The following variables correlated significantly with the first discriminant function: Early Sexual Experience (r = .66), Hostility Toward Women (r = .51), Family Violence (r = .46), Negative Masculinity (r = .45), Acceptance of Interpersonal Violence (r = .45), and Adversarial Beliefs (r = .45). The variables that correlated significantly with the second discriminant function included Sexual Conservatism (r = .57), Rape Myths (r = .51), MMPI Scale 4 (r = .40), Positive Masculinity (r = −.28), and Androgyny (r = −.20). When both the early experience variables and the psychological characteristics variables were used to classify the men into levels of sexual aggression, 44.91% of the cases could be grouped correctly. These data are summarized in TABLE 3.

Current Behavior Block

In step three, the early experience and psychological characteristics variables were forced in as a block, then the current behavior variables were allowed to enter stepwise. The Wilks' lambda of .93 (approximate $\chi^2 = 495.87$, df = 52, $p < .001$) indicated that the five groups differed significantly. The resulting discriminant function accounted

TABLE 3. Blockwise Discriminant Analysis of Levels of Sexual Aggression

Function	Eigenvalue	Percent of Variance	Canonical Correlation	Wilks' Lambda	χ^2	df	p	Classification Rate
Early Experiences Block								
0				.94	194.67	8	.001	
1	.07	94.04	.25	.99	11.92	3	.010	
2	.01	5.96	.06					
								47.21%
Psychological Characteristics Block								
0				.89	324.26	28	.001	
1	.10	86.71	.30	.99	44.81	18	.001	
2	.01	8.67	.10	.99	15.62	10	.111	
								46.23%
Current Behavior Block								
0				.84	495.87	52	.001	
1	.15	83.67	.36	.97	85.48	36	.001	
2	.01	10.03	.13	.99	33.09	22	.061	
								45.74%
Final Model								
0				.85	465.32	36	.001	
1	.15	86.95	.36	.98	64.23	24	.001	
2	.02	9.04	.12	.99	19.82	14	.135	
								46.70%

for 84% of the discriminating power. The canonical correlation of .36 indicated a mild degree of redundancy between the five groups and the first discriminant function; approximately 13% of the variance in the function was accounted for by group membership. After the first function had been derived, analysis of the residuals resulted in a Wilks' lambda of .97 (approximate χ^2 = 85.48, df = 22, p < .001). The canonical correlation of .13 indicated that just 2% of the variance on the second function was redundant with group membership. After the first two functions had been derived, analysis of the residuals indicated no further significant functions. These data are summarized in TABLE 3.

Of the total of 16 variables, only 3 failed to enter the model: Androgyny, Reasoning, and Symbolic Aggression. The following variables correlated significantly with the first discriminant function: Adult Sex behavior (r = .59), Releasers (r = .57), Early Sexual Experiences (r = .55), Hostility Toward Women (r = .41), Negative Masculinity (r = .37), Acceptance of Interpersonal Violence (r = .37), and Violent Aggression (r = .29). The variables that correlated significantly with the second discriminant function included Sexual Conservatism (r = .54), Rape Myths (r = .49), MMPI Scale 4 (r = .36), and Positive Masculinity (r = −.27). When all the variables were used to classify the men into levels of sexual aggression, 45.74% of the cases could be grouped correctly.

Final Model

Using the natural breaks in the sizes of the correlations, the model was reduced to the 9 most powerful variables. Then, the blockwise regression was run exactly as described above with just these 9 variables: Early Sexual Experiences, Family Violence, Hostility Toward Women, Negative Masculinity, Sexual Conservatism, Acceptance of Interpersonal Violence, Rape Myths, Adult Sexual Behavior, and Releasers. The Wilks' lambda of .85 (approximate χ^2 = 465.32, df = 36, p < .001) indicated that the five groups differed significantly. The resulting discriminant function accounted for 87% of the discriminating power. The canonical correlation of .36 suggested a mild degree of association between the five groups and the first discriminant function. Approximately 13% of the variance in the function was redundant with group membership. After the first function had been derived, analysis of the residuals resulted in a Wilks' Lambda of .98 (approximate χ^2 = 64.23, df = 14, p < .001). The canonical correlation of .12 suggested that just 2% of the variance on the second function was accounted for by group membership. After the first two functions had been derived, analysis of the residuals indicated no further significant functions. These data are presented in TABLE 3.

The variables that correlated significantly with the first discriminant function were Releasers (r = .57), Early Sexual Experiences (r = .56), Hostility Toward Women (r = .42) and Acceptance of Interpersonal Violence (r = .37). The variables that correlated significantly with the second discriminant function included Adult Sexual Behavior (r = −.63), Sexual Conservatism (r = .60), Rape Myths (r = .54), Family Violence (r = .40), and Negative Masculinity (r = .37). Using these 9 variables, 46.70% of the cases could be classified correctly. A breakdown of the actual and predicted group membership is presented in TABLE 4.

The group centroids on the two discriminant functions were as follows: sexually nonaggressive (−.21, .01), sexual contact (.33, .10), sexual coercion (.61, −.40), attempted rape (.83, .20), rape (1.14, .18). These data are plotted in FIGURE 1.

TABLE 4. Discriminant Classification of Sexually Aggressive Men

Actual Group	Number of Cases	Sexually Nonaggressive	Sexual Contact	Sexual Coercion	Attempted Rape	Rape
Sexually Nonaggressive	2167	1145 (53%)	227 (11%)	374 (17%)	195 (9%)	226 (10%)
Sexual Contact	293	89 (30%)	54 (19%)	63 (21%)	37 (13%)	50 (17%)
Sexual Coercion	206	36 (18%)	21 (10%)	79 (38%)	27 (13%)	44 (21%)
Attempted Rape	96	15 (15%)	11 (12%)	23 (24%)	25 (26%)	23 (23%)
Rape	128	21 (16%)	14 (11%)	29 (23%)	18 (14%)	46 (36%)

DISCUSSION

The detection of sexually aggressive men is a critical methodological issue. The sampling plan and methods of data collection in the present study were successful in obtaining data from approximately 600 men who admitted perpetrating some act of sexual aggression since the age of 14, including 131 men who reported behaviors that met legal definitions of rape, from a group of 2,972 men. Five levels of self-reported sexual aggression (sexually nonaggressive, sexual contact, sexual coercion, attempted rape, and rape) could be successfully discriminated by subjects' early experiences, psychological characteristics, and current behavior. Most of the discriminating power resulted from the first function on which the groups were arrayed linearly according to the severity of self-reported sexual aggression. Highly associated with this function were a background variable, Early Sexual Experience; two psychological variables, Hostility Toward Women and Acceptance of Interpersonal Violence; and the current behavior variable, Releasers. Men who reported perpetrating severe sexual aggression, as compared to men who reported lesser degrees of sexual aggression, were more likely to have become sexually active at an earlier age and to report more childhood sexual experiences both forced and voluntary. Psychologically, highly sexually aggressive men were typified by greater hostility toward women, which may decrease their sensitivity to their victims' suffering or even encourage further aggression in the face of resistance.[6,15,16] Also, sexually aggressive men were more likely then less sexually aggressive men to believe that force and coercion are legitimate ways to gain compliance in sexual relationships.[19,20] Finally, the more serious the self-reported sexual aggression, the more likely that current behavior was characterized by frequent use of alcohol, violent and degrading pornography, and involvement in peer groups that reinforce highly sexualized views of women.

In short, the results provided support for a developmental sequence for sexual aggression in which early experiences and psychological characteristics establish preconditions for sexual violence. In turn, these preconditions are most likely to be associated with self-reported sexual aggression, when linked to the presence of releasing factors in the current environment. The present results are consistent with Donnerstein's contentions that releasers such as pornography elicit aggressive behavior only among those people where evidence of higher levels of sexual activity and interest can already be seen during childhood.[22] These results support a temporal sequence for the development of sexually aggressive behavior and support our plans to develop structural equation models from these data. In future work, it may be possible to address Malamuth's suggestion that the causal links among the predictor variables be determined, in addition to describing their influences on sexual aggression.[6]

The observation that the groups can be equally well classified by each block of variables suggests that the later blocks fail to add significantly to the prediction of sexual aggression that can be made on the basis of early experiences alone. While the results substantiate a predictive role for both preconditions and releasers of sexual aggression, they suggest that variables pertaining to psychological characteristics and current behavior may provide information that duplicates that which is already available from knowledge of a subject's family background. However, it was noted that although the overall level of accuracy does not vary greatly, the classification of self-reported rapists was most accurate using psychological characteristics alone (41.3% correct vs. 36.4% based on early experiences alone, 32.7% based on current behavior alone, and 36.1% based on the final model).

The results are not as powerful as might be expected if sexual aggression were a simple continuum of behavior where sexual contact represents low sexual violence and rape represents high sexual violence. Even at the extreme level of rape, many classification errors were made. Common sense suggests that there should be differences among men who have perpetrated acts of sexual aggression that differ greatly in severity. However, it is possible that the severity of the sexually aggressive act is an artificial classification that does not correspond directly to important differences among perpetrators of sexual violence. The necessity of future work on the scaling of the sexual aggression factor is clear. Potentially, more than one dimension may be required to account for the variability among sexually aggressive men. For example, Malamuth has suggested that both differences in degrees of inclination to aggress and in actual aggression must be encompassed.[6] Additionally, environmental factors such as the man's perceptions of the avoidance strategies of the victims may also be important determinants of those episodes of sexual violence that proceed to completed rape. The role of such variables will be considered in future analyses.

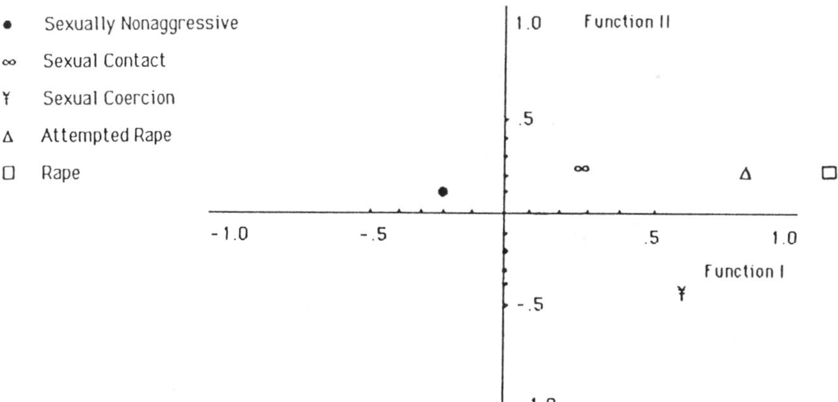

FIGURE 1. Plot of group centroids for groups of sexually aggressive men.

SUMMARY

An approximately representative national sample of 2,972 male students at 32 U.S. institutions of higher education was surveyed regarding their use of several degrees of verbal coercion and physical force to obtain sexual intimacy with women without consent. The most severe form of sexual aggression each man reported was used to classify him into one of five groups: sexually nonaggressive, sexual coercion, sexual contact, attempted rape, or rape. Respondents also provided data that was grouped into three blocks of variables: early experiences (family violence exposure, childhood sexual abuse, age of sexual initiation), psychological characteristics (MMPI Scale 4, Hostility Toward Women, rape supportive beliefs, gender role orientation), and current behavior (alcohol use, pornography use, male bonding, sexual values and activity, conflict tactics). Data were analysed via blockwise discriminant function analysis. Variables were entered following a suggested development sequence. Specifically, all early experience variables were entered first as a block. Then the entire set of psychological characteristics were entered stepwise followed by all the current behavior variables. Variables from all three blocks entered the model. The classification rates have been discussed and the implications of the analyses for future causal models of male sexual aggression considered.

REFERENCES

1. Kilpatrick, D. G, C. L. Best, L. J. Veronen, A. E. Amick, L. A. Villeponteaux & G. A. Ruff. 1985. Mental health correlates of criminal victimization: A random community survey. J. Consult. Clin. Psychol. **53:** 866-873.
2. Koss, M. P., C. J. Gidycz & N. R. Wisniewski. The scope of rape: Incidence and prevalence of sexual aggression and victimization in a national sample of students in higher education. J. Consult. Clin. Psychol. In press.
3. Russell, D. E. H. 1984. Sexual Exploitation: Rape, Child Sexual Abuse, and Workplace Harassment. Sage Publications. Beverly Hills, CA.
4. Johnson, A. G. 1980. On the prevalence of rape in the United States. Signs: J. Women Culture Society **6:** 136-146.
5. Koss, M. P., K. E. Leonard, D. A. Beezley & C. J. Oros. 1985. Nonstranger sexual aggression: A discriminated analysis of the psychological characteristics of undetected offenders. Sex Roles **12:** 981-992.
6. Malamuth, N. M. 1986. Predictors of naturalistic sexual aggression. J. Pers. Soc. Psychol. **50:** 953-962.
7. Finkelhor, D. 1984. Child Sexual Abuse: New Theory and Research. The Free Press. New York, NY.
8. Finkelhor, D. 1981. Four preconditions of sexual abuse: A model. Presented at the National Conference of Family Violence Research, Durham, New Hampshire, June 1981.
9. Koss, M. P. 1987. Hidden rape: Incidence, prevalence, and descriptive characteristics of sexual aggression and victimization in a national sample of college students. *In* Sexual Assault, Vol. 3. A. W. Burgess, Ed. Garland Publishing Company. New York, NY.
10. Office of Civil Rights. 1980. Fall Enrollment and Compliance Report of Institutions of Higher Education. U.S. Department of Education. Washington, DC.
11. Koss, M. P. & C. J. Oros. 1982. Sexual Experiences Survey: A research instrument investigating sexual aggression and victimization. J. Consult. Clin. Psychol. **50:** 455-457.
12. Koss, M. P. & C. J. Gidycz. 1985. Sexual Experiences Survey: Reliability and validity. J. Consult. Clin. Psychol. **53:** 422-423.

13. STRAUSS, M. A. 1979. Measuring intrafamily conflict and violence: The Conflict Tactics (CT) Scales. J. Marriage Fam. **41:** 75-88.
14. AGETON, S. S. 1983. Sexual Assault among Adolescents. Lexington Books. Lexington, MA.
15. CHECK, J. V. P. 1985. The Hostility Toward Women Scale. Diss. Abstr. Int. **45:** 3993.
16. CHECK, J. V. P. 1985. The Hostility Toward Women Scale. Ph.D. dissertation, University of Manitoba, Winnipeg, Canada.
17. GRAHAM, J. R. 1977. The MMPI: A practical guide. Oxford University Press. New York, NY.
18. BURT, M. R. 1978. Attitudes supportive of rape in American culture. Hearing of the 95th Congress, 2nd Session, House Committee on Science and Technology, Subcommittee on Domestic and International Scientific Planning, Analysis, and Cooperation, Research into Violent Behavior: Sexual Assaults: 277-322. U.S. Government Printing Office. Washington, DC.
19. BURT, M. R. 1980. Cultural myths and support for rape. J. Pers. Soc. Psychol. **38:** 217-230.
20. SPENCE, J. T., R. L. HELMREICH & C. K. HOLAHAN. 1979. Negative and positive components of psychological masculinity and femininity and their relationships to self-reports of neurotic and acting out behaviors. J. Pers. Soc. Psychol. **37:** 1673-1682.
21. Ohio Revised Code, Supp. 1980. 2907.01A, 2907.
22. DONNERSTEIN, E. 1984. Pornography: Its effects on violence against women. *In* Pornography and Sexual Aggression. N. M. Malamuth & E. Donnerstein, Eds.: 143-172. Academic Press. New York, NY.

PART III. BIOLOGICAL ISSUES

Introduction to Biological Issues, with Neuropathological Case Illustrations

ANNELIESE A. PONTIUS[a]

Department of Psychiatry
Harvard Medical School
Boston, Massachusetts 02114

Achievement of the ultimate, though still distant, goal of model building can benefit from clinical and biological data, even when the constraints imposed by such data (e.g., small samples) preclude statistical significance. The explanatory power of a model that accommodates such constraints is further enhanced when these clinical-biological data are placed in the context of known basic patterns of biological functioning.

A comparison between animal and human sexual behavior is considered an intermediary bridge between social-psychological and biologically based studies. Nadler's study of sexual aggression in the great apes found increased initiation of copulation ("aggression") under "free access" conditions, where males and females were locked in one cage. From this observation he extrapolates to the human species, concluding that "the potential for male sexual aggression is inherent in our species," and that such aggression is likely to be expressed under social, cultural, and environmental conditions that "reduce the female's prerogatives for refusing sexual overtures." He regards human sexual aggression as neither inevitable nor justified. It would appear that in humans the "pressure" from drives serving the survival of the species is less than the pressure from drives serving the individual's survival.

Langevin and his co-workers discuss the correlation of sadism with biological factors. They report on certain patterns of endocrinological abnormalities in sexual aggressives: the weak androgen, DHEAS, and cortisol tended to be higher, and prolactin tended to be lower in sexual aggressives than in controls. As has been found in other studies, testosterone levels were not significantly different between these groups. With regard to brain abnormalities, Langevin's findings with CT scans suggested the involvement of two brain systems. The right temporal horn was dilated in sadists more frequently than in other sexual aggressives and in controls. Also, some EEG findings suggested temporal lobe epilepsy. These researchers are planning MRI studies to differentiate implicated brain systems.

Freund considers the hypothesis that abnormal human sexual behavior (voyeurism, exhibitionism, toucheurism, frotteurism, preference for rape) constitutes a distortion of a phase of "courtship behavior." He cites as the best-supported hypothesis for the

[a] Address for correspondence: Anneliese A. Pontius, M.D., Associate Clinical Professor of Psychiatry, Department of Psychiatry, Massachusetts General Hospital, Fruit Street, Boston, Massachusetts 02114

causes of these "courtship disorders" that proposed by Madlafousek *et al.*,[1] which suggests that males who prefer to get sexually involved with a strange or unsuspecting woman—as in the case of the courtship disorders and in sadism—cannot readily make the transition from the initial stages of sexual motivation to the later ones connected with high arousal states. An abnormally high potential for arousal is another possible etiological factor. Attempts to correlate these abnormal sexual behaviors with hormonal factors have so far been unsuccessful.

Berlin reports on two studies aimed at determining the biological basis for paraphilic sexual drives. The preliminary results of one, which uses PET scans, suggest that opiate receptor activity in the brain changes in association with sexual arousal. In the other study, involving intravenous injection of gonadotropin releasing hormone, men with pedophilic sexual orientation showed a pathological pattern of gonadotropin release into the blood. Berlin emphasizes the importance of using in such experiments groups of subjects that are homogeneous with respect to their specific form of paraphilic disorder, so as to separate biological and environmental factors. He argues that society should recognize in its treatment of sex offenders that some biological drives cannot be resisted by willpower alone.

Organic treatment of male sex offenders aims at reducing their sexual drive. With surgical castration and stereotaxic neurosurgery ruled out as treatment options, Bradford considers the controversial use of antiandrogens and other hormonal agents—particularly cyproterone acetate (CPA)—to reduce the level of testosterone in the blood.

CLINICAL EXAMPLES IMPLICATING FRONTAL AND TEMPORAL (LIMBIC) SYSTEMS

In illustration of the two brain systems discussed by Langevin, Berlin, and their co-workers, two detailed clinical studies[2] are here summarized. One of these systems implicates an imbalance between the frontal lobe and limbic systems.[3–6] The second case has positive objective test findings (EEGs, brain electrical activity mapping—BEAM, and neuropsychological tests) that suggest left temporal lobe dysfunction.

Patient 1

Mr. U., a white, single teenager had several psychiatric hospitalizations prior to his arrest for assault and battery and assault with intent to commit rape. There was no history of accidents, but he had high fevers as a child. He reported occasional "blackouts"—"a funny feeling in the head—sometimes I just feel kinda dizzy and cannot hear or see things and fall to the ground." During the incident to be described, he had no such feelings. He occasionally wet himself, but he knew nothing about thrashing about, and nobody had ever seen him during a "blackout," even though he had been in several psychiatric hospitals until age fourteen. His parents were separated when he was a child. When he came home from school, his mother used to lock him up in his room so that he would not get into trouble outside fighting with other children and hurting people.

The day of the incident, he escaped from a mental hospital. "I continued to walk." He saw an old woman, maybe seventy-two years old, sitting outside her house. "I asked her for a cigarette." She said, "I haven't any to give you." "The way she said it, in a rejecting tone, made me think she did smoke, but didn't want to give me one, like my mother often didn't give me a cigarette, but she smoked herself. Then I left and came back after about five minutes. That's when I started to hear voices saying, 'Attack her! kill her! fuck her!' and I just did it. I don't know why. I only thought of doing it when I saw her and when I saw her get up and walk, she reminded me of my mother, the way she walked." (He didn't feel any anger against the woman.) "When I walked up to the woman she looked at me in a funny way, like she didn't even know who I was. Then I says 'I'll kill you,' and she got real upset. Then I started to rip her dress off and I took out my penis. I didn't touch her yet with my penis. The neighbor came running over when she screamed. I started punching her in the head and I wanted to rape her." He didn't remember that he put his shirt around her neck, as the police report stated, but admitted that it could have happened.

Presently his sleep began to be interrupted by "very strange dreams," recurring about biweekly. "I'm seeing that old woman [the victim] and I say 'hi!' Then all of a sudden I just start staring at her and staring and staring and I say to her that something reminds me of whom?—my mother! Then I have a blackout in the dream, [laughs] it is crazy." Asked how the blackout feels in the dream, he answers, "It feels psychologically good." Sometimes his dreams are directly. about the victim, and something says, "Fuck her, stab her in the god-damn back!"

He frequently hears female voices, which he experiences as real and ascribes to his mother or to the old female victim, telling him to attack some of the inmates, saying "Stab him!" or "Escape!" "You are just an old plain psycho!" or "I am playing mind games on you."

His "strange dreams" and his hallucinations are reminiscent of several "strange experiences" that he has had since age fifteen and that recur about once a month. "For instance four years ago, I see this nice broad, I said 'hi, how are you doing?' She said 'hi' back. I suddenly stared at her, and it bothered her, and then it was going through my mind, I want to just fuck her. It was like a strange exotic person, somebody inside here [he touches both sides of his forehead] saying it. I was just borne away."

Objective and Neurological Tests

Patient 1's scalp electroencephalogram (EEG) was within normal limits, as were his routine neurological examination, electromyelogram (EMG), and routine laboratory tests, including DRL and tine tests, thyroid tests, and blood urea nitrogen (BUN).

Patient 1 showed positive results on the two tests specifically implicating frontal lobe system dysfunctioning: Trail-Making-Test B[7] and the Clinical Narratives Test,[8–10] both of which revealed an inability to switch the principle of action of an ongoing activity.

Patient 2

Mr. M. is a right-handed white heterosexual single man; a high-school graduate of average intelligence, he is in his early 20s, the father of a 6-year-old son. While baby-sitting for his son's playmate, a boy aged 6, Mr. M. suddenly performed fellatio on the sexually naive boy. Mr. M. did not attack his own son, who was in an adjacent room. This is an intriguing aspect, not explainable by the principles of sociobiology, regarding an "incest taboo" that is applicable only to heterosexual adult partners (to prevent inbreeding).[11]

Mr. M. had no previous history of pedophilia, nor of any homosexual contact; he claimed he never masturbated and felt he needed only sporadic heterosexual contact since age 15. He had not been sexually abused as a child; the beginning of such a potential attempt by an adult male was aborted at the stage of exhibition when Mr. M. was about 8 years old. Around the time of the incident of "rape of a child," as the charge was called, Mr. M. did not feel sexually aroused. He had had some beer and some drugs ("pot" and possibly some cocaine and/or "speed"), but was not drunk and recalled the incident quite well.

The incident was ego-alien to him; he felt intense remorse afterwards, and 2 years afterwards still had nightmares that the boy victim had died from the attack. "Oh no, he is dead! I was still scared about it for a while after I woke up." Other nightmares lingering after awakening were about wolves "tearing people apart." They were very explicit, ripping heads and arms off. I saw lots of blood and other colors, but the wolves did not attack me. I woke up seven times during the night and dreamt the same nightmare again and again." He was sweating profusely, had headaches, and after awakening checked his closets for wolves.

Mr. M. was born with several birth defects involving the left side of his body, including chest, foot, and hand deformities and mild weakness of the sixth and fifth (third branch) cranial nerves. He also suffered head injuries at ages 9 and 13, the latter associated with 1 to 2 weeks' coma. Seven years after the second injury he developed left-sided Jacksonian-type seizures that on rare occasions may have approximated grand mal status. All seizures were fully controlled by Dilantin. He had been seizure free for several years prior to the incident with the boy. He had nocturnal enuresis until age 14 but does not recall ever wetting himself or biting his tongue during any seizures, though these were often followed by drowsiness, intense headaches, and sweating. Up to the present time he would occasionally experience visual hallucinations, see changes in the brightness of lights, see colors, "smell something burning," and experience metallic tastes.

Objective and Neurological Tests

One of several EEGs with nasopharyngeal leads showed temporal lobe dysfunctioning (theta waves), left more than right; brain electric activity mapping (BEAM)[12] implicated the same structures, as did neuropsychological examination.

The neurological examination concludes that he has a history of spells nine years ago reminiscent of focal seizures. "The most recent visual disturbances are less clear in terms of whether they represent seizures or some unusual form of migraines without the accompanying headache or perhaps just visual disturbances relating to poor attention. The EEG abnormality certainly suggests that temporal lobe seizures are a possibility."

The Clinical Narratives Test[8–10] was positive for the frontal lobe specific dysfunctioning of inability to switch his principle of action appropriately during the incident. Further, on Trail-Making-Test B,[7] which requires alternating between sequential numbers and letters, his performance was only between the 25th and 50th percentiles of adults taking the test.

On other neuropsychological testing, he revealed "attention deficits, poor ability to abstract proverbs, missing the point of complex stories, impaired expressive vocabulary, and intratest scatter. His constructions reveal closing in on his drawings, working from left to right on designs, and mild segmentation on complex stimuli. His gestalt recognition was intact. While his overall Memory Quotient was in the average range, he showed impaired memory for narrative material, as well as difficult visual designs."

On the Temporal Lobe Inventory, he obtained self-reported high scores on items concerning personal destiny, hypermoralism, and dependence.

Left fronto-temporal dysfunction with possibly current subclinical seizures was the overall impression of the neuropsychologist. Her conclusions also took into account Mr. M.'s history of seizure disorder, hyperactivity as a youth, nocturnal enuresis up to age 14, irritability, olfactory and gustatory hallucinations, and visual problems, including occasional experience of dimming lights.

DISCUSSION

Two subtypes of limbic system dysfunctioning appear to be illustrated here: Patient 1 can best be classified as an example of the new diagnostic entity *limbic psychotic trigger reaction,*[3–6] while Patient 2 fits quite well into the class of temporal lobe epilepsy. The two subforms of limbic dysfunctioning, TLE and PTR, show a certain overlap in symptomatology with episodic dyscontrol (ED).[13] Such an overlap can be discerned especially with regard to the TLE symptomatology of Patient 2. The symptomatology of Patient 1, however, which was typical of PTR, differed in essential aspects from ED, which has been defined[13] as episodic loss of impulse control not only out of character but also out of context. By contrast, PTR occurs within a specific context[3–6] that became revived to a hallucinatory degree by a probably once-in-a-life-time encounter with the specific trigger stimulus.

In conclusion, detailed inquiry into puzzling acts is indicated when clinical specific pattern detection implicates a dysfunction of the evolutionary old limbic system, be it in relation to the frontal lobe system or to other limbic components.

REFERENCES

1. MADLAFOUSEK, J., M. ŽANTOVSKÝ, Z. HLIŇÁK & A. KOLÁŘSKÝ. 1981. Sexual behavior as a communicative process by which the system of partial motivational states is executed. Cesk. Psychiatry **77:** 377-384.
2. PONTIUS, A. A. 1988. Limbic system-frontal lobes' role in atypical rape. Psychol. Rep. In press.
3. PONTIUS, A. A. 1981. Stimuli triggering violence in psychoses. J. Forensic Sci. **26:** 123-128.
4. PONTIUS, A. A. 1984. Specific stimulus-evoked violent action in Psychotic Trigger Reaction: A seizure-like imbalance between frontal lobe and limbic systems? Percept. Mot. Skills **59:** 299-333.
5. PONTIUS, A. A. 1987. "Psychotic Trigger Reaction": Neuropsychiatric and neurobiological (limbic?) aspects of homicide, reflecting on normal action. Integrative Psychiatry **5:** 116-139.

6. PONTIUS, A. A. 1988. Neuro-psysiological views of "Psychotic Trigger Reaction"—A rejoinder. Integrative Psychiatry. In press.
7. ARMITAGE, S. G. 1946. An analysis of certain psychological tests for the evaluation of brain injury. Psychol. Monogr. **60:** No. 1 (Whole No. 277).
8. PONTIUS, A. A. 1974. Basis for neurological test of frontal lobe system functioning up to adolescence. Adolescence **9:** 221-232.
9. PONTIUS, A. A. & K. F. RUTTIGER. 1976. Frontal lobe system maturational lag in juvenile delinquents shown in narratives test. Adolescence **11:** 509-518.
10. PONTIUS, A. A. & B. S. YUDOWITZ. 1980. Frontal lobe system dysfunction in some criminal actions, as shown in Narratives Test. J. Nerv. Ment. Dis. **168:** 111-117.
11. WILSON, E. O. 1978. On Human Nature. Harvard University Press. Cambridge, MA.
12. DUFFY, F. H. 1985. The BEAM method for neurophysiological diagnosis. *In* Hope for a New Neurology. F. Nottebohm, Ed. Ann. N. Y. Acad. Sci. **457:** 19-34.
13. MONROE, R. R. 1970. Episodic Behavioral Disorders. Harvard University Press. Cambridge, MA.

Sexual Aggression in the Great Apes[a]

RONALD D. NADLER

Yerkes Regional Primate Research Center
Emory University
Atlanta, Georgia 30322

INTRODUCTION

The purpose of this paper is to analyze the data on sexual behavior of three species of great apes for evidence of sexual aggression that might provide a biological perspective on sexual aggression in our own species. Sexual aggression in the context of great ape sexual behavior is defined as the initiation of copulation through intimidation or other forms of coercion, suggesting that the recipient would not copulate of its own free choice. The data considered relate primarily to fully mature individuals. Evidence of sexual aggression is presented for all three species: common chimpanzee, orang-utan, and gorilla; and in all three it is the male that intimidates or coerces the female to copulate.

The approach taken is to (1) present data on the species-typical pattern of mating in the natural habitat (where sexual aggression is relatively rare); (2) consider the altered pattern of mating observed in free-access tests (FATs), the traditional laboratory pair-tests (in which sexual aggression is proposed to be prominent); (3) provide support for an interpretation of sexual aggression in the FATs by examining the complementary data from restricted-access tests (RATs), in which the female regulates sexual access; and (4) discuss the possible implications of these data on our closest phyletic affiliates for a biologically based conceptualization of sexual aggression among human beings.

SEXUAL BEHAVIOR IN THE NATURAL HABITAT

Increased field research on the great apes, especially over the past decade, has provided considerable information on the species-typical patterns of mating in these species. Analysis of these data, moreover, suggests that the particular pattern of sexual interaction characteristic of each species is a function of the extent of intermale

[a]This work was supported in part by NIH Grant RR-00165 from the Division of Research Resources to the Yerkes Regional Primate Research Center and by NIH Grant HD-19060 to the author.

competition for estrous females—that is, the number of males of a particular species in competition for, or available to, a female *at the time of estrus.*[1]

In the multimale mating system of the chimpanzee, in which estrous females mate with essentially all the mature males in the community, intermale competition is high, though nonaggressive, and it is the males that initiate copulation with the performance of a conspicuous courtship display.[2,3] The relatively long 10-14 day period of estrus enables the female to mate with a large number of males before selecting a particular male with which to consort exclusively toward the end of estrus, during the periovulatory phase of the cycle.[4,5]

In the one-male mating system of the gorilla,[6] intermale competition at estrus is minimal, since the parous females of the group mate only with the silver-backed leader.[7] In the absence of intermale competition at the time of estrus, it is the female gorilla that initiates copulation; a relatively short, 2-3-day period of estrus is adequate for reproduction.

Orang-utans live a semisolitary life-style[8-11] in what may be called a "dispersed harem."[12] Since males live in separate home-ranges, there is little or no competition between males at estrus; primarily females initiate copulations.[13-16] The orang-utan, therefore, resembles the gorilla in these respects. However, male home-ranges of orang-utans overlap to some degree, such that females may have more than a single male available at estrus. Concordant with this potentially increased choice in female orang-utans, the period of estrus and mating in this species is slightly longer than that of the gorilla, about 5-6 days. These data support the hypothesis that '. . . differences in reproductive behavior of the great apes . . . can be related to differences between them in the number of males simultaneously competing for and available to estrous females" (p. 308).[1] These data on sexual behavior of the great apes in their natural habitat, moreover, establish the basis for evaluation of their sexual behavior during two types of pair-tests conducted in the laboratory.

SEXUAL BEHAVIOR DURING FREE-ACCESS TESTS IN THE LABORATORY

Chimpanzees were the first species of great ape to be studied in traditional laboratory pair-tests, the free-access test (FAT).[17-19] The term "free-access" is used to denote the condition wherein the male and female are tested in a single cage with both animals freely accessible to each other. The FAT is distinguished from the restricted-access test (RAT), which is initiated with the male and female in separate cages such that only one—in the present context the female—can regulate sexual access (see below). The RAT with female choice was developed in order to assess independently the sexual responsiveness of the female, which in the original studies on the chimpanzee was compromised by an inordinate influence of the male.

The results of the early FATs on the chimpanzee indicated that (1) this species mated primarily during an approximately 10-day midcycle period of estrus, associated with maximal ano-genital swelling of the female; but (2) they also mated at other times in the cycle under certain circumstances. The circumstances under which mating was dissociated temporally from the presumptive time of ovulation included: (1) the partners were unacquainted, uncongenial, or hostile; (2) the male was dominant over the female; (3) the female was timid or defensive; (4) either member of the pair was sexually inexperienced or not completely mature; (5) the male was older or larger than the female; (6) the pair was brought together for testing after being apart for some time; and (7) the pair was brought together for a relatively brief period of time. Under any of these conditions mating *might* occur "... by reason of the dominance or impulsiveness of the male and the desire of the female to avoid risk of physical injury by obeying his command" (p. 34).[17] In a subsequent study of chimpanzees, a similar impression is conveyed: "Completion of the mating pattern by copulation does not necessarily imply female receptivity even in low degree, since the male consort may dominate and command the female, and she may respond defensively, protectively, or accommodatingly *in the experimental mating situation,* whatever her sexual status, desire, or preference" (p. 110).[18]

The foregoing descriptions of the male chimpanzee's influence over the female in matters sexual, as well as other comments of a similar nature in the same articles, clearly suggest an interpretation of male sexual aggression in this species under the conditions of free-access laboratory testing. Male dominance over the female and the inability of the female to avoid and/or escape from the male within the confines of the laboratory cage were the major factors that permitted the males to behave in a sexually aggressive manner.

Subsequent studies on gorillas and orang-utans using the FAT paradigm some 40 years later obtained comparable results. In the case of the gorillas, the data from an initial study were consistent with those obtained in the wild.[20,21] The females primarily initiated sexual interactions, and mating was restricted to a relatively brief, 1-4-day period of maximal tumescence of the perineal labia in the female,[22] subsequently shown to be the periovulatory phase of the menstrual cycle.[23] In a second study, however, copulation in several pairs occurred more frequently than the species-typical frequency per cycle and appeared to reflect male sexual aggression.[24,25] The males, in fact, initiated two-thirds of the copulations recorded in the second study. In one-third of the copulations the males solicited copulation directly by approaching and positioning the female for copulation, whereas in the remaining third male charging and striking out at the female appeared to induce the female to present for copulation. Analysis of female- and male-initiated copulations, moreover, revealed that the females initiated copulations as in the earlier study, during the periovulatory phase, whereas the males primarily accounted for copulations temporally dissociated from ovulation. As in the chimpanzees, therefore, the male gorillas induced the females to copulate at times in the cycle when conception was unlikely to occur, and they did so in a sexually aggressive manner.

The clearest and most conspicuous examples of male sexual aggression in the great apes, however, were observed in FATs conducted with orang-utans.[26] In this species, the male immediately pursued the female at the start of the test, quickly caught the female, and wrestled it to the floor of the cage. The female initially struggled and resisted but was subdued by the larger and apparently stronger male, which then forcibly positioned the female for copulation. In 3 of the 4 pairs tested, moreover, this pattern of forcible copulation was carried out by the males on every day of the cycle!

It should be noted that forcible initiation of copulation has also been reported for male orang-utans in the wild.[9–11,27] In the wild, however, it is the subadult male that behaves in this way. As mentioned above, fully mature males in the wild are generally solicited to copulate by the females and are not often sexually aggressive. The reversion of fully mature males in the FATs to the subadult pattern of sexual aggression appears to result from the female's inability to avoid and/or escape from the male within the limited spatial conditions of the test cage. In all three species of great apes tested in the FAT paradigm, therefore, evidence of male sexual aggression was apparent.

The general pattern of male-initiated copulation by the great apes during infertile phases of the menstrual cycle was, in fact, predicted by Yerkes[18] from his research on the chimpanzees. Yerkes proposed that there were two basic factors involved in the regulation of sexual behavior of mammals: (1) relative brain size and complexity, and (2) the sex of the animal that initiated or controlled the sexual interactions. He proposed that for animals such as the primates, with relatively large, complex brains, sexual activity would in general be less restricted to the time of ovulation then for smaller-brained animals. With respect to the primates per se, he proposed that in species or under conditions in which the female initiated sexual activity, copulation would be restricted to the time of ovulation, whereas when the male was in control, copulation could also occur at times dissociated from ovulation. Although Yerkes did not define the male chimpanzee's nonperiovulatory sexual initiations specifically as sexual aggression, he described them in sufficient detail as to leave little doubt that such definition is entirely appropriate. As indicated above, the case for the gorilla and orang-utan is, if anything, even more convincing.

SEXUAL BEHAVIOR DURING RESTRICTED-ACCESS TESTS IN THE LABORATORY

Although Yerkes hypothesized the relation between male and female sexual initiation and the distribution of mating in the cycle, as described, he was not at all satisfied that his data were adequate to establish the relationship in the chimpanzee. "At present our observational techniques are inadequate. Obviously methods should be developed which render possible measurement of sexual receptivity and responsiveness objectively in the isolated individual" (p. 111).[18] The foregoing quotation relates to Yerkes's specific goal of establishing the phenomenon of estrus in the chimpanzee, which he believed had been compromised in his studies by the male's influence. The development of an objective method for measuring the sexual responsiveness of the female per se can, however, also serve the present goal of establishing male sexual aggression as the basis for the nonperiovulatory mating recorded in the three species of great apes considered here. If objective measurement of female sexual responsiveness confirmed its restriction to the periovulatory phase of the cycle, this would provide further support for the conclusion that the nonperiovulatory copulation recorded in the FATs was indeed due to the male's sexual aggression.

The RAT with female choice was specifically developed for this purpose. With respect to the sexually dimorphic gorilla and orang-utan, female regulation of sexual access was accomplished by reducing the size of the doorway between the male's and female's cages such that only the (smaller) female could pass through it. For the less dimorphic chimpanzee, a similar result was accomplished by training the female to open the door between the male's and female's cages by pressing a lever to a predetermined criterion of lever-presses.

Studies of sexual behavior using the RAT paradigm with female choice have now been completed for the three species of great apes. The data, simply stated, support the hypothesis that female regulation of sexual activity results in a relatively restricted period of copulation closely associated with the presumptive time of ovulation.[28] In the RAT paradigm, male sexual aggression was greatly reduced or eliminated entirely, and apparently, as a result, the pattern of mating more closely resembled the pattern in nature than had been the case during the FATS.

The difference in behavioral interactions between the FATs and RATs was most pronounced in the case of the orang-utans.[29,30] In comparison to the FATs, in which the males forcibly initiated copulation on a near-daily basis, in the RATs the males came to assume an essentially passive role, and the females took over active initiation of copulation. During their initial exposures to the reduced doorway, the males struggled to squeeze through it, with occasional success. Once a size was determined that reliably excluded the male, several of the males then attempted to catch the females after they had entered the males' cage. Strategies and counterstrategies were developed that ultimately led to a cessation of male attempts to catch or trap the female. One interesting point regarding the interactions of the male and female during these first several tests was that the female, once caught, often struggled free from the male and retreated back into its own cage. Although the females had struggled with the males in the FATs, they did so only briefly and quickly ceased resisting, apparently resigned to the inevitable. It appeared in the RATS that the possibility of escaping to their own cage encouraged the females to struggle more and/or discouraged the males from attempting forcibly to restrain them.

Once the options available to the female became apparent to both animals, there was little interaction between them until midcycle. Some of the females remained in their own cage and others made occasional unimpeded excursions into the male's cage. Then, in a number of cases at midcycle the male performed a display that had never been reported before in an orang-utan. The male reclined supine on the cage floor near the doorway with an erection and directed its penis toward the female. The male maintained this position for varying periods of times—in one male for approximately 45 minutes—until the female approached. Eventually the female approached the male and examined its penis, while the male remained essentially immobile. The female then mounted the male's penis and initiated thrusting, in some cases leading to ejaculation. That this rather remarkable display and sexual interaction are not artifacts of laboratory testing but rather are part of the species-typical pattern of mating was confirmed by comparable observations on wild orang-utans.[15,16]

The date on all three species of great apes in the RATs are consistent with the view that the increased mating that occurred in the FATs, especially the nonperiovulatory mating, was (1) due to the male's influence, and (2) contrary to the female's inclinations. As such, these data, combined with more-or-less clear indications of aggressivity in the initiation of copulation by the males in the FATs, support the conclusion that the males' influence in the FATs is appropriately termed sexual aggression, as defined above.

CONCLUSIONS AND IMPLICATIONS

Although sexual aggression is relatively rare among mature great apes in their natural habitats, it does occur to some degree. Tutin and McGinnis,[3] for example, reported two instances of forcible copulation in wild chimpanzees. In both cases, the males trapped females in trees from which the females could not escape. These investigators also noted that the male chimpanzee's courtship display includes elements, such as piloerection, that are also observed in aggressive displays. These data suggest that some degree of male aggressivity is inherent in the species-typical mating pattern of chimpanzees.

Sexual aggression is rare among gorillas in the wild, but at least one example of aggression against a relatively young adult female in estrus has been reported.[31] In this example, the male charged and hit the female in association with mating. Harcourt[31] presented evidence, moreover, that this type of aggressive display could serve several functions, including alerting the females and drawing their attention to the male's "intentions"; it could serve, for instance, as a cue for dispersal at the end of a rest period.

In a subsequent field study by the author, another possible function of the male gorilla's (aggressive) display was suggested (unpublished observations). In the course of observations of more than 20 copulations between one silver-backed leader and two different females over several cycles, more-or-less complete examples of the male display were observed prior to copulation. In most cases, in response to an estrous female's approach, the male merely arose and assumed a tight-lipped, stiff-legged quadrapedal stance, whereupon the female quickly approached closer and presented for copulation. At first, no particular significance was ascribed to the male's behavior. On several occasions following the female's initial approach to proximity, however, the male charged a short distance parallel to the female before assuming the stiff-legged stance. On some fewer occasions, moreover, the male's charge was preceding by chest-beating. These observations, therefore, suggest that the male's display, in more-or-less complete form, can also serve as a signal for the female to present for copulation.

These observations in conjunction with those of Harcourt[31] suggest a role for sexual aggression in the mating of gorillas. With respect to mature and sexually experienced estrous females, it is generally sufficient for the male merely to rise to the stiff-legged stance to stimulate the female to present. In some cases, however, a more conspicuous signal may also be required, such as the charging component of the display. Finally, for a more recalcitrant female, or a relatively inexperienced female such as that described by Harcourt,[31] the complete male display with chest-beating and hitting out at the female may be performed. This interpretation suggests, therefore, that there are aggressive components in the natural pattern of sexual initiative of the male gorilla, similar to the proposal made for the male chimpanzee. Also, as for the chimpanzee, the degree to which the aggressive components are expressed varies with the context in which the mating occurs. When confined in a single cage with the female on a daily basis in the laboratory FATs, the males performed these displays repeatedly on most test days, including hitting out at, and sometimes biting, the females.[24] In both gorillas and chimpanzees, therefore, the species-typical mating pattern includes behavioral elements that serve multiple functions, including a threat of aggression and actual sexual aggression under certain conditions.

Among wild orang-utans, as described above, forcibly initiated copulations are carried out primarily by subadult males. Although fully mature males in the wild typically mate in cooperation with the female, some mature males initiate some copulations in the aggressive manner. The circumstances in which this behavior is exhibited by mature males in the wild has not been described in detail, but it has been described both for subadults in the wild and mature males in the FATs. In the wild, forcibly initiated copulations by subadult males occurred when females were encountered for the first time, or encountered *following a period of separation.*[27] In the FATs, forcibly initiated copulations by adult males occurred on a near-daily basis when each test day was preceded by a period of separation since the previous one. In the orang-utans, therefore, the conditions of testing simulated the conditions in which forcible copulation (by subadult males) occurs in the wild. That forcible copulation was carried out by fully mature males in the FATs appears to reflect the conditions of the FATs, in which the female cannot avoid or escape from the male.

It is possible that adult male orang-utans in the wild cease copulating with females forcibly in part because their large size prevents them from catching the smaller, more mobile females. Since their reduced mobility is a less significant factor in the relatively small space of a test cage, the males are able to pursue the pattern of forcible copulation that probably becomes ineffective under natural conditions.

Various interpretations have been proposed regarding the significance for the species of forcible copulation by subadult male orang-utans in the wild, but there is no clear consensus. One interpretation of possible relevance to present purposes is that this aggressive behavior reflects the limited social experience of these animals. That orang-utans are reared by their mothers in the absence of age-mates distinguishes them from the other great apes, which live in relatively large groups of individuals of both sexes and varied ages. Thus, it is likely that the social learning experiences of orang-utans are less extensive than those of the other great apes, and it is possible that the males learn less aggressive ways of initiating sexual interactions only when their increased size prevents them from pursuing their subadult tactics.

The data on these species of great apes are similar in revealing that (1) sexual aggression is carried out to some extent by males of all these species under natural conditions, albeit relatively infrequently; and (2) sexual aggression occurs at increased frequencies in FATs conducted in the laboratory as a consequence of test conditions that compromise the females options for regulating sexual interactions. These data support the interpretation that sexual aggression to some degree is an inherent characteristic of the behavioral repertoires of our closest biological affiliates and that conditions that render the females vulnerable to such aggression lead to its increased occurrence.

It is apparent because of its occurrence cross-culturally and throughout history that sexual aggression by males is also inherent in the behavioral repertoire of the human species.[32] It is not clear whether extrapolation from the great apes to humans is productive in this context. To the extent that generalization is possible, however, the present analysis suggests that the probability of a human female encountering sexual aggression is directly related to conditions—social, cultural and environmental—that permit the male's dominance over the female to assume the predominant role in the regulation of their sexual interactions and thereby reduce the female's prerogatives for refusing sexual overtures. It is important to note that this interpretation does *not* imply that sexual aggression in our species is inevitable or justified. It is consistent with the view, however, that the *potential* for male sexual aggression is inherent in our species, and that such aggression is likely to be expressed under a variety of conditions unless society and individuals take specific measures to preclude it. The recent passage of laws against sexual harassment in the marketplace and in institutions of higher education—traditional domains of male power and dominance—is consistent with the conclusions derived from research on the great apes.

SUMMARY

Species-typical frequencies of copulation during the menstrual cycle differ among common chimpanzee, orang-utan, and gorilla, but all three species exhibit a midcycle enhancement associated with estrus. Thus, in the natural habitat, chimpanzees mate for 10-14 days, orang-utans for 5-6 days, and gorillas for 2-3 days. In traditional laboratory pair-tests, however, conducted in a single cage with both animals freely accessible to each other, all three species of great apes copulate more frequently than the species-typical pattern. In all three species, moreover, the increased copulation appears to result from increased male sexual initiative (aggression), male dominance over females, and the inability of the female to avoid or escape from the male within the limited spatial conditions of the free-access test. This interpretation is supported by studies using restricted-access tests in which females control sexual access. These data suggest that male sexual aggression in our closest biological affiliates commonly occurs when females are rendered vulnerable to the male by the absence of the normal social constraints and spatial prerogatives typical of the natural habitat. The possible implications of this interpretation for a biological perspective on human sexual aggression are considered.

REFERENCES

1. Harcourt, A. H. 1981. Intermale competition and the reproductive behavior of the great apes. *In* Reproductive Biology of the Great Apes: Comparative and Biomedical Perspectives. C. E. Graham, Ed.: 301-318. Academic Press. New York, NY.
2. van Lawick-Goodall, J. 1968. The behavior of free-living chimpanzees in the Gombe Stream Reserve. Anim. Behav. Monogr. **1:** 161-311.
3. Tutin, C. E. G. & R. McGinnis. 1981. Chimpanzee reproduction in the wild. *In* Reproductive Biology of the Great Apes: Comparative and Biomedical Perspectives. C. E. Graham. Ed.: 239-264. Academic Press. New York, NY.
4. Elder, J. H. 1938. The time of ovulation in chimpanzees. Yale J. Biol. Med. **10:** 347-364.
5. Nadler, R. D., C. E. Graham, R. E. Gosselin & D. C. Collins. 1985. Serum levels of gonadotropins and gonadal steroids, including testosterone, during the menstrual cycle of the chimpanzee (*Pan troglodytes*). Amer. J. Primatol. **9:** 273-284.
6. Schaller, G. B. 1963. The Mountain Gorilla. University of Chicago Press. Chicago, IL.
7. Harcourt, A. H., K. J. Stewart & D. Fossey. 1981. Gorilla reproduction in the wild. *In* Reproductive Biology of the Great Apes: Comparative and Biomedical Perspectives. C. E. Graham, Ed.: 265-279. Academic Press. New York, NY.
8. Davenport, R. K., Jr. 1967. The orang-utan in Sabah. Folia Primatol. **5:** 247-263.
9. MacKinnon, J. R. 1971. The orang-utan in Sabah today. Oryx **11:** 141-191.
10. Rodman, P. S. 1973. Population composition and adaptive organisation among orang-utans of the Kutai Reserve. *In* Comparative Ecology and Behaviour of Primates. R. P. Michael & J. H. Crook, Eds.: 171-209. Academic Press. London.
11. Horr, D. A. 1975. The Borneo orang-utan: Population structure and dynamics in relation to ecology and reproductive strategy. *In* Primate Behavior: Developments in Field and Laboratory Research, Vol. 4. L. A. Rosenblum, Ed.: 307-323. Academic Press. New York, NY.
12. Nadler, R. D. 1981. Laboratory research on sexual behavior of the great apes. *In* Reproductive Biology of the Great Apes: Comparative and Biomedical Perspectives. C. E. Graham, Ed.: 191-238. Academic Press. New York, NY.
13. Galdikas, B. M. F. 1979. Orangutan adaptation at Tanjung Puting Reserve: Mating and ecology. *In* The Great Apes: Perspectives on Human Evolution, Vol. 5. D. A. Hamburg & E. R. McCown, Eds.: 195-233. Benjamin/Cummings. Menlo Park, NJ.
14. Galdikas, B. M. F. 1981. Orangutan reproduction in the wild. *In* Reproductive Biology of the Great Apes: Comparative and Biomedical Perspectives. C. E. Graham, Ed.: 281-300. Academic Press. New York, NY.
15. Schurmann, C. L. 1981. Courtship and mating behavior of wild orangutans in Sumatra. *In* Primate Behavior and Sociobiology. A. B. Chiarelli & R. S. Corruccini, Eds.: 130-135. Springer-Verlag. Berlin.
16. Schurmann, C. L. 1982. Mating behaviour of wild orang utans. *In* The Orang Utan: Its Biology and Conservation. L. E. M. de Boer, Ed. Dr. W. Junk Publ. The Hague.

17. YERKES, R. M. & J. H. ELDER. 1936. Oestrus, receptivity and mating in the chimpanzee. Comp. Psychol. Monogr. **13:** 1-39.
18. YERKES, R. M. 1939. Sexual behavior in the chimpanzee. Hum. Biol. **11:** 78-111.
19. YOUNG, W. C. & W. D. ORBISON. 1944. Changes in selected features of behavior in pairs of oppositely-sexed chimpanzees during the sexual cycle and after ovariectomy. J. Comp. Psychol. **37:** 107-143.
20. NADLER, R. D. 1975. Sexual cyclity in captive lowland gorillas. Science **189:** 813-814.
21. NADLER, R. D. 1976. Sexual behavior of captive lowland gorillas. Arch. Sex. Behav. **5:** 487-502.
22. NADLER, R. D. 1975. Cyclicity in tumescence of the perineal labia of female lowland gorillas. Anat. Rec. **181:** 791-798.
23. NADLER, R. D., C. E. GRAHAM, D. C. COLLINS & K. G. GOULD. 1979. Plasma gonadotropins, prolactin, gonadal steroids and genital swelling during the menstrual cycle of lowland gorillas. Endocrinology **105:** 290-296.
24. NADLER, R. D. & L. C. MILLER. 1982. Influence of male aggression on mating of gorillas in the laboratory. Folia Primatol. **38:** 233-239.
25. NADLER, R. D., D. C. COLLINS, L. C. MILLER & C. E. GRAHAM. 1983. Menstrual cycle patterns of hormones and sexual behavior in gorillas. Horm. Behav. **17:** 1-17.
26. NADLER, R. D. 1977. Sexual behavior of captive orang-utans. Arch. Sex. Behav. **6:** 457-475.
27. RIJKSEN, H. D. 1978. A field study on sumatran orang utans (*Pongo pygmaeus abelii* Lesson 1827). Ecology, Behaviour and Conservation. H. Veenman and Zonen B. V. Wageningen, The Netherlands.
28. NADLER, R. D., J. G. HERNDON & J. WALLIS. 1986. Adult sexual behavior: Hormones and reproduction. *In* Comparative Primate Biology, Vol. 2(A): Behavior, Conservation, and Ecology. G. Mitchell & J. Erwin, Eds.: 363-407. Alan R. Liss. New York, NY.
29. NADLER, R. D. 1982. Reproductive behavior and endocrinology of orang utans. *In* The Orang Utan: Its Biology and Conservation. L. E. M. de Boer, Ed.: 231-248. Dr. W. Junk Publ. The Hague.
30. NADLER, R. D. 1987. Sexual and reproductive behavior of orang-utans. *In* Aspects of the Biology of the Orang-utan. J. H. Schwartz, Ed. Oxford University Press. New York, NY. In press.
31. HARCOURT, A. H. 1979. Social relationships between adult male and female mountain gorillas in the wild. Anim. Behav. **27:** 325-342.
32. BROWNMILLER, S. 1975. Against Our Will. Simon and Schuster. New York, NY.

Sexual Sadism: Brain, Blood, and Behavior

R. LANGEVIN, J. BAIN, G. WORTZMAN, S. HUCKER,
R. DICKEY, AND P. WRIGHT

Department of Psychiatry
Mount Sinai Hospital
Toronto, Ontario M5G 1X5, Canada

Sadism is a bizarre fusion of sexual urges and aggression. Surprisingly little research has been directed to this unusual and dangerous sexual anomaly. This paper focuses on sadists, a group who are preferentially sexually aroused by dominating, controlling, entrapping, terrorizing, and injuring their victims. The cases discussed here satisfy DSM-III criteria, and interrater agreement is over 90%.[1] The sadist, in place of foreplay, desires to entrap his victim so that she is in his power and has no alternative but to do his bidding sexually. The response of the victim—fear, terror, and pleading—is sexually stimulating. In some cases the foregoing features are short-circuited, and the offender immediately attacks and injures the victim. This behavior, also, is sexually exciting, even though there may be no orgasm. For other men, the death of their victim is a prelude to their sexual activity, which may involve intercourse, oral sex, and cunnilingus. The victim's body may be mutilated in a frenzy of excitement and the penis inserted into various cavities of the body that have been carved. The genitals may be removed, and cases of cannibalism have been noted.

BEHAVIOR PATTERNS

There are other features of sadism that are of interest to the forensic psychologist and psychiatrist and may have a bearing on the physiological findings to be noted later. The sadist is similar in many respects to other sexual aggressives (SAs) who are not primarily sadistic in their sexual acts (TABLE 1).

The abuse of alcohol and drugs is common to both groups. Over half of the sex offenders are heavy drinkers; a third are chronic alcoholics. Up to three-quarters have abused nonmedical drugs at some time in their lives. Both groups are criminal, and they have about as many nonsexual crimes as sexual crimes in their history. Common to both groups is poor socialization and disturbed parent-child relationships, in which half of the sexual aggressives' parents are alcoholic and/or violent towards their children. The men show a long history of antisocial behavior, so that approximately 40% of both groups could be labeled "antisocial personality" or the nebulous "psychopath."

Although approximately one-sixth of SAs engage in orgasmic transvestism,[2] the sadists are unique in showing a disturbance in gender identity. This feature has been hinted at by Brittain,[3] who noted an "effeminate tinge" to the sex killer. We have found that most of the sadists who are admitters show either gender indifference or feminine longings. A small number of cases are interested in sex reassignment. For example, Mr. A murdered a woman and had intercourse with the corpse. He then removed the genitals and was contemplating eating them when he was interrupted by a third party and he fled the scene of his crime. He attempted to rape and murder a second woman, but he was apprehended in the act. Upon clinical examination he presented as a very narcissistic individual, and he expressed an interest in sex reassignment surgery. He was particularly eager to have hormones so that he might grow female breasts.

The extreme quality of Mr. A's gender longings is not always witnessed, but it is more frequent than one would expect in a group who are presumably at the hypermasculine end of the aggression spectrum. Many of these men are, of course, psychopaths, and they do not incorporate social roles; so it is to be expected that they also would not incorporate sex roles. Rather, they play along with social roles to suit their own purposes. In some cases, however, there is a genuine gender confusion, indifference, or feminine orientation as commonly seen in transsexuals.

TABLE 1. Clinically Important Features Common to Sadists and Other Sexually Aggressive Men

Alcoholism	53%
Illegal drug use	up to 75%
Criminality (average number of crimes)	
Sex crimes	2.55
Nonsexual violence	1.10
Break and enter	2.33
Other crimes	0.93
Socialization	
Antisocial personality	40%
Parents aggressive and alcoholic	50%

Narcissism is also an interesting feature of sadism that merits closer examination. It may occur specifically in a sexual interpersonal context, or it may be a more global personality characteristic that appears in a wider range of behaviors. For example, some men may enjoy only parading themselves before their terrorized victims, suggesting that their narcissism is specifically sexual in nature. On the other hand, mass or sex killers may enjoy seeing their picture in the newspaper. They may show childish delight in the attention that they receive from authorities for their hideous crimes, suggesting a global narcissism. Evidently, many of these men have little regard for their victims or for human life in general. Arbolita-Florez and Holley[4] have suggested that mass killers are generally sexual sadists. They derive great satisfaction from publicity as well as from the sexual mutilations and/or deaths they cause.

One may expect that such bizarre sexual behavior patterns would be correlated with some biological variables, and indeed we have not been disappointed. We have explored the role of sex hormones and brain abnormalities in a series of studies that will now be discussed.

ENDOCRINE ABNORMALITIES

We have examined sex hormone profiles in 49 cases of sexual aggression and 31 controls to date. The initial study, on 15 SAs and 16 controls, was reported in 1985.[5] The results suggested that the adrenal axis of the endocrine system might be important in sexual sadists and nonsadistic sexual aggressives. The weak androgen, DHEAS, was found to be elevated in sexual aggressives generally over a control group of nonviolent, nonsex offenders matched for age and education. There was a trend for cortisol to be higher and prolactin lower in SAs, as well. It was noteworthy, however, that testosterone (T, hereafter) was not significantly different in these groups, although it has been the hormone most frequently hypothesized to be related to sexual anomalies as well as to aggression in general.[5] There was a trend for the nonsadistic sexual aggressives to have higher levels of T than the sadists or controls. However, the results of sex hormone analyses are frequently confounded in aggressive groups generally because of their high incidence of substance abuse. Only Rada and his colleagues,[6–8] to our knowledge, have taken into account the effect of alcohol or drug use on the hormonal assay. We, also, have attempted to sort the groups into "alcoholics" and "nonalcoholics" based on their history and on the MAST,[9] and into drug abusers and non-drug abusers, based on their history and on the DAST-20.[10] Rada *et al.*[6–8] found a positive correlation of alcohol abuse and the degree of force used in sexually aggressive acts. Langevin *et al.*[5] and Bain *et al.*[11] found that both aggressive sex offenders and nonaggressive nonsex offenders who abused alcohol and drugs tended to have higher T levels, but results were nonsignificant.

The logical avenue to pursue on conclusion of our first study[5] was to (1) replicate on a larger sample DHEAS results, and (2) determine whether the trends to cortisol and prolactin differences would be significant. (3) A further investigation to pursue was the so-called challenge test—that is, to administer ACTH and determine whether the dynamic relationships of hormones on the adrenal axis in rapists would prove significantly different from a control group. On all counts, the use of larger numbers and replication show that these results were negative. Bain *et al.*[11] found that in a sample of 20 sadists—14 nonsadistic sexual aggressives and 15 offender controls—there were no significant differences on nine different hormones: T. androstenedione, estradiol, prolactin, cortisol, DHEAS, LH, FSH, and SHBG. The results of the ACTH test also were not significantly different for the three groups. The results of T analyses have been disappointing, both in sexually aggressive and in nonsexually aggressive men such as murderers and common assaulters.[12–13] It has been suggested that free T might be more suitable to investigate, because it is the biologically active component of total T. However, the reliability and validity of this measure continues to be debated.

Characteristics of some peculiar individuals, however, suggest that there are some endocrine correlates of sexual sadism. In one sadist, LH and FSH levels were five times the normal male limits. The male was small and boyish in stature. Gonadal insufficiency was evident. This young man had a long antisocial history for his 17 years. He would attack women with a knife and cut them while he experienced sexual pleasure. In a second case T levels were very low, and the retarded, sadistic young man showed hypospadias, a congenital abnormality in which the penis does not fuse. This abnormality was surgically corrected when he was 14 years of age. He was examined at 19 years of age, at which time he would attack and strangle women with great sexual excitement. T levels were at a pregenital level in this man. However, he had been removed from Provera only 4 days before venipuncture, and it is not clear whether the Provera caused this low result.

A few physical abnormalities that have been evident in sadists suggest that there had been unusual endocrine involvement at some time. We found two cases of hypospadias. This abnormality is believed to be due to a local T insufficiency, but it is a poorly understood phenomenon. One has to wonder whether there are other body sites where T levels may be too low—for example, in the brain. We have also examined a sadist with gynaecomastia and lactation. This man reported the breast development at puberty. There has been one case of XYY syndrome and another of possible XXY or Klinefelter's syndrome. A complete karyotyping on a random sample of cases has not been undertaken to date.

Although the striking endocrine abnormalities are few in number, they have occurred only in sadists, which makes further research on sex hormones in this group worthwhile. However, sex hormone levels in the peripheral blood seem normal in sexually aggressive men once substance abuse is controlled. Central nervous system levels of sex hormones may prove informative, and the LHRH test is currently being administered.

BRAIN ABNORMALITIES

There have been a number of single case reports and of uncontrolled group studies that suggest that temporal lobe pathology is important in sexual anomalies. As Cummings noted,[14] there are three sexualized effects of temporal lobe brain abnormalities: reduced sexual drive, increased sexual drive, and sexual anomalies. Kolarsky *et al.*,[15] in a well-controlled study, suggested that approximately 18% of temporal lobe epileptics in general manifest some sexual anomaly. Most commonly one sees fetishism, a feature not unusual in sexual aggressives; but other anomalies have been noted.

To date we have examined brain structure and function in a total of 91 SA cases, including 22 sadists and 21 nonsadists as well as 36 offender controls. An additional 48 SA cases have been unclassified because they are nonadmitters, but they were nevertheless clearly guilty of sexually aggressive crimes. They were kept separate so as not to confuse them with admitting cases of sadism and nonsadism. In some instances there have been striking brain abnormalities. FIGURE 1 shows the CT scan of a sexually aggressive male with a left frontal-temporal lobe glioma. This is a slowly growing development that likely has been present from childhood. In conjunction with alcohol abuse, this young man engaged in a bizarre attack on a young girl in a house full of people. He wandered into the house seminude after consuming an unknown amount of beer and hard liquor at a party. The father and brother of the young girl attacked him, and when he was strangled by the father, he suddenly "came to." He was cooperative while the father called the police. Later he could not recall any of these events. FIGURE 2 shows another unusual CT scan of a sadist. It shows gross enlargement of the ventricles. This man was not schizophrenic, but he, also, engaged in bizarre sexual behavior. However, these are atypical cases.

When a large number of men are examined, the overall incidence of gross pathology is no different from that found in a nonsexual nonaggressive offender group (TABLE 2). However, it should be recalled that the temporal lobes in particular have been implicated in unusual sexual behavior. When the temporal lobes specifically are examined, it is the sexual sadists who have right temporal horn dilatation, shown in

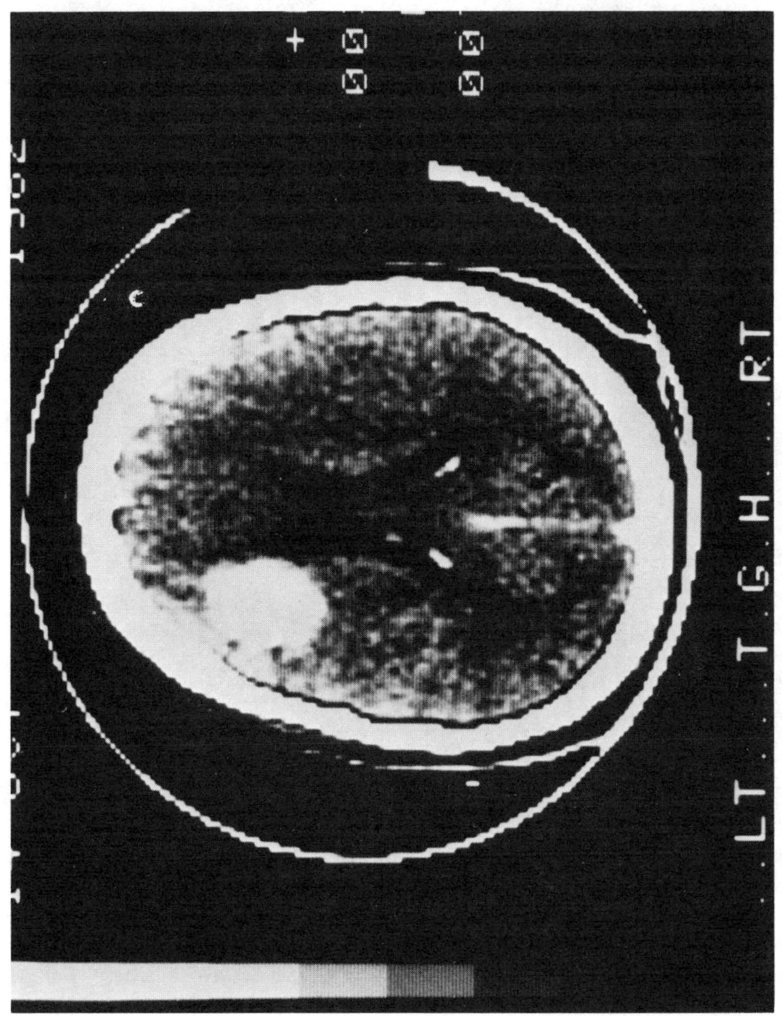

FIGURE 1. CT scan of a sexually aggressive male with a left frontal-temporal lobe glioma.

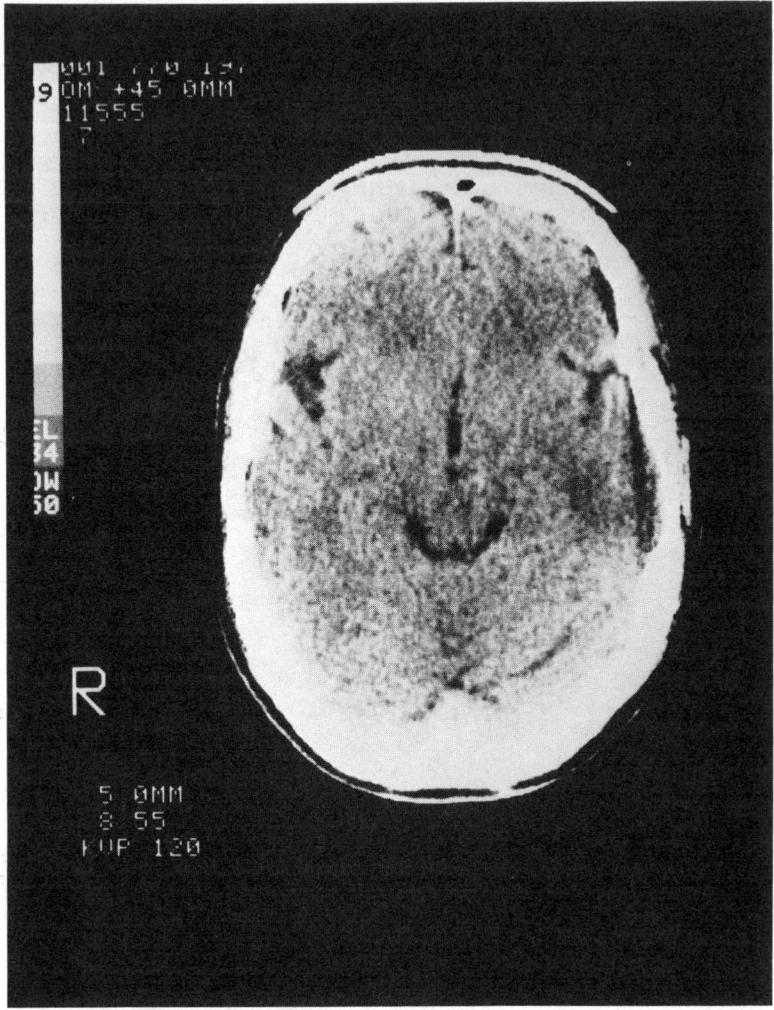

FIGURE 2. CT scan of a sadist, showing gross enlargement of the ventricles.

FIGURE 3. This is a relatively subtle phenomenon, but it has been consistent. Forty-one percent of the sadists show this abnormality, compared to 11% of nonsadistic sexual aggressives and 13% of controls (TABLE 2). The results for the sadists are statistically significant.[1,5]

The results of neuropsychological testing using the Halstead Reitan Battery[5] and the Luria Nebraska Neuropsychological Test Battery[1] suggest that impairment is higher in sexual aggressives than in controls, but the results are not consistent. Using the Reitan Battery,[5] it was found that the sadists showed significantly more impairment overall than the other groups (TABLE 2). Using the Luria Nebraska,[1] the reverse was

TABLE 2. CT Scan and Neuropsychological Test Results for Sadists, Nonsadistic Sexual Aggressives, and Offender Controls

	Percent of Group		
	Sadists	Other Sexual Aggressives	Controls
CT scan			
Any abnormality	50	39	30
Right temporal horn dilatation	41	11	13
Halstead-Reitan			
Significant impairment index	35	8	18
Luria-Nebraska			
Significant impairment	17	70	0

NOTE: For details of studies see References 1, 5, and 16.

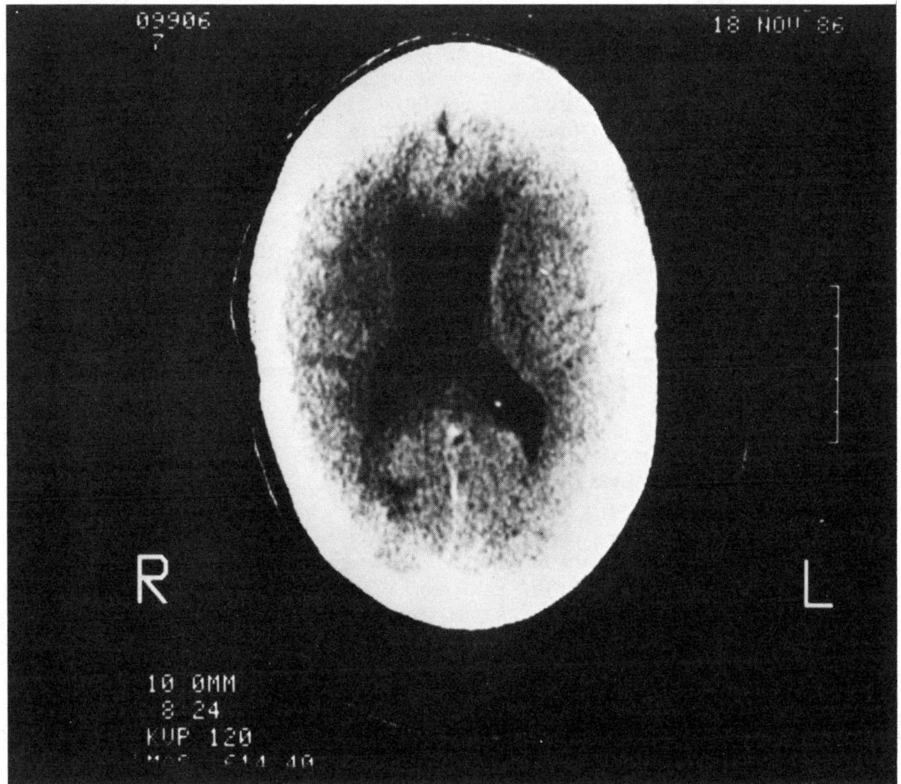

FIGURE 3. CT scan showing right temporal horn dilatation typical of sexual sadists.

the case; that is, nonsadists showed more impairment than sadists or controls. The CT findings, however, have been consistent. They have been checked for reliability with over 90% interrater agreement, and, although they are subtle findings, they suggest that the right temporal lobe is somehow more implicated in sexual aggression than are other areas of the brain. These findings show discriminant validity from aggression in general, in which there are no differences in damage to the temporal lobe versus other areas;[16] from other sexual anomalies, such as pedophilia, in which the left temporal lobe is more implicated;[17] and from substance abuse, where damage tends to be more global. EEG work in progress is directed to extending CT findings. It is possible that overall the EEG will be abnormal in sadists compared to a control group. It is also possible that sexual arousal may activate EEG abnormalities in sadists that are not seen in a control group. Some cases are suggestive of complex partial seizures, that is, temporal lobe phenomena. Case B had brutally beaten and mutilated a women. He performed cunnilingus on the corpse. He attempted to do the same to a second woman, who fought him off, and he was apprehended. A prototype of a narcissist, this man reveled in the attention that he received from the press, the police, and professionals. He repeated his story several times, for a total recording time of 21 hours. During an interview, he expressed the fact that he was sexually excited describing the entrapment and murdering of his victim. The interesting feature of this case is the evidence of witnesses who had seen him in other circumstances. Working in an animal shelter, he had tortured and killed several animals before he was dismissed. A witness who caught him in the act described him as "in a trance, strangling a dog."

We have found some cases of severe head injuries and of epilepsy, but as with endocrine abnormalities, they are the exception and do not explain CT scan or other results. However, the abnormalities detected in sadism are consistent but subtle. Much more work is required before a clear picture of the nature of the anomaly is evident. Current EEG work and MRI scans may help to further understand this phenomenon.

SUMMARY

The behavior of sadists is bizarre and poorly understood. There are gross endocrine and brain abnormalities in a small number of these men. Approximately two-fifths show subtle temporal lobe brain abnormalities that are logically linked to sexual behavior and require further exploration. It would be interesting to explore the interface of the endocrine system and the brain—that is, to determine if there are interactive processes that may be related to the development of sexual anomalies, perhaps early in life as suggested by Kolarsky *et al.*[15] Certainly, biological factors cannot determine whether an individual will act on his sexual impulses. Many psychological factors, such as family background and substance abuse, play a significant role in the dangerousness of the individual. However, it appears that biological factors are noteworthy in sexual sadism. Brain pathology, especially, shows some correlation with force used in offences and likelihood of recidivism,[5] and for this reason alone it merits further study.

REFERENCES

1. HUCKER, S. *et al.* 1987. Cerebral damage and dysfunction in sexually aggressive men. Manuscript in preparation.
2. LANGEVIN, R., D. PAITICH & A. RUSSON. 1985. Are rapists sexually anomalous, aggressive or both? *In* Erotic Preference, Gender Identity and Aggression in Men. R. Langevin, Ed. L. Erlbaum Associates. Hillsdale, NJ.
3. BRITTAIN, R. 1970. The sadistic murderer. Med. Sci. Law **10:** 198-207.
4. ARBOLITA-FLOREZ, J. & H. HOLLEY. 1985. What is mass murder? Psychiatry—The State of the Art, Vol. 6, T. Pichat, P. Berner, R. Wolf & U. Thaw, Eds. Plenum Press. New York, NY.
5. LANGEVIN, R., *et al.* 1985. Sexual aggression: Constructing a prediction equation. *In* Erotic Preference, Gender Identity and Aggression in Men. R. Langevin, Ed. L. Erlbaum Associates. Hillsdale, NJ.
6. RADA, R. T. 1975. Alcoholism and forcible rape. Am. J. Psychiatry **132:** 444-446.
7. RADA, R. T., D. R. LAWS & R. KELLNER. 1976. Plasma testosterone levels in the rapist. Psychosom. Med. **38:** 257-268.
8. RADA, R. T., *et al.* 1983. Plasma androgens in violent and nonviolent sex offenders. Bull. Am. Acad. Psychiatry Law **11:** 149-158.
9. SELZER, M. 1971. The Michigan Alcoholism Screening Test: The quest for a new diagnostic instrument. Am. J. Psychiatry **127:** 1653-1658.
10. SKINNER, H. A. 1982. Drug Use Questionnaire (DAST-20). Addiction Research Foundation. Toronto.
11. BAIN, J., R. DICKEY & R. LANGEVIN. 1987. A comparison of the ACTH test in sexual sadists, other sexual aggressives and offender controls. Manuscript in preparation.
12. BAIN, J. 1987. Sex hormones in killers and assaulters. Behav. Sci. Law In press.
13. BAIN, J. & R. LANGEVIN. 1987. Sex hormones in sadistic sex offenders. Manuscript in preparation.
14. CUMMINGS, J. L. 1985. Clinical Neuropsychiatry. Grune & Stratton. New York, NY.
15. KOLARSKY, A. *et al.* 1967. Male sexual deviation: Association with early temporal lobe damage. Arch. Gen. Psychiatry **17:** 735-743.
16. LANGEVIN, R., M. BEN-ARON, G. WORTZMAN, R. DICKEY & L. HANDY. 1987. Brain damage, diagnosis, and substance abuse among violent offenders. Behav. Sci. Law **5:** 77-94.
17. HUCKER, S. *et al.* 1986. Neuropsychological impairment in pedophiles. Can. J. Behav. Sci. In press.

Courtship Disorder: Is This Hypothesis Valid?

KURT FREUND

Clarke Institute of Psychiatry
University of Toronto
Toronto, Canada M5T 1R8

THE HYPOTHESIS

Voyeurism, exhibitionism, making obscene telephone calls, toucheurism, frotteurism, or an erotic preference for rape in men who are not really sadistic—all have a certain pattern in common, and this may indicate that there is a strong common factor in the etiology of these anomalous behaviors.[1] This conjecture resulted from these considerations:

1. The sequence of activities in the course of typical human sexual interaction can be seen as a succession of four phases.[2] The first phase is initial partner choice, which involves scrutinizing the potential partner visually. The second is pretactile interaction, which involves posturing, smiling, and verbal communication. The third phase involves tactile interaction, and the fourth phase involves genital union.
2. Each of the above-noted anomalous behaviors can be seen as an exaggeration, distortion, or caricature of one of the four normal phases, and if the remaining phases are at all represented in these behaviors, their representation is only vestigial.

These anomalous activities lead to ejaculation either on the spot or later, through masturbation at home as the patient replays these situations in his imagination. Following students of animal behavior, who designate all precopulatory procreative activities as "courtship behavior,"[3,4] I have called the hypothesized anomaly a disturbance of phasing of courtship behavior or, for short, a "courtship disorder."

THE EVIDENCE

If the anomalous behaviors in question have a common etiological factor, one should expect their rate of simultaneous cooccurrence in the same person to be relatively high, and clinical observation appears to indicate that this is so. While the majority of publications on these anomalous patterns do not pose the question of cooccurrence of more than one of these disturbances in the same person, such cooccurrence has been noted by a number of investigators. Taylor[5] observed the combination of exhibitionism and toucheurism. However, he thought the combination was rare. Yalom[6] described cases of cooccurrence of voyeurism, exhibitionism, and rape. Grassberger[7] stated that among subjects arrested for indecent exposure 12% had committed other sexual offenses as well, "rape" in particular.

Gebhard *et al.* cautioned that "while the great majority of exhibitionists do not resort to violence, a minority of perhaps one in ten have attempted or seriously contemplated rape" (p. 399).[8] Rooth[9] and Cabanis[10] (quoted by Rooth) note simultaneous occurrence of exhibitionism, toucheurism, and frotteurism in the same subjects. Paitich *et al.*[11] tested the initially stated hypothesis by investigating the cooccurrence of the anomalous patterns in question by a factor analysis of answers given by a large number of patients to a sexual history questionnaire. Voyeuristic, toucheuristic, and frotteuristic activities, exposing, and rape all clustered together.

There seemed, however, to be substantial differences as to the degree of relatedness of these various anomalous behaviors. We investigated these relationships by comparing cooccurrence of the four behaviors most often mentioned. The subjects for this investigation were charged for, or had themselves volunteered information regarding, voyeuristic activity, toucheuristic activity, exposing, or rape. For reasons that will be obvious later on, we also included in our selection all of our 131 patients who had

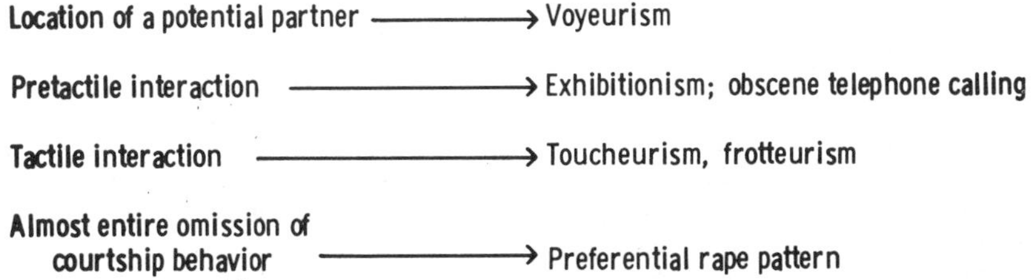

FIGURE 1. Relationships between the normal phases and the various expressions of a courtship disorder. (From Freund *et al.*[12] Reprinted by permission from *Archives of Sexual Behavior.*)

sexually approached an early adolescent girl (12-15 years old). Finally, there were 40 patients who had sexually approached a child less than 12 years old, in addition to approaching an adult female, in an indictable manner. The total group of probands consisted of 950 men: mean age = 29.9 years, SD = 10.3 years, modal education, more than 8 grades completed but less than 12.

Our measure of association between pairs of the anomalous behaviors in question was the percentage of individuals who, in addition to having carried out one of these activities, had also carried out the other anomalous behavior. TABLE 1 shows the percentages of voyeurs who were also toucheuristic, who also had exposed, and who had raped; the percentages of exhibitionists who were also voyeurs, and so on.

The closest relationship appears to be between voyeurism and exhibitionism, the next closest between exhibitionism and toucheurism. TABLE 2 shows that voyeurism occurs rarely just by itself, that it is usually accompanied, in the same person, by another expression of a courtship disorder. Exhibitionism, however, occurs approxi-

TABLE 1. Percentage of Patients with One of the Indexed Anomalies Who Show Evidence of an Additional Such Anomaly[13]

	Additional Anomalies			
Indexed Anomaly	Voyeurism	Exhibitionism	Toucheurism	Rape
Voyeurism		73.5	33.7	18.4
Exhibitionism	27.9		26.4	10.5
Toucheurism	26.6	54.8		16.1
Rape	11.5	17.3	12.8	

mately half the time without the patient's showing any other among these anomalous behaviors. Moreover, if any other among these anomalous activities is accompanied by an additional expression of a courtship disorder in the same patient, the latter is most frequently exhibitionism. Exhibitionism appears, therefore, to be the most typical expression of a courtship disorder.

The low rate of cooccurrence of rape with the other anomalous patterns in question was expected, because from the start—that is, when the courtship disorder hypothesis was first put forward—it was already clear that the preferential rape pattern would account only for a small proportion of rape cases.[12] However, what holds for rape may also apply, to a minor extent, to voyeurism, exhibitionism, and toucheurism as well; and these anomalous patterns may sometimes occur in a context other than a courtship disorder. There is, however, no reason to suppose that, apart from the connection with the preferential rape pattern, this factor would considerably distort the relationships between the other anomalous patterns in question.

The relationships shown in TABLES 1 and 2 are in any case likely to be inaccurate, because apart from the information about the reason of the patient's referral we had to rely preponderantly on his self-report. We have tried to estimate this information loss,[13] but for this purpose only a relatively small subgroup of these patients was available, because only much later were the relevant questions included in the Erotic Preference Examination Scheme we use with outpatients. Our estimate was arrived at by assessing the percentage of individuals accused of, or charged for, voyeuristic or toucheuristic activities, or for exposing, who denied even fantasizing carrying out one of these activities, or dwelling on past occasions when they had indulged in one

TABLE 2. Percentages of Patients with One of the Indexed Anomalies Who Show Evidence of Any One of the Three Other Similar Anomalies[13]

	Voyeurism	Exhibitionism	Toucheurism	Rape
Presence of any one of the other three anomalies, given the indexed anomaly	86.7	48.4	68.5	28.2
Presence of the indexed anomaly, given any one of the remaining three anomalies	19.7	40.1	20.9	13.2

of these activities, or feeling the desire to go out on the street to carry out one of these activities, or masturbating with fantasies or memories of one of these activities.

The subgroup we used had 122 members: mean age = 27.1 years, SD = 9.8 years; modal education, 8 grades completed but less than 12. The percentage of those who denied fantasizing, dwelling on, or desiring about, any of their objectively assessed anomalous sexual activities was 59.8. This suggests a high degree of deliberate underreporting which, in turn, makes it likely that the frequency of cooccurrence of these anomalies is higher than indicated by TABLES 1 and 2.

In attempting to obtain more objective information about the relatedness of the various expressions of a courtship disorder, we used the phallometric method, which assesses the arousal value of potentially erotic stimuli by monitoring during their presentation the subject's penile volume changes.[14–16]

With this method it was shown that (a) patients who suffered from an expression of a courtship disorder other than voyeurism, and who denied voyeuristic activity or tendencies, nonetheless responded more to narratives describing voyeuristic situations than did normal controls; and that (b) exhibitionists who denied toucheuristic activity or tendencies responded more to toucheuristic stimuli than did controls (FIGS. 2 and 3).[12]

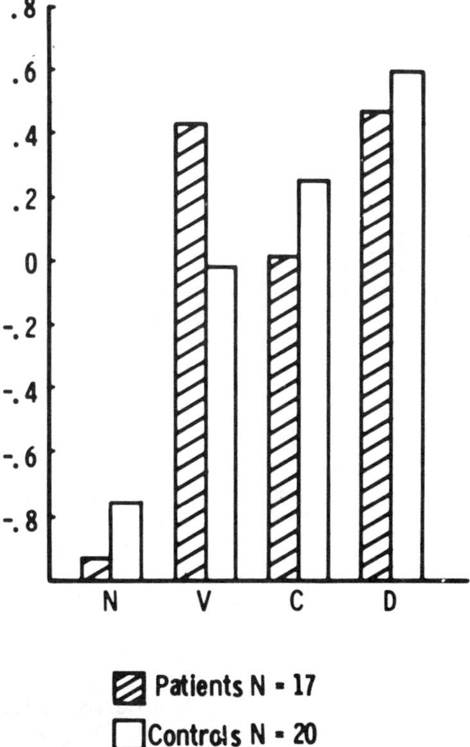

FIGURE 2. The responses of nonvoyeurs. N = sexually neutral situations; V = voyeuristic situations; C = situations of normal tactile interaction; D = situations of intercourse. On the *vertical line* is the mean penile response in Z scores. (From Freund *et el.*[12] Reprinted by permission from *Archives of Sexual Behavior.*)

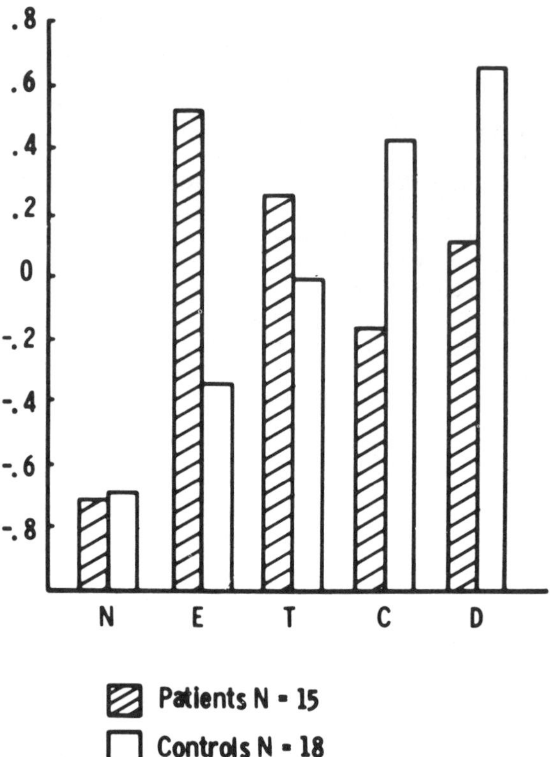

FIGURE 3. The responses of nontoucheurs. N = sexually neutral situations; E = situations of exposing; T = toucheuristic situations; C = situations of normal tactile interaction; D = situations of intercourse. On the *vertical line* is the mean penile response in Z scores. (From Freund *et al.*[12] Reprinted by permission from *Archives of Sexual Behavior.*)

A further experiment compared 11 rape-prone males, who were most likely afflicted with the preferential rape pattern, with 11 sexually normal controls. The dependent measure was penile response to audiotaped narratives that described imaginary scenes in which the examinee engaged in behavior typical of voyeurs, exhibitionists, or toucheurs. Narratives depicting normal tactile interaction (short of intercourse) with a genuinely participating woman, normal intercourse, and nonerotic scenes were also presented. To avoid having sadists in the sample, we included in the experiment only those rape-prone males who did not use greater threats or force than would seem necessary to have the woman submit to the rape.

The rape-prone males responded more to the voyeuristic situations and relatively less to depictions of normal intercourse than did the controls. In respect to toucheuristic situations, there was only a marginal effect in the expected direction.

There was, however, still the possibility that rape proneness in general originates from abnormally high agonistic motivation—that is, from an abnormally strong inclination toward fight and flight behavior—and that even males selected as described differ on this factor from males with the other anomalous behaviors in question. We therefore compared a group of 12 such rape-prone males with 12 males with courtship disorders and 12 normal controls.

The procedure was similar to that in foregoing experiments. However, the test stimuli consisted of narrative descriptions of (1) the imaginary protagonist's pretactile erotic interaction with a woman (talking, smiling, etc.); (2) tactile interaction short of intercourse; (3) coitus; (4) erotically neutral activities. Each of the three erotic stimulus categories was represented by eight narratives, in four of which the woman

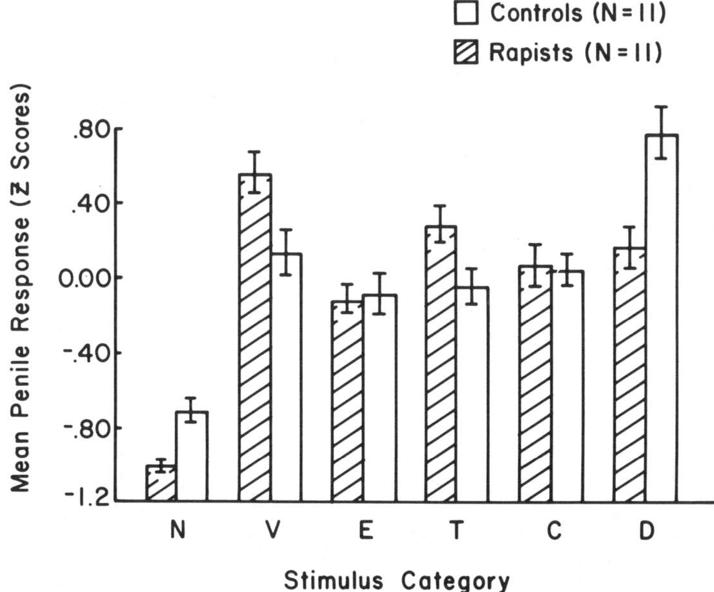

FIGURE 4. Penile responses to situations typical of various expressions of a courtship disorder. Penile responses to stimulus narratives that depict the protagonist in a voyeuristic situation (V); in the situation of exposing (E); in the toucheuristic situation (T); in the situation of tactile sexual interaction short of intercourse (C); in the situation of intercourse (D); in sexually neutral situations (N). The *vertical lines on the bars* indicate standard errors. (From Freund *et al.*[17] Reprinted by permission from *Archives of Sexual Behavior.*)

was depicted as genuinely participating; in the other four she became fearful of the individual. The results of this experiment are shown in FIGURE 5.

Males demonstrating an expression of a courtship disorder other than the preferential rape pattern and males afflicted with this latter pattern both tolerate the presence of an abnormally strong agonistic component in sexual interaction with genital involvement much better than sexually normal males, or even prefer the abnormal sexual interaction because of its inherently stronger agonistic component. This is probably the kind of "sadism" thought of by Glover,[18] Grassberger,[7] Hackett,[19] Hartwich,[20] Karpman,[21] Rooth,[9] and Yalom,[6] whose clinical experience led them to believe that voyeurism and exhibitionism are sadistically motivated.

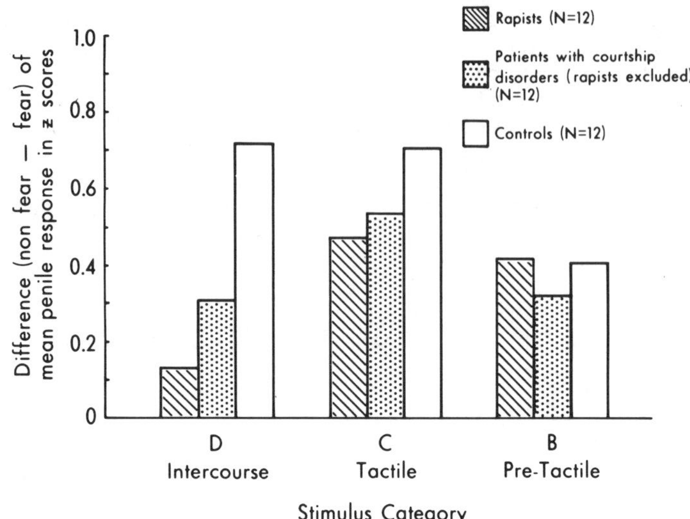

FIGURE 5. Difference between mean penile responses to sexual interaction with a genuinely participating woman and such responses to sexual interaction with a fearful woman. D = the situation of intercourse; C = the situation of tactile interaction short of intercourse; B = the situation of pretactile sexual interaction. (From Freund *et al.* Reprinted by permission from *Archives of Sexual Behavior.*)

According to clinical observation, the anomalous activities in question—and exposing in particular—are conspicuously often, and sometimes exclusively, directed toward early adolescent girls. In the present study this was the case in 19.4% of the patients. Among those who approached early adolescent girls sexually (incest cases excluded), roughly one-third (32.8%) were either exclusively exhibitionists or exposed in addition to demonstrating one or more of the other anomalous patterns. Some patients with a courtship disorder extend the age range of their quasi partners as far as to include children as well as adults.

The proportion of these patients was between 5% and 10%. However, Langevin *et al.*,[22] using the phallometric test, found that exhibitionists do not respond more to children than do sexually normal controls.

POSSIBLE CAUSES

Langevin[23] has given a comprehensive review of current and past conjectures about the causes of the anomalous behaviors in question and of the few experiments carried out to test these suppositions. This makes possible restricting the following hypotheses to those that seem to be the most plausible:

(a) Taking into account the substantial degree of association of the anomalous patterns in question, the simplest alternative to the courtship disorder hypothesis would be a demonstration that—rape excluded—their common cause is a disinclination toward intercourse. This would make the conjecture of a disturbance of phasing superfluous, and the various anomalous patterns could be seen as having developed as a surrogate for intercourse.

The outcome of one of the earlier-mentioned phallometric experiments seemed to suggest this possibility, but what it really showed was the relatively low standing of the erotic value of normal intercourse compared to that of the anomalous activities in these patients. Only a comparison of these patients with normal subjects on responses to narratives depicting each of the four phases of normal sexual interaction can show whether there is a disinclination toward one of these phases. Such a comparison was carried out in 16 exhibitionist and 16 normal controls.[24] FIGURE 6 shows that there was no such primary disinclination toward the intercourse phase.

(b) The outcome of the experiment shown in FIGURE 5 suggested that courtship disorder is associated with either an abnormally high tolerance of, or a preference for, an abnormally strong agonistic component in sexual interaction. One of the probable functions of courtship is suppression of agonistic tendencies in sexual partners.[25,26] However, the question of whether the heightened agonistic level is part of the causation or the sequelae of a courtship disorder was neither asked nor answered by the above study. A study investigating these possibilities further is under way.

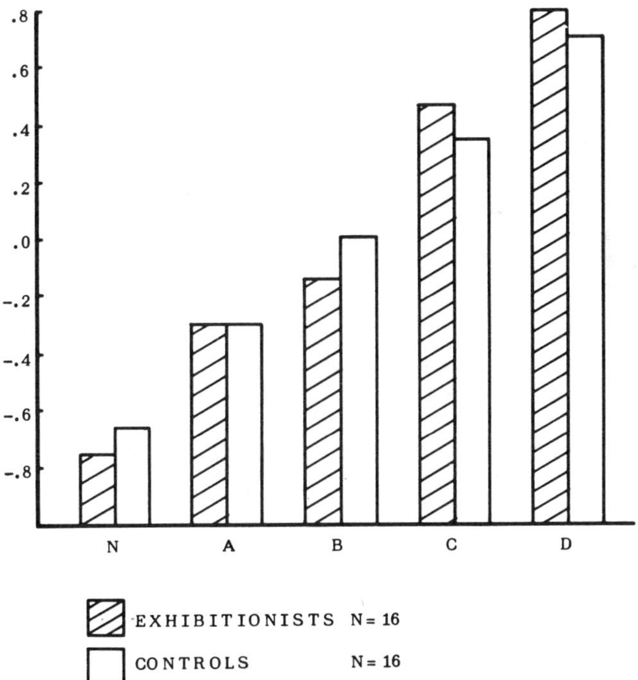

FIGURE 6. Responses to the four phases of normal courtship behavior. N = sexually neutral situations; A = location of a potential partner; B = pretactile interaction; C = tactile interaction; D = intercourse. On the *vertical line* is the mean penile response in Z scores. (From Freund *et al.*[24] *Archives of Sexual Behavior.*)

(c) By far the most promising etiological theory was put forward by Madlafousek *et al.*[27] who proposed that males who prefer to involve a strange and unsuspecting woman in their sexual activities, as is the case in courtship disorder and sadism, do so because they have difficulties with the transition from the initial stages of sexual motivation to the further stages that are connected with high arousal states. These initial stages are evoked by the female's initial "coy" erotic signalization. Such initial signalization is clearly absent in those strange and unsuspecting women who are preferred by these males as the targets of their anomalous sexual activities.

Kolarksy and Madlafousek[28] tested this theory by comparing exhibitionists and normal controls on penile response to the gestures of explicit sexual invitation made by an actress in a filmstrip. As they predicted, the exhibitionists responded more when this scene was not closely preceded by coy erotic signaling by the woman on the screen; that is, coy signaling immediately before the explicit gesture weakened the impact of the explicit gesture. In contrast, the normal controls responded more to the explicitly sexual invitation when it was closely preceded by coy erotic signaling. Fedora *et al.*[29]reported that in a phallometric experiment exhibitionists responded to females in typically nonerotic situations considerably more than did normal controls. While Madlafousek *et al.* proposed their theory only to explain the choice of a stranger as a quasi-partner, it may account—at least partly—for the etiology of courtship disorder.

(d) A different etiological factor—one that would not be in contradiction to the foregoing theory—has sometimes been postulated; namely, that the anomalous patterns in question are due to an abnormally high potential for arousal on the part of such patients.[30] This appears to be borne out by the abnormally high frequency the acted out part of courtship behavior can reach. This hypothesis should lead to physiological investigations. There is a fast-growing body of knowledge about the physiological substrate of sexual behavior of some species of experimental animals. There is not very much pertinent information about humans, however. Two studies have some bearing on this subject. Both measured testosterone level, but only as a kind of first crude orientation. One of these investigations was on exhibitionists,[22] the other on men who raped.[31] The outcome of both studies was negative in respect to the physiological parameters in question. Even a preliminary investigation of this kind, however, should involve a wider spectrum of related compounds and an assessment of rhythms of hormone production. One should also compare patients and controls on their responses to sexual stimulation, according to the experimental paradigm of Pirke *et al.*,[32] who demonstrated a gradual increase in serum testosterone levels in normal males who were viewing explicitly sexual films. The curve of increase of testosterone or gonadotrophic hormone under such stimulation might turn out to be unusual in patients with a courtship disorder. Still another level of physiological phenomena will have to be investigated in the context of courtship disorder—for example, the possibility of a hypersensitivity of certain brain systems to steroid hormones. Investigations of this kind, however, will probably not be feasible in the near future.

DISCUSSION

The initially posed question of whether the concept of courtship disorder is at all valid is still not solved. The evidence is still scant. Much more research will have to be done. One may ask why, under these circumstances, efforts are being made to detect relevant etiological factors. The answer is that common causes may be found for the anomalous behaviors in question that would not hold for other anomalous erotic behaviors, for instance, sadism.

There is also the problem of the instruments used in the earlier-mentioned assessments. The shortcomings of the verbal method have already been discussed. Penile responses are less dependent on degree of cooperativeness or resistance of the assessed individual than is his self-report, but they still can be voluntarily distorted,[14–16] and in phallometric studies like the ones mentioned in the course of this report this is likely to be the main shortcoming. At stimuli that visually or verbally depict a socially disapproved of object or situation, suppression is encountered, particularly with men who are accused of or charged with anomalous sexual behavior. It is therefore likely that the phallometric results discussed in the foregoing are distorted in one direction: stimuli depicting voyeuristic behavior, toucheuristic behavior, rape, and similar disapproved-of situations probably elicited smaller responses than would be the case if all of our patients admitted freely to their anomalous inclinations. Some of these men may even be able to increase their responses to stimuli depicting normal sexual interaction, such as normal intercourse. If the reported differences between patients and controls were nonetheless significant, they would probably be more, rather than less, pronounced if there were no distortion by the patient. On the other hand, if patients afflicted with the preferential rape pattern still respond more to normal intercourse than to rape, we should not feel too comforted by this fact, but should realize that this is most probably an artifact, and that in fact they probably *prefer* to rape.

REFERENCES

1. FREUND, K., H. R. SEELEY, W. E. MARSHALL & E. K. GLINFORT. 1972. Sexual offenders needing special assessment and/or therapy. Can. J. Criminol. Corrections **14**(4): 345-365.
2. FREUND, K. & A. KOLÁŘSKÝ. 1965. Grundzüge eines einfachen Bezugsystems für die Analyse sexueller Deviationen (Basic features of a reference system for considering anomalous erotic preferences). Psychiatrie, Neurologie und medizinische Psychologie **17**(6): 221-225.
3. MORRIS, D. 1954. The reproductive behaviour of the zebra finch. *In* Patterns of Reproductive Behaviour: Collected Papers by Desmond Morris. Desmond Morris, Ed.: 43-88. Jonathan Cape Limited. London.
4. MORRIS, D. 1956. The function and causation of courtship ceremonies. *In* Patterns of Reproductive Behaviour: Collected Papers by Desmond Morris. Desmond Morris, Ed.: 128-152. Jonathan Cape Limited. London.
5. TAYLOR, F. H. 1947. Observations on some cases of exhibitionism. J. Ment. Sci. **93:** 631-638.
6. YALOM, I. D. 1960. Aggression and forbiddenness in voyeurism. Arch. Gen. Psychiatry **3**(2): 305-319.
7. GRASSBERGER, R. 1964. Der Exhibitionismus. Kriminalistik in Österreich **18:** 557-562.
8. GEBHARD, P. H., J. H. GAGNON, W. B. POMEROY & C. V. CHRISTENSEN. 1965. Sex Offenders. Harper & Row. New York.
9. ROOTH, G. 1973. Exhibitionism, sexual violence and paedophilia. Br. J. Psychiatry **122**(571): 705-710.
10. CABANIS, D. 1966. Medizinisch-kriminologische Untersuchung über Exhibitionismus. Unpublished material.
11. PAITICH, D., R. LANGEVIN, R. FREEMAN, K. MANN & L. HANDY. 1977. The Clarke SHQ: A clinical sex history questionnaire for males. Arch. Sex. Behav. **6**(5): 421-436.
12. FREUND, K., H. SCHER & S. HUCKER. 1983. The courtship disorders. Arch. Sex. Behav. **12**(5): 369-379.

13. FREUND, K. & R. BLANCHARD. 1986. The concept of courtship disorder. J. Sex Marital Ther. **12**(2): 79-92.
14. FREUND, K. 1961. A laboratory differential diagnosis of homo- and hetero-sexuality—An experiment with faking. Rev. Czech. Med. **7:** 20-31.
15. FREUND, K. 1963. A laboratory method for diagnosing predominance of homo- or hetero-erotic interest in the male. Behav. Res. Ther. **1:** 85-93.
16. FREUND, K. 1981. Assessment of pedophilia. *In* Adult Sexual Interest in Children. M. Cook & K. Howells, Eds.: 139-179. Academic Press. London.
17. FREUND, K., H. SCHER, I. G. RACANSKY, K. CAMPBELL & G. HEASMAN. 1986. Males disposed to commit rape. Arch. Sex. Behav. **15**(1): 23-35.
18. GLOVER, E. 1964. Aggression and sado-masochism. *In* The Pathology and Treatment of Sexual Deviation. I. Rosen, Ed.: 146-162. Oxford University Press. London.
19. HACKETT, T. P. 1971. The psychotherapy of exhibitionists in a court clinic setting. Semin. Psychiatry **3**(3): 297-306.
20. HARTWICH, A. 1959. Aberrations of Sexual Life after the Psychopathia Sexualis of Dr. R. V. Krafft-Ebing. Staples Press. London.
21. KARPMAN, B. 1954. The Sexual Offender and his Offenses. Julian Press. New York, NY.
22. LANGEVIN, R., D. PAITICH, G. RAMSAY, C. ANDERSON, J. KAMRAD, S. POPE, G. GELLER, L. PEARL & S. NEWMAN. 1979. Experimental studies of the etiology of genital exhibitionism. Arch. Sex. Behav. **8**(4): 307-331.
23. LANGEVIN, R. 1983. Sexual Strands: Understanding and Treating Sexual Anomalies in Men. Lawrence Erlbaum Associates. Hillsdale, NJ.
24. FREUND, K., H. SCHER & S. HUCKER. 1984. The courtship disorders: A further investigation. Arch. Sex. Behav. **13**(2): 133-139.
25. MORRIS, D. 1970. Patterns of Reproductive Behaviour: Collected Papers by Desmond Morris. Jonathan Cape. London.
26. TINBERGEN, N. 1965. Some recent studies of the evolution of sexual behavior. *In* Sex and Behavior. F. A. Beach, Ed.: 1-33. John Wiley & Sons. New York.
27. MADLAFOUSEK, J., M. ŽANTOVSKÝ, Z. HLIŇÁK & A. KOLÁŘSKÝ. 1981. Sexual behavior as a communicative process by which the system of partial motivational states is executed. Cesk. Psychiatry **77:** 377-384.
28. KOLÁŘSKÝ, A. & J. MADLAFOUSEK. 1983. The inverse role of preparatory erotic stimulation in exhibitionists: Phallometric studies. Arch. Sex. Behav. **12**(2): 123-148.
29. FEDORA, O., J. R. REDDON & L. T. YEUDALL. 1986. Stimuli eliciting sexual arousal in genital exhibitionists: A possible clinical application. Arch. Sex. Behav. **15**(5): 417-427.
30. RADA, R. T., D. R. LAWS & R. KELLNER. 1976. Plasma testosterone levels in the rapist. Psychosom. Med. **38**(4): 257-268.
31. EAST, N. W. 1946. Sexual offenders. J. Nerv. Ment. Dis. **103**(6): 626-666.
32. PIRKE, K. M., G. KOCKOTT & F. DITTMAR. 1974. Psychosexual stimulation and plasma testosterone in man. Arch. Sex. Behav. **3**(6): 577-584.

Issues in the Exploration of Biological Factors Contributing to the Etiology of the "Sex Offender," plus Some Ethical Considerations

FRED S. BERLIN

Department of Psychiatry and Behavioral Sciences
The Johns Hopkins University School of Medicine
Baltimore, Maryland 21205

INTRODUCTION

The present paper is intended to be neither a review of the literature nor a summary of research data. Rather, it is intended as a concept paper. The purpose is to explore the conceptual considerations that must first be made if one wishes to learn more about biological factors that may contribute to the occurrence of sexually offensive behaviors. Much of the literature in this area refers to sex offenders, rapists, child molesters, incest offenders, or sexual aggressives. These categories (none of which are diagnoses) may, in the author's judgment, often be far too broad, amorphous, and heterogeneous to allow for a proper examination of the relationship between behavior and biology.

All human experience is influenced by both biology and environment. The ability to speak a language, for example, is biologically based. Human beings can do so, whereas certain other species cannot or, if they can, can do so only in rudimentary form. Which language a given human being speaks, however, be it French, German, or English, is a product of the environment in which he or she was raised. The critical issue in human behavior, then, is ordinarily not whether it is environment or biological constitution that plays the more dominant role. Rather, the question is one of the degree to which each factor is important and of how each exerts its influence. When biology and environment exert their respective roles in influencing human behavior, the subjective mental processes, abilities, and perceptions of a given individual are often the final common pathways through which these influences are experienced and expressed.

The current paper will be subdivided into a number of sections. The first will emphasize the importance of making a differential diagnosis when clinically assessing "sex offenders." It will be argued that failure to make a proper diagnosis may significantly impair one's ability to identify biological factors that may influence the occurrence of sexually inappropriate behaviors. In a later section of the paper some examples will be cited to demonstrate how such diagnoses can enable researchers to address in a more precise manner questions about the relationship between biology and behavior. The final section of the paper will explore some ethical issues that derive from research and clinical practice in this area. It will also address the need to try to integrate moral and scientific conceptual models that attempt to understand and explain human behavior.

DIFFERENTIAL DIAGNOSIS

In general the law defines one as a sex offender simply by considering behavior alone. Thus, if an adult engages in sexual activity with a child, exposes himself publicly, or commits a rape, it is essentially the behavior itself that defines one criminally as a sex offender. Persons can engage in similar behaviors for a variety of reasons. Some sex offenses may be in large part a manifestation of the fact that a given individual recurrently experiences aberrant sexual desires. In other instances the offending behavior may be enacted by an individual possessing a perfectly conventional sexual appetite. Since most human behavior is enacted in response to particular phenomenological or mental experiences (i.e., as a response to thoughts, desires, perceptions, yearnings, and construals), if one is interested in understanding how biology may influence a particular type of human behavior, then one may have to look first at the relationship between biology and particular mental or motivational states. Some examples may help to clarify this point.

Rape is a behavior. By definition it is always a coercive behavior. The consequences of this behavior upon a victim are almost invariably experienced as terribly traumatic. But in knowing the behavior and knowing the consequences of the behavior, does one necessarily know anything whatsoever about what motivated the individual to act in such a fashion in the first place? The answer is no. The motivation of the rapist may have been related predominantly to lust, anger, a psychotically disturbed mind, or a variety of other possibilities. Many rapes are committed by persons who manifest perfectly conventional sexual appetites. Take for example the career criminal who breaks into a house to steal a television set, discovers a woman home alone, finds her to be sexually appealing, and rapes her. Clinically, many examples of this sort are seen. Such a rapist may not be angry at his victim, he may not be sexually driven, he may not be retarded, intoxicated on drugs, or psychotic. His behavior can perhaps best be appreciated as predominantly the product of lack of conscience and lack of an internalized sense of social responsibility. If one were interested in searching for biological factors contributing to the sex offending behavior of this particular type of individual, then one might need to find a population of persons all of whom manifest a substantial lack of conscience (i.e., a population of rapists all of whom meet the psychiatric diagnostic criteria for antisocial personality disorder) who could then be examined for biological similarities. To include the "antisocial rapists" in a group of persons who raped for various other reasons might result in such a heterogeneous group of rapists as to obscure the search for biological factors shared in common.

Another population containing individuals of whom some may rape is the population of mentally retarded. Probably few of us take the time to imagine what it must be like to have the mental age of an eight year old while experiencing the intensity of sexual desires that most of us are aware of as adults. Furthermore, if one has the mental age of an eight year old, how does one persuade an adult to become involved with him or her in a sexually intimate way. Thus clinicians have observed that a mentally retarded individual may persuade or even coerce a child who may be of similar mental age into engaging in sexual activity. Legally this may be classified as rape. If one were to look for a biology associated with this individual's rape behavior, the emphasis here might need to be on a biology related to cognitive deficits.

Clearly many more examples of rape related to a variety of motivational states of which none had anything to do with aberrant sexual drives could be presented. The argument being advanced here is that the possibility of finding a biological basis for a given behavior such as rape is likely reduced in proportion to the heterogeneity of the various motivational and mental states associated with that form of behavior in the population being studied. Furthermore, even if one could find a biological basis for rape amongst persons manifesting antisocial personality disorder, mental retardation, or a variety of other factors unrelated to aberrant sexual drives, this would still not account for the fact that some individuals manifesting such conditions commit sex offenses, whereas others do not.

Perhaps, then, the search for biological factors associated with sexually offending behaviors might prove more fruitful if one were to focus more closely on those persons whose sex-offending behaviors seem more closely tied to aberrations of the biologically based sexual drive itself. In order to explore this possibility further, it might be helpful to look first at the ways in which persons differ from one another in the sexual sphere.

DIFFERENCES IN HUMAN SEXUALITY

It is a myth to suggest that all persons are created equal. Certainly there ought to be universal equality of opportunity, and decent persons should all be thought of as possessing equal moral worth. However, we are not all equal in a variety of ways, to the extent that equal means the same. One way in which we are not the same is in the area of sexuality. Persons differ from one another sexually in at least four ways: (1) in terms of the kinds of *partners* they find to be sexually appealing, (2) in terms of the kinds of *behaviors* they find to be erotically arousing, (3) in *intensity* of sexual desire (and thus conversely, perhaps, in the difficulty they may experience in resisting sexual temptations), and (4) in their *attitudes* about whether or not they should try to resist.[1]

Each of us can describe a gender of partner and an age range of partner that we find to be appealing in a sexual way. The author, for example, is a man who is attracted exclusively to females rather than to males. Although he might find a broad age range of females to be appealing in a sexual way, he is not attracted to 4-year-old females, nor is he attracted sexually to 80-year-old females. Thus he does not refrain from having sex with young children only because he is a moral person. He is simply not tempted sexually by young children.

Other persons, when asked to describe the gender and age range of partners to whom they are attracted sexually, or even romantically, describe something quite different from the example just given. Some persons, for instance, report that they are not at all attracted sexually to adults, be they male or female, but that they must recurrently resist the temptation of becoming involved with children.

If a man is attracted exclusively to boys in a sexual way, he is said to have a fixated (or exclusive) homosexual pedophilic orientation. If he is attracted exclusively to girls, he is said to have a fixated (or exclusive) heterosexual pedophilic orientation. If he is attracted exclusively to both boys and girls, he is said to have a fixated (or exclusive) bisexual pedophilic orientation. Pedophilic sexual orientations are found almost exclusively in males.

Some persons who are very much tempted by children in a sexual way do report having some degree of erotic attraction to adults as well. This can raise a question as to why, if these persons are not attracted *exclusively* to children, they do not simply choose to be intimate with adults instead. Sex can be looked at in many ways, but what it is in one sense is a biological appetite, and such appetites can have within them various tastes. A person can finish a big turkey dinner and still have difficulty resisting the temptation to have dessert. Similarly, a person who is attracted sexually to both adults and children (such a person is said to have regressed or nonexclusive pedophilic orientation) can have sex with an adult, but this does not do anything to erase the fact that he may still continue craving sexually for children as well. The fact that persons experience different sexual desires does not make them any better or any worse morally than others, just different.

Sometimes, because persons experience recurrent sexual attractions of the sort that cause them to feel distressed, impair function, or could cause harm if enacted, these attractions are acknowledged by way of a psychiatric diagnosis.[2] This diagnosis is done both to enable researchers to learn more about why persons experience such unconventional erotic desires and to enable clinicians to develop better ways of providing psychological assistance if it is needed. TABLE 1 lists some of the major categories of the psychiatric disorders known as the paraphilias.[2] Each of these represents a condition in which persons experience either recurrent sexual attractions towards partners of the sorts society generally considers unacceptable (e.g., children) or a condition in which persons experience recurrent sexual urges to engage in behaviors society generally considers unacceptable (e.g., public genital exhibition).

TABLE 1. Major Subcategories of Paraphilic Disorders (DSM III)

1. Pedophilia
2. Zoophilia
3. Fetishism
4. Exhibitionism
5. Sexual Sadism
6. Sexual Masochism
7. Voyeurism
8. Transvestism

Considering these different forms of erotic phenomenology to be psychiatric conditions does involve a value judgment. It is important to recognize, however, that value judgments are inherent in all medical diagnoses. Cancer and respiration are both simply biological processes. However, we diagnose and label cancer because we do not like it and thus we want to learn more about it so as to be able to change it. In our society cutting the penis of an unanesthetized child with a scalpel is called circumcision and is not considered sexual abuse. Kissing the child on the penis would be.

As noted above, in evaluating sex offenders one can distinguish a group of individuals whose behaviors are due to a variety of motivations and psychological factors that have nothing to do with the presence of aberrant sexual drives of the sort just described. In these nonparaphilic cases, searching for biological factors correlated with the offending behavior may need to involve a focus of attention on a biology unrelated to differences in human sexuality. On the other hand, when the behavior in question does seem intimately related to differences in erotic phenomenology, focusing more directly on biological factors thought possibly relevant to differences in sexual appetite may be crucial.

In this connection one needs to be careful to diagnose or categorize by similarities in mental and motivational state rather than grouping persons by means of labels that are determined simply on a behavioral or relationship basis. *The terms "incest," "child molester," "sex offender," and "sexual aggressor" are not diagnostic terms.* Father-daughter incest may be nonpedophilic. A father who has sex with his 14-year-old stepdaughter may have a perfectly conventional sexual orientation. On the other hand, the father who recurrently engages in sex with his 4-year-old daughter may indeed have a pedophilic sexual orientation. Alternatively, he might be behaving in this fashion in response to delusions or hallucinations. Thus, looking for biological factors associated with incest or child molestation—categories that likely involve a great heterogeneity of motivational and mental states—might prove more difficult than searching for biological factors associated with a more homogeneous population of persons who share a pedophilic sexual orientation.

Finally, it might be noted that knowing about the types of sexual desires a person experiences tells one absolutely nothing else about the individual himself. Thus we do not know, for example, simply by determining that a person is attracted exclusively to young children, whether he is temperamentally aggressive or nonaggressive. Similarly, one could easily arrive at misleading conclusions in knowing that a man has committed a rape. Any man is physically capable of committing a rape, but the average man is not so aroused sexually by recurrent thoughts of rape to the point where he has repeatedly to fight off the urge to commit rape. Persons who do experience such recurrent erotic urges may as a consequence rape and yet be temperamentally nonviolent. Thus the term sexual aggressor can in one sense be quite misleading. The biology associated with temperamental violence and the biology associated with antisocial traits may be very different from the biology associated with the various paraphilic conditions. This is an important point because so much of the literature that currently exists looks for the presence or absence of biological pathologies in sex offenders, rapists, or child molesters rather than first making the kinds of diagnostic distinctions that the author is suggesting here may be crucial when doing research in this area.

ETIOLOGY

If the arguments made thus far are valid, then discussions of etiology must first define the nature of the condition requiring an etiological explanation. If it is true that sometimes sex offenses are a manifestation of mental retardation, temperamental hostility, drug and alcohol abuse, and a variety of other factors, then one would need to search for etiological correlates related to each of these possibilities in trying to understand better the spectrum of sexually offensive behaviors. Clearly this would constitute a monumental task.

In discussing etiology here the author will focus on a much narrower question: why is it that individuals experience particular sorts of erotic desires? As noted above, some persons are sexually attracted to adults, while others are sexually attracted to children. Traditionally this matter has been approached from a moral standpoint, labeling the former virtuous and the latter sinful. However, this question can also be approached as a matter for legitimate scientific inquiry. Those attracted sexually to children may, of course, be at increased risk of committing a sex offense.

Perhaps the first point that ought to be made in discussing why persons experience particular types of sexual desires should be to emphasize that they do *not* do so as a consequence of a voluntary decision. The author did not *decide,* because he is a good person, to become a man who is sexually attracted to women. Rather, in growing up he *discovered* that this was the nature of his sexual orientation. In our society this certainly makes life less problematic.

Men who are sexually attracted to children are not this way because they *decided* that they wanted to be so. Rather, in growing up they discovered that this was the nature of their sexual orientation. Making such a discovery about oneself in our society can lead to conflict, anguish, and difficulty. Stating that such persons are this way because they are bad and that we know they are bad because they are this way simply attaches a label, which then masquerades as an explanation.

If the sexual desires that one experiences are not, then, the consequence of a voluntary decision, what etiological factors are of significance? Before discussing the biological factors, to keep a proper balance the author would like first to touch briefly upon the issue of environmental influences. Perhaps it should be noted at this point that sexual orientation is much like language. The capacity to learn a language is biologically determined, whereas which language one speaks is related to life experiences. Once language has been acquired, however, regardless of the degree to which biology or environment played a role, that language cannot through psychological methods be erased. Once a man is attracted sexually to women, or conversely to children, again, regardless of whether this is due predominantly to biology or environmental influences, such attractions cannot simply be made to go away.

If one looks at all persons who smoke, thankfully most smokers do not develop lung cancer. On the other hand, if one looks at a group of persons who do have lung cancer, particularly squamous-cell carcinoma of the lung, most are smokers. Therefore, one can rightfully conclude that smoking is associated with an increased prevalence of that disorder.

If one looks at a group of children who have been active sexually with adults, thankfully most do not grow up to develop a pedophilic sexual orientation. However, Groth and others have shown that if one looks at a group of men who do have a pedophilic sexual orientation, the overwhelming majority were active sexually with adults during childhood.[3] Thus, if one wishes to use words such as victim and victimizer, it appears that many men with pedophilic sexual orientations are in fact simply the former victims of sexual abuse during childhood, grown up. It appears, then, that having been sexually active with an adult during childhood, especially for a boy, is an example of one type of environmental influence that seems to increase the risk of developing an aberrant sexual appetite such as pedophilia.

Persons do not ordinarily become interested in sex initially as a result of reading a book that tells them that this is a good idea. No father ever had to sit down with his son in order to teach him how to obtain an erection. Rather sexual drive is rooted in biology. Therefore it is just as reasonable to ask whether some persons may experience aberrant sexual drives because of biological factors as it is to ask whether this might be so as a consequence of certain life experiences. The author will briefly describe two studies intended to explore this issue, emphasizing the importance of doing such research by employing a homogeneous subgroup of individuals diagnosed as having a specific form of paraphilic disorder rather than a more heterogeneous group of child molesters, rapists, or sexual aggressives.

Philosophers have pondered for centuries the relationship between the mind as subjective experience and the brain as a biologically functioning organ. Technologies are now being developed that may enable scientists to study this relationship in a way not previously possible. One such technology is known as positron emission tomography, or PET scanning.[4]

In conducting PET scanning, researchers inject a small amount of radioactively labeled material into a peripheral vein. The radioactivity level is very low and considered safe. That material then passes through the circulation of the body, affording it an opportunity to bind to chemical receptors in various organs to which it may possess an affinity. A Geiger-counter-type device connected to a computer can then be placed around a given body region. Such a device can be put around the head if one is interested in detecting the amount of binding of such radioactively labeled material to chemical receptors in the brain. The computer can then determine which areas of the brain, if any, have concentrated amounts of the radioactively labeled substance injected.

By conducting PET scanning twice, for example while persons are in a nonaroused and then in an aroused sexual state, one can look for changes in chemical activity in the brain that may be associated with each of these two different mental states, respectively. If one could identify in this fashion neurochemical activity that correlates with sexual arousal, one could then address the issue of whether or not the same or different types of chemical activity patterns are associated with sexual arousal in persons who manifest paraphilic as opposed to conventional sexual appetites. The identification of chemical changes in the brain that might correlate with erotic appetites of the sort that increase the risk of committing a sexual offense could have implications of both scientific and moral importance.

Drs. Jim Frost and Helen Mayberg, the author, and others have now begun a series of studies of this sort at the Johns Hopkins Hospital with the financial aid of a grant from The Harry Frank Guggenheim Foundation (New York, New York). Currently, approximately 20 individuals have been PET scanned in both a sexually nonaroused and aroused state.[5] Scanning has been done after injecting radioactively labeled carfentanil, a mild opiate known to bind to the same chemical receptors in the brain to which other opiates bind.

It is still too soon to know whether or not differences will be detectible that can distinguish between persons with paraphilic and those with nonparaphilic sexual appetites. However, preliminary results do suggest that opiate receptor activity does change in the brain in association with sexual arousal. These changes appear to be greater in certain areas of the brain known to contain opiate receptors and less in other areas of the brain, even though they, too, contain such receptors. The greatest change in this type of chemical activity in the brain during sexual arousal appears to occur in the thalamus.

The results reported here should be considered preliminary. The important point that the author wishes to stress is that this type of research, intended to look for biological correlates in brain associated with sexually offending behavior, may depend heavily upon properly diagnosing similarities in the motivational or mental states out of which such behaviors may emerge. Such research would likely have less probability of proving fruitful if one were to try to look for common biological changes in the brains of sex offenders whose motivations to act may have been quite varied and perhaps not in any way related to differences in sexual appetite per se.

A second example that further emphasizes this point emerges out of a study conducted by Gaffney.[6] In that study Gaffney looked at three groups of individuals. Group 1 was a group of sex offenders all of whom shared a pedophilic sexual orientation. Group 2 was a group of sex offenders who did not meet the diagnostic criteria for pedophilia. Group 3 was a group of individuals who had no history of sex-offending behavior at all. Gaffney injected men in each group with an intravenous bolus of gonadotropin releasing hormone. He then looked at the pattern of release of gonadotropins from the pituitary gland in the brain in response to that injection. Men manifesting a pedophilic sexual orientation showed a pathological pattern of gonadotropin release into the blood stream, whereas men in the other two groups did not. The point to be emphasized here is that had Gaffney lumped all of the sex offenders together in that study, the finding of biological pathology that was detectable in the group of men with pedophilic sexual orientations might well have been obscured.

ETHICAL CONSIDERATIONS

It was stated above that persons do not decide voluntarily the nature of their own sexual appetites. Thus it seems difficult to see how a person could be considered blameworthy because he is sexually attracted to children. However, it could be argued that although it is not his fault that he is sexually attracted to children, it is still his responsibility to resist succumbing to such temptations. The author agrees with this, but what is the evidence when it comes to biologically based drives, such as the sexual drive, that persons can invariably control their behaviors simply by making up their minds to do so?

An interesting investigation by Wirth and Folstein relates to this issue.[7] They studied a group of persons on renal dialysis necessitated by serious kidney disease. The dialysis procedure made these individuals thirsty, but they were asked by their physicians to limit fluid intake between dialysis sessions because excessive fluid intake could endanger their health. In legal terms the law laid down by the physician stated, "do not drink too much fluid between dialysis sessions." Potentially the penalty for disobeying could have been death. Folstein and Wirth reported almost all of these patients *did* drink excessive fluid between dialysis sessions. The degree of excessive fluid consumption was proportional to the degree to which the dialysis procedure caused thirst. In general, the more discomforted the individual was made by virtue of the intensity of his thirst, the more fluid he consumed. Biologically based thirst, rather than impaired morals, seemed to account best for these people's failure to obey the "law" as prescribed by their physicians.

McHugh reported an intriguing series of studies of animals demonstrating that even when attempts were made to fool the animal by changing the texture and mix of food ingested, most still consumed the same number of calories each day.[8] It was as though nature was in effect determining daily caloric intake. This may help explain why literally millions of people spend so much money each year in an attempt to diet. Many persons in trying to keep their weight down may in a sense be fighting nature. The person trying to diet often promises himself to eat less. As he becomes increasingly more discomforted by hunger, however, he may begin to rationalize, telling himself, "a little food won't matter." He may then *premeditatedly* go to the refrigerator, take some food, and ingest it, after which he may become disgusted with himself, promise never again, but repeat the cycle as his appetite intensifies.

Many of us would like to believe that we can do anything we want simply by making up our own minds to do so. The law generally makes that assumption, and for good reason. Otherwise, any criminal could come into a court room arguing that he was overcome by feelings of intense greed that were more than he could handle. Thus he might contend that he should not be held criminally responsible. For this reason society often must assume that persons can control themselves through will power and their own efforts. The only problem with this assumption when it comes to biologically based drives, such as hunger, thirst, or sex, is that it may not always be true.

The author has treated a number of "sex offenders" with antiandrogenic medication who, prior to such treatment, contended they were so discomforted by their sexual cravings they sometimes could not resist succumbing.[9] Most moral conceptual models of behavior suggest that persons should be able to control themselves by the proper application of will power. Scientific conceptual models may question whether or not, when it comes to biologically based drives such as the sexual drive, this can invariably be done.

If, indeed, some persons at times cannot control themselves by will power alone, and they are not believed because of an unwillingness to acknowledge that this could be so, progress towards making available to such persons treatment programs that might help may be deterred. Stating with moral certainty that persons should be able to control themselves sexually does not prove that they all can.

In the criminal justice system blameworthiness does not depend upon an act or the consequences of that act alone, but upon mental state as well. For example, if we know that person number 1 became angry at person number 2, went home, got a gun, and shot him, we know the behavior and we know the consequences of that behavior. Do we, however, know whether or not that person should be considered blameworthy. The answer is, not necessarily. Suppose we now find out that person number 1 is three years old. The knowledge that he has the mental age of a three year old changes our concept of blameworthiness, even though the behavior and its consequences remain unchanged. In the State of Maryland on at least four separate occasions, a judge or jury has decided not to hold a person with a paraphilic sexual disorder criminally responsible, based upon evidence that the disorder impaired the capacity of the individual in question to conform his behavior to the requirements of the law.

Society has not given much thought as to how it might better integrate moral and scientific conceptual models that try to explain human sexual behavior. Morally, most would agree that sexual activity between an adult and a child in our society is improper. However, arguing that persons with pedophilic sexual orientations are that way because they are evil simply begs the question. There is little reason to believe that the desires that they experience should be, or can be, punished away by means of incarceration. When it comes to biologically based drives, including the sexual drive, there is clearly a need to try to better integrate legitimate issues of moral concern with emerging scientific knowledge and inquiry. Some sex offenders, in spite of their behavior, may not be evil or bad people. Perhaps in some instances the key to better understanding sex-offending behavior may be tied more to biology and science than to theories of evil or moral corruption. The author believes that these are issues deserving of careful thought, consideration, and further investigation.

REFERENCES

1. Berlin, F. S. & E. K. Krout. 1986. Pedophilia: Diagnostic concepts, treatment, and ethical considerations. Am. J. Forensic Psychiatry **7:** 13-30.

2. AMERICAN PSYCHIATRIC ASSOCIATION. 1978. Diagnostic and Statistical Manual of Mental Disorders, 3rd Edition. Task Force on Nomenclature and Statistics of American Psychiatric Association. Washington, D.C.
3. GROTH, A. N. 1979. Men Who Rape. Plenum Press. New York, NY.
4. TER-POGOSSIAN, M. A., M. E. RACHLE & B. E. SOBEL. 1980. Positron Emission Tomography. Sci. Am. **10:** 169-181.
5. FROST, J. J., H. S. MAYBERG, F. S. BERLIN, R. BEHAL, R. F. DANNALS, J. M. LINKS, H. T. RAVERT, A. A. WILSON & H. N. WAGNER, JR. 1986. Alteration in brain opiate receptor binding in man following sexual arousal using C-11 carfentanil and positron emission tomography. J. Nucl. Med. **27**(6): 1027.
6. GAFFNEY, G. S. & F. S. BERLIN. 1984. Is there a hypothalamic-pituitary-gonadal dysfunction in paedophilia? Brit. J. Psychiatry **145:** 657-660.
7. WIRTH, J. B. & M. S. FOLSTEIN. 1982. Thirst and weight gain during maintenance hemodialysis. Psychosom. **3:** 1125-1134.
8. MCHUGH, P. R. & T. H. MORAN. 1978. Accuracy of the regulation of caloric ingestion in the Rhesus monkey. Am. J. Physiol. **23:** R29-R34.
9. BERLIN, F. S. & C. F. MEINECKE. 1981. Treatment of sex offenders with antiandrogenic medication: Conceptualization, review of treatment modalities, and preliminary findings. Amer. J. Psychiatry **138:** 601-607.

Organic Treatment for the Male Sexual Offender

JOHN M. W. BRADFORD

Forensic Service
Royal Ottawa Hospital and
Department of Psychiatry
University of Ottawa
Ottawa, Ontario K1Z 7K4, Canada

Organic treatments for the male sexual offender are used for the reduction of sexual drive in men who are sexually aggressive and have poor control over their sexual behavior. They are also used in the treatment of the paraphilias, such as pedophilia, where although sexual aggression may not be a problem, sexual control is poor and the behavior is likely to result in conflict with the legal system. There are three main types of organic treatments: antiandrogens and other hormonal treatments; surgical castration; and stereotaxic neurosurgery. Stereotaxic neurosurgery is of only theoretical interest, as it is highly unlikely that this technique is going to play any major role in the treatment of sexual offenders in North America.[1] Surgical castration is similarly mainly of academic interest but is important because of its close relationship to the antiandrogen and hormonal treatments; in addition it provides follow-up studies of postcastration recidivism rates.[2–4]

CASTRATION

Castration is the surgical removal of the testicles in man. The testicle is the principal site of androgen production and is responsible for 95% of the body's total testosterone (T) production. Androgen deficiency and a decline in sexual behavior are results. The rate of decline is variable, but it is usual for ejaculation to be affected first, then erections, and lastly copulatory behavior.[5] Castration has been widely used to treat sexual offenders because of this effect.[6–8] Various studies of postcastration recidivism rates have reported substantial reductions in the rate of reoffence.[2–4, 6–8] There are four main studies in this area: Langeluddeke (1963), Cornu (1973), Bremer (1959), and Stürup (1968).[7] Large numbers of individuals were studied for follow-up periods of up to 20 years.[7] Langeluddeke (1963) reported on over 1000 sexual offenders followed for between 6 weeks and 20 years and reported that the recidivism rate fell from over 80% to 2.3%.[8] Cornu (1973) examined 127 castrated sexual offenders released for 5 years and found a recidivism rate of 4.1% compared to a prior rate over 75%. He also reported on a comparison group that had been offered castration and refused. This group showed a precastration recidivism rate of 66% and a postrelease rate of 54%. Bremer (1959) described over 200 castrates with a diverse number of paraphilias and psychiatric diagnoses and found a postcastration recidivism rate of 2.9% with between 5 and 10 years' follow-up.[2] Stürup (1968) summarized a follow-up study of over 900 castrates with a 30 year follow-up period and documented a recidivism rate of 2.2%.[3,4] This was reduced to 1.1% when further review took place.[3,4,7,8] Ortmann (1980, 1984a, 1984b) has studied the recidivism rates of castrated sexual offenders in Denmark.[7,9,10] He analyzed a number of previous studies and found that castration was mostly used in rapists and homosexual pedophiles. Selection for castration appears to have been based on the presence of sexual aggression (rape) or a perceived poor prognosis and potential dangerousness. The castrated sexual offenders therefore differed from other sexual offenders with regard to paraphiliac behavior as well as age, marital status, occupation, and to a certain extent psychiatric diagnosis. Heim and Hursch (1979) have criticized the methodology used in the calculation of recidivism rates; nevertheless, castration does appear to have a substantial effect on recidivism rates (see TABLE 1).

As already mentioned, the effect of castration is the reduction of available androgen, specifically T but also dihydrotestosterone (DHT). T is converted to DHT in various target organs. T is the most important of the sex hormones influencing sexual behavior in males. Both T and DHT have an effect at the androgen receptors. The sensitivity of the androgen receptors in the central nervous system determines male sexual behavioral patterns, provided there is sufficient T above a specific individually determined threshold. The androgens, specifically T and DHT, have a high affinity for a receptor protein in the cytoplasm of the receptor cells. These receptors have differing affinities for the two principal androgens. When a steroid androgen molecule reaches the receptor, a steroid receptor complex is formed, and this then migrates into the nucleus. A full review of these complicated biochemical events is beyond the scope of this paper. The androgen receptors are found in the various androgen-sensitive target organs. Androgen receptors are present in the prostate, seminal vesicles, and epididymis, where DHT is preferentially received. Androgen receptors in the limbic system, specifically the anterior hypothalamus, respond to T. In summary, the effect of castration is to make less androgen available at the receptors without affecting the sensitivity of the receptors or causing a receptor blockade. This mechanism of action is substantially different from that of the antiandrogens, such as cyproterone acetate (CPA), but is similar to the hormonal agents.

TABLE 1. Recidivism Rates following Castration[8,34]

Studies	Follow-up Period	n	Pre-Rate[a]	Post-Rate[b]
Langeluddeke (1963)	20 yr.	1036	84%	2.3%
Cornu (1973)	5 yr.	127	76.8%	4.1%
Bremer (1959)	5-10 yr.	216	58%	2.9%
Stürup (1972)[c]	30 yr.	900		2.2%

[a] Refers to the recidivism rate prior to castration.
[b] Refers to the recidivism rate after castration.
[c] Mostly rapists.

The Role of Testosterone in Sexual Aggression

There is considerable research at the present time attempting to identify the violent sexual offender. One approach has been to establish and validate various typologies of rape and sexual aggression against children.[11-13]

There has also been promising work on the sexual arousal patterns of rapists. This work, pioneered by Abel and his coworkers, found that rapists showed higher arousal responses to rape than to mutually consenting sexual acts with adult females in standard audiotape narratives.[14,15] They developed a Rape Index (RI), which was the ratio of penile response to rape compared with the response to mutually consenting sexual intercourse. An Aggressive Index (AI) was developed, comparing penile responses to nonsexual aggression and consenting sex narratives. This was modified by Quinsey and Chaplin (1982, 1984).[16,17] Further research has confirmed their findings.[18,19] Similar principles have been extended to the assessment of child molesters.[20] Research in this area is ongoing.[21]

The relationship of T to aggressive sexual behavior in man has also been extensively researched since 1971. Various studies have shown positive correlations between plasma T levels and sexual aggression as measured by questionnaires on aggression.[22–32] In a recent study of 146 sexual offenders an association was found between plasma T and violence. The classification of "no" (n = 23), "low" (n = 101) and "high" (n = 22) violence groups was on the basis of manifested violent behavior rather than on the use of questionnaires on aggression. In the "high" violence group there was sexual aggression to the point at which there was additional physical injury caused by the perpetrator beyond the sexual act itself. Sexually motivated homicide and attempted homicide and sadistic rape and child molesting formed the "high" violence group. The "no" violence group were mostly nonviolent pedophiles and some exhibitionists. Further, the "high" violence group had a mean plasma T level that was at the upper limit of the normal range (mean 29.6 nmol/l, SD 5.84). The normal range is 10-30 nmols/l, with a sensitivity of 0.3 nmol/l and a coefficient of variation of 10%. The normal range is standardized on the mean and 2 standard deviations (SD) from the mean. This differed at statistically significant levels from the "no" violence (mean 23.8 nmol/l, SD 6.11) and the "low" violence (mean 22.8 nmol/l, SD 7.05) groups. Plasma T levels in the three groups were studied using analysis of covariance (ANCOVA) procedures with age as a covariate and using the Neuman-Keuls multiple comparison technique. After controlling for the effect of age, the plasma T was significantly different among the violence classifications ($F = 7.08, p = .001$). Results of the multiple comparison tests indicated that plasma T in the "high" violence group was significantly greater than in either the "low" or the "no" violence groups. Penile tumescence tests using standard audiotape narratives developed by Abel and his co-workers were also studied, but these tests did not discriminate between the groups.[14,15] The RI was higher for the rapists than for the other paraphilias when the sample was grouped by sexual deviation rather than by catagories of violence, but not at statistically significant levels. Only the AI of the rapists under suppress instructions differed significantly from the other groups of sexual deviants.[33]

ANTIANDROGENS AND HORMONAL AGENTS

The antiandrogen and hormonal treatment of sexual offenders is a pharmacological method of reducing the sexual drive and consequently affecting the sexual behavior of sexual offenders. It has always been assumed that the direction of the sexual drive was unaffected by such treatment, although recent work with the antiandrogen cyproterone acetate (CPA) shows differential effects on sexual arousal patterns with a reduction of pedophilic sexual arousal but less affect on sexual arousal to adult mutually consenting heterosexual intercourse.[34] Hormonal agents, starting initially with estrogens, have also been used for sexual drive reduction.[35–37] The hormonal agent that has received most attention in the treatment of sexual offenders in North America is medroxyprogesterone acetate (MPA). A number of studies have now been completed that show its usefulness in the treatment of sexual offenders, although a specific affect in the treatment of sexual aggression is not described.[38–44]

MPA's mechanism of action works principally through the induction of testosterone-A-reductase in the liver, thereby accelerating the metabolism of T. This progestational agent affects the plasma and production rate of T through an increased clearance rate from the plasma.[45] In addition it has an antigonadotrophic effect.[45] It also has some effect in competing with the androgens at the androgen receptors.[45] A detailed review of MPA is beyond the scope of this paper.

Cyproterone acetate (CPA) is the first commercially available antiandrogen. CPA has antiandrogenic, antigonadotrophic, and progestational effects.[46] Its principal mode of action, as is that of the true antiandrogens, is on the androgen receptors. The androgen receptor response is disrupted by CPA. CPA blocks the intracellular T uptake, the intracellular metabolism of the androgens, as well as the receptor binding.[47] CPA appears to have a main effect on receptors that have a high affinity for DHT.

TABLE 2. Side Effects of CPA Treatment[49]

Time after Treatment	Side Effect
0-2 months	Serum testosterone decreased; erections decreased; ejaculate decreased; spermatogenesis decreased; sexual fantasies decreased; fatigue; hypersomnia; activity decreased; neurasthenia; depression; sexual drive decreased; psychopathology that is accompanying high sexual drive normalizes (i.e., labile affect, inner restlessness); negative nitrogen balance; weight gain
At 3 months	Nitrogen balance returns to normal; calcium and phosphate metabolism normalizes
6-8 months	20% chance protracted and temporary gynecomastia; decrease in body hair; increase in scalp hair; decrease in sebum secretion

There are pure antiandrogens, such as cyproterone (i.e., without the acetate radical) and flutamide (nonsteroidal); when these are administered, an androgen deficit is registered, and there is presumably an outpouring of luteinizing hormone releasing hormone (LHRH), luteinizing hormone (LH), and an increase in T.

CPA has a number of therapeutic indications in males. It is used for treatment of carcinoma of the prostate and for treatment of the paraphilias. In females it has been used for the treatment of hirsutism, alopecia and associated acne, and seborrhea. It has also been used in the treatment of idiopathic precocious puberty in children.

CPA has both desirable and undesirable side effects.[48] The side effects affecting sexual behavior are desirable in the treatment of the paraphilias. The side effects are to a large degree dose dependent. Manifestation of the side effects also has some temporal relationships[49] (see TABLE 2).

There are some theoretical risks to CPA treatment that are highly unlikely to occur at the dosage levels used to treat the paraphilias. There is the possibility of liver dysfunction, as small rises in serum bilirubin have been found in the first 6 weeks of treatment.[50,51] Animal research has shown that adrenal suppression can occur. Parallel findings are reported in children treated for precocious puberty. The evidence for any similar findings in adults is equivocal. Feminization effects depend on the relative levels of plasma androgens and estrogens. It has been the author's experience with CPA that plasma T levels can be allowed to rise to the normal range without any recurrence of the paraphiliac behavior. This decreases the likelihood of feminization taking place.

Many patients treated with CPA report a feeling of calm as a result of the treatment. This appears to be specifically related to a reduction of anxiety and irritability.[49,52] The reduction in irritability appears to be part of a general reduction in psychopathological symptoms found during treatment with CPA.[49,52]

The important effects on sexual behavior are the rationale for the use of CPA in the treatment of the paraphilias. These effects are a reduction in sexual interest and sexual drive, also a reduction of sexually deviant fantasy and behavior.[49]

Clinical Studies of CPA Treatment

The first clinical studies of CPA were reported from Germany. Laschet and Laschet (1971) reported on over 100 men who were treated, half of whom were sexual offenders. The duration of treatment varied from 6 months to over 4 years. The effects were reversible in about 6 weeks. The paraphilias treated were paedophilia, exhibitionism, sexual aggression including lust murder, incest, and fetishism. The largest group were exhibitionists. In about 5% of cases there was a complete elimination of all deviant behavior even after treatment with CPA was terminated. Undesirable side effects included fatigue, transient depression, weight gain, and some episodes of gynecomastia. No specific effect against sexual aggression was reported. The effect of CPA on hypersexuality was emphasized.[53]

Ott and Hoffet (1968) reported on the treatment of 26 sexual offenders with CPA. The treatment was successful in all cases except three. One case of severe organic brain syndrome failed to respond to treatment, and two treatment failures were caused by inadequate dosage and poor compliance. No specific effect against sexual aggression was described.[54]

Mothes *et al.* (1971) reported on the successful treatment of a large number of sexually deviant men.[55]

Cooper *et al.* (1972) reported on use of CPA in the treatment of hypersexuality in a 40-year-old male. He had been involved in incest with a daughter. In addition to this he also had multiple sexual deviations. He was treated with CPA for 21 days and followed up for 8 weeks posttreatment. There was a rapid reduction in erections, sexual fantasy, and sexual urges. Three weeks after cessation of treatment, sexuality had returned to pretreatment levels. No unwanted or toxic side effects were reported.[56]

Bancroft (1974) compared CPA and ethinyl estradiol in a double-blind comparison study of 12 patients. CPA reduced the plasma T, luteinizing hormone (LH), and follicle-stimulating hormone (FSH), whereas estradiol caused a rise in plasma T as well as LH.[57,58] Various measures of sexual activity as well as erectile responses to a variety of erotic stimuli were obtained. There were no significant differences between the two drugs on any of the erectile measures. As compared to the no-treatment phase, both drugs significantly lowered self-report measures of sexual activity. Self-rated responses during penile tumescence testing were significantly lowered by CPA but not by oestradiol. CPA had a similar but weaker effect on erectile responses.[57,58]

Davies (1974) treated 50 patients with CPA over a 5-year period. Many different types of paraphilias were treated; in addition 16 recidivist sexual offenders were treated. The 50 patients were described as hypersexual. No recidivism occurred on treatment or during 3 years follow-up after cessation of treatment. The 16 recidivists were convicted of sexual assaults against women and children. Ten hypersexual homosexual males were successfully treated, with a reduction in sexual activity, although the direction of the sexual drive was not affected. A number of chromosomal abnormalities were also treated, including an XYY-syndrome boy with a long history of sexual aggression and hypersexuality. The CPA caused a dramatic improvement in both his physical and sexual aggression. Two sadomasochistic men also improved considerably on CPA. No significant undesirable side effects were reported during the 5 years of the trial. Two patients developed slight gynecomastia.[59]

Laschet and Laschet (1975) reported on the treatment of 300 patients with CPA over periods of 2 months to 8 years. Oral and depot preparations of CPA were used. Dosage range for the oral CPA was 50 to 200 mg/day, while the depot CPA was given at either one- or two-week intervals in a dosage range of 300 mg to 600 mg per injection. The side effects are listed in TABLE 1. Contraindications given for CPA treatment included any debilitating illness, thrombophlebitis, and unstable diabetes mellitus. An additional 25 patients followed for up to 5 years did not recidivate when treatment was discontinued. A normalization of LH and FSH between the 8th and 15th month if the dosage was an average of 100mg per day was noted. Spermatogenesis returned to normal at this time. It was reported that cases of organic brain damage leading to sexual deviation can be only partially treated with CPA. It was also reported that CPA is not effective in aggression that is not sexually related.[49]

Cooper (1981) completed a placebo-controlled study of treatment with CPA in 9 patients. Sexual arousal and sexual drive were both reduced and appeared to correlate with plasma testosterone levels. The effects of CPA were noted to be reversible.[60]

CPA has been extensively studied at the Sexual Behaviors Clinic of the Royal Ottawa Hospital and the University of Ottawa. A double-blind placebo crossover trial of the use of CPA in the treatment of sexual deviation is presently underway; the results of the first 19 cases have been reported.[52] In addition a single case study with repeated measures showed that CPA caused a significant reduction in sadistic and aggressive arousal responses in a sadistic homosexual pedophile.[34] This particular case was a long-standing behavioral treatment failure. Further, for the first time a differential effect of CPA on sexual arousal patterns was reported.[34] CPA clearly reduced the arousal to pedophilic stimuli and also improved the ability to suppress that arousal when instructed to do so. The arousal to mutually consenting adult heterosexual intercourse was not affected to the same extent, resulting in a net increase in this "normal" sexual arousal response.[34] The double-blind placebo crossover study includes 12 sexual offenders with high rates of recidivism—a mean of 2.5 previous convictions per offender. CPA significantly reduced T, LH, and FSH during the active treatment phase as compared to placebo and baseline phases. ($p < .001$, ANOVA). Sexual arousal was measured by standard penile tumescence techniques. The sexual arousal to a visual color slide stimulus preselected by the subject for its erotic potential was used as well as the response to 2 minutes of covert sexual fantasy. Active drug reduced the response to the slide ($p < .01$, ANOVA) as well as the response to fantasy ($p < .001$, ANOVA) as compared to placebo. Significant reduction in psychopathology, sexual interest, and sexual activity were also found. More detailed study of individual sexual activity showed active drug reduced sexual tension, sexual fantasies, libido, sexual potency, nocturnal emission, spontaneous erections in the morning, and masturbation—at statistically significant levels as compared to baseline and placebo. Irritability and aggressiveness as measured by the Buss Durkee Hostility Inventory total score was reduced by active drug, but not at statistically significant levels. CPA did, however, significantly reduce the levels of psychopathology on the Brief Psychiatric Rating Scale (Overall and Gorham). This plus the reduction of anxiety, irritability, restlessness, and sexual tension suggests that CPA has an effect on sexual aggression. In the second phase of this study the effects of CPA on the patterns of sexual arousal to standard audiotape narratives used in the assessment of child molesters has also been examined.[15,20] In an initial analysis only the baseline and active drug treatment phases were considered. Nineteen subjects were classified as a "high" T group ($n = 9$, mean 34 nmol/l, range 29-46 nmol/l) and a "low" T group ($n = 10$, mean 20.9 nmol/l, range 14.2-24.9 nmol/l). The mean ages for the two groups were not statistically different. Analysis of the T level alone by group ("low" T/"high" T) across phases (baseline/active) yielded a significant group by treatment interaction ($F = 44.08$, $p < .001$ ANOVA). While baseline T levels were different for the 2 groups $t = -7.49$ $p < .001$), treatment levels were not ($t = -.76$, not significant). Baseline to treatment T levels were significantly different for the 2 groups ($t = 10.7$, "low"; $t = 18.7$, "high"; $p < .001$ ANOVA). Analysis of the 3 major arousal responses assessed (pedophilic, nonphysical coercion [pedophilic], and assault [pedophilic]) yielded a significant effect for type of stimulus ($p < .01$ or $p = .005$). There was also

TABLE 3. Recidivism Rates Following CPA Treatment[7,34]

Studies	Follow-up Period	n	Pre-Rate[a]	Post-Rate[b]
Horn (1973)	1-4.5 yr	33	100%	0%
Fahndrich (1974)	3 yr	14	93%	0%
Davies (1974)	3 yr	16	100%	0%
Appelt *et al.* (1974)	1.5 yr	6	100%	16.7%
Jost (b) (1974)	4 yr	10	100%	0%
Jost (a) (1975)	3 yr	11	54%	0%
Baron *et al.* (1977)	1 yr	6	50%	0%

[a] Refers to the recidivism rate prior to CPA treatment.

[b] Refers to the recidivism rate after CPA treatment. Corrected for poor patient compliance, inadequate dosage, and inadequate information on relapse.

a significant 3-way interaction between T group, phase, and type of response ($p < .01$). Within the interaction, significant differences between baseline and treatment responses were found on the pedophilic response for the "low" T group ($p < .05$) and on the assault response for the "high" T group ($p < .05$). There appears to be some evidence that CPA affects the sexual arousal responses of sex offenders and that the degree and nature of the effect is influenced by the type of stimulus presented and also by plasma T levels prior to treatment.[61]

CPA has an important role to play in the treatment of sexual offenders. It is well documented that CPA can substantially reduce recidivism rates; and CPA appears to have an effect on aggression that is sexually driven (see TABLE 3).

REFERENCES

1. BRADFORD, J. M. W. 1985. Organic treatments for the male sexual offender. Behav. Sci. Law **3**(4): 355-375.

2. BREMER, J. 1959. Asexualization—A Follow Up Study of 244 Cases. Macmillan. New York, NY.
3. STÜRUP, G. K. 1968. Treatment of sexual offenders in Herstedvester, Denmark: The rapists. Acta Psychiatr. Scand. Suppl. **204**(44): 5-61.
4. STÜRUP, G. K. 1972. Castration: The total treatment. *In* Sexual Behaviors: Social, Clinical and Legal Aspects. H. L. P. Resnik & M. E. Wolfgang, Eds.: 361-382. Little Brown. Boston, MA.
5. BANCROFT, J. 1983. Human Sexuality and Its Problems. Churchill Livingstone. Edinburgh.
6. LE MAIRE, L. 1956. Danish experiences regarding the castration of sexual offenders. J. Crim. Law, Criminol. Police Sci. **47:** 295-310.
7. ORTMANN, J. 1980. The treatment of sexual offenders, castration and antihormone therapy. Int. J. Law Psychiatry **3:** 443-451.
8. HEIM, N. & C. J. HURSCH. 1979. Castration for sexual offenders: Treatment or Punishment? A review and critique of recent European literature. Arch. Sexual Behav. **8:** 281-304.
9. ORTMANN, J. 1984a. How castration influences on relapsing into sexual criminality among Danish males. Unpublished manuscript.
10. ORTMANN, J. 1984b. How antihormone treatment with cyproterone acetate influences on relapsing into sexual criminality amongst male sexual offenders. Unpublished manuscript.
11. GROTH, A. N. 1979. Men Who Rape: The Psychology of the Offender. Plenum Press. New York, NY.
12. GROTH, A. N., A. W. BURGESS & L. L. HOLMSTROM. 1977. Rape: Power, Anger, and Sexuality. 1977. Am. J. Psychiatry **134:** 1239-1243.
13. RADA, R. T. 1978. Classification of the Rapist. *In* Clinical aspects of the Rapist. R. T. Rada, Ed.: 117-132. Grune & Stratton. New York, NY.
14. ABEL, G. G., D. H. BARLOW, E. BLANCHARD & D. GUILD. 1977. The components of rapist's sexual arousal. Arch. Gen. Psychiatry **43:** 895-903.
15. ABEL, G. G., E. BLANCHARD, J. BECKER & A. DJENDEREDJIAN. 1978. Differentiating sexual aggressives with penile measures. Crim. Justice Behav. **5:** 315-332.
16. QUINSEY, V. L. & T. C. CHAPMAN. 1982. Penile responses to nonsexual violence among rapists. Crim. Justice Behav. **9:** 372-381.
17. QUINSEY, V. L. & T. C. CHAPMAN. 1984. Stimulus control of rapist's and non-sex offender's sexual arousal. Behav. Assessment **6:** 169-176.
18. BARBAREE, H. E., W. L. MARSHALL & R. D. LANTHIER. 1979. Deviant sexual arousal in rapists. Behav. Res. Ther. **17:** 215-222.
19. DAVIDSON, P. R. & P. B. MALCOLM. 1985. The reliability of the rape index: A rapist sample. Behav. Assessment **7:** 283-292.
20. ABEL, G. G., J. BECKER, W. MURPHY & B. FLANAGAN. 1981. Identifying dangerous child molesters. *In* Violent Behavior: Social Learning Approaches to Prediction, Management and Treatment. R. B. Stuart, Ed. Brunner-Mazel. New York, NY.
21. MALAMUTH, N. M., J. V. P. CHECK & J. BRIERE. 1986. Sexual Arousal in Response to Aggression: Ideological, Aggressive and Sexual Correlates. J. Pers. Soc. Psychol. **50(2):** 330-340.
22. BRADFORD, J. M. W. 1983. Research on sex offenders. *In* The Psychiatric Clinics of North America, Vol. 6(4). R. L. Sadoff, Ed.: 715-733. W. B. Saunders Company, Philadelphia, PA.
23. BRADFORD, J. M. W. & D. MCLEAN. 1984. Sexual offenders, violence and testosterone: a clinical study. Can. J. Psychiatry **29:** 335-343.
24. PERSKY, H., K. D. SMITH & G. K. BASU. 1971. Relation of psychologic measures of aggression and hostility to testosterone production in man. Psychosom. Med. **33:** 265-277.
25. KREUZ, L. E. & R. M. ROSE. 1972. Assessment of aggressive behavior and plasma testosterone in a young criminal population. Psychosom. Med. **34:** 321-332.
26. MEYER-BAHLBURG, H. F. L., R. NAT, D. A. BOON, M. SHARMA & J. A. EDWARDS. 1974. Aggressiveness and testosterone measures in man. Psychosom. Med. **36:** 269-274.
27. EHRENKRANZ, J., E. BLISS & M. H. SHEARD. 1974. Plasma testosterone: Correlation with aggressive behavior and social dominance in man. Psychosom. Med. **36:** 469-475.
28. BROWN, W. A. & G. H. DAVIS. 1975. Serum testosterone and irritability in man. Psychosom. Med. **37:** 87.

29. RADA, R. T., D. R. LAWS & R. KELLNER. 1976. Plasma testosterone levels in the rapist. Psychosom. Med. **38:** 257-268.
30. MONTI, P. M., W. A. BROWN & D. D. CORRIVEAU. 1977. Testosterone and components of aggressive and sexual behavior in man. Am. J. Psychiatry **134**(6): 692-694.
31. OLWEUS, D., A. MATTSSON, D. SCHALLING & H. LOW. 1980. Testosterone, aggression, physical and personality dimensions in normal adolescent males. Psychosom. Med. **42:** 253-269.
32. SCARAMELLA, T. J. & W. A. BROWN. 1978. Serum testosterone and aggressiveness in hockey players. Psychosom. Med. **40:** 262-265.
33. BRADFORD, J. M. W., A. PAWLAK & D. BOURGET. 1987. Sexually aggressive offenders. Manuscript in preparation.
34. BRADFORD, J. M. W. & A. PAWLAK. 1987. Sadistic homosexual pedophilia: Treatment with cyproterone acetate—a single case study. Can. J. Psychiatry **32**(1): 22-30.
35. FOOTE, R. M. 1944. Diethylstilbestrol in the management of psychopathological states in males. J. Nerv. Ment. Dis. **99:** 928-935.
36. GOLLA, F. L. & S. R. HODGE. 1949. Hormone treatment of sexual offenders. Lancet **i:** 1006-1007.
37. WHITTAKER, L. H. 1959. Oestrogens and psychosexual disorders. Med. J. Aust. **2:** 547-549.
38. HELLER, C. G., W. M. LAIDLAW & H. T. HARVEY *et al.* 1958. Effects of progestational compounds on the reproductive processes of the human male. Ann. N. Y. Acad. Sci. **71:** 649-655.
39. MONEY, J. 1970. Use of androgen depleting hormone in the treatment of male sex offenders. J. Sex Res. **6:** 165-172.
40. MONEY, J. M., C. WIEDEKING, P. A. WALKER & D. GAIN. 1976. Combined antiandrogen and counselling program for treatment of 46, XY and 47, XYY sex offenders. *In* Hormones, Behavior and Psychopathology. E. Sachar. Ed.: 105-120. Raven Press. New York, NY.
41. WIEDEKING, C., J. MONEY & P. A. WALKER. 1979. Follow up 11 XYY males with impulsive and/or sex-offending behavior. Psychol. Med. **9:** 287-292.
42. WALKER, P. A. & W. J. MEYER. 1981. Medroxyprogesterone acetate treatment for paraphiliac sex offenders. *In* Violence and the Violent Individual. J. R. Hays, T. K. Roberts & K. S. Solway, Eds.: 353-373. S. P. Medical and Scientific Books. New York, NY.
43. GAGNE, P. 1981. Treatment of sex offenders with medroxyprogesterone acetate. Am. J. Psychiatry **138**(5): 644-646.
44. BERLIN, F. S. & C. F. MEINECKE. 1981. Treatment of sex offenders with antiandrogenic medication: conceptualization, review of treatment modalities, and preliminary findings. Am. J. Psychiatry **138**(5): 601-607.
45. SOUTHREN, A. L., G. G. GORDON, J. VITTEK & K. ALTMAN. 1977. Effect of progestagens on androgen metabolism. *In* Androgens and Antiandrogens. L. Martini & M. Motta, Eds.: 263-279. Raven Press. New York, NY.
46. LIANG, T., J. L. TYMOCZKO, K. M. B. CHAN, H. C. HUNG & S. LIAO. 1977. Androgen action: Receptors and rapid responses. *In* Androgens and Antiandrogens. L. Martini & M. Motta, Eds.: 77-89. Raven Press. New York, NY.
47. MAINWARING, I. P. 1977. Modes of action of antiandrogens: A survey. *In* Androgens and Antiandrogens. L. Martini & M. Motta: 151-161. Raven Press. New York, NY.
48. CHAPMAN, M. G. 1982. Side effects of antiandrogen therapy. *In* Androgens and Antiandrogen Therapy. S. L. Jeffcoate, Ed.: 169-178. John Wiley & Sons. New York, NY.
49. LASCHET, U. & L. LASCHET. 1975. Antiandrogens in the treatment of sexual deviations of men: J. Steroid Biochem. **6:** 821-826.
50. NEUMANN, F. 1977. Pharmacology and potential use of cyproterone acetate. Hormone Metabolic Res. **9:** 1-13.
51. CREMONOCINI, C., E. VIGINATI & A. LIBROIA. 1976. Treatment of hirsutism and acne in woman with two combinations: cyproterone acetate and ethinyloestradiol. Acta Europ. Fertil. **7:** 299-314.
52. BRADFORD, J. M. & W. A. PAWLAK. 1986. Double-blind placebo crossover study of cyproterone acetate in the treatment of sexual deviation. Submitted for publication.

53. LASCHET, U. & L. LASCHET. 1971. Psychopharmacotherapy of sex offenders with cyproterone acetate. Pharmakopsychiatr. Neuro-Psychopharmakol. **4:** 99-104.
54. OTT, F. & H. HOFFET. 1968. The influence of antiandrogens on libido, potency and testicular function. Schweiz. Med. Wochenschr. **98:** 1812-1815.
55. MOTHES, C., J. LEHNERT, F. SAMIMI & J. UFER. 1971. Schering symposium uber sexual deviationen und ihre medikamentose Behandlung. Life Sci. Monogr. **2:** 65.
56. COOPER, A. J., A. A. ISMAIL, A. L. PHANJOO & D. L. LOVE. 1972. Antiandrogen (Cyproterone Acetate) therapy in deviant hypersexuality. Br. J. Psychiatry **120:** 59-63.
57. BANCROFT, J., G. TENNENT, K. LOUCAS & J. CASS. 1974. The control of deviant sexual behaviour by drugs: 1. Behavioral changes following Oestragens and Anti-androgens. Br. J. Psychiatry **125:** 310-315.
58. MURRAY, M. A. F., J. H. J. BANCROFT, D. C. ANDERSON, T. G. TENNENT & P. J. CARR. 1975. Endocrine changes in male sexual deviants after treatment with anti-androgens, oestragens or tranquilizers. J. Endocrinol. **67:** 179-188.
59. DAVIES, T. D. 1974. Cyproterone Acetate for male hypersexuality. J. Int. Med. Res. **2:** 159-163.
60. COOPER, A. J. 1981. A placebo controlled study of the antiandrogen cyproterone acetate in deviant hypersexuality. Compr. Psychiatry **22:** 458-464.
61. BRADFORD, J. M. W. & A. PAWLAK. 1987. The treatment of child molesters with cyproterone acetate. Manuscript in preparation.

Introductory Comments

D. RICHARD LAWS

Florida Mental Health Institute
University of South Florida
Tampa, Florida 22612

Following the conclusion of this symposium, I was speaking with presenter Bill Marshall about what we had heard. "Ten years ago," I said, "we wouldn't have heard what we did today. This is the first sex offender treatment conference I've attended where there was more agreement than disagreement on issues and data."

For me the New York Academy of Sciences conference was a watershed, a recognition that it was all coming together at last. The data emerging over nearly 20 years had seriously thinned out, if not eliminated, the major noncontenders, and it appeared that we had, at last, a realistic but probably somewhat limited treatment model for sex offenders. The papers presented in this symposium lend support to that conclusion. The centerpiece of that model appears to be cognitive-behavior therapy primarily directed at elimination of cognitive distortions related to sexual and social activities, and self-management in high-risk situations. This core model is supplemented by a wide variety of interventions, including behavior therapy to reduce deviant sexual arousal, a variety of treatments for social competency, anger management, stress reduction, assertiveness training, sex education, human sexuality, lifestyle modification, and training of coping skills. Increasingly it is recognized that accountability for treatment effects is mandatory. We now find treatment progress being monitored by self-report, reports of significant others, penile plethysmography, and periodic readministration of treatment outcome measures. Most important, perhaps, is the recognition that it is what happens *after* the delivery of the treatment package that is critical. Consequently, long-term follow-up is now considered essential. Sexual deviation can be managed, but it is unlikely to go away. There is no "technofix" for this problem. As one of the presenters put it, therapy may formally end, but "maintenance is forever."

Everybody talks about the menace of the adolescent sex offender, but hardly anyone does anything about it. Presenter Judith Becker and her colleagues *are* doing something about it. She presents some early findings from a multicomponent adolescent program, modified from an adult model developed by Abel, Becker *et al.* over a number of years. Importantly, an adult model worked equally well with adolescents, handily demolishing the "But they're just boys!" objection. Outcome data on changes in sexual response are presented, although the authors note that more comprehensive measures are needed.

William Farrall and Robert Card present new information on a computer-managed sexual arousal assessment developed by the senior author. The paper is somewhat contentious on several issues, and many researchers and clinicians will disagree with the assertions and conclusions. Especially interesting to me were their comments about the need for cognitive scaling of sexual arousal that could be related to physiological measures, development of stimulus materials that will maximize what they call a "discriminant" sexual response rather than just large erectile responses, and the concurrent use of other physiological measures, in this case Galvanic Skin Response.

The popular cognitive-behavior therapy, relapse prevention, is emerging as a major sex offender treatment. Presenter Janice Marques was one of the first clinicians in the United States to see the potential of this treatment, and she describes an institutional treatment program based on this model. A trend is developing to offer sex offender treatment in confinement, and many states are watching California's program as a possible model. Readers will note that this is a very comprehensive program that operates on many different levels. Importantly, Marques recognizes the importance of aftercare, and the contracting with community providers is a nice touch and quite a realistic one, given the burden of operating the main program. Sadly, aftercare extends for only one year, and then follow-up is confined to examination of official records. This limited hands-on follow-up was a result of constraints on state funding.

As usual, presenters William Marshall and Howard Barbaree demonstrate their sensitivity as clinicians as well as scientific rigor in their description of one of the longest running (and still developing) outpatient sex offender programs in North America. Readers will be impressed at the way these investigators manage to get inside the manifest issues of what is going on in the areas of deviant sexual behavior and social competence. Especially notable is the broad scope the authors give to social competence that goes well beyond the usual reports. Their outcome data are impressive, as is the length of the follow-up periods. Note in particular their refusal to rely upon official records as a reliable source of recidivism data.

Presenter Gene Abel and his colleagues provide data on his recently completed prospective study of treatment of child molesters. This is an unusual and welcome presentation. It is devoted to identifying specific client characteristics that predict dropping out of treatment and recidivating one year posttreatment. Essentially, the message is that the more heterogeneously deviant the client, the less likely he is to be successful in treatment. Optimists beware!

William Pithers and his colleagues have the advantage of working with sex offenders both within and outside of confinement, often being able to follow the client from the former to the latter situation. Pithers, like Marques, is one of the pioneers in applying relapse prevention treatment to sex offenders. The paper reports numerous modifications of the original Marlatt model. Especially interesting are the data reported on the analysis of sequential precursors to the commission of sexual aggression. In terms of dealing with client expectations for treatment outcome, note the program's hard-nosed "management is possible, cure is not" stance. This was one of the first programs to adopt this nontraditional position.

In summary, these papers inform us about the state of the art, and the news is good. However, the bad news is that very few of these offenders will come to official attention and be offered treatment. Therefore, our efforts would be more efficiently focused on early identification and treatment of the adolescent sex offender. Such efforts could more easily truncate development of the chronic, intractable disorder that, despite our optimism, we still too frequently see.

An Outpatient Treatment Program for Child Molesters[a]

W. L. MARSHALL AND H. E. BARBAREE

Department of Psychology
Queen's University
Kingston, Ontario, Canada K7L 3N6

In this paper our main aim will be to describe our outpatient treatment program for child molesters, although we will also briefly report tentative outcome data. The program began operation in 1973, with 18 patients being seen in the initial year. Included in the patient sample were child molesters (nonfamilial as well as familial offenders), rapists, exhibitionists, voyeurs, obscene telephone callers, and various other deviants. Over the years the number of patients has grown considerably, and the main thrust of this increase has been a rise in the number of child molesters. In 1985, a total of 95 patients were seen, with 62 of these being child molesters; during 1986 up to the end of October, over 100 child molesters were assessed, with approximately 40 percent entering treatment. The demographics and offense histories of those entering treatment do not differ from those who are simply assessed, although there are obviously other differences. Of those who are not treated, approximately 40 percent refuse the offer of treatment, usually because they continue to maintain their innocence, while the rest are unable to accept the treatment offer either because they are jailed (few of these return after release to be treated) or because their home is so far away as to make attendance impossible. Every effort is made to persuade all patients to enter treatment, and no one is refused entry regardless of his offense history, intelligence, or other personal features. Since there is no charge to patients, lack of funds is not an obstacle to entering treatment.

Over the years we have reported progressive changes in our program[1–4] that reflect an increase in the range of problems targeted in assessment and treatment, with a shift away from an exclusive focus on deviant sexual preferences. Our most recent report[5] detailed the comprehensive nature of our current approach, but described its application to sexual aggressors (including rapists and the more vicious child molesters), whereas the program outlined herein is more specifically tailored to the needs of the full range of child molesters, and it has been expanded accordingly.

In designing a program that will accommodate the heterogeneity of problems displayed by child molesters, our intention is to identify those various features that research has indicated are relevant to the maintenance of the unacceptable sexual behaviors of these men. Research, however, is not the only source of inspiration for our program's design. In the first place the publication of research findings typically lags behind practice, which tends to be heavily informed by clinical experience. Second, most of the research that might be relevant to decisions concerning treatment design is of the comparative group paradigm. Here, a group of nonoffenders is typically

[a]This work was supported by The Child Abuse Prevention Program of the Ontario Ministry of Community and Social Services.

compared with a group of offenders on some aspect of their functioning. If the groups differ, it is concluded that this indicates a need to normalize the offenders on the behavior in question. On the other hand, if there are no group differences, it is concluded that the feature in question is not in need of treatment. The logic of this argument is faulty for at least two reasons. While there may not be group differences, there might very well be individual differences, with some of the offenders being seriously deficient in the feature under examination. Alternatively, even if there are few individual differences between or within groups, a degree of deficiency in some of the offenders may nonetheless be functionally related to their misbehavior. For example, we[6,7] found little in the way of social skill differences between sex offenders and controls matched for intelligence, age, education, and socioeconomic status. However, in a substantial proportion of our patients, there is a clear functional relationship between social deficits and the probability of their engaging in aberrant sexual acts. Research aimed at discerning functional relationships would be far more helpful than the current emphasis on demonstrating group differences. In any case, the content of our program is a product of both research findings and clinical evaluations that focus more on discerning functional relationships than on determining group differences.

The program, as we noted, is quite comprehensive, covering as it does various aspects of sexual functioning and a number of features of social competence. It is not to be understood, however, that all patients are considered to be deficient in all these respects. Assessments focus on this broad range of problems and any other problems that may be raised by the patient, and only those where deficiencies are apparent are addressed in treatment for that individual. There is, therefore, an inbuilt flexibility in the program that is meant to meet the expectation on our part that each client will be unique and must be treated as such.

THE TREATMENT PROGRAM

Two general areas of functioning are targeted in our program: (1) sexual behaviors; and (2) social competence. These areas each encompass a variety of behaviors and cognitions, the most salient of which are described in the outline provided below of the assessment and treatment program. Given our understanding of the uniqueness of individual patients, it follows that occasionally we see patients with problems additional to those listed below. In these cases we attempt to determine whether or not these additional difficulties are functionally related to the maintenance of the aberrant sexual behavior, and if so we address these problems in treatment. We are guided in our functional analyses by a consideration of the possible facilitative effect on sexual misbehavior of three classes of problems: (1) those that place the man under stress, since evidence indicates that stress increases the probability that various deviant or dysfunctional behaviors will occur;[8] (2) those behavioral deficiencies that restrict access to engaging in appropriate sexual interactions or that render such interactions unsatisfying; and (3) those actions or states that disinhibit the constraining nature of internalized social rules. These are, basically, the guides by which we determine the functional relevance of all the problems we have listed below, and we extend this approach to the inclusion of any relevant, but idiosyncratic, feature of an individual patient.

These men are, obviously, distinguished by behavioral aberrations, and this is what brings them to treatment; but it is our operating assumption that such behaviors are maintained by a variety of problems. All of these problems affect the probability that child molestation will occur, either directly—in, for example, the case of deviant sexual desires; or indirectly—by either denying access to appropriate partners (e.g., heterosexual/heterosocial anxiety), or by increasing stress in the patient's life (e.g., marital discord), or by disinhibiting whatever social controls are in place (e.g., alcohol intoxication). In fact many of these problems increase the probability of offending through all these routes. In that sense the division of these presenting problems into sexual or social is arbitrary. This is done simply for ease of description; these problems should not be, and cannot be, dealt with independently in treatment.

Sexual Problems

The most obvious sexual problem concerns the fact that these men molest children. However, this behavior cannot be directly assessed or recreated in therapy, for both ethical and practical reasons. It is often assumed[9] that laboratory-assessed sexual preferences are valid indicators of overt sexual activities, and support for this assumption has been derived from criterion group differences in preferences. If this claim is true, then the outcome of these laboratory assessments could serve as the indicator of overt sexual behavior. Unfortunately, the studies that have been taken to attest to the external validity of these measures have, again, been based on comparative group research, which ignores possible within-group differences. These within-group differences may be far more relevant to understanding and treating these offenders than any group average index might be. To illustrate this possibility, let us briefly describe our recent investigations of the sexual preferences of child molesters.

We have described[10] the laboratory assessment of the sexual preferences of child molesters and outlined the group averages for father-daughter incest offenders, heterosexual nonfamilial child molesters, and a matched group of nonoffenders. The averaged responses of the incest offenders did not markedly differ from those of the controls (a finding that essentially replicates earlier research),[11] while the nonfamilial offenders showed a bimodal distribution of preferences, with peak arousal to children and adults but little arousal to adolescents. Such profiles would encourage us to ignore sexual preferences in the treatment of incest offenders and would also direct us to focus only on reducing deviant arousal in the nonfamilial offenders with a corresponding neglect of any need to increase arousal to adults in these men. However, subsequent analyses of each individual's preferences[12] revealed that only 12.5% of the nonfamilial offenders had a profile that matched the group average, while 40% of the incest offenders failed to discriminate children from adults. Such analyses indicate very clearly that decisions about treatment targets must be based on individual configurations of problems rather than on some assumed commonality across all child molesters. These individual analyses revealed that deviant sexual preferences, or a failure to be inhibited by the young age of some females, is a common enough problem amongst both familial and nonfamilial child molesters. Treatment programs, therefore, must have a component that deals with this in those cases where deviant sexual preferences are evident. Our treatment program has such a component.

Various procedures have been described that aim to decrease deviant arousal or to increase appropriate sexual interests. We prefer behavioral techniques, partly because we believe the evidence is somewhat stronger in support of their efficacy compared with physical or medical strategies,[13] but also because they more readily promote self-control in the patients.

While most reports of therapy outcome using behavioral approaches have focused on the evaluation of one procedure in isolation, we believe that a combination of procedures is likely to be more effective. Indeed, in our earlier reports[14] we have always used a combined package to shift deviant interests to more acceptable preferences. In targeting deviant arousal, our current program combines electrical aversive conditioning,[15] conducted in the laboratory, with satiation therapy,[16] modified as a home-practice program. In addition each patient carries smelling salts (nonperfumed versions), which he uses to eliminate deviant thoughts elicited in his day-to-day environment; when a deviant thought occurs, he places the salts close to his nose and takes a quick deep inhalation. These three procedures combine in ways that seem as practically sensible to our patients as they do to us by: (1) decreasing arousal to deviant visual and verbal prompts (aversive conditioning); (2) reducing the attractiveness of deviant fantasies during masturbation (satiation); and (3) eliminating the occurrence of deviant thoughts elicited by the sight of children or by daydreams (the smelling salts).

We have modified the satiation procedure from our original description largely as a response to wise informal counsel offered by Drs. Gene Abel, Jack Annon, and Richard Laws. We now have patients carry out the procedure in the natural circumstances where masturbation typically occurs, rather than in the laboratory. Patients are encouraged to use appropriate fantasies (which, if necessary, we provide) until they ejaculate, after which they generate variations on their deviant theme out loud. This is certainly more readily acceptable to patients and appears, from both our own within-treatment data and that collected by Abel, Annon, and Laws, to be an effective strategy. Of course, the practice of associating appropriate fantasies with masturbation to ejaculation matches what has been described as either orgasmic reconditioning[17] or masturbatory conditioning,[18] both of which aim at increasing arousal to appropriate sexual behaviors. While this latter aspect of our procedures is popular with clinicians, it cannot be said to have strong empirical support.[19]

In addition to our focus on changing sexual preferences by the combination of these three procedures, we also give attention to various other features of sexuality that we believe contribute to the maintenance of deviant acts. For instance, many of these men have sexual relations with adult females that they deem to be unsatisfactory. Sometimes this results from restricted sexual practices that do not include much in the way of precoital preparatory behaviors, and that emphasize getting the act over and done with quite quickly. These are much the same features that Masters and Johnson[20] describe as characterizing dysfunctional sexual relations. While only a few of our patients have identified actual dysfunctions (usually impotence or premature ejaculation), most claim that sex with their current partner is unsatisfying. Our treatment goal here is to expand their sexual repertoire and help them to identify just what it is they are seeking in sexual encounters. In our experience most males (deviant or otherwise) characteristically see physical release as the goal of sex, although they often claim to be dissatisfied despite regularly having orgasms during intercourse. We believe that sex serves many other purposes for most males, including a reduction in stress-induced tension as well as providing an affirmation of their sense of masculinity. Indeed, for many men sex appears to be the prime source of their self-esteem.[21] In addition, many males count a woman's willingness to have sex with them as an indication of her commitment to the relationship.

In order to address these issues in treatment, we provide sex education (which emphasizes common sexual practices and positive attitudes toward sex rather than instruction in the biological aspects of sex) and counseling, both on an individual basis and within a group format. This counseling process follows the features usually identified with cognitive therapy;[22] it involves identifying and challenging present assumptions, considering the possible consequences of such assumptions, offering alternative views of sex, and illustrating the likely consequences of these alternatives. Where necessary, patients are referred to other services for concurrent treatment of any sexual dysfunctions.

We also deal with the distorted ideas these men hold about the value of their sexual involvement with children on both the victims and their own family (or the rest of their family, in the case of incest offenders). Associated with this, we examine the views these men have regarding the role their victims play in the offense. Typically, child molesters believe their victims are seductive and wish to have sex with them, and they are convinced that these children benefit from the experience. Similarly, they expect their families to accept, and forget quite quickly, the evidence of their deviance. These issues are faced within an individual and group counseling context; the processes match those described above.

These men often make other inappropriate attributions about responsibility for their actions, blaming, for example, intoxication, stress, sexual deprivation, and their own molestation as children as factors that caused them to act inappropriately. Here, we attempt to shift their attributions to self-responsibility, while at the same time having them recognize that these factors are influential only if allowed to be. Accordingly, in addition to altering these views, we teach them ways to deal with and avoid stress, and we provide brief sexual counseling (or direct them elsewhere for more prolonged counseling if necessary).

Social Competence

Originally our focus in the area of social competence was limited to improving conversational skills with appropriate adult partners, reducing anxiety in the presence of such partners, and training in assertiveness.[1,4] Assertiveness training emphasizes not simply standing up for one's rights, but also expressing positive feelings and controlling anger. These components have been retained with the conversational skills training and have been expanded to include perceptions of the partner's emotions and interests[23] and efforts to encourage and reward the partner's responses.[24] Within this context we also attempt to develop more general empathic skills, which, of course, are salient to many of the other issues raised in treatment. In this sense there is some redundancy in our treatment processes. These aspects of behavior are modified through role-playing, group discussion, and training in relaxation as a self-control strategy.[25]

We also provide brief relationship training, since these men typically report dissatisfaction with their current partner, and frequently their relationship seems to be dysfunctional and stressful. Our brief relationship therapy is modeled after Jacobson and Dallas's[26] marital counseling and emphasizes conflict resolution, effective communication, and shared leisure activities. We believe the latter is particularly important, because an absence of constructive or enjoyable spare-time activities frequently gives rise to thoughts of sex with children as a diversion from boredom. Accordingly, we encourage our patients to develop a greater range of leisure interests, both shared with their partners and individually pursued.

It is also apparent that many of our patients experience severe financial stress, so we either provide abbreviated budgeting counseling or send them to a local agency that specializes in such skills training. Also, many of our patients are poor at job search and secure skills and find it difficult to hold a job. Again, our counseling on these issues is brief, but if more protracted training is needed, we direct them to other agencies in the community that are skilled in these matters.

Finally, we attempt to teach patients ways to control their behavior when intoxicated. For instance, we caution them to insure before using intoxicants that they will not be without adult company when they become intoxicated. Most of these men either drink alone, or they leave friends once they become intoxicated. Once they are alone and intoxicated, the probability of seeking out children for sex appears to increase markedly. We have observed similar disinhibitory processes in the responses of normal males to forced sex.[27] If the use of intoxicants is chronic or at addictive levels, we refer these patients to a local addiction treatment center.

OUTCOME

In an earlier paper[28] we drew attention to the need in treatment studies to evaluate the changes produced by treatment in those features of the patient that are thought to underlie the problem behavior, in addition to estimating reductions in the deviant acts. The former is meant to determine whether or not the procedures employed have been effective in changing the targeted behaviors (e.g., deviant sexual preferences, inappropriate beliefs and attributions, low sense of masculinity, dysfunctional sexual and marital relations, poor social skills, ineffective use of leisure time, abuse of intoxicants). We then should evaluate whether or not such changes are related to a reduction in child molestation, which is, after all, the main goal of treatment.

We now have underway a comprehensive evaluation of our program along the lines outlined above, but data relevant to this will not be available for some time. However, since our program began in 1973, we have been able to collect recidivism data on 117 patients who did or did not receive treatment. Amongst the untreated patients, the main reasons for not entering treatment were either that they lived too far away for regular attendance to be feasible, or they were incarcerated and by the time they were released they had changed their minds about entering any outpatient program. In addition, as we noted earlier, some 40% of our untreated patients refused the offer of treatment. However, none of these men who refused treatment were involved in the evaluation. Thus our untreated group all agreed that they had a problem and indicated a desire to receive treatment, but were unable to access treatment in our program. In fact, most of the incarcerated men were given some form of treatment during their jail term. Obviously this does not represent the ideal untreated comparison group, but clinical concerns about protecting society would preclude deliberately withholding treatment from some patients in order to enable random assignment to treated or untreated groups. Therefore, unless we accessed the group of patients who were assessed but not treated, we would not be able to provide estimates of base-rate recidivism.

It should be remembered that our treatment program has evolved over the past 13 years; the presently evaluated treated patients did not receive all of the components of our most recent comprehensive package. Accordingly, we selected for evaluation only those treated patients who received approximately the same set of components from our package. All these patients were given the same procedures to alter sexual preferences, and all of them received social skills training, including anxiety reduction and training in assertiveness, conversational skills, and relationship skills. We also addressed issues concerned with financial management, use of leisure time, and alcohol or drug use. Essentially, what was omitted from our present program were attempts to enhance empathy and to modify distorted cognitions and to correct misattributions. Furthermore, all of the evaluated patients were seen individually rather than within a group format. We make no apologies for these earlier variations on our present program, as we are constantly evolving our treatment approach based on both research results and continuing clinical experience. Nevertheless, this report of outcome cannot be construed as a thorough test of the present program but should be, if anything, an underestimate of its effectiveness.

Our basis for determining recidivism did not rely simply on official records, since these have been criticized[29] as seriously underestimating reoffense rates. In addition to having access to official records that indicate all charges as well as convictions and that record all offenses committed in North America, we were provided with information from the unofficial files of local police stations and Children's Aid Societies in the towns where the majority of our offenders lived. We also attempted to get reports from our patients' live-in partners or parents, indicating, amongst other things, how well the patient could account for his time. Unfortunately, the return of these reports has been slow, and we have not yet collected sufficient to justify adding them to our data. So far they have not contradicted recidivism estimates derived from the other sources. In this sense, however, our outcome evaluation is incomplete; since we have attempted to put together descriptively what we have at present, this report is a tentative account of the effectiveness of our program. A more complete data set will allow a more complete description of the population and will permit us both to subcategorize patient groups and to examine the relationship between various indices and outcome. For present purposes we will simply put all our patients into treated and untreated categories and ignore their specific diagnoses.

Data from 53 untreated patients and 64 treated patients entered the evaluation. The average follow-up period was 42.13 months (range 9-113 months) for the untreated patients, and 44.31 months (range 9-117 months) for the treated group. Follow-up months are corrected for incarceration, so they are in fact months spent out of institutional settings with access to children. This means that the follow-up period for the untreated subjects was actually longer than for the treated group.

Recidivism figures revealed an overall rate of 32% of the untreated group who reoffended, compared with 14% of the treated patients. In terms of number of offenses, those untreated men who reoffended molested 27 ($\bar{x}$ = 1.59 per offender) children after discharge, whereas the treated patients molested 13 ($\bar{x}$ = 1.44 per offender). TABLE 1 describes the outcome data in more detail. As can be seen from this table, whether or not the offender had completed intercourse with one of his victims was a strong predictor of recidivism in the two groups of heterosexual offenders. In these offenders, while treatment did not reduce recidivism in the intercourse offenders to levels comparable to those who did not have intercourse with their young victims, the proportional reduction in repeat rates was at least equivalent if not greater. Nevertheless, the most sexually intrusive offenders are clearly the most problematic, treated or untreated. We are in the process of analyzing these data further. The results so far are clearly encouraging, although we apparently still have a long way to go before we are able to eliminate child molestation in these offenders.

A final interesting point to our recidivism data concerns the fact that, overall, the official records underestimated recidivism quite substantially. In terms of the 26 men who recidivated, only 11 were identified officially. As for the number of victims, the official records indicated 15, while the unofficial information revealed that an additional 25 children had been molested. Our sources of information, then, suggested far higher recidivism figures than the official police records, and these differences were equally apparent for the treated and the untreated patients.

TABLE 1. Recidivism Rates as Percentages of Each Group

	Untreated			Treated		
	Intercourse[a]	Nonintercourse	Total	Intercourse[a]	Nonintercourse	Total
Heterosexual child molesters	83 (n = 6)	23 (n = 13)	42 (n = 19)	30 (n = 10)	12 (n = 17)	19 (n = 27)
Homosexual child molesters	40 (n = 5)	43 (n = 7)	42 (n = 12)	14 (n = 7)	14 (n = 7)	14 (n = 14)
Incest offenders	27 (n = 11)	9 (n = 11)	18 (n = 22)	18 (n = 11)	0 (n = 12)	9 (n = 23)

[a] Offenders so classified completed intercourse (vaginal or anal) with at least one of their victims.

REFERENCES

1. MARSHALL, W. L. 1971. A combined treatment method for certain sexual deviations. Behav. Res. Ther. **9:** 292-294.
2. MARSHALL, W. L. 1973. The modification of sexual fantasies: A combined treatment approach to the reduction of deviant sexual behavior. Behav. Res. Ther. **11:** 557-564.
3. MARSHALL, W. L. & R. D. MCKNIGHT. 1975. An integrated treatment program for sexual offenders. Can. Psychiatr. Assoc. J. **20:** 133-138.
4. MARSHALL, W. L. & S. WILLIAMS. 1975. A behavioral approach to the modification of rape. Q. Bull. Br. Assoc. Behav. Psychother. **4:** 78.
5. MARSHALL, W. L., C. M. EARLS, Z. SEGAL & J. DARKE. 1983. A behavioral program for the assessment and treatment of sexual aggressors. *In* Advances in Clinical Behavior Therapy. K. Craig & R. McMahon, Eds.: 148-174. Brunner/Mazel. New York, NY.
6. SEGAL, Z. & W. L. MARSHALL. 1985a. Heterosexual social skills in a population of rapists and child molesters. J. Consult. Clin. Psychol. **53:** 55-63.
7. SEGAL, Z. & W. L. MARSHALL. 1985b. Self-report and behavioral assertion in two groups of sexual offenders. J. Behav. Ther. Exp. Psychiatry **16:** 223-229.
8. DOHRENWEND, B. S. & B. P. DOHRENWEND. 1974. Stressful Life Events: Their Nature and Effects. Wiley. New York, NY.
9. EARLS, C. M. & W. L. MARSHALL. 1983. The current state of technology in the laboratory assessment of sexual arousal patterns. *In* The Sexual Aggressor: Current Perspectives on Treatment. J. G. Greer & I. R. Stuart, Eds.: 336-362. Van Nostrand Reinhold. New York, NY.
10. MARSHALL, W. L., H. E. BARBAREE & D. CHRISTOPHE. 1986. Sexual offenders against female children: Sexual preferences for age of victims and type of behavior. Can. J. Behav. Sci. **18:** 424-439.
11. QUINSEY, V. L., T. C. CHAPLIN & W. F. CARRIGAN. 1979. Sexual preferences among incestuous and nonincestuous child molesters. Behav. Ther. **10:** 562-565.
12. BARBAREE, H. E. & W. L. MARSHALL. 1987. Erectile responses amongst heterosexual child molesters, father-daughter incest offenders and matched nonoffenders: five distinct age preference profiles. Submitted for publication.
13. QUINSEY, V. L. & W. L. MARSHALL. 1983. Procedures for reducing inappropriate sexual arousal: An evaluation review. *In* The Sexual Aggressor: Current Perspectives on Treatment. J. G. Greer & I. R. Stuart, Eds.: 267-289. Van Nostrand Reinhold. New York, NY.
14. MARSHALL, W. L. 1974. A combined treatment approach to the reduction of multiple fetish-related behaviors. J. Consult. Clin. Psychol. **42:** 613-616.
15. MARSHALL, W. L. 1985. Electrical aversion. *In* Dictionary of Behavior Therapy Techniques. A. S. Bellack & M. Hersen, Eds.: 114-117. Pergamon Press. New York, NY.
16. MARSHALL, W. L. 1979. Satiation therapy: A procedure for reducing deviant sexual arousal. J. Appl. Behav. Anal. **12:** 10-22.
17. MARQUIS, J. N. 1970. Orgasmic reconditioning: Changing sexual choice through controlling masturbatory fantasies. J. Behav. Ther. Exp. Psychiatry **1:** 263-271.
18. ABEL, G. G., E. B. BLANCHARD & J. V. BECKER. 1978. An integrated treatment program for rapists. *In* Clinical Aspects of the Rapist. R. T. Rada, Ed.: 161-214. Grune & Stratton. New York, NY.
19. CONRAD, S. R. & J. P. WINCZE. 1976. Orgasmic reconditioning: A controlled study of its effects upon the sexual arousal and behavior of adult male homosexuals. Behav. Ther. **7:** 155-166.
20. MASTERS, W. H. & V. E. JOHNSON. 1970. Human Sexual Inadequacy. Little, Brown. Boston, MA.
21. SCHIMEL, J. L. 1974. Self-esteem and sex. *In* Sexual Behavior: Current Issues. L. Gross, Ed. Spectrum Publications. Flushing, NY.
22. BECK, A. T., A. J. RUSH, B. F. SHAW & G. EMERY. 1979. Cognitive Therapy of Depression: A Treatment Manual. Guilford. New York, NY.

23. MORRISON, R. L. & A. S. BELLACK. 1981. The role of social perception in social skill. Behav. Ther. **12:** 69-79.
24. FISCHETTI, M., J. P. CURRAN & H. W. WESTBERG. 1977. Sense of timing: A skill deficit in heterosexual-socially anxious males. Behav. Modification **1:** 179-194.
25. GOLDFRIED, M. R. 1971. Systematic desensitization as training in self-control. J. Consult. Clin. Psychol. **37:** 228-235.
26. JACOBSON, N. S. & M. DALLAS. 1981. Helping married couples improve their relationship. *In* Behavior Modification: Principles, Issues, and Applications. W. E. Craighead, A. E. Kazdin & M. J. Mahoney, Eds.: 379-398. Houghton Mifflin. Boston, MA.
27. BARBAREE, H. E., W. L. MARSHALL, E. YATES & L. LIGHTFOOT. 1983. Alcohol intoxication and deviant sexual arousal in male social drinkers. Behav. Res. Ther. **21:** 365-373.
28. MARSHALL, W. L., G. G. ABEL & V. L. QUINSEY. 1983. The assessment and treatment of sexual offenders. *In* Sexual Aggression and the Law. S. N. Verdun-Jones & A. A. Keltner, Eds.: 41-52. Criminology Research Centre, Simon Fraser University. Burnaby, B.C., Canada.
29. QUINSEY, V. L. 1983. Prediction of recidivism and the evaluation of treatment programs for sex offenders. *In* Sexual Aggression and the Law. S. N. Verdun-Jones & A. A. Keltner, Eds.: 27-40. Criminology Research Centre, Simon Fraser University. Burnaby, B.C., Canada.

Measuring the Effectiveness of Treatment for the Aggressive Adolescent Sexual Offender[a]

JUDITH V. BECKER,[b,c] MEG S. KAPLAN,[c] AND RICHARD KAVOUSSI [c]

[b]*Sexual Behavior Clinic*
New York State Psychiatric Institute

[c]*Department of Psychiatry*
College of Physicians and Surgeons
Columbia University
New York, New York 10032

INTRODUCTION

The exact incidence of sex crimes committed by adolescent offenders is unknown. Available incidence figures from victim reports and arrest statistics indicate that approximately 20% of all rapes and 30% to 50% of child molestation cases were perpetrated by adolescent offenders.[1,2] Adolescent offenders engage in other deviant sexual behaviors involving victims that do not meet the criteria for forcible rape or child molestation, including telephone scatalogia, frottage, and exhibitionism.

Ageton conducted a survey using a national probability sample of male adolescents aged 13 to 19.[3] Sexual assault, for the purpose of her study, was defined as forced sexual behavior, including contact with sexual parts of the body. Exhibitionism and any other act that was not a "hands on" experience were excluded. Of a sample of 863 adolescent males, the rate of sexual assaults per 100,000 adolescent males ranged from 5,000 to 16,000. The incidence rates varied as a function of the definition of sexual assault and whether one relied on arrest or self-report data of the offenders.

Even though we do not know the exact incidence figures for sexual crimes committed by adolescents, we do know that the average adolescent sexual offender may be expected to commit 380 sex crimes during his lifetime.[4] This is based on data of adult offenders who began committing sexual crimes as adolescents. If sex crimes are to be reduced, it is imperative that effective treatment strategies be developed and implemented with adolescent sexual offenders.

Treatment approaches have been described in the scientific literature for adult offenders, including those based on a biological model;[5,6] and a community program for incest offenders.[7] More recently a behavioral approach for adult sex offenders based on social learning theory has been utilized. This approach has a major focus of teaching the adult sex offender control over his deviant sexual interest pattern.[4,8,9]

[a]This work was supported by a grant from the New York State Division of Criminal Justice.

Programs that treat adolescent sexual offenders are described in the literature.[10,11] However, there are no controlled outcome studies designed to evaluate the effectiveness of treatment programs for adolescent sexual offenders. Such studies have been difficult to conduct because ethics dictate that one cannot have a randomly assigned no-treatment control group. Self selection and the fact that some youth are mandated to receive treatment while others elect to are also sources of bias in evaluating treatment effectiveness.[12]

The purpose of this paper is to describe a community-based outpatient treatment program for male adolescent sexual offenders and therapy outcome for those adolescents who completed treatment and a posttreatment evaluation.

METHOD

Subjects

The subjects for this study were 24 adolescent males who sought evaluation and treatment at the Sexual Behavior Clinic of the New York state Psychiatric Institute. Subjects ranged in age from 13 to 18 ($\bar{x}$ age 15.6). Sixteen subjects (67%) were black, seven (29%) were Hispanic, and one (4%) was Caucasian. Referral sources included probation (7 subjects or 29%), legal aid (6 subjects or 21%), courts (6 subjects or 21%), division for youth (2 subjects or 8%), and others (3 subjects or 13%).

For 21 of the adolescents (88%), this was the first arrest for a sexual crime, one adolescent (4%) had been arrested on two occasions, and two adolescents (8%) had never been arrested for sexual crimes. Only two of the adolescents (8%) had no prior arrests for nonsexual crimes.

Of the 24 subjects, 23 (96%) had no history of psychiatric hospitalization. Twenty-two (92%) reported no family history of psychiatric hospitalization.

All subjects had engaged in a hands-on nonconsensual sexual activity with another person. TABLE 1 represents a distribution of the victims of the 24 subjects by age and sex of victims. The 24 subjects had victimized a total of 47 victims. The majority of victims were younger than 13 years of age (36 victims).

All subjects were nonpsychotic. All subjects and their parents signed a consent form indicating their willingness to participate in the clinical research project.

Procedure

All subjects underwent a structured clinical interview, which focused on specific demographic characteristics, numbers and types of deviant acts committed, and number of victims. Subjects also completed a battery of paper-and-pencil tests (results will not be reported here) and underwent a psychophysiologic assessment of their sexual interest patterns.

The psychophysiologic assessment evaluated the extent of the subjects' deviant sexual interest patterns. Each subject underwent direct measurement of his erection response while listening to two-minute audiotaped descriptions of paraphilic behavior.

TABLE 1. Distribution of Victims of 24 Adolescent Sex Offenders by Age and Sex of Victims

		Mean No. of Acts	
Age of Victim	Sex of Victim	Self-Report	Referral Source
8 or less	Female (n = 9)	0.56 (0.53)	1.11 (0.33)
	Male (n = 11)	2.36 (2.94)	1.36 (0.92)
9-12	Female (n = 8)	28.75 (78.90)	1.50 (1.41)
	Male (n = 8)	2.63 (0.92)	1.38 (1.06)
13-18	Female (n = 6)	26.50 (37.09)	0.17 (0.41)
	Male (n = 2)	2.00 (1.41)	12.50 (16.26)
Adult	Female (n = 3)	38.33 (53.93)	0.33 (0.58)
	Total (n = 47)		

Each subject was instructed to place a mercury-in-rubber strain gauge (D. M. Davis, Inc.) around his penis. This was done in the privacy of a sound-attenuated room. The audiotaped stimuli involved descriptions of sexual activity between a male adult and either a male or female child victim. They varied along a continuum of violence, from a child initiating a sexual interaction, to a mutually consenting interaction, to progressively more coercive descriptions of sexual interaction with a child, including a physical, nonsexual attack. There were two additional audiotapes describing mutually consenting sexual activity between two adults.

All subjects were given aggression ratings based on the referral source report of how much coercion the victim reported during the commission of the crime. A rating of 0 equals no coercive or aggressive behavior; 1 equals verbally aggressive/coercive behavior; 2, a threat of physical aggression; 3, physically aggressive behavior; 4, threat of a weapon; 5, use of a weapon; and 6 is excessive physical behavior beyond that which is needed to commit the crime.

After evaluation, subjects entered a structured cognitive behavior treatment program that is a modified version of the treatment program described by Abel *et al.*[4] The components of the treatment program are as follows:

Component 1. Each subject underwent eight 30-minute sessions of verbal satiation in the laboratory. Verbal satiation is a therapeutic technique adapted from Marshall's procedure.[13] It teaches the offender how to use deviant thoughts in a repetitive manner to the point of satiating himself with the very stimuli that he may have used to become aroused. There are three differences from Marshall's procedure that we felt were necessary in working with adolescents. First, the subjects did not masturbate during the session. Second, because over 95% of our subjects deny having any deviant fantasy, the therapist provides the subject with a deviant phrase to repeat during the session. The phrase is based on the referral source's report of the nature of the deviant act. Third, while repeating the deviant phrase, the subject is required to look at a slide depicting a deviant target (young girl or boy).

Following the satiations, and for some subjects while they were still in the process of completing the satiations, subjects participated in a group orientation session. During the orientation session, the cotherapists (one male and one female) informed the subjects that during the following sessions they would learn appropriate ways of relating to people, that each subject was there because he had engaged in a sexual behavior that society proscribed, and that he would be taught how not to engage in that behavior in the future.

Component 2. The second treatment component consists of four 75-minute group sessions held weekly. The sessions focus on cognitive restructuring, a procedure that assists the subject in confronting his rationalizations about why it was okay for him to engage in deviant sexual behavior. The majority of sex offenders know that their deviant behavior is contrary to the morals and ethics of our society, yet they give themselves permission to engage in such behavior. These "permission giving statements" are cognitive distortions used by offenders to justify their behaviors.

Subjects are confronted with their cognitive distortions via role playing. Subjects are asked to play the roles of members of the victim's family, the victim, or criminal justice personnel, while the therapist role-plays the individual with cognitive distortions. The patient then has to confront the beliefs presented by the therapist. This process of role reversal is highly effective in helping the sex offender to understand the inappropriateness of his thinking.

Component 3. The third component consists of one 75-minute group session during which the therapist explains covert sensitization, which is utilized to disrupt the behaviors that are antecedent to the offender's actually coming into contact with his victim. The procedure involves having the offender imagine and verbalize on tape the various feelings or experiences that lead him towards committing a deviant sexual act and then immediately bringing to mind very aversive images that reflect the negative consequences of proceeding in that direction. Following the initial group session, subjects are required over the next three weeks to complete eight 15-minute covert sensitization audio tapes at the clinic during the group time.

Component 4. The fourth component consists of four 75-minute sessions of social skills training to help the adolescent learn the requisite skills to relate in a functional manner to peers, and to increase their comfort and skill in interpersonal communication by role playing.

Component 5. The fifth component consists of four 75-minute sessions of anger control training. The majority of subjects use and condone physical aggression as the major form of problem resolution. The subjects are taught alternative means of problem solving through role-playing.

Component 6. The sixth component consisted of sex education and values clarification. Subjects are taught about sexual myths, adolescent sexual development, and appropriate sexual behavior.

Component 7. The seventh component is two 75-minute sessions of relapse prevention, which consist of listing the situations that present risks to them and learning to identify and cope with any urges or deviant thoughts they might experience in the future.

One week following the completion of treatment, subjects undergo a clinical interview, paper-and-pencil testing, and repeat psychophysiologic assessment.

RESULTS

Outcome data is presented separately for those subjects who had engaged in inappropriate sexual behavior with males versus females, because to date research has not looked at diagnostic categories separately.

Male Victims

There were eleven subjects who had been referred to us for inappropriate sexual behavior with males; and of these eleven subjects, four had used verbal coercion or threats, and seven had used physical or excessive physical coercion. FIGURE 1 presents the pre- and posttreatment data. For those four subjects who had used verbal coercion, the mean erection response to the verbal coercion cue was 77% pretreatment and 16.8% posttreatment. For these four subjects, the mean erection response to the physical coercion cue was 73.5% pretreatment and 33.8% posttreatment; to the sadism cue, the pretreatment mean was 53.3% and the posttreatment mean was 31.8%. To a pure assault cue devoid of sexual contact, the pretreatment mean was 37.3% and 3% posttreatment.

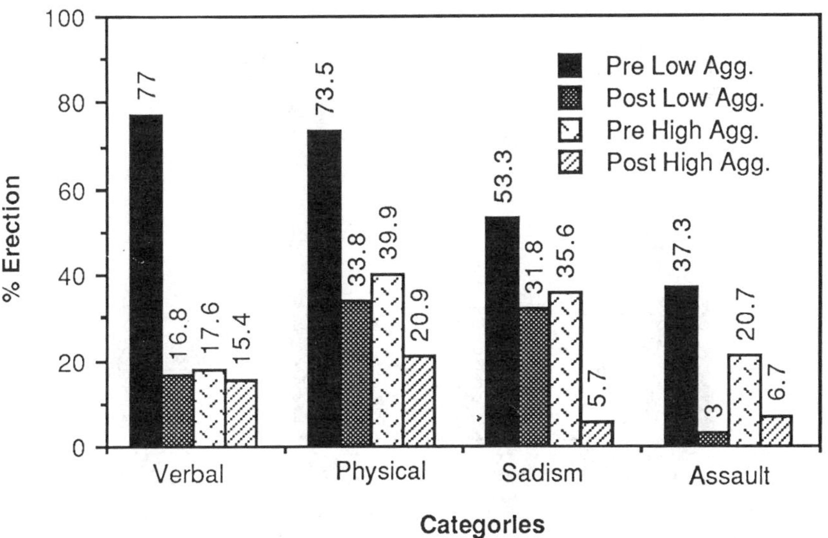

FIGURE 1. Pre- and post-Rx measures: male pedophilic cues.

The seven subjects who had used physical or excessive physical coercion showed less arousal to the verbal aggression cue pretreatment (17.6%) and an erection response of 15.4% posttreatment. Contrary to our expectations, the more physically aggressive group showed less of an erection response pretreatment to the aggressive cues than did the verbally aggressive group: 39.9% to physical coercion, 35.6% to sadism, and 20.7% to assault. However, the physically aggressive group did evidence posttreatment changes in erection measures: 15.4% to verbal coercion, 20.9% to physical coercion, 5.7% to sadism, and 6.7% to assault. For the eleven subjects who had male victims, there was a decrease in arousal posttreatment that was statistically significant at the $p < .01$ level, $F = 9.79$ (1,9), using a repeated measures ANOVA.

Female Victims

There were 13 subjects who had been referred for inappropriate sexual behavior with females (see FIG. 2). One subject had used verbal coercion, and 12 subjects had used physical coercion. For the one subject who had used verbal coercion, his erection response to the verbal cue pretreatment was 42%, compared to 85% posttreatment. To the aggression cue, his pretreatment versus posttreatment erection response was 80% versus 33%; to sadism, 23% versus 95%; and to assault cues, 0% versus 28%. This subject unexpectedly evidenced an increase in erection responses posttreatment.

Changes in erection response did occur in the expected direction for those 12 subjects who had utilized physical or excessive physical coercion against female victims. For the verbal coercion cue, mean erection response went from 30.8% pretreatment to 15.8% posttreatment; for the physical aggression cue, from a mean of 38.1% to 20.2%; and for the sadism cue, from a mean of 40.6% to 24.2%. A small change occurred in erectile measurement to the assault cue: 18.6% pretreatment versus 14.5% posttreatment. However, these decreases in arousal were not statistically significant at the $p < .05$ level.

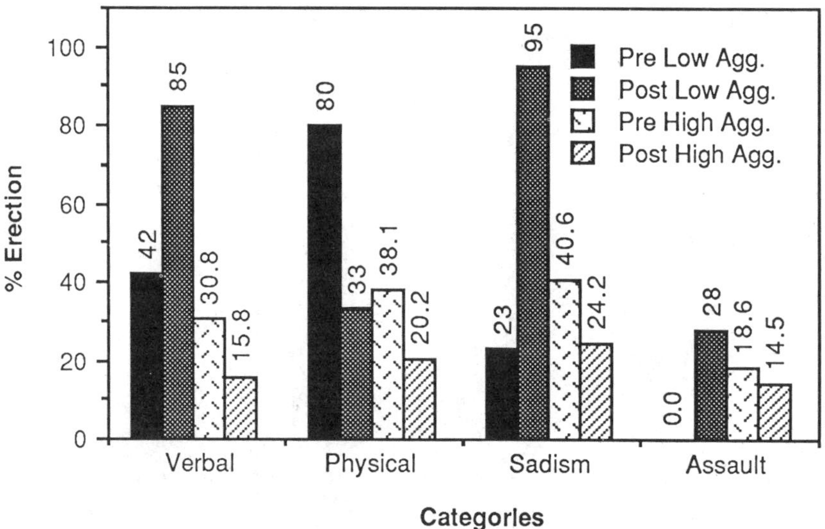

FIGURE 2. Pre- and post-Rx measures: female pedophilic cues.

DISCUSSION

The results of the present study suggest that for the subjects who were involved with male victims the treatment was successful in assisting them to reduce their arousal to deviant sexual stimuli. Although there was evidence that this was also true for those adolescents who had been involved with female victims, it was not demonstrated statistically. Some of the reasons that no significant difference was found in pre- and posttreatment responses with adolescents who engaged in deviant sexual acts with females could be due to the fact that the adolescent is still aroused to female genitalia or the female body, or due to insufficient specificity of the cues. The standard deviations were extremely high, which indicates variability of response.

As noted above, one subject experienced more arousal posttreatment. At a posttreatment follow-up interview, the subject reported that he felt that he was not at risk for reoffending, and he had no deviant fantasies. We felt this subject required further treatment, but attempts to bring the subject in for further follow-up sessions were unsuccessful. Surprisingly, those youngsters who reported utilized only verbal coercion demonstrated a higher erectile response to the physically aggressive cues than did those who utilized physical aggression. There are several possible explanations for this finding. It is possible that the adolescents who used verbal aggression did not find it necessary to escalate to physical aggression because the verbal aggression was sufficient to obtain compliance. Perhaps these adolescents were physically larger, or their victims were weaker. An alternative hypothesis is that the youngsters who used physical aggression attempted to suppress their arousal in the laboratory pretreatment to conceal the extent of their arousal to physical aggression. Another possible explanation is that it is more difficult to change arousal patterns within the same gender.

The results from this study cannot be generalized to other populations, since the adolescents in this study were for the most part inner-city minority youngsters. This population does not reflect all adolescent sexual offenders, since our referrals are from the criminal justice system.

There are problems in psychophysiologic assessment. Studies have found that adult males can voluntarily control erection responses; however, this is an unresolved issue with adolescent males. Reliability and validity also have not been established with an adolescent population. A third problem is stimulus consideration—specifically, the audio stimulus material used in this study. No data exists with a comparison group of normal adolescents.

Variability was also evidenced in individual responses to the deviant stimulus material. Some subjects experienced considerable erectile response to the deviant cues, while others evidenced minimal response. The data presented represented the means of each subject category. Clinical relevance lies in the interpretation of each individual case. This variability may be due to the fact that the adolescent subjects were in various stages of puberty and therefore differed with respect to physical development (penis size), and testosterone level. This was not a controlled study in that subjects were not assigned to a notreatment condition for ethical reasons.

Our study found that a cognitive-behavioral treatment program was effective in reducing inappropriate sexual arousal in adolescent offenders who were involved with male victims. Research on adolescent sex offenders is at a very early stage of development. Future studies need to compare deviant sexual arousal to consensual sexual arousal with appropriate peers. Further controlled therapy outcome research needs to be designed to investigate which forms of therapy are effective for adolescent offenders. Analyses of specific treatment components also need to be conducted.

Psychophysiologic assessment of arousal in the laboratory should not be the only criteria for determining the efficacy of treatment outcome, but should be combined with other measures of treatment outcome, such as ratings of social skills, anger control, and appropriate interactions with peers. Finally, long-term follow-up studies are needed to determine if treatment gains are maintained.

SUMMARY

This paper has described a cognitive-behavioral outpatient treatment program for adolescent sexual offenders. The multicomponent treatment program consists of verbal satiation, cognitive restructuring, covert sensitization, social skills training, anger control training, sex education, and relapse prevention sessions. Data has been presented on 24 adolescents who completed treatment. Results indicated that adolescents involved with male victims significantly decreased deviant sexual arousal pre- and posttreatment, as measured by penile plethysmography. For those adolescents who molested female victims, a decrease in deviant arousal was also evidenced, although it was not statistically significant.

REFERENCES

1. Brown, F. J., T. J. Flanagan & M. McLeod. Eds. 1984. Sourcebook of Criminal Justice Statistics. Washington, D.C.
2. Deisher, R. W., G. A. Wenet, D. M. Paperny, T. Clark & P. Fehrenbach. 1982. Adolescent sexual offense behavior: The role of the physician. J. Adolescent Health Care, **2:** 279-286.
3. Ageton, S. 1983. Sexual Assault among Adolescents. Lexington Books. Lexington, MA.
4. Abel, G. G., J. V. Becker, J. Cunningham-Rathner, J. Rouleau, M. Kaplan & J. Reich. 1984. The Treatment of Child Molesters: A Manual. Unpublished manuscript.
5. Bancroft, J. A., G. Tennet, G. Loveas & J. Cass. 1974. The control of deviant sexual behavior by drugs: Behavioral changes following estrogens and antiandrogens. Br. J. Psychiatry **25:** 310-315.
6. Berlin, F. S. & C. Meinecke. 1981. Treatment of sex offenders with antiandrogenic medication: Conceptualization, review of treatment modalities, and preliminary findings. Am. J. Psychiatry, **138:** 601-607.
7. Giarretto, H., A. Giarretto & S. Sgroi. Coordinated community treatment of incest. *In* Sexual Assault of Children and Adolescents. A. Burgess, A. Groth, L. Holmstrom & S. Sgroi, Eds. Lexington Books. Lexington, MA.
8. Bandura, A. 1973. Aggression: A Social Learning Analysis. Prentice-Hall. Englewood Cliffs, NJ.
9. Abel, G. G., M. Mittelman & J. V. Becker. 1985. Sex offenders: Results of assessment and recommendations for treatment. *In* Clinical Criminology: Current Concepts. H. Ben-Aron, S. Hucker & C. Webster, Eds. M. & M. Graphics. Toronto.
10. Knopp, F. 1982. Remedial Intervention in Adolescent Sex Offenses: Nine Program Descriptions. Safer Society Press. Syracuse, NY.
11. Otey, E. M. & G. D. Ryan. 1985. Adolescent Sex Offenders, Issues in Research and Treatment. U.S. Department of Health and Human Service. Washington, DC.
12. Davis, G. E. & H. Leitenberg. 1987. Adolescent sex offenders. Psychol. Bull. In press.
13. Marshall, W. L. 1979. The modification of sexual fantasies: A combined treatment approach to the reduction of deviant sexual behavior. Behav. Res. Ther. **11:** 557-564.

Predicting Child Molesters' Response to Treatment

GENE G. ABEL,[a,b] MARY MITTELMAN,[c] JUDITH V. BECKER,[d] JERRY RATHNER,[d] AND JOANNE-L. ROULEAU [a]

[a]*Department of Psychiatry*
Emory University School of Medicine
Atlanta, Georgia 30322

[c]*New York University Medical Center*
New York, New York 10016

[d]*Sexual Behavioral Clinic*
New York State Psychiatric Institute
New York, New York 10032

Sex crimes constitute a significant portion of assaults in the United States. Although rape crisis counseling centers have been established throughout the country, little attention has been paid to the perpetrators of these sexual assaults. This appears to be especially problematic, since prevention of sex crimes requires a reduction of these offenses at their source, the perpetrators. Researchers have only recently begun to examine who the paraphiliac is, what crimes he commits, what his treatment needs are, and how to go about providing treatment to meet those needs.[1,2] This study attempts to predict the outcome of treatment for a group of child molesters, all of whom were outpatients who voluntarily participated in a behavioral therapy treatment program[3] to reduce their likelihood of recommitting sexual crimes. The most critical aspects of treating paraphiliacs is to predict which paraphiliacs will stay in treatment once treatment is initiated, and which paraphiliacs will recidivate once they have completed their treatment. By answering these two important questions, we can increase the incentives for staying in treatment for those paraphiliacs unlikely to complete treatment, and we can identify the paraphiliacs who need more extensive supervision or additional treatment, to be certain that recidivism will remain low.

Although clinical lore has suggested various means of predicting treatment outcome for paraphiliacs, no prospective control study has attempted to predict the paraphiliac's response to treatment during or after completion of treatment. A number of potential obstacles have prevented such a study. First, such an outcome study must evaluate a paraphiliac population that has the opportunity to recidivate, that is, an outpatient sex offender population. It is impossible to evaluate treatment effectiveness of an inpatient population, since opportunities for recidivism are exceedingly low or non-existent, and assessment methods must, therefore, rely upon indirect measures of likelihood to recidivate.

[b]Present address: Behavioral Medicine Institute, Paces Pavilion, Suite 202, 3193 Howell Mill Road, NW, Atlanta, Georgia 30327-4101.

Second, studies of recidivism must evaluate a homogeneous group of sex offenders, since there is tremendous variability in the frequency of sex crimes across different diagnostic categories of paraphiliacs.[4] Evaluating heterogeneous groups of sex offenders increases the risk of obtaining spurious results. Third, obtaining a valid measure of recidivism is especially difficult with sex offenders, since they frequently falsify their recidivism rates in order to escape reincarceration. Because paraphiliacs are aware of the possibility of severe consequences should they report their recommission of sex crimes even to a therapist, they are reluctant to report them. Rearrest records of paraphiliacs (and other criminal offenders) are also notoriously invalid as measures of recidivism. Many sex crimes are not reported. Many of those reported, are never pursued to arrest. Of those few where arrests occur, offenders often plea bargain to lesser crimes. As a result the arrest records appear to have limited value in assessing a paraphiliac's response to treatment.

Three aspects of the treatment program these subjects underwent were unique: the extensive steps taken to protect the confidentiality of the molesters' recidivism information; the use of a homogeneous group of paraphiliacs (pedophiles only); and the program's use of an outpatient treatment setting, where recidivism could be evaluated during and after treatment.

The goals of this study are to determine if pedophiles' pretreatment demographic characteristics or the type of child molestations they committed could predict their completing behavioral treatment or their recidivating after treatment had been completed.

METHOD

I. Subjects

The subject population has been extensively described elsewhere.[5] In brief, 192 nonincarcerated pedophiles entered treatment. They were young (average age 34.7 years) and representative of all socioeconomic backgrounds and religions. The racial distribution closely paralleled the racial mix of New York City. In addition they were fairly well educated and were referred to the treatment program by the criminal justice system or by mental health facilities, or they came on their own in response to various media advertisements. None were required by the court to enter the treatment.

II. Structured Clinical Interview

Clinical interviews to determine the subjects' paraphilic interest and behaviors lasted from one to five hours. They specifically targeted the history of deviant behavior, focusing on age of onset of deviant arousal, frequency of types of paraphilic acts, number of victims, use of drugs and alcohol, and use of pornographic material. The subjects' demographic characteristics and individual motivation to enter treatment were also collected.[3] All interviews were conducted by research staff with greater than five years' experience interviewing paraphiliacs.

III. Experimental Design

A multiple baseline design across subjects was used with an A-B sequence within subjects to evaluate the effect on each component of the treatment program on dependent variables. The multiple baseline across subjects also involved different orders, in the sequence of treatment components.

Not all subjects were treated at the same time. For example, Group 1 started with Component 1 followed by Component 2 or 3. Their final component was whichever treatment component they had not received. Group 2 started with Component 2 followed by Component 3 or 1, and Group 3 started with Component 3 followed by Component 1 or 2. The 192 subjects were divided into 19 groups, each receiving the various sequences of the treatment program.

IV. Procedure

The treatment program consisted of thirty 90-minute sessions, given in a group format. Sessions were held weekly. There were ten sessions for each of the three components.[6]

Component 1: Decreasing Deviant Arousal. Five sessions were devoted to teaching the subjects how to control their deviant behavior by pairing thoughts of aversive consequences with thoughts of the chain of events preceding their paraphilic behavior (covert sensitization). Five sessions were devoted to teaching the patients to eliminate their deviant sexual fantasies by satiating themselves with their most erotic paraphilic fantasies (masturbatory satiation).

Component 2: Sex Education / Sex Dysfunction and Cognitive Restructuring. This component consisted of five sessions devoted to increasing the subject's level of sexual knowledge and treating any specific sexual dysfunctions, and five sessions devoted to altering distorted attitudes or beliefs that supported the offender's inappropriate sexual behavior with children.

Component 3: Social and Assertiveness Skills Training. Five sessions were devoted to increasing the subject's social competence with adults and five sessions were devoted to the teaching of appropriate assertive (expression of feelings) skills with adult partners.

Following each of these components of treatment, recidivism was evaluated using the Structured Clinical Interviews described above. Assessment was repeated at 6 and 12 months following treatment.

RESULTS

I. Predicting Dropping Out of Treatment

Of 192 pedophiles entering treatment, 30 dropped out after the first 10 treatment sessions, 27 after the second 10 treatment sessions, and 10 after the third 10 treatment sessions, so that by the end of treatment 67 (34.9%) had dropped out of treatment and 125 (65.1%) had completed the 30 weeks of treatment. Subjects were questioned at the time of dropping out as to why they had left treatment. Of these 50.7% simply refused to continue treatment without a specific reason, 23.9% could not be reached to be questioned, 10.4% had been incarcerated (for crimes committed prior to entering this study), 7.5% were terminated by the investigators because of their disruptive behavior during treatment, 4.5% either became psychotic or their alcoholism became too problematic for them to finish treatment, and 3.0% moved out of state.

A few subjects were so disruptive to the treatment groups that they had to be terminated by the experimenters. Some individuals, for example, with passive-aggressive personalities consistently refused to carry out treatment assignments; some individuals who had been previously arrested with ample evidence of deviant sexual interest yet consistently denied having any deviant interest. One individual with a prior diagnosis of paranoid schizophrenia and marginal adjustment tentatively attempted treatment, but within a few sessions it became apparent that his schizophrenia precluded his participation. Two other patients dropped out because of chronic alcoholism.

Student's *t*-tests were computed in an attempt to identify significant differences between those who dropped out versus those who did not drop out during treatment.

TABLE 1. Pressure on Subjects to Participate in Treatment Program

Amount of Pressure to Participate	Completed Rx		Dropped Rx		Entered Rx	
	n	%	*n*	%	*n*	%
None	64	68.1	30	31.9	94	100.0
Slight	36	69.2	16	30.8	52	100.0
Moderate	17	70.8	7	29.2	24	100.0
Heavy	7	41.2	10	58.8	17	100.0
Extreme	1	20.0	4	80.0	5	100.0
Total	125	65.1	67	34.9	192	100.0

NOTE: Student's $t = -2.3$ ($p < .05$).

A number of factors did not differentiate between the groups, including age, race, Hollingshead social class, marital status, education, employment status, religious preference, and source of referral to the treatment program. Surprisingly, a number of pedophilic behavior characteristics, as reported prior to entering treatment, also failed to discriminate between the groups. The degree of motivation for seeking treatment, identified treatment goals, the frequency of pedophilic acts just prior to entering treatment, the lifetime number of pedophilic acts or victims, and self-reported current ability to control pedophilic urges all failed to discriminate those who would drop out from those who would not.

Only three characteristics significantly differentiated those who would drop out: (1) the amount of pressure the subject was under to participate in treatment, (2) the diagnosis of an antisocial personality, and (3) the lack of discrimination in the choice of sexual victim or paraphilic act.

TABLE 1 shows the self-reported amount of pressure subjects felt they were under to participate in the treatment program. In spite of this being a voluntary program, 17 patients felt under heavy pressure and 5 under extreme pressure to participate.

TABLE 2. Subjects Entering Treatment Program: Age and Gender of Target

	Gender of Target							
	Female Only		Male Only		Male and Female		Total	
Age of Target	*n*	%	*n*	%	*n*	%	*n*	%
Child only	26	13.5	11	5.7	17	10.5	54	28.1
Adolescent only	19	9.9	3	1.6	2	1.0	24	12.5
Child and adolescent	30	15.6	16	8.3	68	35.4	114	59.4
Total	75	39.1	30	15.6	87	45.3	192	100.0

Ten and 4 of these respective groups dropped out of treatment,which was significant at the $p < .05$ level.

Nineteen of the 192 subjects entering treatment had a diagnosis of antisocial personality; 10 of these dropped out during treatment (and an additional 5 during follow-up), which was significant at the $p < .01$ level.

A large portion (69.2%) of subjects entering treatment had histories indicating they had committed acts against more than one age category (victims less than 14 years of age or victims 14 to 17 years of age) or gender category (females versus males). Sixty-eight subjects (35.4%) had targets in both categories and both gender categories (see TABLE 2).

Surprisingly, the number of categories of age and gender of pedophilic targets prior to treatment predicted dropping out of treatment. All 30 offenders who dropped out during the first 10 weeks of treatment had committed acts against both males and females and against both children and adolescent victims. More than half of the subjects who dropped out before the end of the 30-week treatment showed this same multiplicity of diagnoses, which was significant at the $p < .0001$ level (see TABLE 3).

Subjects could also be grouped according to whether they had committed actual "hands-on" assaults of children or whether their sex crime had been "hands-off" such as, exhibitionism or voyeurism. Here again, those whose child molestation involved only the hands-on offense or a hands-off offense had low levels of dropping

TABLE 3. Subjects Who Dropped Out of Treatment Program: Age and Gender of Target

	Gender of Target							
	Female Only		Male Only		Male and Female		Total	
Age of Target	*n*	%	*n*	%	*n*	%	*n*	%
Child only	3	4.5	5	7.5	6	9.0	14	20.9
Adolescent only	6	9.0	1	1.5	1	1.5	8	11.9
Child and adolescent	3	4.5	3	4.5	39	58.2	45	67.2
Total	12	17.9	9	13.4	46	68.7	67	100.0

NOTE: $\chi^2 = 32.2$, df $= 8$, $p < .0001$.

TABLE 4. Predicting Dropping Out of Treatment Program: Type of Behavior

	Type of Behavior							
	Hands-On Only		Hands-Off Only		Hands-On and Hands-Off		Total	
Stay or Drop	*n*	%	*n*	%	*n*	%	*n*	%
Stayed in Rx	95	76.0	6	85.7	24	40.0	125	65.1
Dropped Rx	30	24.0	1	14.3	36	60.0	67	34.9
Total	125	100.0	7	100.0	60	100.0	192	100.0

NOTE: $\chi^2 = 24.5$, df = 2, $p < .0001$.

out of treatment, whereas those subjects who committed both hands-on and hands-off molestations had a much higher drop out rate ($p < .0001$) (see TABLE 4).

After combining these various characteristics, it was found that 88.9% of subjects who dropped out of treatment had committed acts both against males and females, against both children and adolescents, and in both hands-on and hands-off categories of child molestation. These findings were significant at the $p < .0001$ level.

The characteristic of the relationship of the offender to his victim also significantly predicted dropping out of treatment. No pedophile who had committed only incest dropped out of treatment, 29.1% of those committing only nonincestuous pedophilia dropped out, while 60.0% of individuals committing both incestuous and nonincestuous pedophilia dropped out of treatment, which is significant at the $p < .0001$ level (see TABLE 5).

When age and gender of target was combined with both incestuous and nonincestuous offenses, 88.1% of those offenders who had both male and female and child and adolescent targets and who also committed incestuous and nonincestuous acts dropped out, which was significant at the $p < .0001$ level.

Combining all the multiplicities of target characteristics, it was found that 35 subjects had committed pedophilic acts against males and females, children and adolescents, and incest and nonincest victims, using hands-on and hands-off molestation. Almost all of them (32 subjects, or 91.4%) dropped out of the treatment program. Of the 157 subjects who did not report such multiplicity of behaviors before treatment, only 22.3% dropped out of the treatment program.

TABLE 5. Predicting Dropping Out of Treatment Program: Relationship of Subject to Target

	Relationship of Subject to Target							
	Incest Only		Nonincest Only		Incest and Nonincest		Total	
Stay or Drop	*n*	%	*n*	%	*n*	%	*n*	%
Stayed in Rx	21	100.0	61	70.9	43	50.6	125	65.1
Dropped Rx	0	0.0	25	29.1	42	60.0	67	34.9
Total	21	100.0	86	100.0	85	100.0	192	100.0

NOTE: $\chi^2 = 20.8$, df = 2, $p < .0001$.

A discriminant function analysis was performed to estimate the extent to which staying in treatment and dropping out of treatment could be predicted on a linear combination of variables found to be significantly different in the two groups. The variables that significantly discriminated staying in from dropping out of treatment were, in order of statistical importance: (1) committing both hands-on and hands-off pedophilia, (2) committing pedophilic acts against both males and females and both children and adolescents, (3) committing pedophilic acts against both incest and nonincest victims, (4) being under more pressure to enter treatment, and (5) having an antisocial personality diagnosis. Such a discriminant function analysis could correctly classify 72.4% of subjects entering treatment as to whether they would drop out of treatment based upon pretreatment characteristics.

Discussion

It was not surprising that subjects who felt they were under considerable pressure to enter treatment were more likely to drop out of treatment, especially when they realized that participation was truly voluntary and that no consequences would result should they drop out. It should also not be surprising that individuals with antisocial personality are more likely to drop out of treatment, since a characteristic frequently seen in such personalities is manipulativeness of others to get what they want. In this situation, admission to a treatment program was probably helpful to them at the moment; and as soon as they had satisfied someone by their entrance into treatment, they quickly terminated the treatment program.

More interesting was the finding that multiplicity of targets of child molestation was so significant at differentiating drop outs. A possible interpretation of the latter finding is that pedophiles who lack discrimination as to the characteristics of their behavior (molesting boys and girls, young children and adolescents, family members and nonfamily members, and with touching and nontouching of the victim) have developed a number of rationalizations to explain all of their various paraphilic behaviors and are therefore better able to justify their continued molesting and drop treatment. By contrast, when a molester has limited the characteristics of who or how he will molest, it may mean that he has set limits on his behavior with children. As such he accepts that there are some behaviors with some children that are inappropriate and he is therefore more likely to remain in treatment to learn control over his molesting behavior.

II. Predicting Recidivism within the First Year after Treatment

Twelve of the 98 subjects who were evaluated one year after the end of treatment had recidivated. Marital status was the only demographic characteristic that differentiated between subjects who had committed pedophilic acts within one year after treatment and those who did not. Those who were married or separated but not divorced were less likely to recidivate, while those who were divorced or single were more likely to recidivate.

The characteristics that did not differentiate recidivist from nonrecidivist included age, race, Hollingshead social class, education, employment status, religious preference, motivation for seeking treatment, frequency of pedophilic acts before entering treatment, lifetime number of molestations or sexual victims, and reported self-control over pedophilic behavior before entering treatment.

Those who recidivated were less likely to endorse the goals of the behavioral treatment program, which include decreasing pedophilic behavior, increasing sexual arousal to adults, learning to assert oneself, increasing communication skills with adults, and making one's behavior more socially acceptable. Goals that did not discriminate the two groups significantly were the objectives of decreasing the risk of rearrest, gaining control over pedophilic arousal, increasing sexual knowledge, decreasing cognitive misbeliefs about pedophilia, obtaining a lifelong plan for controlling pedophilic arousal, and improving relationships with one's family.

A final area that differentiated between recidivists and nonrecidivists was that recidivists were more likely to have more varied pedophilic behavior and targets than nonrecidivists. Nine of the 12 subjects who committed pedophilic acts after treatment had reported that prior to treatment they had committed acts against both males and females, and both children under 14 and adolescents 14 to 17 years of age. Two of the remaining three subjects who reported recidivism had committed crimes in either two age categories or two gender categories. As indicated in TABLE 6, the multiplicity of child and adolescent, and male and female victims was significant at the $p < .01$ level at predicting recidivism.

Examining whether pretreatment pedophilic behaviors involved hands-on, hands-off, or a combination of both categories of molestation revealed that those offenders committing both hands-on and hands-off behavior had significantly higher recidivism than those who did not ($p < .01$). When the multiplicity of age categories, gender categories, and hands-on versus hands-off categories of pedophilic behavior were combined, the combination proved to be a very significant predictor of recidivism, with $p < .0001$ (see TABLE 7).

Although pedophilic behavior involving incestuous and nonincestuous acts predicted dropouts from treatment, it was not significant at predicting recidivism during the one year following treatment.

A discriminant function analysis to ascertain the extent to which recidivism could be predicted with information obtained before treatment revealed a number of variables that significantly discriminated those who recommitted pedophilic acts after treatment from those who did not. In order of decreasing statistical importance, these were (1) committing pedophilic acts against both males and females, and both children and adolescents (a dichotomous variable), (2) failure to list as a treatment goal increasing communication with adults, (3) committing both hands-on and hands-off pedophilic acts (a dichotomous variable), (4) being divorced (a dichotomous variable), and (5) committing pedophilic acts against both incest and nonincest victims (a dichotomous variable). Having committed pedophilic acts against both males and females, and both children and adolescents was exceedingly effective on its own at predicting recidivism. This one variable predicted 9 of the 12 recidivists as well as 73 of the 86 subjects who were not recidivists, correctly classifying 83.7% of all subjects. All five variables together were only slightly more effective, correctly classifying 85.7% of subjects (see TABLE 8).

Discussion

It is impossible, given the design of this study, to explain why endorsing the various treatment goals, being married or separated, and not having multiple pedophilic

TABLE 6. Pedophiles Who Recidivated within One Year after Treatment by Age and Gender of Target before Treatment

Age of Target	Gender of Target: Female Only		Male Only		Male and Female		Total	
Child only (%)[a]	19	(19.4)	5	(5.1)	10	(10.2)	34	(34.7)
Recidivated (%)[b]	1	(8.3)	0	(0.0)	1	(8.3)	2	(16.7)
Adolescent only (%)[a]	10	(10.2)	1	(1.0)	1	(1.0)	12	(12.2)
Recidivated (%)[b]	0	(0.0)	0	(0.0)	0	(0.0)	0	(0.0)
Child and adolescent (%)[a]	18	(18.4)	12	(12.2)	22	(22.4)	52	(53.1)
Recidivated (%)[b]	0	(0.0)	1	(8.3)	9	(75.0)	10	(83.3)
Total (%)[a]	47	(48.0)	18	(18.4)	33	(33.7)	98	(100.0)
Recidivated (%)[b]	1	(8.3)	1	(8.3)	10	(83.3)	12	(100.0)

NOTE: $\chi^2 = 22.9$, df = 8, $p < .01$.

[a] Percentage of total number of pedophiles evaluated one year after end of treatment (98).

[b] Percentage of total number of pedophiles who recidivated (12).

TABLE 7. Predicting Recidivism in 12 Months after Treatment: Age and Gender of Target and Type of Behavior

	Age and Gender of Target and Type of Behavior					
	Male and Female Child and Adolescent Hands-On and Hands-Off		Other Combinations of Age and Gender of Target and Type of Behavior		Total	
Recidivism	*n*	%	*n*	%	*n*	%
No	3	37.5	83	92.2	86	87.8
Yes	5	62.5	7	7.8	12	12.2
Total	8	100.0	90	100.0	98	100.0

NOTE: $\chi^2 = 15.7$, df = 1, $p < .0001$.

behaviors or targets led to subjects' having low recidivism rates. A number of obvious interpretations, however, are possible.

Being married indicates a greater possibility that the pedophile not only was attracted to young children, but also to adult sexual partners. This might have made treatment to eliminate attraction to young children more feasible, since an alternate means of expressing one's sexual feelings already existed. Another possibility is that a married or separated individual is more likely to be surrounded by significant others who encourage the molester to be successful in treatment, by reinforcing societal standards of not being sexually involved with children, by supporting the idea of staying in treatment for one's deviant behaviors, and possibly by supporting the molester's treatment reports of socially acceptable behaviors such as "I have not been involved with children since treatment began."

Recidivism was low in subjects endorsing the treatment goals of the therapy program prior to entering treatment. The treatment goals that predicted no recidivism were those stressing the importance of eliminating attraction to children, while maintaining or increasing attraction and involvement with adults. These goals suggest that being involved with sexual partners other than children was a high priority and, therefore, that subjects with such goals were more likely to give up involvement with children. These goals were a major focus of the treatment. If treatment was effective, its goals were likely to be reached, with a good fit between what subjects wanted and what they achieved.

TABLE 8. Classification Results: Discriminant Function Analysis of Prediction of Recidivism in Year after Treatment

		Predicted Group Membership			
		No Recidivism		Recidivism	
Actual Group	Number of Cases	*n*	%	*n*	%
No recidivism	86	74	86.0	12	14.0
Recidivism	12	2	16.7	10	83.3

The most intriguing question is why subjects with multiple pedophilic behaviors or targets were more likely to recidivate. One interpretation is that since all subjects received the same amount of therapy time to decrease any deviant arousal, those with a greater variety of arousal patterns to decrease got less treatment devoted to each category of arousal, so treatment was less effective. Another, more plausible, explanation might be that subjects with multiple paraphilic behaviors or targets are qualitatively different from those with fewer behaviors or targets, because the former have a more serious "dose" of paraphilic interests and behaviors. In that respect, they have a more serious problem than paraphiliacs with only limited deviant behavior. Further support is given to the latter interpretation by the prior finding that a multiplicity of paraphilic behaviors and targets predicted dropping out of treatment.

Irrespective of the interpretation of why child molesters with multiple pedophilic behaviors or targets are more likely to recommit molestation, these results indicate that whom the child molester is attracted to and the category of child molestation he participates in are significant at predicting recidivism. Proper categorization of these characteristics is therefore important in predicting recidivism. Unfortunately, our current system of categorization fails to include a categorization system as detailed as that which accurately predicts recidivism. Although the molester's gender preference is incorporated in the DSM-3 diagnoses,[7] targeting children under 14 or adolescents 14 to 17, participating in hands-on versus hands-off child molestation behavior, and molesting victims within the family and/or outside the family are not categories of child molestation currently differentiated.[8] However, since predicting recidivism is exceedingly important in the clinical management of the child molester, this more refined classification is indicated.

A problem of obtaining such information is that our current laws makes it nearly impossible for the molester to reveal such information truthfully, since such revelations could lead to the therapist's reporting the criminal behavior and subsequent criminal charges. This conflict between the reporting laws and obtaining important information needs resolution.

Predicting who will drop out of treatment will better help the clinician organize a treatment more palatable to those likely to drop out. Predicting those who recidivate will also help the clinician identify those pedophiles who need closer supervision, more extensive treatment, and/or more thorough evaluation for other problems needing treatment beyond those provided in this behavioral treatment package. The goal of treatment programs for pedophiles is to prevent child molestation at its source, the perpetrator. The better we understand the perpetrator, his treatment, and his response to treatment, the more effective we will be in our ultimate goal of preventing child molestation.

REFERENCES

1. ABEL, G. G. & J.-L. ROULEAU. 1987. Outpatient treatment of sex offenders. *In* Handbook of Outpatient Treatment of Adults. M. E. Thase, B. A. Edelstein & M. Hersen, Eds. Plenum. New York, NY.
2. QUINSEY, V. L. 1977. The assessment and treatment of child molesters: A review. Can. Psychol. Rev. **18:** 204.
3. ABEL, G. G. 1986. The Treatment of Child Molesters. Final Report. Grant RO1MH36347. National Institute of Mental Health. Rockville, MD.
4. ABEL, G. G., J. V. BECKER, J. CUNNINGHAM-RATHNER, M. S. MITTELMAN & J.-L. ROULEAU. 1987. Multiple paraphilic diagnoses among sex offenders. Submitted for publication.

5. Abel, G. G., J. V. Becker, M. S. Mittelman, J. Cunningham-Rathner, J.-L. Rouleau & W. L. Murphy. 1987. Self-reported sex crimes of non-incarcerated paraphiliacs. J. Interpers. Violence **2:** 3.
6. Abel, G. G., J. V. Becker, J. Cunningham-Rathner, J.-L. Rouleau, M. Kaplan & J. Reich. 1984. Treatment of Child Molesters. Department of Psychiatry, Emory University School of Medicine. Atlanta, GA.
7. American Psychiatric Association. 1980. Diagnostic and Statistical Manual of Mental Disorders. 3rd ed. American Psychiatric Association. Washington, DC.
8. Abel, G. G. 1987. Paraphilias. *In* The Comprehensive Textbook of Psychiatry. 5th ed. H. I. Kapler & B. S. Sadock, Eds. Williams & Wilkins Publishers. Baltimore, MD.

The Sex Offender Treatment and Evaluation Project: California's New Outcome Study

JANICE K. MARQUES

California State Department of Mental Health
Sacramento, California 95814

In 1981, the California State Legislature passed a law that repealed existing statues providing for the commitment of mentally disordered sex offenders to state hospitals and required that sex offenders be delivered to the Department of Corrections after sentencing.[1] Although this legislation eliminated the option of direct commitment to state hospitals, it did allow for the voluntary transfer of certain sex offenders to the Department of Mental Health for inpatient treatment during the last two years of their prison terms. The state hospital program for these offenders was to be "established according to a valid experimental design in order that the most effective, newest and promising methods of treatment of sex offenders may be rigorously tested." Subsequent legislation limited the experimental program to 50 beds and required that formal reports on treatment outcomes be submitted biennially to the Legislature until the termination of the program in 1991.[2] In 1985, the Department of Mental Health initiated the Sex Offender Treatment and Evaluation Project, a six-year clinical research program designed to meet the two goals specified in the legislative mandate: (a) the development and operation of a small, innovative treatment unit for sex offenders; and (b) the rigorous evaluation of the effectiveness of the treatments provided in the experimental program. In this paper, the Project's design, treatment model, and evaluation methods will be presented, and the results of the first 18 months of operation will be described.

PROJECT DESCRIPTION

In order to achieve the two goals of the Project, the operation of an innovative treatment unit and the evaluation of its effectiveness, two separate but interrelated projects are conducted under the direction of a Project Director in Sacramento. The Treatment Project is housed on a 46-bed treatment unit at Atascadero State Hospital, the Department of Mental Health's most secure treatment facility. The treatment staff includes a Treatment Director; one psychiatrist; three clinical psychologists; three clinical social workers; six social work associates; two rehabilitation therapists; and 28 nursing personnel, most of whom are psychiatric technicians. This team is responsible for the assessment and treatment of Project participants during their inpatient stay. The Evaluation Project is located in the Department's central office in Sacramento and is staffed by research professionals and assistants who are responsible for the screening and selection of participants and for measuring program fidelity and treatment outcomes.

Design

The treatment program's effectiveness will be measured by comparing the postrelease activities of three matched groups of subjects:

1. *Treatment Group.* An experimental group consisting of sex offenders who have volunteered to participate and are randomly selected for the Treatment Project at Atascadero State Hospital.
2. *Volunteer Control Group.* A group of sex offenders in prison who volunteer but are not randomly selected for treatment (a control for the factor of voluntarism). These offenders are matched to the Treatment Group members on the basis of type of offense, criminal history, and age.
3. *Nonvolunteer Control Group.* A second control group of prisoners who are matched with the other groups on the basis of type of offense, criminal history, and age, but who do not volunteer for treatment.

Subjects

The study participants are male inmates from the California Department of Corrections who have been convicted of one or more violations of Penal Code sections pertaining to rape and child molestation. Inmates who have offended only in concert (e.g., gang rape) or only against consanguine victims (incest) are not included. The study is also limited to those who: (a) are between 18 and 30 months of their release from incarceration; (b) are between 18 and 60 years of age; (c) have no more than two prior felony convictions; (d) acknowledge commission of the offense(s) for which they are incarcerated; (e) have an IQ of over 80; (f) can speak English; (g) do not have a psychotic or organic mental condition; and (h) are not so medically debilitated as to require skilled nursing care.

Since the hospital program is designed to treat offenders for approximately two years and is required by statute to end in 1991, it is anticipated that three groups (a total of about 130 subjects) will be treated during the six-year life of the Project.

Procedure

Participants are involved in four phases of the Project: (a) subject selection; (b) treatment; (c) aftercare; and (d) follow-up.

Subject Selection Phase

Selection of participants begins with the identification and screening of subjects in the Department of Corrections. Project staff visit the 11 institutions that house sex offenders and review the prison records of potential subjects to determine which inmates meet the Project's eligibility criteria. Screened inmates are then scheduled for an interview session, in which the Project is explained in detail and the informed consent of volunteers is obtained. A brief mental status interview is also conducted by a licensed clinician at this time, in order to detect any undocumented organic, psychotic, or other disqualifying conditions present in the volunteers.

After inmate screening is completed, Evaluation Project staff match pairs of candidates within the volunteer pool on the variables of: (a) age of subject; (b) type of offense(s) committed; and (c) criminal history (number of prior felony convictions). Assignment of one member of each pair to the Treatment Group and one member to the Volunteer Control Group is then made on a purely random basis. Finally, members of the third group, the Nonvolunteer Control Group, are selected from a matched group of inmates who learned of the Project but did not elect to participate.

Treatment Phase

During this phase, members of the Treatment Group participate in an intensive treatment program at Atascadero State Hospital for approximately two years (a range of 18 to 30 months). The theoretical orientation of the experimental program is Relapse Prevention (RP), an innovative self-control approach recently developed in the field of addictive behaviors[3] and adapted for use with sex offenders.[4–6] RP is a multimodal and prescriptive approach specifically designed to help clients maintain behavioral changes by anticipating and coping with the problem of relapse. As applied with Project participants, RP provides a framework within which a variety of behavioral, cognitive, educational, and skill-training approaches are prescribed in order to teach the sex offenders how to recognize and interrupt the chain of events leading to relapse, or reoffense. The focus of both assessment and treatment procedures is on the specification and modification of the steps in this chain, from broad characterological factors and cognitive distortions to more circumscribed skill deficits and deviant sexual arousal patterns.

The hospital program begins with a two-month orientation and assessment period, in which the offender is assisted in making the transition from prison to hospital, and completes an extensive battery of pretreatment measures. The assessment techniques include standardized tests, structured exercises, and direct behavioral measures designed to accomplish three tasks:

1. Analysis of High-Risk Situations. The core of the RP assessment process is the identification of the circumstances that threaten the offender's sense of self-control and increase the probability of relapse. Assessment techniques used to identify high-risk situations include self-monitoring (of fantasies, urges, or other precursors), guided relapse fantasies (in which the offender imagines and describes future situations that could provoke relapse), and structured exercises designed to analyze the chain of events that preceded prior offenses. The analysis of offense chains is a tedious and time-consuming process that begins with the offender starting at the crime and moving back in time, identifying each significant step preceding the offense. This is first done for events and behaviors, then the affective components and cognitive steps (decisions and interpretations) are added. Each step is also evaluated to determine its relative importance in moving the offender toward the commission of an offense. Although this process is considered here as an assessment technique, it should be emphasized that the construction, analysis, and revision of the cognitive-behavioral chain leading to relapse is an ongoing process that continues throughout the RP program.

2. Assessment of Coping Skills. Since a given situation is "high risk" only to the extent that the offender has difficulty coping with it, several assessment procedures are used to determine the areas of strength and weakness in his coping abilities. Again, the analysis of the sequence of events preceding past or fantasized relapses is a primary source of information, since coping failures are integral parts of these offense chains. The subject's coping repertoire is also assessed by self-efficacy ratings, a procedure in which the offender is presented with a list of common high-risk situations and is asked to rate each according to how difficult it would be to cope with the situation without offending, or moving closer to an offense. Finally, Project staff are developing a behavioral assessment tool based on the Situational Competency Test from the field of alcoholism.[7] In this procedure, the offender responds in a role-playing format to descriptions of common problem situations.

3. Identifying Specific Determinants and Early Antecedents. The comprehensive assessment of sex offenders requires that the relative importance of various common determinants of sexual deviance be determined. First, each Treatment Group member receives a thorough psychophysiological assessment of his sexual arousal patterns in the Project's sexual behavior laboratory. In this procedure, a variety of deviant and nondeviant stimuli (slides, audiotapes, and videotapes) are used to identify the offender's sexual arousal profile and to measure his ability to exert self-control over his sexual responses. These behavioral data, supplemented by self-report measures such as the Multiphasic Sex Inventory,[8] assess the role of deviant sexual arousal and interests in the subject's offense chain.

Other common determinants are addressed in the intake assessment battery by measures of sexual knowledge and attitudes, hostility, social skills, attitudes toward women, and cognitive distortions. Finally, the role of more general characterological and life-style factors is determined by a variety of standard psychological inventories, offender autobiographies, and measures of empathy, self-esteem, and locus of control.

Based on the assessment results, a structured program is prescribed specifically to address the offender's identified precursors of relapse. The primary treatment structure is the Core Relapse Prevention Group, which is led by a pair of therapists (psychiatric technician and either psychologist, psychiatrist, or social worker), and meets for an hour each weekday throughout the program. The highly structured group is the setting in which the cognitive-behavioral offense chains are constructed and used to integrate other program components into a system specifically designed to enhance control and prevent relapse for each individual offender. The goals of the Core RP Group are to have the participant: (a) recognize the decisions and conditions that place him at risk for reoffending; (b) avoid or effectively cope with these high-risk situations; (c) restructure his interpretation of "urges"; (d) reduce the likelihood that a "lapse" (e.g., return to deviant fantasies) will result in a full-blown relapse (reoffense); and (e) learn that the prevention of relapse is an ongoing process in which he must take an active and vigilant role.

In addition to this intensive RP training, Treatment Group subjects participate in a wide range of other treatment activities designed to modify various determinants of sexual offending. All offenders are required to attend and complete pre- and posttreatment measures for the following groups: Sex Education, Human Sexuality, Relaxation Training, Social Skills, Stress Inoculation, and Lifestyle Modification. A prerelease class designed to prepare the offender for "life on the streets" is also mandatory for participants. Other groups are provided by the Project on a prescriptive basis, and include: Substance Abuse, Depression Management, Anxiety Management, Anger Management, Cognitive Restructuring, Victimization (for offenders who have also been victims), Assertiveness Training, and Covert Conditioning. Appropriate pre and post measures are administered for each of these specialty groups.

In addition to these group activities, each participant has three hours of individual counseling, six hours of structured leisure activities, and four hours of rehabilitation therapy each week. Individual behavior therapy sessions in the sexual behavior laboratory are also conducted on a prescriptive basis for offenders evidencing deviant sexual arousal patterns. The most frequently used interventions in the lab are orgasmic reconditioning and olfactory aversion.

Since control subjects are in correctional settings that allow them to reduce their sentences by earning work credits, similar work opportunities, credits, and compensation are provided for Treatment Group participants. In all, most participants have a 30-hour work assignment and approximately 24 hours of program activities per week.

The primary evaluation Project tasks during the Treatment Phase involve the measurement of treatment process and in-treatment changes. Treatment process is monitored by self-report and direct observation, and assessment measures focus on whether the Core RP Group members are indeed identifying offense chains and learning to use basic RP interventions. In-treatment changes are measured globally by readministration of the pretreatment assessment battery described above, and by pretreatment to posttreatment changes in variables relevant to speciality groups (e.g., Situational Competency Test scores before and after the Substance Abuse Group) or individual treatment components (e.g., sexual arousal patterns before and after orgasmic reconditioning). In addition to allowing evaluators to measure in-treatment changes and determine the outcomes of various interventions, these assessment data will help identify the major predictors of community success and recidivism among treated subjects. Exiting Treatment Group members, including drop-outs, also complete a comprehensive exit interview and an anonymous program evaluation instrument designed to measure the relevance and impact of the Treatment Project. Finally, these subjects are trained in the randomized response procedure,[9] which will be used to supplement official records of recidivism during the Project's aftercare period. Randomized responding is a statistically-based technique designed to ascertain group differences while protecting the identity of individual subjects.

Volunteer Control Group members receive no treatment services from the project during the Treatment Phase, but are interviewed by Evaluation Project staff just before their release from prison. These individuals are paid to participate in a 90-minute session, which includes: (a) a description of their postrelease situations, including work, housing, social supports, and plans (if any) for treatment; (b) self-report measures of their deviant sexual interests and the cognitive distortions that facilitate offending; (c) self-efficacy ratings for a number of common high-risk situations; and (d) estimates regarding the intensity of their past illegal activities. Training in the randomized response procedure is also provided during this session.

Members of the Nonvolunteer Control Group, since they did not consent to be a part of the Project, do not participate in any assessment or treatment activities during the Treatment Phase.

Aftercare Phase

California sex offenders are routinely placed on parole for a period of at least one year following their release from incarceration. For Treatment Group members, attending two sessions a week in the Sex Offender Aftercare Program (SOAP) is a condition of parole for the first year. SOAP services are contracted, and may be provided by a state aftercare program, a county mental health center, or a private clinician, depending on the specific clinical and geographical needs of the offender. Aftercare clinicians are individually trained by Project staff to provide an extended version of the RP program that is tailored to meet the needs of the paroled offender. Sessions focus on "boosting" treatment effects; that is, enhancing the participant's understanding of RP concepts, practicing the skills learned in the program, and testing nondeviant lifestyles. Most SOAP sessions are individual; however, providers with ongoing groups may have Project participants for one group and one individual session per week. Depending on the treatment needs of the offender, aftercare may also include family interventions, drug testing, and/or follow-up laboratory sessions in which deviant sexual arousal is monitored and treated. All SOAP services are provided at no cost to the subject.

Project staff receive quarterly reports from aftercare providers, and are obligated to notify the Department of Corrections in the event of treatment failure, significant parole violation, or evidence of reoffense. Members of the two control groups are also on parole during this period, and may be revoked (i.e., returned to custody) if parole conditions are violated.

At the end of the one-year aftercare period, Treatment and Volunteer Control Group members will participate in structured interviews conducted by Evaluation Project staff. Again, Volunteer Controls will be paid for their participation. The interview protocol has not been developed at this time, but will focus on the same topics as the prerelease session described above; that is, descriptions of the offender's life situation, deviant sexual interests, and perceptions of self-efficacy. Also in this session, specific questions about whether the subject has reoffended during the aftercare period will be asked, using the randomized response procedure.

Follow-up Phase

This phase overlaps the Aftercare Phase, and lasts for five years following the release from incarceration of all study participants (Treatment, Volunteer Control, and Nonvolunteer Control group members). In this period, information will be gathered on a periodic basis from the Department of Justice concerning contacts between participants and the criminal justice system. When documented contacts do occur, local criminal justice agencies will be asked to provide data on the nature and context of the offense, victim characteristics, and other pertinent variables.

PROGRESS AND INITIAL FINDINGS

Results of Subject Selection

Since the Project began in 1985, information on the sex offender population in Corrections has been reviewed on a quarterly basis, and staff have visited all 11 institutions housing potential participants. The number of incarcerated sex offenders during the Project period has averaged 4800 inmates, but most of these men failed to meet the eligibility criteria listed earlier. The most common reason for ineligibility was that the offender's remaining sentence exceeded 30 months. The next most common reason for disqualification was a remaining sentence of less than 18 months, followed by: low IQ (below dull normal), incest offense only, denial of offense, psychosis, pending warrants or holds, severe medical conditions, inability to speak English, three or more prior felony convictions, offense committed in concert, age over 60, and organicity.

In order to describe the eligible offender pool and the differences between volunteers and nonvolunteers, data from the prison records of 106 volunteers and a sample of 135 nonvolunteers were analyzed. As classified by instant offense, this pool of eligibles consisted of 80 rapists (33%), 102 heterosexual child molesters (43%) and 59 homosexual child molesters (24%). A comparison of the demographic characteristics and criminal histories of these three offense groups revealed only the following significant differences: (a) rapists were younger, more violent, and ethnically more diverse (i.e., nonwhite) than the other groups, and were most likely to victimize strangers; (b) heterosexual child molesters were most likely to offend against stepchildren; and (c) homosexual child molesters had higher IQs and more prior sex offense convictions than the other two groups.

Comparisons made between the volunteers and nonvolunteers also revealed few significant differences. No evidence was found, for example, that volunteering for the Project was related to ethnicity, education, employment status, number of prior felony convictions, number of prior arrests and convictions for sex offenses, prior treatment in a program for sex offenders, or marital status, although there was a tendency for married offenders to volunteer less frequently than unmarried men. A clearly significant finding was that rapists and offenders over 40 were less likely to volunteer for the Project. Offenders with below-average IQs were also overrepresented in the nonvolunteer sample, but the overall mean and median intelligence estimates did not differ between the two groups. The only offenders overrepresented in the volunteer group were homosexual child molesters, particularly those with prior felony convictions.

Characteristics of the First Treatment Group

In its first 18 months of operation, the Treatment Project admitted 53 participants, 40 of whom were child molesters and 13 of whom were rapists. Seven participants (5 molesters and 2 rapists) dropped out of the program during this time, and two (1 molester and 1 rapist) were involuntarily returned to the Department of Corrections, because they created severe management problems during their hospital stays. The demographic and clinical characteristics of the 44 offenders who have remained in the program will be described in this section.

The Treatment Group includes 20 heterosexual child molesters, 14 homosexual child molesters, and 10 rapists. Of the child molesters, 85% are Caucasian, 6% are Black, 6% are Hispanic, and 3% are other minorities. Among rapists, however, only 50% are Caucasian, with Blacks (30%) and Hispanics (20%) making up the other half. The oldest group is the heterosexual molesters (average age 37.6), and the youngest is the rapist group (average age 30.2), with the homosexual molesters in between with an average age of 35.5. The modal marital status of the homosexual molesters and rapists is single (50% and 60% respectively), while 80% of the heterosexual molesters are divorced or separated. Over three-quarters of the offenders have high school degrees, and a majority were employed at the time of arrest.

Although several Treatment Group members have no criminal histories, half of the heterosexual molesters and two-thirds of the rapists and homosexual molesters have at least one prior felony conviction. When only prior sex crimes are considered, the homosexual offenders have the most extensive histories, with 64% having a prior arrest for a sex offense. In contrast, only 40% of the rapists have been previously arrested for a sex crime.

Psychophysiological data collected in the pretreatment assessment period indicated that 59% of the group had a pattern of deviant sexual arousal when they started the program. Nineteen percent were not responsive in the laboratory setting, and 22% showed a nondeviant pattern of arousal.

Every rapist in the program has a history of alcohol or drug abuse, and 80% were using alcohol or drugs at the time of the offense. Over half (56%) of the child molesters have a history of this problem, and 26% were drinking or using drugs when they committed their crimes.

Nearly all (94%) of the child molesters in the Treatment Group have an Axis I diagnosis of paraphilia, and a similar proportion of rapists have "other psychosexual disorder, aggressive sexuality" as their primary diagnosis. While 65% of the molesters have no Axis II diagnosis, a majority of rapists have Axis II diagnoses of antisocial or borderline personality disorders. The most common MMPI profile in the Treatment Group is either 4-8 or 8-4 (20%), and over two-thirds of the group have scores over 60 on these two scales.

The intellectual functioning (full-scale IQs) of the heterosexual child molesters and rapists is quite similar, with 88% of those tested falling within the average range. The homosexual molesters are more diverse intellectually, with 31% testing below average, 46% average, and 23% above average. Cognitive distortions, particularly those that facilitate or justify offending, are extremely common in this group. For example, the Justification Scale scores from the Multiphasic Sex Inventory indicate that all of the homosexual molesters, 80% of the rapists, and 78% of the heterosexual molesters show at least a "marked justification" of their sexual deviance. This group is also notably external in their perceived locus of control, with two-thirds of the group scoring as more external than the average prison inmate.[10]

At this time, only two participants have completed the posttreatment assessment battery; as a result, in-treatment changes cannot be reported. By the end of 1987, a majority of this first group will have completed the hospital program and will be in the Project's aftercare phase.

SUMMARY AND CONCLUSIONS

The Sex Offender Treatment and Evaluation Project is a six-year clinical research program specifically mandated by the California State Legislature. Objectives of the project are: (a) to operate an innovative state hospital unit for sex offenders who volunteer for treatment during the last two years of their prison terms, and (b) to evaluate the effectiveness of the methods used in the experimental program. The treatment model is Relapse Prevention, a prescriptive and multimodal approach designed to train offenders to interrupt and control the chain of events leading to relapse (recidivism). Treatment effectiveness will be measured by comparing the 5-year recidivism rate for treated subjects with the rates for two control groups: (a) matched volunteers who were randomly assigned to a no-treatment group; and (b) a matched group of inmates who qualified for the program but did not volunteer. At this time, 44 sex offenders (34 child molesters and 10 rapists) are in the experimental treatment program. A majority of this first group of subjects will be released from the hospital in 1987.

REFERENCES

1. California Laws. 1981. Chapter 928, codified as California Penal Code Sections 1364 and 1365.
2. California Laws. 1982. Chapters 1529 and 1549, amending California Penal Code Sections 1364 and 1365.
3. MARLATT, G. A. & J. R. GORDON, Eds. 1985. Relapse Prevention: Maintenance Strategies in the Treatment of Addictive Behaviors. Guilford. New York, NY.
4. PITHERS, W. D., J. K. MARQUES, C. C. GIBAT & G. A. MARLATT. 1983. Relapse prevention with sexual aggressives: A self-control model of treatment and maintenance of change. *In* The Sexual Aggressor: Current Perspectives on Treatment. J. G. Greer and I. R. Stuart, Eds.: 214-239. Van Nostrand Reinhold. New York, NY.
5. MARQUES, J. K., W. D. PITHERS & G. A. MARLATT. 1984. Relapse prevention: A self-control program for sex offenders. Appendix to: J. K. Marques. An Innovative Treatment Program for Sex Offenders: Report to the Legislature in Response to 1983/84 Budget Act Item 4440-011-001. California State Department of Mental Health. Sacramento, CA.
6. NELSON, C., M. MINER, J. MARQUES, K. RUSSELL & J. ACHTERKIRCHEN. Relapse prevention: A cognitive-behavioral model for treatment of the rapist and child molester. J. Soc. Work and Human Sexuality. In press.
7. CHANEY, E. F., M. R. O'LEARY & G. A. MARLATT. 1978. Skill training with alcoholics. J. Consult. Clin. Psychol. **46:** 1092-1104.
8. NICHOLS, H. R. & I. R. MOLINDER. 1984. Multiphasic Sex Inventory Manual. Author. Tacoma, WA.
9. FOX, J. A. & P. E. TRACY. 1986. Randomized Response: A Method for Sensitive Surveys. Sage. Beverly Hills, CA.
10. NOWICKI, S. 1983. Manual for the Adult Nowicki-Strickland Locus of Control Scale. Unpublished.

Relapse Prevention of Sexual Aggression

WILLIAM D. PITHERS, KENNON M. KASHIMA, GEORGIA F. CUMMING, LINDA S. BEAL, AND MAUREEN M. BUELL

Vermont Treatment Program for Sexual Aggressors
Vermont Department of Corrections
South Burlington, Vermont 05403

An intriguing pattern emerges when one examines the period of time between a "vow of abstinence" (e.g., smoking cessation, dieting) and the first "transgression" or lapse. In many instances, the initial 90 days of abstinence pose an unusually high risk of relapse. An early meta-analysis of relapse data revealed that nearly 66% of all relapses occurred within the first 90 days after the end of treatment.[1] The probability of relapse decreased markedly after that period.

Marlatt and Gordon[2] observed that the traditional interpretation of the similarity in relapse rates across substances had been that the substances were equally addictive. They proposed an alternate conception, which maintained that "there may be common behavioral and cognitive components associated with relapse, regardless of the particular 'addictive substance' involved." An analysis of the initial relapses of 311 clients (problems drinkers, smokers, heroin addicts, compulsive gamblers, and overeaters) revealed that three high-risk situations—negative emotional states, interpersonal conflict, and social pressure—were the primary determinants of 71% of the relapses regardless of the substance abused.[3]

It is interesting to note that the first nine months after discharge is the period marked by the highest recidivism rate for sex offenders.[4] The longer period prior to the relapse of sex offenders may be attributed to the more severe violations of social norms inherent in their acts and the greater penalties imposed for their behavior than for the relapse of a substance abuser.

Pithers, Buell, Kashima, Cumming, and Beal[5] analyzed precursors to offenses of 136 pedophiles and 64 rapists (see TABLES 1 and 2). In contrast to the analysis performed with substance abusers, which examined the immediate precursor to relapses,[3] we looked at multiple determinants of sexual aggression in an effort to identify a relapse process occurring over a longer time. Eighty-nine percent of the subjects ($n = 177$) reported experiencing strong emotional states prior to relapse. Ninety-four percent of the rapists ($n = 60$) recalled experiencing an intense anger, which had been precipitated in a majority of cases by interpersonal conflict. Pedophiles more frequently recalled having felt anxious (46 percent; $n = 63$) or depressed (38 percent; $n = 52$), generally as a consequence, or cause, of prolonged social disaffiliation. (Since many offenders reported experiencing more than one precursive negative emotion, the sum of individual precursors exceeds 100%.)

In analyzing precursors, a common sequence of changes that ultimately led to a sexual offense was often found. The first change in the relapse process from the clients'

TABLE 1. Immediate Precursors to Sexual Aggression

Precursor	Percentage of Sample	
	Rapists	Pedophiles
Anger		
At event	3	3
Interpersonal conflict	3	4
Generalized, global	88	32
Anger towards women	77	26
Anxiety	27	46
Assertive skills deficit	42	23
Boredom	45	28
Cognitive distortions	72	65
Compulsive overworking	0	8
Depression	3	38
Deviant sexual fantasies	17	51
Disordered sexual arousal pattern	69	57
Divorce	2	2
Driving car alone without destination	17	1
Emotionally inhibited/overcontrolled	58	51
Interpersonal dependence	30	48
Low self-esteem	56	61
Low victim empathy	61	71
Opportunity (e.g., finding a hitchhiker)	58	19
Peer pressure	2	3
Personal loss	6	14
Personality disorder	61	35
Photography as new hobby	0	4
Physical illness	14	6
Planning of sexual offense	28	73
Pornography use	2	7
Psychiatric hospitalization	0	7
Sexual knowledge deficit	45	52
Social anxiety	25	39
Social skills deficit	59	50
Substance use/abuse		
Alcohol	42	23
Other substances	14	7

typical functioning was affective. They referred to themselves as "feeling moody," or "brooding." The second alteration involved fantasies of performing the aberrant sex act. Fantasies were converted into thoughts, often cognitive distortions, in the third step of the relapse process. Offenders frequently devised rationalizations for their behaviors that minimized the effects of their soon-to-be-committed acts. These distortions often attributed inaccurate properties to potential victims, effectively objectifying women or ascribing adult characteristics to children. As fantasies and thoughts continued, the offenders engaged in a process of passive planning, cognitively refining the circumstances that would permit commission of a sexual offense. Often, passive planning was accomplished during masturbatory fantasies. In the final step of the relapse process, the plan was manifested behaviorally. Minimal substance use was noted as an occasional immediate precursor to abuse, particularly among rapists.

In this relapse process, the earliest sign of increasing danger involved affect. The relapse process entailed a distinct sequence of functional alterations: affect-fantasy-thought (cognitive distortion)-passive planning-behavior. Thus, the relapse processes of sexual offenders and other forms of compulsive behavior reveal specifiable precursors that may be addressed during treatment to enhance maintenance of change.

Many theorists propose that sexual offenses, particularly rapes, are "impulsive" acts. While many offenses may appear "impulsive" upon first inspection, we argue that a closer examination reveals a different conclusion. In our analysis of precursors

TABLE 2. Early Precursors to Sexual Aggression

Precursor	Percentage of Sample	
	Rapists	Pedophiles
Cognitive impairment (IQ < 80)	9	10
Divorce (more than 5 years before act)	14	15
Exposure to violent death of human or infrahuman	22	2
Familial chaos	86	49
Late sexual experience (older than 25 at initial activity)	0	4
Limited education (< grade 9 completed)	44	26
Maternal absence/neglect	41	29
More than one prior sex offense	14	17
More than one known victim	30	60
Parental marital discord	59	45
Paternal absence/neglect	59	54
Physically abused as child	45	7
Pornography use (habitual)	14	33
Precocious sexuality (<12 years at time of first act of penetration not considered abuse)	14	30
Prior arrest for nonsexual offense	44	15
Sexual anxiety	39	58
Sexual dysfunction	11	11
Sexual victimization		
Prior to age 12	5	56
Between ages 12 and 18	11	6
Use of female prostitutes	30	8

to assaults,[5] more than half of all offenders appeared emotionally overcontrolled. Frequently, these men left a hostile interaction without expressing anger. Over time, as they brooded about the incident, their animosity grew. Some offenders in our sample had harbored hatred from a single event for a decade. Although they failed to express anger at the appropriate moment, eventually their continual amplification of emotion led to a later explosive release. Since this outburst, or assault, was temporally so far removed from the instigating event, the behavior might appear situationally noncontingent, or "impulsive." In reality, however, the act was not impulsive at all, but motivated by a delayed emotional response.

Empirical evidence indicates that psychological treatment modalities are effective in inducing beneficial modifications of behaviors, including those in the sexual arena.

Unfortunately, short-term benefits often fail to become long-term changes. A major therapeutic concern with sexually aggressive clients involves assisting them to maintain changes after termination of formal treatment.

Treatment of sex offenders often implicitly communicates the notion that successful psychotherapy results in elimination of attraction to deviant sex acts or objects. If successful treatment permanently eliminated deviant sexual preferences, relapse rates of sex offenders would be low. Such is clearly not the case. While reconviction rates for sex offenders are lower than those of the general criminal population, repetition of sex offenses is not an infrequent occurrence.[6] Recidivism data have been used to argue that efficacy of treatment for sexual offenders has not been proved.[7] Rather than attributing sexual reoffending to ineffective treatment, the therapeutic goals for sex offenders may require examination. The anticipated consequence of treatment that is most likely to lead to reoffense may be that successful therapy *should eliminate* fantasies about a deviant sex object or act.

Few therapists who have experience working with sex offenders regard the sexual aggressor as "curable." No existing therapeutic intervention eradicates, across time and situations, the offender's sexually deviant fantasies.

However, many sex offenders enter treatment believing that therapy will affect a "cure." When suffering from physical maladies in the past, a trip to the physician and ensuing medication usually led to elimination of the disorder. Treatment has been something done to him, rather than an activity requiring his active involvement. Thus, the sex offender may enter treatment for sexual deviance with similar expectations about a quick fix that makes few personal demands.

Unfortunately, treatment programs promote the offender's belief in the possibility of "cure" by failing to prepare clients for the likelihood of lapses (i.e., a return to the moods, fantasies, and thoughts associated with the relapse process). Similarly, institutionally based treatment programs, functioning without associated outpatient follow-up groups, promote the deceptive assurance that treatment ends upon discharge. Clients who leave therapy with such misconceptions are primed for relapse. Fortunately, options exist that enhance maintenance of therapeutic gain.

Marlatt[8] devised an intervention model, "Relapse Prevention" (RP), that is designed to enhance maintenance of change of compulsive behaviors. Pithers, Marques, Gibat, and Marlatt[9] modified the RP model for application with sexual offenders. RP is specifically designed to help clients maintain control of a problem behavior over time and across situations.

What determines whether an individual will successfully avoid relapse? RP proposes that the determinants of relapse are embedded in the following process (see FIG. 1). First, we assume that the individual experiences a sense of perceived control while maintaining abstinence, and that this perception of self-control grows until the person encounters a high-risk situation. Broadly speaking, a high-risk situation is one that threatens the individual's sense of control and thus increases the risk of relapse. If an individual in a high-risk, stressful situation is able to perform a successful coping response (e.g., resisting an urge to perform a sexually aggressive act or resolving an argument), the probability of relapse decreases. But what happens if an individual fails to cope successfully with a high-risk situation? A likely result is a decreased sense of control and a helpless feeling of "It's no use, I can't handle it." If these reactions occur in a situation containing cues associated with the prohibited behavior (such as the availability of a potential victim), the stage is set for a probable relapse. This is particularly the case if the person also holds positive expectancies about the immediate effects of performing the prohibited behavior. A rapist might focus on the immediate effects of performing a sexual assault, such as a feeling of power and release of hostile emotions, rather than keeping in mind the full ramifications of the act.

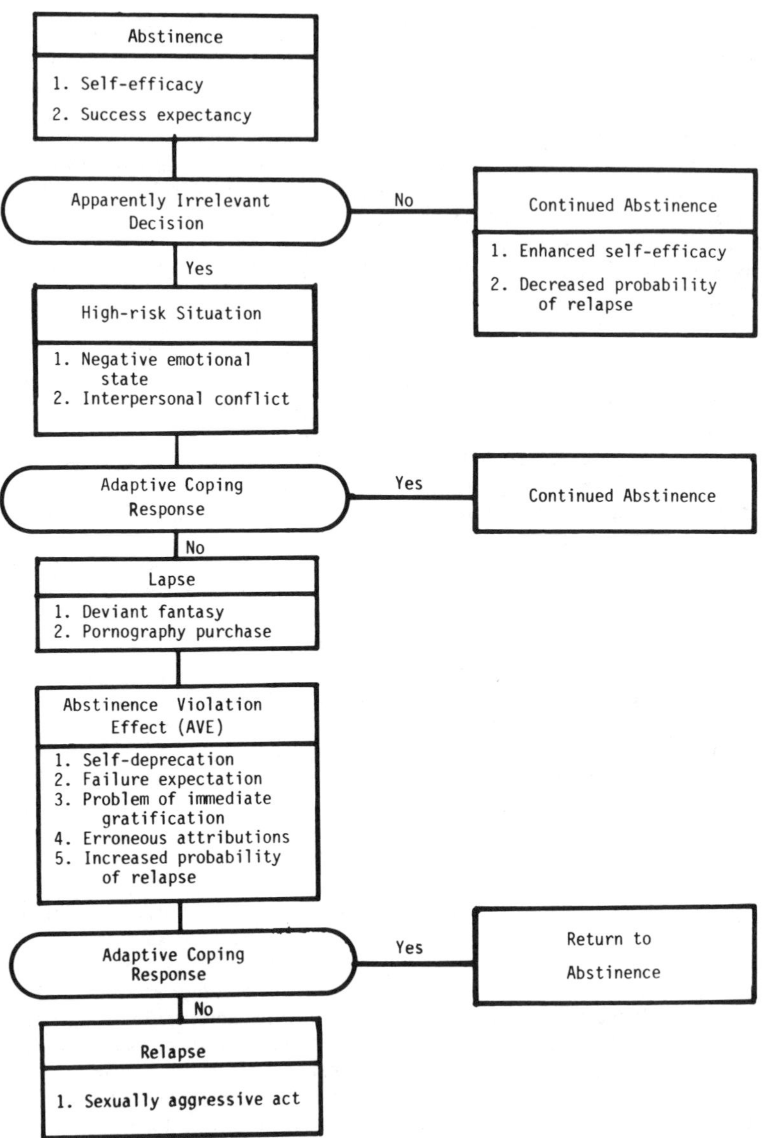

FIGURE 1. A cognitive-behavioral model of the relapse process.

In the sequence of precursors discovered to precede sexual aggression (i.e., affect-fantasy-thought (cognitive distortion)-planning-behavior), the first stage that discriminates most sex offenders from other individuals is the predominance of fantasies involving sexual aggression. Therefore, for most sexual offenders, the first occurrence of *fantasy* about performing a sexually aggressive act may be considered the initial *lapse.* Recurrence of sexually aggressive *behaviors* is defined as a *relapse.* Treatment under the RP model provides clients with skills to enable interruption of the relapse process at the earliest possible point in order to reduce the likelihood that a sexual offense will recur.

Whether or not a lapse becomes a relapse depends on a number of factors, one of which is called the abstinence violation effect (AVE). A major source of the AVE is a conflict between the individual's previous self-image as an abstainer and his recent experience of the prohibited behavior (e.g., a deviant sexual fantasy). To the extent that the person views a lapse as a personal failure, his expectancy for continued failure increases, and the chances of a full-blown relapse also grow.

In the above discussion, the relapse process is depicted from the point at which a person encounters a high-risk situation. It is important to note, however, that the RP model also examines events which precede the high-risk situation. Although some sex offenders relapse in situations that would have been difficult to anticipate, the majority appear to set the scene for relapse by placing themselves into high-risk situations.

One can covertly set up a relapse by making a series of apparently irrelevant decisions (AID), each of which represents another step toward a tempting, high-risk situation. A case study illustrates this process.[10] On vacation in California, a compulsive gambler (currently abstinent) decided to see the "amazingly blue waters" of Lake Tahoe on his way home to Seattle. Unfortunately, this AID led him across the California-Nevada border into a high-risk situation. By the time he "found himself" in downtown Reno needing change for a parking meter, his relapse was almost inevitable. By putting himself in an extremely tempting situation, the gambler could indulge, claiming he was overwhelmed by external circumstances.

The preceding case example of the relapse process leads directly into the RP approach to treatment. While there is very little a sex offender can do to avoid relapse in a "Downtown Reno" situation, he can accept responsibility for initiating the chain of events that got him there in the first place. He can learn to recognize the conditions that precede relapse and be prepared to intervene before it is "too late."

RP begins by dispelling misconceptions that the client may have regarding the outcome of treatment and describing more realistic goals. RP continues with an assessment of the client's high-risk situations, which are the conditions under which relapse has occurred or is likely to occur. Also included in the initial assessment is an evaluation of the client's coping skills, since any situation can be considered high-risk only to the extent that the person has difficulty coping with it. After high-risk situations have been identified, an intervention program is designed to train the client how to minimize lapses and to keep lapses from snowballing into a full-blown relapse.

In introducing RP to clients, we emphasize development of realistic expectations about therapy and encourage an active, problem-solving approach on the part of the client. We explicitly inform clients that no cure exists for their disorder. Clients are told that treatment will diminish their attraction to deviant sexual behaviors, but that fantasies about these behaviors are likely to recur at least momentarily in the future. Clients are informed that return of a deviant fantasy does not signify that they are necessarily going to reoffend, and that a critical part of treatment involves learning what to do when they feel drawn to deviant sexual activity again. We instruct clients that they will discover a variety of situations in which they make seemingly unimportant decisions that actually lead them closer to offending again, or which take them away from that danger. They are encouraged that developing ability to recognize these situations and enact alternatives will reduce the likelihood of acting out their deviant fantasy.

RELAPSE PREVENTION ASSESSMENT PROCEDURES

Since the RP approach to treatment is highly individualized, thorough assessment of the client's needs is required. The assessment phase of the RP program includes three major tasks: (1) analysis of the client's high-risk situations (including the decisions that create those situations); (2) assessment of the client's skills for coping with identified high-risk situations; and (3) identification of specific determinants and early antecedents of the client's deviant or aggressive acts. Several methods may be used to identify the conditions, both internal and external, that increase the threat of relapse for a given offender. These include self-monitoring, direct observation, and self-report measures.

Assessment of High-Risk Situations

Self-Monitoring

Self-monitoring is useful if the offender is still performing the problem behavior (e.g., exposing himself), or still experiencing precursive moods and fantasies (e.g., masturbating to sexually aggressive themes). The following information should be recorded at the time a client experiences an urge to perform a deviant act: time of day, description of internal events (thoughts and feelings which accompanied the urge), external situation, and a numerical rating of the individual's consequent mood. A thorough examination of these self-monitoring records may reveal a pattern of situations in which the behavior most often occurs or is associated with the greatest psychological need.

Direct Behavioral Observation

Physiological measurement of the client's sexual response to auditory or visual depictions of various offense scenarios may reveal high-risk factors (i.e., a deviant pattern of sexual arousal) that the client has not recognized or reported. Such measurements also provide information about the relative strength of a client's nondeviant sexual interests, information which may be useful in developing alternatives to relapse.

Self-Report Measures

In a RP-structured interview, clients provide detailed descriptions of circumstances associated with past offenses. Again, both situational and personal (cognitive and affective) antecedents should be identified, and AIDs made en route to the offense should be explored. Once the client begins to recall AIDs he has made, the pace with which he remembers them will accelerate. By integrating information from the client's self-monitoring record, direct observational data, and the AIDs that he recalls during a structured interview, the constellation of situations posing a high-risk of relapse may be envisioned.

Assessment of Coping Skills

Since a given situation represents risk only to the extent that the offender is unprepared to cope with it, assessment includes measures of his coping abilities. The therapist uses a combination of behavioral and self-report measures to obtain a profile of the client's strengths and weaknesses in coping. These measures include the Situational Competency Test, self-efficacy ratings, and relapse fantasies.

Situational Competency Test

In this test, the client is asked to respond to descriptions of common problem situations. The client's response is later scored along a number of dimensions. A problematic situation is considered to exist whenever the client is unable to formulate a coping response, articulates a strategy that is unlikely to be successful, or verbalizes a response only after a prolonged latency.

Self-Efficacy Ratings

In this procedure, the client is presented with a long list of specific high-risk situations, each of which he rates (on a seven-point scale) according to how difficult or easy it would be to cope with the situation without experiencing a lapse. The assumption is that motivated clients are often the best predictors of their own relapse episodes, an assumption which has been supported by studies of substance abusers.[11]

Relapse Fantasies

In this procedure, the client is asked to provide a fantasized account of a possible future relapse. By reviewing these fantasies with the client, the absence of adaptive coping responses and use of maladaptive coping behaviors can be noted. Occasionally, offenders will become agitated due to the heightened guilt and responsibility they feel as AIDs and high-risk situations preceding their acts are detailed. It is sometimes necessary to indicate that the intent of recursively detailing these factors is to enable enhanced recognition and coping, not to heighten guilt and induce helplessness. Exacerbation of guilt usually dissipates as the focus of treatment shifts from identifying AIDs and high-risk situations to developing coping strategies for these factors.

Assessment of Determinants of Sexual Aggression

Assessment is not complete until the client and therapist have generated hypotheses regarding why the client's response to a stressful situation involved a sex offense instead of some other (even maladaptive) coping response.

A variety of tools are available to help the therapist and client assess the specific determinants of the client's deviant or aggressive behaviors. The structured interview, for example, can be used to explore the relative importance of a number of common determinants, such as extreme hostility toward women, deficient social and sexual skills, sexual dysfunction, and deviant patterns of sexual arousal (excessive arousal to deviant themes or deficient arousal to nondeviant themes). To assess these determinants, the direct measurement methods described previously should be used if available. If not, self-report instruments such as the Clarke Sexual History Questionnaire[12] should be employed, along with self-monitoring records, to assess the relative importance of these determinants.

In addition to identifying the client's specific determinants, complete assessment should include exploration of "early antecedents," factors in the client's lifestyle that appear to be significant predisposing influences. Examples of such predispositions include lack of empathy, victim stancing, unrealistic expectations of others, rigid defensive structures, a sense of worthlessness, and excessive power needs.

RELAPSE PREVENTION TREATMENT PROCEDURES

Since Relapse Prevention is designed to be an individualized, prescriptive program, it is important that the client assume a responsible role in determining the pace and content of both the assessment and treatment phases. A variety of intervention procedures are included in a comprehensive RP program. FIGURE 2 illustrates how these treatment components correspond to the various precursors of relapse. The interventions are divided into two groups: (1) procedures designed to help the client avoid lapses; and (2) procedures designed to minimize the possibility of a lapse precipitating a relapse.

Avoiding Lapses

The first step in teaching a client to avoid lapses is a straightforward extension of the assessment process: recognizing the chain of precursive events involved in the relapse process. As the client becomes more skilled in analyzing his own behavior, he will discover more subtle decisions that led to high-risk situations. Continued self-monitoring of thoughts, fantasies, and urges (along with descriptions of antecedents and consequences of these events) sensitizes the client to recognize important patterns in his behavior. Study exercises, using case examples of the "Downtown Reno Effect," help the client discover how one can covertly plan an offense by making a series of AIDs. These examples are explored in both group and individual sessions. As a result of these exercises, the client and therapist should be able to identify a discrete point in the relapse process that will be considered the client's "lapse." For most offenders, the lapse will be one of the cognitive steps—fantasy, thought (cognitive distortion), planning—that precede commitment of an offense. For others, the lapse may be an

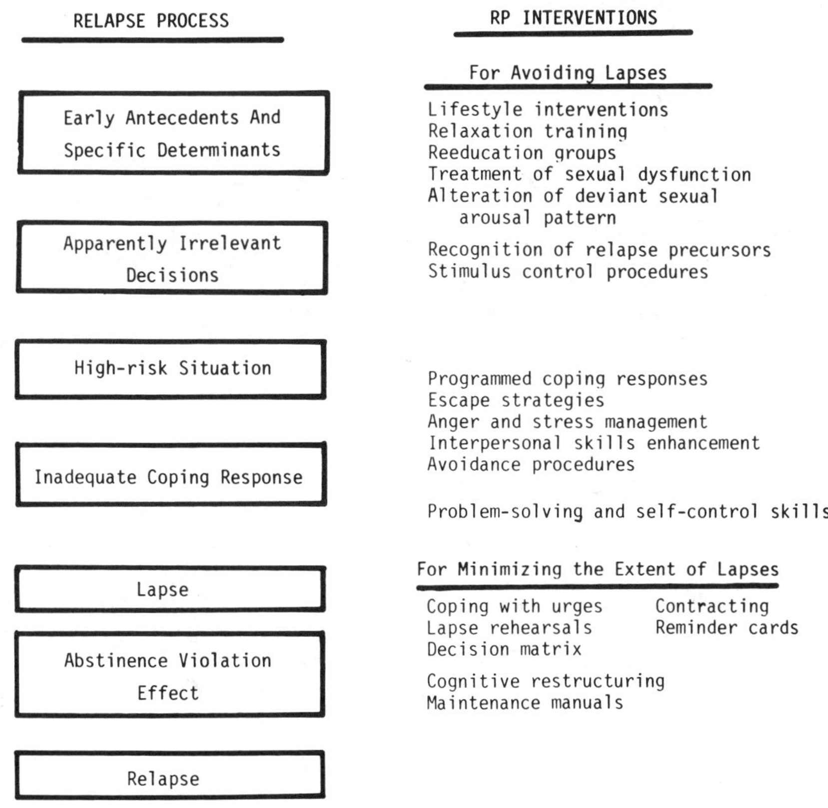

FIGURE 2. Treatment components to disrupt the relapse process.

emotional state (e.g., intense anger toward a potential victim), a behavior (e.g., "cruising"), or a combination of behavioral and cognitive events (e.g., buying child pornography and fantasizing).

Most sex offender treatment programs require clients to identify a "warning signal" that will alert them to imminent reoffenses. "Warning signal" and "lapse" are similar concepts. In contrast to most therapeutic models, however, RP maintains that clients can engage in activities to minimize the frequency of lapses (e.g., identifying AIDs and high-risk situations). In addition, RP proposes that clients can enhance self-control by analyzing, and learning from, lapses (rather than responding with alarm and hiding them from therapists). Finally, RP programs clients with specific procedures for keeping lapses from becoming reoffenses. Unfortunately, many other interventions leave clients unprepared to respond adaptively when a "warning signal" is detected. They know they are in trouble, but have no notion of what to do.

In the RP model, once a lapse is identified, the client and therapist analyze the situations and decisions that preceded it. Lapses are viewed not as signs of therapeutic failure but as opportunities to learn. By carefully examining the factors that led to a lapse and modifying coping strategies to deal with them, an offender may develop enhanced self-management skills.

Stimulus Control Procedures

To the extent that the client's relapse process includes external stimuli that can be eliminated, he can exercise control by removing these from his everyday environment. If a pedophile's deviant fantasies are elicited by the presence of child pornography, he should remove these cues from his surroundings.

Avoidance Strategies

Avoidance strategies can be useful in the early stages of treatment. A pedophile whose daily drive to work takes him by an elementary school can easily travel by another route.

Escape Strategies

Until the client has mastered coping skills necessary for high-risk situations, he should be "programmed" to escape. Escape responses can be programmed by having the client overlearn them by repeatedly rehearsing the behaviors in a variety of situations. Again, these strategies should be designed for the earliest point in the relapse process that the offender can recognize. A client who is programmed to get out of situations that precede a lapse is likely to be more successful than one who waits for a "Downtown Reno" situation to develop. Previous research using the Situational Competency Test has demonstrated that the adequacy of a coping response appears less important in preventing relapse than the speed with which the response is emitted.[13]

Specific Coping Skills

Although some lapses can be prevented by training the client to recognize, avoid, and escape risk situations, successful maintenance also requires the acquisition of additional programmed coping responses and problem-solving skills.

Programmed Coping Responses

The development of adaptive coping responses for risk situations always begins with problem-solving sessions. The client initiates the problem-solving procedure by describing his highest-risk situation in detail. Once the situation has been described fully, brainstorming is used to generate a large number of potential coping responses. Potential consequences of each option are listed to evaluate whether that response would have the desired effect of lessening the likelihood of relapse. The most effective, feasible coping response is then selected for performance. Focusing on the thought processes that the client follows in performing the problem-solving strategy is important in providing clues that suggest additional problem areas for further exploration (e.g., an unrealistic approach to life, grandiose expectations).

Continued practice of the coping behaviors should be conducted throughout the client's treatment. Practice of these behaviors resembles the repetitive drills used by athletic coaches who strive to have their players respond "instinctively" in important situations. These "instinctive" reactions actually result from intensive programming. By practicing over time, the client will perform the programmed coping response in many situations and moods, enhancing generalization.

Interpersonal Skills

Acquisition of effective interpersonal skills is an important part of the RP program for many sex offenders. For some, basic skills necessary for establishing and maintaining relationships with adults are deficient. Others show deficits in sexuality skills, are unable to communicate effectively, erroneously interpret the meaning of social cues, or are severely inhibited by anxiety in interpersonal encounters. Lack of assertive behaviors is another common social skill deficit that appears as a precursor to relapse. Many sex offenders, particularly rapists, are unable constructively to express feelings to others, and react to interpersonal conflict with unexpressed anger, which is later overexpressed in aggressive outbursts.

Anger and Stress Management

Since negative arousal states are common precursors of relapse, skills for managing these affective antecedents are important coping strategies for many offenders. For pedophiles, social anxiety appears to be a frequent antecedent; for rapists, anger is the more common precursor. Our general approach to management of negative arousal states is stress inoculation training, a cognitive-behavioral program that has been successfully applied to problems of anxiety[14] and anger.[15]

Coping with Urges

As with other compulsive behaviors, the performance of sexually deviant acts is typically characterized by some type of immediate gratification (e.g., a restored sense of power and control, relief from tension). Negative consequences (e.g., guilt, decreased self-esteem, social disapproval, arrest and incarceration) are typically delayed. Selectively recalling the positive aspects of offenses, while neglecting the negative aftereffects (for both the victim and himself), increases the probability of recurrence of the deviant act. Positive outcome expectancies for the immediate effects of a behavior become especially potent when the client is faced with a high-risk situation and is beginning to feel unable to cope effectively. Under such conditions, the client may experience a strong urge to commit a deviant act. We teach the client that his overall response to sexual aggression is biphasic in nature. The initial sense of gratification is frequently followed by a delayed negative effect. Clients are also taught to use self-statements to disrupt the urge. Inclusion of aversive outcomes in self-statements enhances their potency in counteracting urges.

Another technique that assists the client in coping with urges is the decision matrix. In creating a decision matrix, the client is presented with a three-way table ($2 \times 2 \times 2$ matrix) in which the following factors are listed: the decision to perform a deviant act or to refrain from doing so; the immediate and delayed consequences of each decision; and, within each of the former categories, the positive and negative effects involved (see FIG. 3). The client and therapist work together to complete each of the eight cells of the matrix, listing outcomes that the client feels would have the greatest impact on his decision making. The client should assign numerical ratings to each of the positive and negative outcomes to illustrate their relative importance.

Modification of Specific Determinants of Lapses

As was emphasized previously, the RP program would be incomplete if it did not address specific determinants of sexual aggression. The most important "response relevant" interventions are behavior therapy procedures designed to alter deviant arousal patterns that are critical precursors to relapse for many offenders. The importance of including behavioral assessments (i.e., penile plethysmography) and interventions with sexual aggressors has been emphasized by many experts in this field.[16–19] As a general rule, we employ treatment procedures that are direct, simple, and transferable to the client's home (e.g., masturbatory satiation, orgasmic reconditioning, olfactory aversion, etc.).

	IMMEDIATE		DELAYED	
	POSITIVE	NEGATIVE	POSITIVE	NEGATIVE
TO REFRAIN	1. Increased self-efficacy (+75) 2. Social approval (+20) 3. Respect of spouse (+50) 4. Respect of children (+30) 5. No harm to victims (+65)	1. Denial of gratification (-8) 2. Momentary anger (-30) 3. Frustation (-15)	1. Enhanced self-control (+75) 2. Increased social approval (+35) 3. Respect of spouse (+50) 4. Maintenance of friendships (+40) 5. Avoidance of jail (+45) 6. Less treatment (+5)	1. Denial of gratification (-9) 2. Residual anger (which becomes less in time)(-20)
TO PERFORM	1. Immediate gratification (+20) 2. Release of anger (+15) 3. Sense of power (+30)	1. Social censure (-80) 2. Guilt (-30) 3. Loss of self-respect (-20) 4. Harm to victim (-60) 5. Risk of injury (-10) 6. Possiblility of getting caught (-90)	1. Continued gratification (+20)	1. Social censure (-40) 2. Guilt (-25) 3. Loss of self-respect (-20) 4. Identity of offender (-80) 5. Lasting harm to victim (-40) 6. Loss of spouse (-90) 7. Imprisonment (-40) 8. Public disclosure (-70)

FIGURE 3. Decision matrix for coping with urges.

Interventions for Early Antecedents

The final set of interventions is designed to modify "early antecedents," the global predispositions that have been determined by the client and therapist to contribute to lapses. A wide range of techniques are included in this component, such as didactic sessions on human sexuality, victim confrontations for offenders who lack empathy or refuse to take responsibility for the full extent of their crimes, and cognitive restructuring techniques to correct "thinking errors" that support the offender's interpersonal aggression.[20] "Reeducation Groups," as described by Groth,[21] may be employed to address the most common early antecedents.

MINIMIZING THE EXTENT OF LAPSES

Specific RP procedures have been developed to prepare the client to cope with lapses by applying some cognitive and behavioral "brakes" so that a lapse does not become a relapse. First, we teach the client behavioral skills to moderate lapses. Second, in order for these moderating skills to be successful, we instruct the client in cognitive restructuring procedures to cope effectively with the various components of the AVE. Third, lapse rehearsals may be staged to practice skills he has acquired to handle the occurrence of a lapse. Finally, an individualized maintenance manual is constructed to provide the offender with general reference material, specific refresher exercises, and emergency coping strategies to use if all else fails and he is on the brink of relapse.

CONCLUSIONS

RP serves as a comprehensive training program designed to help sex offenders avoid reoffenses. An abbreviated form of RP may be used as a supplemental package to enhance and extend effects of other treatment approaches. In any case, the basic premise of the RP model is that clients should *be prepared;* that is, they should be able to recognize AIDs, avoid or effectively cope with high-risk situations, restructure interpretation of urges, and prevent a lapse from creating a full-blown relapse.

No final therapy session is conducted under the RP model. RP is not an activity that a sex offender completes. Offenders who believe that their treatment ends with the termination of formal therapy have failed to learn the crucial lesson that *maintenance is forever.* The client who has adequately learned the RP philosophy will continue his own therapy every day of his life.

The Vermont Treatment Program for Sexual Aggressors represented the initial application of RP with sex offenders.[22] The relapse rates of clients involved in this program are presented in TABLE 3. Based on these data, RP would appear to be a highly effective method of assisting sexual aggressors to avoid violating another's safety. The program is also highly cost-effective. Only $60,850 was appropriated for

TABLE 3. Efficacy of RP in Maintenance of Change in Convicted Pedophiles and Rapists

	Rapists	Pedophiles	Total
Offenders in outpatient therapy > 1 year	18	101	119-
Relapses	2	3	5
Total	20	104	124-
Relapse rate[a]	10%	3%	4%

[a] Relapse is defined as conviction for another sexual offense. Two relapses occurred within 2 months after start-up of outpatient treatment groups; a third relapse took place 3 weeks after offender's parole officer permitted him to discontinue treatment against therapists' advice.

the 15 outpatient therapy groups associated with the Vermont Treatment Program for Sexual Aggressors in 1986. The initial outcome data have motivated other states[22] to adopt RP as a central component of their treatment programs.

REFERENCES

1. HUNT, W. A., L. W. BARNETT & L. G. BRANCH. 1971. Relapse rates in addiction programs. J. Clin. Psychol. **27:** 455-456.
2. MARLATT, G. A. & J. GORDON. 1980. Determinants of relapse: Implications for the maintenance of change. *In* Behavioral Medicine: Changing Health Lifestyles. P. O. Davidson & S. M. Davidson, Eds. Brunner/Mazel. New York, NY.
3. CUMMINGS, C., J. GORDON & G. A. MARLATT. 1980. Strategies of prevention and prediction. *In* The Addictive Behaviors: Treatment of Alcoholism, Drug Abuse, Smoking, and Obesity. W. R. Miller, Ed. Pergamon Press. New York, NY.
4. FRISBIE, L. 1969. Another Look at Sex Offenders in California. Research Monograph No. 12. California Department of Mental Hygiene. Sacramento, CA.
5. PITHERS, W. D., M. M. BUELL, K. M. KASHIMA, G. F. CUMMING & L. S. BEAL. 1987. Precursors to sexual offenses. Paper presented at the Association for the Advancement of Behavior Therapy for Sex Abusers, Newport, Oregon.
6. STURGEON, H., J. TAYLOR, R. GOLDMAN, D. HUNTER & D. WEBSTER. 1979. Report on Mentally Disordered Sex Offenders Released from Atascadero State Hospital in 1973. Atascadero State Hospital. Atascadero, CA.
7. BRECHER, E. M. 1978. Treatment Programs for Sex Offenders. U. S. Government Printing Office. Washington, D.C.
8. MARLATT, G. A. 1982. Relapse prevention: A self-control program for the treatment of addictive behaviors. *In* Adherence, Compliance, and Generalization in Behavioral Medicine. R. B. Stuart, Ed. Brunner/Mazel. New York, NY.
9. PITHERS, W. D., J. K. MARQUES, C. C. GIBAT & G. A. MARLATT. 1983. Relapse prevention with sexual aggressives: A self-control model of treatment and maintenance of change. *In* The Sexual Aggressor: Current Perspectives on Treatment. J. G. Greer & I. R. Stuart, Eds. Van Nostrand Reinhold. New York, NY.

10. MARLATT, G. A. & J. R. GORDON. 1985. Relapse Prevention. Guilford Press. New York, NY.
11. CONDIOTTE, M. M. & E. LICHTENSTEIN. 1981. Self-efficacy and relapse in smoking cessation programs. J. Consult. Clin. Psychol. **49:** 648-658.
12. LANGEVIN, R. 1983. Sexual Strands: Understanding and Treating Sexual Anomalies in Men. Lawrence Erlbaum Associates. Hillsdale, NJ.
13. CHANEY, E. F., M. R. O'LEARY & G. A. MARLATT. 1978. Skill training with alcoholics. J. Consul. Clin. Psychol. **46:** 1092-1104.
14. MEICHENBAUM, D. 1977. Cognitive-Behavior Modification. Plenum Press. New York, NY.
15. NOVACO, R. W. 1977. Stress inoculation: A cognitive therapy for anger and its application to a case of depression. J. Consult. Clin. Psychol. **45:** 600-608.
16. ABEL, G. G., E. B. BLANCHARD & J. V. BECKER. 1978. An integrated treatment program for rapists. *In* Clinical Aspects of the Rapist. R. Rada, Ed. Grune & Stratton. New York, NY.
17. LAWS, D. R. & C. A. OSBORN. 1983. How to build and operate a laboratory to evaluate and treat sexual deviance. *In* The Sexual Aggressor: Current Perspectives on Treatment. J. G. Greer & I. R. Stuart, Eds. Van Nostrand Reinhold. New York, NY.
18. QUINSEY, V. L. & W. L. MARSHALL. 1983. Procedures for reducing inappropriate sexual arousal: An evaluation review. *In* The Sexual Aggressor: Current Perspectives in Treatment. J. G. Greer & I. R. Stuart, Eds. Van Nostrand Reinhold. New York, NY.
19. ROSEN, R. C. & J. C. FRACHER. 1983. Tension-reduction training in the treatment of compulsive sex offenders. *In* The Sexual Aggressor: Current Perspectives in Treatment. J. G. Greer & I. R. Stuart, Eds. Van Nostrand Reinhold. New York, N.Y.
20. YOCHELSON, S. & SAMENOW, S. 1976. The Criminal Personality, Vol. 1: A Profile for Change. Jason Aronson. New York, NY.
21. GROTH, A. N. 1983. Treatment of the sexual offender in a correctional institution. *In* The Sexual Aggressor: Current Perspectives on Treatment. J. G. Greer & I. R. Stuart, Eds. Van Nostrand Reinhold. New York, NY.
22. PITHERS, W. D. 1982. The Vermont Treatment Program for Sexual Aggressors. Vermont Department of Corrections. Waterbury, VT.
23. MARQUES, J. K., W. D. PITHERS & G. A. MARLATT. 1984. An Innovative Treatment Program for Sex Offenders. California Department of Mental Health. Sacramento, CA.

Advancements in Physiological Evaluation of Assessment and Treatment of the Sexual Aggressor

WILLIAM R. FARRALL

Farrall Instruments, Inc.
Grand Island, Nebraska 68802-1037

ROBERT D. CARD

Clinic for Counseling & Psychotherapy, Inc.
Salt Lake City, Utah 84103

INTRODUCTION

For nearly twenty years the author has been involved in the development of reliable penile measuring equipment and stimulus materials used by many clinicians in the evaluation, assessment, and treatment of sexual offenders. The coauthor has been actively involved in assessing and treating a wide variety of sex offenders. In the summer of 1987, while attending a workshop on improving the accuracy of tumescence monitoring at Farrall Instruments, he became convinced that technology and psychological theory had advanced to the point where major advances could be made. In later discussions the two authors decided the combined expertise they could jointly bring to bear on some major problems in physiological assessments might provide some useful answers. One of the major concerns was that approximately 20% of known offenders show no arousal to any sexual stimuli. The other concern was that some known offenders show almost the same degree of tumescence for deviant and nondeviant stimuli, but this is not reflected in their behavior. A pilot study, composed of a mixture of 30 known offenders and a few presumed nonoffenders, has been completed. This preliminary study, which uses a procedure very different from presently used techniques, shows what the authors consider to be great promise in solving both of the previously noted problems, while shedding light on some other issues related to tumescence recording.

Before discussing this "marriage" of clinician to technology, a very abbreviated review of the method and the major theoretical and technical issues will be presented for those who are not familiar with penile assessment of sexual aggressors. Following this will be a discussion on an innovative approach to stimulus materials and how this approach, when assisted by computer-controlled stimulus presentation, data collection, and analysis, can potentially improve the accuracy and effectiveness of physiological assessments of the sexual aggressor. We will also suggest some implications for future research.

PENILE PLETHYSMOGRAPHIC EVALUATIONS: GENERAL INFORMATION

At this point in time there is a wide consensus that the most valid and reliable measure of the male sexual response is the penile response or tumescence.[1] The plethysmograph is a recording device that measures change in tumescence of the male penis in response to a sexual stimulus. Beyond this general statement great diversity exists in relation to how to evaluate the tumescence of the penis in relation to a particular stimulus. These issues will be briefly addressed in the paragraphs to follow. Plethysmographic evaluation of male tumescence is most widely used in assessing the sexual response of offenders to assist the courts in dictating conditions in the disposition of each individual offender. The plethysmograph can also be used to measure change in response to deviant and normal stimulation across treatment time as well as to provide biofeedback to the client during the course of treatment in the development of voluntary self-control.[2] During evaluations a discriminant response is the major goal; in treatment a differential response to a particular class of stimulus across time is the goal.

ASSESSMENT PROCEDURES

The client is seated in a comfortable chair in a small private room, which is sometimes equipped with a one-way mirror. The client places a device called a transducer around the shaft of the penis. The types of transducers and their relative values will be discussed below. The transducer produces a change in electrical resistance across a Wheatstone bridge as erection occurs. This very small change in resistance is amplified, and the changes are recorded on a strip chart recorder, or these changes are converted through an analog to digital converter, processed digitally in the computer, and recorded via the computer printout. The stimulus materials to which the individual is expected to respond can be auditory, visual, or some combination of both. Typically, stimulus materials are generally alternated with detumescent times. The total assessment time may range from one to two hours. Prior to the evaluation, some clinicians require the client to masturbate to full tumescence, or he is shown sexually stimulating materials to produce what is thought to be full tumescence, in order to provide a measure of response to the assessment materials based on a percentage of maximum. Other clinicians rely on the individual's responses to various types of materials, using the individual as his own control by the difference in his responses to deviant versus "normal" stimulus materials.

It is essential to point out what a penile evaluation can and cannot do. First, the penile tumescence plethysmograph is not a sexual "lie detector." It will not tell whether or not a suspected offender has actually offended, nor will it tell if the offender is certain to offend again or to not offend. In other words, it cannot be used to search for probable offenders in the general public. However, properly obtained and interpreted, the penile evaluation can generally make it possible to determine the gender preference, age preference, and in many cases the type of sexual activity of interest to both an offender and a nonoffender. This is obtained by noting the relative level of sexual response to various types of stimulus materials. A recent survey for the New York Council of Churches revealed that 27% of the adult sex offender treatment programs and 12% of the juvenile sex offender treatment programs are currently using penile tumescence recording as part of their treatment program.[3]

Second, tumescence recording should not be used as the only method of determining information about a person's sexual preference and sexual activities. Undoubtedly the best measure of this information is based in the history of the person's sexual behavior as verified by legal and/or historical records. The plethysmograph, however, provides valuable material corroborating or disconfirming the individual's self-reports and, as stated earlier, it can be used in evaluating change. Denial is a common component in the mental makeup of sexual offenders. At times tumescence recording has suggested sexual fantasies at variance with the individual's self-report. The tumescence recording is frequently more accurate than the individual's denial.

DATA COLLECTION AND INTERPRETATION

No assessment procedure that permits varying interpretations serves to advance any scientific field of endeavor. One of the major problems in the reliable interpretation of tumescence recordings is the wide variety of recording equipment, the nonstandardization of the stimulus materials, and a lack of systemization in the collection of data.

Several kinds of transducers are available, and each type has its group of clinical and/or research users and nonusers, for a variety of reasons to be discussed later. Amplification equipment varies from the simplest to the most sensitive and sophisticated. Sensitivity from one piece of equipment to another is impossible to compare. Some equipment has been designed by amateur electronics engineers and has dangerous design flaws; other equipment has been designed by trained biomedical engineers and includes adequate shock protection in case of component failure.

Recording devices are equally unstandardized. Some equipment has no way of relating the sensitivity of the equipment to the amplitude of the responses produced by the recording equipment. The recording equipment used by some clinicians and researchers produces a graph that is so small that fine interpretations of variances in response are impossible. For the most part, however, there is no reliable way to compare the response from one type of pen-recorded strip chart to another. Even computerized collection of data does not help much in this regard. For example, Dr. Card's original (1982) computerized data collection was programmed to sample data of 5-second intervals, and full scale reading went from 0-255 units. Other programs currently being used can select data points from four per second to a variety of longer units, and the printout is based on a full scale reading of 0-100.

INTERPRETATION OF PLETHYSMOGRAPHIC RESPONSES

Researchers and clinicians using different systems are left to their own devices to interpret what a particular response might be. Many researchers and clinicians use audio stimulus materials. Audio materials are generally found to be more stimulating sexually than visual materials. Most clinicians and researchers, if they use audio materials, develop their own and reluctantly pass them from one clinician to another.

While it is true that these audio materials do have stimulus value in assessing the responses of deviant individuals, the authors know of no standardized audio stimulus materials that are generally available, nor do they know of any audio stimulus materials that have been evaluated to see how they discriminate the responses of the deviant individuals from those of "normal" individuals. This seems to be a major flaw, because there is no way of knowing how many false positives will be included in the supposedly deviant population being tested. Second, audio materials generally seem to have been constructed to be blatantly sexual, in order to produce the maximum arousal value possible. In the view of the authors this compounds the problem of including false positives in the deviant population. Some of the audio materials heard by the authors have appeared to be so specifically written and so blatantly sexual as to be pornographic in nature. This narrowness may result in detection of only a narrow range of offenders, leaving others equally guilty undetected. In addition, the blatancy of the materials may be so offensive to religiously inclined individuals as to reduce or eliminate compliance to test conditions. Religiosity is a major characteristic of many sex offenders.[4]

Visual stimuli are generally conceded to be less arousing than auditory stimuli. Most of the visual stimuli in use are 35-mm slides that have been collected by individual researchers. Farrall Instruments has a large and varied collection of slides. Exposure time to slides varies greatly from one researcher to another. The quality of the picture itself and of the sexual object and/or activity portrayed varies enormously, further compounding the difficulty of comparing results from one researcher or clinician to another. One of the most serious problems in the use of visual stimulus materials is that current federal and state child pornography laws make the taking and possession of pictures of a nude minor illegal and punishable by law. Thus, it is extremely difficult to obtain a set of visual stimulus materials that is both stimulating and legally obtained.

Some researchers and clinicians are using audio-visual stimulus materials presented through a video recorder and TV screen. Appropriate materials are extremely difficult to find and usually are obtained through the pornographic market. When recording the responses of a client to moving-picture stimuli, it is difficult if not impossible to correlate the individual's response to anything more than his response to a particular gender and age of stimulus object.

It has long been recognized that sophisticated offenders can control their erections and often alter their response during assessment. Less knowledgeable offenders may learn from the assessment experience or are coached by those who have previously been assessed. Critics of assessments point this out to undermine the validity of the procedure. Provided that an assessor is able to detect faking, such attempts may be of great diagnostic significance. For instance, such attempts may be related to a character disorder, denial, prognosis for treatment in a particular setting, or progress in treatment. Results of our pilot study suggest a way to detect dissimulation even by inexperienced examiners.

TRANSDUCERS

A key element in penile tumescence monitoring is the transducer. As mentioned earlier, a transducer is a mechanical device that transforms minute changes in circumference of the penis into resistance changes measured across a Wheatstone bridge.

The minute resistance changes are amplified and sent to a recording device such as a pen on a chart recorder, or, in the case of a computer, the resistance analog changes are converted to a changing digital signal, which is recorded on a recording device by the computer.

There are three basic types of penile transducers in use today. The first is called the Barlow Gauge. It is a very lightweight, flexible, stainless-steel clip, which surrounds the shaft of the penis. Flexion of this clip during tumescence creates a resistance change across resistors glued to the saddle of the transducer. This device is reliable and easily sterilized. The Mercury and Indium-Gallium transducers consist of a very thin column of an electrically conductive substance sealed inside a flexible tube. The tube is light and flexible enough to be almost unnoticable by the wearer when it is placed around the shaft of the penis. Both the Mercury and Indium-Gallium transducers produce resistance change by narrowing of the conductive substance as the tube stretches and thins during tumescence.

A basic problem with all three gauges is that they are nonlinear across the full range of flexion. An average deviation from linearity of 10-15% can be expected with any of the measuring devices mentioned above, unless calibration of the gauge and linearization of the data are done.

A number of researchers attempt to measure the full range of tumescence of each client by measuring the flaccid penis and then obtaining the upper limits of tumescence by having the client stimulate himself to full erection or by exposing the client to highly stimulating pornographic video tapes until, theoretically, maximum tumescence is obtained. The difference between flaccid and "maximum" arousal thus obtained is considered to be 100% arousal, and it is theorized that any change in tumescence observed during later testing can be scaled on the basis of some percentage compared to 100% tumescence.

The authors have some difficulty with this 100% scaling procedure. First, the transducers, as mentioned previously, are not linear. Hence, a change percentage of 23% at the lower or middle part of the tumescent range will not necessarily have the same scaling as 23% obtained at the top part of the range. Figures reported in this way tend to be misleading. Second, some subjects observed in the RESULTS OF THE PILOT STUDY section of this report show client expectations producing greater test responses after exposure to prior stimulation materials. Introducing the client to stimulating materials or having the client masturbate to full erection prior to testing is likely to create an elevated response during the testing proper. This could be especially problematic, depending on whether the deviant or the normal stimulus material is presented first; the materials presented later will likely be artificially elevated because of prior stimulation.

We are aware of further difficulties in the concept of 100% scaling. We have not seen any studies that provide that tumescent change from flaccid to full erection is a linear function. Is a millimeter change in circumference of the penis at the beginning of the arousal cycle equal to one millimeter change in circumference at the peak of arousal? To complicate the matter even further, we know of no study that has demonstrated that there is a linear *cognitive* scaling method for measuring arousal. For example, can the client report subjective arousal change across time as a linear function (which it probably is not) and then relate this change to a consistent unit of change as related to tumescence? Because of the scaling problems inherent in the transducers, stimulus materials, and the penile response itself, we tend to favor a comparative form of scaling, using the individual's own response as the control. We are not alone in reaching this conclusion. Earls and Marshall have both raised these questions.[5]

THE ARRIVAL OF MICROCOMPUTERS ON THE TUMESCENCE MONITORING SCENE

At least 25 computer-assisted tumescence monitoring systems are in use in Canada and the United States. Drs. Abel, Bradford, and Card were among the early users of computers. This is not just another computer fad but a perfect application of the use of the power of the computer not only to process data but to give precise control of stimulus presentation. For the first time automated scoring and retrieval capabilities of the computer make it relatively easy for a therapist to compare an offender's progress throughout therapy and further to compare particular offenders to similar offenders in a wide variety of treatment settings.

Mass production of the personal computer has reduced the cost of a powerful system, making it possible for the most advanced technology to be placed in the office of even the private practitioner. The small laboratory can now have far more analytical power than research laboratories using multichannel polygraphs could even four years ago. A number of research projects using this increased analytical power are already underway in the offices of private practitioners. Preliminary findings indicate that with improved procedures, a wealth of previously unseen data about the offender can be gathered. Unfortunately there are three major factors that the authors feel are standing in the way of realizing the full potential of computer-assisted assessment and therapy: lack of standardized procedures, inadequate and unstandardized stimulus materials, and lack of attention to some basic theoretical issues.

STIMULUS MATERIALS

There is a considerable disagreement in the literature regarding the results of penile tumescence recording for the assessment of sexual aggressors. This is partly due to each therapist using a different set of stimulus materials. At a National Institute of Mental Health meeting in January of 1986, Farrall[6] proposed a large study of the response of a wide range of offenders and nonoffenders to a standardized set of audio and visual stimuli. Thirty groups in the United States and Canada have agreed to participate in this study. It is hoped that this will generate a large data base that will give basic response patterns of the various types of offenders and normals. This will be an important first step in standardization of stimulus materials.

About six months ago the authors met in Dr. Card's office in Salt Lake City for an extended brainstorming session relative to the technical problems involved in penile assessment procedures and some possible ways to address these problems. Dr. Card has worked exclusively with audio-visual materials presented at first by 8-mm film projection. The visual motion picture stimuli have been replaced with video moving picture stimuli. He was greatly impressed by the data collection, analysis, and stimulus control capabilities of Farrall's Computer Assisted Therapy™, (CAT-200) System controlled by the software program developed by Farrall Instruments, but he was less than impressed by the 35-mm still slides and the lack of availability of what he considered to be adequate audio stimulus materials. Out of this meeting emerged a proposal on the part of Dr. Card to produce and pilot a new concept in stimulus material, with Farrall consulting and providing the 35mm still slides that Dr. Card would use to transfer to a VHS video format. The results of the pilot study have met and exceeded the greatest expectations of either of the authors. A careful analysis of the early results of the pilot study provide some early suggestions for solutions to many technical problems in the collection and analysis of data collected via the penile plethysmograph.

THE METHOD

The authors theorized that it was more important to develop stimulus materials that maximize a *discriminant* response than a maximal response. By focusing on a discriminant response rather than a maximum response, problems of equal units of scaling and problems of nonlinearity of response and transduction can be minimized or eliminated entirely.

FIGURE 1. Typical computer assessment system in operation.

It was theorized that if audio materials could be designed to cue into the sexual offender's mental set leading into the deviant act, a response could be "seasoned" that would be discriminant if the "seasoned" response were enhanced or triggered by immediately following focused visual stimuli. It was theorized further that the nonoffender would not cue into, or be "seasoned" by, the audio materials and would be less likely to respond to the focused visual materials. To enhance the likelihood that an offender would cue into his particular stimulus set, the audio materials would have to be written to be suggestive rather than prescriptive so as to elicit a response to a wide range of personal feelings and activities, into which the offender could project himself.

Dr. Card drew on his extensive experience in treating sex offenders to place himself in the position of the offender. Scripts were written beginning with the probable mental set of the offender followed by a series of decisions and activities leading up to the act itself. The audio stops short of the deviant act, leaving the presentation of the pictures to confirm or deny the presence or absence of a sexual response pattern to the particular stimulus sequence being presented. Fifteen 132-second stimulus sequences were developed and recorded on a VHS format. Segments included an initial nonsense script and pictures to acquaint the client with the testing procedure, thirteen segments involving a wide variety of deviant sexual activities focused on male/female victims over a wide age range, and an adult heterosexual sequence. Some coercive and permissive sequences are included in the thirteen deviant segments. Examples of deviant audio segments are as follows:

Stimulus Set #10, CHILD MOLEST, Female Victim 3-8 years old.

> I really like little kids. They like me too. They always seem to want to climb on my knee or play horsie with me. I feel so good when I see them come running to me when I go into the room. They want to climb on my lap and wriggle around and cuddle up to me. They're so soft and cute. I hope she wants to sit on my lap today. She's the cutest one. I feel so good when I'm there. I just want to touch her a bit. Maybe we can do it in the other room. It feels good when she squirms around. Maybe she'll want to touch it. I could get her to do some things if we played some games. She seems to know all about it so it can't hurt her.

Stimulus Slides are from Farrall Instruments slides #XX-31, XX-37, XX-42, XX-45.

Stimulus Set #13, ADULT HETEROSEXUAL, Adult Female.

> I'm really having a hard time concentrating on my work today. She's wearing that tight sweater again. If she comes over here once more and bends over my desk I'm not sure I can keep from grabbing them. I can almost feel the excitement if I could push my face between them. Get a hold of yourself! She looks almost as good from the back. Can't keep my eyes off her butt as she walks past. I can almost feel my hands running along that soft body. No wonder I'm so horny! I haven't had it for days. The last time we got it on was wonderful! I've got to get some tonight. I can almost feel her squirming with excitement at the touch of my hands.

Stimulus Slides are from Farrall Instruments slides #M-46, M-55, TTT-67, TTT-72.

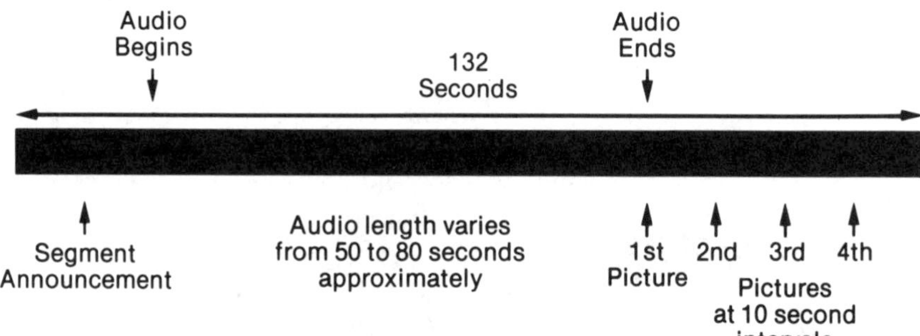

FIGURE 2. Stimulus time sequence chart.

The structure of each 132-second segment is shown in FIGURE 2. From the beginning of the segment to the beginning of the pictures the TV monitor is colored red. The pictures become increasingly erotic.

The penile response printout to these stimulus materials was enhanced by a trace that multiplies the penile response by a factor of five. We theorized that the response to the stimulus materials would be very small, and that the $\times 5$ trace would be helpful in detecting very small changes. We have since dropped the $\times 5$ trace, because the client response to the stimulus materials was so good that the $\times 5$ trace quickly disappeared off the scale.

The penile response is offset 10/100 units high to allow for observation of possible "turn off" or decremental responses to some stimulus sequences.

The client's Galvanic Skin Response (GSR) was also input to the CAT-200 system and printed out simultaneously with the penile response to the stimulus segments. It was hypothesized that this response would correlate with cueing in to the stimulus sequences and possibly provide a means to detect attempts to control responses or fake no response.

RESULTS OF THE PILOT STUDY

We feel we can report some preliminary findings at this time, because we acknowledge the tentativeness of our findings based on a very small sample. However, we feel we can report what we are finding using the client as his own control. Further, we are refining and expanding our pilot study into a full-scale research study.

FIGURES 3a and 3b show the response of a 35-year-old male who molested a 5-year-old female. The printout in FIGURE 3a is his response to a stimulus set of a 6-year-old. The printout in FIGURE 3b is his response to an adult female stimulus set. Response to the consenting child shows that the offender did cue into the audio and, when the slides were presented, produced an incremental response. With the adult female stimulus set, the audio produced some turn off, but the slides did elicit a response. Note that the response was considerably less than the response to the child's stimulus set. The differential response between the child's stimulus set and the adult set shows an interest in activity with children. Another dramatic indicator is the length of time to detumefy after the end of the stimulus set. In this case detumescence took 149 seconds for the child's set and 31.5 seconds for the adult set. It will be noted that the bottom line running across the chart is a recording of the penile response. A much more jagged line above it, which follows the general contour of the penile response, magnifies the penile response by five times. However, to allow for responses that may reduce instead of increase, the recording level is begun at a scale reading of 10. This places the times-five reading at 50, and the times-five magnification quickly goes off scale with a minimal degree of arousal. Following the stimulus presentation, detumescent data is collected for 30 seconds. Note in FIGURES 3a and 3b that where the client responds to the deviant materials, his sexual response continues or rises during this 30-second detumescence period, while nonresponders tend to remain steady or drop off very quickly.

The trace toward the top two-thirds of the scale in FIGURE 4 is the Galvanic Skin Response (GSR). Initial indications are that the GSR will be valuable in detecting faking or attempts to fake. When a male attempts to voluntarily control his sexual response, he generally sucks in his stomach and holds his breath. This is the response

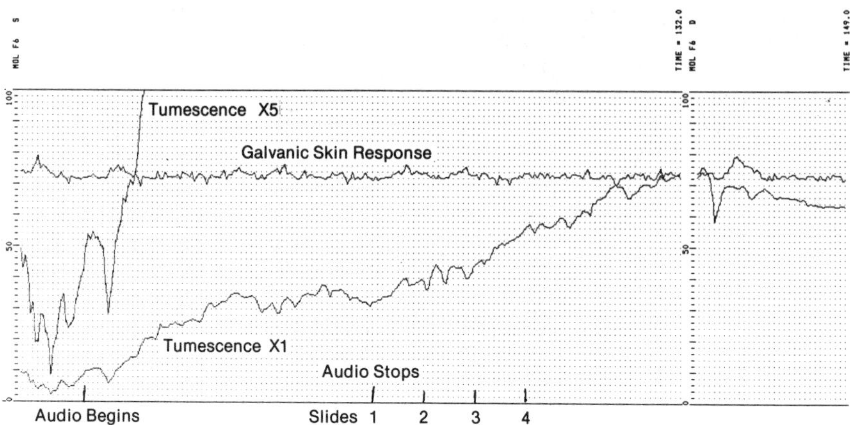

FIGURE 3a. Response of a 35-year-old male who molested a 5-year-old female. Stimulus was 6-year-old consenting female. Farrall Slide numbers XX-31, XX-37, XX-42, XX-45.

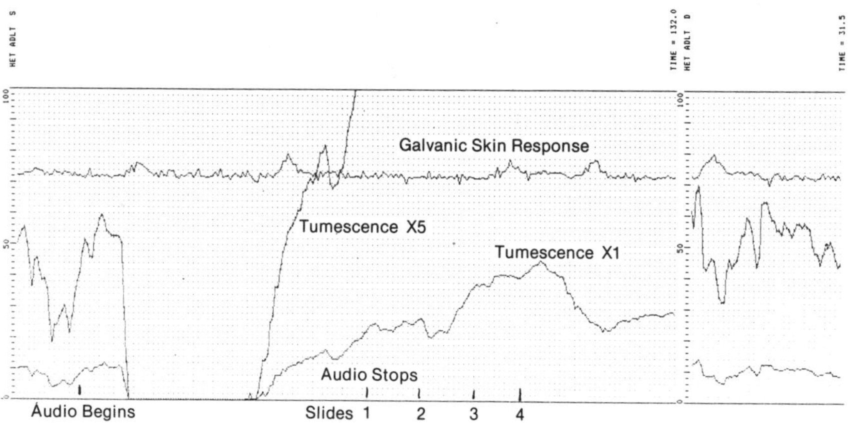

FIGURE 3b. Response of a 35-year-old male who molested a 5-year-old female. Stimulus was consenting heterosexual adult. Farrall Slide numbers M-46, M-55, TTT-67, TTT-72.

that tends to generate a powerful GSR. By being able to correlate spikes on the GSR with sudden depressions in the penile response, attempts to control in this manner can be detected. Note in FIGURE 4 how closely the downward spikes in the GSR are correlated with sudden depressions in the penile response.

The pilot study has produced some further interesting findings. For example, we have determined that the client's mind set when he enters the testing situation can have an effect on his response to the stimulus materials. This was discovered when it was noted that one individual produced a strong penile response to the baseline stimulus set. The baseline stimulus set is identical in format to the sexual stimulus sets except that the audio materials are totally meaningless and the pictures do not even have a human figure in them; they are only pictures of outdoor landscapes. Nevertheless, the client's mind set produced a sexual response because he was expecting to find something sexually stimulating occurring from the outset of the testing.

We also noted that a sexual response to one set of stimulus materials appears to condition a sexual response to the following set of materials. This was noted with an individual who had responded sexually to a set of materials. In the succeeding set a strong sexual response occurred as soon as the TV screen indicated another stimulus set had commenced, but before any stimulus materials had been presented.

An interesting and potentially useful finding was that some individuals respond almost exclusively to audio materials, while others respond almost exclusively to visual materials. The nature of the format of the stimulus materials, however, can enable one to obtain a discriminant response in spite of his being primarily an audio or a visual responder.

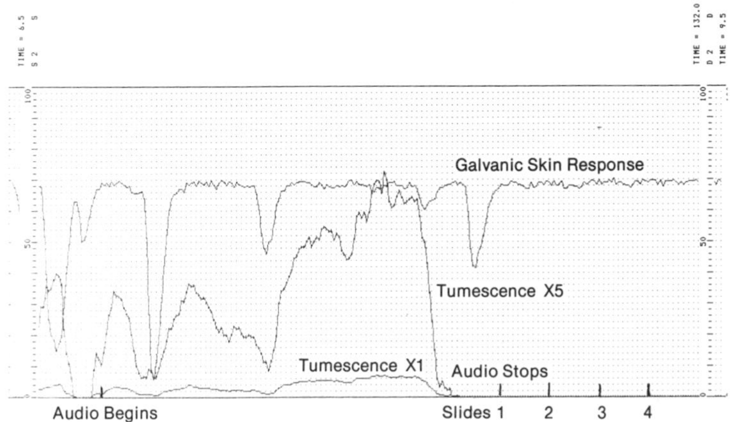

FIGURE 4. Response of a 41-year-old male who molested a 10-year-old female. Client had been taught biofeedback self-control as part of therapy. Farrall Slide numbers BB-55, BB-45, BB-50, BB-56.

FUTURE DIRECTIONS

The authors feel they are prepared at this point to refine the stimulus materials and engage in a major experimental study. In this study they hypothesize the following:

1. Individuals who cue into a particular classification of "generic" audio materials will be likely to respond sexually to these materials.
2. If an individual cues into the audio materials, the presentation of the visual materials will tend to enhance the sexual response.
3. An individual who cues into the audio and visual materials will take longer to detumify than the individual who does not.

4. The individual who has a fantasy life consistent with the stimulus materials will require a longer *total* detumescent time before the next presentation can continue.
5. Using a regression equation involving degree of change of tumescence to the audio stimulus plus degree of change through the visual presentation plus the rate of detumescence during the recorded 30-second detumescent period plus total length of time before the next stimulus sequence can be shown will result in a figure that is highest for an individual whose fantasy life is primarily in one stimulus area as contrasted to another. The authors suspect that the computer will enable us rapidly to arrive at a computation of a figure for each stimulus sequence and allow for a ranking of responses to all of the stimulus sequences.
6. The GSR will provide a means of detecting attempts to falsify a plethysmograph record, and it may also be used to develop an additional component for the regression equation. Similarly, the authors plan to include a self-report in each of the stimulus segments, to obtain a measure of the individual's ability to recognize his own responses and to provide a possible measure of defensiveness or denial.

The authors are in the process of editing the audio materials so that they will be of identical length, making the various stimulus sequences as comparable as possible. The authors expect to develop stimulus materials into a complete testing sequence to address some of the major features of maturational age rather than chronological age, providing a clearer discrimination between stimulus materials. The authors plan to tie these materials more closely to the computer to provide absolute control of timed sequences and to be able to indicate precisely on the printout the point at which some physiological response occurs in relation to a stimulus event. They expect the entire evaluation to occupy approximately one hour in length, making it more cost-effective for use in the private clinical setting.

The authors' purpose in presenting this paper was to outline some of the major problems in obtaining valid assessments of the sexual aggressor. They feel that with the introduction of the computer to present and analyze suitably discriminant sexual stimuli, many of the problems inherent in utilizing penile plethysmography can be resolved. They have presented a new method of combining the advantages of both audio and still-picture stimuli during assessments of sexual aggressors in a way to facilitate a discriminant response. By standardizing data collection and analysis methods to standardized stimulus materials, data transportation from center to center will be facilitated, resulting in comparable input from many sources. The authors hope they are providing a small, but significant, step in this direction.

REFERENCES

1. Quinsey, V. L. & W. L. Marshall. 1983. Procedures for reducing inappropriate sexual arousal: An evaluation review. *In* The Sexual Aggressor: Current Perspectives on Treatment. J. G. Greer & I. R. Stuart, Eds.: 267-289. Van Nostrand Reinhold Company. New York, NY.
2. Card, R. D. 1982. Biofeedback in the treatment of sexual deviation. Am. J. Clin. Biofeedback **5:** 31-42.
3. Knopp, F. H., J. Rosenberg & W. Stevenson. 1986. Report on nationwide survey of juvenile and adult sex-offender treatment programs and providers. Safer Society Press. Syracuse, NY.
4. Toobert, S., K. F. Bartelme & E. S. Jones. 1959. Some factors related to pedophilia. Int. J. Soc. Psychiatry **4:** 272-279.

5. Earls, C. M. & W. L. Marshall. 1983. The current state of technology in the laboratory assessment of sexual arousal patterns. *In* The Sexual Aggressor: Current Perspectives on Treatment. J. G. Greer & I. R. Stuart, Eds.: 336-362. Van Nostrand Reinhold Company. New York, NY.
6. Farrall, W. R. A Proposal for guidelines for P & P assessment. Presented at the Assessment and Treatment of Sexual Offenders Conference of the National Mental Health Institute, Tampa, Florida, February 1986.

Victims of Sexual Aggression: Introduction

JOYCE THOMAS

Division of Child Protection
Children's Hospital
National Medical Center
Washington, D.C. 20010

The pain, suffering, misfortunes, and other problems of sexual victimization of both adults and children are harsh realities that we have witnessed all too often in our professional practice. The number of victims continues to grow; each situation seems more overwhelming than the previous one; there is massive public awareness of the problem of sexual victimization. These factors make clinical intervention and decision making very complex. The victims of rape, incest, and other forms of sexual molestation come from all social strata, all racial and ethnic groups, and all geographic areas. We still do not know the true dimensions of the problem; estimates vary a great deal. In 1985 reports of sexual abuse of children increased more dramatically and quickly than did reports of physical abuse and neglect of children. A survey of 50 states indicated a consistent trend toward the more frequent reporting of sexual victimization of children in 1985 than five years earlier.

Critical documents such as the President's Task Force on Victims of Crime Report (1983), the Attorney General's Task Force on Family Violence (1984), and the Surgeon General's Workshop on Violence and Public Health (1985), as well as thousands of professional articles all point to the importance of expanding our understanding of the problem of victimization in order to improve treatment of and services to victims.

Today workers in the field of victimization are moving toward a consensus regarding "what to do" and "what to look for." Experience has shown that assessment of victimization has several stages: first, determining the immediate reactions to the crime; second, looking at the impact in order to determine the type of treatment needed; and third, looking at the long-term effects in order to judge the future needs of the client. In addition, developmental issues are seen as important in understanding and treating child victims of sexual abuse. The research articles in this part by Drs. Ann Burgess, Ellen Frank, Jon Conte, John Briere, Dean Kilpatrick, and Martha Burt address a variety of research issues related to adult and child victims of sexual assault.

Victims of crime pose a tremendous challenge to service providers—a challenge to transcend traditional roles, to interact and cooperate with different agencies, and above all to handle cases with compassion, sensitivity, and skill. While many sexually victimized individuals may not suffer extensive or major physical trauma, almost all experience various forms of psychological or emotional disturbance as a direct result of the victimization. Our knowledge of clinical assessment, appropriate treatment, the effects of sexual aggression on adults and children, as well as the coping strategies of survivors, has been greatly enhanced by empirical research. Basic descriptive research also plays an important role in providing information about the problems and special needs of victims of sexual assault. It is hoped that this information will serve as a basis for programs for victims.

The article by Ann Burgess *et al.* focuses on 41 men who were victimized as children. The article examines the possible link between sexual exploitation of male children and the later pattern of behavior described as serial rape. Dr. Burgess points out the importance of establishing a clear definition of sexual abuse, providing early intervention, and understanding the long-term effects of sexual abuse on male children in order to break the cycle of abuse. This is vital as we attempt to describe and understand the incidence, prevalence, and effects of sexual abuse on young male children. Factors such as the reluctance of male victims to discuss their victimization and the underreporting of child sexual abuse affect the victim-to-victimizer linkage.

The article by Ellen Frank *et al.* attempts to address the issue of treatment impact on recovery of the rape victim. Dr. Frank examines the implications and impact of various treatment approaches. In addition to specific information about the assault, biographic and psychiatric information was gathered to assist in the assessment process. The significance of short-term treatment to reduce immediate distress and thus reduce the secondary consequences of rape trauma was documented.

The next two articles specifically document the short- and long-term impact on children of sexual victimization. In the first of these articles Dr. Conte examines the effects of sexual victimization on 369 children 4 to 17 years of age seen at the Sexual Assault Center of Harborview Medical Center in Seattle between September 1983 and May 1985. A comparison group of children were recruited from day-care centers, churches, youth groups, and other community agencies. The study explores the perceptions of parents, behavioral variations in victimized children, and the implications of these factors in lessening the impact of the abuse on the child. Dr. Conte's findings are significant to both social welfare/child protection decisions and the need for special early treatment for child victims. Dr. Briere's study had two specific goals: first, to replicate earlier studies on the effects of childhood sexual trauma on adult mental health problems; and second, to look at the relationship of specific effects of certain aspects of the abuse experience. His findings reinforce other studies that document the harmful effects of childhood sexual abuse and the increased or varied symptoms associated with specific abuse acts, such as ritualization or intercourse.

The remaining two articles in this section specifically address the act of rape. Dr. Kilpatrick focuses on the additional legal and attitudinal problems associated with marital and acquaintance rape. The data suggest that victims are more likely to be raped by persons known to them than by strangers. There appears to be no difference between rape committed by strangers and rape committed by husbands and boyfriends with respect to the immediate and long-term physical and psychological impact of the assault. The article further documents the devastation of the female victimized by domestic sexual violence. In the final article of this section Drs. Burt and Katz research the issue of "coping strategies." They define "coping" as efforts made in response to stimuli experienced as threatening or stressful and the process of reducing the anxiety of the experience.

In looking at the issue of victimization, it is important to note that recent major social changes have influenced research on family violence. There have been increased awareness and concern about the rights of women and children. In addition, social scientists and the general public have become increasingly sensitive to violence as a result of the Vietnam War, assassinations of political leaders, civil and political disruptions, and rising homicide rates. The emergence of the Women's Movement highlighted problems of battered women. The identification of the Battered Child Syndrome by C. Henry Kempe alerted us to the issues of abused children. As a result of these social changes, different approaches to studying victimization have emerged.

One must keep in mind that such matters as ethical issues, concerns about confidentiality, and poor sampling often served as barriers to the study of sexual victimization. Many conceptual, methodological, and interpretative problems characterized research on sexual victimization during the late 1970s and early 1980s. Major problem areas include the defining of child sexual abuse and other forms of sexual victimization nominally and operationally and the nonuse of comparison groups. Research in the 1970s sought to refute the myths about victimization. The field has matured tremendously since that time.

Serial Rapists and Their Victims: Reenactment and Repetition[a]

ANN W. BURGESS,[b] ROBERT R. HAZELWOOD,[c] FRANCES E. ROKOUS,[b] CAROL R. HARTMAN,[d] AND ALLEN G. BURGESS[e]

[b]*University of Pennsylvania School of Nursing*
Philadelphia, Pennsylvania 19104

[c]*Behavioral Science Unit*
FBI Academy
Quantico, Virginia 22135

[d]*Graduate Program in Psychiatric Mental Health Nursing*
Boston College
Chestnut Hill, Massachusetts 02167

[e]*Boston University School of Management*
Boston, Massachusetts 02115

INTRODUCTION

Considerable attention has been paid to the study of child abuse since 1960,[1] and in particular, child sexual abuse in the past decade.[2] While child sexual abuse as it affects females has gained visibility within the last few years,[3,4] the issue of boy victimization has only recently surfaced.[5] Of the many debates in the study of this social problem as it relates to males, three of the most prominent issues include the definition, prevalence, and the long-term effects of sexual abuse of males.

Definition of Sexual Abuse

The first issue asks: What is a useful definition of sexual abuse of boys? In reviewing child sexual abuse studies (both sexes) from the victim's perspective, Wyatt and Peters[6] describe similarities and differences in the definitions used in terms of upper age limit for defining child sexual abuse, the criteria used to define a sexual experience as abusive, the inclusion or exclusion of experiences involving age peers, and the use of the different criteria for incidents occurring during adolescence. The studies reviewed for definition include Finkelhor's (1979) nonprobability sample of 530 women and

[a]This work was supported in part by Department of Justice, Office of Juvenile Justice and Delinquency Prevention Grant Number 84-JN-K010.

266 male students in six New England Colleges and Universities[7] and his 1984 probability sample of 185 male and 334 female parents of children 6 to 14 years of age in the Boston area;[5] Russell's 1983 probability sample of 930 women;[8] and Wyatt's[9] multistage stratified probability sampling with quotas of 126 Afro-American and 122 white women representing Los Angeles County. An example of the impact of definitions are the prevalence rates from one study that used a definition of abuse slightly less restrictive than that used by other researchers; recalculation, based on the definitions of other researchers, resulted in a 14% decrease in the number of individuals identified as abused. While this is a substantial change, Wyatt and Peters[10] argue that definition accounts for only a portion of the discrepancy in prevalence rates, suggesting that other methodological differences need to be examined with regard to their impact on prevalence rates.

Prevalence of Boy Sexual Abuse

The second issue asks: How frequently does sexual abuse occur in boys? In reviewing prevalence studies specifically on boy victimization, Finkelhor[5] cautions us on the methodological limitations in the scant data available. In the Bell and Weinberg study of homosexuality in San Francisco[11] a control group of 284 heterosexuals were interviewed, and 2.5% reported a "prepuberty sexual experience with a male adult involving physical contact." This is comparable with Bell and Weinberg's[12] homosexual sample's percentage of 4.9% with such a boyhood experience. When Finkelhor used a definition fairly consistent with the one used by Bell and Weinberg on his Boston survey of 185 fathers of children ages 6 to 14,[5] he found 3.2% of the fathers reporting such an experience.

Sociologists Risin and Koss[13] conducted a survey representing an approximated representative national sample of male students in higher education, with one of their research goals being to look at the issue of the sexual abuse of boys. Self-reports of childhood sexual experiences obtained from 2,972 men indicate that 7.3% of the men reported a childhood experience that met at least one of the following three criteria for sexual abuse: (1) existence of age discrepancy between the child and perpetrator, (2) use of some form of coercion to obtain participation by the victim, and/*or* (3) a perpetrator who was a caregiver or authority figure. Although the results are limited in generalizability to other students, this group represents 25% of all persons in the United States aged 18-24.[14]

Impact on Sexually Abused Boy

The third issue asks: What happens to the abused boy when he grows up? Finkelhor's review of studies reporting child sexual abuse notes that large numbers of boys show up in general surveys and police-based studies, rather than clinic-based studies.[5] Thus, it is not surprising that the long-term effects of boyhood victimization might be found in studies of sex offenders. Using a nonprobability sample of 348 men incarcerated for a sexual assault, Groth[15] through interview and/or clinical records, reported on sexual trauma in the life histories of rapists and child molesters. Sexual trauma was operationally defined as any sexual activity witnessed or experienced that was emotionally upsetting or disturbing to the subject. As a comparison group, 62 male law-enforcement officers were sampled. Evidence of some form of sexual trauma between ages 1 and 15 was found in the life histories of 30% of the sex offenders ($n = 309$) and in 3% of the life histories of police officers ($n = 62$).

In a study by Seghorn, Boucher, and Prentky[16] of the incidence of childhood physical and sexual abuse in a sample of incarcerated rapists ($n = 97$) and child molesters ($n = 54$), four major findings were that: (1) the incidence of sexual assault in childhood among child molesters was higher than the incidence of such abuse reported in the literature, (2) the incidence of sexual assault in childhood among child molesters was over twice as high as its incidence among rapists, (3) rapists were three times more likely to be victimized by a family member than were child molesters, and (4) when a sexual assault did occur, it was associated with many other indices of familial turmoil and instability.

Conceptual Framework for Project

The study reported here is part of a larger project examining the possible linkage of childhood sexual abuse to juvenile delinquency and criminal behavior in population samples of victims and victimizers. As Finkelhor notes, one of the most important components of a successful research design is a conceptual framework to guide the design.[2] We would emphasize that a framework is critical in analyzing qualitative data.

Major efforts have been exerted by researchers and clinicians to develop models to explain the impact of sexual abuse on children. Sociologists Finkelhor and Browne[17] have proposed a model for analyzing the experience of sexual abuse in terms of four trauma-causing factors, called traumagenic dynamics: traumatic sexualization, stigmatization, betrayal, and powerlessness. These dynamics are believed to "alter the child's cognitive and emotional orientation to the world, and create trauma by distorting a child's self-concept, worldview, and affective capacities" (p. 180)[17]

The Linkage Project has focused on the first of these trauma-causing factors, traumatic sexualization. As such, the conceptual framework of informational processing of trauma was developed for the project because of the lack of explicated or tested frameworks for understanding the linkage between child sexual victimization and level of adjustment.[18] Data were analyzed for this paper within the specific psychodynamic concepts of trauma theory of (1) intrusive repetitions and (2) denial described by Horowitz[19] as labels for two extremes of responses to stressful life events. Although great controversy has surrounded the concept of trauma originally described by Breuer and Freud in their Studies on Hysteria,[20] clinicians seem to agree that after a traumatic event, there is a compulsive tendency to repeat some aspect of the experience.[21-23] To quote Horowitz:

> This involuntary repetition includes the recurrence of thoughts and especially images about the stress event, of feelings related to the original experience, and of behavioral reenactments of parts of the experience itself. . . . The trauma may be symbolically repeated over and over again. Finally, there are several repetitive physiological responses to stress . . . (pp. 15-16).[23]

A psychodynamic conceptual model used by Green[24] to explain the trauma of child physical abuse describes how the defensive efforts of the child fail when the impact of the trauma critically damages the defensive functions of the ego. Green states:

> The damaged or weakened ego then resorts to a driven, compulsive repetition and reenactment of the traumatic elements . . . The repetition compulsion, then, may be regarded as the ego's last line of defense against traumatic stimulation. Its success or failure to achieve mastery will depend on the strength of the ego, in relation to the magnitude of the traumatic event (pp. 150-151).[24]

Green observes this model of trauma to be consistent with Benjamin's[25] and Bellak, Hurvich, and Gediman's concept of the stimulus barrier as an active, adaptive ego function, and Brody and Axelrad's[27] view of the receptive and integrative functions of the protective shield.

Our clinical research interest was directed to these concepts with the serial rapist data because of the emerging data on sex offender fantasies[28] and the work by FBI agents with criminal profiling in isolating crime scene patterns[29,30] In another Linkage Project sample, we compared sexual murderers with a history of child sexual abuse with murderers without a history, and found that the former reported earlier rape fantasies, aversion to peer sex, and multiple paraphilias of zoophilia and sexual sadism.[31]

With the serial rapist population, we were particularly interested in the clinical question of whether childhood sexual abuse was an antecedent in the deviant sexuality noted in sex offenders.[16] This paper reports on childhood physical and sexual abuse in serial rapists, the reenactment of boyhood abuse, and the repetition of sexually aggressive behaviors.

METHOD

Subjects

The sample consists of 41 serial rapists, who were incarcerated in twelve different states at the time of interview (Maryland, Kentucky, Oklahoma, New Mexico, Utah, Arizona, Colorado, Idaho, California, Oregon, Michigan, and Montana). Each rapist committed at least ten rapes, exhausted all forms of appeal, and voluntarily participated in the study through signing a human subjects consent form and being interviewed by FBI agents.

Data Collection

The data collection consisted of a face-to-face interview with two special agents from the Behavioral Science Unit of the Federal Bureau of Investigation. Thirty-seven of the interviews were taped and transcribed; the shortest interview was 4½ hours, the longest 12½ hours. A 79-page questionnaire was completed by the agents from the review of pre- and postsentencing records and the interview. In addition to extensive background information, complete data were obtained on the first, middle, and last rape offense. As a result of the methods of data collection, both qualitative and quantitative data were available for analysis.

Procedure

The data for this study includes the analysis of the following variables: childhood physical and sexual abuse, evidence of reenactment of abuse, and evidence of repetition of criminal behavior of forcible rape.

The variable of physical abuse was ascertained if there was congruence between the answer of yes to physical abuse on the protocol and in the interview with the FBI agent as to the subject's description of patterns of discipline and parental aggression.

Acknowledging that investigators have questioned the validity of self-reported sexual behavior and speculating that most boy sexual abuse would not be documented in records, it was determined that additional methods would have to be taken to ascertain the presence of sexual trauma in the childhood histories. Thus, the procedure was to routinely ask, during the interview, if the subject had even been sexually abused. In most instances the answer was no. An immediate follow-up question was, "At what age and with whom did you have your first sexual experience with another person?" A panel of special agents and clinicians then determined if the experience met the criteria for sexual abuse and then classified the experiences according to a level of abuse.

Scoring Procedures

The experience was classified as sexual abuse if one of the following three criteria, based on the criteria recommended by Finkelhor and Hotaling,[32] was present: (1) some form of force or coercion was used to obtain the participation of the victim (i.e., gifts or money, threats to hurt or punish, use of power over victim, actual physical force); (2) there was an age discrepancy of at least 5 years between the child and the other person; and (3) the other person was a caregiver or an authority figure (i.e., parent, teacher, coach, babysitter, family member, stepparent).

Those experiences deemed sexually abusive were then subjected to classification by level of abuse, using a classification system adapted from Burgess and Holmstrom[33] and reported by Risin and Koss.[13] The three mutually exclusive classes of sexual abuse, from the most serious and directly experienced, are: (1) forced sex or penetration, (2) exploitive sex, and (3) witnessing sexual events deemed stressful or stimulating. These categories are defined as follows.

- *Forced or penetration* experiences are those in which oral or anal intercourse, attempted or completed, is achieved; ejaculation is not necessary; the legal term of rape is often used to characterize this type of experience.

- *Exploitive* situations are those in which another person sexually fondles the boy, or the boy is requested to touch or stroke another person's sex organs; the exploiter uses a variety of methods to lure, entice, or seduce the child into sexual activity.
- *Witnessing* disturbing sexual situations are those in which the boy views sexual activity or another person's sex organs, is requested to do something sexual, or exhibits his sex organs at another person's request and reports it confusing or disturbing.

Five raters classified sexually abusive experiences into these categories. Agreement was 90%. Consensus was reached for the remaining 10%. Total agreement was 100%.

Reenactment

Reenactment is the direct replication of the abuse experience. Reenactment was determined from the interview data of the subjects' memories of their earliest sexual experiences and their first self-initiated sexual venture. Evidence of reenactment included examples of sexual activity and assertive behaviors with family, acquaintances, and/or strangers. The details of the earliest sexual experience, not coded for level of abuse, were compared to the details of their memories of their earliest sexually assertive behaviors. Thus, reenactment was a behavioral match or a clear symbolic reference to the abuse. If either or both were present, reenactment was affirmed.

Repetition

Repetition is a fixed pattern of rape behaviors that has its roots in the reenactment experience and constructed memories of the abuse experience. Repetition was inferred from the details of what the rapist did to contact and control his victim, the characteristics of the offense itself, and aspects of postoffense behavior. The behavioral reoccurrence of these acts in subsequent rapes establishes the phenomenon of repetition.

RESULTS

Sample

The ages of the 41 men in the sample range from 23 to 55 years, with a mean of 35.2. The majority (85%) are white, 12% are black, and 2% are Hispanic. The educational level of the sample ranges from 5 years of schooling to 17 years, with an average of 11.3 years. Seventeen percent of the men report no degrees held, including high school. While 61 percent of the men claim a high school diploma as their highest degree, 22 of the 25 men received this degree through equivalency testing. The remaining 22 percent claim a college degree (associates 12%, bachelors 10%).

The annual income at the last day worked ranges from $5,000 to $52,000, with an average of $16,446. Just under half of the men (46%) describe themselves as lacking job stability or chronically unemployed. Questions about preadult institutionalization history reveal that 41% of the men had spent time in a detention center, 26% in a mental health facility, 15% in a state home or orphanage, 8% in a foster home, and 4% in a boarding or military school.

Physical Abuse

Out of 40 cases with data, 15 (37.5%) had evidence that the subject was physically abused by parents or dominant caretakers. Offenders reported being whipped, beaten, and suffering broken bones for a variety of perceived infractions. Sometimes the offender's description illustrated out-of-control rage of the parent:

> It would start out with a small spanking and then he'd end up throwing the strap down and using his hands or whatever he could put his hands on. In fact, I've been through four or five prisons and the only scars I got on my body I got from my father at home.

This offender recalled the beatings starting as early as age 3 or 4. The effect of this beating is illustrated by this offender's intrusive thinking, his fantasizing of his own violent aggression, and his denial of the fantasy:

> After he'd get through with me, I'd go off by myself and I'd think about fixing him so he didn't ever do me like that again. . . . In fact, one time when I was nine or ten, we were out hunting and it was just after a severe whipping that he gave me and he was in front of me and I had this gun and I was behind him and I thought how easy it would be just to squeeze the trigger and take him out. Just say it was an accident, that I tripped. When it got down to squeezing the trigger, I actually loved him too much to do it.

Sexual Memories Defined as Abusive

One of the most noteworthy findings in this study is that 56.1% (23 of 41) of the rapists had been sexually abused in either a forced (16) or exploitive (7) manner as a child. An additional 8 (19.5%) reported the most serious level of abuse as witnessing a sexually disturbing event. Ten of the rapists (24.4%) could not recall any sexually abusive events.

Recalculating these figures with only abused subjects, the numbers become quite dramatic: 74.2% (23 of 31) of the rapists had one or more sexual experiences of either the forced or exploitive type. The highest level of abuse of 8 (25.8%) was witnessing. Of the 23 who were either forced or exploited, 10 (43.5%) reported only a single occurrence, while 13 of this group (56.5%) had multiple occurrences with

TABLE 1. Number of Different Abusers by Type of Assault of 41 Serial Rapists

Number of Abusers	Forced Only	Exploited Only	Witnessed Only	Forced and Exploited	Forced and Other	Exploited and Other	All Three
1	7	3	5	—	—	—	—
2	0	1	2	3	2	1	—
3	0	0	1	0	2	1	0
4	0	0	0	0	0	1	1
5	0	0	0	0	0	0	1
Totals	7	4	8	3	4	3	2

the same abuser. As noted in TABLE 1, 16 of the 31 (51.6%) had more than one abuser. Brief examples of each level of abuse follow.

Forced Sex

One offender recounted an experience at a movie theater at age 7. A man sitting two seats away from him asked if he wanted to make three dollars by unzipping his pants. The boy, after refusing, moved to another seat across the theater. The man followed and offered him two dollars to be allowed to perform oral sex on him. The boy accepted and allowed the act every weekend (for payment) for approximately one year. This example suggests a compliant boy who is confused and pressured by the money into a startling forced experience. The intrusive thinking and fixation about the homosexual experience carried over into his adult life. He described living two lives: he lived a heterosexual life on the "side of tracks of his home town" and drifted to the "other side of the tracks" for sex with a transvestite.

Exploitive Sex

At around age 8, the subject was playing with friends. An older boy took him into the woods, exposed his penis, and asked the boy to touch it. The offender reported both touching and masturbating the boy.

Witnessing Disturbing Sex

One offender recalls seeing his mother nude with various male partners in the home following his parents' divorce, when he was between 7 and 10 years old. After his mother remarried, when he was a 14-year-old boy, he made a pinhole in the wall, through which he would peer to watch his mother and stepfather engage in sex. He would masturbate and feel excited, angry, and jealous.

Gender of Abuser in Most Serious Level of Abuse

When studying the gender of the aggressor in the most serious level of abuse, penetration, one notes the predominance of males ($n = 16$). For both the exploited and witnessing level of abuse, males and females were implicated equally as abusers; however, only witnessing has both males and females as abusers. The most forceful abuse was perpetrated by males (51.6%). When TABLE 2 is interpreted across levels of abuse, the figures indicate that almost half (48.4%) are male, followed by one-third females (32.3%), and 12.9% are both men and women (6.5% no data).

Relationship of Abuser in Most Serious Level of Abuse

In examining the relationship of abuser by level of abuse, TABLE 3 indicates that it is just as likely for the boy to experience forced sex with a stranger (45%) as with someone in the family (45%); 10% of the abusers who are not in the family are known to the boy. Exploitive sex is predominantly with known people (50%), with family members accounting for 33% and strangers 8% of the incidents. Strangers appear not to be involved in the level of witnessing; rather the relationship is family (75%) or known (25%).

As far as the totals are concerned, the largest percentage of all levels of sexual abuse occurs within the family (48.4%); sexual abuse by a known perpetrator and that by strangers both account for 22.6% of the incidents.

Reenactment

As shown in TABLE 4, slightly over half of the offenders (51.6%) had direct experiences of reenactment when they were preadolescent, usually with younger children. The most common pattern was for the subjects to molest children in their neighborhood (50%), in their family (25%), or "girlfriends" (25%). It is important to note that the offenders reflected in TABLE 4 did not identify themselves as sexually assertive, nor did they associate the details of their earliest sexual experiences with their own sexual abuse.

One offender with 19 rapes and 11 convictions described two abusive situations

TABLE 2. Gender of Aggressor in Highest Level of Abuse

Gender	Forced	Exploited	Witnessed	Total
Male	10	3	2	15 (48.4%)
Female	4	4	2	10 (32.3%)
Both	0	0	4	4 (12.9%)
No data	2	0	0	2 (6.5%)
Total	16	7	8	31

TABLE 3. Relationship of Abuser in Most Serious Level of Abuse

Relationship	Forced	Exploited	Witnessed	Total
Family	6	2	7	15 (48.4%)
Known	3	3	1	7 (22.6%)
Stranger	5	2	0	7 (22.6%)
No data	2	0	0	2 (6.5%)
Total	16	7	8	31

that occurred around age 6, the year he lived with his grandmother after his parents divorced. On several occasions during the daytime, the maternal grandmother would call him to bed, and they would lay face to face. She never made any overt sexual contact with him, but he remembered feeling uncomfortable. The second situation involved his finding the football of two teenage boys and taking it to them with the hope of playing. Rather, one of the teenagers knocked him down and pinned him to the ground while the other boy grabbed his genitals. This offender then remembers a game he and his best friend played when he was 8-10 years old:

> We used to play this game; it was like tag and hide-and-seek. We would find girls, catch them, tie them up and put them in our club house. The rules of the game were that we could do anything we wanted to them.

In his first assaults, which began at age 19, he would grab women's breasts and fondle them. In later assaults he would tie the victim's hands, fondle her breasts, ejaculate on her, and leave.

Repetition

The repetition of sexually aggressive behaviors was found to begin at adolescence with the onset of rape fantasies and rape behaviors. The majority of offenders (n = 39) reported an age of first rape fantasy. This age was as early as 8 and as late as 28 years, with a mean of 16.9 years.

One offender describes the sequence of his fantasy development, a quiescent phase, and his fantasy's reactivation to action. His first recalled rape fantasy was at age 14:

> There was this rape scene in [the book] and I remember getting really turned on by that . . . I used to read it all the time then I got to sort of acting out in my room . . . just sort of playing it out, thinking about it. It didn't go beyond that; it sort of just died. Must have been dormant. I was about 16 or 17 when I first started to go out, not with the intent of committing a rape. I'd go into houses at night or early in the morning . . . houses right across the street. I'd look at the woman's bra or panties, just sort of explore the house. I'd leave . . . not take anything. That went on for a couple of years. Then I did that more and more . . . Then I got my driver's license and began driving . . . My first attempt at a sexual assault was when I was about 19 . . . I got an image of grabbing her, feeling her breasts and taking off.

Rape fantasies were found to occur within a shorter time period (3.7 years average) after witnessing a sexually disturbing event than after either exploited (5.8 years average) or forced sex (8.5 years).

The 41 serial rapists reported 837 rapes and 401 attempted rapes of strangers, for which there were 200 convictions. The hidden rape statistics from these subjects' early and midadolescent age period, during the reenactment phase, account for an additional 100 known victims (e.g., siblings, cousins, neighborhood girls, and dates). The number of rapes of strangers committed by those in the sample ranged from 10 to 59, with a mean of 30 per offender. The period of time during which the offenders raped before being arrested for the first time ranged from three months to twelve years. Additionally, over two-thirds (68%) of the serial rapists had histories of voyeurism.

DISCUSSION

The Victims of the Serial Rapists

The critical finding of this study is the overwhelming number of victims of these serial rapists. The earliest victims, determined through reconstruction of reenactment of early sexual abuse, were younger siblings, neighborhood children, girlfriends, and acquaintances. In adolescence the offenders continued this behavior with their dates, and as young adults many admitted to spouse and partner rapes. Very few of these rapes of known victims were reported to authorities. That 41 men could continue this socially deviant behavior in their stranger rapes to over 1200 victims is a sobering commentary on the effectiveness of our juvenile system, mental health system, and judicial system in case findings, reporting, investigating, and treating rape cases.

Is Boy Sexual Abuse Underacknowledged?

In an effort to address the saliency of early sexual victimization to raping behavior with a comparison sample, we took figures of boy sexual abuse reported by sociologists Risin and Koss in their study of 2,972 male college students.[13] This comparison sample was chosen for several reasons: (1) it represented an approximated national sample

TABLE 4. Reenactment of Abuse on Earliest Victims of Serial Rapists

Category	Number	(%)
Direct reenactment	16	(51.6)
Known	8	
Sister	4	
Girlfriend	4	
No reenactment determined	15	(48.4)

of men between ages 18 and 24, a time developmentally when male rape behavior is often reported; (2) the data had been judged for most serious or highest level of abuse; and (3) the men had been asked about their own sexually aggressive behaviors, which were then judged as rape and/or coercive. In this college sample, of the 7.3% (n = 216) who reported an abusive sexual experience before the age of 14, exhibition was the most serious for 34.7%, with fondling accounting for 34.7% and penetration the most serious incident for 30.7%. According to Risin and Koss,[13] 4.4% (n = 131) of the 2,972 men reported perpetrating since the age of 14 acts that met strict legal definitions of rape; 3.3% of the men reported acts that met the legal definition of attempted rape; acts constituting sexual coercion were reported by 7.2%, and acts constituting sexual contact were reported by 10.2%, for a total of 25.1%. Virtually none of these men were involved in the criminal justice system.

Compared to the college sample, this study of serial rapists shows levels of abuse that are reversed, with the most serious level of abuse being penetration for 51.6% of those abused. There is a difference of 20.9% between the college and rapist sample. In the rapist sample, the second most serious level of abuse was fondling for 32.2% and exhibition for 25.8%.

As compared to the college sample, our data suggest that the serial rapist had a higher level of abuse (forced sex) and that abuse more often involved incest and family members (48.4% vs. 22.2%). This finding, also reported by Seghorn *et al.*,[16] suggests that the family system of the rapist was too weakly organized to be able to guide and direct the sexual and aggressive development of the boy.

Both men and women play a role in the socialization of the male child regarding sexual behavior. Although the rapist sample, as compared to the college male sample, reports lower percentages of woman as abuser (32.3% vs. 47.1%), it is noteworthy that the female as abuser is reported in both samples.

A possible reason for the underacknowledgment of women as abusers is the early expectation and identification of the male as being sexually active regardless of the context. There is an inclination to joke about the boy who is sexually initiated by the older girl. There are bemused smiles when one hears of the 11-year-old male being met at the door by the attractive drunk nude mother of a playmate. The arousal, anxiety, inadequacy, humiliation, disillusionment, and instability that the boy confronts under such circumstances is discounted.

Finkelhor[5] suggests three factors that may explain the underreporting of the sexual abuse of boys: (1) boys grow up with the male ethic of self-reliance; (2) boys have to grapple with the stigma of homosexuality when an adult male has abused them; and (3) boys may have more to lose from reporting their victimization experiences.

The importance of understanding early sexual abuse of a boy as trauma is linked to his developing characteristics and beliefs. When a female is a sexual aggressor to a boy, several cognitive shifts occur. First, the boy has to change traditional thinking that only males initiate and seek out sexuality to a belief that females are equally aggressive sexually. The thinking that females are to be valued and protected becomes confused, and the predatory nature of the woman is highlighted in the males mind. The young boy derives an image of females as being imperious, if not lustful and insatiable in their sexual interests and demands.

This belief system gathers support and reinforcement in family situations where there is divorce and the mother has frequent male partners. Several rapists in this study volunteered their feelings about observing sexually explicit behaviors between mother and male partners in the home.

When the exploiter is a male, there is perplexity for the boy. There may be a new awareness of homosexual activity. There may be confusion over being betrayed by a male adult and intensifications of fear that the male is not to be trusted. This betrayal puts them in an unstable state regarding their own maleness and affective life, all of which becomes framed in an uncontrollable urge to do something. Under these circumstances the young boy experiences himself as not being protected by the female, in some instances experiencing the female as complicit in his abuse by the older male.

Detecting Boy Sexual Abuse

Could the abuse experienced by these boys have been detected even without their disclosing it? Probably not, given our times; but with new knowledge on child sexual abuse, we suggest that reenactment is a key observation.

Reenactment, a trauma response to victimization, has been noted most clearly in the play of very young children.[18,34,35] Play reenactment supports the notion of the intrusive imagery and the preoccupation with sexual matters and aggression. The play begins to bind the symptoms of stress and trauma (sex and aggression) that constitute preoccupation with what had happened.

Consider the following case, coded as reenactment. One rapist described memories he regarded as sexual, in which an aunt, while bathing him in a tub, would fondle his penis. This occurred several times. He recounts going to the home of a male school friend at around age 11 or 12 and finding his friend's mother (who was in her 30s) "drunk and nude, lying on a couch." His young friend ran from the scene, leaving the offender, who found himself intrigued by what he saw and highly excited. He states that she called him over to her and, when he approached, took hold of his hand, moved it across her body, and thrust it between her legs. He reported that he found this exciting and inserted his fingers into her. He thought that it was wrong and that he should leave, but then he leaned over and kissed her on the buttocks. With that, she "popped me in the ears." This action startled and frightened him, and he ran from the house feeling "scared to death," fearful that his mother and father would be informed, realizing he had done something wrong but feeling he did it because he wanted to. He remembers being upset, confused, and scared. He knows that these are the same feelings he has every time he rapes.

One can accept the experience at face value as the offender reports it—that this woman invited some type of sexual contact with the young boy, and in his curiosity he continued the activity and she startled him with her movements to rebuff. Alternatively, one can speculate that the two boys came home, found a partially clothed woman sleeping, and saw liquor bottles and an empty glass. The friend left in embarrassment, while the offender became curious and excited and began to explore her body, only to have her wake up and box him in the ears. However one regards this incident, it is important to note that each boy behaves differently. The level of excitement in one boy (the offender) is remembered as feelings of fright and confusion over right and wrong. This emotional state seems to be central to his raping behavior as an adult male.

Repetition

The juvenile behaviors noted in this group of serial rapists focused on an array of secretive acts of stealing underwear from sisters or clotheslines or entered homes—all for mastubatory fantasy. Sometimes the juvenile would just spy inside the house and take nothing. As one offender put it: "I used to like to break in when the husband and wife would be sleeping and just sneak around." He even called his behavior "symbolic penetration."

The onset of rape fantasies represented the earliest observations of the juvenile's crystalizing of sexually aggressive behaviors. The repetition of the fantasies did not result in resolution of his inner tension; rather, repetition became a prototype for the early rape behaviors.

As time advances, each of the rapes carried out by the offenders augments their criminal patterns. They make adjustments as to how they obtain their victims. They perfect ritualistic characteristics of maintaining control and extracting whatever they want from the victim. While the rape behavior gains in skill and elaborateness, it tends to maintain key characteristics. As a matter of fact, it is these key characteristics that give a modus operandi to the rapist.[36] While a learning set operates in repeated rapes, it has little to do with the resolution of the internal tension that we suggest has its origins in the early abuse. We suggest that this internal state may account for the ultimate escalation of violence.

Critical Intervening Variables for Sexual Violence

What role does boy sexual abuse play in adult rape behavior? Although this study was designed as a preliminary, exploratory project, it suggests that early sexual abuse in and of itself does not explain the sexually aggressive behaviors of rapists. Studies indicate a variety of response patterns in sexually abused children,[17,37] of which identification with the aggressor is only one.

This study provides descriptive data on several combinations that cluster to create a state of disinhibition in men who serially rape. One important interacting set of variables addresses family pathology and violence. The blurring of multiple types of childhood abuse—physical, sexual, and neglect—has been cited as a critical variable by Seghorn *et al.*[16]

Another variable is peer violence, either on a one-to-one basis or in a gang. Studies support the critical role of violent homes as an intervening variable in delinquency and criminal behavior.[38,39] The research on gang behavior and sexual activity is minimal. In this sample, several anecdotal examples surfaced, one of which is illustrative of this point. One offender reported the following:

> We watched the older boys picking up girls and not letting them go; we were like the little guys tagging along. They would run us off but we would sneak back. The guys would take the girls to the back of the hill and beat on them. We'd hear screams. I remember the guys had this girl down. They took her clothes off and wouldn't give them back until she gave in. Another time my father went down with a gun and brought the girl back.

This example illustrates the offender, as a boy, identifying with the violence of his peers versus the consideration of his parents for the girl. The choice was his; he chose his peers. Repetition was noted in his description of his middle rape offense as a gang rape.

In the context of an unresponsive, erratic social context that sanctions and condones exploitation of others, abuse may well play a part in fixing characterlogical defenses of the traumatized child. Even when children are removed from disorganized or violent homes and neighborhoods, institutional care may be equally problematic. We heard ample testimony to this. Early stress and trauma compounded by these other salient events may account for what Horowitz[19] suggests as posttraumatic characterlogical disorders. It was striking to observe the state of entitlement and justification shown by these offenders. Their narcissism reflects a cognitive set that centers all life on the subject, with minimal attachment to others and to social values of community and responsibility for the rights and property of others.

In summary, the data suggest that early sexual abuse is responded to by reenactment behavior as an attempt to manage the confusion and stress generated by the sexual activities. This behavior is either ignored or responded to in a punitive manner; neither response addresses the underlying trauma of exploitation. The child is unable to regulate his own arousal behavior. Furthermore, he has an inordinate preoccupation with sex and sexually stimulating aggressive thoughts. These evolved for these young men into what we call their first rape fantasies. There has usually been a parallel movement in spying activities, obscene phone calls, and secretive exploits into the lives of nearby females and children. For this group, soon after the establishment of the rape fantasy, the first rapes (as defined by the offender) occurred. There is now a crystalization and patterning of the rape behavior to the predatory stance. Such behavior tends to repeat itself and become, in the process, refined; the thoughts become elaborated, and stylized patterns emerge. We suspect that the original hyperarousal manifested during the period of reenactment behavior has become channeled into a more organized pattern of rape. The connection between the rape behavior and early abuse, sexual and physical, is not always made by the offender; rather, there is a total absorption and involvement in the rape behavior, which begins to cycle: there is a rape, the experience is reflected upon and developed, it serves as an arousal level, which then motivates and propels the rapist to repeat the rape. Each repetition of a rape insures mastery and control of each element of the rapist's own abuse, and is destined to be irreversible.

PRACTICAL IMPLICATIONS: STOPPING THE RAPES AND PREVENTING VICTIMIZATION

The first order of business is to stop the rapes in order to prevent additional victims. This can be done by: (1) intervention and finding cases of the early reenactment of the child victim; (2) juvenile authorities attending to the troubled boy from the disorganized and chaotic home; (3) institutions providing protection and treatment for children and juveniles; (4) mental health professionals acknowledging child sexual victimization and providing treatments to deal with the trauma.

Law enforcement agents have a pragmatic task in dealing with serial rapes: to find a suspect as quickly as possible to reduce anxiety in a community. It will be helpful for police to know that the majority of serial rapists are probably married and have a history of peeping and fetish burglary that can be related to other crimes. For example, police can tie certain crimes together, as, for example, fetish burglary with rape. Since it appears that the reenactment phase is closest to the offender's own type of abuse, police should take seriously complaints of juveniles who are sexually molesting family members and/or acquaintances.

There is a rigidity to the patterning of the crime scene of rapists. We find that elaborate crime activity may actually be preparatory to selecting and controlling victims. We have underestimated the role of spying or voyeuristic behavior. There is investigative evidence that voyeuristic behavior may escalate to breaking and entering and targeting victims. Sometimes the rapist operates by selecting the victim and then by spying on her, observing her over time in order to become familiar with an area that renders the victim vulnerable. We have to reexamine the notion that breaking and entering and fetish burglary are simply for drug money or mischief of some sort. These crimes may be the precursor to more physically violent activity or a dress rehearsal for the rape fantasy.

Consider the following case. A 30-year-old serial rapist admitted to raping approximately 25 women in one particular geographic location in a major city. He revealed that his behavior included multiple offenses of spying and burglaries as well as rape since age 16, and that he improved with experience. He would use the spying and burglaries to familiarize himself with a home and its surroundings, in order to custom design a fantasy of his rape of the victim. Thus, to him the woman would not be a stranger (as he would be to her), because of his fantasy rehearsal. Indeed, this rapist admitted to seeing one of his victims in a store several months after the rape and noted her wearing a plaid dress that he remembered from a family photograph hanging on her wall when he burglarized and spied on her apartment several times prior to the rape. This statement by the rapist provides insight as to the type of detailed information he would obtain. It is important to note that this information in no way aroused any sympathy or empathy in him; rather, it provided power and control over the victim and an incorporation of the victim into himself, to make him seem all-knowing and all-powerful. In the rape, he forbids his victims to talk, and he blindfolds them, indicating his need for and skill in gaining ultimate control in order to carry out the rape fantasy. He will not allow anything to break through the organized perceptions he has of his victim and what he is doing. As a matter of fact, it could be potentially lethal for any victim to challenge his control, because he cannot tolerate any interruption that may stop or inhibit his actions toward a victim. From talking with one of his victims, we surmise that his skill in intimidating and terrorizing women was expert, resulting in severe fear imprinting to his victims.

As clinicians routinely ask questions relating to early sexual memories, they need to differentiate reenactment behavior from peer activity. This requires sensitivity in judging dominant/submissive relationship patterns and methods of control and intimidation. Family therapists need routinely to assess families for incest behaviors and to be alert to the fact that there may be multiple family members committing incest when one disclosure is made. It is crucial to insure that young children are protected from sexually aggressive older siblings.

In conclusion, the number of unreported victims from this sample of 41 serial rapists is substantial. Even if the victim-to-victimizer linkage existed for these 41 men alone, the inability to correct the reenactment and early rape behavior of these men as boys or juveniles cost enormous suffering to over 1300 child and female victims, their families, and their communities.

SUMMARY

The major finding in this study of 41 serial rapists is the large numbers of reported and unreported victims. For over 1200 attempted and completed rapes, there were 200 convictions. The hidden rapes or earliest nonreported victims of these men as boys and adolescents were identified from their families, their neighborhood, and their schools.

Examining the possible link between childhood sexual abuse and criminal behavior in this sample of 41 serial rapists, 56.1% were judged to have at least one forced or exploitive abuse experience in boyhood, as compared to a study of 2,972 college males reporting 7.3% experiencing boyhood sexual abuse. Looking within the abused samples, 56.1% of the rapists reported forced sex, compared to the college sample's 30.4%. Also, the rapist sample revealed higher rates of family member as abuser (48.4%), compared to 22.2% for the college sample. Retrospective reconstruction of the sexual activities and assertive behaviors of these men as boys reveals that 51% of the boys reenact the abuse as a preadolescent with their earliest victims being known to them (48% as neighborhood girls), family (25% as sisters), or girlfriend (25%). The onset of rape fantasies in midadolescence (mean age 16.9) crystalizes the earlier sexually initiated behaviors into juvenile behaviors of spying, fetish burglaries, molestations, and rapes. Repetition of these juvenile behaviors set their criminal patterns on strangers—their next group of victims.

To reduce victimization, serial rapists need to be identified early and stopped. This means acknowledging and reporting boy sexual abuse. This includes being sensitive to the reenactment behaviors noted in the initiated activities of abused children, which in turn need to be differentiated from peer play. Closer attention needs to be paid to families with incest behavior to insure that younger children are protected. Adolescents showing early repetitive juvenile delinquent behaviors must be assessed for physical and sexual abuse, and intervention must be planned to deal with the victimization. In the investigation and apprehension of serial rapists, law enforcement might pay closer attention to fetish burglaries and the spying, secretive behaviors that serve as the prototype for rape behavior.

REFERENCES

1. Helfer, E. & C. H. Kempe. 1968. The Battered Child. University of Chicago Press. Chicago, IL.
2. Finkelhor, D. 1986. A Sourcebook on Child Sexual Abuse. Sage Publications. Beverly Hills, CA.
3. Rush, F. 1980. The Best Kept Secret: Sexual Abuse of Children. Prentice-Hall. Englewood Cliffs, NJ.
4. Herman, J. 1982. Father-Daughter Incest. Harvard University Press. Cambridge, MA.
5. Finkelhor, D. 1984. Child Sexual Abuse: New Theory and Research. Free Press. New York, NY.
6. Wyatt, G. E. & S. D. Peters. 1986. Issues in the definition of child sexual abuse in prevalence research. Child Abuse and Neglect **10:** 21-30.
7. Finkelhor, D. 1979. Sexually Victimized Children. Free Press. New York, NY.
8. Russell, D. E. H. 1983. The incidence and prevalence of intrafamilial and extrafamilial sexual abuse of female children. Child Abuse and Neglect **7:** 133-146.

9. WYATT, G. E. 1985. The sexual abuse of Afro-American and White American women in childhood. Child Abuse and Neglect **9:** 507-519.
10. WYATT, G. E. & S. D. PETERS. 1986. Methodological considerations in research on the prevalence of child sexual abuse. Child Abuse and Neglect. In press.
11. BELL, A. & M. WEINBERG. 1978. Homosexualities. Simon and Schuster. New York, NY.
12. BELL, A. & M. WEINBERG. 1981. Sexual Preference: Its Development among Men and Women. Indiana University Press. Bloomington, IN.
13. RISIN, L. I. & M. P. KOSS. 1987. Sexual abuse of boys: Prevalence and descriptive characteristics of childhood victimization. J. Interpers. Violence **2**(3): 309-319.
14. U. S. DEPARTMENT OF CENSUS. 1980. U. S. Government Printing Office. Washington, DC.
15. GROTH, A. N. 1979. Sexual trauma in the life histories of rapists and child molesters. Victimol. **4**(1): 10-16.
16. SEGHORN, T. K., R. A. PRENTKY & R. J. BOUCHER. 1987. Childhood sexual abuse in the lives of sexually aggressive offenders. J. Am. Acad. Child Adolescent Psychiatry **26:** 262-267.
17. FINKELHOR, D. & A. BROWNE. 1986. Initial and long-term effects: A conceptual framework. *In* A Sourcebook on Child Sexual Abuse. D. Finkelhor, Ed. Sage Publications. Beverly Hills, CA.
18. HARTMAN, C. R. & A. W. BURGESS. 1986. Child sexual abuse: Generic roots of the victim experience. J. Psychother. Fam. **2**(2): 77-87.
19. HOROWITZ, M. J. 1986. Stress Response Syndromes, 2nd ed. New York, NY.
20. BREUER, J. & S. FREUD. 1954. Studies on hysteria. Standard Edition, Vol. 2: 1-17. Hogarth Press. London.
21. FREUD, S. 1958. Remembering, repeating and working through. Standard Edition, Vol. 12: 145-150. Hogarth Press. London.
22. FREUD, S. 1962. Beyond the pleasure principle. Standard Edition, Vol. 18: 1-68. Hogarth Press. London.
23. HOROWITZ, M. J. 1976. Stress Response Syndromes. Jason Aronson Inc. New York, NY.
24. GREEN, A. H. 1985. Children traumatized by physical abuse. *In* Post-Traumatic Stress Disorder in Children S. Eth & R. S. Pynoos, Eds. American Psychiatric Press. Washington, DC.
25. BENJAMIN, J. 1965. Developmental biology and psychoanalysis. In Psychoanalysis and Current Biological Thought. N. Greenfield & W. Lewis, Eds.: 57-80. University of Wisconsin, Madison, WI.
26. BELLAK, L., M. HURVICH & H. GEDIMAN. 1973. Ego Functions in Schizophrenia, Neurotics, and Normals. John Wiley & Sons. New York, NY.
27. BRODY, S. & S. AXELRAD. 1966. Anxiety, socialization, and ego formation in infancy. Int. J. Psychoanalysis **47:** 218-229.
28. PRENTKY, R. A., A. W. BURGESS & D. L. CARTER. 1986. Victim response by rapist type: An empirical and clinical analysis. J. Interpers. Violence **1**(1): 73-98.
29. RESSLER, R. K., A. W. BURGESS, J. E. DOUGLAS, C. R. HARTMAN & R. B. D'AGOSTINO. 1986. Sexual killers and their victims: Identifying patterns through crime scene analysis. J. Interpers. Violence **1**(3): 288-308.
30. DOUGLAS, J. E., R. K. RESSLER, A. W. BURGESS & C. R. HARTMAN. 1986. Criminal profiling from crime scene analysis. Behav. Sci. Law **4**(4): 401-421.
31. RESSLER, R. K., A. W. BURGESS, C. R. HARTMAN, J. E. DOUGLAS & A. MCCORMACK. 1986. Murderers who rape and mutilate. J. Interpers. Violence **1**(3): 273-287.
32. FINKELHOR, D. & G. HOTALING. 1984. Sexual abuse in the national incidence study of child abuse and neglect: An appraisal. Child Abuse and Neglect **8:** 22-23.
33. BURGESS, A. W. & L. L. HOLMSTROM. 1974. Rape: Victims of Crisis. Brady. Bowie, MD.
34. PYNOOS, R. S. & S. ETH. 1985. Children traumatized by witnessing acts of personal violence: Homicide, rape, or suicide behavior, *In* Post-Traumatic Stress Disorder in Children S. Eth & R. S. Pynoos, Eds. American Psychiatric Press. Washington, DC.
35. TERR, L. 1981. Forbidden games: Post-traumatic child's play. J. Am. Acad. Child and Adolescent Psychiatry **20:** 741-760.

36. HAZELWOOD, R. R. 1987. Analyzing the rape and profiling the offender. *In* Practical Aspects of Rape Investigation. R. R. Hazelwood & A. W. Burgess, Eds. Elsevier. New York, NY.
37. BURGESS, A. W., C. R. HARTMAN, M. P. MCCAUSLAND & P. POWERS. 1984. Children and adolescents exploited through sex rings and pornography. Am. J. Psychiatry **141**(5): 656-662.
38. LYSTAD, M. 1986. Violence in the Home: Interdisciplinary Perspectives. Brunner/Mazel. New York, NY.
39. STRAUS, M. A., R. J. GELLES & S. K. STEINMETZ. 1980. Behind Closed Doors: Violence in the American Family, Doubleday. New York, NY.

Immediate and Delayed Treatment of Rape Victims[a]

ELLEN FRANK, BARBARA ANDERSON, BARBARA DUFFY STEWART, CONSTANCE DANCU, CAROL HUGHES, AND DEBORAH WEST

Department of Psychiatry
School of Medicine
University of Pittsburgh
Pittsburgh, Pennsylvania 15213

Early descriptions of the response to rape victimization indicated that while some rape victims made a relatively rapid and complete recovery following the assault experience, others had more prolonged difficulties.[1,2] Furthermore, these studies suggested that most victims continued to experience residual fears and problems many months, and even years, afterward.

The three large empirical studies of rape victims conducted in the last six years at first appear to contradict these early descriptions. Each of the major assessment studies found greatly elevated symptom levels in recent victims and highly significant differences between victims and matched controls at initial assessment.[3–5] When followed over a year's time, subjects tended to show marked improvement. Indeed, a first reading of the findings in the repeated-assessment-only studies, in which scores on standardized assessment instruments for depression, fear, anxiety, and social adjustment were used as outcome measures, would suggest that recovery from rape occurs within a few months and is largely a function of the passage of time.[3,5]

A major source of confusion in the attempt to understand recovery from rape trauma is the lack of clarity concerning the role that treatment intervention may or may not play in the process. Few research groups have attempted systematic treatment trials with rape victims. Kilpatrick's initial study (personal communication, 1981) included a treatment trial that began three months after the initiation of the assessment study. Relatively small numbers of subjects were sufficiently symptomatic at the three-month point to justify a course of treatment. Thus, the number of subjects entered into treatment proved too few to permit statistical analysis. In a subsequent study, Kilpatrick compared a Brief Behavioral Intervention Procedure (BBIP), Repeated Assessment, and Delayed Assessment and was unable to find significant differences among the three groups.[6] Ledray (personal communication, 1985) compared Supportive Crisis Counseling with Goal-Oriented Counseling and found goal-setting superior to support; however, she presents no evidence to demonstrate that the groups did not differ prior to treatment.

We have compared subjects who were randomly assigned to either Cognitive Behavior Therapy or Systematic Desensitization and, while both groups of subjects

[a]This study was supported in part by Grants MH29262 and MH30915 from the National Institute of Mental Health.

showed highly significant pre-post improvement, few differences were observed *between* the two treatment modalities.[7–9]

A comparison of results from the assessment-only studies[3,5,10] with the assessment-and-treatment studies[6–9] would suggest that active treatment intervention does not have a powerful impact on the rate or extent of recovery, especially as measured by comparisons of group means on standardized instruments. When viewed more closely, however, it appears that substantial numbers of subjects in each of the assessment-only studies continued to show elevated symptoms when compared with subjects in treatment studies. Calhoun's research group found 26% of their victimized subjects reporting "mild to severe" depression at one year, as compared with 17% of control subjects.[11] However, among the subjects we have studied, who were treated with either Cognitive Therapy or Systematic Desensitization and assessed on a repeated basis, fewer than 15% would still be rated as depressed at one year, making them more comparable to nonvictimized controls than to untreated victims.[9] The Atlanta researchers have also reported data on the social adjustment of their subjects.[5] While their untreated subjects hover between the "fair" and "good" level of adjustment on the Social Adjustment Scale at four months, by three months the treated subjects in our study cluster around the "very good" adjustment level.[9]

All the assessment-only studies of recent victims that have included follow-up components point to the symptomatic recovery that takes place over the course of the first three to four months following a rape experience, both in terms of those symptoms measured by standardized self-report instruments and those measured by clinical scales.[3,5,10,12,13] The equivocal results of the few systematic treatment studies, coupled with the recovery seen in the assessment-only studies, suggest that further attention should be paid to the question of what role treatment intervention plays in the recovery from rape and what the timing of such intervention should be.

The present paper addresses this question by examining the relative levels of initial symptomatology and the relative amounts of symptomatic improvement seen in two groups of systematically treated rape victims: one group seeking help for the first time several months after the assault and a second group, which made immediate contact with a rape crisis center and began treatment within days or weeks of the assault.

METHOD

Study Design

Subjects were referred to the investigators by the Allegheny County Center for Victims of Violent Crime or Pittsburgh Action Against Rape between September of 1978 and June of 1985. Within a week to ten days of making contact with one of these rape crisis centers, each potential subject was asked by her crisis center advocate whether she would be willing to be contacted by a counselor from a research project at the University of Pittsburgh that offered counseling to victims of sexual assault. If a potential subject agreed, she was then contacted by one of the three clinicians associated with the project. The counselor explained that the project involved participation in a fourteen-session treatment protocol and the completion of a battery of assessment measures initially, at the end of treatment, and at subsequent follow-up sessions. All participating subjects signed a consent form outlining the requirements of their participation. Treatment consisted of either Systematic Desensitization or Cognitive Behavior Therapy.

Assessment Measures

Biographic and psychiatric history data, as well as information on the assault incident were gathered using the Demographic, Assault, and Psychiatric History Interview Schedule (DAPHIS), a structured interview guide designed by project staff. Measures of current functioning included the Beck Depression Inventory,[14] a 21-item self-report measure; the Spielberger State-Trait Anxiety Inventory,[15] a 40-item self-report instrument; a modified version of the Veronen-Kilpatrick Fear Survey Schedule,[16] a 120-item self-report inventory; the Janis-Field Feelings of Inadequacy Scale,[17] a 23-item self-report scale measuring self-esteem; and the Social Adjustment Scale-II (SAS-II),[18] a structured interview designed to collect background information and to assess functioning in four specific role areas (work, household, external family, and social/leisure) as well as overall social functioning. The SAS-II interviews were conducted by the project counselors, tape-recorded, and subsequently rated by raters who were blind to the subjects' treatment condition and who had been trained to an acceptable level (.85) of interrater agreement. Finally a Target Complaints Assessment was employed as another primary measure of treatment efficacy.[19] Subjects were asked to list the three most disturbing rape-related problems (target complaints) that they had been experiencing since the assault. Subjects then indicated a severity score from 0 ("not at all troubled by problem") to 7 ("very severely troubled by problem") for each of the target complaints noted. As some subjects listed fewer than three target complaints, the ratings were averaged to yield a mean target complaint score for each individual at each assessment, thus permitting comparisons across subjects.

Treatment Interventions

Systematic Desensitization

Systematic Desensitization (SD), a procedure designed to reduce or eliminate maladaptive anxiety and its behavioral correlates, should be an optimal treatment for the fears that develop subsequent to a rape experience. Since this treatment was formally introduced by Wolpe,[20] it has been subjected to extensive experimentation; the literature concerning its efficacy is voluminous.[21,22] Although Systematic Desensitization has been found to be an effective treatment for many behavioral disorders, it applies best to those complaints in which the cues for fear or anxiety are easily pinpointed.

Once a subject's specific fears or avoidance behaviors were identified through the Target Complaints Assessment, she was taught progressive muscle relaxation in the first three sessions.[23,24] In relaxation training, the subject learned to alternately tense and relax various muscle groups until she achieved a state of relaxation or calm.

Usually at the fourth visit, the subject was asked to turn her attention again to her list of three target complaints resulting from the rape.

Each subject's target complaints were broken down into specific scenes or examples of the problem, and the subject rated each of the scenes on a scale ranging from 0 (no anxiety) to 10 (intense anxiety). The component scenes of each problem were then arranged in a hierarchy, from the least anxiety-provoking event to the most anxiety-provoking event. This method of hierarchy construction individualizes the treatment process and conforms to the early recommendations of Wolpe.

During treatment, the subject imagined each scene in each hierarchy while in a relaxed state, beginning with the least distressing scenes. When the subject experienced anxiety, she signaled and stopped imagining the scene. Each scene was presented twice, until the subject had imagined each item in the hierarchy without anxiety. If a subject had several hierarchies, the clinician was free to decide whether it was advisable to complete one hierarchy at a time or it was less anxiety-provoking to present one scene from each hierarchy during a session. In order that all sessions end on a positive note, no session terminated with a scene that elicited anxiety. If necessary, less distressing scenes were presented to accomplish this goal.

Cognitive Behavior Therapy

Cognitive Behavior Therapy (CBT)[25] is a directive, time-limited psychotherapy that has been demonstrated to be at least as effective as tricyclic antidepressants in treating serious depression[26] and has also been shown to be an effective treatment for fear and anxiety.[27] Its mechanisms of change are made explicit from the outset of treatment, and each treatment session is intended to reinforce the patient's understanding of how the treatment works. The essence of the change sought as a result of CBT is increased control (in particular, of cognitive processes), a goal entirely consistent with our perception of the needs of recent rape victims.

An individual's cognitions filter past, present, and future experience through preexisting assumptions or beliefs about the world. Cognitive therapy techniques are designed to help individuals identify and test the reality of distorted and dysfunctional beliefs, referred to as "automatic negative thoughts" by Beck.[25] The three phases of CBT, involving groups of treatment techniques appropriate to their differing goals, progress from concrete to abstract interpretations of the problem.

Group I cognitive techniques challenge maladaptive thinking with homework tasks that change behavior and encourage novel thinking about specific situations and behaviors. Homework includes: (1) *a weekly activity schedule,* on which the subject records her daily activities hour by hour and rates the amount of "mastery" or "pleasure" she experienced from the activities listed in her log; (2) *graded task assignments,* in which the subject undertakes a series of tasks to reach a goal she considers difficult or impossible (e.g., going out alone). Beck *et al.*[28] argue that experiences that give a distressed individual a sense of mastery or pleasure reduce discomfort and automatic negative thoughts.

In using CBT with rape victims, we took into account the fact that both depression and anxiety have been successfully treated with cognitive techniques.[27,28] Once again, subjects were asked to identify up to three target complaints that had become sources of distress since the assault. Therapists then targeted those complaints in each phase of CBT treatment, emphasizing those tasks, activities, and thoughts that the subject identified as particularly distressing to her. Guided by responses to the activity schedule, therapists designed graded task assignments to increase the level of activity, to upgrade the quality of activity, or to enable gradual approach to situations or tasks avoided since the assault.

Early in treatment, the weekly activity schedule was also used to identify situations that elicited automatic negative thoughts. Both during the explanation of the rationale for cognitive therapy and during the early treatment sessions, the therapists listened carefully for statements that had the characteristics of an automatic negative thought. These statements typically included an absolute, such as "always," "never," "only," or "none" and were usually statements about the subject herself, her world, or her future. The therapist labeled these statements as automatic thoughts and explained how the subject could record such thoughts when they occurred, along with the situations that elicited them and the feelings that resulted, on the daily record of automatic negative thoughts.

In the second phase of treatment, therapist and subject worked together to identify the cognitive distortion that gave rise to each automatic thought recorded and to construct a rational, adaptive response. These are the Group II techniques of CBT; they form the core of the treatment process.

Some subjects eventually moved onto the third (Group III) phase of treatment, in which the subject explored her basic assumptions about the world. Basic assumptions are common themes that unify a client's automatic negative thoughts; they are resistant to change because they are supported by numerous automatic thoughts. In our project, subjects who had a prior history of difficulties with depression and were in need of exploring their basic belief systems accounted for only 20% of the cognitive therapy subjects.

Therapists

Project therapists were experienced female clinical psychologists or psychiatric social workers specifically trained in both Cognitive Behavior Therapy and Systematic Desensitization. Trainers were clinicians with extensive experience in the respective therapies (Maria Kovacs, Ph.D. for Cognitive Behavior Therapy; Samuel M. Turner, Ph.D. for Systematic Desensitization) who continued to provide on-going supervision to project counselors throughout the first three years of study.

Subjects

Of the approximately 253 referrals to whom the study was presented, 54.5% agreed to participate. Although psychological assessment data could not be obtained for nonparticipants, none of their demographic characteristics and none of the variables characterizing the nature of their rape experiences differed significantly from those subjects who agreed to enter the study.

Prior to initial assessment, consenting subjects were assigned to treatment on a random basis. A total of 71 subjects were assigned to Cognitive Behavior Therapy, and 67 were assigned to Systematic Desensitization. Fifty immediate-treatment seekers were assigned to CBT, and 49 were assigned to SD. Of those, 34 CBT subjects and 26 SD subjects completed treatment. The rate of treatment completion did not differ for the two groups ($\chi^2_{(1)} = 2.313$, $p = .128$). Among the late-treatment seekers, 21 were assigned to CBT, of whom 14 completed treatment; 18 were assigned to SD, of whom 10 completed treatment. Again the rate of treatment completion did not differ across modalities ($\chi^2_{(1)} = .506$, $p = .477$). Immediate-treatment seekers were not significantly less likely to complete treatment than late-treatment seekers ($\chi^2_{(1)} = .010$, $p = .920$). The treatment results discussed in the present paper are based on the 84 subjects who completed the fourteen-week protocol.

Demographic characteristics of the subjects are presented in TABLE 1. Like most cohorts of rape victims that have been studied to date,[4,5,29] these women were typically young and single. Although the proportion of white to black subjects is higher than in most studies, it is consistent with Pittsburgh-area demographics. Information on the rape experiences (TABLE 2) and psychiatric histories (TABLE 3) also suggest comparability with other populations of rape victims studied thus far.[11,30]

Subjects who sought immediate treatment were similar to those who sought treatment several months postassault on all demographic features (age, race, marital status, employment status, work role, income, and education) examined except living arrangement. Immediate-treatment seekers were more likely to live alone ($\chi^2_{(1)} = 6.15$, $p < .05$). More important, there were no statistically significant differences in the psychiatric histories of the immediate- versus late-treatment seekers. Finally, there were no differences with respect to the nature of the rapes they experienced in terms of such characteristics as location of assault, number of assailants, use of weapon, and degree of physical violence. As we have reported elsewhere,[31] the late-treatment seekers were, however, less likely to report that they had attempted to defend themselves at the time of the assault ($\chi^2_{(1)} = 3.91$, $p < .05$). Within the two groups (immediate- and late-treatment seekers), there were no significant differences between those subjects assigned to CBT and those assigned to SD on any demographic, psychiatric history, or rape situation variable.

When the results for all subjects completing Cognitive Behavior Therapy were compared with the results for all subjects completing Systematic Desensitization, we found no significant differences on any of the self-report measures or any of the measures of social adjustment with respect to either absolute end-of-treatment scores or change scores. Neither the multivariate tests examining all self-report instruments together and all SAS scores together nor the univariate tests examining individual instruments revealed any differences between the treatments.

We then hypothesized that the treatments might be differentially effective with depressed versus anxious subjects; however, when we attempted to identify subjects by depressed versus anxious symptom picture, we were unable to do so. In the subjects we have studied, rape trauma appears to produce a global elevation on all measures of symptomatology, yielding high correlations between even those measures that seem conceptually unrelated (TABLE 4). If the two treatments we have employed do not appear to function differently but are both associated with highly significant symptom reduction, a key question becomes whether the global reduction in symptomatology observed is a function of the treatment interventions provided. In order to address this question, the present paper describes the results of treatment with 60 women entering treatment within a few weeks ($\overline{X} = 20.1$ days; range = 2 to 30 days) of their assault experience and 24 women who did not contact a crisis center until several months later and began treatment approximately four months postassault ($\overline{X} = 128.7 \pm 77.7$; range = 44 to 365 days). Multivariate Analyses of Variance (MANOVAs) were used to examine differences between immediate- and late-treatment seekers on self-report measures of symptomatology and on social adjustment. Univariate Fs are

TABLE 1. Demographic Characteristics of Immediate-Treatment Seekers and Late-Treatment Seekers

	Immediate-Treatment Seekers (n = 60)	Late-Treatment Seekers (n = 24)
Age (in years)		
Mean	23.3 ± 7.4	23.4 ± 6.0
Race		
White	79.2%	81.7%
Black	20.8%	18.3%
Religion		
Catholic	31.8%	41.4%
Protestant	45.5%	41.4%
Other	22.7%	17.2%
Education		
High school or less	50.0%	34.8%
Post-high school	50.0%	65.2%
Marital status		
Single	90.0%	83.3%
Married	10.0%	16.7%
Living arrangement		
Parents	44.3%	45.8%
Mate[a]	13.1%	20.8%
Roommate	6.6%	12.5%
Alone	21.3%	0.0%
Other	14.8%	20.8%
Income		
Less than $10,000	44.9%	40.0%
$10,000-$20,000	36.4%	55.0%
Over $20,000	18.2%	5.0%
Employment status		
Unemployed	54.1%	50.0%
Employed	45.9%	50.0%

[a] Includes marital partners and other males living with subjects by consensual agreement.

reported as an aid in assessing specific outcome variables following the finding of a significant multivariate F.

RESULTS

Although the late-treatment seekers entered the treatment protocol four months later, on the average, than the immediate-treatment seekers, their overall initial symptomatology was higher ($F(5,78) = 3.94$, $p < .003$) than that of those subjects assessed within a few weeks of the assault. Post-hoc comparisons indicated that this difference was accounted for primarily by the higher levels of trait anxiety ($F(1,82) = 8.61$, p

$< .004$). Immediate- and late-treatment seekers were not significantly different on measures of social adjustment at initial assessment ($F(5,55) = 1.55$, $p = 0.188$), nor on levels of distress associated with target complaints ($t(74) = .51$, $p = .61$) (See TABLE 5).

If comparisons are made between immediate-treatment seekers at their posttreatment assessment and late-treatment seekers at their initial assessment (which represent comparable time points in relation to the assault), the two groups differ significantly ($F(5,77) = 6.48$, $p < .000$) on all measures; however, when comparisons are made between end-of-treatment scores for both groups, there are no differences between the groups on absolute levels of self-reported symptomatology ($F(5,69) = 1.97$, $p = .094$), on absolute levels of social adjustment ($F(5,44) = 0.18$, $p = .970$), or on mean levels

TABLE 2. Frequency of Selected Rape Situation Characteristics for Immediate- and Late-Treatment Seekers

	Immediate-Treatment Seekers ($n = 60$)	Late-Treatment Seekers ($n = 24$)
Location		
Victim's home	27.9%	27.5%
Vehicle	26.2%	8.3%
Actor's home	19.7%	29.2%
Street	11.5%	16.7%
Other	14.8%	8.3%
Relationship of actor to victim		
Known	48.3%	70.8%
Unknown	51.7%	29.2%
Weapon employed by actor		
Yes	41.0%	30.4%
No	59.0%	69.6%
Victim beaten or tortured		
Yes	39.3%	37.5%
No	60.7%	62.5%
Victim's life threatened		
Yes	47.5%	43.5%
No	52.5%	56.5%
Victim's family or friends threatened		
Yes	13.6%	21.7%
No	86.4%	78.3%
Victim attempted to defend self		
Yes	66.1%	39.1%
No	33.9%	60.9%
Nature of actor's approach		
Blitz[a]	60.0%	65.2%
Con[b]	40.0%	34.8%
Victim's perception of situation prior to attack		
Safe	79.3%	90.5%
Dangerous	20.7%	9.5%

[a] Burgess and Holmstrom[29] define a "blitz" rape as one in which there is no preparation for the attack and no participation on the part of the victim.

[b] Burgess and Holmstrom[29] define a "con" rape as one in which there is some enticement of the victim into the situation in which she is finally victimized.

TABLE 3. Frequencies of Selected Psychiatric History Characteristics of Immediate- and Late-Treatment Seekers

	Immediate-Treatment Seekers ($n = 60$)	Late-Treatment Seekers ($n = 24$)
Previous psychiatric treatment		
Yes	36.1%	47.8%
No	63.9%	52.2%
Suicidal ideation		
Never	32.8%	34.8%
Prerape only	32.8%	13.0%
Postrape only	16.4%	30.4%
Pre- and postrape	18.0%	21.7%
Suicide attempts		
Never	75.4%	77.3%
Prerape	24.6%	22.7%
Postrape	0%	0%
Pre- and postrape	0%	0%
Psychiatric family history		
Yes	27.3%	24.1%
No	72.7%	75.9%

of distress from the Target Complaints identified at the beginning of treatment ($t(60) = .49, p = .627$) (See TABLE 6). Finally, as illustrated in TABLE 7, when delta scores were calculated, no differences were observed in the amount of change associated with treatment intervention in the two groups; however, the percentage of change on each measure is substantial for both groups.

TABLE 4. Correlations[a] among Symptom Measures in 84 Rape Victims

	Beck Depression Inventory	Spielberger State Anxiety	Spielberger Trait Anxiety	Modified Fear Survey	Janis-Field Feelings of Inadequacy
Beck Depression Inventory	1.00	0.52	0.49	0.31	−0.52
Spielberger State Anxiety		1.00	0.38	0.27	−0.30
Spielberger Trait Anxiety			1.00	0.45	−0.65
Modified Fear Survey				1.00	−0.59

[a] Correlations are all significant at $p < .01$.

DISCUSSION

Although the data presented above do not offer a final answer to the question of what role treatment plays in the recovery from rape, they do shed considerable light on this issue. As Kilpatrick[3] and Atkeson[11] have both demonstrated, subjects who are exposed to repeated assessment but not to treatment still show lower levels of symptoms at each assessment point when compared to subjects exposed to a first assessment at that time point. While some of the change observed in the repeated-assessment subjects may be accounted for by subjects' adaptation to the assessment measures ("instrument decay"), these results suggest that simply having contact with

TABLE 5. Initial Assessment Scores for Immediate- and Late-Treatment Seekers

	Immediate-Treatment Seekers (n = 60)	Late-Treatment Seekers (n = 24)
Beck Depression Inventory		
$\bar{x}$	20.5	23.9
SD	10.3	12.2
Spielberger State Anxiety		
$\bar{x}$	53.7	50.9
SD	14.3	13.6
Spielberger Trait Anxiety		
$\bar{x}$	48.2	56.5
SD	12.1	10.1
Fear Survey		
$\bar{x}$	311.6	321.7
SD	73.3	61.8
Janis-Field Self-Esteem		
$\bar{x}$	61.9	60.2
SD	15.8	15.2
Target Complaints		
$\bar{x}$	5.5	5.7
SD	1.2	1.2
SAS II Work		
$\bar{x}$	2.5	1.8
SD	1.2	1.4
SAS II Household		
$\bar{x}$	1.9	2.1
SD	1.0	1.2
SAS II External Family		
$\bar{x}$	1.8	1.9
SD	1.2	1.3
SAS II Social/Leisure		
$\bar{x}$	2.4	2.6
SD	1.2	0.9
SAS II General Adjustment		
$\bar{x}$	2.5	2.6
SD	0.9	0.8

clinicians or assessors produces some additional improvement over what would be expected solely as a result of the passage of time since the assault.

The late-treatment seekers we have studied differ from the delayed-assessment subjects seen in the Charleston and Atlanta studies in that they *sought* contact with a rape crisis center as a result of their distress, while Kilpatrick's[3] and Atkeson's[11] delayed-assessment subjects presumably were *recruited* on the basis of simply having had a rape experience at a time point comparable to that of the repeated-assessment subjects. When assessed systematically, the late-treatment seekers we have studied displayed a symptom complex comparable in quality to, and at least as severe as, that seen in the immediate-treatment seekers we have studied. Their initial assessment profiles represent incontrovertible evidence that for at least some rape victims the passage of time is not associated with recovery from rape trauma.

When exposed to the same systematic treatments as were offered to the immediate-treatment seekers, these subjects showed comparable symptom reduction over a com-

TABLE 6. Posttreatment Scores for Immediate- and Late-Treatment Seekers

	Immediate-Treatment Seekers (n = 60)	Late-Treatment Seekers (n = 24)
Beck Depression Inventory		
$\bar{x}$	7.8	9.7
SD	8.2	8.3
Spielberger State Anxiety		
$\bar{x}$	38.0	38.6
SD	11.9	11.9
Spielberger Trait Anxiety		
$\bar{x}$	39.5	44.1
SD	11.9	9.4
Fear Survey		
$\bar{x}$	231.6	266.4
SD	75.1	86.3
Janis-Field Self-Esteem		
$\bar{x}$	74.9	74.5
SD	16.2	15.1
Target Complaints		
$\bar{x}$	2.6	2.8
SD	1.7	1.3
SAS II Work		
$\bar{x}$	1.3	1.3
SD	0.9	1.3
SAS II Household		
$\bar{x}$	1.2	1.4
SD	1.0	1.1
SAS II External Family		
$\bar{x}$	1.2	1.2
SD	1.0	1.2
SAS II Social/Leisure		
$\bar{x}$	1.3	1.3
SD	1.2	1.1
SAS II General Adjustment		
$\bar{x}$	1.4	1.4
SD	0.9	1.0

TABLE 7. Delta Scores for Immediate- and Late-Treatment Seekers

	Immediate-Treatment Seekers (n = 60)	Late-Treatment Seekers (n = 24)
Beck Depression Inventory		
$\bar{x}$	12.5	11.7
SD	9.7	17.3
Spielberger State Anxiety		
$\bar{x}$	15.8	13.0
SD	16.7	17.7
Spielberger Trait Anxiety		
$\bar{x}$	12.4	12.4
SD	8.6	13.2
Modified Fear Survey		
$\bar{x}$	53.8	37.8
SD	46.0	42.6
Janis-Field Self-Esteem		
$\bar{x}$	12.3	14.2
SD	13.8	14.0

parable time period on all measures, as well as comparable improvement in social adjustment. These results, then, argue against the notion that the improvement seen in the immediate-treatment seekers can be explained solely on the basis of spontaneous remission or improvement simply as a result of the passage of time. What remains unclear is precisely what constitute the curative factors in the treatments offered. This question is of particular relevance in light of the failure to find the anticipated differences between Cognitive Behavior Therapy and Systematic Desensitization.

When the present study was first conceptualized, no empirical studies of the psychological response to rape had been carried out. It was anticipated, on the basis of the descriptive studies available, that rape reactions could be accurately categorized along traditional diagnostic lines.[29,32] Thus, it was expected that those rape victims who presented with depression would respond more favorably to Cognitive Behavior Therapy, while those who presented with phobic reactions would respond best to Systematic Desensitization. While many of the subjects we have studied do meet criteria for major depressive disorder,[8,9,33] and for generalized anxiety disorder and/or phobic disorder,[34] what we have observed in the subjects we have studied is the existence of a distinct symptom complex (consistent with current diagnostic thinking, as represented in DSM-III and DSM-IIIR), specific to traumatic reactions, that includes features of depression, phobia, and anxiety. The high correlations among all the measures selected for this study suggest the presence of a global traumatic reaction that would not be expected to respond differentially to a treatment that targets depression (and anxiety) versus one that targets phobia (and anxiety). The comparable improvement in this global traumatic reaction seen in both the immediate- and late-treatment seekers suggests that systematic intervention aimed at reducing distress from specific target complaints identified by a rape victim is helpful whenever it is instituted.

The question, then, of when to institute treatment becomes one of ethics. In the best of all possible worlds, short-term treatment would be made available immediately to all victims experiencing distress, thus minimizing the amount of time they must spend in the distressed state and preventing the frequently observed secondary consequences of rape trauma, including quitting or being fired from one's job, dropping out of school, or changing residence, all of which add to the victim's distress and to the difficulty of treatment.

REFERENCES

1. Burgess, A. W. & L. L. Holmstrom. 1974. Rape: Victims of Crisis. Robert Brady Co. Bowie, MD.
2. Queen's Bench Foundation. 1975. Rape Victimization Study. Queen's Bench Foundation. San Francisco, CA.
3. Kilpatrick, D. G., L. Veronen & P. A. Resick. 1979. The aftermath of rape: Recent empirical findings. Am. J. Orthopsychiatry **49:** 658-669.
4. Frank, E., S. Turner & B. D. Stewart. 1980. Initial response to rape: The impact of factors within the rape situation. J. Behav. Assessment. **2(1):** 39-53.
5. Resick, P. A., K. S. Calhoun, B. M. Atkeson & E. M. Ellis. 1981. Social adjustment in victims of sexual assault. J. Consult. Clin. Psychol. **49(5):** 705-712.
6. Kilpatrick, D. G. 1984. Treatment of fear and anxiety in victims of rape. National Center for the Prevention and Control of Rape, Final Report, Grant No. MH29602. National Institute of Mental Health. Rockville, MD.
7. Frank, E. & B. D. Stewart. 1982. The treatment of depressed rape victims: An approach to stress-induced symptomatology. *In* Treatment of Depression: Old Controversies and New Approaches. P. Clayton, Ed.: 309-330. Raven Press. New York, NY.
8. Frank, E. & B. D. Stewart. 1983. Treating depression in victims of rape. Clin. Psychol. **36(4):** 95-98.
9. Frank, E. & B. D. Stewart. 1984. Depressive symptoms in rape victims: A revisit. J. Affective Disorders. **7:** 77-85.
10. Calhoun, K. S., B. M. Atkeson & P. A. Resick. 1982. A longitudinal examination of fear reaction in victims of rape. J. Counseling Psychol. **29:** 655-661.
11. Atkeson, B. M., K. S. Calhoun, P. A. Resick & E. M. Ellis. 1982. Victims of rape: Repeated assessment of depressive symptoms. J. Consult. Clin. Psychol. **50(1):** 96-102.
12. Calhoun, K. S., B. M. Atkeson & P. A. Resick. 1979. Incidence and patterns of depression in rape victims. Presented at the meeting of the Association for Advancement of Behavior Therapy, San Francisco, California, December 1979.
13. Kilpatrick, D. G., L. Veronen & P. A. Resick. 1979. Assessment of the aftermath of rape: Changing patterns of fear. J. Behav. Assessment **88:** 101-105.
14. Beck, A. T., C. H. Ward, M. Mendelsohn, J. Mock & J. Erbaugh. 1961. An inventory for measuring depression. Arch. Gen. Psychiatry **4:** 561-571.
15. Spielberger, C., R. Gorsuch & R. Luschene. 1970. The State-Trait Anxiety Inventory. Consulting Psychologists Press. Palo Alto, CA.
16. Veronen, L. J. & D. G. Kilpatrick. 1980. Reported fears of rape victims: A preliminary investigation. Behav. Modification. **4:** 383-396.
17. Janis, I. L. & P. B. Field. 1959. Sex differences in personality factors related to persuasibility. *In* Personality and Persuasibility. C. I. Hoveland & I. L. Janis, Eds. Yale University Press. New Haven, CT.
18. Schooler, N. R., G. Levine, J. B. Severe, B. Brauzer, A. DiMascio, G. L. Klerman & V. B. Tauson. 1980. Prevention of relapse in schizophrenia: An evaluation of fluphenazine decanoate. Arch. Gen. Psychiatry **37:** 16-24.
19. Battle, C. C., S. D. Imber, R. Hoehn-Saric, A. R. Stone, E. R. Nash & J. D. Frank. 1966. Target Complaints as criteria of improvement. Am. J. Psychother. **20(1):** 184-192.
20. Wolpe, J. & P. J. Lange. 1964. A Fear Survey Schedule for use in behavior therapy. Behav. Res. Ther. **2:** 27-30.
21. Paul, G. L. 1969. Outcome of systematic desensitization. Controlled investigation of individual treatment, technique variations, and current status. *In* Behavior Therapy: Appraisal and Status. C. M. Franks, Ed. McGraw-Hill. New York, NY.

22. RIMM, D. C. & J. C. MASTERS. 1979. Behavior Therapy: Techniques and Empirical Findings. Academic Press. New York, NY.
23. JACOBSON, E. 1938. Progressive Relaxation. University of Chicago Press. Chicago, IL.
24. JACOBSON, E. 1970. Modern Treatment of Tense Patients. Charles C. Thomas Press. Springfield, IL.
25. BECK, A. T. 1972. Depression: Causes and Treatment. University of Pennsylvania Press. Philadelphia, PA.
26. RUSH, A. J., A. T. BECK, M. KOVACS & S. HOLLON. 1977. Comparative Efficacy of Cognitive Therapy and Pharmacotherapy in the Treatment of Depressed Outpatients. Cognitive Ther. Res. **125:** 433-441.
27. BECK, A. T. & G. EMERY. 1979. Cognitive therapy of anxiety and phobic disorders. Center for Cognitive Therapy, University of Pennsylvania. Philadelphia, PA.
28. BECK, A. T., A. J. RUSH, B. F. SHAW & J. EMERY. 1979. Cognitive Therapy of Depression. The Guilford Press. New York, NY.
29. BURGESS, A. W. & L. L. HOLMSTROM. 1974. Rape trauma syndrome. Am. J. Psychiatry **131:** 981-986.
30. MCCAHILL, I., L. MEYER & A. FISCHMAN. 1979. The Aftermath of Rape. Lexington Books. Lexington, MA.
31. STEWART, B. D., C. HUGHES, E. FRANK, B. ANDERSON, K. KENDALL & D. WEST. 1987. The aftermath of rape: Profiles of immediate and delayed treatment seekers. J. Nerv. Ment. Dis. In press.
32. SUTHERLAND, S. & D. J. SCHERL. 1970. Patterns of response among victims of rape. Am. J. Orthopsychiatry. **40:** 503-511.
33. FRANK, E., S. TURNER & B. DUFFY. 1979. Depressive symptoms in rape victims. J. Affective Disorders. **1(4):** 269-277.
34. FRANK, E. & B. P. ANDERSON. 1987. Psychiatric disorders in rape victims: Past history and current symptomatology. Compr. Psychiatry. In press.

The Effects of Sexual Abuse on Children: Results of a Research Project[a]

JON R. CONTE

School of Social Service Administration
The University of Chicago
Chicago, Illinois 60637

The effects of childhood sexual experiences on children and adults victimized as children have been an interest of mental health professionals since Freud pondered a connection between the hysterical illness of eighteen patients and their reports of sexual contact with adults during childhood. Although the number of reports dealing with some aspect of this interest has greatly increased of late, there has been a steady flow of publications over the last thirty years or so. (For reviews see References 1-3.)

Until very recently much of the literature describing the effects of sexual abuse has consisted of clinical reports in which the presumed effects are anecdotally presented, often in relatively small samples, without actual measurement of the effects reported. While such reports are useful in providing a context for discovery, without measurement or control procedures they fail to demonstrate with any certainty what the actual functioning of children is and what may account for such functioning.

The data reported here were collected as part of a study funded by the National Center for the Prevention and Control of Rape at the National Institute of Mental Health, and resulted from a collaborative effort of the School of Social Service Administration at the University of Chicago and the Sexual Assault Center (SAC) at Harborview Medical Center in Seattle. The project's purpose was twofold: (1) to describe the effects of sexual abuse on children, and (2) to identify factors associated with differential effects. This report will present a general summary of the major findings of the project, which describe the effects of sexual abuse. (See References 5 and 7 for reports on factors associated with variation in effect.) More detailed reports on the project data are otherwise available.[4-6]

METHODOLOGY

Children 4 to 17 years of age seen at SAC between September 1983 and May 1985 and believed to have been sexually abused were eligible for the study. Children who had been removed from their homes and placed in substitute care; whose parent(s)

[a]This work was supported in part by Grant MH37133 from the National Institute of Mental Health.

refused permission for participation in the study; or whose parent was regarded by the social worker as emotionally unable to complete data collection (e.g., because of extreme emotional upset) were excluded from the study. Children were also excluded if the agency social worker believed that abuse had not occurred. Data were collected at or near the time of disclosure of the abuse from the child's parent (nonoffending), the social worker, and the child, if she or he was over twelve years of age. Data were also collected from the parent twelve months later.

During the time of the study, when a parent brought a child to SAC, she was asked to complete the Child Behavior Profile (Profile), which asked the parent to indicate how characteristic certain behaviors were of the child and to provide other information about the child and family for use in comparing the samples (e.g., amount of support available to the child). After the social worker interviewed the child, parent, and (on occasion) others, the nature and process of the study were reviewed with the parent. Data were not collected on parent refusal rates or on the number of cases ruled out by the social workers. However, of the total number of cases (1338) eligible for the study during the study period and meeting all study criteria (age, victim not removed from home, and parent or significant other of the child available to complete data collection), all instruments were completed on 369 (28%).

The assessment process varied in terms of number of interviews and persons interviewed, depending on the case. Within seven days of the last appointment, social workers completed a 38-item Symptom Checklist and a Clinical Assessment Form (CAF). The CAF summarized information about a large number of aspects of the abuse and abuse context that might be associated with a more severe impact of abuse (e.g., the relationship between victim and offender or the victim's coping during the abuse). Social workers completed the Checklist based on interviews with the child, parent, and collateral contacts.

A community comparison sample was recruited from day care centers, churches, youth groups, and other community agencies. Comparison sample parents were asked to complete a modified Profile. Parents in both the abused and community comparison groups were contacted twelve months after first completing the Profile and asked to complete a follow-up questionnaire, Child Behavior Profile II (Profile II). Profile II questionnaires varied between the samples, with the abused sample providing information on the comparison variables, a 110-item behavior checklist, and information about intervention since intake at SAC.

Samples

Abused Sample

The sample of abused children consisted of 369 children. Of these, 76% (280) were female, and 24% (89) were male. The average age of children in the study was 9.1 years. Caucasian children constituted 83% of the abused sample, Blacks 8.4%, Hispanics 2.4%, Asians 1.9%, and Native Americans 3%.

The Abuse Experience. Child victims in this sample had been abused in 95% of the cases by a male, in 4% by a female, and in 1% by both a male and female offender. Of the offenders, 70% were Caucasian. Children were abused by a wide range of adults. The offender was a stranger to the child in only 3.8% of the cases. An acquaintance of the child or family was the offender in 30%, a natural parent in 16%, stepparent or adoptive parent in 11%, other relative in 23%, babysitter in 7% (other in 7% of the cases).

The time during which child victims were abused varied considerably. In working with young children it is often difficult to determine exactly when the abuse started. Some children may not remember a time when it did not take place. Others may have a sense it began when they were young, but not know an exact date. Because of this difficulty in determining duration of abuse, our definition of duration combines time and frequency of abuse. Of the child victims in this sample, 25% were abused one time, 44% for a limited period, and 25% chronically (6% missing). Children were seen at the Sexual Assault Center relatively recently after the last assault: 15.4% of the children were seen within 48 hours of the last assault, 14.1% 2 days to 2 weeks, 25.7% 2 weeks to 6 months, and 17% more than six months since the last assault (27% unknown). Information about how long ago the last incident of abuse took place is often difficult to get from children, especially young children at the beginning of professional contact. This explains the large number of unknowns on this variable.

Community Comparison Sample

Children were recruited from the Seattle community to serve as a comparison group for the sexually victimized children. The recruitment of the comparison group turned out to be considerably more difficult than originally anticipated. Many community agencies (e.g., schools and youth groups) were reluctant to allow parents to be approached to give permission for their children to serve as comparison subjects. Finally a research assistant was hired to make in-person contacts with parents at day care centers, churches, youth groups, and other community agencies.

Parents were asked by the research assistant to complete a modified version of the Child Behavior Profile, containing descriptive information on their child and family and the same behavior items as completed by the parents of sexually abused children.

In addition to collecting demographic information on the abused and community comparison groups, other descriptive information was also collected on both samples. For example, parents were asked to indicate whether certain significant life events had occurred in their child's life any time in the previous year and, if it had, whether the parent believed the event was stressful for the child.

As can be seen in TABLE 1, the differences between abused and not-abused samples on these twelve demographic and other comparative variables are all significant, except for age of child.

RESULTS

Reliability

At the time of the study, it was the policy of the Sexual Assault Center not to ask clients to engage in activities which had no direct meaning or utility for them.

Consequently, reliability studies were difficult to conduct. Several reliability studies were completed by obtaining the participation of other sexual abuse programs. For example, in a small study ($n = 19$) in which mothers of children who were abused by fathers or stepfathers completed the Profile at two points in time two weeks apart, the 19 test-retest reliabilities representing the agreement between the two times these parents completed the Profile ranged from .44 to .85, with a mean of .67. Test-retest reliability of the social worker Symptom Checklist and Clinical Assessment Form yielded reliability coefficients ranging from .63 to .87 ($\bar{x}$ = .69). In two studies in which social workers were asked to read and complete the Symptom Checklist and CAF on two case reports, interrater reliabilities varied. The correct response was defined as the response given by the majority of social workers (agreement that a factor was not present in the cases was not included as an agreement, since agreement of nonoccurrence would inflate the estimate of reliability). A score of 1 would indicate that the social worker had completed the Checklist and CAF in complete agreement with the majority opinion. Resulting estimates of individual social workers' agreement with the consensus definition of the correct response in the first study ranged (n = 6) from .86 to .64 ($\bar{x}$ = .80) and in the second study ($n = 5$) from .87 to .63 ($\bar{x}$ = .79).

Effects of Abuse as Seen at Intake/Disclosure

Symptom Checklist

The average number of symptoms (from the 38-item Symptom Checklist) exhibited by abused children in this sample was 3.5. There was considerable variation in number of symptoms across the sample: 27% had four or more, 13% three, 14% two, 17% one, and 21% no symptoms. TABLE 2 presents the proportion of abused children exhibiting each of the symptoms. Data on the Symptom Checklist was not available for comparison subjects at intake/disclosure.

Child Behavior Profile

Items from the parent-completed Profile were scored with higher scores, indicating more of a problem for that item. Forty items were dropped due to little variation (e.g., 84% of abused and 92% of nonabused children were described as "never" sexually active; 97% of the abused and 100% of the nonabused children were described as "never" having tried to kill themselves. The 70 behaviors from the Profile for the abused sample were factor analyzed, using principal axis factoring with varimax rotation, resulting in 8 factors: poor self-esteem, aggressive, fearful, conscientious, difficulty in concentration, withdrawal, acting out, and anxious to please/tries too hard. A summary score (parent total score) was created by adding the ratings for the 70 items. As is often the case with behavioral checklists, the factor analysis was somewhat disappointing. The 8 factors account for 43% of the variance among the items, and the commonalities tend to be low, ranging from 0.15 to 0.67. Most of the commonalities are below 0.5.

TABLE 1. Comparison of Abused and Not-Abused Children

	Abused	Not Abused	Significance
Education of parent			
Professional	2%	20%	
4 years college	8%	30%	
1-3 years college	32%	34%	
High-school grad.	38%	15%	Mann-Whitney *U*
10-11 years	13%	1%	$w = 75410.5$
7-9 years	7%	—	$p = .001$
Less than 7 years	1%	—	
Family income (thousands)			
Over $60	2%	7%	
$50-$59	2%	8%	
$40-$49	4%	17%	Mann-Whitney *U*
$30-$39	15%	19%	$w = -9.8$
$20-$29	25%	24%	$p = .001$
$10-$19	19%	18%	
Less than $10	32%	6%	
Number of dependents on family income	3.9	3.6	$t = 2.45, p = .02$
Number of children	2.5	1.9	$t = 6.52, p = .001$
Marital status of child's parents			
Married/living with someone	53%	72%	$Chi^2 = 40.7$
Separated	15%	4%	$p = .001$
Divorced	24%	16%	
Not married/living with someone	8%	7%	
Mean age of child	8.8	8.1	$t = 1.81$ NS
Sex of child			
Male	22%	42%	$Chi^2 = 30.5$
Female	78%	57%	$p = .001$
Mean number of stressful events	2.0	1.2	$t = 6.72, p = .001$
Mean number of events rated as stressful	1.2	0.7	$t = 6.03, p = .001$
Mean negative parent outlook	0.97	0.63	$t = 4.26, p = .001$
Mean social desirability score	5.4	4.8	$t = 3.97, p = .001$
Mean negative parent outlook	0.97	0.63	$t = 4.26, p = .001$
Mean social desirability score	5.4	4.8	$t = 3.97, p = .001$
Mean support index	8.3	9.4	$t = 6.68, p = .001$

A series of clinical dimensions were created from items on the Profile, due to the relatively poor results of the factor analysis and some discomfort that in conducting the factor analysis it was necessary to delete information describing many of the problems thought to be clinically important in understanding the functioning of abused children. Characteristics of children from the original 110-item Profile, were conceptually grouped into clusters based in part on the factor analysis, clinical judgement, and the clinical literature on child sexual abuse. This resulted in twelve dimensions of child behavior. Items were included in only one dimension, except for the last dimension (posttraumatic stress), which was made up of some items in other dimensions. Differences between abused and nonabused children on the twelve clinical dimensions are all statistically significant. TABLE 3 presents the differences between abused and not-abused comparison children on each of the factors, dimensions, and parent total score. (See Reference 6 for more information on Profile factors and dimensions.)

TABLE 2. Proportion of Abused Sample Exhibiting Checklist Symptoms

Symptom	% Present	% Previously Present
Panic/anxiety attacks	5.7	1.6
Behavioral regression	13.8	5.4
Runs away/takes off	2.7	3.5
Excessive autonomic arousal	4.6	0.5
Depression	18.7	1.1
Withdrawal from usual activity or relations	15.2	5.7
Sexually victimizes others	3.0	0.8
Generalized fear	11.7	2.2
Suicidal attempts	1.9	2.2
Body image problems	7.9	1.4
Repressed anger/hostility	19.2	0.5
Daydreaming	13.8	2.7
Major problems with police	0.3	0.3
Eating disorders	0.8	0.3
Psychotic episode	—	—
Overly compliant/too anxious to please	13.8	0.3
Drug/alcohol abuse	2.2	1.1
Age-inappropriate sexual behavior	7.9	1.4
Hurts self physically	1.4	0.5
Minor problems with police	3.3	0.5
Fearful of abuse stimuli	30.1	5.4
Suicidal thoughts or actions	5.7	1.4
Psychosomatic complaints	10.0	3.8
Ritualistic behavior	1.1	0.3
Indiscriminate affection giving or receiving	6.5	0.5
Low self-esteem	32.8	0.5
Places self in dangerous situations	4.9	—
Violent fantasies	2.4	0.3
Emotional upset	22.8	3.5
Prostitution	0.8	0.5
Obsessional, repetitive/recurrent thoughts	5.4	0.8
Shoplifting/stealing	2.2	0.5
Nonacademic school behavior problems	9.2	1.6
Nightmares/sleep disorders	20.1	9.2
Inability to form/maintain relationships	8.7	0.5
Academic problems	15.4	1.9
Aggressive behavior	14.4	1.4
Inappropriate/destructive peer relationships	7.0	0.5

Follow-Up

Twelve months after the first contact with the Sexual Assault Center, the adult who completed the intake/disclosure Child Behavior Profile (usually the child's mother) was contacted by mail and asked to complete a follow-up questionnaire, Child Behavior Profile II. Parents from the comparison group who completed the Profile at time 1 were also contacted by mail and asked to complete the Profile II twelve months after time 1.

The follow-up contact was intended to provide information about the functioning of abused children twelve months after disclosure of the abuse and to identify factors

TABLE 3. Differences between Child Functioning for Abused and Not-Abused Children at Intake/Disclosure for Profile Factors, Dimensions, and Parent Total Score

Measure	Abused	Not Abused	*t*	*p*
Factors				
Self-esteem	.34	−.38	9.7	.001
Aggression	.11	−.11	3.1	.01
Fearful	.18	−.30	6.6	.001
Conscientious	.21	−.23	6.1	.001
Concentration problems	.13	−.10	3.6	.001
Withdrawal	.08	−.10	2.7	.01
Acting out	.006	−.08	1.4	NS
Anxious to please/tries too hard	.05	−.06	1.7	NS
Dimensions				
Concentration problems	19.9	15.9	10.26	.001
Aggressive	16.3	12.9	9.4	.001
Withdrawn	16.6	13.7	9.0	.001
Somatic complaints	10.2	8.1	10.9	.001
Character/personality	6.2	21.5	9.7	.001
Antisocial	20.6	18.5	7.7	.001
Nervous/emotional	31.8	24.9	13.0	.001
Depression	18.2	15.8	11.5	.001
Behavioral regression	14.1	12.2	6.3	.001
Body image/self-esteem problems	12.2	9.7	9.7	.001
Fear	15.3	13.1	6.3	.001
Posttraumatic stress	46.6	36.3	13.5	.001
Parent total score	167.4	135.5	13.3	.001

in the child and family's life after disclosure (e.g., a police interview of the child, the child's mother working to support the family, or the offender removed from the home) that might be associated with differential reactions of the abuse.

The Profile II for the abused sample asked the parent to describe events since intake associated with sexual abuse (e.g., whether the child testified in court, the parent's reaction to the abuse, feelings for the offender, and changes experienced by the child and family), certain of the control variables from the time-1 Profile (e.g., number of stressful life events experienced by the child since intake), and two measures of child functioning. The 110 items describing behavioral characteristics of the child (Profile) were repeated in the same form as used in the time-1 Profile. A parent version of the Impact Checklist (Checklist II) was also constructed. This version provided either more explanation or used nontechnical terms to describe each of the 38 symptoms on the original social-worker-completed Checklist (e.g, the problem *inability to form/maintain relationships* from the social-worker-completed checklist became *developing relationships that are unhealthy or destructive* on the parent-completed checklist).

The Profile II for the comparison sample asked the parent to provide current (at the time of completion) information on the control variables (e.g., amount of support available to family) and to complete the Symptom Checklist (Checklist II) and the 110-item behavioral description of the child.

Several weeks after the parent was contacted by mail and asked to complete the follow-up Profile II, a reminder post card was sent to the same address, offering help in completion of the questionnaire or offering a second questionnaire if the original had been misplaced. In a few cases second copies were requested. No assistance was requested.

Completed questionnaires were obtained from 198 cases in the abused sample (54% of the time-1 subjects) and 165 of the comparison cases (52% of the original time-1 sample).

While a direct assessment of the child, family, and situation at follow-up by the social workers would have provided a professional and perhaps different view than that available from the child's parent, this was not feasible as part of this study. Bringing the abused child back to the Sexual Assault Center for such an assessment was regarded by the SAC staff as potentially traumatic, as it risked reminding the child of events that may have been forgotten or psychologically resolved. Consequently, only the parent's view is available at follow-up.

Who Responded at Follow-Up?

Although the response rate for both abused and comparison samples is larger than originally anticipated, it is important to understand how subjects who completed the follow-up may differ from those who did not. For example, if the parents of more damaged victims refused to complete the Child Behavior Profile II, then conclusions drawn from an analysis of the behavioral data at follow-up would be biased in favor of less damaged victims. Several analyses were undertaken to determine the extent to which those subjects who completed the Profile II might differ from those who refused to participate in the follow-up. As can be seen in TABLE 4, the differences are limited, and in general the responders and nonresponders are similar on demographic and other comparative data. The major difference between time 1 and time 2 on these variables is that those who responded to the follow-up had significantly younger victims and fewer children in the family. Respondents also had higher indexes of support available to the family and were more likely to have higher family incomes.

Impact Checklist

TABLE 5 presents the proportion of abused and not-abused children exhibiting each of the Checklist II symptoms. These data were provided by the child's parent,

TABLE 4. Differences between Responders and Nonresponders in Abused Sample at Follow-Up on Data Available at Intake

Variable	Nonresponders	Responders	t	p
Age of victim (years)	9.2	8.5	1.96	.05
Sex of victim				
Male	24%	21%	$Chi^2 = .48$	
Female	76%	79%	$p = .48$	
Number of children in family	2.6	2.4	2.06	.04
Number of significant life events child exposed to	2.1	1.8	1.51	.13
Number of events rated as stressful	1.3	1.1	.97	.33
Parent tendency to have a negative outlook on life	.93	1.04	−.88	.38
Family Support Index	7.9	8.6	−2.70	.007
Parent tendency to give socially appropriate response	5.5	5.3	.91	.36
Education of Parent			Mann-Whitney	
Professional	2%	2%	$U = 9790.5$	
4 years college	9%	8%	$p = .64$	
1-3 years college	30%	32%		
High-school graduate	35%	39%		
10-11 years	17%	11%		
7-9 years	6%	7%		
Less than 7 years	1%	1%		
Family income (thousands)			Mann-Whitney	
Over $60	5%	12%	$U = 9790.5$	
$50-$59	3%	12%	$p = .002$	
$40-$49	10%	21%		
$30-$39	22%	21%		
$20-$29	17%	20%		
$10-$19	20%	13%		
Less than $10	23%	2%		
Marital status of parent				
Married	47%	58%		
Separated	19%	12%	$Chi^2 = 8.2$	
Divorced	26%	22%	$p = .08$	
Not married	8%	8%		

TABLE 5. Proportion of Abused and Not-Abused Children Exhibiting Each of 38 Symptoms at Follow-Up

	Abused (n = 198)	Not Abused (n = 165)
Suddenly gets panic or anxiety attacks	23.8	7.9
Acts younger than age (e.g., begins using bottle, wetting bed)	26.5	8.5
Runs away/takes off	14.1	5.5
Depressed, sad, or withdrawn	47.0	15.8
Stays away from usual activities or relationships	14.6	4.2
Sexually victimizes others	3.8	0.0
Fearful (e.g., afraid of leaving home)	20.0	6.1
Attempts suicide	4.3	0.0
Does not like how his/her body looks, distorted body image, constantly worries about body odor and appearance	21.6	5.5
Holds anger inside	32.4	9.7
Daydreams, unable to remember things, unable to concentrate on a task	30.8	14.5
Serious problems with police (robbery, assault)	1.1	0.0
Problems with eating (not able to eat at all or unable to keep food in stomach)	10.3	3.0
Hears voices or is out of touch with reality	2.2	0.0
Tries too hard to please or does things just to please	22.2	12.1
Problems with drugs and alcohol	2.7	1.8
Hurts self physically (e.g., hitting arm against wall until it is cut or bruised)	4.3	1.8
Less serious problems with police (shoplifting, vandalism)	4.9	1.8
Fearful of certain places, situations, or people	36.2	18.2
Thinks or talks about suicide	13.5	3.0
Complains about stomach aches, headaches, or other pains	43.2	30.3
Activities or behaviors that are performed over and over in a ritualistic manner	8.1	1.8
Gives affection to or receives it from any person, even someone the child does not know well	14.1	7.9
Places self in dangerous situations (takes unnecessary risks)	10.8	3.0
Dreams or fantasizes about the use of physical force to solve problems	13.5	7.3
Emotionally upset (e.g. crying a lot or easily, very sensitive)	53.0	18.8
Prostitution	2.2	0.0
Unable to stop thinking about or going over in mind certain thoughts	16.8	5.5
Problems with shoplifting or stealing	7.0	2.4
Problems with school that are not related to school performance (e.g., behavior problems, getting into trouble)	21.6	4.8
Problems with sleeping or nightmares	31.5	6.7
Problems with making and keeping friends	30.4	4.2
Problems at school that are related to school performance (e.g., grades)	25.0	9.7
Problems with aggressive behavior (e.g., hits, yells at people, breaks things)	38.6	16.4
Develops relationships that are unhealthy or destructive	8.7	1.2
Low self-esteem or low belief in his/her abilities	41.8	20.0
Acts in a sexual manner or is preoccupied with sexual talk	14.1	1.8
Easily startled by unexpected noise or light	22.3	3.0

not the social worker. Children in the abused sample exhibited a mean of 7.4 of these symptoms, while children in the community comparison sample at time 2 exhibited a mean of 2.6 symptoms ($t = 9.59$, 273 df, $p = .001$). Comparison of Checklist II data and Checklist I data should be made quite cautiously, since they were collected in the first case by children's parents and in the second case by professional social workers.

Profile II

TABLE 6 presents follow-up data indicating the differences between abused and not-abused samples on each of the Profile II factors, dimensions, and parent total score II. As can be seen in the table, none of the differences between abused and not-abused children at follow-up are significantly different on the Profile II factors. The differences for the conceptually created dimensions and parent total score are all significantly different. In the case of the dimensions and parent total score, the differences are all in the direction of the abused children exhibiting more problematic functioning.

TABLE 6. Differences between Child Functioning for Abused and Not-Abused Children at Follow-Up on Profile Factors, Dimensions, and Parent Total Score

Measure	Means		t	p
	Abused	Not Abused		
Factors				
Self-esteem	.0007	.03	−.031	.7
Aggression	.03	−.054	.85	.4
Fearful	−.07	−.04	−.27	.8
Irrational/lacking confidence	−.07	−.05	−.17	.8
Concentration problems	−.04	−.02	−.24	.8
Withdrawal	−.03	−.06	.30	.8
Acting out	.0008	.002	−.01	.9
Anxious to please/tries too hard	−.01	.008	−.27	.8
Dimensions				
Concentration problems	18.6	15.3	5.6	.0001
Aggressive	15.7	12.3	6.57	.0001
Withdrawn	16.4	13.1	6.89	.0001
Somatic complaints	9.5	8.0	5.55	.0001
Character/personality style	26.8	20.1	8.06	.0001
Antisocial	20.86	18.4	4.81	.0001
Nervous/emotional	30.2	23.7	8.34	.0001
Depression	18.1	16.1	6.01	.0001
Behavioral regression	13.2	11.0	5.53	.0001
Body image/self-esteem problems	12.3	10.4	5.03	.0001
Fear	14.7	11.4	6.68	.0001
Posttraumatic stress	44.5	34.1	8.38	.0001
Parent total score	160.5	129.7	8.03	.0001

TABLE 7. Differences between Child Functioning for Not-Abused Children at Intake/Disclosure and Follow-Up on Profile Factors, Dimensions, and Parent Total Score

Measure	Intake	Follow-Up	*t*	*p*
Factors				
Self-esteem	−.39	.04	−7.16	.0001
Aggression	−.15	−.04	−1.91	.06
Fearful	−.35	−.08	−4.76	.0001
Conscientious	−.23	−.04	−3.81	.0001
Concentration problems	−.15	−.03	−2.31	.02
Withdrawal	−.15	−.03	−1.93	.05
Acting out	−.10	−.01	−1.93	.06
Anxious to please/tries too hard	−.002	−.01	.24	.80
Dimensions				
Concentration problems	15.8	15.3	2.06	.04
Aggressive	12.9	12.3	2.67	.008
Withdrawn	13.5	13.0	2.08	.04
Somatic complaints	8.1	9.0	.73	.46
Character/Personality	21.3	20.8	1.44	.15
Antisocial	18.36	18.4	− .24	.81
Nervous/emotional	24.8	33.8	2.579	.01
Depression	15.9	16.1	−1.03	.3
Behavioral regression	12.0	11.0	6.16	.0001
Body image/self-esteem problems	9.7	10.4	−3.67	.0001
Fear	12.9	11.5	6.68	.0001
Posttraumatic stress	35.8	34.1	3.63	.0001
Parent Total Score	133.9	129.7	2.73	.007

Change from Intake/Disclosure to Follow-Up

Both abused and not-abused children exhibited significant changes in behavior from time-1, to time-2 assessments. TABLE 7 presents Profile and Profile II data indicating the change from time 1 (intake/disclosure) to time 2 (follow-up) for the not-abused comparison group for each of the Profile factors, dimensions, and parent total score. There are nonsignificant changes on a number of variables. Changes on Profile factors are all in the direction of not-abused children exhibiting less problematic behavior. Changes on Profile dimensions are in the direction of a decrease in problematic functioning, except for *nervous/emotional* and *body image/self-esteem problems,* which indicate that comparison children reflected an increase in these dimensions at follow-up. The decrease in parent total score II indicates an overall significant reduction in problematic functioning for the comparison sample from time-1 to time-2 assessments.

TABLE 8 presents data describing the changes in functioning from time 1 (intake/disclosure) to time 2 (follow-up) for abused children. As can be seen in the table, change in functioning as measured by Profile II factors is significantly different for five of eight factors. The change is in the direction of less problematic functioning at follow-up. Seven of twelve dimensions reflect a significant change from time 1 to time 2. The direction of change on the dimensions indicates movement toward reduced problematic functioning. The change from time 1 to time 2 on the parent total score is significant and in the direction of an overall reduction in problematic functioning.

Note should be made that changes in certain of the factors (*withdrawal, acting out,* and *anxious to please/tries too hard*) and dimensions (*withdrawn, character/personality style, acting out, depression,* and *body image/self-esteem problems*) are not significantly different. This means that abused children on these measures of child functioning were functioning at follow-up at levels similar to those at the time of intake/disclosure.

TABLE 8. Differences between Child Functioning at Intake/Disclosure and Follow-Up on Profile Factors, Dimensions, and Parent Total Score: Abused Children

Measure	Intake	Follow-Up	*t*	*p*
Factors				
Self-esteem	.40	.02	5.58	.0001
Aggression	.12	−.01	2.21	.03
Fearful	.26	−.09	4.36	.0001
Conscientious	.17	−.02	2.83	.005
Concentration problems	.14	−.02	2.27	.03
Withdrawal	.01	−.04	.72	.47
Acting out	.09	.02	1.13	.26
Anxious to please/tries too hard	−.09	−.005	−1.13	.26
Dimensions				
Concentration problems	20.1	18.6	3.99	.0001
Aggressive	16.8	15.8	2.70	.008
Withdrawn	16.7	16.5	.50	.621
Somatic complaints	10.2	9.5	3.57	.0001
Character/personality	26.5	27.0	− .95	.35
Antisocial	20.3	20.7	−1.09	.28
Nervous/emotional	32.9	30.4	4.19	.0001
Depression	18.2	18.1	.36	.72
Behavioral regression	14.6	13.3	4.26	.0001
Body image/self-esteem problems	12.1	12.3	− .66	.512
Fear	15.5	14.7	2.08	.04
Posttraumatic stress	47.7	43.6	4.68	.0001
Parent Total Score	168.9	160.5	3.05	.003

The Abused Child's Experience

Parents of children in the abused sample were asked to describe a range of information about the child, the abuse, and events taking place since intake/disclosure. Highlights of this information (see Reference 7 for more complete discussion of these data) include:

- Most of the abuse is revealed because the victim either told the parent (37%) or told someone else (23%) about the abuse.

- The involvement of professionals in these cases varied considerably. For example, 72% of children were interviewed by police or prosecutors, 70% by Child Protective Services, 45% received a medical exam, only 14% testified in court, and 26% had been to some kind of legal proceeding.

- Almost 8% of children were removed from the home by Child Protective Services.

- Ten percent of children were temporarily placed by the parent in an out-of-home placement.

- In 32% of the cases the offender was living in the home with the child at the time of the abuse, and in 21% of the total cases the adult offender lived away from the home for some time as a result of the disclosure.

- Almost 43% of the offenders continue to deny the abuse at the time of the follow-up.

- The number of changes (e.g., mother began working) experienced by sexually abused children after intake/disclosure varied (56% of those sampled had 0 changes, 20% had 1, 12% 2, 8% 3, 3% 4, and 4% 5 or more).

- At the time of the follow-up 52% of the victims had no contact with the offender who abused them.

- The amount of counseling/therapy victims received varied considerably. Over 15% received no mental health service. The average number of months of mental health service received by abused children was 3.6.

Demographic Differences between Samples

Since the abused and comparison samples differed on a number of the control variables (e.g., negative outlook), the differences between samples cannot be taken as evidence for the effects of sexual abuse. To shed some light on the importance of these differences, data for the abused sample and the ten comparative variables were entered in a series of multiple regression analyses with each of the Profile factors and clinical dimensions, and with the Profile-based Parent Total Score and the Checklist-based Social Worker Score as dependent variables. The resulting regression equations indicate that a number of the comparative variables are associated with variation in the dependent measures. Most notable in this regard are the number of life stresses experienced by the child, the age of the child, and a tendency for the child's parent to have a negative outlook on life. Depending on the specific measure of child functioning, the control variables in the final regression equations explain between 3% and 28% of the variance.

A second set of regressions were run on the combined abused and comparison samples, entering first the control variables in the previous equations and then entering the sample dummy (i.e., whether the child was abused or not abused). The sample dummy remains in the regression equation explaining a significant amount of the remaining variance (after controlling for demographic and other differences between samples) on all measures, except on the following factors: *aggressive, withdrawal, acting out,* and *anxious to please/tries too hard.* This indicates that for most measures of child functioning reported here, the observed differences in the functioning of abused and nonabused children are not solely attributable to differences between samples on the control variables used in the study.

DISCUSSION

These data present a number of implications for clinical practice and research on sexual victimization of children. Several of these will be highlighted in the remainder of this paper.

Sexually abused children are perceived by their parents as behaving differently than children who have not been sexually abused. While this study cannot rule out parent bias as a possible source of some of this behavioral difference, preliminary evidence suggests that the observed differences hold when controlling for such parent variables as *social desirability response set* and a *parent's tendency to have a negative outlook on life.* Although the range of child functioning is limited by the nature of the measures employed in the research, still, abuse appears to effect a number of quite different clusters of behaviors (e.g., somatic behaviors vs. concentration).

The experience of this research project also raises a number of issues for future research efforts. I am increasingly convinced that broad-band multi-item, multifactor measures of child behavior/functioning are not all that useful in understanding the effects of sexual abuse. There are a number of problems with such measures. To begin with, the factors vary considerably in terms of behavioral specificity, and many are too abstract to be useful clinically. For example, one of our factors is *self-esteem problems* and includes items such as *feels inferior* or *is self-critical.* From a clinical point of view it is of little use to know that a victim "feels inferior" or "is self-critical." To intervene effectively, one must understand specifically *how* a victim feels inferior to others or is self-critical. Some victims feel different or less deserving than others: they feel the abuse has made them different, or they feel responsible for their own abuse because they did not disclose it earlier.

Another problem with broad measures of functioning is that they often lack any conceptual or theoretical foundation. A simple listing of broad areas of functioning does not lead directly to intervention. Recent work has begun to group behaviors into various conceptual schemes. For example, Berliner and Wheeler suggest a social learning model that groups victim behaviors into those indicative of anxiety or maladaptive learning.[8] Browne and Finkelhor[9] have suggested a traumagenic model, in which both trauma-producing factors (traumatic sexualization, stigmatization, betrayal, and powerlessness) and specific problems associated with each dynamic are presented. Burgess *et al.*[10] have outlined an information-processing or posttraumatic stress model for understanding the effects of sexual abuse. Although these various models are still in development, they offer important advantages to simple listing of impacts of abuse in that they direct attention toward clinical interventions.

Another problem with broad measures of child functioning is that many descriptions of broad aspects of functioning are limited to observable behavior. As such, they may ignore many of the most severe consequences of sexual victimization. Direct contact with victims points out that the overwhelming assault victimization is to the child's and adult survivor's world of meaning. Considerable energy in treatment is spent in trying to come to some understanding "why me?" or "why did he do this to me when he said he loved me?" This attack on the victim's world of meaning or "assumptive world"[11] has been addressed by several individuals working with adult survivors of sexual abuse,[12,13] but has not been well addressed by those working with children, nor is it adequately addressed in current measures of child functioning.

To be able to design abuse-sensitive interventions, that is, treatment that deal directly with the problems in living that are directly associated with abuse and abuse-related experiences, a new area of research on the effects of sexual abuse is needed. This research will need to identify the mediators between abuse and abuse-related experiences, and problems in living. Many of these mediators are likely to be cognitive aspects of human functioning. For example, it is not clear why victims are more likely to have relationship problems than are other people needing help. Something is altered by the abuse experience; this alteration leads to inability or difficulty in maintaining healthy relationships. Clinical speculation can identify a number of potential mediating variables.

Perhaps adults victimized as children see themselves as unworthy or incapable of relationships with people they perceive as good or healthy. Some victims who have not recovered from the trauma of a destructive relationship may try to recreate it again and again in the hopes of gaining some mastery over it or having it end differently than in their childhood. These are matters of some importance clinically, since the nature of therapy is likely to vary depending on whether the target of intervention is a victim's self-perceptions or a victim's need to recreate an abusive relationship. These may also be interrelated.

Research on the effects of sexual abuse has come a long way since the Army anecdotal clinical reports. Current efforts to describe the effects of abuse in terms of broad aspects of human functioning are likely to give way to efforts to understand how abuse affects more specific psychological processes that are more strategically linked between the abuse and abuse-associated factors and problems later in adult life. There is a solid foundation for this work.

REFERENCES

1. CONTE, J. R. 1985. The effects of sexual abuse on children: A critique and suggestions for future research. Victimol. **10**(1-4): 110-130.
2. BROWNE, A. & D. FINKELHOR. 1985. The traumatic impact of child sexual abuse: A conceptualization. Am. J. Orthopsychiatry **55:** 530-541.
3. MRAZEK P. & B. MRAZEK. 1981. The effects of child sexual abuse: Methodological considerations. *In* Sexually Abused Children and Their Families. P. Mrazek & B. Mrazek, Eds.: 235-246. Pergamon. New York, NY.
4. CONTE, J. R. & J. R. SCHUERMAN. 1987. The effects of sexual abuse on children: A multidimensional view. Child Abuse and Neglect. **11:** 201-211.
5. CONTE, J. R. & J. R. SCHUERMAN. 1987. Risk factors associated with the impact of sexual abuse. J. Interpers. Violence **2:** 380-390.
6. CONTE, J. R. & L. BERLINER. 1988. The impact of sexual abuse on children. *In* Handbook on Sexual Abuse of Children. L. E. A. Walker, Ed. Springer. New York, NY. In press.

7. CONTE, J. R. 1987. Follow-up results on the impact of sexual abuse on children. Submitted for publication.
8. BERLINER, L. & J. WHEELER. 1988. Treating the effects of sexual abuse. J. Interpers. Violence **2:** 415-434.
9. BROWNE, A. & D. FINKELHOR. 1986. The impact of child sexual abuse: A review of the research. Psychol. Bull. **99:** 66-77.
10. BURGESS, A. W., C. R. HARTMAN, W. A. WOLBERT & C. A. GRANT. 1987. Child molestation: Assessing impact in multiple victims. Arch. Psychiatric Nurs. **1**(1): 33-99.
11. JANOFF-BULMAN, R. & I. FREIZE. 1983. A theoretical perspective for understanding reactions to victimization. J. Soc. Issues **39:** 1-17.
12. JEHU, D., C. KLASSAN & D. GAZAN. 1985-1986. Cognitive restructuring of distorted beliefs associated with childhood sexual abuse. J. Soc. Work Hum. Sexuality **4:** 49-69.
13. DONALDSON, M. & R. GARDNER. 1985. Diagnosis and treatment of traumatic stress among women after childhood incest. *In* Trauma and Its Wake: The Study and Treatment of Post-traumatic Stress Disorder. C. Figley, Ed.: 356-377. Brunner Mazel. New York, NY.

The Long-Term Clinical Correlates of Childhood Sexual Victimization

JOHN BRIERE [a]

Department of Psychiatry
University of Southern California School of Medicine
Los Angeles, California 90033

Despite the contention of some clinicians and researchers that sexual child abuse is not necessarily traumatic or harmful,[1–3] most recent studies indicate that sexual victimization during childhood produces both short- and long-term psychological effects. In their comprehensive review of over 35 studies, most of which were published or presented since 1980, Browne and Finkelhor conclude that "sexual abuse is a serious mental health problem, consistently associated with very disturbing subsequent problems in some important portion of its victims."[4] Among other difficulties, it appears that women sexually abused as children are more likely than their nonabused peers to report depression, guilt, feelings of inferiority, and low self-esteem,[5–9] interpersonal problems, delinquency, and substance abuse,[5,7,9–11] suicidality,[5,12,13] anxiety and chronic tension,[5,6,12,14] sexual problems,[5,7,10,15,16] and a tendency toward revictimization in adulthood.[5,17,18] These findings appear to be relatively stable across a variety of groups (i.e., clinical, university student, and community samples), and may hold for both males and females.[19]

Until very recently, in what may be referred to as the "first wave" of sexual abuse research, investigators devoted considerable time and energy to "effects research"—documenting that adults with histories of childhood sexual abuse have more mental health problems than similar adults with no such history. As reflected in the Browne and Finkelhor[4] review, this goal has been more or less accomplished. What remains in this area may be described as the "second wave" of investigation—determining the actual relationship between aspects of the abuse (what Finkelhor[20,21] refers to as "traumagenic" factors) and specific psychological symptomatology. Such data are important, since they (a) offer clinicians and others a greater understanding of abuse-related symptom development, potentially leading to more specific and effective treatment procedures, and (b) increase our ability to identify and treat sexual abuse victims who are specifically "at risk" for certain types of problems (e.g., suicidality or substance abuse) later in life, by virtue of the specific type(s) of trauma they experienced. Finally, such research is "good science," increasing our ability to explain and predict sexual victimization effects. Unfortunately, as noted by Browne and Finkelhor,[4] "only a few studies on the effects of sexual abuse have had enough cases and been sophisticated enough methodologically . . . [to study traumagenic factors] empirically," and little consensus has been reached regarding specific abuse-effects relationships.

[a] Address for correspondence: Department of Psychiatry, LAC-USC Medical Center, 1934 Hospital Place, Los Angeles, California 90033.

The present study was undertaken in order to replicate "first wave" studies on the "effects"[b] of childhood sexual abuse, and attempt a "second wave" analysis of the relationship of these specific effects to certain aspects of the abuse experience. With regard to the second goal, a sufficient number of former sexual abuse victims were obtained to permit the use of multivariate techniques, thereby allowing a more detailed study of the longterm sequelae of sexual victimization. Specifically, canonical correlation analysis was applied to the sexual abuse subgroup data. This statistical procedure allows for the simultaneous consideration of multiple abuse and effects variables, and is able to determine multiple, independent sources of variance between these variable sets.

The abuse characteristics examined in the present study (e.g., duration of sexual abuse, presence of intercourse, presence of incest) were those identified in some research[6,9,12,13,18,22] (although not in others) as having specific impacts on psychological functioning. In addition, based on clinical experience, a new abuse variable—"bizarreness"—was included in the present analysis. Reflecting the presence of rituals (e.g., "black magic" rites, symbolic or pseudoreligious ordeals), especially repugnant acts (e.g., anal or vaginal insertion of objects, forced sexual contact with animals), or multiple perpetrators per act (e.g., sex rings, "orgies," gang rape), this form of abuse is thought by many clinicians to produce especially severe longterm effects,[23] despite the absence of empirical data in this area. Finally, the present study included aspects of psychosocial or behavioral functioning (e.g., substance addiction, suicidality, revictimization), as opposed to solely "mental health" variables, since fewer studies have been conducted on the former.

Based on the above, the hypotheses of the current investigation were (a) that a variety of psychological problems would be more common among abused than non-abused subjects, (b) that among subjects with a history of sexual abuse, certain aspects of their victimization experience would have had specific traumatic impact, thereby increasing levels of psychological difficulty, and (c) that abuse involving bizarre features would be especially associated with psychological symptoms and problems.

METHOD

Subjects

Subjects in the present study were 195 female clients of an outpatient crisis intervention service, described in more detail in an earlier paper on sexual abuse and suicidal behaviors.[13] This sample consisted of a preponderance of former sexual abuse victims relative to the number of never-abused subjects (133 vs. 61, respectively), in order to allow for a more detailed and multivariate study of sexual abuse effects. The average age of the entire sample was 27 years, with nonabused subjects being an

[b] It may not be entirely appropriate to refer to mental health correlates of sexual abuse as "effects," since these sequelae may be a function of some "third" set of variables, such as family environment or socio-economic status. A number of studies, however, have found that various abuse-effects relationships either remain after other relevant variables have been controlled, or vary as a function of abuse-specific events.[6,9,17,22,24,25]

average of 3.3 years older than abused subjects. Forty-three percent had never been married, 31% were married or living as married, and 26% were divorced or separated.

Sexual abuse in this study was defined as sexual contact (ranging from fondling to intercourse) on or before age 16, with someone 5 or more years older. Within the sexual abuse subsample, 43% of subjects reported sexual contact with a parent or stepparent (parental incest), 77% had experienced oral, anal, or vaginal intercourse during the abuse, and 56% were also physically abused (violent parental contact beyond spanking). "Bizarre abuse," which included reports of ritualistic sexual contact, multiple simultaneous perpetrators, use of animals, insertion of foreign objects, and/or sexual torture, occurred on at least one occasion in 17% of all sexual abuse subjects. The mean lifetime number of sexual abuse perpetrators per victim was 1.8, and the average duration of sexual abuse per victim was 5.9 years.

Procedure

Analysis of the clinical effects of sexual abuse proceeded in three stages. At stage 1, discriminant function analysis was used to compare abused and nonabused subjects on a number of variables: scores on the dissociation, sleep disturbance, sexual problems, and anger subscales of the Crisis Symptom Checklist[5] (CSC), history of rape or sexual assault during adulthood (since age 16), client reports of self-mutilatory behavior (cutting or burning of body parts without suicidal intent), and an overall measure of previous suicidal behavior (0 = no history of suicide attempts; 1 = low lethality attempts only; 2 = at least one moderately lethal suicide attempt, but no highly lethal suicide attempts; 3 = at least one highly lethal suicide attempt in the past).

Stages 2 and 3 involved the use of, respectively, canonical and simple correlation analysis of abuse effects within the sexual abuse subsample. In stage 2, canonical correlation analysis examined the relationship between characteristics of the abuse (presence of intercourse, bizarreness of abuse, and lifetime number of sexual abuse perpetrators) and the clinical variables listed at stage 1. Although multivariate techniques are appropriate for samples of this size ($n = 133$), the standardized weighting coefficients may be somewhat unstable for sample sizes of less than two or three hundred. For this reason, the canonical structure coefficients were interpreted as meaningful only when the absolute value of c was at least .40 (a relatively conservative criterion).

In stage 3, simple correlations were calculated for those abuse and effects variables found meaningful at stage 2, in order to allow a post-hoc evaluation of the canonical results. Given the number of correlations, the minimum p value for statistical significance was set at .01.

RESULTS

Discriminant Function Analysis

Discriminant analysis, using the CSC scales and other effects variables to predict childhood history of sexual abuse, was highly significant, $Rc = .53$, $\chi^2(9) = 62.10$,

$p < .0001$. The discriminant structure coefficients and univariate ANOVA results indicated that former sexual abuse victims scored higher on the dissociation, sleep disturbance, sexual problems, and anger scales of the CSC, reported more alcoholism and drug addiction, were more likely to have been raped or sexually assaulted as an adult, had been more suicidal in the past, and reported more self-mutilation than subjects with no self-reported sexual abuse history (see TABLE 1).

Canonical Correlation Analysis

Canonical analysis of abuse and effects variables within the subsample of sexually abused subjects revealed two significant canonical variates; Roots 1 through 5; F (54,606) = 1.66, $p < .003$; Roots 2 through 5: F (40,522) = 1.51, $p < .03$. Inspection of the structure coefficients for the first variate indicated a relationship between longer periods of sexual abuse, concommitant physical abuse, bizarre sexual abuse, and multiple perpetrators, and five effects variables: sexual problems, alcoholism, drug addiction, rape or sexual assault during adulthood, and suicidality. The second variate suggested that abuse involving sexual intercourse was related to dissociation and suicidality (see TABLE 2).

Simple Correlation Analysis

Characteristic of the abuse situation correlated with a number of effects variables. As indicated in TABLE 3, bizarre abuse was associated with sexual problems, anger, and alcoholism; concurrent physical abuse was related to alcoholism, drug addiction,

TABLE 1. Discriminant Function Analysis Using Effects Variables to Predict Sexual Abuse Status

Effects Variables	$\bar{x}$ Abused (n = 133)	$\bar{x}$ Nonabused (n = 61)	ANOVA F (1,193)	ANOVA $p <$	c^{str}[a]
Dissociation	.53	.29	26.18	.0001	*.59*
Sleep problems	.76	.60	11.85	.0007	*.40*
Sex problems	.65	.40	27.23	.0001	*.60*
Anger	.49	.32	11.54	.0008	*.39*
Alcoholism	.28	.03	17.23	.0001	*.48*
Drug addiction	.32	.08	14.26	.0002	*.44*
Sexual assault	.43	.13	18.52	.0001	*.50*
Self-mutilation	.08	.00	5.53	.0197	*.27*
Suicidal lethality	1.11	.42	16.02	.0001	*.46*

[a] Discriminant structure coefficients, considered meaningful (italicized) if $|c| > .25$.

TABLE 2. Canonical Correlation Results for Abuse and Effects Variable Sets

Variable	Variate Number 1	Variate Number 2
Abuse variable set		
Incest	−.22	.35
Duration	*−.47*	.06
Concurrent physical abuse	*−.63*	−.39
Intercourse	−.29	*−.75*
Bizarreness	*−.70*	.22
Lifetime number of perpetrators	*−.63*	.24
Effects variable set		
Dissociation	−.21	*−.61*
Sleep disturbance	−.39	.00
Sex problems	*−.45*	−.06
Anger	−.39	.27
Alcoholism	*−.58*	.12
Drug addiction	*−.66*	.06
Sexual assault	*−.51*	.05
Self-mutilation	−.39	.39
Suicidal lethality	*−.58*	*−.54*

NOTE: Canonical structure coefficients considered meaningful (italicized) if $|c| > .40$.

and suicidality; abuse involving intercourse was correlated with sexual problems and suicidality; and multiple perpetrators was associated with drug addiction.

DISCUSSION

The results of the current investigation, as do those of other recent studies, offer strong support for the notion that sexual abuse in childhood produces long-term psychological problems. Former sexual abuse victims scored higher on four scales of the Crisis Symptom Checklist, reported greater substance addiction and self-destructiveness, and were more likely to be sexually revictimized as adults.

Given such data and the focus of the current study, the issue then becomes whether such effects are the general results of victimization per se, or specific aspects of sexual abuse are traumatic above and beyond any general abuse effects. According to the present canonical and simple correlation results, certain abuse characteristics are, in fact, associated with certain psychological problems and symptoms. The first canonical variate suggests that extended sexual abuse, victimization involving bizarre acts, multiple perpetrators, and concommitant physical abuse may produce a variety of psychological problems; whereas the second variate indicates that, in addition to these effects, sexual intercourse during abuse may result in especially high levels of dissociation and suicidality. The presence of such relationships is all the more significant given the likelihood of decreased validity coefficients in this case—arising from the limitations inherent in a "within group" analysis of this type (e.g., increased subject homogeneity and restriction of range in the dependent variables).

It was hypothesized at the outset that sexual victimization involving rituals or especially repugnant acts ("bizarre abuse") would be associated with significantly higher levels of trauma. Both the canonical and simple correlation results support this hypothesis—in fact, in both cases the highest coefficients were those reflecting the relationship between bizarre abuse and psychological effects. According to the simple correlation results, bizarre abuse was associated with sexual problems, anger, and alcoholism; whereas the canonical results suggest that bizarre abuse is one of several variables that combine to produce especially negative effects. Although the basis for the aversive impact of bizarre abuse cannot be ascertained from the present data, it is likely that such events produce "stigmatization," described by Finkelhor and Browne[21] as "the negative connotations . . . that are communicated to the child around the experiences and that then become incorporated into the child's self-image." Specifically, it has been the author's clinical experience that if a child is exposed to especially high levels of humiliation and disgust (e.g., as a result of forced sexual acts

TABLE 3. Simple Correlations between Abuse and Effects Variables

Variable	Duration	Concurrent Physical Abuse	Parental Incest	Intercourse	Bizarre Abuse	Number of Perpetrators
Dissociation	−.05	.17	−.15	.17	.08	−.07
Sleep disturbance	.15	.09	−.02	.03	.12	.08
Sex problems	.04	−.01	.06	.22[a]	.29[b]	.15
Anger	.00	.02	−.03	−.05	.24[b]	.14
Alcoholism	−.02	.21[a]	.00	−.04	.22[a]	.18
Drug addiction	.20[a]	.19[a]	.08	.06	.17	.20[a]
Sexual assault	.11	.18	.08	.02	.15	.10
Self-mutilation	.14	.10	.13	−.11	.09	.14
Suicidality	.17	.27[c]	−.03	.22[b]	.06	.15

[a] $p \leq .01$.
[b] $p \leq .005$.
[c] $p \leq .001$.

with animals or with other children, or through vaginal insertion/masturbation with objects), the child may come to the conclusion that she or he must "deserve" such treatment, and therefore must be as disgusting and abhorrent as whatever was done to her or him[23] (see Jehu, Klassen, and Gazan[26] for other common attributions and assumptions made by victims of severe sexual abuse). Such cognitions may be especially prevalent when the former victim finds herself/himself in (even slightly) similar situations later in life (hence the sexual problems noted earlier), and may motivate self-destructive thoughts and feelings.[13,20,21]

As is apparent from the canonical results, most abuse variables (all except incest) and many effects variables (all but sleep problems, anger, and self-mutilation) are meaningfully related, suggesting that—as indicated earlier—certain aspects of abuse are significantly traumagenic. Viewed from another perspective, however, the specificity of individual abuse variable effects may be questioned. With the exception of intercourse and two effects variables—dissociation and suicidality—most abuse and effects variables load (or nearly load) on the same canonical variate, suggesting a broader cause-and-effect relationship than might have been hypothesized. Instead of specific relationships between individual abuse and effects variables, the canonical results point to a general "traumagenic" abuse factor and a general "negative impact" effects factor, which are strongly associated. Such a lack of specificity suggests that abuse-related symptom development may proceed in response to the general aversiveness of various types of sexual victimization, rather than as a reaction to certain events.

The exception to this phenomenon may be the relationship of intercourse to dissociation and suicidality. These variables formed their own orthogonal variate, indicating their distinctness from the general abuse-effects relationship described above. As suggested elsewhere,[6] abuse-related dissociation may serve as a defense against emotional and physical pain, wherein the victim learns to escape sensory input by cognitively disengaging or "going away" during aversive experiences. The current data support this possibility, since dissociation was associated with intercourse during sexual abuse (an extremely intrusive and painful event for a child) and—marginally—concommitant physical abuse. The presence of suicidality on this variate is intriguing, since suicide has also been described as a type of escape behavior (in fact, a complete dissociation) for some sexual abuse victims.[13,27]

In summary, data from the present study reinforce the findings of other studies with regard to the probable harmfulness of childhood sexual abuse. These data also suggest that there may be a general "traumagenic" process in sexual abuse, which can be triggered by a number of abuse-related events or processes. Whether sexual abuse produces long-term effects in the absence of these characteristics cannot be answered by the current findings, although it is the author's hypothesis that sexual abuse is traumatic per se, becoming even more destructive in the presence of certain characteristics such as bizarreness and extended duration. Finally, the present data indicate that sexual intercourse during abuse (and perhaps concommitant physical abuse) is specifically associated with later dissociation and suicidality.

Because of the multivariate nature of the present study and the only moderate sample size, the data reported here should be replicated with other samples—preferably using equivalent statistical techniques. To the extent that the findings can be generalized, however, the current study indicates the complexity of the sexual victimization process. Further study of traumagenesis in sexual abuse can only increase our understanding of abuse-related symptomatology, potentially leading to more effective interventions for the sexual abuse victim.

ACKNOWLEDGMENT

The author thanks Marsha Runtz, M.A., for her considerable assistance with this study.

REFERENCES

1. Rascovsky, M. & A. Rascovsky. 1950. On consumated incest. Int. J. Psycho-Anal. **31:** 42.
2. Constantine, L. L. 1982. Effects of early sexual experiences: A review and synthesis of

research. *In* Children and Sex: New Findings, New Perspectives. L. L. Constantine & F. M. Martinson, Eds.: 117-144. Little, Brown. Boston, MA.
3. HENDERSON, J. 1983. Is incest harmful? Can. J. Psychiatry **28:** 34-39.
4. BROWNE, A. & D. FINKELHOR. 1986. Impact of child sexual abuse: A review of the research. Psychol. Bull. **99:** 66-77.
5. BRIERE, J. & M. RUNTZ. 1987. Post Sexual Abuse Trauma: Data and implications for clinical practice. J. Interpers. Violence. **2:** 367-379.
6. BRIERE, J. & M. RUNTZ. 1988. Symptomatology associated with childhood sexual victimization in a non-clinical adult sample. Child Abuse and Neglect. **12:** 51-59.
7. HERMAN, J. 1981. Father-Daughter Incest. Harvard University Press. Cambridge, MA.
8. GOLD, E. 1986. Longterm effects of sexual victimization: An attributional approach. J. Consult. Clin. Psychol. **54:** 471-475.
9. PETERS, S. D. 1987. Child sexual abuse and later psychological problems. J. Interpers. Violence. In press.
10. COURTOIS, C. 1979. Characteristics of a volunteer sample of adult women who experienced incest in childhood or adolescence. Diss. Abstr. Int. **40:** 3194A-3195A.
11. RUNTZ, M. & J. BRIERE. 1986. Adolescent "acting out" and childhood history of sexual abuse. J. Interpers. Violence. **1:** 326-33.
12. BAGLEY, C. & R. RAMSAY. 1985. Disrupted childhood and vulnerability to sexual assault: Longterm sequels with implications for counselling. J. Soc. Work Hum. Sexuality, **4:** 33-48.
13. BRIERE, J. & M. RUNTZ. 1986. Suicidal thoughts and behaviors in former sexual abuse victims. Can. J. Behav. Sci. **18:** 413-423.
14. SEDNEY, M. A. & B. BROOKS. 1984. Factors associated with a history of childhood sexual experiences in a nonclinical female population. J. Acad. Child Psychiatry. **23:** 215-218.
15. MEISELMAN, K. 1978. Incest: A Psychological Study of Causes and Effects with Treatment Recommendations. Jossey-Bass. San Francisco, CA.
16. JEHU, D., M. GAZAN & C. KLASSEN. 1984-1985. Common therapeutic targets among women who were sexually abused. J. Soc. Work Hum. Sexuality **4:** 46-69.
17. FROMUTH, M. E. 1986. The relationship of childhood sexual abuse with later psychological and sexual adjustment in a sample of college women. Child Abuse and Neglect **10:** 5-15.
18. RUSSELL, D. E. H. 1986. The Secret Trauma: Incest in the Lives of Girls and Women. Basic Books. New York, NY.
19. BRIERE, J., D. EVANS, M. RUNTZ & T. WALL. 1987. Are there sex differences in the longterm effects of child sexual abuse? Presented at the Third National Family Violence Research Conference, Durham, New Hampshire, July 6-9, 1987.
20. FINKELHOR, D. 1987. The trauma of child sexual abuse: Two models. J. Interpers. Violence. **2:** 348-366.
21. FINKELHOR, D. & A. BROWNE. 1985. The traumatic impact of child sexual abuse: A conceptualization. Am. J. Orthopsychiatry **55:** 530-541.
22. FINKELHOR, D. 1979. Sexually Victimized Children. Free Press. New York, NY.
23. BRIERE, J. 1988. The Sexual Abuse Survivor: A Psychotherapy Manual. Springer Publishing Co. New York, NY. In press.
24. TSAI, M., S. FELDMAN-SUMMERS & M. EDGAR. 1979. Childhood molestation: Variables related to differential impacts on psychosexual functioning in adult women. J. Abnorm. Psychol. **88:** 407-417.
25. WYATT, G. E. & M. R. MICKEY. 1987. Ameliorating the effects of child sexual abuse: An exploratory study of support by parents and others. J. Interpers. Violence **2:** 403-414.
26. JEHU, D., M. KLASSEN & M. GAZAN. 1985-1986. Cognitive restructuring of distorted beliefs associated with childhood sexual abuse. J. Soc. Work Hum. Sexuality **4:** 49-69.
27. REICH, J. W. & S. E. GUTIERRES. 1979. Escape/aggression incidence in sexually abused juvenile delinquents. Crim. Justice Behav. **6:** 239-243.

Rape in Marriage and in Dating Relationships: How Bad Is It for Mental Health?[a]

DEAN G. KILPATRICK, CONNIE L. BEST, BENJAMIN E. SAUNDERS, AND LOIS J. VERONEN

Department of Psychiatry and Behavioral Sciences
Medical University of South Carolina
Charleston, South Carolina 29425-0742

Even a cursory examination suggests that victims of marital and date rape suffer the additional burdens of legal and attitudinal discrimination as compared to victims of stranger rape. After considerable study, the Attorney General's Task Force on Family Violence Report[1] concluded that there has been a long-standing tendency for the general public and for the criminal justice system to treat victims of violent crimes, such as rape, perpetrated by family members or loved ones less favorably than victims of identical crimes committed by strangers. One example of discrimination against marital rape victims is the marital exclusion in the criminal rape statutes of many states, which specifically states that rape cannot occur between husband and wife, because the wife is presumed to have given perpetual consent for sexual relations upon taking the marriage vows. Another example is the fact that crime victim compensation statutes in many states exclude from eligibility victims whose assailants reside in the same household as the victim. Thus, marital rape victims cannot receive compensation for treatment of physical or psychological injuries sustained in an attack by their husbands.

Perhaps an even more devastating form of discrimination is that many people, sometimes including the victims themselves, do not define attacks as rape unless the assailant is a stranger. As Burt[2] and others have shown, the general public holds stereotypes about rape, including the belief that virtually all rapes are committed by strangers. Koss[3] as well as Kilpatrick and Veronen[4] have shown that these stereotypes and beliefs extend to victims themselves. Both these investigators asked representative samples of college students (Koss[3]) and adult women in the general population (Kilpatrick and Veronen[4]) whether they had ever had experiences involving nonconsensual completed oral, anal, or vaginal intercourse in which the assailant had used force or threat of force. This type of experience would be legally defined as rape in most jurisdictions, unless the statute in that jurisdiction contained a marital exclusion. A substantial proportion of respondents in both studies reported having had one or more experiences that met the legal definition of rape, but responded negatively when asked if they had ever been raped. Koss[3] refers to such women as unacknowledged rape victims. In both the Koss[3] and the Kilpatrick and Veronen[4] studies, the probability

[a]This work was partially supported by a grant from the National Institute of Justice, No. 84-IJ-CX-0039.

that a rape incident would be unacknowledged was higher if the assailant was *not* a stranger to the victim. Thus, victims themselves often fail to define an experience as rape if they have the misfortune to have been attacked by a husband or date.

Two negative consequences of victims' and the general public's failure to define nonstranger attacks as rape are: (a) victims are less likely to report such rapes to police (Koss[3]); and (b) victims who do report such rapes to police might expect to receive less sympathetic treatment from the criminal justice system. Criminal prosecutors often state that they are reluctant to prosecute marital or even date rape cases because of concerns that juries will not believe that a women could be raped by a husband or boyfriend. It goes without saying that rape cases not reported to police or not effectively prosecuted result in a major injustice being done to the victim, the assailant, and to society in general.

What assumptions might account for this discrimination against married and date rape victims? One assumption, already alluded to, is the tendency of most people not to believe that marital and date rape even exist. Among those people who believe that marital and/or date rape exist, a second possible reason for discrimination is an assumption that marital and date rape occurs rather infrequently in comparison to stranger rape. Thus, some people might believe that marital and date rape are not important, because there are fewer victims affected by these types of nonstranger rape than by stranger rape. A third possible reason for discrimination is that people might assume that marital and date rapes have a less severe psychological impact on the victims' mental health. Given the potential negative consequences for victims and for society itself of discrimination against marital and date rape victims, it is important to determine the extent to which any of these assumptions are supported by empirical data.

A methodologically sound study examining this question should meet the following criteria.

1. The rape victim sample should be as representative as possible of the population of interest. Since many victims do not report to police or seek services from agencies, samples from these sources cannot be presumed to be representative of all rape victims. Similarly, samples recruited via media advertisements cannot be presumed to be representative.
2. Victimization survey methodology should be used, in which members of a representative sample are screened for possible rape experiences. As Koss[3] noted, these screening questions must include descriptions of the behavioral elements that would constitute rape (i.e., nonconsent, use of force or threat of force, and completed sexual activity involving penetration), rather than simply ask women if they have been raped.
3. Descriptive data must be gathered about the objective and the subjectively-perceived violence of rape incidents as well as about the offenders' relationship to the victims.
4. A comparison group of nonvictims must be included in the study design, if any inferences are to be made about the psychological impact of rape upon the victims' mental health. Without being able to show that victims differ from nonvictims on relevant mental health variables, it is difficult, if not impossible, to make inferences that rape produces a negative impact on mental health.
5. Measures of mental health problems should have acceptable psychometric characteristics.
6. If the focus of interest is the long-term mental health effects of rape, at least one assessment must be conducted sufficiently long after the rape to permit

assessment of long-term effects. Ideally, study designs should be longitudinal rather than retrospective, although the practical and economic problems associated with conducting a large longitudinal study are considerable.

7. Data on the prevalence of marital, date, and stranger rape cases should be determined.
8. The objective and subjective violence of the three kinds of rape cases should be compared.
9. The mental health problems of victims and nonvictims should be compared.
10. The extent to which marital, date, and stranger rapes are associated with victims' long-term mental health problems should be determined, by conducting within-victim-group comparisons on mental health problem variables upon which victims and nonvictims have been shown to differ.

No published study to date has met all of these criteria. Although it is not without problems, a general-population victimization survey conducted by Russell[5] provides reasonably good data on the prevalence of marital, date, and stranger rape. However, the Russell study's assessment of mental health problems was extremely weak. Koss[3] conducted an excellent study of rape among college students at a large midwestern university, but collected minimal data on mental health consequences. Other investigators have studied marital rape within the context of marital violence situations, using nonrepresentative samples (e.g., Frieze[6] and Doron[7]). One study that controlled for nonsexual violence also used nonrepresentative clinical and convenience samples.[8] Other studies, using clinical samples, have examined the effects of rape on psychological adjustment as a function of victim/assailant relationship, with generally negative results.[9–14] However, Ellis, Atkeson, and Calhoun[15] distinguished between stranger versus nonstranger rape and reported victims of strangers to be more anxious, depressed, and socially dysfunctional than victims of nonstrangers. It is noteworthy that these authors also reported stranger rapes to be characterized by more violence and more sudden onset than nonstranger rapes, thus suggesting victim perceptions of violence as a potential covariate of psychological adjustment. The importance of a victim's subjective distress during the assault as a predictor of long-term adjustment was suggested by Girelli *et al.*[16]

The current study was specifically designed to correct most of the methodological problems of the kind present in existing studies and thereby to permit the gathering of sound empirical data concerning the adequacy of the aforementioned assumptions about differences among marital, date, and stranger rapes. Specific attention was focused on careful measurement of current mental health problems associated with rape and on determining whether such problems differ as a function of the assailant's relationship to the victim.

METHOD

Subjects

Subjects were 43 adults (age 18 or older) female victims of completed rape and 96 adult female nonvictims of completed rape, other sexual assault, aggravated assault, robbery, or burglary. All subjects were drawn from a sample of 391 adult women who had participated in a large National Institute of Justice-funded study designed to determine the lifetime prevalence of several types of criminal victimization experiences and to explore relationships among victimization experiences, current psychological functioning, and current and lifetime mental health disorders. The 43 rape victim subjects were selected on the basis of the following criteria: (1) they had experienced a completed rape; (2) that completed rape was either the only crime they had experienced or it was subjectively judged by the victim to be the "worst" crime if more than one crime had been experienced; and (3) that completed rape involved an assailant who was the victim's husband, her boyfriend, someone the victim had never seen before, or someone she had seen before but did not know well. In order to be defined as completed rape, an experience must have involved the use of force or threat of force by the assailant, occurred without the victim's consent, and included a completed act of sexual penetration of the victim's vagina, anus, or mouth. Nonvictims had never been victims of completed rape, other types of sexual assault, aggravated assault, robbery, or burglary.

Sampling Procedure

The 139 subjects in the present study were drawn from 391 participants in the larger National Institute of Justice-funded project, who were in turn drawn from a National Institute of Mental Health-funded telephone survey of a representative sample of 2004 adult female residents of Charleston County, South Carolina conducted by Louis Harris and Associates. The methodology and results of the parent Louis Harris survey are described in detail elsewhere.[17] A major objective of the survey was to locate a representative sample of women to participate in an in-depth, in-person follow-up study of lifetime victimization, current psychological functioning, and mental health problems. When asked about their willingness to consider participating in the follow-up study, 1467 women responded affirmatively and provided the interviewer with their first name.

Because of unavoidable delays, at least 18 months and as long as 30 months passed between participation in the telephone survey and attempts to recontact respondents. It was possible to contact 933 (63.6%) of the 1467 potential participants. Of those contacted, 399 (42.8%) agreed to participate and completed all assessment procedures. Data from 8 of these subjects was excluded from the study; interviewers judged their data to be invalid because of extreme confusion and/or inability to comprehend the meaning of assessment questions. Thus, the final sample size for the National Institute of Justice (NIJ) follow-up study was 391.

Representativeness of NIJ sample

Briefly stated, the more representative the NIJ sample is of the Charleston County population, the greater is the ability to generalize findings. Since the Louis Harris sample was representative, we compared the demographic characteristics of the 391 members of the NIJ sample with those of the 2004 members of the Louis Harris sample. Comparisons were based on characteristics at the time of the 1983 Louis Harris survey.

The NIJ sample members were significantly younger than Louis Harris sample members (M = 39.8 years vs. M = 42.0 years; $t(390) = -3.02, p < .01$). Whites (non-Hispanic) were significantly overrepresented in the NIJ sample (72.9% vs. 66.1% $z = 3.03, p < .005$), and NIJ sample members had significantly higher household incomes than did Louis Harris sample members (percent of samples with incomes over $35,000 per year was 19.2% and 13.4% respectively; $z = 2.91, p < .005$). Thus, it appeared that the NIJ sample was somewhat demographically biased, although these biases were small in nature.

Assessment Measures

The assessment battery consisted of two structured interviews and four paper-and-pencil tests; the latter will not be described, since they were not used in the current study. The first structured interview gathered data about the respondent's lifetime experience with completed rape, several other types of sexual assault, aggravated assault, robbery, and burglary. In addition to screening questions about these victimization experiences, this interview gathered data about: (1) the respondent's current age, marital status, racial status, educational status, and household income; (2) characteristics of the crime incident (e.g., the assailant's identity and relationship to the victim, the victim's cognitive appraisal of whether she was in a life-threatening situation during the incident, the extent of physical injuries sustained), and (3) the victim's age at the time of the incident and how many years ago the incident occurred.

The Mental Health Problem Interview represents a slight modification of the Diagnostic Interview Schedule,[18] a structured interview designed to gather data enabling the interviewer to determine whether a respondent meets the American Psychiatric Association's Diagnostic and Statistical Manual of Mental Disorders (DSM-III) criteria for diagnosing current and lifetime prevalence of the following mental health disorders: (1) major depressive episode, (2) agoraphobia, (3) social phobia, (4) simple phobia, (5) panic disorder, (6) obsessive-compulsive disorder, (7) posttraumatic stress disorder (for victims only), and (8) disorders of sexual desire and/or sexual functioning. In this paper the only mental health problems to be examined were current major depressive episode, social phobia, obsessive-compulsive disorder, and sexual dysfunction. This interview was completed by clinical psychologists who were blind to the respondent's victimization status until the posttraumatic stress disorder section of the interview.

Procedure

Participants were contacted via telephone, informed about the study, and were scheduled for assessment by one of the three female research assistants. After agreeing to participate, they were informed that they would receive $25.00 to partially compensate them for their participation. During the in-person assessment, a research assistant completed the incident classification interview for each respondent.

Information was obtained about up to three separate crime incidents per respondent; the first crime, the most recent crime, and any crime that was worse than the first or most recent. Only 96 (24.6%) of the 391 women in this sample were defined as nonvictims, because they had never experienced completed rape, other forms of sexual assault, aggravated assault, robbery, or burglary. The remaining 275 women (75.4% of respondents) had been victims of one or more crimes. Of these, 91 respondents had been victims of at least one rape (23.3% of the sample). There were a total of 101 separate rape cases.

RESULTS

To provide data on the relative prevalence of marital, date, and stranger rape, the proportion of total rape cases involving each type of assailant was determined (see TABLE 1). Husbands were assailants in 23.8% of the 101 rape cases. Assailants were identified as dates (boyfriends or exboyfriends) in 16.8% of all rape cases. Other nonstranger assailants were responsible for 38.6% of these rape cases. Assailants never

TABLE 1. Percentage of Total Rape Cases Involving Husband, Date, and Stranger Assailants

Type of Assailant	Number	Percentage
Husband	24	23.8%
Date	17	16.8%
Stranger	21	20.8%
Other	39	38.6%
Total Cases	101	100.0%

seen before or not known well by the victim accounted for 20.8% of all rape cases. Thus, of all the rapes in the sample, 40.6% were committed by husbands or dates, nearly twice as many as those committed by strangers.

The assumption that husband and/or date rapes were objectively and subjectively less dangerous than stranger rapes were examined by comparing the percentage of total husband, date, and stranger rape cases ($n = 60$) in which the victim sustained a physical injury as a result of the rape or thought that she might have been killed or seriously injured during the rape. The percentage of victims in each assailant group having sustained physical injuries during the rape is presented in TABLE 2.

Assaults by dates and by husbands were somewhat more likely than assaults by strangers to result in the victim's sustaining a physical injury, although a chi-square analysis indicated that these differences were not statistically significant. Data on the percentage of rape cases in which the victim's cognitive appraisal of the rape situation involved the possibility of death or serious injury by type of assailant is presented in TABLE 3. Date rapes were most likely to produce a subjective cognitive appraisal of life threat or injury, while husband and stranger assaults were less likely to have done so. Chi-square analysis indicated that these differences were not statistically significant.

The next stage of analysis compared the prevalence of current mental health

TABLE 2. Percentage of Rape Cases by Type of Assailant in Which Victim Sustained Physical Injury

Type of Assailant	Sustained Physical Injury		
	Yes	No	Not Sure
Husband	45.8%	51.2%	3.0%
Date	46.7%	53.3%	0.0%
Stranger	38.1%	61.9%	0.0%

problems of the 43 rape victims whose rape was their only crime or their worst crime and whose assailant in that crime was a husband, date, or stranger to that of the 96 nonvictims. As inspection of TABLE 4 indicates, a significantly higher percentage of rape victims than nonvictims currently met the diagnostic criteria for major depressive episode, social phobia, and sexual dysfunction. The rate of current obsessive disorder did not differ significantly for victims and nonvictims.

The final set of analyses was designed to investigate the assumption that the prevalence of current mental health problems of victims assaulted by strangers might be higher than that among victims assaulted by husbands or dates. Prior to conducting these analyses, victims were separated into groups based on type of assailant and compared with respect to two possibly confounding variables: (a) current age and (b) number of years since the rape occurred. Analyses of variance indicated that there were statistically significant differences across victim groups on both variables. With respect to current age, victims assaulted by strangers ($M = 42.4$, SD = 11.7) or by husbands ($M = 41.4$, SD = 13.3) were significantly older than victims assaulted by a date ($M = 30.0$, SD = 6.1; $F(2, 40) = 3.91, p < .05$). There was also a significant difference in the length of time since the assault occurred for rapes committed by strangers ($M = 21.9$, SD = 16.4), husbands ($M = 12.7$, SD = 10.9), or by dates ($M = 9.8$, SD = 4.3; $F(2,400 = 3.91, p < .05$). Thus, within-victim-group analyses focusing on the degree of current mental health problem might be confounded by victims' current age and length of time since the rape, unless these variables are controlled statistically. Thus, the final analysis was a multivariate analysis of covariance (MANCOVA) in which type of assailant was the independent variable, current age and length of time were covariates, and the current presence or absence of major depressive episode, social phobia, obsessive-compulsive disorder, and sexual disorders were the dependent variables. Results of the MANCOVA indicated that there were no significant differences in current mental health variables as a function of assailant type both controlling for and not controlling for victim current age and number of years since the rape ($F(8, 74) = 1.28$, based upon Wilks lambda). Univariate analyses

TABLE 3. Percentage of Rape Cases by Type of Assailant in Which Victim Thought She Might Be Killed or Seriously Injured

Type of Assailant	Thought She Might Be Killed	
	Yes	No
Husband	41.6%	58.4%
Date	53.3%	46.7%
Stranger	38.1%	61.9%

of covariance and chi-square analysis conducted on each of the dependent variables confirmed this finding, in that there were no significant differences attributable to assailant type on any of the dependent variables.

DISCUSSION

The results detailed above not only offer little support for the common assumptions about marital and date rape, but directly contradict them. The notion that marital or date rape occurs only infrequently and affect very few victims is strongly refuted by these data. Nearly twice as many women had been raped by husbands or boyfriends as by strangers. Clearly, if the occurrence of sexual assault is at epidemic levels, these results suggest that marital and date rape are the leading edge of the problem. The public perception of rape being committed only by strangers in remote places late at night is a fallacy. These data indicate that a victim is most likely to be attacked by someone very close to her.

TABLE 4. Percentage of Rape Victims and Nonvictims Currently Experiencing Each Mental Health Problem

Type of Mental Health Problem	Rape Victims	Nonvictims	χ^2	p
Major depressive episode	11.6%	1.0%	5.69	.01
Social phobia	14.0%	2.1%	5.68	.01
Obsessive-compulsive disorder	7.2%	2.1%	0.88	.35
Sexual dysfunction	30.2%	11.5%	6.07	.01

The assumption that rape by a husband or boyfriend has a less severe immediate impact on the victim also was not supported. Victims are no more likely to be physically injured if assaulted by a stranger than by a spouse or date. Indeed, although the differences are not statistically significant, in this sample women assaulted by husbands and boyfriends were actually more likely to sustain physical injury. There were also no differences in the way in which victims subjectively judged the danger of the attack. Again, though the differences were not statistically significant, in this sample women assaulted by a husband or boyfriend were more likely to think they might be killed or injured than those raped by strangers. Therefore, there appear to be no differences in the immediate physical or psychological impact of the assault between those committed by husbands, boyfriends, or strangers.

The long-term impact of rape is also apparent in these data. Despite the fact that on average it had been nearly 15 years since the sexual assault had occurred, there were still significant and substantial differences in the psychological functioning of rape victims and nonvictims. Even after this long period of time, victims were 11 times more likely to be clinically depressed, 6 times more likely to be severely fearful in social situations, and 2½ times more likely to experience sexual dysfunction than were nonvictims. And, though the difference was not statistically significant, in this sample victims were over three times as likely to have obsessive-compulsive disorder than nonvictims. Discovering differences of this magnitude long after a sexual assault occurred is indicative of the severity of the impact of rape.

There was no evidence to support the assumption that rape by a husband or boyfriend had less severe long-term psychological consequences than rape by a stranger. Multivariate analysis revealed that women assaulted by spouses or dates were just as likely as those assaulted by strangers to be depressed, fearful, obsessive-compulsive, and sexually dysfunctional years after the assault. Common assumptions about women assaulted by strangers having a more difficult time adjusting to the event than women raped by husbands and boyfriends appear to be incorrect.

The best conclusion at this time is that the impact of rape is severe whether the assailant is a stranger, husband, or boyfriend. There are no differences in either the immediate or long-term effects of rape based upon the role of the perpetrator. Therefore, an assumption that rape by a husband or date somehow has a less severe impact on the victim appears to be simply incorrect.

These results have several implications for future research, clinical intervention, public and professional education, and public policy. Clearly, more research attention should be devoted to marital and date rape. These results suggest that over 40% of all rapes are perpetrated by husbands and boyfriends, yet the majority of the research literature concerns stranger rape. Future research efforts should reflect the prevalence of this problem.

At the same time clinical programs should recognize the unique relational dynamics of marital and date rape. While marital and date rape victims may have many of the same psychological problems as stranger rape victims and benefit from the same types of therapy, their relationship to the assailant must be taken into account in clinical intervention. Treating these victims while ignoring or making assumptions about their relationship to the perpetrators may have negative effects. Also, as described above many marital and date rape victims do not identify the violent event as a rape or themselves as victims. Consequently, they may present with what appear to be common psychiatric disorders and not describe a victimization experience as an important etiological or precipitating event. Current problems may be related to a past or recent unacknowledged sexual assault. Therefore, educating clinicians to take a careful victimization history that respects the victims' appraisal of possible past experiences while gathering relevant facts should be emphasized.

Public and professional education on the severity of the impact of marital and date rape is a critical need. Both the public and professional community should be made aware of the prevalence of marital and date rape, that it is not infrequent but one of the most common forms of sexual assault. Also, public and professional education should describe what is known about the lack of differences in the psychological consequences of marital, date, and stranger rape. Through significant public education, incorrect assumptions about marital and date rape can be challenged. Through professional education, services to marital and date rape victims may be improved.

Finally, public policy should reflect the reality of marital and date rape. Marital exclusion clauses in sexual assault laws carry many false assumptions. The idea that rape cannot occur in marriage because the wife has given perpetual sexual consent is rooted in the supposition that rape is strictly a sexual act between two people. Though rape obviously is sexual, it is primarily a violent crime with severe consequences for the victim, as these data demonstrate. The assumption that violence in families is somehow less harmful or less severe is also refuted by the data. If anything, the opposite is true. Public policy and the legal process should recognize marital and date rape for the violent crime that it is.

REFERENCES

1. ATTORNEY GENERAL'S TASK FORCE ON FAMILY VIOLENCE. 1984. Final Report, September 1984. U.S. Government Printing Office. Washington, DC.
2. BURT, M. R. 1980. Cultural myths and supports for rape. J. Pers. Soc. Psychol. **38**(2): 217-230.
3. KOSS, M. P. 1983. The scope of rape: Implications for the clinical treatment of victims. Clin. Psychol. **36:** 88-91.
4. KILPATRICK, D. G., & L. J. VERONEN. 1984. Assessing victims of rape: Methodological issues. Final Report, Grant No. R01 MH38052. National Institute of Mental Health. Rockville, MD.
5. RUSSELL, D. E. H. 1982. The prevalence and incidence of forcible rape and attempted rape of females. Victimol. **7:** 81-93.
6. FRIEZE, I. 1983. Investigating the causes and consequences of marital rape. Signs **8**(3): 532-553.
7. DORON, J. 1980. Conflict and violence in intimate relationships: Focus on marital rape. Presented at a Meeting of the American Sociological Association, New York, New York, 1980.
8. HANNEKE, C. R., N. M. SHIELDS & G. J. MCCALL 1986. Assessing the prevalence of marital rape. J. Interpere. Violence. **1:** 350-362.
9. ATKESON, B. M., K. S. CALHOUN, P. A. RESICK & E. M. ELLIS. 1982. Victims of rape: Repeated assessment of depressive symptoms. J. Consult. Clin. Psychol. **50:** 96-102.
10. BECKER, J. V., L. J. SKINNER, G. G. ABEL & E. C. TREACY. 1982. Incidence and types of sexual dysfunctions in rape and incest victims. J. Sex Marital Ther. **8:** 65-74.
11. FRANK, E., S. M. TURNER & B. D. STEWART. 1982. Initial response to rape: The impact of factors within the rape situation. J. Behav. Assessment **2:** 39-53.
12. KILPATRICK, D. G., L. J. VERONEN & C. L. BEST. 1985. Factors predicting psychological distress among rape victims. *In* Trauma and Its Wake. C.R. Figley, Ed.: 113-141. Brunner/Mazel. New York, NY.
13. MCCAHILL, T. W., L. C. MEYER & A. M. FISCHMAN. 1979. The Aftermath of Rape. Lexington Books, D.C. Heath. Lexington, MA.
14. RUCH, L. O. & S. M. CHANDLER. 1983. Sexual assault trauma during the acute phase: An exploratory model and multivariate analysis. J. Health Soc. Behav. **24:** 174-185.
15. ELLIS, E. M., B. M. ATKESON & K. S. CALHOUN. 1981. An assessment of long-term reaction to rape. J. Abnorm. Psychol. **90:** 263-266.
16. GIRELLI, S. A., P. A. RESICK, S. MORROEFER-DVORAK & C. K. HUTTER. 1986. Subjective distress and violence during rape: Their effects on long-term fear. Violence and Victims **1**(1): 35-46.
17. KILPATRICK, D. G., C. L. BEST, L. J. VERONEN, A. E. AMICK, L. A. VILLEPONTEAUX & G. A. RUFF. 1985. Mental health correlates of criminal victimization: A random community survey. J. Consult. Clin. Psychol. **53:** 866-873.
18. ROBINS, L. N., J. D. HELZER, J. CROUGHAN & K. S. RATCLIFF. 1981. The National Institute of Mental Health diagnostic interview schedule: Its history, characteristics, and validity. Arch. Gen. Psychiatry **38:** 381-389.

Coping Strategies and Recovery from Rape

MARTHA R. BURT AND BONNIE L. KATZ

The Urban Institute
Washington, D.C. 20037

INTRODUCTION

A substantial body of research has developed in recent years documenting the immediate and short-term (up to one year) symptomatic reactions to a rape experience.[1,2] Much less work has been done on long-term patterns of response, and even less research has directly addressed the coping strategies women use as they struggle to come to terms with the rape experience over the years after acute symptoms wane, or the relationship between coping efforts and the recovery process. Burgess and Holmstrom's work[3,4] is a rare exception; Meyer and Taylor[5] have recently published results of a new study that adds to our understanding of coping patterns following rape.

In this paper we present a set of coping scales derived from our research data on the coping patterns found in 113 women who are 1 to 14 years postrape; initial reports of these data have previously been presented. The selection of items for our questionnaire, as well as our interpretation of results, are informed by previous theoretical and empirical research, some of which we will review. Our primary interest lies in systematically documenting the real patterns that are observed in women as they cope with rape over time, and specifically as their recovery progresses. Doing so should enable us to identify the most adaptive coping approaches and to utilize this information in counseling rape victims. In addition, this information will add to our understanding of the dynamics of the recovery process.

In studying coping efforts, it is important to define what we are talking about. We view "coping" as comprising efforts made in response to stimuli experienced as threatening or stressful—efforts aimed both at reducing the anxiety that those stimuli create and at reducing the interference of the stimuli with one's capacity to function. Lazarus and Folkman[7] divide coping strategies into two large domains—problem-focused and emotion-focused coping. Problem-focused coping is directed at helping the person manage or solve the problem, and can involve strategies directed at the environment (e.g., altering environmental pressures, barriers, resources, procedures) and also strategies directed inward (e.g., learning new skills, developing new standards of behavior, or changing one's level of aspiration). Women who have been raped may have used problem-focused coping strategies during the rape itself, and may also define the process of recovery in such a way that the future represents a series of tasks to get through or accomplish. Cast in the light of problem-focused coping, recovery is seen largely as a performance to be achieved.

Emotion-focused coping strategies are directed at helping the individual accept or handle events that have happened and situations that are chronic and cannot be altered. The recognition of such strategies as important coping resources is crucial because, as Lazarus and Folkman point out,[7] coping is too often confused with mastery. Some events and circumstances simply cannot be mastered, but must be lived with or endured. Emotion-focused coping strategies—reconceptualizing the situation, selective attention, narrowing or minimizing strategies, avoidance, venting anger and other emotion, or seeking emotional support—may promote good adjustment more than repeated attempts to change a past event or ongoing real stressor. Rape victims may rely heavily on this type of coping strategy, both during the rape itself and throughout the process of recovery. Women for whom these strategies dominate see recovery, and probably the actual assault, as something to be endured.

People typically use both types of strategies together in response to stressful incidents.[7] They alternate between retreat and vigilance, between emotion-focused and problem-focused coping, in increasingly lengthy cycles until the incident is absorbed and integrated into their view of themselves and their world. In this formulation, Lazarus and Folkman's view is very similar to Horowitz's[8] formulation of posttraumatic stress responses. Horowitz posits that coping efforts rely on denial, numbing, and other "emotion-focused" techniques to allow the self to become aware of a catastrophe in regulated doses, small enough so that one can handle and absorb them. Recovery, in his formulation, is the process of revising one's world view little by little until it has changed to incorporate the reality of what happened.

The specific content of the work of recovery has been explored extensively in social psychological research on coping with traumatic victimization.[9–12] Silver and Wortman[11] reviewed this research and concluded that stage theories of coping are largely unsupported by empirical evidence, but that cognitive processes are prominent among the mechanisms used in adjusting to many types of catastrophe, including rape. Janoff-Bulman[9] has asserted that the impact of traumatic victimization results largely from its destruction of three particular cognitive assumptions about the world. These are (1) belief in personal invulnerability, (2) perception of the world as meaningful and having a just order, and (3) a view of oneself as positive. These assumptions are usually not in conscious awareness until they are shattered, and then the individual confronts the extent to which she depends on these tenets in order to function in and cope with daily life. Taylor[12] describes three dimensions that are equivalent to these, and argues that they are cognitive illusions that are necessary for healthy adjustment to life. Accordingly, she regards recovery from traumatic victimization primarily as the task of reestablishing these illusions/assumptions.

While coping theory provides the framework for guiding our exploration of coping with rape, we are also interested in how our data relate to previous research on adjustment following rape. Burgess and Holmstrom[3,4] collected interview data that enabled them to organize into categories women's qualitative descriptions of coping with their own rapes. These researchers described these coping approaches as either successful or maladaptive, depending on the women's self-reported length of time to recovery. They found that victims who used one or more conscious defense mechanisms to reduce anxiety recovered the fastest. Those most frequently reported by their sample (81 women, four to six years postrape) were: explanation (aimed at understanding why the rape happened), minimization (viewing what happened to them as better than other possible scenarios), suppression (avoiding thinking about the rape), and dramatization (extensive expression of feelings about or discussion of the rape incident). Burgess and Holmstrom[4] also found that women who adopted action-oriented behaviors, such as changing residence or traveling, were likely to have recovered faster. The "maladaptive" patterns they described were: decreased activity (staying at home, for instance), withdrawal from people, and substance abuse. They concluded that there were, then, particular strategies for coping with rape that seemed to yield a faster recovery.

Burgess and Holmstrom reported the first empirical data available regarding the relationship between other factors and the speed of recovery. They found that women who had lost a family member more than two years prior to the rape recovered more quickly than those who had not, suggesting a few alternate explanations. These women may have had a real life trauma to use as a basis for comparing the magnitude of the rape trauma, and thereby more easily gained a healthy perspective on the role of the rape in their lives. In addition, they are likely to have developed coping skills in managing the earlier death that they could rely on postrape. They also knew that they had survived the previous trauma, which may have added to their confidence in their capacity to handle the rape. Burgess and Holmstrom[9] also reported that women who showed positive self-esteem recovered faster than did those with negative self-esteem. Women took longer to recover when they had experienced a prior victimization, when they had chronic economic stress, and when they lacked social support.[3]

Meyer and Taylor[5] have made an important contribution to this beginning effort to understand the relationship between a traumatic victimization, the coping behaviors that follow, and the recovery process. They explored women's coping approaches and whether particular coping styles are associated with particular "outcomes." Their subjects were 58 women, ages 16-42 (one subject was 76) who had been raped within the past two years (a median of 16 weeks had passed since the rape). They constructed a coping questionnaire based on Burgess and Holmstrom's[4] reports of qualitative data on coping efforts following sexual assault. Meyer and Taylor used factor analyses of their coping questionnaire to derive seven coping scales, which they labeled as follows: suppression, minimization, stress reduction, activity, precautionary behavior, withdrawal, and remaining home.

Meyer and Taylor also described four categories that classified 73% of the responses given to an open-ended question asking women what they had done to feel better since the rape. Women said they sought counseling (45% of respondents mentioned this), used precautionary behaviors (36%), talked to friends and family about the rape (27%), and/or made life changes such as moving or quitting work (18%). Meyer and Taylor, like Burgess and Holmstrom, found that certain coping approaches were associated with relatively better adjustment postrape. They used factor-analytically derived scales of depression, fear, and sexual dissatisfaction as their indicators of adjustment. Using precautionary safety measures was significantly correlated with less sexual dissatisfaction, and practicing specific stress reduction techniques was significantly associated with less depression and less fear. Women who remained home and those who withdrew from the world were more likely than those who did not to exhibit depression. Women who remained home also reported higher fear levels. Although Meyer and Taylor measured outcomes primarily in terms of symptomatology rather than using a broader view of recovery, they nonetheless have provided us with a basis for comparing our own theoretical constructs and empirical evidence.

We expected to find a variety of coping patterns across individuals, while still finding some strategies to be used by all (or most) rape victims. Given our understanding of coping efforts as being triggered by experienced stress, we expected that higher levels of stress indicators and negative symptomatology (e.g., fear, anxiety, depression) would be associated with more active coping. We expected that the passage of time would yield increased integration and acceptance of the rape, more firmly reestablished "cognitive illusions," and a feeling of increased recovery. Accordingly, we hypothesized that coping efforts would, in general, decrease as more time elapsed postrape, and as women were experiencing less distress. In addition, we anticipated finding that there would be some differences between the types of coping strategies used most often immediately postrape and those used as recovery progressed. Specifically, we expected to see more use of "negative" coping techniques—self-destructive behaviors, avoidance, or restrictive strategies—initially, and more use of "productive" techniques—for example, talking about it or cognitive reframing—as time elapsed.

Even as we were collecting data (i.e., conducting 80 lengthy interviews with rape victims), we were struck by our qualitative impressions that women did in fact exhibit their own distinctive coping styles across time, but still that most women—especially in the immediate postrape period—relied on similar coping tactics in response to the extreme stress of the rape. Before analyzing the quantitative data, we wrote down our sense of several "pure forms" of coping that some subset of our respondents seemed to exhibit. We interviewed "avoiders," who used sleep, distracting activities, forgetting, ignoring, and sometimes alcohol and drugs to "make the rape go away." We talked with "back to business" women, who used the very real role responsibilities they had as sole breadwinner or manager/executive to help pull themselves back together in a very short time period. We had "sturdy battlers," who were determined to face the rape and their feelings about it, and work their way *through* their feelings to achieve resolution and perspective. There were also some women whose basic style seemed to be "ingestion"—of food, cigarettes, alcohol, drugs, and rape center telephone reassurance—to allay (but not necessarily work through) the anxiety of their feelings. Finally, we saw some women whose lives were so generally chaotic that the rape was just one more, albeit severe, blow added to an already overflowing sea of troubles.

There were, of course, the majority of women who were not "pure types," and even the most single-minded of our respondents used a range of coping tactics to help them absorb the impact of the rape. The analysis reported here explores the patterns respondents reported to us on Likert-type scales. In the discussion we will return to our predata analysis impressions to see how well the quantitative data bear them out.

METHOD

The methodology of this study, and the questionnaire instrument from which the present data derive, have been described in more detail by Burt and Katz.[6] Very briefly, 113 adult rape victims participated in this study; 80 completed both questionnaires and interviews; 33 did only questionnaires. All data reported here come from the self-administered questionnaires completed by 113 women. Women were recruited from five rape crisis centers in the Washington-Baltimore area (69% of the sample) and newspaper announcements (31% of the sample). Data were collected between February and June, 1985. Sample characteristics are described by Burt and Katz.[6] Respondents took approximately 2 hours to complete the questionnaire instrument, which they received through the mail. If they were also to receive an interview, the questionnaire was completed before the interview took place.

The data reported in this paper come from an instrument titled "How I Deal with Things," which contained 33 items describing different behaviors often used when coping with a rape (or with other traumatic events). A factor analysis of the instrument, its psychometric properties, test-retest and internal consistency reliability, and validity correlates, are described in Burt and Katz.[6] We obtained a five-factor solution following equimax rotation, and labeled the factors as follows: 1. Avoidance; 2. Expressive; 3. Nervous/Anxious; 4. Cognitive; and 5. Self-Destructive. TABLE 1 gives the factor structure, showing the items on each factor that achieved a factor loading of .4 or higher.

For each item on the "How I Deal with Things" instrument, respondents answered on 7-point scales, where 1 = never, 2 = rarely, 3 = sometimes, 4 = half the time, 5 = often, 6 = usually, and 7 = always. They gave two sets of answers—one for how they dealt with the rape in the weeks and months immediately after it occurred, and a second set for how they deal with the rape now. For the average respondent, these two sets of answers referred to time periods separated by approximately 3.5 years.

The data reported in this paper are *unit-weighted scale scores* based on the five factors that emerged from the factor analysis. To create these scores, the items loading .4 or higher on the factors were selected to comprise the scales. Respondents' numerical answers to each item on the scale were summed (with reversals where appropriate) to create the scale scores. This procedure was applied twice—once for the responses pertaining to coping behaviors immediately following the rape ("then" scores), and once for coping behaviors currently in use ("now" scores). This procedure is the same as any subsequent researchers would follow in creating scale scores from our factor structure.

RESULTS

The factor structure of the instrument, "How I Deal with Things" proved quite interpretable. Factor analysis yielded five factors (avoidance, expressive, nervous/anxious, cognitive and self-destructive) that tapped many aspects of the coping patterns we had informally observed during interviews. We turn first to the pattern of coping over time, aggregating data over all respondents. Then we look at correlations among the coping scales at single time points and between "then" and "now." Finally, we explore several scale profiles of individuals we had identified as relatively "pure types" on the basis of interview material.

TABLE 2 gives the means and standard deviations for the five unit-weighted coping scales measuring coping "then," and for the five scales measuring coping "now." FIGURE 1 depicts these results in graphic form. *T*-tests of paired comparisons performed on the difference between means for each then-now pair of scales indicated that all differences are significant at $p < .0003$ or better (df = 112).

As FIGURE 1 shows, respondents report using all five coping tactics represented by the coping scales somewhere between "sometimes" and "often" during the period immediately following the rape. The most frequent behaviors reported were avoidance and cognitive coping tactics. With the exception of expressive behaviors, which alone *increased* with the passage of time, all other coping behaviors were significantly reduced from their immediate prerape levels by the time the respondents participated in the research. This pattern is very interesting, since it reinforces our belief that recovery involves gaining comfort with the fact of having been raped, and being able to gain distance and perspective on the assault. Being able to tolerate talking about the assault without its causing great distress or anxiety is one indicator of recovery. The results shown in FIGURE 1 support this conception of recovery.

TABLE 3 gives the zero-order correlations among scale scores on the five scales

TABLE 1. Factors Emerging for "Coping: How I Deal with Things"[a]

Factor 1: Avoidance

θ^* = .745; % variance explained = 11.0; test-retest = .830.

4. Sleeping a lot and trying not to think about what happened.
7. Avoiding people, places, or situations that remind you of the rape.
13. Trying to forget that the rape ever happened.
14. Trying to ignore all thoughts and feelings about the rape.
15. Blaming yourself for what happened, going over all the things you did wrong, holding yourself responsible for the assault, or chewing yourself out for having been "so dumb."
28. Getting more involved in your religion, changing religions, or becoming more religious.
32. Keeping busy and trying to distract yourself from being bothered by the rape experience.

Factor 2: Expressive

θ^* = .706; % variance explained = 9.6; test-retest = .676.

2. Taking concrete actions to make positive changes in your life.
8. Giving yourself permission to feel your feelings and considering *any* feelings to be "okay."
10. Directly showing your feelings when you are with others—actually crying, screaming, expressing confusion, etc.
11. Talking to family and friends about your feelings.
12. Doing things for yourself just because they make you feel good.
22. Examining your life activities, relationships, and priorities, and getting rid of things that aren't really important to you.
24. Telling yourself and/or others that you are determined not to let the rape ruin your life or make you a victim forever, and that you are not going to let the rape defeat you emotionally.

Factor 3: Nervous/Anxious

θ^* = .695; % variance explained = 9.2; test-retest = .720.

3. Changing your habitual ways of doing things, for example, things in your daily routine.
4. Sleeping a lot and trying not to think about what happened.
9. Crying, screaming, or giggling a lot when you are by yourself.
10. Directly showing your feelings when you are with others—actually crying, screaming, expressing confusion, etc.
16. Snapping at people for no apparent reason, generally feeling irritable, or feeling like you are about to explode.
25. Eating or smoking cigarettes a lot more than usual.
29. Talking to a therapist or counselor (including psychologists, psychiatrists, or social workers) about your experiences.
30. Taking prescription drugs (like Valium) to help yourself relax.
33. Staying inside your house or apartment, and going out as little as possible.

Factor 4: Cognitive

θ^* = .684; % variance explained = 9.0; test-retest = .779.

1. Trying to rethink the situation and to see it from a different perspective.
5. Finding out more information about sexual assault and other women's experiences.
6. Going over the rape situation again and again, trying to figure out why it happened and exactly what happened at each point.
7. Avoiding people, places, or situations that remind you of the rape.

TABLE 1. Continued

18. Trying intellectually to understand what happened to you and why you have felt the ways you have.
26. Going over all the things you did that were "good" and helped you get through the rape alive.
29. Talking to a therapist or counselor.

Factor 5: Self-Destructive

θ^* = .650; % variance explained = 8.2; test-retest = .740.

8. Giving yourself permission to feel your feelings and considering *any* feelings to be "okay". (−)[b]
15. Blaming yourself for what happened, going over all the things you did wrong, holding yourself responsible for the assault, or chewing yourself out for having been "so dumb."
16. Snapping at people for no apparent reason, generally feeling irritable, or feeling like you are about to explode.
20. Drinking a lot of alcohol or taking other drugs more than usual.
21. Getting yourself into dangerous or risky situations more than you usually would.
25. Eating or smoking cigarettes a lot more than usual.
27. Thinking about killing yourself.

[a] n = 113; first unrotated factor: θ = .892; variance explained = 22.4%; test-retest = .735.
[b] Item loads negatively.

for coping then and the five scales for coping now. A correlation of ± .185 is significant at $p < .05$, two-tailed. Looking first at the correlations within a single time period ("then" in the upper left quadrant or "now" in the lower right quadrant), we can see that the strongest associations occur among scales 1, 3, and 5 (avoidance, nervous/anxious, and self-destructive). Scale 2 (expressive) is the scale least highly intercorrelated with the others; it is most strongly associated with scale 4 (Cognitive), and it correlates *negatively* with scale 5 (self-destructive), significantly for the period immediately following the rape and nonsignificantly for the present time. However,

TABLE 2. Means and Standard Deviations for Coping Scale Scores (n = 113)

Factor	Number of Items	Mean	Standard Deviation
"Then"			
1	7	28.05	10.14
2	7	26.45	8.41
3	9	31.22	10.97
4	7	28.75	9.91
5	7	22.94	8.81
"Now"			
1	7	19.95	9.64
2	7	29.89	8.31
3	9	23.32	9.68
4	7	23.34	8.97
5	7	16.16	6.86

scale 4 (cognitive) correlates at least as strongly with scale 3 (nervous/anxious) as it does with scale 2 (expressive) both "then" and "now," indicating that cognitive coping mechanisms can be used in conjunction with more than one other coping pattern.

Turning now to the issue of continuity of coping styles across time in the upper right quadrant of Table 3, the data suggest both continuity and diversity. For all

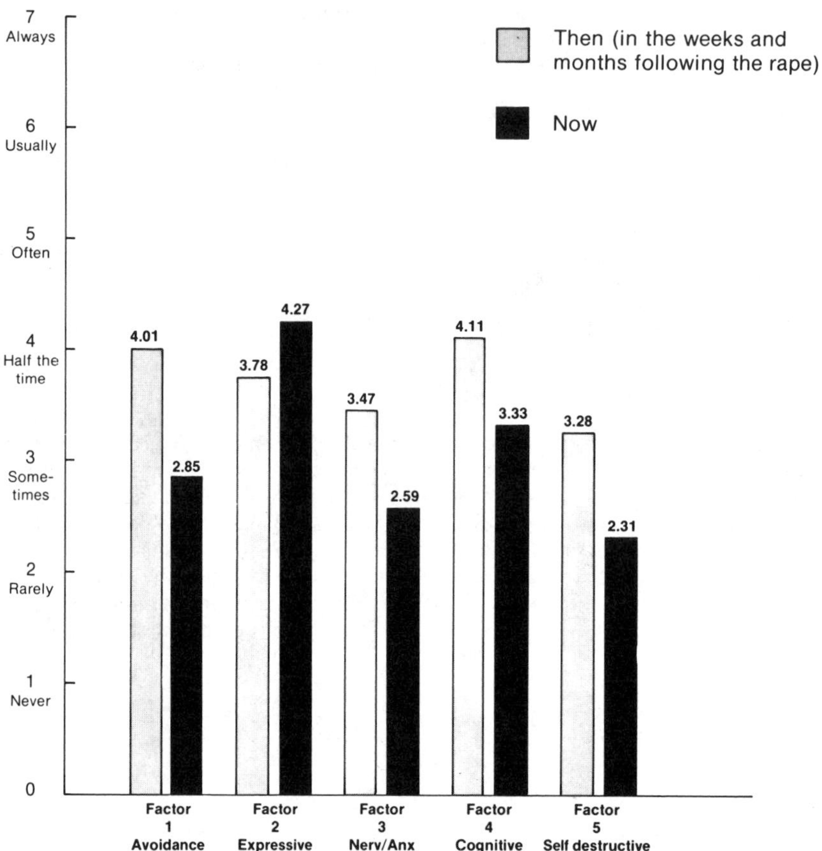

FIGURE 1. Comparison of scores on 5 coping factors, then and now ($n = 113$). The means have been divided by the number of items on the scale to yield the average item response, which is readily interpretable according to the verbal anchors associated with the scale's 7 points. All then and now comparisons of means for the same factor are significant at $p < .0003$ or better.

scales but scale 4, correlations are highest between the same scale score "then" and "now" (rather than between a score on one scale "then" and a score on a different scale "now"). Scale 4 "then" correlates about equally with scales 2 and 4 "now." Scale 2 is again the most distinctive, correlating significantly only with itself in the "then-now" figures. This suggests perhaps that expressive behavior is a less common

TABLE 3. Zero-Order Correlations among Coping Scale Scores ($n = 113$)

	"Then"					"Now"				
	1	2	3	4	5	1	2	3	4	5
"Then"										
1	—	−.065	.449	.212	.596	.551	.256	.319	.361	.348
2	—	—	.289	.504	−.286	.082	.224	.006	−.039	.002
3	—	—	—	.566	.521	.371	.388	.406	.255	.310
4	—	—	—	—	.050	.109	.215	.056	.188	−.005
5	—	—	—	—	—	.333	.187	.338	.212	.465
"Now"										
1	—	—	—	—	—	—	.392	.552	.493	.441
2	—	—	—	—	—	—	—	.434	.481	−.099
3	—	—	—	—	—	—	—	—	.590	.579
4	—	—	—	—	—	—	—	—	—	.259
5	—	—	—	—	—	—	—	—	—	—

NOTE: A correlation of ± .185 is significant at $p < .05$, two-tailed.

style and one which maintains its integrity more over time, whereas the behaviors represented by the other scales (especially 1, 3, and 5) may be more interchangeable and overlapping.

It is also possible that women who use expressive coping strategies initially keep using them, and do not rely as much on the addition of other strategies. We believe, from our counseling experience with rape victims, that the ability to express feelings about the rape is *necessary* for most women if they are to achieve fully-integrated recovery. We also know (from TABLE 2 and FIGURE 1) that expressive coping tactics are the only ones to increase over time, a pattern we take as indicative of coming to grips with the rape experience. We would tentatively interpret the patterns of coping strategies revealed by our data as suggesting that expressive behaviors are perhaps a more constructive route to recovery than avoidance or some of the other coping tactics we measured. One final note in this vein: women exhibiting more mature levels of ego development, as measured by Loevinger's[13] ego development scale, showed significantly lower current use of avoidance ($r = -.234$), nervous/anxious ($r = -.255$), and self-destructive behaviors ($r = -.234$) ($n = 102$, $p < .05$).

Additional evidence regarding the productive, or positive, attributes of an expressive coping style comes from research on the relationship between coping and somatic illness. Pennebaker and his colleagues[14,15] have suggested that people who express their feelings about a traumatic event are less likely to develop later health problems than are those who do not. They studied individuals who had lost a spouse due to sudden, unexpected death, and found a significant negative correlation between the rate of health complaints and both the amount of rumination and the extent of discussion about the death.[14] In addition, a negative correlation existed between the extent to which subjects discussed their spouses' death and the amount they ruminated about the loss. Despite the small sample size and the authors' reservations about drawing firm conclusions, this evidence suggested that the more people confided in others, the better they adjusted to their sudden traumatic loss (assuming good health as an indicator of adjustment).

This suggestion was strengthened by a second study, in which college student subjects wrote essays describing either a personally traumatic event or a trivial topic; students who wrote about the traumatic event were told to focus either on their feelings about the event, the objective facts of the incident, or a combination of the two. Pennebaker and Beall[15] found that writing about earlier traumatic experiences was associated with short-term increases in physiological arousal and long-term decreases in health problems. Specifically, the expression of *emotions* about the trauma seemed to be the key; subjects who wrote only about objective facts were no different as a group from those who were assigned trivial topics.

Pennebaker and his colleagues' work suggests that cognitive strategies that do not address and work through the emotional aspects of a trauma's impact do not have the long-term benefits that the processing of emotions appears to have. The authors believe that the emergence of health problems when a trauma is not discussed with others is related to the active behavioral inhibition that becomes necessary in order to hide the emotional impact of the event from others.

Previous analysis of our data set revealed that all coping behaviors (including expressive ones) are elevated when respondents report high negative symptomatology, such as fear, anxiety, depression, and intrusive thoughts,[6] and are thus farther from recovery. In addition, Katz and Burt[16] have shown that four of the five coping scales measuring current coping behaviors show significant positive relationships with current levels of generalized guilt and self-blame. This association is strongest for self-destructive behaviors ($n = 113$, $r = .342$, $p < .0003$) and next strongest for avoidance behaviors ($n = 113$, $r = .234$, $p < .02$). Expressive strategies are the only coping behaviors *un*associated with current generalized guilt and self-blame (as measured by a factor score from a self-perception instrument).

In addition, previously unreported data for a self-blame measure specific to the rape itself[a] shows very strong relationships among self-blame for the rape immediately after it happened and coping strategies in the weeks and months immediately following the rape. The percent of blame for the rape attributed to self correlated positively with avoidance (.472), nervous/anxious (.294), and self-destructive (.497). Further, self-blame correlated *negatively* with expressive coping behaviors in the immediate postrape period (−.203) ($n = 85$, $p < .05$ for all).

Our data also reveal that 45% of the women moved (changed residence) within the first year following the assault. It is difficult to interpret this finding in the context of the high mobility of young women in today's society, but it is worth noting that other researchers have reported a similar postrape phenomenon. Both Burgess and Holmstrom[4] and Meyer and Taylor[5] cite this as a common coping strategy, one that is often associated with better postrape adjustment. It seems probable, however, that moving is not in itself curative, but that its significance depends upon what other coping tactics accompany it. Moving might, for example, represent avoidance of the rape and of confronting the feelings that it evokes. On the other hand, moving could be a realistic and pragmatic means for reducing fear or reestablishing a sense of self-direction, thereby facilitating the woman's ability to mobilize other coping strategies in dealing with the rape.

Individual Profiles

We were interested in whether the women we had identified on the basis of their interviews as relatively "pure types" in their coping styles would reveal different profiles on the coping scales, as they should if the scales measure what we were observing qualitatively. FIGURE 2, showing a somewhat more clinical use for these data, gives eight individual profiles of women who seemed quite distinct. We initially identified the persons profiled in FIGURE 2 as "back to business" women, "chaotic life" women, "sturdy battlers," and an "ingester."

These profiles *are* quite different. The "sturdy battlers" (graphs E, F, and G) all used more expressive tactics initially than the other 5 women, and tended to maintain or increase their expressiveness regarding the rape. They also made high use of cognitive tactics, especially at first. They tended to be relatively low on self-destructive behaviors, although two of the three used the less extreme forms of avoidance early in their recovery process.

The "back to business" respondents (graphs A and B) showed generally low levels of symptomatology overall, although graph B shows substantial early use of avoidance and cognitive strategies. Both were low in expressive behaviors. Interestingly, they reported quite different times to recovery. The person in graph A said it took her 24 months to recover, but she reported little active *effort* associated with this passage of time. The woman in graph B reported a recovery time of one month, but also indicated substantial levels of avoidance and of cognitive work during that period. Neither showed much coping behavior of any variety at present, reflecting their conviction that they have nothing left to cope with.

[a] "Take 100% of the blame for the rape, and distribute it among the rapist, society, yourself, and "other," for how you feel at present, and for how you felt immediately after the rape."

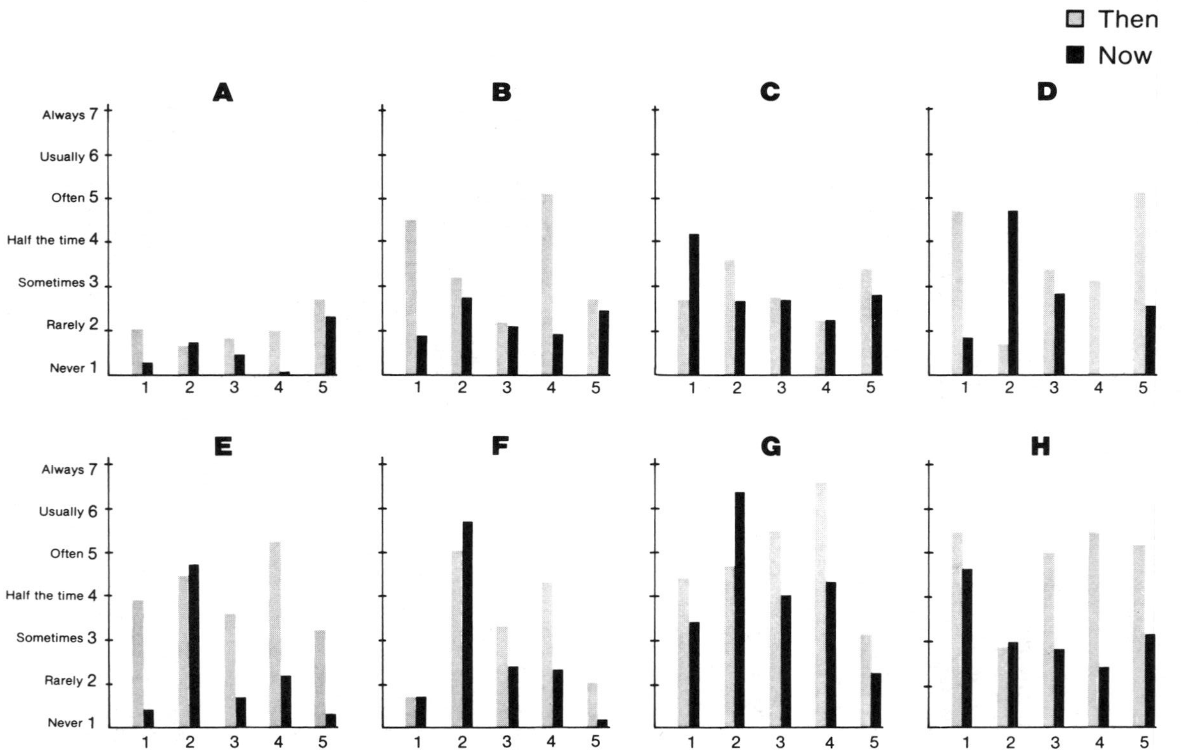

FIGURE 2. Selected individual profiles using coping scales. Factors (*numbers along horizontal axes*) are as follows: 1 = Avoidance; 2 = Expressive; 3 = Nervous/Anxious; 4 = Cognitive; 5 = Self-Destructive. Individuals profiled were initially identified as follows: graphs **A** and **B** = "back to business" women; **C** and **D** = "chaotic life" women; **E, F,** and **G** = "sturdy battlers"; **H** = "ingester."

Among those women whose lives appeared to us chaotic with or without the rape (graphs C and D), one (graph C) showed relatively low use of all coping tactics, and very little change between the time immediately postrape (18 months before the interview) and the time of the interview. She also reported a 1-month recovery time. The women in graph D appeared to be among the most changeable of our respondents, reporting very different behaviors at different times. We later learned that she had a psychiatric diagnosis for which such behavioral flip-flops were the norm.

The final graph (H) in FIGURE 2 displays the coping behaviors reported by an "ingester." As expected, avoidance, nervous/anxious, and self-destructive behaviors were very high after the rape, and expressive behaviors were low and remained so. She did initially also use cognitive tactics, but never felt that the explanations she believed with her head made any difference in how she felt, so she dropped them. She made over 80 rape hotline calls over the course of a year, and drank a lot of alcohol.

DISCUSSION

We have shown that a new measure of strategies for coping with a rape experience produces scales with reasonable internal consistency, high interpretability, and construct validity. These scales represent specific coping tactics that include both the emotion-focused and problem-focused domains posited by Lazarus and Folkman.[7] Our empirically-derived scales are somewhat different from the coping classifications derived by Burgess and Holmstrom[3,4] and the scales derived by Meyer and Taylor.[5] Our scales broadly characterize different types of coping approaches; used together they can, as we have demonstrated, describe the distinctive coping patterns seen in individual victims. Consistent with previous research are our findings that active coping behavior is associated with higher symptom levels. One difference that would be worth exploring in future research is that Meyer and Taylor[5] did not find activity, suppression, or minimization strategies to be associated with higher symptomatology, but we did find such a relationship with all our scales, including both avoidance and cognitive.

Our interpretation of the coping scales we have derived and the roles in recovery of particular coping patterns gains support from the work of Pennebaker and his colleagues.[14,15] In particular, their work affirms the importance of coping techniques that involve expression, both by themselves and in conjunction with cognitive and other strategies. Their work is also consistent with our view that the recovery process involves the integration of affective and cognitive elements of rape impact. Continued research on the specific coping strategies of rape victims and their relationship to postrape adjustment will help to elucidate the exact mechanisms with which the work of recovery is accomplished. One particular facet of recovery that we should understand better is the means by which basic cognitive assumptions about the world are reestablished,[10] as well as the relationship between this cognitive aspect and other recovery tasks.

We hope that in future applications the scales will have some predictive and clinical utility, as we believe they do now. Whether the aim is to assess the general level and types of coping within a group of rape victims, or to develop an individual profile of coping tactics, these new measures should be useful. Future research with these scales and their wider use should also help to elaborate the interrelationship of coping patterns and other recovery indicators. Such information will be extremely valuable in counseling rape victims, as it will make it possible to encourage women to utilize those techniques that are known to yield better adjustment.

REFERENCES

1. BURT, M. R. & B. L. KATZ. 1985. Rape, robbery and burglary: Responses to actual and feared criminal victimization, with special focus on women and the elderly. Victimol. **10**(1-4): 325-358.
2. ELLIS, E. M. 1983. A review of empirical rape research: Victim reactions and response to treatment. Clin. Psychol. Rev. **3**(4): 473-490.
3. BURGESS, A. W. & L. L. HOLMSTROM. 1978. Recovery from rape and prior life stress. Res. Health Nurs. **1**(4): 165-174.
4. BURGESS, A. W. & L. L. HOLMSTROM. 1979. Rape: Crisis and Recovery. Brady Publishing. Bowie, MD.
5. MEYER, C. & S. E. TAYLOR. 1986. Adjustment to rape. J. Pers. Soc. Psychol. **50**(6): 1226-1234.
6. BURT, M. R. & B. L. KATZ. 1987. Dimensions of recovery from rape: Focus on growth outcomes. J. Interpers. Violence. **2**(1): 82-90.
7. LAZARUS, R. S. & S. FOLKMAN. 1984. Stress, Appraisal, and Coping. Springer. New York, NY.
8. HOROWITZ, M. 1976. Stress Response Syndromes. Jason Aronson, Inc. New York, NY.
9. JANOFF-BULMAN, R. 1985. The aftermath of victimization: Rebuilding shattered assumptions. *In* Trauma and Its Wake. Charles Figley, Ed. Brunner/Mazel. New York, NY.
10. JANOFF-BULMAN, R. & I. H. FRIEZE. 1983. A theoretical perspective for understanding reactions to victimization. J. Soc. Issues **39**(2): 195-221.
11. SILVER, R. L. & C. B. WORTMAN. 1980. Coping with undesirable life events. *In* Human Helplessness. J. Garber and M. E. P. Seligman, Eds. Academic Press. New York, NY.
12. TAYLOR, S. 1983. Adjustments to threatening events: A theory of cognitive adaptation. Am. Psychol. **38**(11): 1161-1173.
13. LOEVINGER, J. 1970. Measuring Ego Development. Jossey-Bass. San Francisco, CA.
14. PENNEBAKER, J. W. & R. C. O'HEERON. 1984. Confiding in others and illness rate among spouses of suicide and accidental-death victims. J. Abnorm. Psychol. **93**(4): 473-476.
15. PENNEBAKER, J. W. & S. K. BEALL. 1986. Confronting a traumatic event: Toward an understanding of inhibition and disease. J. Abnorm. Psychol. **95**(3): 274-281.
16. KATZ, B. L. & M. R. BURT. 1988. Self-blame in recovery from rape: Help or hindrance? *In* Rape and Sexual Assault, Vol., 2. Ann. W. Burgess, Ed. Garland Press. New York, NY.

Introduction: Social Policy

ELI H. NEWBERGER

Family Development Study
Children's Hospital
Boston, Massachusetts 02115

and

Department of Pediatrics
Harvard Medical School
Boston, Massachusetts 02115

Notwithstanding the documentation of human sexual aggression for as long as we have had a history of mankind, the subject has been cloaked in mystery and shrouded by the veils over sexuality until recent times. Periodically, human sexual aggression has been rediscovered. Limiting our capacity to perceive this problem has been a set of values and assumptions about families and family life. These include notions of women, men, and their relation to children—notions that embrace religious and cultural stereotypes.

In late 19th-century Vienna, for example, as the historian Larry Wolfe points out in his forthcoming book *Postcards from the End of the World* (Atheneum, 1988), the newspapers read by the intelligentsia were full of cases involving rape, sexual victimization, and child abuse. Yet, curiously, when Freud presented his "seduction theory" to his medical colleagues, he was ridiculed. Freud reformulated his theory, and reports of physical and sexual victimization in childhood came to be understood as artifacts of fantasy. This reformulation was in keeping with a Victorian ideal of family life that denied the possibility of physical and sexual aggression between and among its members.

It was a combination of political forces, a women's movement, and a victims' rights movement that peeled open the eyes of professionals to sexual aggression as a prevalent problem. Impressive, too, is the extent to which its reality continues to be denied.

The papers in this session treat forthrightly the main issues in society's acknowledgment and approach to human sexual aggression. They leave the reader with a sense of admiration for the courageous individuals who brought the problem to credible visibility. As Lenore Walker puts it, "victims whose individual voices were disbelieved or ignored became loud enough to be heard when they joined together." Walker directly addresses key issues for women and for children: rights and clinical realities. She leaves no question as to where she stands on the value of legal interventions for the victim. There is a therapeutic benefit in advocacy, she notes, and claims can be made against professionals as well as offenders.

Frederick Green points to the fantasy of the ideal American family that appeared to bear on the veto by President Richard Nixon of the 1973 Child Development Act, and he connects it with the currently prevailing notion that families should first be protected from intrusions by agents of the state. He calls for a focus on children and a rethinking of the relationship between the home as a private place and the interests of the larger community.

Sexual assault legislation has been the subject of substantial efforts at reform, and these efforts are the subject of the paper by Jeanne Marsh. She notes that notwithstanding the saliency of these issues, rigorous policy research has been lacking. It is the legal framework that defines "those wise restraints which keep men free," to paraphrase the encomium with which the Harvard president confers degrees to new graduates of its law school. Marsh notes that the law has been one of the most important devices to effect social change in the field of sexual aggression. An initiative in one area—rape, for example—may lead to a useful set of initiatives in other areas—for example, domestic violence and sexual abuse of children.

Two Canadian contributors note the significance of law reform in coming to terms with the meaning of sexual offenses. Duncan Chappell notes that the 1977 reformulation of rape as a crime of violence was a major theoretical breakthrough that led to important reform. This took place, however, only after five years of discussion. Chappell points to the paucity of data available on the national level in Canada as a major deterrent to effective action. He reviews the survey data, which suggest a high prevalence of victimization among males and females, as was also found by surveys conducted in the United States. The lively interplay between feminist thought and patriarchal institutional and political tradition is emphasized in this interesting discussion.

Certainly the most provocative paper in this series is that offered by Cyril Greenland. He presents his view of the "sordid history" of efforts by politicians and professionals to control sexuality for religious and political purposes. He raises directly the ethical questions associated with consent for intrusive treatments of prisoners, focusing especially on the routine use of phallometry. He notes the opprobrium that attaches to the private parts of our body, counterposing the ideals of behavior to the stigma in the notion that "sexuality exists in the penis." These papers should inspire thought and inform serious action on behalf of both sex offenders and victims.

The Impact of Forensic Issues on Women's Rights

LENORE E. A. WALKER

Walker & Associates
Denver, Colorado 80209

INTRODUCTION

The changes in sexual assault laws, procedures for processing cases, as well as social norms have increased the number of victims who are involved in some form of litigation, including being a witness in a criminal prosecution of a sex offender or in an administrative hearing against a licensed professional, a plaintiff in a civil tort action, and a party in a divorce or juvenile court action. For many sexual assault victims, most of whom are women, this is their first encounter with the legal system. Although this increased involvement in litigation has had a positive impact on women's rights in general, individual women have reported feeling as though they were being victimized a second time.[1,2,3] This paper will review the history of rape litigation, the gains made in women's legal and social rights, and current forensic issues as they impact on individual victims and on women's rights in general.

BRIEF HISTORY OF SEXUAL ASSAULT PROSECUTION OF ADULT VICTIMS

The crime of rape, historically believed to have a sexual imperative, often seemed to place the burden of proof on the victim to demonstrate that she did not deserve to be assaulted. Any deviation in her life style from the strict expectations of the "proper" daughter, wife, or mother role, such as walking alone downtown late at night, wearing seductive clothing, prior sexual activity or fantasies, or angry feelings demonstrated about a former lover were seen as somehow provoking the attacker. These themes have been passed down for as long as we have records. Brownmiller[2] suggests that the fear of being raped by many men pushed otherwise reluctant women into monogamous marriages: monogamous, that is, on the woman's part. Adulterous women and prostitutes were seen as causing their own victimization; they, like wives, were considered "rape-proof."[4]

Two changes were necessary before these archaic concepts could be overturned. First was the change in viewing rape as a crime of violence, not passion. Second was the change in viewing women as independent, not extensions of their fathers', husbands', or sons' property. Both of these changes occurred in the 1960s, resulting in new criminal laws that revised prosecution procedures.

The woman's movement of the late 1960s and early 1970s took on rape as a major issue in its overall campaign to eradicate men's violent behavior against women. Recognition of the similarity of victims' experiences became apparent as hospital emergency and treatment programs, rape crisis centers, and trauma counselors began reporting these experiences.[5] Victims whose individual voices were disbelieved or ignored became loud enough to be heard when they joined together. The legal admonition about the credibility of a woman's claim of rape was questioned and then changed. The victim's sexual history was excluded from trial evidence, unless a showing was made of its relevance. This is often referred to as the rape shield law. Corroboration of the victim's truthfulness by another witness (who was rarely available, given the private nature of the crime), polygraph examination and intense cross-examination by the police, or evidence of having defended herself became unnecessary.

Broad-based public education informed victims of these changes. The new victim/witness support and advocacy programs established within prosecutors' offices persuaded more women victims who reported crimes to become witnesses if arrests were made.[6]

Simultaneous with the growth of services to rape victims came the legislative reform believed necessary to meet the burdens of proof in cases that go to trial. The single act of forcible rape became changed to several different acts of sexual assault, based on the intent of the perpetrator and the seriousness of the act. Any coercive act toward sexual parts of the body, not just penetration, became labeled a violent crime. Although this change was seen as important to increasing convictions, especially since it also allows for adjustment of penalties corresponding to the degree of sexual assault, neither the victim's psychological injuries nor her perception of dangerousness are adequately handled.

In spite of good intentions, the law still perpetuates many of the old difficulties, with some victims being stigmatized, and others being considered better victims for the purpose of criminal prosecution. There is still difficulty in introducing expert-witness testimony to bolster the victim's credibility, a problem to be discussed later. So even though there have been major changes in attitudes toward sexual assault, in women victims' credibility, and in the legal arena, more change is needed.

WOMEN'S LEGAL RIGHTS

The changes discussed previously indicate how intricately woven together the legal and social changes in attitudes toward women have been. For example, the economic and political rights of women helped assert women's independent status. Owning their own property meant that women could seek redress for any injuries inflicted upon them, rather than depending upon the men in their lives. In the criminal justice system, the victim is only a witness in a crime against the state. This concept is hard for many victims to understand. Since they were the ones hurt, they believe it is their case! The new victim impact statements now required when the rapist is sentenced have helped victims feel more a part of the system.[7] Prosecution and incarceration of the rapist are outcomes most victims would prefer. Statistics at Washington's Center for Women Policy Studies suggest that fewer than one in ten rapes are reported, about 10% of those go to trial, and only 16% of those win a conviction.

Even with the reforms in rape prosecution, women are discouraged by long delays in trial, little control over the process, and not being allowed their own choice of attorney to represent their rights. Prosecution is even less of a deterrence to sex offenders in those states where they are given minimal sentences. For example, in Colorado it is not uncommon for sex offenders to spend an average of 2 ½ years in prison. This may be less time than it takes for the victim to heal psychologically.

WOMEN'S SELF-DEFENSE AND SEXUAL ASSAULT

One of the changes that has come along with the changing norms is the acceptance of women who use violence to fight back. The two cases upon which newer modifications in self-defense laws have been based both involved women who were prosecuted for defending themselves. In *People v. Garcia,* the famous California case in which Inez Garcia got a gun, went out to look for, shot, and killed one of the men who had raped her earlier, she was acquitted on the grounds of self-defense. So too, in the case of Joan Little, who took the ice pick that the warden of the prison in which she was serving time (for an unrelated crime) was using to try to coerce her into performing oral sex on him, and stabbed him. She, too, was found not guilty because of self-defense.[11] Other cases of justifiable homicide for self-defense have occurred with battered women who kill their abusers, usually before the violence escalates or in the middle of a beating. Many of the women were sexually as well as physically abused by their abusive partners. This is a new area of law in which expert witnesses have played an important role in explaining women's behavior to judges and juries. It expands the stereotyped image of a victim to include being an aggressor in order to protect her life. Not all cases are won easily. Women who do not display "good" victim characteristics, engage in sexual or other acting-out behaviors, or display outbursts of anger at times are more likely to be convicted. In a Colorado case, the judge agreed to admit rape trauma syndrome testimony by an expert witness on behalf of a defendant who had killed the man who had just sexually assaulted her; but the judge ruled that the expert witness could then be questioned about the defendant's sexual history, which otherwise would be considered irrelevant! No expert testimony was offered, and the woman was convicted of manslaughter and sentenced to five years in prison!

CIVIL ACTIONS

The civil courts have been an arena in which women have had more control and legal rights. They are the plaintiffs who bring the action, whether it is against the perpetrator directly or against a third party for failing to provide a safe environment for women. Lawsuits against perpetrators often win empty judgments, especially if the rapist is serving time in jail. But such judgments assure the woman that should the rapist ever achieve economic stability, she will have first claim on his property. To some women, the vindication that occurs is often more important than the money won. Such women make a stand that supports all women's claims that they are independent and valued members of society who are entitled to compensation should a man decide to harm them by sexual assault made possible by others' negligence or willful disregard of caution. The showing of harm that must be made is detailed below.

Some feminist scholars believe that economic deprivation may be even more of a deterrent to rape than the threat of criminal prosecution.[8,9] Obviously, if the man does have property, which is commonly the case with acquaintance, date, and marital rapes, economic loss could be devastating to him. The threat of such loss may, indeed, persuade men to recognize the need for them to stop should a woman say no to their sexual advances. It is interesting to note the difference in women's and men's perceptions of consent to sexual intercourse. Typically the man translates the woman's weak *no* to mean *yes,* unless she puts up a big struggle. Women, however, fear that a big struggle might make the man more angry and use up the energy they need to stay alive. Changes in criminal rape statutes had to occur before civil laws could recognize the different levels of forcible rape as well.

On a larger, community level third-party civil actions have held those providing services to women liable for failure to protect them when there was foreseeable harm. Lawsuits against landlords, motel owners, shopping malls, parking lots, and government properties all are based on some kind of liability and often assert theories such as negligence, breach of contract, warranties of habitability, and housing ordinances. Even product liability can be asserted as a contributing factor. The sexual assault of singer Connie Francis that was made possible by a defective sliding glass door lock in a New York City Howard Johnson's motel helped bring this type of lawsuit to public awareness when she won a $2,550,000 jury award for her damages.[10] It has not been uncommon for insurance companies to settle for policy-limit awards (often as much as $500,000) rather than taking the chance of a higher jury award.[11]

Juries simply reflect the community norm. Civil cases can be resolved with a lower standard of proof than the "beyond a reasonable doubt" standard in criminal courts. For some women such trials are an important part of their healing process.

Other actions, also, have indicated that social norms are swinging over to support the victim's right to be safe in her community. Sexual crimes committed in places of employment have caused employers to be sued for negligent hiring and supervision as well as opportunity to commit crime.[12,13] Lawsuits claiming a violation of civil rights have been won against police for negligence in responding to reports of crime and for failure properly to protect a victim when they leave the crime scene without making an arrest.[14] While opponents to this new legislation claim unforeseeability and cite psychological studies on prediction of violence[15] to support their position, many assaults on victims known to their assailants were, indeed, predictable.[16]

Another area of litigation that has recently gained popularity is civil tort actions against family members. Battered women have filed civil tort actions against their abusive mates for both physical and sexual assault. The removal of interspousal tort immunity, which was originally instituted to protect family tranquility, has permitted these actions in civil cases; while the elimination of the marital rape exemption in criminal law allows both criminal and civil filings. In some jurisdictions, filing divorce and personal injury cases simultaneously is used as a strategy to gain a more equitable financial settlement from the person who caused the violence. It is interesting that legislators once saw the need to protect families by including spousal immunity when, in fact, families were often destroyed anyhow, by the man's abusive behavior. The combined voices of battered women and child abuse and rape victim advocates have changed this imperative. Today, the woman's legal right to be safe in her own home supercedes the man's right to rule his family behind closed doors. Family privacy no longer can come at the expense of individual rights.

CONFLICTS WITH CHILDREN'S RIGHTS

The state has taken the right to protect the child in lieu of the parent when the parent is unable to do so. The Uniform Children's Code, which the majority of the states have adopted, sets forth the means to protect the child who is in danger of harm. While this code for the most part does allow for the protection of children, its reunification-of-the-family clause in the preamble has been used by most juvenile courts to justify returning unrestricted visitation and custody to the abusive parent without regard for the potential of further abuse. This most often occurs with children who have been victims of incest. Women have been the primary parent for most children, and they have the greater opportunity to either protect or harm the child. Unfortunately, when the child protection system intervenes on behalf of a child, it frequently becomes antagonistic to the mother, putting her at odds rather than regarding her as an ally to help the child.

Mothers who themselves have been victims of rape or battery may be accused of not adequately protecting their child, should physical or sexual abuse be disclosed; or, if no overt physical or sexual abuse can be proved, they may be considered vengeful when they try to protect the children from being alone with their father.[17] Women frequently find themselves as codefendants in dependency and neglect petitions, even when they did not know child sexual abuse had occurred. The newer research on pedophiles and incestuous fathers supports women's and children's insistence that it is the incest perpetrator who is obsessed with sex, has few internal controls, may demonstrate deviant arousal patterns with children, and invests a great deal of energy in maintaining secrecy.[18,19]

Women are more likely to lose custody of their children when child abuse reports are made but cannot be proved.[20] In divorce actions, women in danger of being beaten by husbands are frequently forced to coparent and live in the same neighborhood as the husband, under the misguided notion that it is in the best interests of the child to have equal access to both parents, even if there is a high likelihood that the father will harm either mother or child.[17] The probability that this action places children at greater risk to exhibit violent behavior and become physically, sexually, or psychologically abusive themselves has been found to be 700 times greater for males.[21] These legal developments represent a loss of rights to women and perhaps even to children.

CLAIMS AGAINST PROFESSIONALS

As sexual abuse became more clearly defined and women's credibility in making claims became enhanced, sexual exploitation by professionals in a position of trust came to light. As in other areas of sexual assault, the relationship between offender and victim, rather than physical aggression, is used to force compliance. Although this occurs in all professions, documentation is available only for pediatricians,[22] psychiatrists,[23] and psychologists.[24] Student-faculty sexual exploitation has also been documented.[25]

Legal cases against professionals can be filed in criminal, civil, and administrative courts of law. The criminal and civil actions are similar to those already reported. The administrative hearing to delicense the professional is a way of protecting the public. Usually the attorney general of the state prosecutes this type of case, with a hearing officer acting as judge and the licensing board acting as jury. Rape shield laws, which keep irrelevant evidence of the victim's history from being admitted, do not apply in these cases. In fact, few of the rules of evidence in other proceedings apply. For those victims who have gone through the criminal trial, the administrative hearing, which usually follows after all the professionals' appeals and legal remedies have been exhausted, can become a redramatization of the whole event, this time with no legal representation and no legal protection.

INSURANCE INDUSTRY RESPONSE

The insurance industry, which operates as a for-profit business, has attempted to curb its liabilities in courts of law. Juries have made it clear by the size of their awards that insurance companies must assume liability. If they choose to insure businesses, homes, and professionals, then they must accept the responsibility of a lifestyle of androcentric design that places women and children at risk of harm.

The creativity of attorneys who look for "deep pockets" to sue when women and children have been sexually abused has been interesting. Homeowners' insurance has been used when a case for negligence can be asserted. Baby-sitters who unknowingly expose a child to a teen-age sex offender could be considered negligent. If they knew about his aggressive tendencies, it would more likely be considered an intentional tort for not taking protective action. A mother who tells the minister that her husband is sexually abusing their child may be considered negligent if she follows the religious leader's advice to pray for forgiveness and go on with their family life rather than look further for help. A woman soliciting door to door can sue a man who invites her in allegedly to make a donation and then sexually assaults her. In all three cases, homeowners' insurance has been found liable for the harm committed on the property they insure. A mental health professional who is court-ordered to supervise a father's visitation of his children may be considered negligent if he didn't realize the man's potential dangerousness, but guilty of malpractice if he intentionally left them alone and the child was reassaulted. Even with these actual case examples, it is not always clear who has what financial liability or how that decision is made.

Civil lawsuits rarely go to trial; malpractice insurance companies frequently settle out of court. However, more insurance companies are excluding sexual conduct with clients from coverage or placing limits, such as the $25,000 in the American Psychological Association policy. Women's rights are being compromised by these cutbacks.

It is certainly more therapeutic for a sexual assault victim to believe that the attack was someone else's liability, and not her fault. The large judgments need to be understood on a public policy level. Even though insurance companies—most of which have shouldered the responsibility of a society not designed for the convenience or safety of its female members—complained, lobbied, and won legislative limits to their financial liability, civil lawsuits have not abated. It is now more difficult for a victim to find an attorney to represent her. Even smaller awards will make the point that women now have legitimate roles in all areas of society. And, as long as men sexually assault women and children, society must take moral, financial, and social responsibility for not trying to stop it this behavior, either in its designs for living and public places, in its child raising, which does not prevent the transmission of violence, or at the time a crime is committed, by giving compensation to the victim.

CLINICAL FORENSIC ISSUES

Psychological Impact of Sexual Abuse on Victims

The psychological literature on the negative impact of sexual assault on a victim has expanded during the past decade. Burgess and Holmstrom's[26] classic article on rape trauma syndrome provided the framework against which other empirical studies have documented harm. For example, Kirkpatrick, Veronen, and Resick[27] have measured fears, anxiety, depression, and healing times of rape victims; Burt and Katz[28] have measured perceptions of rape myths, recovery and coping skills of victims; and Conte and Berliner[29] have measured the impact of children's sexual abuse. Finkelhor and Browne[30] provide a good review of the literature on child sexual abuse trauma. Russell[31] documents the incidence and prevalence rate of child sexual abuse, as well as traumatic effects still reported by women who had been sexually abused as children.[32] This literature is used by forensic expert witnesses who testify in criminal, civil, or other legal cases. It can help guide other experts in estimating prognosis and the cost of damage, which can be estimated using special tables prepared for personal injury cases.

At Walker & Associates, we have assembled a rape notebook with over 50 adult sexual assault articles and a child sexual abuse notebook with a similar group. These notebooks are made available to attorneys with whom we consult. They help provide educational information so the attorney can adequately prepare the case. They also have the side effect of helping the attorney believe the victim; that her experiences are similar to others' gives her credibility and legitimacy in the attorney's viewpoint. This impacts positively on the attorney's treatment of the client, who then begins to have greater trust and provides more relevant information. In child sexual abuse cases, we encourage attorneys to obtain the National Institute of Justice publication, *When the Victim Is A Child,*[33] which outlines the major legal issues and social science data about a child's credibility, competency, memory, and behavior. The admissibility issues around hearsay evidence when a child will or will not testify are also discussed. Long[34] discusses application of these issues, legal precedents, and use of expert witnesses to overcome them.

Rowland[35] writes about the use of experts' presenting rape trauma syndrome testimony at criminal trials. Prosecutors use such testimony to support the credibility of the victim. While some jurisdictions have admitted such testimony, particularly to rebut a defense assertion of consent,[36] others have ruled that it is too prejudicial to the defendant.[37,38] In civil trials, however, where the issues concern damages as well as liability, evidence of posttraumatic stress disorder,[39] the diagnostic category under which rape trauma syndrome is subsumed, is admissible. A new category, Self-Defeating Personality Disorder (originally called Masochistic Personality Disorder) has been added to the appendix of the 1987 revision of the American Psychiatric Association's *Diagnostic and Statistical Manual of Mental Disorders,*[40] despite the fact that no empirical evidence could be found to demonstrate its validity and despite the objections of every other mental health group. Posttraumatic stress disorder lends itself to misdiagnosis under this new category.

Measurement of Rape Trauma Syndrome

Psychologists and other clinicians can measure the victim's psychological injury from sexual assault with precision. Use of fear surveys, personality inventories, anxiety and depression measures, along with standard clinical interviews compiling history and current functioning provide objective evidence of the trauma. At Walker & Associates we try to conduct an assessment every three to four months as a way of recording areas where there is progress and areas that are not responsive. This permits the victim to utilize crisis intervention or psychotherapy without postponing her healing until after the trial. In civil cases the delays can cause up to four-year waits until trial. If objective test data and behavioral checklists can be presented at trial, often in charts and other visual forms, even those victims who have healed can still demonstrate damages. These data augment the standard expert witness testimony by allowing juries to understand how psychologists come to professional opinions.

In child sexual abuse cases it is neither feasible nor necessary repeatedly to measure psychological injury. Here documentation on videotape of the evaluation, which should include a developmental baseline, examination of the child's story through the proper use of props (usually anatomically explicit dolls), control of the amount of specificity in questioning the child, and test of the child's ability to recover from the telling of the traumatic incident(s) are most helpful.[41]

Protection of Raw Data and Confidentiality Issues

The rules of evidence that guide the conduct of a trial allow the opposite side to obtain the materials upon which a professional bases his or her opinion. If the psychologist or other mental health professional expects to testify at trial, attempts will be made to find out the results of the evaluation, either by deposition, report, or informal discussion. It is usually inappropriate to participate in informal discussions without a lawyer present, as a psychologist rarely understands all the rules of evidence. Most of the time the raw data are demanded, again either through informal requests or through a formal request called a *subpoena ducas tecum.* Ethical codes of most professionals, including psychologists, call for the protection of raw data. Turning it over to an attorney, untrained in its interpretation, is likely to harm a client. Thus, it is appropriate to request a hearing before the judge, to which the raw data is brought in a sealed envelope. At that hearing be prepared to refer to the part of the Administrative Code under which a license is granted that cites adherence to the profession's Ethical Code and, for psychologists, the Standards for Providers of Psychological Services.[42] I offer to turn raw test data over to another psychologist trained in its administration and interpretation. Sometimes it becomes necessary to hire an attorney to represent the psychologist's rights.

In cases where rape victims have undergone psychotherapy to heal from their abuse, it is common to demand the therapist's progress notes. Courts are beginning to understand that victims need confidentiality in order to trust the therapist and thus to heal. State supreme court decisions are limiting the opposing side's access to those records, frequently relying on the trial court judge to use a balancing test between the victim's rights to privacy and a confidential relationship with a therapist and the accused's right to know in order to prepare a defense. *State of Colorado v. Bond*[43] is typical of these supreme court decisions. In Colorado, it is unusual for a judge to allow therapy notes to be turned over to the defense if a good showing is made at a hearing, although therapists can be asked to prepare a report or give testimony at a deposition. Full discussion of these legal issues with the client is important at the beginning of therapy, as well as at appropriate later times.

ISSUES OF CONFLICT BETWEEN THERAPY AND LITIGATION

There are a number of issues of conflict that can arise during treatment of a individual litigant. For rape victims, it is expected that those who effectively utilize the crisis into which they have been inadvertently placed by the assault will make changes in their life-style. For some women this may mean a greater push towards independence, perhaps as a counter to the overwhelming fearfulness initially experienced by most victims. They may adopt a feminist philosophy, and they may act out their fear and anger at the rapist by using it as a catalyst to display anger towards all men. Or they may deal with their sexual dysfunction by indiscriminate sexual behavior or even a discrete affair. All of these behaviors are not unusual for rape victims, but can be detrimental to their lawsuit. The sex-role stereotyped standards of behavior for women are still the yardstick against which victims are judged, and a display of unexpected behavior is harmful.

In one civil case, a client contracted herpes from an unknown sex partner. The defense learned of it through medical records they had obtained and tried to use it to attack her character and credibility. The offender had already been convicted on criminal charges. In another case, a married rape victim was placed under surveillance by the insurance company, and her amorous behavior in a car with her secret, married lover was videotaped. Threats were made to show this videotape to her unsuspecting husband at the trial if she did not accept a significantly lower financial settlement than that suggested by a settlement judge. In that case, I was careful to testify at deposition that her sexual dysfunction occurred with her husband. Had they asked me if the damages extended to an extramarital affair, I would have been in a difficult position. I had discussed the options with the client prior to my testimony, but neither of us told her attorney, who was understandably chagrined by his lack of knowledge. The client also chose not to disclose her affair to the psychologists who performed the evaluations for both plaintiff and defense. The surveillance, of course, undermined her entire credibility, even though she was assaulted in a public facility and severely injured physically as well as sexually. These are difficult decisions.

In civil cases the rape shield laws do not apply, so the defense can hire mental health professionals and require the victim to participate in the examination. This procedure tests the woman's shaky belief in herself and can retraumatize her, causing acute crisis-stage symptoms to be reexperienced. It can also cause her to question her trust in her therapist, especially when evaluators make negative comments about treatment progress in their reports. In one case, a psychiatrist criticized a psychologist's treatment of a client's panic disorder without the adjunct of chemotherapy. The client perceived medication as giving up her control to heal. Since such a belief in one's own reempowerment is an appropriate goal of therapy for rape victims, allowing her to make an informed decision about medication is an appropriate therapy management decision. However, the attorney insisted that without a trial on the drugs, the woman could be accused of malingering in the lawsuit! Thus, a lawsuit can dictate otherwise contrary therapy decisions.

Therapeutic Benefits of Litigation

Despite the difficulties cited, sexual assault victims often make great therapeutic gains upon conclusion of a civil lawsuit, no matter what the outcome. The ability to put forth her experience in a public arena helps overcome the woman's feelings of stigmatization. The money she might be awarded rarely motivates the victim; she is more interested in stopping the abuser. For example, even when a professional does not lose his license to practice, victims believe they are put on notice that should he sexually abuse another woman, he will be caught again. Victims also believe they warn all women to be wary of this man when they accuse him publicly.

Unlike the situation in a criminal trial, where the rapist can go free on a legal technicality such as improper police interrogation or preservation of evidence, in a civil case the woman has only herself or her lawyer to blame for poor case preparation or management. Another point of contention is the many biased judges and jurors who lie; but victims accept that even better than attorneys and forensic psychologists do, as part of the risk in using the system. In one case, two out of six jurors admitted during deliberations that they lied on voir dire when asked if they had ever been raped. One of those jurors persuaded the others not to find for liability against a motel owner because she was raped too, and it did not cause her permanent damage! Another juror felt guilty after the verdict came down against the plaintiff and called to give the attorney this information. The judge refused to grant a mistrial, because of his erroneous belief that sexual assaults experienced long ago could not be expected to have a major impact on a juror's deliberations. The importance of the fact that one-third of the jurors did not tell the truth escaped his analysis. The victim was disappointed at the outcome, but so glad to get the case out of her life that its disposition alone was therapeutic.

CONCLUSIONS

Changes in the criminal prosecution of sexual abuse cases have paralleled changes in social attitudes toward rape victims. As rape became defined as a crime of violence, the need for women to demonstrate their good virtue became less necessary in criminal actions where rape shield laws, which create a presumption of irrelevancy of a victim's sexual history, were passed. Newer police procedures of collecting evidence and rape crisis center advocates support has enhanced the credibility of victims. However, despite the changes, rape prosecutions are still difficult to win. Civil actions, where there is a lower standard and more control by the victim, have increased. Victims are winning large financial awards against perpetrators and third parties who fail to provide a safe environment for women. It is hoped that these cases will encourage communities to design living and public spaces so that women can be better protected from violent men. Despite the many victories for women's rights, sexual assault victims are still held to stereotyped sex roles. "Good" victims are those who follow the "correct" advice and heal without engaging in potentially embarrassing behaviors. "Bad" victims, as always, are women who act out sexually and do not conform their behavior to approved societal standards.

Forensic psychologists and other mental health professionals can provide consultation, evaluation, therapy, and expert witness testimony in sexual assault litigation. Protection of raw test data and progress records needs to be zealously guarded by forensic experts. The courts seem to agree by placing limitations on the opposing sides' access to these records if it will damage the client's therapy. Battles are still being fought within the mental health profession to avoid misdiagnosis of rape victims. Therapy management may be influenced by litigation. Victims need a lot of support while going through the stressful process of litigation, if there are to be major therapeutic gains at its conclusion.

NOTES AND REFERENCES

1. BOCHNAK, E. 1980. Women's Self Defense Cases. Michie & Co. Charlottesville, VA.
2. BROWNMILLER, S. 1975. Against Our Will: Men, Women, and Rape. Simon & Schuster. New York, NY.
3. SCHNEIDER, E. & S. JORDAN. 1978. Representation of women who defend themselves in response to physical or sexual assault. 15 Harvard C.R.-C.L. Law Rev. **623:** 645-46.
4. HEIDENSOHN, F. 1985. Women and Crime. University of Cambridge. Cambridge, England.
5. KLINGBEIL, K. 1986. Interpersonal violence: A hospital based model from policy to program. Response **9**(3): 6-9.
6. PRESIDENT'S COMMISSION ON VICTIMS OF CRIME. 1983. Final Report. President's Commission on Victims of Crime. Washington, D.C.
7. U. S. CONGRESS. 1984. The Victim Compensation Act.
8. Recourse for rape victims: Third party liability. 1981. Harvard Women's Law J. **4:** 1.
9. Civil law suits for sexual assault: Compensating rape victims. 1982. Golden Gate Law Rev. Women's Law Forum **8:** 479.
10. Garzilli v. Howard Johnson's: 419 F. Supp. 1210 EDNY.
11. The Institute for Study of Sexual Assault, 403 Ashbury Street, San Francisco CA 94117, publishes a listing of judgments and settlements.
12. The liability of an employer for the willful torts of his servants. Chi-Kent Law Rev. **45:** 1.
13. Police liability for negligent failure to prevent crime. 1981. Harvard Law Rev. **94:** 821.
14. *Thurmond v. Torrington,* City of Torrington, Connecticut (1985).
15. SHAH, S. A. 1980. Dangerousness: Conceptual, prediction and public policy issues. *In* Violence and the Violent Individual. Ritlays & Solway, Eds.: 151-178. S.P. Medical and Scientific Books. New York, NY.
16. SONKIN, D. T. 1986. Clairvoyance vs. common sense: Therapist's duty to warn and protect. Violence and Victims **1**(1): 7-22.
17. WALKER, L. E. A. 1986. Domestic violence and visitation and child custody determination. *In* Domestic Violence on Trial. D. J. Sonkin, Ed. Springer. New York, NY.
18. ABEL, G. G., J. V. BECKER, W. D. MURPHY & B. FLANAGAN 1981. Identifying dangerous child molesters. *In* Violent Behavior: Social Learning Approaches to Prediction, Management and Treatment. R. B. Stuart, Ed.: 116-137. Brunner/Mazel. New York, NY.
19. WOLF, S. C., J. R. CONTE & M. ENGLE-MENIG. 1988. Community treatment of adults who have sex with children. *In* Handbook on Sexual Abuse of Children. L. E. A. Walker, Ed. Springer. New York, NY. In press.

20. CHESLER, P. 1986. Mothers on Trial. McGraw Hill. New York, NY.
21. KALMUSS, D. 1984. The intergenerational transmission of marital aggression. J. Marriage Fam. **51**(4): 11-19.
22. NEWBERGER, C. M. & E. H. NEWBERGER. 1986. When the pediatrician is a pedophile. *In* Sexual Exploitation of Patients by Health Professionals. A. W. Burgess & C. R. Hartman, Eds. Praeger. New York, NY.
23. STONE, A. 1976. The legal implications of sexual activity between psychiatrists and patient. Am. J. Psychiatry **133:** 1138-1141.
24. BOUHOUSTOS, J. C. 1984. Sexual intimacy between psychotherapists and clients: Policy implications for the future. *In* Women and Mental Health Policy. L. E. A. Walker, Ed.: 207-277. Sage. Beverly Hills, CA.
25. POPE, K. 1986. Research and laws regarding therapist-patient sexual involvement: Implications for therapists. Am. J. Psychother. **40**(4): 564-571.
26. BURGESS, A. & L. HOLSTROM. 1974. Rape trauma syndrome. Am. J. Psychiatry **131(9):** 981-986.
27. KIRKPATRICK, D. G., L. VERONEN & J. P. A. RESICK. 1979. Assessment of the aftermath of rape. J. Behav. Assessment **2**(1): 133-148.
28. BURT, M. R. & B. L. KATZ. 1985. Rape, robbery, and burglary: Responses to actual and feared criminal victimization with special focus on women and the elderly. Victimol. **10**(1-4): 325-358.
29. CONTE, J. R. & L. BERLINER. 1988. The impact of sexual abuse on children: Empirical findings. *In* Handbook on Sexual Abuse of Children. L. E. A. Walker, Ed. Springer. New York, NY. In press.
30. FINKELHOR, D. & A. BROWNE. 1988. Assessing the long term impact of child sexual abuse. *In* Handbook on Sexual Abuse of Children. L. E. A. Walker, Ed. Springer. New York, NY. In press.
31. RUSSELL, D. H. 1983. The incidence and prevalence of intrafamilial and extrafamilial sexual abuse of female children. Child Abuse and Neglect **7:** 133-145.
32. RUSSELL, D. H. 1984. Sexual Exploitation: Rape, Child Abuse and Workplace Harassment. Sage. Beverly Hills, CA.
33. WHITCOMB, D., E. R. SHAPIRO & L. D. STELLWAGEN. 1985. When the Victim Is a Child: Issues for Judges and Prosecutors. U. S. Department of Justice/National Institute of Justice. Washington, D.C.
34. LONG, G. 1988. Legal issues in child sexual abuse: Criminal and dependency and neglect cases. *In* Handbook on Sexual Abuse of Children. L. E. A. Walker, Ed. Springer. New York, NY. In press.
35. ROWLAND, J. 1985. The Ultimate Violation. MacMillian. New York, NY.
36. *State v. Marks,* 647:2nd 1292.1982.
37. *State v. Saldana,* 324:N.W.2d 227.1982.
38. 1986. Comment. The use of rape trauma syndrome as evidence in a rape trial: Valid or invalid? Lake Forest Law Rev. **21:** 121.
39. AMERICAN PSYCHIATRIC ASSOCIATION. 1980. Diagnostic and Statistical Manual of Mental Disorders. 3rd ed. American Psychiatric Association. Washington, DC.
40. AMERICAN PSYCHIATRIC ASSOCIATION. 1987. Diagnostic and Statistical Manual of Mental Disorders. Rev. 3rd ed. American Psychiatric Association. Washington, DC.
41. WALKER, L. E. A. 1988. New techniques of assessment and evaluation of sexually abused children using anatomically "correct" dolls and videotape techniques. *In* Handbook on Sexual Abuse of Children. L. E. A. Walker, Ed. Springer. New York, NY. In press.
42. AMERICAN PSYCHOLOGICAL ASSOCIATION. 1985. Biographical Directory. American Psychological Association. Washington, DC.
43. Bond v. District Court In & For Denver. County, Colorado. 1984. 682 P 2d 33.

The Treatment and Maltreatment of Sexual Offenders: Ethical Issues

CYRIL GREENLAND

Centre of Criminology
University of Toronto
Toronto, Ontario, Canada M5S 1A5
and
School of Social Work
McMaster University
Hamilton, Ontario, Canada

The invitation to present a paper on ethical issues concerning the treatment of sex offenders provides unlimited opportunities for giving offence and making enemies of distinguished colleagues. But, having accepted the challenge, I am obliged to address these issues as vigorously as possible. My main concerns will be discussed under two broad headings. The first is the use and abuse of penile tumescence measurement, or phallometry. My second and even greater concern is with the reductionist attempts to locate the causes of sexual aggression within the individual rather than within the structures of our society and its values. Since they are of primary importance, the sociopolitical issues will be considered first. The rest of this paper examines the ethical issues relating to the treatment of sex offenders in prisons and prison-like settings and with the application of phallometrics to captive populations.

Considering the imminent threat of global disaster generated by the totally insane decisions of our government to spend $900 billion (US)[1] ($1.7 million every minute) on weapons of mass destruction, is it sensible to limit our professional concerns to the psychobiology of sexual aggression while ignoring the much greater sources of danger? Can we be sure that there is no causal connection between the increased propensity to rape and the threat of nuclear annihilation? And will future generations of historians, if there are any, regard our preoccupation with sexual aggression as another droll example of "fiddling while Rome burns"? If they are well informed, our future historians will know that" . . . it is precisely at times such as these, when we live with the possibility of unthinkable destruction, that people are liable to become dangerously crazy about sexuality."[2]

The main point to be made here is that, like the religious disputes of earlier times, which acquired immense symbolic value, sexuality is another vehicle for displaced social anxiety. There is, I think, good reason to believe that the high level of social anxiety in North America is exacerbated by a confluence of powerful social forces, including feminism, religious fundamentalism, and the advent of victims'-rights organizations. Combined with the prevailing mood of neoconservatism, these disparate movements have, in turn, stimulated the demand for retributive justice and for stricter penal sanctions, including the return of capital punishment.

At times like these, when there is so much anxiety about sexuality, as a professional community we should avoid adding fuel to the fire of "moral panics," which are cynically exploited by the news media. Our conference organizers may have inadvertently contributed to the hysteria by including in the program highly emotive expressions such as "child molester" and "sexual aggression." While they make gut-wrenching headlines, lacking precision, these pejorative terms are clearly inappropriate for the purposes of scientific discourse. I suspect that these essentially journalistic expressions were chosen to emphasize the social relevance of the topics under discussion and, in this way, to pry scarce research funds from government coffers or from private agencies. However, before succumbing to the current hysteria about sexual offenders, perhaps we should remember our earlier involvement with similar "social menaces": the mentally retarded; moral defectives; and sexual psychopaths who, because they seemed to threaten the stability of society, were institutionalized, punished, and deprived of normal human rights.

The sordid history of previous attempts to co-opt physicians and psychologists to control sexuality for religious and political purposes has been well documented by Haller and Haller[3] and others.[4] It may, however, be useful to remind you of the heroic contributions of former colleagues who: (1) devised painful cures for the "scourge" of masturbation; (2) institutionalized mentally retarded children on the basis of "scientifically" validated but quite spurious I.Q. tests; (3) selected many thousands of patients and prisoners for compulsory sexual sterilization; (4) trained healthy women to have mature vaginal instead of inferior clitoral orgasms; (5) leucotomized rebellious "acting-out" adolescents; and, most recently, (6) employed aversive conditioning in court-ordered settings to generate heterosexual feelings and relationships in homosexual men. Except to note the virtual absence of ethical standards in the application of these therapeutic interventions, there is, I think, no need to labor the point.

Having drawn attention to some of the lessons of the past, I will return briefly to the search for a psychobiological explanation of rape and other forms of sexual aggression. While there are pathological conditions that may exacerbate the propensity to rape, the research of Quinsey[5] and Langevin *et al.*[6] indicate that rapists are, for the most part, not unlike other men of the same age, socioeconomic level, and educational status. The differences, if any, are not to be found in raised testosterone levels or phallometric responses, but in disturbed childhood experiences, early histories of antisocial behavior, poverty, slum-dwelling, and membership in marginal minority groups. Although there is strong evidence that the skillful use of phallometry on cooperative subjects can differentiate the "sadistic" from the "opportunistic" rapist, the predictive value of these measurements is still far from perfect.

With this background in mind, the rest of this paper will be concerned with ethical problems and issues relating to the assessment and treatment of sex offenders, especially in prisons or otherwise under compulsion. Having withdrawn from direct involvement with sex offenders,[7] I will contribute to the debate,[8] "not by providing answers but by the discovery of problems where none was previously thought to exist."

ETHICAL ISSUES

Ethics are concerned with abstract moral principles, their codification and application. Writing from the perspective of psychiatry and the treatment of sex offenders, Bancroft[9] claims that ethical guidelines serve a threefold purpose: "1. to protect the patient from exploitation, incompetence, and the pressure to conform; 2. to uphold the rights of that patient, his entitlement to make decisions about his own life and to have access to information that is important to his welfare; and 3. to foster, by the psychiatrist's own behavior, desirable social attitudes and actions." Although somewhat paternalistic, Bancroft[9] provides a useful outline of the key concerns in respect to ethics of research and treatment of sex offenders. The basic elements consist of free and informed consent, including the right to withdraw consent without any penalty; professional confidentiality; acceptability of treatment; and professional competence. Although these standards are or should be mandatory in university-based research, their application to involuntary patients or prisoners, who are not strictly free to enter into consensual relationships, is problematical.

At least two types of problems arise in prisons and court-mandated treatment centers. The first concerns consent, which will be considered later. The second concerns the role of the therapist as a double agent. Discussion on this issue can be focused on the question "Who is the client?"[10,11] A particularly difficult aspect of this problem, for social workers, physicians, nurses, and psychologists employed in prisons, is the conflict between their professional and their Correctional Officer roles. A poignant example of this problem is provided by a psychologist employed in an American correctional facility. He wrote:[12]

> Correctional settings are unique in that they clearly define *security* as the first responsibility of *all* employees and this frequently conflicts with the psychologist's role. My position is that I am first a correctional worker, and though I try to avoid conflicting situations, there are occasions when my job is similar to the correctional officer's, e.g. shakedowns, riots and disturbances, disciplining inmates' infractions, etc. My observations of many correctional psychologists' failures is that they see their correctional role as quite different from other employees' and gradually they lose credibility and the confidence of fellow employees.

This valuable statement reveals, albeit naively, the process by which professionals absorb the prevailing ethos of the institution and its values. Unfortunately, the prevailing ethos in many prisons, rewards toughness on the part of the guards and servility of the inmates. While few prisoners are able to avoid degrading experiences at the hands of their keepers, the worst abuses and terror is reserved for the sex offenders, who are the pariahs of the correctional system. In these circumstances, the application of humane treatment philosophies, which depend on mutual trust and respect, is extremely difficult to sustain. The difficulty is, of course, compounded by the remote locations of prisons and prison hospitals, and the reluctance of well-qualified professionals to practice in essentially hostile environments.

Having made the point that the maintenance of ethically sound therapeutic relationships is likely to be compromised in prisons and prison-like institutions, I can now return to the doctrine of "free and informed consent." Due mainly to the dreadful revelations concerning the medical atrocities conducted by Nazi physicians in World War II, informed consent has become the hallmark of ethical treatment and research, at least in the Western world. However, as Bancroft[9] points out, the possibility of undue influence by the threat of punishment or the removal of privileges is so great as to make "free and informed" consent an unattainable ideal in the treatment of prisoners. An additional problem is that ethical research guidelines usually insist that the subjects must be totally free to withdraw their consent at any time without prejudice. Colleagues with experience in correctional settings will appreciate that refusal to participate in treatment and research is, to say the least, unlikely to improve the inmate's prospects of upgrading his status. Displays of independence and lack of cooperation are also unlikely to be rewarded by the Parole Board, which determines the inmate's fitness for release.

It should be obvious by now that treatment and research involving imprisoned sex offenders is fraught with difficulties. Including among them is the chronic shortage of well-qualified professionals and the sense of alienation and isolation that so many of them endure. This is confirmed by a recent survey of forensic psychiatrists employed in institutions.[13] Similar depressing information was presented in a national study of psychologists employed in the United States criminal justice system in 1976.[10] In presenting this information, my aim is not to condemn our colleagues who, often at great personal cost, continue to provide essential clinical services in prisons and maximum security hospitals. They will, I am sure, be the first to recognize the extreme difficulty of maintaining ethically sound standards of practice, and the risks of being co-opted by the demands of security and the punitive attitudes of the custodial staff. In these circumstances it is difficult to resist being concerned about the qualifications, experience, and supervision of staff who are permitted to use aversive conditioning on prisoners. I also wonder to what extent biomedical research and treatment is being conducted under the rules of the World Medical Association, following the Helsinki Declaration of 1975. This states:[14] '. . . bio-medical research involving human subjects should be conducted only by scientifically qualified persons under the supervision of a clinically competent medical person. The responsibility for the human subject must always rest with a medically qualified person and never rest on the subject of the research, even though the subject has given his or her consent."

In order to consider the question of "acceptability of treatment," we must start with the guidelines of the World Psychiatric Association,[15] also known as the Hawaii Declaration. Rule 2 states: "Every patient must be offered the best therapy available and be treated with the solicitude and respect due to the dignity of all human beings and to their autonomy over their own lives and health."

This means not only protecting inmates from physical harm, but also guarding them against the loss of dignity, exploitation, and moral degradation. In relation to these ethical standards, it is difficult to avoid the conclusion that at least some of the current methods of investigating and treating sex offenders are probably unethical. For this reason, "Aversion therapy" should never be employed without the person's free and informed consent, which may not be possible in prisons. Similarly, while "covert sensitization" techniques are not beyond reproach, "shame aversion" therapy[16] involving humiliation and moral degradation must be considered unethical as well as potentially dangerous. Commenting on shame aversion techniques, Langevin,[17] for example, says: "The therapist has to be careful to ensure that the patient is not depressed. The humiliation and 'shame' may add to his existing feelings and backfire. Only a few cases are reported in the literature and one transvestite, who seemed depressed, attempted suicide after the treatment session."

Unlike shame aversion, which deliberately insults human dignity, the routine use of penile tumescence measurement, is much more insidious in its effects and open to widespread abuse. Since it is a form of search and seizure, involving intrusions into the person's most private parts, without consent it may well breach the Canadian Charter of Rights and Freedoms, Section 8.[18] Also, as Langevin[10] and Quinsey[19] point out, although it is a valuable research tool, phallometry is not an exact science. Even with normal volunteers, it is not always possible to determine the significance of erectile movements. For example, normal law-abiding men sometimes respond to pedophilic and rape-scene stimulation. Phallometry with incarcerated offenders is also open to criticism because, according to Langevin,[17] many of them can and do fake penile reactions. "Thus," he writes, "we are forced to deal only with voluntary and honest research participants at present. This is perhaps the most serious limitation of penile measurement but, in spite of that, it is still the best measure available of erotic preference." However, despite Langevin's plea for caution, phallometry continues to be used on captive populations of sex offenders. For example, in a recent report of a study of "post conviction" sex offenders, which reminds me of medieval accounts of the interrogation of heretics under the Spanish Inquisition, the author[20] claims that: "positive erectile response data . . . allowed 32 percent to stop denying their sexual proclivities." However, "20 percent continued to deny even when confronted with positive arousal data." It does not appear to have occurred to the author that at least some of these data might be "false positives." Our colleagues seem to be equally oblivious to the fact that, in some prisons, being identified as a sex offender may be little short of a death sentence.

The painful fact that many sex offenders are viciously assaulted and killed while serving prison sentences leads us finally to the ethics of preserving professional confidentiality. In the best of times, laying bare one's most private thoughts about sexual feelings and desires is difficult and not without an element of risk. Doing so in a hospital or a prison may be ill-advised, if not extremely dangerous. This is so because it is virtually impossible for the therapist to guarantee that the information provided will be treated in absolute confidence. This problem is particularly acute in prisons, because phallometric reports and other intimate disclosures, to the therapist or in the course of group therapy, are usually made available to the parole board. Since this type of information quickly becomes public property, it is not unheard of for sex offenders, even those in protective custody, to become the victims of blackmail, or worse.

CONCLUSIONS

While I was preparing this paper, a colleague asked me what I was writing. When I told her, she became quite angry and said ". . . it would be more useful if you were at least as concerned with protecting the rights of rape victims and sexually abused children." Since my explanation failed to convince her of my good intentions, I still feel oppressed by her reproach. But even more depressing is the unspoken assumption that prompt and equally brutal retaliation would ease the victim's pain and make the streets safer for women and children. Thus it is difficult to avoid concluding that many feminists believe that sex offenders should be severely punished, as if they were obstreperous children, in order to return them and the rest of mankind to some preexisting state of innocence and social harmony. Apart from the fact that retributive justice—giving the offender his just deserts—only increases the overall risks of interpersonal aggression, the danger is that in the process of scapegoating, the real causes of violence in our society will, once again, be concealed. Therefore, as a professional group we should do everything in our power to avoid perpetuating the myth that punishing or treating identified sex offenders will, by itself, solve the rape crisis.

My final remarks concern the preoccupation with phallometry and the behavioral approaches to the identification and treatment of sex offenders. It is worth remembering that from ancient times Christian theologians, also, regarded the penis as evil and a shameful reminder of our animal natures. The fact that we call them private parts, which must never be exposed in public, adds to our fear and anxiety. The fear persists because, just as men in the Western world believe that the head is the seat of the soul, they are equally deluded in thinking that sexuality exists in the penis. This may explain our longstanding anxiety about its size and the current zeal to find causes of sexual aggression in this frequently measured but highly overrated appendage.

REFERENCES

1. The Globe and Mail, Toronto, 30 Dec. 1986.
2. RUBIN, G. 1985. Sex and violence. CBC Radio, Ideas Program, Toronto. October 31, 1985.
3. HALLER, J. S. & R. M. HALLER. 1974. The Physician and Sexuality in Victorian America. University of Illinois Press. Urbana, IL.
4. GREENLAND, C. 1974. What every young doctor should know about sex. Med. Aspects Hum. Sexuality **4**(11): 5-29.
5. QUINSEY, V. L. 1984. Sexual aggression: Studies of offenders against women. *In* Law and Mental Health: International Perspectives, Vol. 1. D. Weisstub, Ed. Pergamon Press, New York, NY.
6. LANGEVIN, R., D. PAITICH & E. RUSSON. 1985. Are rapists sexually anomalous, aggressive, or both? *In* Erotic Preference, Gender Identity, and Aggression in Men. R. Langevin, Ed.: 17-34. Lawrence Erlbaum Associates. Hillsdale, NJ.
7. GREENLAND, C. 1984. Dangerous sexual offender legislation in Canada 1948-1977; an experiment that failed. Can. J. Criminol. **26**(1): 1-12.
8. SCHAFER, A. 1986. Are hospital ethicists doing a worthwhile job? The Globe and Mail, Toronto, December 9, 1986.
9. BANCROFT, J. 1981. Ethical aspects of sexuality and sex therapy. *In* Psychiatric Ethics. S. Bloch & P. Chodoff, Eds. Oxford University Press. Oxford, England.
10. MONAHAN, J. 1980. Who is the Client? The Ethics of Psychological Intervention in the Criminal Justice System. American Psychological Association. Washington, DC.
11. NORTON, W. A. 1981. Ethics and the work of psychologists in the field of criminal justice. *In* The Ethics of Psychological Research J. D. Keehn, Ed.: 39-49. Pergamon Press. Oxford, England.
12. CLINGEMPEEL, W. S., E. MULVEY & N. D. REPUCCI. 1980. A national study of ethical dilemmas of psychologists in the criminal justice system. *In* Who is the Client? J. Monahan, Ed.: 30. American Psychological Association. Washington, DC.
13. HARRY, B. 1986. Panel on Institutional Psychiatry. Am. Acad. Psychiatry Law Newsl. **11**(3): 13.
14. WORLD MEDICAL ASSOCIATION. 1975. Declaration of Helsinki. *Quoted from* Psychiatric Ethics. S. Bloch & P. Chodoff, Eds.: 347. Oxford University Press. Oxford, England. 1981.
15. WORLD PSYCHIATRIC ASSOCIATION. 1977. Declaration of Hawaii. *Quoted from* Psychiatric Ethics. S. Bloch & P. Chodoff, Eds.: 350. Oxford University Press. Oxford, England. 1981.
16. SERBER, M. 1974. Shame aversion therapy. Behav. Ther. Exp. Psychiatry **1**: 219-221. *Quoted in* J. Bancroft. 1981. Ethical aspects of sexuality and sex therapy. *In* Psychiatric Ethics. S. Bloch & P. Chodoff, Eds.: 175. Oxford University Press. Oxford, England.
17. LANGEVIN, R. 1983. Sexual Strands: Understanding and Treating Sexual Anomalies in Men. Lawrence Erlbaum Associates. Hillsdale, NJ.
18. Canadian Charter of Rights and Freedoms. A Guide for Canadians. Section 8, 1982. Minister of Supply and Services. Ottawa.
19. QUINSEY, V. L. 1973. Methodological issues in evaluating the effectiveness of aversion therapies for institutionalized child molesters. Can. Psychol. **14**(4): 350-361. *Quoted in* R. Langevin. 1983. Sexual Strands: Understanding and Treating Sexual Anomalies in Men. Lawrence Erlbaum Associates. Hillsdale, NJ.
20. TRAVIN, S. 1986. Sexual offences. Am. Acad. Psychiatry Law Newsl. **11**(3): 12.

Law Reform, Social Policy, and Criminal Sexual Violence: Current Canadian Responses

DUNCAN CHAPPELL[a]

School of Criminology
Simon Fraser University
Burnaby, British Columbia

> I was not surprised to find very little research and only a handful of published articles dealing with human sexuality in Canada. We had relied almost completely on the American output of books, booklets and research. . . . Canada is still conservative in the open discussion of many of the critical issues dealing with sexuality. This may not be a negative aspect but rather a cautious positive aspect of our country.[1]

Scarcely a decade has passed since Benjamin Schlesinger provided this assessment of the Canadian approach to the topic of human sexuality as part of his introduction to the first book devoted to the study of sexual behavior in Canada. Yet today this description is in need of substantial modification, for there has been a rapid and, on occasion, dramatic change in Canadian attitudes towards the identification and discussion of critical issues associated with sexuality, especially sexual aggression.

This change, which is still ongoing, has been stimulated by at least four significant developments in Canadian society. First and foremost among these has been the emergence and sustained growth of the women's movement. Like their American cousins, Canadian feminists have focused public attention upon many discriminatory laws and practices, including those concerned with sexual violence against women.[2] This attention, which began in the early 1970s, has contributed to the passage in the 1980s of major revisions to Canada's uniform and codified criminal laws relating to sexual assault.[3]

A second and closely associated development influencing change has been the work of the Law Reform Commission of Canada (LRCC). Established by the federal government in 1970, the LRCC has spent much of its time formulating and presenting for public discussion a set of far-reaching proposals for the updating of the nation's Criminal Code.[4] These proposals have extended to the area of sexual offences, such as rape.[5]

A third development of enormous importance and significance has been the creation of a Canadian Charter of Rights and Freedoms.[6] The Charter, which came into effect only in 1984, has already begun to open to the scrutiny of the courts a number of critical issues dealing with human sexuality, including methods of responding to sexual violence.[7] This form of judicial review is very familiar to Americans, but in Canada

[a]Present address: Australian Institute of Criminology, P.O. Box 28, Woden, ACT 206, Australia.

the newly established and very extensive interpretative powers given by the Charter to the courts remain matters of some controversy and uncertainty.

The fourth and final development of significance has been the extensive attention given in Canada in the 1980s to child sexual abuse and pornography. Reflecting similar trends in the United States during this period, numerous feminists have joined forces with community groups—many of them conservative in outlook—to press for protective legislation to curb the incidence of child sexual molestation and pornography. These public concerns have not gone unheard by Canadian legislators. In 1980 the federal government established a committee, chaired by an academic, Dr. Robin Badgley (the Badgley Committee), to report on the problems of sexual offences against children.[8] The Badgley Committee's mandate was subsequently extended to include consideration of the problems of juvenile prostitutes and pornography. The Committee finally reported its findings in 1984, after conducting a most comprehensive program of research and public consultation. Meanwhile, a further committee was formed by the federal government in 1983 to report upon the problems of prostitutes and pornography with special concentration upon adults, but also with regard to young people. This committee, chaired by a practicing attorney, Paul Fraser Q.C. (the Fraser Committee), also conducted an extensive research and consultation program, before reporting its findings in 1985.[9]

For the cross-national audience for this paper, what has been said so far has two main objectives: first, to explain why Schlesinger's statement requires modification; and second, to provide for those who may be unfamiliar with many events occurring across the forty-ninth parallel some background to the discussion that now follows of more specific law reform and social policy in Canada affecting issues of direct interest and concern to this Conference on Human Sexual Aggression. This discussion is of necessity selective, and centered around three topics that remain controversial in Canada—namely, the definition, incidence and prevalence, and prevention of criminal sexual violence. Since Canada shares with the United States, and several other jurisdictions, many similar cultural and legal traditions, including English common law, it is also hoped that this discussion will place in some comparative perspective a number of current questions of concern to policy makers.

DEFINITION

Until 1983, Canada's legal definition of criminal sexual violence was very much shaped by common law. The Canadian Criminal Code, which first codified the criminal laws as they existed in 1892, adopted the common law definition of the crime of rape.[10] As is now widely known, this definition provided that a male person committed rape when he had nonconsensual intercourse with a female person who was not his wife.[11] This intercourse was established only by the penetration of the male's penis into the woman's vagina. Attempted rape was also proscribed, together with buggery, and bestiality.

In addition to these common law crimes, the Criminal Code—in Part IV dealing with "Sexual Offences, Public Morals and Disorderly Conduct"—also incorporated a range of lesser statutory offences, like indecent assault of a female or male, gross indecency, sexual intercourse with females who were feeble minded or under the age of 14, and incest.[11] Of these sexual offences, only those involving rape, attempted rape, or some other form of assault were concerned in a legal sense with any type of potentially violent, nonconsensual sexual behavior.

The range and definition of sexual offences contained in the Canadian Criminal Code remained relatively unchanged for almost a century. It was not until the general awakening of the women's movement in North America in the 1970s that any serious criticism of these offences began to be offered. The nature of this criticism, and the names of those involved in the leadership of the campaign that developed to change substantive, procedural, and administrative aspects of rape laws across the continent are now well known and documented.[12] In Canada much of the credit for prompting questions about these laws can be attached to Lorenne Clark and Debra Lewis[2] and their seminal research on the way in which the Canadian criminal justice system administered existing rape legislation. Building upon the theoretical perspectives of rape developed by other feminist writers, such as Brownmiller[13] and Griffin,[14] Clark and Lewis concluded that rape was inappropriately classified and considered to be a sexual offence. Rather, rape was a crime of violence and:

> The primary legislative change which must be made is the deletion of rape from the 'Sexual Offences' section of the Criminal Code. New assault offences should be created to define prohibited behaviour, on the basis of principles which acknowledge the full equality of men and women.[2]

This conclusion was presented in 1977. In 1978 the LRCC published a Working Paper on Sexual Offences (WP 22),[15] which outlined a comprehensive set of proposals to simplify and modernize this area of the criminal law. These proposals included amalgamation of the offences of rape and indecent assault to a new and single offence of sexual assault.[15] This new offence would be committed by a person who without consent had "sexual contact" with another. Sexual contact was said to include "any touching of the sexual organs of another or the touching of another with one's sexual organ that is not accidental and that is offensive to the sexual dignity of that person."[15] The questions of whether there had been penetration, and whether force had been used, was to be taken into account only in sentencing.

Subsequent public discussion of WP 22 led to criticism of this new proposed offence on the ground that it failed to recognize an important distinction between mere touching of sexual organs and actual sexual aggression. Responding to this criticism, the LRCC, in a final report on sexual offence reform, recommended that two distinct types of sexual assault be recognized, depending upon whether or not violence or threats were used.[16] These offences would be called, respectively, sexual interference (punishable by a maximum of 5 years' imprisonment) and sexual aggression (punishable by a maximum of 10 years' imprisonment).

A further five years was to elapse before major reform was finally achieved of Canada's rape laws. Changing a single area of a national criminal law seems on this occasion to have been a much more complex, cumbersome, and time-consuming process than affecting the revision of state-based rape laws like those prevailing throughout the United States. Significant numbers of United States' jurisdictions had made significant changes to their rape laws during the 1970s, and by 1980 all of the American states had considered, and most secured, rape law reform of some type.[17] This American experience was watched closely by Canadian exponents of rape law reform, with particular interest being shown in the most innovative and far-reaching revisions made to Michigan's rape laws.[18] The so called "Michigan model" was undoubtedly influential in determining the ultimate shape of Canada's new sexual assault law, which came into effect in January 1983.[18]

The sexual assault legislative package eventually endorsed by the Canadian parliament encompassed many of the general philosophies espoused by feminists such as Clark and Lewis, and the LRCC. The new legislation has created a triad of sexual assaults: simple sexual assault (with 10 years' imprisonment as a maximum punishment); sexual assault with a weapon, threats to a third party, or causing bodily harm (14 years' imprisonment); and aggravated assault (life imprisonment).[19] These gender-neutral offences now encompass many forms of sexual molestation not previously reached by the old crime of rape. They have been accompanied by a series of changes to procedural and evidentiary rules intended to facilitate the prosecution of sexual assault cases.[19]

More will be said below about the perceived impact of these changes. But under this definitional head it must be noted that substantial controversy continues about the scope of the new sexual assault law, and particularly about the meaning of the word "sexual" in the context of an assault. No legislative assistance has been provided in defining this word, and Canadian courts have expressed widely varying opinions on the subject.[20] Among these has been the 1984 decision of *Chase v. R.* in the New Brunswick Court of Appeal,[21] where it was ruled that the forcible touching of a 15-year-old girl's shoulders and breasts by a 40-year-old male was not sexual. Sexual assault, according to this court, was limited to the application of force involving the sexual organs of another, or the touching of another with one's sexual organs. Breasts were secondary sexual characteristics, not primary sexual organs. A failure to make this distinction could lead, said the court, to the absurd possibility that the touching of a man's beard, or the stealing of a midnight kiss, would constitute sexual assault.

Just what the word *sexual* means will have to be resolved finally by the Supreme Court of Canada, but the failure of the legislature to specify in clear terms what types of behavior it wished to incorporate in the new sexual assault provisions has now allowed judicial discretion to determine social policy in this area. Canadian feminists have been quick to suggest that this discretion is often guided by the same patriarchal beliefs that produced such unsatisfactory results under the old rape laws.[22] If any lesson is to be learned from this recent Canadian experience, it is that these beliefs remain highly resistent to change.[23] Accordingly, the opportunity for the exercise of judicial and other forms of discretion in the criminal justice system should be minimized by avoiding the use of vague words and phrases in the drafting of new sexual assault laws.[20]

A further concern that has emerged about the definitional scope of the 1983 sexual assault law related to the adequacy of its protection of children and youths who are victims of sexual offences. The Badgley Committee, in a comprehensive review of the legislative framework associated with sexual offences, reached the conclusion that the 1983 reforms failed "to deal adequately either with the peculiar vulnerabilities of children or with the very different reality of child as opposed to adult sexual abuse."[8] The committee felt that this inadequacy stemmed from the "age old practice of using a legal framework designed for adult sexual victims in purporting to deal with child sexual victims."[8] An extensive set of proposals for law reform to remedy these perceived deficiencies was advanced by the Badgley Committee, but these recommendations have yet to be acted upon by the federal government.

INCIDENCE AND PREVALENCE

One of the stated objectives of Canada's new sexual assault laws has been to encourage better reporting and prosecution of this type of crime.[11] Simplifying and modernizing the law in this area and providing greater protection to the victims of sexual assault during the adjudication process will, it is hoped, encourage many more victims to assist in the detection, conviction, and deterrence of those responsible for acts of sexual violence.

Despite the laudable nature of this objective, determining whether or not it has been achieved is an extremely difficult and frustrating task, since the statistical information available to evaluate this and other types of impact of the new laws is seriously deficient. One major limitation is that the series of official crime statistics maintained by Statistics Canada has, since the passage of the new sexual assault laws in 1983, ceased to include separate information regarding the gender of sexual offence victims or to maintain the previous distinctions between rape and indecent assault.[24] Thus most comparisons of trends in sexual assault offences before and after 1983 based on this data source are largely meaningless. However, one recent attempt has been made to compare aggregate totals of all of the old sexual offences previously reported separately with those that are now labeled simply as sexual assaults.[25] This analysis suggests that there was a significant increase in 1983 in the overall number of sexual assaults reported by victims to the police, and that the new law may therefore have achieved one of its intended consequences. It remains to be seen whether this trend will continue.

Trends in the incidence of sexual offences in Canada prior to 1983 were reviewed in some detail by the Badgley Committee. Examining crime statistics between 1890 and the early 1970s, the committee found that the reported occurrence of all types of sexual offences declined for several decades prior to the 1970s.[8] Throughout the period under consideration, indecent assault was the most frequently reported offence, with the ranking of second place varying between sexual intercourse with a minor, rape, seduction, and "other sexual offences."

Although it was able to discern general trends like these from historical statistical data, the Badgley Committee was scathing in its overall assessment of the quality of the information systems available in Canada in this area. The committee stated:

> that existing official statistical reporting systems (police, homicides, corrections, disease classification, child protection services) are virtually worthless in serving to identify the reported occurrence and circumstances of child sexual abuse. Without exception, all of these statistical reporting systems are so seriously flawed that they do not provide even rudimentary information about the victims of sexual offences, whether they are children, youths or adults.[26]

Seeking to overcome this information gap the Badgley Committee instituted an extensive research program of its own, which included the conduct of a unique National Population Survey of Canadians to determine their experience with unwanted sexual acts.[8] The principal and most controversial findings to emerge from this survey were that about one in two Canadian females and one in three males claimed to have been the victims of such acts. In most cases (four out of five) these experiences were said to have first occurred while the victim was a child or youth. When asked about the types of unwanted sexual acts that took place, survey respondents reported a significant number of sexually aggressive behaviors, including the unwanted touching of "a sex part" (23.5 percent of females; 12.8 percent of males) and attempted or completed sexual attacks (22.1 percent of females; 10.6 percent of males).

These National Population Survey results suggest that unwanted and often assaultive sexual acts are far more prevalent in Canadian society than most informed observers previously suspected. The results also indicate that only a fraction of this sexual behavior comes to the attention of public agencies like the police. In the case of the National Population Survey respondents who said they were the victims of unwanted sexual acts, only 1 in 11 females and 1 in 14 males made contact with a law enforcement agency.[8] Clearly, a change in the reporting behavior of victims like these could have a significant effect on official crime statistics. At present, the most frequent explanations given by victims for not reporting include being too ashamed; feeling that the matter is too personal; and, in the case of females, being fearful of the person responsible for the unwanted act.[8] It seems rather unlikely that the simple passage of the new sexual assault laws in 1983 has by itself overcome major concerns like these. Instead, more intensive and long-term community education programs are almost certainly required to inform Canadians who are or may become the victims of sexual crimes of the reasons why reporting this behavior can be beneficial for them and society at large. For many victims, one very important personal benefit may be the availability of professional assistance to alleviate both the psychological and physical traumas caused by a sexual assault or related offence.

PREVENTION

The provision of various types of services for victims of such crimes as sexual assault is becoming a more common practice in Canada.[27] It is one of the ways in which society can assist in ameliorating the plight of those unfortunate enough to be victimized in this way as well as encouraging such persons to become involved in the task of preventing future crimes. The general search for effective methods of preventing sexual assaults continues in Canada, as it does in many other societies. Among the measures that have been suggested or implemented in Canada, one deserves brief mention here. In an attempt to change long-entrenched beliefs about the appropriate role and status of women in society, which many feminists consider productive of a climate conducive to the commission of sexually violent acts, a concerted attack is being mounted upon pornography. In 1978 the Justice and Legal Affairs Committee of the Canadian House of Commons described pornography as material that:

> is exploitative of women—they are portrayed [in it] as passive victims who derive limitless pleasure from inflicted pain, and from subjugation to acts of violence, humiliation and degradation. Women are depicted as sexual objects whose only redeeming features are their genital and erotic zones which are prominently displayed in minute detail[28]

As noted earlier, both the Badgley and Fraser Committees were asked by the federal government to consider the impact of pornography upon Canadian society during the 1980s. Each committee reviewed the substantial and rapidly growing body of research results, produced largely by psychologists, relating to pornography and its purported effects on human behavior. The Badgley Committee, which was concerned with the effects of pornography upon children, concluded that this research contained "insufficient evidence . . . to show that children were or were not harmed by exposure to sexually explicit materials."[8] The Fraser Committee, which investigated the general effects of pornography, said that "the research on this topic is so inadequate and chaotic that no consistent body of information has been established."[9]

These Canadian conclusions about the message to be drawn from research on the effects of pornography stand in marked contrast to those offered more recently by the U.S. Attorney General's Commission on Pornography, which found that:

> when clinical and experimental research was focused particularly on sexually violent material, the conclusions have been virtually unanimous. . . . The research . . . shows a causal relationship between exposure to material of this type and aggressive behavior[29]

Although reaching these diametrically opposed conclusions about the utility and meaning of largely identical bodies of social science research, the Canadian and American inquiries each recommended the introduction of similar and extensive controls over the production and distribution of pornographic materials because of their harmful effects. These recommendations have received a mixed response in Canada. In the view of some feminists the recommendations would, if implemented, assist in the difficult task of changing male attitudes towards women and lead to a reduction in the level of sexual violence in Canadian society.[30] Other feminists have suggested that the recommendations do not go far enough, or that they divert attention from the real causes of sexual inequality and violence.[31] There is also concern, in some feminist groups, among others, that the suggested controls over pornography would impose severe restrictions on the freedom of expression in Canada.[32] Caught in the midst of this controversy, and with a generally conservative constituency to assuage, the current federal government in Canada has yet to establish a clear position on its approach to dealing with pornography.

THE FUTURE

To an unprecedented and historical degree Canadians have for more than a decade been engaging in a far-reaching examination of their own sexuality. A very visible and current symbol of this fresh approach can be found in the internationally acclaimed Canadian movie *The Decline of the American Empire.*[33] Filmed in Quebec by Denys Arcand, the movie consists largely of a witty and at times sad conversation about sex among a group of Montreal intellectuals.

But this new-found freedom, which has brought with it an extensive and indigenous academic literature on a range of critical issues associated with such subjects as rape,[34] child sexual abuse,[35] and pornography,[36] has still to coalesce into a coherent and acceptable set of social policies relating to sexual violence. Substantial reliance has been placed to date upon the revision of specific criminal laws to deal with aspects of the problem, but, as has been indicated, dissatisfaction with the judicial interpretation and protective reach of these laws remains. It has also been suggested that far too much reliance and attention has been attached to legislative and other traditional approaches to reform in this area. The Badgley Committee's report, for example, has been severely criticized by Clark[37] for failing to consider why it is that males are overwhelmingly responsible for the sexual violence occurring in Canadian society. Since the committee did not consider this question, what reason do we have, says Clark,

> to believe that the recommendations it puts forward would, if implemented, solve the problem? For surely the point is not merely to give better assistance to the victims once

> they are victims, or even to ensure greater detection and/or conviction or treatment of offenders. Rather we must try to eliminate the underlying causes of disturbed male sexuality which produces the primary problem in the first place. . . . It is naive to believe that a problem of such dimensions can be cured without fundamental social change.[37]

Clark's statement will certainly be endorsed by all concerned with the dismantling of patriarchy wherever it occurs. In the long term in Canada some assistance with this dismantling process may come from the Charter and its equality provisions.[6] In the short term, however, more immediate results must be sought from the new sexual assault laws and related reforms. The statement by Schlesinger with which this paper began referred to the "cautious positive aspect" of the past Canadian approach to sexuality. In a pluralist society such as Canada some caution will continue to be a beneficial quality when decisions come to be made about the control of pornography and similarly controversial issues. Freedom of expression, like many other civil liberties, has often had a more fragile environment in which to blossom in Canada than in the United States.[38] The new and potentially fertile soil cast into this environment by the Charter should therefore encourage the close scrutiny of any future legislation that purports to impose various forms of censorship in Canada under the guise of preventing sexual violence. The facilitation of still more, rather than less, discussion of human sexuality in Canada would seem to offer the most promising approach to understanding and preventing sexual aggression.

REFERENCES

1. Schlesinger, B. 1977. Introduction. *In* Sexual Behaviour in Canada. B. Schlesinger, Ed. University of Toronto Press. Toronto.
2. Clark, L. M. G. & D. J. Lewis. 1977. Rape: The Price of Coercive Sexuality. The Women's Press. Toronto.
3. Boyle, C. L. M. 1984. Sexual Assault. The Carswell Company. Toronto.
4. Law Reform Commission of Canada. 1977. Report. Our Criminal Law. Minister of Supply and Services Canada. Ottawa.
5. Law Reform Commission of Canada. 1977. Report on Sexual Offences. Minister of Supply and Services Canada. Ottawa.
6. Constitution Act. 1982. Schedule B. Part 1. Canadian Charter of Rights and Freedoms.
7. Boyle, C. L. M., M. Bertrand & C. Lacerte-Lamontagne. 1985. A Feminist Review of Criminal Law. Minister of Supply and Services Canada. Ottawa.
8. Committee on Offences against Children and Youths. 1984. Report. Minister of Supply and Services Canada. Ottawa.
9. Special Committee on Pornography and Prostitution. Pornography and Prostitution in Canada. Minister of Supply and Services Canada. Ottawa.
10. Backhouse, C. B. 1983. Nineteenth century Canadian rape law 1800-92. *In* Essays in the History of Canadian Law, Vol. 2. D. H. Flaherty, Ed.: 201-236. University of Toronto Press. Toronto.
11. Osborne, J. A. 1985. Rape law reform: The new cosmetic for Canadian women. *In* Criminal Justice Politics and Women: The Aftermath of Legally Mandated Change. C. Feinman, Eds.: 49-64. The Haworth Press. New York, NY.
12. Geis, G. 1977. Forcible rape: An introduction. *In* Forcible Rape. The Crime, the Victim, and the Offender. D. Chappell, R. Geis & G. Geis, Eds.: 1-44. Columbia University Press. New York, NY.
13. Brownmiller, S. 1975. Against Our Will. Men, Women and Rape. Simon and Schuster. New York, NY.
14. Griffin, S. 1971. Rape: The all-American crime. Ramparts, September 1971: 26-35.

15. LAW REFORM COMMISSION OF CANADA. 1978. Working Paper 22. Criminal Law. Sexual Offences. Minister of Supply and Services Canada. Ottawa.
16. LAW REFORM COMMISSION OF CANADA. 1978. Report on Sexual Offences. Minister of Supply and Services Canada. Ottawa.
17. BIENEN, L. 1980. National developments in rape reform legislation. Women's Rights Law Reporter **6**(3): 171-213.
18. BACKHOUSE, C. & L. SCHOENROTH. 1983. A comparative survey of Canadian and American rape law. Canada-United States Law J. **6:** 48-88.
19. CHAPPELL, D. 1984. The impact of rape legislation: Some comparative trends. Int. J. Women's Stud. **7**(1): 70-80.
20. RUEBSAAT, G. 1985. The New Sexual Assault Offences: Emerging Legal Issues. Department of Justice Canada. Ottawa.
21. *Chase v. R.* (N.B.). 1984. 40 C.R. (3d).: 282-287.
22. BOYLE, C. 1985. Annotation. Chase v. R. (N.B.): 282-283.
23. MARSH, J. C., A. GEIST & N. CAPLAN. 1982. Rape and the Limits of Law Reform. Auburn House Publishing Co. Boston, MA.
24. STATISTICS CANADA. 1986. Canadian Crime Statistics, 1985. Minister of Supply and Services Canada. Ottawa.
25. RENNER, K. E. & S. SAHJPAUL. 1986. The new sexual assault law: What has been its effect? Can. J. Criminol. **28**(4): 407-413.
26. COMMITTEE ON SEXUAL OFFENCES AGAINST CHILDREN AND YOUTHS. 1984. Sexual Offences Against Children in Canada. Summary. Minister of Supply and Services Canada. Ottawa.
27. CANADIAN FEDERAL-PROVINCIAL TASK FORCE ON JUSTICE FOR VICTIMS OF CRIME. 1983. Report. Minister of Supply and Services Canada. Ottawa.
28. HOUSE OF COMMONS STANDING COMMITTEE ON JUSTICE AND LEGAL AFFAIRS. 1978. Report on Pornography. Minister of Supply and Services Canada. Ottawa.
29. U.S. ATTORNEY GENERAL'S COMMISSION ON PORNOGRAPHY. 1986. Final Report. U.S. Government Printing Office. Washington, DC.
30. MCLAREN, J. 1986. The Fraser Committee: The politics and process of a special committee. *In* Regulating Sex. An Anthology of Commentaries on the Findings and Recommendations of the Badgley and Fraser Reports. J. Lowman, M. A. Jackson, T. S. Palys & S. Gavigan, Eds.: 39-54. Simon Fraser University. Burnaby, B.C., Canada.
31. DIAMOND, S. 1986. Childhood's end: Some comments on pornography and the Fraser Committee. *In* Regulating Sex. An Anthology of Commentaries on the Findings and Recommendations of the Badgley and Fraser Reports. J. Lowman, M. A. Jackson, T. S. Palys & S. Gavigan, Eds.: 143-158. Simon Fraser University. Burnaby, B.C., Canada.
32. BOYD, N. 1986. Sexuality, gender relations and the law: The limits of free expression. *In* Regulating Sex. An Anthology of Commentaries on the Findings and Recommendations of the Badgley and Fraser Reports. J. Lowman, M. A. Jackson, T. S. Palys & S. Gavigan, Eds.: 127-142. Simon Fraser University. Burnaby, B.C., Canada.
33. STOLER, P. 1986. Sex and success in Montreal. Time **128**(26): 61.
34. CLARK, L. M. G. & S. ARMSTRONG. 1979. A Rape Bibliography with Special Emphasis on Rape Research in Canada. Minister of Supply and Services Canada. Ottawa.
35. SCHLESINGER, B., Ed. 1986. Sexual Abuse of Children in the 1980's. Ten Essays and an Annotated Bibliography. University of Toronto Press. Toronto.
36. LOWMAN, J., M. A. JACKSON, T. S. PALYS & S. GAVIGAN, Eds. 1986. Bibliography. *In* Regulating Sex. An Anthology of Commentaries on the Findings and Recommendations of the Badgley and Fraser Committee Reports.: 215-223. Simon Fraser University. Burnaby, B.C., Canada.
37. CLARK, L. M. G. 1986. Boys will be boys: Beyond the Badgley Report, a critical review. *In* Regulating Sex. An Anthology of Commentaries on the Findings and Recommendations of the Badgley and Fraser Reports. J. Lowman, M. A. Jackson, T. S. Palys & S. Gavigan, Eds.: 93-106. Simon Fraser University. Burnaby, B. C., Canada.
38. FRIEDENBERG, E. Z. 1980. Deference to Authority: The Case of Canada. M. E. Sharpe. White Plains, NY.

What Have We Learned about Legislative Remedies for Rape?

JEANNE C. MARSH

The School of Social Service Administration
The University of Chicago
Chicago, Illinois 60637

At 5:30 in the morning, 13 July 1974, near the close of a marathon session, the Michigan legislature signed a bill entitled "Criminal Sexual Conduct." The small group of reformers who had lobbied all night for the bill saw it as a "wrenching change from the old state law, . . . the first comprehensive attempt by a state to break away from century-old myths and legal traditions surrounding the crime of rape."[1] And when the bill passed, one particularly disgruntled legislator shook his fist at the reformers in the gallery and said, "Keep your legs crossed ladies, we will be back next year."[2] Sure that they had accomplished an important reform, the activists were cautious, nevertheless, in their predictions of the law's likely impact:

> While our Michigan reformers must have done something right to so upset the traditionalists, I would nevertheless caution the enthusiasts against the belief that an untested law can be a model law. Its carefully chosen words may say what many of us want a fair law to say. But we do not yet know if in practice it will help to right what is so desperately wrong. More than a legal reform, the Michigan law is an experiment in which we hope to learn how a major revision in the criminal code can deter, control, publicize, and *equalize the treatment* of a very destructive set of acts against human beings.[1]

Since that morning in July 1974, all 50 states have made some modification in their sexual assault laws. Further, enough empirical analyses and legal critiques have been completed so that it is possible to take stock of what we have learned about the utility of legal remedies for the problem of rape. It is the purpose of this paper to review recent sexual assault legislation, to examine what we have learned about the character and impact of these legislative changes, and to discuss the implications of our findings for policy research and policy making.

Four questions are central in any policy evaluation, and will provide an organizing framework for our discussion. What was the nature of the reform, and what changes or *effects* might logically be anticipated? What were the measurable effects? Were the reforms, in fact, implemented? And if there were changes, what aspects of the reform appear to be responsible for the changes? Research to date has focused primarily on documenting the impacts of reforms, but, in addition, there have been some analyses of implementation.

NATURE AND GOALS OF THE REFORMS

Traditional common law relevant to rape reflects a view of women as a form of male property whose value is determined by premarital chastity and marital fidelity. According to this system, any evidence, past or present, of lack of chastity is sufficient proof of "reduced value." Therefore, only one degree or category of rape is required and recognized. A women either is or is not "despoiled." Further, she is expected to "resist to the utmost" to protect her social status. Finally, this view restricts definitions of the crime to the penetration of female victims by male perpetrators.

The view of the social status of women and the nature of the crime implicit in the reformed laws is quite different. An individual's right to choose to engage in sexual activity is protected as a personal right. By taking this view, laws shift causal attribution from the victim to the offender, making rape more consistent with other crimes. For example, a victim's past sexual history or previous decisions regarding sexual activity are deemed irrelevant to the current situation. In some statutes when sexual penetration or contact is accompanied by force, nonconsent is assumed. Many laws explicitly define a continuum of violent sexually assaultive behavior. In some states, a husband can be convicted of raping his wife. Further, the laws acknowledge that victims can be both male and female.

Thus, the provisions in sexual assault legislative reforms represent a fundamental redefinition of the crime—from an infringment of a property right to a violation of a personal right. Implicit in the legal changes is a revised view of the position of women in society—from male property to individuals deserving of having their safety and security protected. Further, an individual's right to choose to engage in sexual activity is protected as a personal right. In addition, the reforms represent a change in legal methodology—from an absolute approach based on fixed categories to a relativistic approach in which seriousness is determined by amount of coercion used, injury inflicted, and the vulnerability of the victim.[3]

Although women's rights activists were the main force behind the reform of rape laws, they forged a powerful coalition with two other groups: those interested in the codification of state criminal laws and those interested in crime control.[4,5] This coalition explains in part the fact that rather sweeping reforms were passed in many states with unusual swiftness.[4]

The reforms implemented to address these goals vary by state. As Loh has noted,[4] there are three major issues in any system of forcible rape law: (1) the definition of the crime, i.e., the legal standards for criminalization and the degrees, if any, of culpability; (2) rules of evidence with respect to corroboration of the complaining witness's complaint and the admissibility of the complaining witness's past sexual history; and (3) a penalty structure. Comprehensive reforms address each of these aspects; narrow reforms tend to focus on rules of evidence—particularly limitations on the admissibility of evidence about the complaining witness's past sexual history (rape shield provisions).

Although reforms have taken place in virtually every state, research examining their impact has been limited to three states. To date, four studies have been completed examining the impact of revised criminal sexual conduct laws: two evaluating the impact of the Michigan reform;[5,6] one assessing the effects of the Washington reform;[4] and one examining the impact of the revisions in California.[7] The reforms in Michigan and Washington are comprehensive reforms, since they include major redefinitions of the crime and changes in rules of evidence and in the penalty structure. The California revision is less sweeping, including primarily a rape shield provision (limiting evidence of the complainant's past sexual history) and changes in the penalty structure. More detailed descriptions of reforms in these states and others is available elsewhere.

In addition to the research, there have been a number of legal critiques of rape law reform, including most recently those by Haxton[9] and Estrich.[10] Fundamentally, Haxton claims reforms have gone too far and Estrich claims they have not gone far enough. These critiques will be discussed in relation to the research findings. The suggestions of these authors will be viewed in terms of empirical evidence about the impact of rape law reform.

What were the goals of the reforms? They have been both symbolic and instrumental in character. Among the most widely articulated are the following: (1) to increase reporting, arrest, and conviction rates; (2) to "normalize" the handling of sexual assault cases—to bring legal standards for rape in line with those for other violent crimes; (3) to exercise control over decisions made in the criminal justice system; (4) to protect victims from demeaning treatment at trial by limiting cross-examination; (5) to sensitize and educate society about the position and rights of women.

However, analyses of reforms reveal that their most central and consistent goal was to enhance prosecution—to increase conviction rates. This goal was the shared interest of all the groups promoting reform. Its achievement is a central criterion of the success of the reforms. Additionally, the desire to normalize the crime significantly motivated the activities of reformers. Most of the research and comments have focused on these two goals. The purpose of this paper is to assess the extent to which these goals have been met and thus to enhance our understanding of the gains achievable through legal reform.

LEGAL IMPACT STUDIES: VIEWS FROM MICHIGAN, WASHINGTON, AND CALIFORNIA

Careful analyses of studies evaluating reforms in the three states reveal similar findings. The research provides insight on the effects of legislative reform on the outcome of criminal justice procedures—report, arrest, and conviction rates—and on the process itself. These two aspects of the research are considered in the next section of the paper. Further, the available research incorporates two types of comparisons: comparisons *over time* (before and after a reform) and comparisons *over crime* (examining the relation between rape and other serious crimes). A third comparison, *across jurisdictions,* is implicit in this analysis of research on reforms in three different states.

Before describing the actual empirical findings, the effects of legislative reform that were anticipated are worth noting. A study conducted shortly after the Michigan reform was implemented gathered impressionistic evidence from judges and prosecutors suggesting that the law was viewed as too complex, particularly with respect to the degree structure. Respondents were dubious that criminal justice officials could work with such refined definitions. Further, respondents perceived that the law had little direct effect on charging decisions. Finally, they predicted that if the charging was the same before and after the law reform, convictions probably would remain unchanged as well.[11]

Impact on Disposition

Two studies examined the impact of the law on case disposition—on reports, arrests, and convictions before and after the reforms: Marsh, Geist and Caplan in Michigan;[5] and Loh in Washington.[4] These studies vary in terms of design and source of data.[a] Further, they represent findings of the impacts of two different laws in two different states. Nonetheless, there is some consistency in the direction of the results, as shown in TABLE 1.

Reports, Arrests, and Convictions

Both studies reveal that the arrest rate has changed very little as a result of the law reform. The results show a small increase resulting from implementation of the Michigan law, a reform that has been described as one of the most "radical" reforms.

TABLE 1. Crime Statistics before and after Criminal Sexual Conduct Law Reforms in Washington and Michigan

	Washington (from Loh[3])		Michigan (from Marsh, Geist, and Caplan[5])	
	Prereform	Postreform	Prereform	Postreform
Charging/report	51%	51%	43%	47%
Convictions/charge				
As charged	37%	56%	10%	20%
For a lesser offense	35%	15%	20%	8%
Acquittals/dismissals	23%	28%	20%	19%

The fact that the law had a minimal impact on arrests was explained in both studies by the fact that prosecutors still base decisions to seek warrants on winability, that is, whether or not the case is likely to result in a conviction. Although laws have clarified evidentiary requirements, the characteristics of cases that make them more or less credible to a prosecutor probably have not changed. As long as the nature of cases remains the same and prosecutors rely on the same fact patterns to determine whether or not to prosecute, charging is likely to be minimally influenced by a change in the statute.

The most significant impact of law reform is revealed in the conviction statistics. In both states, the law reform resulted in a significant increase in convictions as

[a] The data for the Washington study were based on 445 rape complaints filed by police with the King County prosecutor from 1972 to 1977. Under the old law (before June 30, 1975) 208 cases were filed; and 237 cases were filed under the new law (after July 1, 1975). The cases were obtained from prosecutor and police files. The Michigan crime statistics were based on UCR statistics for the entire state collected by the Michigan State Police between 1972 and 1978. Prereform and postreform statistics were based on time-series analysis of 44 months of data.

charged and a significant decrease in convictions for a lesser offense, with very little change in the overall conviction rate. This effect can be seen very clearly in the time-series data from the Michigan study (FIG. 1). Loh[3] has described this as the "truth-in-labeling" effect, since it indicates that rape charges that previously resulted in convictions for reduced charges, such as "assault," are now resulting in convictions on the original sexual assault charge. This is a significant effect, since it means that offenders will be "blamed" for the crime they committed and will carry the social stigma attached to serious sexual assault crimes.

A third study tracked changes in the disposition of rape cases and other serious

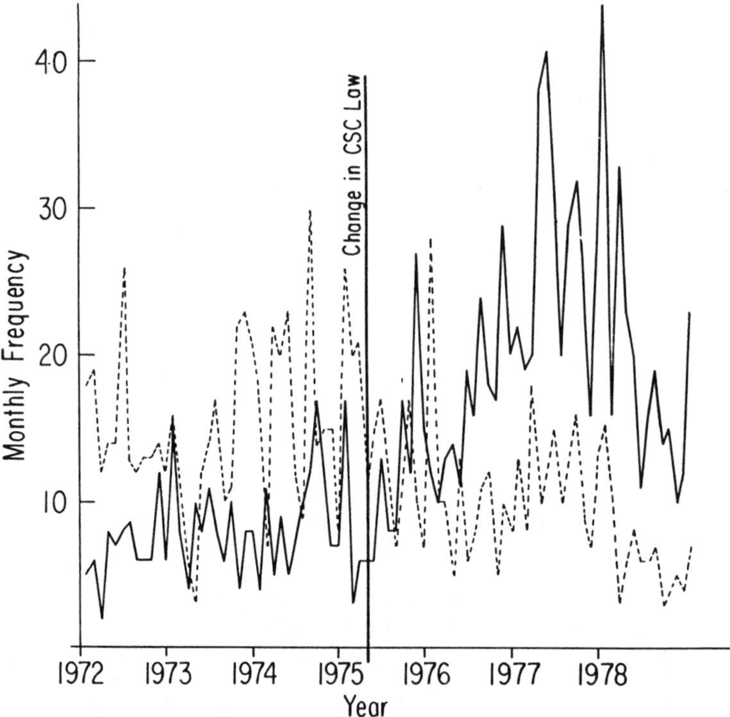

FIGURE 1. Total monthly CSC 1 convictions as charged (*solid line*) and for a lesser offense (*broken line*) for criminal sexual assault in Michigan.

crimes in California after the implementation of reform provisions.[7] These reforms were different from the reforms in Michigan and Washington in that they were part of more general reforms in criminal law and procedure rather than changes made specifically with respect to the crime of rape.[7] As noted previously, the revisions in California were narrow, focused primarily on limitations of evidence of complainants' past sexual history and on the penalty structure. The study examined arrests, convictions, and prison sentences for rape and several other serious crimes from 1975 through 1982. A weakness in the study is its failure to clarify the specific reform provisions or the times they were implemented in relation to the data collected. Several legal revisions were made during the data collection period, including evidentiary provisions beginning in 1974 and new sentencing provisions in 1976, 1978 and 1979.[8] Because he used a "post-test only" or "during" design, Polk is in a weak position to make causal attributions about the impact of the laws. Unfortunately, he fails to note this limitation in his discussion of results.

Nevertheless, the findings on this study are consistent with those of Loh[8] and Marsh, Geist and Caplan.[5] There were no changes in the arrest rate over time, but there was an increase in the proportion of convictions per arrest relative to other serious crimes. Polk also found large increases in the proportion of prison sentences per convictions for 1976, 1978, and 1979—years in which mandatory prison terms and mandatory minimums were implemented. Although the results of this study are generally consistent with the results of others, it is not possible to draw many conclusions. First, the reforms in California were relatively narrow, incorporating a rape shield provision and changes in the penalty structure. Basic social psychological research has documented the importance of rape shield laws for shifting the attributions of blame in rape trials from the victim to the defendant.[12] However, relatively few cases actually go to trial. Indeed, Polk notes that only 20% of convictions in California are achieved through jury trial. Further, rape shield statutes are relevant during trial only when the defense is consent. Research by Reskin *et al.*[13] has shown that consent is the primary defense in less than one-third of rape trials. Therefore, a major effect would not be expected from this type of reform. A larger effect could be expected from mandatory sentencing provisions, and the data do seem to support such an effect. Second, as noted previously, conclusions are weakened by the fact that data were collected only *after* the implementation of the evidentiary changes. Further, only descriptive statistics were used to compare trends in rape cases with those of other serious crimes. No statistical standards were imposed for judging the importance of the changes.

Impact on Case Processing: "Normalizing" the Handling of Sexual Assault Cases

A study by Caringella-MacDonald[6] focused directly on criminal case processing of rape cases and nonrape assault cases before and after the reform in Michigan. Results from her study, supported by findings from Loh[4] and Marsh, Geist, and Caplan,[5] suggest that legislative reform has had limited impact on the processing of sexual assault cases. Caringella-McDonald's study focused on the objective of the law reform in Michigan to "normalize" the treatment of sexual assault cases, that is, to bring the handling of these cases more in line with the handling of assaultive crimes not sexual in nature. As mentioned previously, much of the rhetoric surrounding the reform in Michigan was concerned with "recriminalizing" the crime of rape.

To analyze the extent to which the Michigan law achieved this objective, Caringella-McDonald analyzed 132 criminal sexual conduct (CSC) cases and 285 nonsexual assaults handled in the Kalamazoo County Court during 1981 and 1982, five years after the reformed law was implemented in Michigan. She found that, with some notable exceptions, the handling of sexual assault crimes was basically consistent with the handling of other assaultive crimes. In fact, there was some evidence that CSC cases were handled with greater solicitousness than other crimes. For example, arrest warrants were authorized slightly more frequently for CSC than for non-CSC assaults (67% versus 54%) even though the CSC cases appeared fundamentally weaker from a convictability standpoint. Victims in the CSC cases offered weaker resistance and had more credibility problems; they were more often assaulted by someone with whom they were acquainted; there were fewer witnesses in CSC cases: weapons were less frequently present; and, overall, there was less evidence in CSC cases. Not surprisingly, prosecutors judged the probability of conviction to be lower in CSC cases. Nevertheless, the actual conviction rates in the two types of cases *were not significantly different.* Further, although CSC cases were plea bargained or acquitted/dismissed more frequently (50% and 34% respectively) than other violent assaults (45% and 27%), these differences were not significant. Caringella-McDonald concludes that the objective of eliminating unique requirements and standards have been met, but differential case treatment still exists. Victims of CSC crimes are less frequently considered credible; and although police and prosecutors suggested the use of bad judgment and victim precipitation in a very small number of cases overall, they did so to a significantly higher degree in CSC cases.

Findings from the Loh study[4] shed some light on findings from Caringella-McDonald. He found that five considerations that influenced the charging decision before the legislative reform in Washington remained important after the reform: use of physical force, social interaction between the suspect and victim, corrobative evidence, victim credibility, and race. So although reforms may have been successful in altering formal evidentiary requirements, they have not altered the factors considered by police and prosecutors when assessing convictability. Given this understanding and the Caringella-McDonald finding that CSC cases are weaker according to (informal) conventional convictability standards, it is noteworthy that Caringella-McDonald found CSC crimes authorized slightly more frequently than other violent assaults.

To summarize, data on the implementation of reformed criminal sexual assault laws reveal that the evidentiary provisions of the reformed laws are being carried out. In this respect, the reformers' efforts to "normalize" the handling of this crime have been successful. Nevertheless, these new provisions exert little influence on the way the police and prosecutors judge the strength of cases. They consider aspects of the case that may not be important according to formal standards of evidence. This does not seem to have an adverse effect on case disposition, however. Although Loh[4] found no difference in charging rate before and after reform, and Marsh, Geist, and Caplan[5] found only a slight increase after reform in Michigan, both Loh and Marsh, Geist and Caplan found increases in convictions as charged after the laws were implemented. Thus, the reforms have been successful according to the most central criteria: increases in convictions.

How do we account for the increase in convictions as charged, particularly when little change has been documented in official reporting and arrest statistics? Interviews with criminal justice officials in the Marsh, Geist, and Caplan study may provide some insight. Improved conviction rates were linked by respondents to specific features of the law that refined the definition of the crime (25%) or clarified evidentiary requirements, either restrictions on past sexual history evidence (44%) or changed resistance and consent requirements (26%). These officials' responses suggest that the legal provisions in the law provided tools that enabled them to identify, gather, and use relevant evidence to achieve convictions. Although prosecutors may still consider factors that are not relevant according to the law when deciding whether and how to charge a case, legal definitions and evidentiary guidelines may provide the tools necessary to achieve a conviction once the case is charged.

There is an additional explanation for the increase in conviction rates. Anecdotal and some empirical evidence suggests that prosecutors have felt increased pressure to pursue sexual assault cases and to achieve convictions. The passage of the law reform represented both a symbolic and a substantive change in the handling of sexual assault cases. Its meaning did not elude criminal justice officials. One respondent in the Marsh, Geist, and Caplan study reported that "women are important now." Pragmatically, the complexity and comprehensiveness of the law required many police officers and prosecutors to focus on the new law in order to learn and apply its various provisions. Some jurisdictions even set up special units for prosecuting sexual assault crimes. Thus, the increase in convictions may have been less a function of specific provisions and more a function of the streamlined bureaucratic response resulting from the increased attention and emphasis placed on the handling of this crime.

LEGAL CRITIQUES OF LEGISLATIVE REFORM

The adequacy, appropriateness, and meaning of revised statutes have been analyzed by legal scholars, as well as by social scientists. Two of the most recent legal critiques, both of which consider the empirical evidence reviewed here, provide a picture of the current debate on rape legislation. One discussion[9] suggests that revised legislation may push accepted constitutional limits; a second[10,14] indicates that "model" legislation, such as the Michigan reform, does not go far enough.

Haxton[9] focuses on the constitutionality of rape shield statutes. He argues that by categorically excluding evidence that may be highly relevant to the defense, rape shield statutes interfere with the defendant's exercise of constitutional rights. He provides numerous examples of instances in which categorical exclusion would make a statute unconstitutional. He also discusses various *appropriate* reasons for excluding evidence, such as conflicting constitutional rights of witnesses and defendants; or instances in which the government wishes to protect witness' privacy to insure fairness, or to regulate trials to influence conduct outside the courtroom. He concludes that these provisions are not "facially" unconstitutional, but that trial judges must be vigilant to recognize those "rare occasions" when sexual conduct evidence is so probative that rape shield statutes are unconstitutional. This discussion is noteworthy because the interests of witnesses in rape cases are acknowledged and discussed in a manner without precedent in legal discussions of fifteen years earlier. Further, when the new laws were passed, reformers acknowledged that the constitutionality of rape shield provisions remained to be tested. The direction of discussion as well as the fact that the provision has held up under appeal suggest that constitutionality is becoming established.

Estrich[10,14] reviews revisions in the laws and the evidence of their impact and concludes that the reforms are neither radical nor effective enough. Her argument is premised on the idea that "power and powerlessness are not gender neutral in our society. When women are the victims, gender is an issue that should not be avoided."

She focuses exclusively on "simple" rape—coercive sex in the absence of violence. She is critical of the reforms (a) for relabeling the crime of rape as sexual assault; (b) for expanding the definition beyond intercourse; and (c) for shifting the focus of the prosecution from the victim. She believes that relabeling the crime obscures the unique indignity of rape. She states that gender neutrality suggests that rape law should take into account the different ways men and women understand force and consent. She believes that expanding the definition beyond intercourse is irrelevant to what she sees as the most difficult problems occasioned by simple rape. In short, she is critical of those aspects of the reform that the original reformers identified as the most innovative and important.

Estrich describes a fundamental public policy debate related to rape: the controversy as to whether rape should be considered sex or violence. On the "rape as sex" end of the continuum are found both the radical feminists who consider all sex as coercive in a society where men dominate, and the radical traditionalists who respect the need of men to have their sexual drives satisfied. On the "rape as violence" end are the early rape law reformers, "liberal" feminists, and those who believe that sex is fundamentally inconsistent with violence. Estrich places herself somewhere between these extremes (but closer to the rape-as-violence end) specifically because of her concern for the woman who is forced to engage in sex against her will by a man who does not resort in violence. Her solution, her "new answer" is to shift the focus of the legislation back to the victim and to define consent so that when a woman says "no" to sex, her word is respected by the law. She would at the same time focus on the man for a broader definition of force that includes threats and misrepresentation and considers intent. She promotes a return to gender-specific laws and the use of the term "rape" in place of the more gender-neutral "sexual assault" or "criminal sexual conduct."

Inherent in Estrich's critique of reformed rape laws is a feminist search for an appropriate understanding of the construct of equality. Original reformers of the law sought to achieve equal protection under the law through gender neutrality and provisions that would bring the handling of this crime in line with the handling of other violent crimes. Their approach was to pursue a standard of formal equality that promotes similar treatment for similarly situated individuals. They argued that victims of rape should receive the same treatment as victims of other violent assaultive crimes. Estrich basically rejects this approach in favor of one that emphasizes the special meaning and impact of the crime on women. The difficulties for feminists in identifying an appropriate standard are discussed by Becker.[15] She argues that it is not worthwhile to attempt to find one general standard of equality that can be applied to all women's problems; rather, we should seek particular solutions to particular kinds of problems—typically through piecemeal legislative change. Adapting her view, it may be possible to acknowledge the gains achieved for crimes of violent rape through the application of a formal equality standard, while at the same time promoting further reforms with respect to "simple" rape using a different standard.

A basic element in Estrich's critique of recent reforms is an effort to ignore or discredit the empirical evidence related to the impact of reforms. In her review of the impact studies, she minimizes or casts doubt on the effects of the laws documented in the research and provides a global summary of the reforms as "ineffective."[b] She is correct that the reforms have had very little impact on crimes of rape not accompanied by overt force. However, she fails adequately to distinguish the differential impacts of the reforms on the various degrees of the crime. Further, her analysis fails to distinguish between reforms of different character and intensity and between analytic

[b] In footnote 242[10] Estrich explains her view that in the Marsh, Geist, and Caplan study[5] the "dimensions of improvement in conviction rates are not clear." Her questions reveal a failure to note that the conclusion of an increase in convictions was based on an interrupted time-series analysis of the number of convictions for criminal sexual conduct before and after the reform in Michigan was implemented. Such an analysis is a statistically rigorous way to assess changes in trend and level before and after the reform, controlling for the factors, such as reports and arrests, that contribute to the level of convictions. The main threat to the validity of such an analysis is the possibility that the effect, i.e., the increased convictions, could have been caused by an event other that the passage of the law that occurred simultaneously with its implementation. This threat was ruled out when no effect-causing event could be identified. For further discussion of this analysis, the reader is referred to Cook and Campbell.[16] Estrich further comments on the high post reform conviction rates achieved in Detroit. Marsh, Geist, and Caplan commented on these high rates in their text, noting that they were best explained by the high priority placed on sexual assault crimes by the Wayne County prosecutor and a special Sex Crimes Unit during this period.

strategies of varying rigor and validity. Of particular concern, the modifications in the laws that she promotes are contraindicated by research evidence. For example, officials in Michigan attributed improved conviction rates in CSC 1 to the redefinition of the crime and the modification in the resistance and consent requirements. Estrich would return to a more traditional definition of the crime and change the consent requirements that these officials found helpful.

There is no question that Estrich's "new answers" contribute to the debate on appropriate remedies for rape. Further, they provide a useful vehicle for clarifying a feminist concept of equality. Nonetheless, it is important not to diminish or distort what we have learned about legal remedies for rape in an effort to push the debate further.

WHAT HAVE WE LEARNED?

There are a number of lessons that can be derived from our experience with legislative reform in the area of rape—some substantive, some methodological. The most salient concern is whether the reforms accomplished their objectives. To summarize the state of our knowledge about legal remedies for rape: First, it appears that comprehensive reforms—those that alter the definition of the crime, the rules of evidence, and the penalty structure—*can* have a specific measurable effect resulting in increases in convictions as charged. However, even the comprehensive reforms appear to have very little effect on reporting and arrest rates. Second, although officials adhere to the reform provisions of the law, extralegal considerations, such as judgments about victim credibility, are influenced very little by the reforms in the law. They continue to influence case disposition as much as they did before the reforms and as much as they do in other serious crimes. Decisions made in the criminal justice system are influenced by the new laws to the extent that specific provisions are in place. Analyses of the implementation of the laws reveal that decision makers adhere to the letter, if not always the spirit, of the law. Finally, the passage and existence of reformed rape laws has strengthened and supported a broader social movement to accord women increased rights and respect. Rape laws, in concert with and clearly resulting from women's growing political influence, have helped achieve a broader understanding that "women are important now." Thus, there *are* effects from reforms, some instrumental and measurable, others symbolic and less easily measured.

In general, the effects appear to be related to the nature of the reform, with the strongest effects achieved through the most intense intervention. The fact that the reform in Michigan was a comprehensive revision, a wrenching change from the past, appears to be important to its success. The type of effect achieved appears very much related to the specific character or provisions of the intervention. For example, officials cited the definition of the crime and the modified evidentiary requirements as important to increasing conviction rates. They cited provisions prohibiting past sexual history evidence as valuable for improving victim experience. We can conclude that legal remedies for rape can make a difference, but the effect achieved depends on the specific nature and intensity of the reforms.

Legislative reform in the area of sexual assault was promoted by feminists concerned with women's rights. The strongest critiques of the reforms come from feminists as well—"radical" feminists, according to some categorizations, who view male domination of women's reproductive capacity as the fundamental source of women's oppression. In Susan Brownmiller's classic book *Against Our Will: Men, Women and Rape*[17] she identifies the ability of men to rape women as the beginning of male oppression. This position, articulated in another classic article by Susan Griffin, "Rape: The All-American Crime,"[18] served to place rape and rape law reform at the center of the feminist political agenda. Even though the widespread reform in rape laws could be viewed as a victory for the women's movement, rape and its remedies remain controversial. The critiques of the reforms and of the research on the reforms reflects the debate.

Two lessons on the role of social science in the development of public policy are reinforced here.[19] First, in a pluralistic society policy decisions are influenced primarily by interest groups and critical events. Decisions are only minimally influenced by relevant knowledge. Because most policy choices are value choices, information, even if it were perfect and complete, could not provide an adequate basis for policy decisions. Further, social issues are seldom resolved through a single policy or program. Rather, changes are most effectively accomplished through multiple and varied approaches that are modified incrementally. Often in the process, societal perceptions of a problem change and influence the direction of the policy efforts. Thus, the policy process is value-laden, incremental, and adaptive. Social science has a role to play in the process. Specifically, social scientists can build models to understand and explain social phenomena. Perhaps more important, social scientists can use scientific discipline to collect accurate and reliable facts about the nature of social problems and the consequences of attempting to intervene.

In the ongoing debate on rape and its remedies, research evidence suggests that the goals of past efforts have in many ways been addressed, that we can expect specific effects from efforts to alter legislation in this area. As the debate continues and various policy options are implemented, research should continue to articulate the types of effects that can be expected from specific interventions, carefully distinguishing between performance and politics.

ACKNOWLEDGMENT

The author wishes to thank Mary Becker of The University of Chicago Law School for her helpful comments on this paper.

REFERENCES

1. BENDOR, J. 1976. Justice after rape: Legal reform in Michigan. *In* Sexual Assault: The Victim and the Rapist. M. J. Walker & S. L. Brodsky, Eds.: 150. Lexington Books. Lexington, MA.
2. MICHIGAN TASK FORCE ON RAPE. 1978. Personal Communication.
3. LOH, W. 1981. What has the reform of rape legislation wrought? J. Social Issues **37**(4): 28-52.
4. LOH, W. 1980. The impact of common law and reform rape statutes on prosecution: An empirical study. Washington Law Rev. **55:** 543-652.
5. MARSH, J. C., A. GEIST & N. CAPLAN. 1982. Rape and the Limits of Law Reform. Auburn House. Boston, MA.

6. Caringella-MacDonald, S. 1985. The comparability in sexual and nonsexual assault case treatment: Did statute change meet the objective? Crime and Delinquency **31**(2): 206-222.
7. Polk, R. 1985. Rape reform and criminal justice processing. Crime and Delinquency **31**(2): 191-205.
8. Beinen, L. B. 1980. Rape IV. Women's Rights Law Rep. **6** (3 Supplement): 1-61.
9. Haxton, D. 1985. Rape shield statutes: Constitutional despite unconstitutional exclusions of evidence. Wisconsin Law Rev. 1219-1273.
10. Estrich, S. 1986. Rape. Yale Law J. **95**(6): 1087-1142.
11. Reich, J. & D. Chappell. 1978. Forcible Rape: Final Project Report. National Institute for Law Enforcement and Criminal Justice. Washington, DC.
12. Borgida, E. & N. Brekke. 1985. Psychological research on rape trials. *In* Research Handbook on Rape and Sexual Assault. A. Burgess, Ed.: 313-342. Garland Publishing. New York, NY.
13. Reskin, B., M. Matthews, S. Sanford, C. Visher & G. LaFree. 1980. Study of jury verdicts in sexual assault cases: Some preliminary findings. Presented at the Annual Meeting of the American Society of Criminology, San Francisco, California, October, 1980.
14. Estrich, S. 1987. Real Rape. Harvard University Press. Cambridge, MA.
15. Becker, M. E. 1986. Prince Charming: Abstract Equality. Supreme Court Review.
16. Cook, T. D. & D. T. Campbell. 1979. Quasi-Experimentation: Design and Analysis Issues for Field Settings. Rand McNally. Chicago, IL.
17. Brownmiller, S. 1975. Against Our Will: Men, Women and Rape. Simon and Schuster. New York, NY.
18. Griffin, S. 1971. Rape: The all-American crime. Ramparts, September 1971: 26-36.
19. Marsh, J. C. 1985. Obstacles and opportunities in the use of research on rape legislation. *In* Social Science and Social Policy. R. L. Shotland & M. M. Mark, Eds.: 295-310. Sage. Beverly Hills, CA.

Human Sexual Aggression: Social Policy Perspective

FREDERICK C. GREEN

School of Medicine
George Washington University
Washington, D.C. 20024

I have been assigned the task of examining human sexual aggression from a social policy perspective. Because of my professional background as a pediatrician with a long-standing interest in the clinical management and policy issues related to child maltreatment and their at-risk families, I feel most comfortable in focusing my remarks on those social policies that relate to sexual aggression directed towards children. Specifically, I intend to consider those social policies and practices that impact on the capacity of individuals, families, and communities to cope with the multifaceted syndrome of child sexual abuse, its precursors, and management.

The question that must be addressed is: Do current social policies enhance or diminish the vulnerability of children as targets of sexual aggression?

I find it very difficult to address this subject two days after a federal budget was submitted to Congress that purportedly reflects the priorities and policies to be pursued by our government in the coming year. Further, recognizing the causal relationship between stress and violence in all forms, and the reality of the significant economic and social stress with which our poor, unemployed, working poor, and middle income citizens are coping, one must wonder how in touch our leadership is with the realities of living on a modest or frugal income. At best it is ignorance, at worst insensitivity or callousness.

For those of you who are not aware of the contents of the proposed 1988 federal budget, let me point out that the proposed major slashes in funding will be in housing, urban development, mass transit, public health, welfare, adult and vocational education, student loans, and the clean water program. Nutrition programs for the poor, such as school lunch, food stamps, and school breakfast, are also in jeopardy. You may or may not agree with me that these are undesirable initiatives; however, I simply suggest that you consider the proposed cuts and how they relate to the welfare of people, then decide whether you believe these proposals have any relevance to the topic at hand.

Gil[1] suggests that "social policies are guiding principles or courses of action adopted and pursued by societies and their governments as well as institutions" designed to "influence . . . (a)[the] quality of life in that society; (b) . . . the circumstances of living of individuals and groups [in] that society; (c) . . . the nature of intrasocietal relationships among individuals, groups and society as a whole."

Social policies are not monolithic and unchanging but are dynamic, varying at the national, state, and community levels, with interacting and reciprocal effects at each level. Such policies tend to be modified and shaped by an "unceasing process of intergroup conflicts of interest and competition in the political arena where supposedly every group of citizens have equal opportunities and equal civil and political rights to promote their special interests."[2] Of course this is not the case, since our society is composed of groups of unequals based on social class, ethnicity, age, and economic status. This is an age of unbridled spending by political action committees—such as the gun lobby and the American Medical Association—to achieve their goals.

Thus, it would seem axiomatic that those policies that tend to polarize a population on the basis of the aforementioned social groups—such as school busing, abortion rights, and affirmative action—have the potential to stimulate intergroup rivalry and thus create a milieu supportive of enhancing and perpetuating violence and aggression. This is not to say that controversial issues should not be considered and discussed; what I am saying is that when they are considered, firm and fair leadership must be exercised with prudence, in order to mitigate undesirable, violent confrontations. Such confrontations teach children that bigotry and violence are acceptable forms of behavior under certain circumstances.

Since the political arena is the most visible forum in which the social policies of our nation are shaped, let me share with you what I consider to be the most significant events that are relevant to our concerns.

The decade of the seventies was a period of transition from the "liberalism" of the sixties to the "conservatism" of the eighties. It was a period of sharpening debate between those who favored a strong central government and those who favored stronger state governments; those who supported social welfare entitlements and those who favored stricter regulations on such entitlements; those who considered the direct provision of human services a legitimate role of government and those who favored the transference of this role to the private sector of society. This struggle was exacerbated by an escalating national debt and spiraling inflation.

In the midst of this period of transition, there were two pieces of federal legislation that deserve mention because they impinged on the vulnerability of children and made statements on the degree to which government could protect and support the rights of children being reared under less-than-ideal circumstances.

The first was the Child Development Act of 1973. This was bipartisan legislation designed to provide access to affordable, high-quality day-care service to allow poor mothers to work. This legislation was vetoed by President Nixon, who used such pejorative phrases as "an alien concept contrary to the American ethos," and "a sovietizing of our children." His veto was sustained, and the result of that veto is still being felt, as no similar legislation has been introduced since. Thus the care and nurturing of children outside of their natural home was deemed suspect.

In fairness, this veto represented the beliefs of a vocal and substantial segment of our society that saw such legislation as an attack on the sanctity of the American family. In their ideal world, and in the dreams and fantasies of too many of our legislators, the world of American children is one that consists of a dyad of loving and caring parents capable of meeting all the nurturing needs of their children—physical, emotional, economic, and social. If poor and single-parent families existed, they were apparently seen as aberrations of the norm, undeserving of the largesse of the greater society. Lindner describes this as the "myth of family self-sufficiency."[3]

The second piece of legislation—The Child Abuse Prevention Act of 1974 (P.L. 93-247)—was enacted into law, but not without significant opposition. Opponents of this legislation saw it as an intrusion by "bureaucrats" into the family. Further, it was their belief—shared by many—that parents, kin, and other child-care providers were incapable of intentionally killing, maiming, or sexually assaulting children, especially their own. As one high governmental official told me in 1973, "this child abuse stuff is nothing more than the figment of the psychiatrists' imagination." Some imagination!!

As we entered the eighties, our national priorities and postures shifted to far less government regulation; to a deemphasis of social programs and far greater emphasis on defense spending; to privatization of many former government programs; and to a "trickle-down" economic theory. Since responsibility was shifted to states for the provision and delivery of human services, intense competition developed at community levels for a share of the substantially decreasing resources to meet such needs. Thus, although things seemed to be improving at the macro or national level, the milieu of the less affluent urban and rural areas were—and are becoming increasingly—stressful, with persistently high unemployment, poor housing, and all of the other trappings of poverty. Accompanying this has been the predictable increase in the use and abuse of alcohol and other drugs to escape reality; but also, because of the disinhibiting effects of alcohol and drugs, violence and sexual aggression against children has increased. Finkelhor's[4] construct concerning the etiology of child sex abuse included the ability of adult offenders to overcome both internal and external inhibitions against sexually assaulting children.

As one who has been both directly and indirectly involved with the management of child abuse offenders, I must conclude that current practices do little to strengthen such offenders' inhibitions or decrease their motivation to seek out children for sexual experiences, unless they happen to come under the care of one of a few excellent programs. All too often they are detained and paroled with little or no mandated therapy or rehabilitation. Some offenders avoid any penalties, and therefore therapy, because legal technicalities concerning the acceptability of hearsay evidence allowed them their freedom. Fortunately, this is less common today, because many states now accept such evidence.

Our national preoccupation with sex, particularly as reflected in the print and electronic media, cannot be overlooked as contributing to an "ecology of deviance"[5] that heightens the vulnerability of children to sexual assault and increases the prevalence of adolescent child bearing and child rearing. Parenthetically, I consider any sexual overtures made to children by adults, whether violent or flatteringly persuasive, as human sexual aggression. For me to think otherwise would be to accept the premise that children are the aggressors in their own victimization.

E. and C. Newberger[6] observe that the commercial acceptance of and emphasis on children as sex objects implies a broad base of either overt or "latent" pedophilia in our population. We need only observe such commercial exploitation in the sale of jeans, diet foods, and fragrances.

Commercial television has seldom shown an aversion to displaying sexual activity between consenting and nonconsenting adults; at least we have been spared from seeing such activity between adults and children. This is not the case, however, with X-rated video cassettes and some cable television, where children can be seen as sex partners with other children and adults. Without elaboration, let me note that the print media also contributes to this sexual preoccupation.

Finally, the mind-set that the sanctity of the home, regardless of the damage to the child, must remain inviolate is counterproductive to the identification of at-risk children and families. This thinking has been a deterrent, even to some of our child-care professionals, to identifying and reporting children at grave risk for sexual abuse, simply because the offending parents are members of their same clubs and churches and are of the same social class and are therefore incapable of such deviance. Until these ideas and the myth of family self-sufficiency are disavowed, the victimization of children will continue, abetted by myopic social policies.

In summary, I believe that the vulnerability of children to human sexual aggression has been increasing in the last decade due to fragmented[7] and inadequate social programs and ambiguous and callous social policies—policies that spawn escalating violence in communities by polarizing individuals and groups on the basis of social class, ethnicity, sex, and nationality. Further dependence on the private sector of society to meet the unmet need of the most vulnerable in our communities is both futile and callous.

REFERENCES

1. GIL, D. 1973. Unravelling Social Policy. Schenkman Books. Cambridge, MA.
2. STARR, P. 1983. The Social Transformation of American Medicine. Basic Books. New York, NY.
3. LINDNER, E. 1979. The All-American Family Myth. J.C. Penny Forum, Spring/Summer 1979.
4. FINKELHOR, D. 1984. Child Sexual Abuse: New Theory and Research. Free Press. New York, NY.
5. STEADMAN, H. 1986. Predicting violence leading to homicide. Bull. NY Acad. Med. **26**(5).
6. NEWBERGER, E.& C. NEWBERGER. 1984. Sex with Children: Toward a Moral Policy. Presented at the National Conference on Sexual Abuse of Children, Washington, D.C., April 1984.
7. JOHNSON, A. S. 1978. Toward an inventory of federal programs with direct impact on families. Staff Report, Family Impact Seminar. George Washington University. Washington, DC.

Subject Index

Index of Contributors